TREATING COMPLEX TRAUMATIC STRESS DISORDERS

TREATING COMPLEX TRAUMATIC STRESS DISORDERS
An Evidence-Based Guide

Edited by
CHRISTINE A. COURTOIS
JULIAN D. FORD

Foreword by Judith L. Herman

Afterword by Bessel A. van der Kolk

THE GUILFORD PRESS
New York   London

© 2009 The Guilford Press
A Division of Guilford Publications, Inc.
72 Spring Street, New York, NY 10012
www.guilford.com

Printed in the United States of America

This book is printed on acid-free paper.

Last digit is print number: 9   8   7   6   5   4   3   2

The authors have checked with sources believed to be reliable in their efforts to
provide information that is complete and generally in accord with the standards
of practice that are accepted at the time of publication. However, in view of the
possibility of human error or changes in medical sciences, neither the authors, nor
the editor and publisher, nor any other party who has been involved in the
preparation or publication of this work warrants that the information contained
herein is in every respect accurate or complete, and they are not responsible for any
errors or omissions or the results obtained from the use of such information. Readers
are encouraged to confirm the information contained in this book with other sources.

Library of Congress Cataloging-in-Publication Data

Treating complex traumatic stress disorders : an evidence-based guide / edited by
Christine A. Courtois, Julian D. Ford.
    p. ; cm.
Includes bibliographical references and index.
  ISBN 978-1-60623-039-8 (hardcover : alk. paper)
1. Post-traumatic stress disorder.   2. Psychic trauma.   I. Courtois, Christine A.
II. Ford, Julian D., 1951–
[DNLM: 1. Stress Disorders, Traumatic—therapy.   2. Evidence-Based Medicine.
3. Psychotherapy—methods.   4. Stress Disorders, Traumatic—drug therapy.
WM 172 T7838 2009]
  RC552.P67T763 2009
  616.85′21—dc22

                                                            2008030409

To Tom, the wind beneath my wings

—C. A. C.

For my beloved daughters—Julie, Shelly, Lindy, and Jessa—my role models for resilience

—J. D. F.

About the Editors

Christine A. Courtois, PhD, is a psychologist in private practice in Washington, DC. She is cofounder and past Clinical and Training Director of The Center: Posttraumatic Disorders Program at the Psychiatric Institute of Washington, and past Codirector of the Maryland Psychological Association's Post-Doctoral Institute on Psychological Trauma (2007–2008). Dr. Courtois has authored three books, *Recollections of Sexual Abuse: Treatment Principles and Guidelines* (1999), *Adult Survivors of Child Sexual Abuse: A Workshop Model* (1993), and *Healing the Incest Wound: Adult Survivors in Therapy* (1988); she has also published numerous articles and chapters on related topics. Among her recent awards are the 2007 University of Maryland College of Education Alumni Outstanding Professional Award; the 2007 Outstanding Contributions to Professional Practice Award from Division 56 (Psychological Trauma) of the American Psychological Association; the 2006 Lifetime Achievement Award from the International Society for the Study of Trauma and Dissociation; and the 2005 Distinguished Contribution to the Psychology of Women Award from the Committee on the Psychology of Women of the American Psychological Association. Dr. Courtois routinely conducts professional training locally, nationally, and internationally on topics related to traumatic stress.

Julian D. Ford, PhD, is Associate Professor of Psychiatry at the University of Connecticut School of Medicine and Director of the University of Connecticut Health Center Child Trauma Clinic and Center for Trauma Response Recovery and Preparedness. He has developed the Trauma Affect Regulation: Guide for Education and Therapy (TARGET) treatment model for adult, adolescent, and child traumatic stress disorders, and conducts research on psychotherapy and family therapy, health services utilization, psychometric screening and assessment, and psychiatric epidemiology. Dr. Ford has coedited two other recent books, *Treating Traumatized Children: Risk, Resilience, and Recovery* (with Danny Brom and Ruth Pat-Horenczyk, 2008) and *The Encyclopedia of Psychological Trauma* (with Gilbert Reyes and Jon D. Elhai, 2008).

Contributors

John Briere, PhD, is Associate Professor of Psychiatry and Psychology at the University of Southern California, Director of the Psychological Trauma Program at Los Angeles County–USC Medical Center, and Codirector of the Miller Children's Abuse and Violence Intervention Center–USC Child and Adolescent Trauma Program, National Child Traumatic Stress Network. A past president of the International Society for Traumatic Stress Studies, he has been designated a "highly cited researcher" by the Institute for Scientific Information.

Daniel Brown, PhD, is Associate Clinical Professor in Psychology at Harvard Medical School and has a private practice in Newton, Massachusetts. He has worked with the assessment and treatment of trauma and abuse for 30 years. Dr. Brown is the author of 14 books; coauthor, with Alan W. Scheflin and D. Corydon Hammond, of *Memory, Trauma Treatment, and the Law* (1998); and a recipient of the Guttmacher Award from the American Psychiatric Association and American Academy of Psychiatry and the Law for an outstanding contribution to forensic psychiatry. He has worked in the courts for over 20 years as an expert witness on trauma and abuse cases. In the last 10 years he has been developing attachment-based treatment protocols for patients with major dissociative and/or personality disorders.

Laura S. Brown, PhD, ABPP, practices feminist therapy and forensic psychology in Seattle. Her most recent book, *Cultural Competence in Trauma Therapy: Beyond the Flashback*, was published in 2008. Dr. Brown is the founder and director of the Fremont Community Therapy Project, a low-fee training clinic.

James Caringi, PhD, MSW, is Assistant Professor at the School of Social Work, University of Montana. He has extensive clinical, teaching, and research experience in the areas of complex trauma and vicarious trauma.

Marylene Cloitre, PhD, is the founding director of the Institute for Trauma and Stress at the New York University Child Study Center, and the Cathy and Stephen Graham Professor of Child and Adolescent Psychiatry. She is also a research scientist at the Nathan S. Kline Institute for Psychiatric Research. Dr. Cloitre is the coauthor (with Lisa R. Cohen and Karestan C. Koenen) of *Treating Survivors of Childhood Abuse: Psychotherapy for the Interrupted Life* (2006).

Christine A. Courtois, PhD (*see* "About the Editors").

Roger D. Fallot, PhD, is a clinical psychologist and Director of Research and Evaluation at Community Connections, a private, not-for-profit mental health and human services agency in Washington, DC. He is a contributing author to and coeditor (with Maxine Harris) of *Using Trauma Theory to Design Service Systems* (2001). Dr. Fallot consults widely on the implementation of trauma-informed services and on trauma services for male survivors of physical and sexual violence.

Janina Fisher, PhD, is a licensed clinical psychologist, an instructor at the Trauma Center in Boston, and a faculty member at the Sensorimotor Psychotherapy Institute. She is also past president of the New England Society for the Treatment of Trauma and Dissociation, former Director of the International Society for the Study of Trauma and Dissociation, an EMDR International Association Credit Provider, and a former instructor at Harvard Medical School.

Victoria M. Follette, PhD, is Foundation Professor and Chair of the Department of Psychology at the University of Nevada, Reno. She is a clinical scientist with an interest in the mechanisms of change in psychotherapy for trauma survivors. Additionally, Dr. Follette's work is focused on issues related to resiliency and risk for revictimization. She is the coauthor of *Finding Life Beyond Trauma* (2007) and coeditor of *Integrated Behavioral Healthcare* (2001), *Cognitive-Behavioral Therapies for Trauma* (2006), *Mindfulness and Acceptance* (2004), *Acceptance and Change* (1994), and *Scientific Standards of Psychological Practice* (1995).

Julian D. Ford, PhD (*see* "About the Editors").

Diana Fosha, PhD, is the developer of accelerated experiential–dynamic psychotherapy (AEDP) and the Director of the AEDP Institute in New York City. She is the author of *The Transforming Power of Affect: A Model for Accelerated Change* (2000); coeditor, with Daniel Siegel and Marion Solomon, of *The Healing Power of Emotion: Perspectives from Affective Neuroscience, Development, and Clinical Practice* (2009); and has authored articles on transformational process and trauma treatment. A DVD of her AEDP clinical work has been released by the American Psychological Association, as part of its Systems of Psychotherapy Video Series.

A. Steven Frankel, PhD, ABPP, JD, is a certified clinical and forensic psychologist and an attorney at law. He has been on the faculty of the University of Southern California for over 35 years and is currently Clinical Professor of Psychology. He served as Adjunct Professor of Law at Loyola Law School (Los Angeles) and is now Adjunct Professor at Golden Gate University School of Law. Dr. Frankel has taught courses on health care policy, regulation of health care practice, and mental disorder and the law. He won the USC Award for Teaching Excellence early in his academic career and has authored over 50 articles and book chapters.

Lori Galperin, MSW, LCSW, is an accomplished clinician in the fields of marital and sexual dysfunction, and sexual compulsivity, trauma, and eating disorders, lecturing nationally and internationally on these topics. She has authored several journal articles and book chapters in these areas. Ms. Galperin is trained in various modalities, including the internal family systems approach, and maintains many professional affiliations and clinical designations. Over the past 15 years, Ms. Galperin has treated several thousand inpatients and trained more than 100,000 clinicians throughout the United States, Canada, and Europe.

Kari Gleiser, PhD, is a senior faculty member at the AEDP Institute, and recently became a supervisor/trainer at the Trauma Center in Boston. She specializes in applying accelerated experiential–dynamic psychotherapy to the treatment of complex trauma, dissociative disorders, and personality disorders in her private practice in Hanover, New Hampshire.

Steven N. Gold, PhD, is Professor and Founding Director of the Trauma Resolution and Integration Program at the Nova Southeastern University's Center for Psychological Studies. He is the author of the book *Not Trauma Alone* (2000); founding coeditor of the *Journal of Psychological Trauma* (previously the *Journal of Trauma Practice*); a past president of the International Society for the Study of Trauma and Dissociation; and president-elect of the American Psychological Association Division of Psychological Trauma as well as founding editor of the Division's journal, *Psychological Trauma: Theory, Research, Practice, and Policy.*

Michelle S. Grennan, MA, is currently enrolled in the clinical psychology doctorate program at Long Island University and, along with Lewis A. Opler, is one of the coauthors of the Symptoms of Trauma Scale.

Maxine Harris, PhD, is CEO for Clinical Affairs and cofounder of Community Connections. She is also the Executive Director of the National Capital Center for Trauma Recovery and Empowerment. Dr. Harris is the author of numerous articles and several books, including *Trauma Recovery and Empowerment: A Clinician's Guide to Working with Women in Groups* (1998) and *The Twenty-Four Carat Buddha and Other Fables: Stories of Self-Discovery* (2003).

Judith L. Herman, MD, is Clinical Professor of Psychiatry at Harvard Medical School and Director of Training at the Victims of Violence Program at The Cambridge Hospital. She is the author of two award-winning books, *Father–Daughter Incest* (1981) and *Trauma and Recovery* (1992). Dr. Herman has lectured widely on the subject of sexual and domestic violence. In 2007 she was named a Distinguished Life Fellow of the American Psychiatric Association.

Katherine M. Iverson, PhD, is a clinical scientist with a special interest in the conceptual understanding and treatment of survivors of interpersonal trauma. She is currently a postdoctoral fellow at the National Center for Posttraumatic Stress Disorder, Women's Health Sciences Division, Boston VA Health Care System.

Christie Jackson, PhD, is a licensed cognitive-behavioral therapist who completed postdoctoral training in dissociative disorders and trauma at McLean Hospital/Harvard Medical School. In addition to posttraumatic stress disorder, her research and clinical interests include personality disorders, dialectical behavior therapy, and working with first responders and other populations vulnerable to trauma.

Susan M. Johnson, EdD, is Professor of Psychology at the University of Ottawa and Research Professor at Alliant University in San Diego. She is also Director of the Ottawa Couple and Family Institute and the International Center for Excellence in Emotionally Focused Therapy. Dr. Johnson's latest book is *Hold Me Tight: Seven Conversations for a Lifetime of Love* (2008).

Philip J. Kinsler, PhD, FACFE, is Adjunct Assistant Professor of Psychiatry at Dartmouth Medical School. He is former president of the New Hampshire Psychological Association and former chair of the New Hampshire Board of Examiners of Psychology and Mental Health Practice. For many years, Dr. Kinsler's psychotherapy practice has been focused on survivors of complex trauma, and he writes, teaches, consults, and trains other professionals in this area.

Kore Nissenson, PhD, is a clinical psychologist specializing in cognitive-behavioral therapy for anxiety and depression. Her research interests focus on clinical treatment of adults with a history of childhood abuse.

Pat Ogden, PhD, is a pioneer in somatic psychology and the founder/director of the Sensorimotor Psychotherapy Institute, an internationally recognized school specializing in somatic–cognitive approaches for the treatment of posttraumatic stress disorder and attachment disturbances. She is a clinician, consultant, international lecturer and trainer, and coauthor (with Kekuni Minton and Clare Pain) of *Trauma and the Body: A Sensorimotor Approach to Psychotherapy* (2006).

Lewis A. Opler, MD, PhD, is Professor of Clinical Psychiatry at Columbia University. He has over 200 publications, including the Positive and Negative Syndrome Scale. Dr. Opler is presently developing and testing a new scale, the Symptoms of Trauma Scale, designed to measure change in symptom severity in persons being treated for trauma, including complex posttraumatic stress disorder.

Sandra C. Paivio, PhD, is Professor and Head of the Psychology Department at the University of Windsor in Canada. She has specialized in psychotherapy research, particularly research evaluating the efficacy and processes of change in emotion-focused therapy for complex trauma. Dr. Paivio is coauthor (with Leslie S. Greenberg) of the book *Working with Emotions in Psychotherapy* (1997) and author of the forthcoming book *Emotion-Focused Therapy for Complete Relational Trauma: An Integrative Approach*. She also is the author of numerous articles, conference presentations, and clinical workshops; has been extensively involved in clinical training of both graduate students and professionals; and maintains a part-time private practice. Most recently, her work has involved practice and training in emotion-focused therapy applied to refugee trauma.

Laurie Anne Pearlman, PhD, a consultant on psychological trauma, has published numerous articles and coauthored several books, including *Trauma and the Therapist* (1995). She speaks nationally and internationally on direct and vicarious psychological trauma. Dr. Pearlman serves as president of the Trauma Research, Education, and Training Institute; as senior psychological consultant to the Headington Institute; and on the practice committee of the American Psychological Association's Trauma Division and the Complex Trauma Task Force of the International Society for Traumatic Stress Studies. She has collaborated with Ervin Staub on peace building and trauma recovery in Rwanda since 1999. Dr. Pearlman has received awards for her clinical, scientific, and media contributions from the Connecticut Psychological Association, the International Society for Traumatic Stress Studies, and the American Psychological Association.

William Saltzman, PhD, a clinical psychologist, has been on staff with the UCLA Trauma Psychiatry Program since 1995. In that capacity, he has developed, implemented, and evaluated a series of domestic and international programs for children and families impacted by war; community violence, school shootings, and traumatic death; the World Trade Center attack; the aftermath of hurricanes in Florida and New Orleans; and wartime deployment (FOCUS Project). Dr. Saltzman is Professor of Counseling at California State University, Long Beach, where he is Director of the Master's Program for Marriage and Family Therapy. Since 2001, he has also been a staff member of the National Center for Child Traumatic Stress at UCLA, where he codirected the School Intervention Unit.

Mark F. Schwartz, ScD, is a licensed psychologist, Adjunct Professor in the departments of Psychiatry and Neurology at St. Louis University School of Medicine, and former Executive Director of the Masters and Johnson Institute and Inpatient Treatment Programs, nationally recognized for their innovative treatment with trauma survivors. Over the past 25 years, Dr. Schwartz has achieved national recognition for his contributions in a variety of clinical areas, including the treatment of intimacy disorders, marital and sexual dysfunction, sexual compulsivity, sexual trauma, and eating disorders. He lectures nationally on these topics and has authored numerous articles and book chapters. Dr. Schwartz is on the editorial board of the *Journal of Eating Disorders* and directs the Castlewood Treatment Center for Eating Disorders and Trauma, and the Relational and Sexual Therapy Program of Missouri.

Richard C. Schwartz, PhD, is president of the Center for Self Leadership in Oak Park, Illinois, and the developer of the internal family systems model. A former Associate Professor in the Department of Psychiatry at the University of Illinois at Chicago, he is author or coauthor of six books, including *Internal Family Systems Therapy* (1995).

Joseph Spinazzola, PhD, is the Executive Director of the Trauma Center at Justice Resource Institute in Brookline, Massachusetts, and a Research Associate in the Division of Psychiatry at Boston University School of Medicine. He oversees, with Bessel van der Kolk, the Trauma Center's Research Department and Community Treatment and Services site of the National Child Traumatic Stress Network. Dr. Spinazzola is the Co-Principal Investigator of a Centers for Disease Control and Prevention-funded randomized clinical trial of a trauma-informed, improvisational theater-based tertiary prevention program for urban youth exposed to relationship violence. He specializes in the assessment and treatment of complex adaptation to childhood trauma in adolescents and adults and has professional interests in the areas of forensic evaluation, identity development, and giftedness.

Kathy Steele, MN, CS, is in private practice and is Clinical Director of Metropolitan Counseling Services in Atlanta, Georgia. She is president of the International Society for the Study of Trauma and Dissociation. She is coauthor, with Onno van der Hart and Ellert Nijenhuis, of *The Haunted Self: Structural Dissociation of the Personality and Treatment of Chronic Traumatization* (2006).

Onno van der Hart, PhD, is Honorary Professor of Psychopathology of Chronic Traumatization at Utrecht University, Utrecht, The Netherlands, and a psychologist/ psychotherapist at the Sinai Mental Health Center, Amstelveen, The Netherlands. He is a past president of the International Society for Traumatic Stress Studies and coauthor, with Ellert Nijenhuis and Kathy Steele, of *The Haunted Self: Structural Dissociation and the Treatment of Chronic Traumatization* (2006).

Bessel A. van der Kolk, MD, is Medical Director of the Trauma Center in Brookline, Massachusetts; Professor of Psychiatry at Boston University School of Medicine; and Director of the National Child Traumatic Stress Network Community Program. He is past president of the International Society for Traumatic Stress Studies. Dr. van der Kolk has published extensively on the impact of trauma on development, the psychobiology of trauma, diagnostic issues, and treatment outcome.

He is currently funded by the National Institutes of Health to study the effects of yoga on posttraumatic stress disorder (PTSD), by the Centers of Disease Control and Prevention to investigate the use of theater groups in traumatized adolescents, and by private foundations to study the effects of neurofeedback and sensory integration on PTSD and dissociative disorders.

Foreword

Judith L. Herman

Sometimes the whole is greater than the sum of its parts.

The beauty of the complex posttraumatic stress disorder (PTSD) concept is in its integrative nature. Rather than a simple list of symptoms, it is a coherent formulation of the consequences of prolonged and repeated trauma. When I first proposed the concept (Herman, 1992a), it was an attempt to bring some kind of order to the bewildering array of clinical presentations in survivors who had endured long periods of abuse. The concept gained sufficient recognition that it was subjected to field trials in the fourth edition of the *Diagnostic and Statistical Manual of Mental Disorders* (DSM-IV; American Psychiatric Association, 1994). I was privileged to be part of the PTSD Working Group for DSM-IV, and so had a chance to participate in these studies.

The data seemed promising: my co-investigators and I found that somatization, dissociation, and affect dysregulation—three cardinal symptoms of complex PTSD—were found particularly in survivors of childhood abuse, less commonly in those abused in adolescence or adulthood, and rarely in people who had endured a single acute trauma that was not of human design. Moreover, these three groups of symptoms were highly intercorrelated (van der Kolk et al., 1996). We thought this demonstration of the prevalence and internal consistency of the diagnosis would constitute a strong argument for its inclusion in the DSM, and the PTSD Working Group agreed. Unfortunately, we were overruled at higher levels. The argument against inclusion of a separate diagnosis, as I understood it, went something like this: "We can't include complex PTSD as part of the trauma spectrum because it does not fit neatly under the category of anxiety disorders. It might fit equally well under dissociative disorders, or somatization disorders, or even personality disorders." This was, of course, exactly the point.

Though relegated to the "Associated Features" of PTSD in the DSM-IV (American Psychiatric Association, 1994), the concept of complex PTSD, nevertheless, took on a life of its own. I like to think that this was because it was congruent with a vast body of clinical observation and experience, and it helped clinicians make sense of what they were observing. It also helped patients make sense of themselves.

These days, when I teach about complex PTSD, I always begin with the social ecology of prolonged and repeated interpersonal trauma. There are two main points to grasp here. The first is that such trauma is always embedded in a social structure that permits the abuse and exploitation of a subordinate group (see Chapter 9). The predominance of women among patients who meet criteria for complex PTSD starts to make sense when one understands the insidious pervasiveness of violence against women and girls (Tjaden & Thoennes, 1998). The second point is that such trauma is always relational. It takes place when the victim is in a state of captivity, under the control and domination of the perpetrator.

Violence is but one among an array of methods that a perpetrator uses to establish domination over a victim. Others include using threats, control of bodily functions, capricious enforcement of petty rules, and random intermittent rewards; isolating the victim; and forcing the victim to engage in activities that are degrading or immoral. These methods break down normal capacities for self-regulation, autonomy, and initiative; they humiliate the victim and undermine the victim's closest relationships. These methods are cross-cultural and international; they are used because they work (Amnesty International, 1973). The symptoms later observed in survivors often make sense when one understands the methods of coercion to which they have been subjected.

If the victim is a child, and the perpetrator, as is most commonly the case, is a parent, a close family member, or a primary role model such as a teacher, coach, or religious leader, the absence of a protective parent or the presence of passive bystanders is felt as palpably as the presence of the perpetrator. Abuse is compounded by neglect, when others fail to notice or intervene. It seems increasingly clear that the pathological changes in relationship and identity seen in survivors reflect the disruptions in attachment that almost always attend childhood abuse (see Chapter 6). The "characterological" features of complex PTSD start to make sense if one imagines how a child might develop within a relational matrix in which the strong do as they please, the weak submit, caretakers seem willfully blind, and there is no one to turn to for protection.

What kind of "internal working models" (Bowlby, 1973) of self, other, and relationship would be likely to develop under such circumstances? This thought experiment turns out to be quite useful clinically. One begins to understand the survivor's malignant self-loathing, the deep mistrust of others, and the template for relational reenactments that the survivor carries into adult life. Forming a therapeutic alliance becomes somewhat easier if the clinician understands at the outset why the patient might be unable to imagine a relationship that is genuinely caring, freely chosen, fair to both parties, mutually attuned, and mutually rewarding. It becomes the therapist's task, then, to model, explain, and engage the patient in such a relationship, knowing that initially the patient will perceive this as another likely setup for betrayal.

The past decade has seen the flowering of clinical innovation in the psychotherapy field, with the development of many new evidence-informed treatment models addressing the core manifestations of complex PTSD. The wealth and diversity of therapeutic approaches are well represented in this comprehensive volume. Increasingly there are signs of cross-fertilization, with clinicians from different schools of thought and practices borrowing from one another. We are still in a period of experimentation; it is far too early to make any kind of judgment about which treatment approaches might be the most effective for which patients. Nevertheless, some constants seem to be emerging.

First, many authors cite the importance of recognizing areas of strength and resilience, even in the most severely traumatized individuals, as this will constitute the basis for forming a therapeutic alliance (Harvey & Tummala-Narra, 2007). One of the many advantages of group therapy for this population (see Chapter 20) is that group members are called upon to give supportive feedback to one another, and in the process discover that they have something of genuine value to give (Mendelsohn, Zachary, & Harney, 2007). Couple (Chapter 18) and family systems (Chapter 19) therapies also provide opportunities for survivors to discover or build healthy relationships and new working models for trust and security within their most immediate relationships.

Second, there does seem to be a consensus about the central importance of developing a trusting and truly collaborative, rather than authoritarian, treatment relationship. Most authors also recognize that forming such a relationship is particularly challenging because of the abuse survivor's capacity to engage the therapist in relational reenactments. The difficulties of maintaining a well-bounded therapeutic frame and the risks of vicarious traumatization are now well understood, as are the prescriptions for therapists' self-care and self-reflection (Chapters 8 and 10).

Beyond the notion of collaboration or mutuality, many authors invoke some concept of an observing therapeutic alliance, that is, a relationship within which the patient develops an "observing ego," or the capacity to "mentalize" (Fonagy, Gergely, Jurist, & Target, 2002). Examples in this volume are many. Experiential psychotherapy invokes a state of "metatherapeutic" processing of emotions and thoughts within a "dyadically regulated" relationship (Chapter 14). Contextual psychotherapy (Chapter 11) and sensorimotor psychotherapy (Chapter 15) invoke "mindfulness" as a central premise, and internal family systems therapy (Chapter 17) invokes an inner dialogue between various parts of the patient's personality and a curious, compassionate "self," allied with the therapist.

Finally, most current treatment approaches make use of a tripartite model of recovery stages (Herman, 1992b). The task of the first stage is to establish safety; the task of the second stage is to come to terms with the trauma story;

and, finally, that of the third stage is to repair and enlarge the survivor's social connections. This sequence has always seemed commonsensical to me, and apparently most of the authors in this volume have agreed.

Of course, these stages are not meant to be applied rigidly. In early recovery, for example, issues of safety and self-care always take priority, but this does not mean that the subject of trauma should be avoided. On the contrary, patients in early recovery often benefit greatly from trauma-informed treatment. Acknowledging the trauma and naming its consequences begin the process of meaning making. Survivors come to understand, often for the first time, that their symptoms make sense in the context of a formative relationship of coercive control. This understanding is a powerful antidote to the feelings of malignant shame and stigma that afflict so many survivors. What one does *not* do in early recovery is any form of "exposure" therapy. Coming to terms with the trauma story must await the development of some sort of secure base in the present from which the past can be safely approached.

These conceptual stages can be applied to group as well as individual psychotherapy. At the Victims of Violence Program (in the Department of Psychiatry at Cambridge Health Alliance), we have developed a wide array of time-limited groups, ranging from an "entry-level" Stage 1 group, the trauma information group, which has minimal screening requirements or demands for commitment, to a trauma-focused Stage 2 group, the trauma recovery group, which has careful screening requirements and demands a high level of commitment from group members. The former is a psychoeducational group with weekly topics and homework assignments similar to those described in this volume in the trauma recovery and empowerment model (Chapter 20). The latter is a goal-focused group in which trauma narratives are shared and empathic feedback is cultivated (Herman & Schatzow, 1984). Treatment manuals and reports of outcome data are in preparation.

On the horizon are studies that further refine the concept of complex PTSD in light of basic science findings from neurobiology and developmental psychology. The current state of the field is well summarized in Chapter 2. Also on the horizon, I hope, are even more cooperative ventures integrating different treatment models. In this regard, the congruence between features of complex PTSD and borderline personality disorder (BPD), first documented almost 20 years ago (Herman, Perry, & van der Kolk, 1989), may now have increasing importance from a practical standpoint, because of recent clinical advances in the treatment of BPD.

For example, in a remarkable 8-year follow-up study of a randomized controlled trial, Bateman and Fonagy (2008) demonstrated that a psychodynamic, "mentalization"-based treatment program was much more successful than treatment as usual for patients with BPD. Their model was both more intensive and of longer duration than most current manualized treatments for complex PTSD; it called for 18 months of intensive day treatment, followed by 18 months of biweekly group psychotherapy. I believe this study may ultimately define a new standard of care for BPD. It leads me to wonder about developing similarly intensive, multimodal treatment models for complex PTSD.

But that is for the future. In the meantime, it makes sense to pause and reflect on how far the field has come in less than two decades, and to represent the state of current knowledge in the field of complex traumatic disorders. This is the task that these editors and authors have set for themselves. This volume captures the intellectual excitement of a field in rapid development. Or perhaps, I should say, of multiple fields, intersecting in surprising and unforeseen ways. It also captures the spirit and passionate commitment of the many contributing authors, researchers, and clinicians who have devoted their professional lives to the project of survivors' recovery.

REFERENCES

American Psychiatric Association. (1994). *Diagnostic and statistical manual of mental disorders* (4th ed.). Washington, DC: Author.

Amnesty International. (1973). *Report on torture.* New York: Farrar, Straus & Giroux.

Bateman, A., & Fonagy, P. (2008). Eight-year follow up of patients treated for borderline personality disorder: Mentalization-based treatment vs. treatment as usual. *American Journal of Psychiatry, 165,* 631–638.

Bowlby, J. (1973). *Attachment and loss: Vol. 2. Separation: Anxiety and anger.* New York: Basic Books.

Fonagy, P., Gergely, G., Jurist, E. L., & Target, M. (2002). *Affect regulation, mentalization, and the development of the self.* New York: Other Press.

Harvey, M. R., & Tummala-Narra, P. (Eds.). (2007). *Sources and expressions of resilience in trauma survivors: Ecological theory, multicultural practice.* New York: Haworth Press.

Herman, J. L. (1992a). Complex PTSD: A syndrome in survivors of prolonged and repeated trauma. *Journal of Traumatic Stress, 5,* 377–391.

Herman, J. L. (1992b). *Trauma and recovery.* New York: Basic Books.

Herman, J. L., & Schatzow, E. (1984). Time-limited group therapy for women with a history of incest. *International Journal of Group Psychotherapy 34,* 605–616.

Herman, J. L., Perry, J. C., & van der Kolk, B. A. (1989). Childhood trauma in borderline personality disorder. *American Journal of Psychiatry, 146,* 490–495.

Mendelsohn, M., Zachary, R., & Harney, P., (2007). Group therapy as an ecological bridge to new community for trauma survivors. In M. R. Harvey & P. Tummala-Narra (Eds.), *Sources and expressions of resilience in trauma survivors: Ecological theory, multicultural practice* (pp. 227–244). New York: Haworth Press.

Tjaden, P., & Thoennes, N. (1998). *Prevalence, incidence, and consequences of violence against women: Findings from the National Violence against Women Survey.* Research in Brief. Washington, DC: U. S. Department of Justice.

van der Kolk, B. A., Pelcovitz, D., Roth, S., Mandel, F., McFarlane, A., & Herman, J. L. (1996). Dissociation, affect dysregulation and somatization: The complexity of adaptation to trauma. *American Journal of Psychiatry, 153*(Festschrift Suppl.), 83–93.

Acknowledgments

We are most grateful to many colleagues—too many, unfortunately, to mention all by name. We are deeply appreciative of the insights and expertise contributed to this book by each of the chapter authors, whose enthusiasm and tolerance of our timelines and editing were heroic. We especially thank the comembers of the International Society for Traumatic Stress Studies Complex Trauma Task Force for their guidance and support: Pam Alexander, John Briere, Marylene Cloitre, Laurie Pearlman, Onno van der Hart, and Bessel van der Kolk, along with Bonnie Green who impaneled this group during her presidential year.

We and our field owe a special debt of gratitude to Judy Herman, a true pioneer in this area. And we sincerely thank, for their dedicated work in advancing the science and treatment of complex traumatic stress disorders, the leadership and members of the International Society for the Study of Trauma and Dissociation, the International Society for Traumatic Stress Studies, Division 56 (Psychological Trauma) of the American Psychological Association, and the National Child Traumatic Stress Network.

We also wish to acknowledge the ongoing support from our respective family and friends. They have provided each of us with countless gifts of wisdom, patience, and encouragement that have helped to make this book possible and that have added immeasurable meaning to our lives.

Contents

Introduction

Christine A. Courtois
Julian D. Ford

This book provides a practical framework and a variety of evidence-based approaches for the conceptualization, assessment, and psychotherapeutic and psychopharmacological treatment of complex traumatic stress disorders. It is intended primarily for clinicians within the mental health and behavioral health professions who evaluate and treat traumatized children and adults, and for clinical researchers and graduate-level trainees in those professions (e.g., psychology, psychiatry, counseling, social work, marriage and family therapy, addiction treatment). However, it is also applicable to medical practitioners, attorneys, police, and other forensic and criminal justice personnel who work directly with trauma survivors or consult with and refer to mental health colleagues who treat psychological trauma.

In this book, we address a special subpopulation of survivors of psychological trauma, namely, those whose traumatic experiences were compounded in a number of significant ways, many of which "add insult to injury" and cause a more compounded response. We define *complex psychological trauma* as involving traumatic stressors that (1) are repetitive or prolonged; (2) involve direct harm and/or neglect and abandonment by caregivers or ostensibly responsible adults; (3) occur at developmentally vulnerable times in the victim's life, such as early childhood; and (4) have great potential to compromise severely a child's development. The sequelae of such exposure are equally complex and include states, features, conditions, and phenomenology, including severe problems with emotion dysregulation, dissociation, somatic distress, and identity and relational disturbance and spiritual alienation. Although some of these may not be severe enough to meet formal criteria for a psychological disorder,

1

we nevertheless refer to them here in aggregate form as *complex traumatic stress disorders.*

Traumatization of this type is extreme due to its nature and timing: In addition to often being life-threatening or physically and sexually assaultive and violating, emotionally terrifying or horrifying, and psychologically, physiologically, and somatically overstimulating and dysregulating, it is typically chronic rather than one-time or limited, occurs over the course of childhood development, and has high potential to compromise the child's maturation, self/personality development (including positive self-worth), and basic trust in primary relationships. Complex traumatic stress disorders therefore go well beyond what is defined as the classic clinically significant definition of what is traumatic (Criterion A) and beyond the triad of criteria (intrusive reexperiencing of traumatic memories, avoidance of reminders of traumatic memories and emotional numbing, and hyperarousal in Criteria B–D) that make up the diagnosis of posttraumatic stress disorder (PTSD) in the text revision of the fourth edition of the *Diagnostic and Statistical Manual of Mental Disorders* (DSM-IV-TR; American Psychiatric Association, 2000). Complex traumatic stress disorders also routinely include a combination of other DSM-IV-TR Axis I and Axis II (personality) disorders and symptoms, Axis III physical health problems, and severe Axis V psychosocial impairments. Core problems in need of treatment include affect dysregulation, structural dissociation, somatic dysregulation, impaired self-concept and self-development, and disorganized attachment patterns, *in addition to* symptoms of PTSD and any other associated conditions and comorbidities.

As a result, complex traumatic stress disorders tend to be difficult to diagnose accurately and to treat effectively. This book provides practicing clinicians and clinical researchers with an overview and contemporary practice guidelines and protocols for conceptualizing, assessing, and treating these traumatic aftereffects and their developmental elaborations and complications. It presents current approaches to the conceptualization, assessment, psychotherapy, and pharmacotherapy for complex traumatic stress disorders. As research and clinical knowledge bases relevant to the treatment of clients with complex trauma histories continue to evolve, we expect that the exact features that characterize complex traumatic stress disorders and the relevant assessment and treatment protocols will change in response to them. However, issues identified here are likely to remain those that clinicians will continue to encounter and treat in these individuals, regardless of the specific diagnoses or assessment and treatment methodologies they use. Thus, the approaches to conceptualizing, assessing, and treating clients with complex trauma histories, and the guidelines for professional practice management and self-care presented in this book can provide a lasting foundation on which clinicians and researchers may build new discoveries well into the future.

Throughout the book, real-life composite case examples are provided to illustrate the treatment of complex traumatic stress disorders. We begin with two such cases.

Case A: Charles

This 47-year-old man of mixed racial background (African–Caribbean American) grew up in a Midwestern city, the son of working-class parents whose own parents had immigrated to the United States. Charles's parents had recurrent violent episodes organized around conflict regarding his father's heroin use and his mother's devout Catholicism. These began well before Charles was born (and had occurred as long as his older brother and sister could recall), and all the siblings, including Charles, had repeatedly witnessed and tried to intervene on their mother's behalf. They all learned painfully that intervening did nothing but increase their father's brutality, which was then directed at them, as well as their mother. Stress in the family also escalated periodically when Charles's father began, without notice or concern for their welfare, to leave the family for weeks and then months at a time, absences that began when Charles was quite young. From early on, Charles's mother took solace in him, frequently pouring out her heart to him and relying on him as her "savior" and "main man" when he would do things to take care of her. Charles became a particular target of his father's anger whenever he returned to the home, in part due to his mother's reliance on and special relationship with him. This often resulted in beatings of Charles and his siblings that his father blamed on him. In adolescence, Charles's mother continued to favor him and began to sexualize their relationship, causing him great anguish and confusion, especially when he became sexually aroused by their encounters.

Despite all, Charles was able to do well enough in school and athletics to escape the home periodically as an adolescent and to leave permanently when he joined the military at age 17. However, he had persistent nightmares and episodes of rage that led to his medical discharge from the military and to difficulty maintaining friendships and developing a satisfying and mutual intimate relationship. He has worked for 25 years in a skilled manufacturing job, and was referred for treatment by the company Employee Assistance Program (EAP) because of conflict with a work supervisor. Charles expresses distress and great difficulty being around this female supervisor, whom he describes as "controlling, critical, and demanding" to such an extent that he can hardly contain feelings of rage that have built up over a 2-year period. Always a punctual and hardworking employee prior to this period, Charles has been increasingly inconsistent about attendance and has been making errors that he attributes to "feeling sick, headaches and stomachaches all the time" and to "spacing out, like I'm just not there" while at work. His drinking, normally moderate, has increased at an alarming rate, making him terrified that he will be "just like his old man." His distress and desperation are palpable, and he feels he has no one who understands or can help him. He is thinking of a "geographic cure" that would involve leaving the security of his job and potentially putting his hard-earned retirement at risk.

Case B: Tina

This 31-year-old Japanese American woman has been hospitalized two times in the past 6 months for depression and suicidality, complicated by bursts of energy consistent with Type II manic–depressive illness and hearing voices telling her to kill herself. She is a successful attorney with 5 years' experience in a large firm specializing in family law, and has been married for 8 years to a journalist. The couple has two children, a 7-year-old boy and a 2-year-old girl. Tina grew up in an intact, upper middle socioeconomic status (SES) family that she describes as healthy and loving, with two older brothers to whom she feels close. Tina was a star student and athlete, devoted to gymnastics until she had a serious accident at a meet. During her recovery, she revealed that her coach had been sexually molesting her since she was 6 years old. Her parents filed charges, and the coach was fired and sentenced to probation after a very public trial in which Tina testified against him—unfortunately, other girls on the team accused her of "making up the story" and, in turn, they and their parents ostracized Tina and her parents. Tina views these events as catalysts for becoming an attorney and for her chosen area of specialization. Apart from several months of family therapy at the time of the trial and brief experimentation with marijuana as a teenager, she denied having any treatment or psychiatric history or potentially problematic substance use until she experienced postpartum depression following her daughter's birth. In the intervening 2 years, Tina has experienced escalating symptoms of dysphoria, culminating in the severe recent affective and potentially psychotic symptoms and suicidality, as well as medically unexplained severe exhaustion and blackouts, in which Tina's husband describes her as markedly different. She has also returned to the use of marijuana to cope and to keep her calm.

Commentary: Although different in many ways, these two people are alike in ways that are consistent with a complex traumatic stress disorder formulation. Each experienced traumatic betrayal in childhood by adults who should have been trustworthy. Charles's father's heroin addiction set the stage for physical and emotional abuse and domestic violence, as well as incest, and left Charles neglected and unattended by his most significant male role model, and used and abused by his most significant female role model. Tina's abuse by her coach was different, in that it was premeditated, intentional, and involved "grooming" (false acts of apparent kindness and encouragement) to entrap her as a victim and to keep her silent. Although some adults were supportive when the traumas occurred, both individuals were unprotected/neglected/blamed and psychologically overburdened by caregivers: Charles, by his mother, who alternately parentified/sexualized him or failed to intervene with his abusive and neglectful father; and Tina, by parents who were unaware of the molestation and mistakenly (albeit understandably) trusted the coach. As a result, Charles and Tina developed neither a consistently secure working model of caring relationships nor a positive identity or self-trust, although Tina appears to have had a foundation of more secure attachment with her parents in her earliest childhood (prior to the abuse) that Charles may never have had. Tina's parents in fact showed her in many ways that they genuinely loved and believed in her, but tragically made the mistake of trusting an apparently upstanding adult rather than their child. In contrast, Charles struggled with the dilemma of wanting to love his parents despite their extremely limited ability to love and care for him. As a result, Charles finds his mother "hard to take in more than small doses; she's so in my face and needy all the time," and rather than feeling secure in his relationship with his parents, he instead wishes he could have had a "normal" mother and an attentive, involved father.

Consistent with these traumatic disruptions in their lives and their self- and relational development, Charles and Tina are experiencing significant problems with emotion regulation (e.g., Charles's feelings of suspiciousness and rage; Tina's dysphoria and hypomania), dissociation (e.g., Charles's "spacing out" and extreme shifts in ego state; Tina's blackouts and mood changes), somatization (e.g., Charles's headaches/stomachaches; Tina's exhaustion/fatigue), and the use of substances to cope with/suppress overwhelming emotions. Both have been triggered by different but seemingly innocuous or even happy life events (i.e., Charles's upset at work with his female supervisor, and the birth of Tina's daughter). These problems escalated, and posttraumatic and other symptoms emerged in delayed fashion in response to these changes in each of their interpersonal constellations. They grew from no discernable impairment to life-threatening (and possibly marriage, childrearing, and career-damaging) symptoms for Tina, and from chronic low-level social isolation to potentially harmful (vocationally and legally) reactive aggression for Charles. Both individuals view themselves as damaged and view significant relationships as betrayals, abandonment, or frankly abusive. Both feel detached from not only people but also spiritual help or guidance. They view primary relationships as chronically empty or inadequate (for Charles), or as irreparably conflicted and unstable (for both Charles and Tina). Additionally, Tina is fearful about having a daughter and worries about whether she will be able to keep her daughter safe from abuse such as she suffered. She now worries about whether her daughter is safe with her husband, something she never worried about with her son. Many of these and other features characterize complex traumatic stress disorders, and although they may not appear with as much clarity or intensity in every case as in these composite examples, they are familiar to most clinicians who treat this population.

Although numerous assessment and treatment protocols have been developed that a clinician might draw upon in working with Charles or Tina, the range and complexity of the difficulties they experience present several daunting challenges. Pharmacotherapy or intensive placements (e.g., inpatient, day treatment, or intensive outpatient admissions) might help them to stabilize and to come safely through periods of crisis, as well as prepare them for ongoing psychotherapy. However, patients such as Charles or Tina often become caught in a "revolving door" scenario, in which repeated trials of different medications and psychiatric placements lead to only transient stabilization and are followed by further (often escalating) crises or declines in functioning. If less restrictive approaches (e.g., weekly individual and group outpatient psychotherapy) are used, progress tends to be very gradual and often limited by apparent impasses (e.g., never seeming able to "get on with life" and cope autonomously with waves or peaks and troughs of anxiety or dysphoria) that often deteriorate into new crises. If focal therapeutic interventions such as cognitive restructuring, anxiety management skills training, or exposure therapy for traumatic memories are attempted, the patient may become overwhelmed and go into crisis, or shut down and seem unable to engage in the process without avoidance, dissociation, or simply giving up.

The critical problem is that even the best-validated evidence-based psychiatric and psychotherapeutic interventions for anxiety disorders (including PTSD) and affective disorders—as well as for their common comorbidities, such as substance use and eating, personality, behavioral (e.g., anger or attention-deficit/hyperactivity disorder), and relational disorders—often seem either ineffective or potentially iatrogenic. Or the patient simply never seems "ready" to engage in, cope with, and benefit from these treatments. This book does *not* take the position that extant evidence-based psychiatric and psychotherapeutic assessments and interventions are simply inappropriate for patients with complex trauma histories and complex traumatic stress disorders. Instead, the editors and authors present an array of approaches to clinical assessment and treatment that includes carefully designed adaptations of familiar evidence-based protocols and, in addition, a number of novel assessment tools and therapeutic models developed specifically to address the complexities of severe posttraumatic impairment in children and adults. Readers can draw from this wide selection of methods and models the specific tools and approaches that best suit their own clinical style and the needs of each unique patient.

OVERVIEW OF THE BOOK

This book addresses in three sections the clinical challenges that arise in treating complex trauma survivors like Charles or Tina. Each chapter identifies conceptual and clinical challenges, and provides either a clinical framework (Part I) or specific assessment or treatment models (Parts II and III) to address the identified challenges.

Part I provides an overview based on *available evidence-based practice recommendations* (American Psychological Association, 2006) for complex traumatic stress disorders and their assessment and treatment. Chapter 1 (Ford & Courtois) provides an expanded definition and description of complex traumatic stress disorders and specifically differentiates the traumatic stressor from posttraumatic responses. It further discusses ways of conceptualizing complex trauma disorders as distinct from other types of posttraumatic disorders. Chapter 2 (Ford) reviews preclinical and clinical research studies that are relevant to therapists' understanding of complex trauma and its adverse effects on neurodevelopment, attachment, emotion regulation, and information processing. Chapter 3 (Ford & Cloitre) provides an overview of practice principles and treatment modalities for psychotherapy of children and adolescents, building on recent research and publications by the Complex Trauma Workgroup of the National Child Traumatic Stress Network (NCTSN) (Cook et al., 2005; *www.nctsnet.org*). Chapter 4 (Courtois, Ford, & Cloitre) provides a parallel best practice guide for treating the effects of complex traumatic stress disorders in adults, building on the work of the Complex Trauma Task Force of the International Society for Traumatic Stress Studies (ISTSS) (Ford, Courtois, van der Hart, Nijenhuis, & Steele, 2005; van der Kolk & Courtois, 2005) and its individual members (Alexander, 1993; Briere, 2004; Cloitre, Cohen, & Koenen, 2006; Courtois, 1999; Ford, 2005; Pearlman & Saakvitne, 1995; van der Hart, Neijenhuis, & Steele, 2006; van der Kolk, 2002).

Chapter 5 (Briere & Spinazzola) provides a clinical strategy for selecting and deploying evidence-based assessment instruments with children, adolescents, and adults with complex trauma-related symptoms and impairments. It includes discussion of the special challenges of assessing traumatized individuals and suggests strategies and conditions for conducting the assessment. Chapter 6 (D. Brown) elaborates on the challenges involved in the assessment of complex traumatic stress disorders, describing a theory-driven strategy for multi-instrument assessment of attachment style, complex trauma history, and resultant complex traumatic stress symptoms and impairments.

Chapter 7 (Steele & van der Hart) offers a different perspective, that of structural dissociation, describing it as a core dimension of complex traumatic stress disorders and further discussing approaches to treatment that are applied within a sequenced hierarchy. Chapter 8 (L. Brown) provides a cultural competence model that clinicians may apply to individualize their approach to assessment and treatment of complex traumatic stress disorders in ways that develop and sustain a working alliance with clients of each gender and different ethnocultural, socioeconomic, geographic, and other backgrounds. Chapter 9 (Kinsler, Courtois, & Frankel) shifts the focus to the experience of the dyadic relationship between client and therapist, and provides an overview and guidance for dealing with the relational and professional practice challenges and risks involved in the treatment of clients with complex traumatic stress disorders. Chapter 10 (Pearlman & Caringi) expands the focus on the clinician, examining the nature of vicarious traumatization in relation to clients with complex traumatic stress disorders and proactive approaches to self-care.

Part II describes seven specialized treatment approaches for adults with complex traumatic stress disorders. (Therapeutic models for the treatment of children and adolescents with complex traumatic stress disorders are in an early stage of development; therefore, they are not described beyond the overview provided by Ford & Cloitre in Chapter 3.) In each chapter in Part II, the authors follow a prescribed format that introduces their method, including its clinical rationale, theoretical foundation, and available evidence base; describes key practical clinical features of the method as applied to the treatment of complex traumatic stress disorders; provides a simulated transcript of treatment interspersed with commentary on the method to explain the clinical tactics along with their application; and summarizes key clinical parameters for the specific model of treatment for complex traumatic stress disorders.

Chapter 11 (Gold) describes *contextual therapy*, created by the author to address the developmental and attachment/relational deficits resulting from pervasive abuse and family dysfunction. Chapter 12 (Jackson, Nissenson, & Cloitre) describes three models of *contextual behavior trauma therapy*, including acceptance and commitment therapy, dialectical behavior therapy, and functional analytic psychotherapy. Chapter 13 (Follette, Iverson, & Ford) describes *cognitive-behavioral therapy* models that have been shown to be efficacious or promising for the treatment of the affect and interpersonal dysregulation that routinely characterizes complex traumatic stress disorders. Chapter 14 (Fosha, Paivio, Gleiser, & Ford) describes two *experiential and emotion-focused psychotherapy* models for the treatment of complex traumatic stress disorders, accelerated experiential–dynamic psychotherapy and emotion-focused treatment for trauma. Chapter 15 (Fisher & Ogden) describes *sensorimotor psychotherapy*, a treatment that focuses on the physiological, sensory, and nonverbal behavior changes associated with complex traumatic stress disorders, and that utilizes body awareness–based interventions. Chapter 16 (Opler, Grennan, & Ford) provides an overview of pharmacotherapy options for the treatment of PTSD and complex traumatic stress disorders, and discusses the necessity for a working alliance between psychopharmacologist and client, and including the treating therapist.

Part III addresses systemic and group approaches to psychotherapy for complex traumatic stress disorders. As in Part II, chapters are structured around an introduction to the method and its rationale, description of clinical features and techniques, a review of its empirical substantiation, and application to a clinical case study. Chapter 17 (Schwartz, Schwartz, & Galperin) describes a systems-based, one-to-one psychotherapy for complex traumatic stress disorders that addresses structural dissociation (see Steele & van der Hart, Chapter 7), the *internal family systems* model. Chapter 18 (Johnson & Courtois) describes *emotionally focused therapy* for couples, an experiential, attachment-based approach to couple therapy in which one or both partners have complex traumatic stress disorders. Chapter 19 (Ford & Saltzman) describes two *family systems therapy* approaches to the treatment of complex traumatic stress disorders, including an adaptation of Trauma Affect Regulation: Guidelines for Education and Therapy (TARGET) and Families Overcoming and Coping Under Stress (FOCUS). *Group therapy* approaches to complex traumatic stress disorders, presented in Chapter 20 (Ford, Fallot, & Harris), focus on the Trauma Recovery and Empowerment Model (TREM) for adult survivors of complex trauma with comorbid severe and chronic mental illness.

REFERENCES

Alexander, P. C. (1993). The differential effects of abuse characteristics and attachment in the prediction of the long-term effects of sexual abuse. *Journal of Interpersonal Violence, 8*, 346–362.

American Psychiatric Association. (2000). *Diagnostic and statistical manual of mental disorders* (4th ed., text rev.). Washington, DC: Author.

American Psychological Association. (2006). *American Psychological Association Presidential Task Force on Evidence-Based Practice.* Washington, DC: Author.

Briere, J. (2004). *Psychological assessment of adult posttraumatic states: Phenomenology, diagnosis, and measurement* (2nd ed.). Washington, DC: American Psychological Association.

Cloitre, M. C., Cohen, L. R., & Koenen, K. C. (2006). *Treating survivors of childhood abuse: Psychotherapy for the interrupted life.* New York: Guilford Press.

Cook, A., Spinazzola, J., Ford, J. D., Lanktree, C., Blaustein, M., Cloitre, M., et al. (2005). Complex trauma in children and adolescents. *Psychiatric Annals, 35,* 390–398.

Courtois, C. A. (1999). *Recollections of sexual abuse: Treatment principles and guidelines.* New York: Norton.

Ford, J. D. (2005). Treatment implications of altered neurobiology, affect regulation and information processing following child maltreatment. *Psychiatric Annals, 35,* 410–419.

Ford, J. D., Courtois, C. A., van der Hart, O., Nijenhuis, E., & Steele, K. (2005). Treatment of complex post-traumatic self-dysregulation. *Journal of Traumatic Stress, 18,* 437–447.

Pearlman, L. A., & Saakvitne, K. W. (1995). *Trauma and the therapist: Countertransference and vicarious traumatization in psychotherapy with incest survivors.* New York: Norton.

van der Hart, O., Nijenhuis, E. R. S., & Steele, K. (2006). *The haunted self: Structural dissociation and the treatment of chronic traumatization.* New York: Norton.

van der Kolk, B. A. (2002). Assessment and treatment of complex PTSD. In R. Yehuda (Ed.), *Treating trauma survivors with PTSD* (pp. 127–156). Washington, DC: American Psychiatric Association Press.

van der Kolk, B. A., & Courtois, C. A. (2005). Editorial: Complex developmental trauma. *Journal of Traumatic Stress, 18*(5), 385–388.

PART I

OVERVIEW

The chapters that make up this section provide an overview of complex trauma and conceptualizations, assessment, and treatment of complex traumatic stress disorders. Chapter 1 defines complex trauma and describes different approaches to characterizing complex traumatic stress disorders. Recent findings regarding the neurobiological and developmental substrates of complex trauma and complex traumatic stress disorders are introduced in Chapter 2. The following two chapters introduce evidence-based best practices for the treatment of complex traumatic stress disorders in children and adolescents (Chapter 3), and in adults (Chapter 4). Chapter 5 provides an overview of evidence-based assessment methods and strategies for clinicians working with complex trauma survivors, and Chapter 6 describes a unique case series illustrating the utility of an attachment framework for the understanding and assessment of the sequelae of complex trauma. The issues involved in assessing and treating dissociative aspects of complex traumatic stress disorders are discussed in Chapter 7. Guidelines for approaching complex trauma survivors in a culturally competent manner, developing a working alliance and managing clinical and professional risks, and addressing vicarious trauma with professional self-care are provided, respectively, in Chapters 8–10 in Part I. These call for increased awareness and sensitivity on the part of the therapist to the relationship and the process of treatment, as well as the specific content of each session. The therapist must also attend to issues of professional capacity and self-care in the course of this treatment. There is a clear ethical imperative (as well as a risk management justification) for the therapist to remain attentive to his or her own values, biases, and mental health to conduct the treatment with sensitivity, respect, and an ongoing capacity to offer the client a secure and well-bounded connection.

CHAPTER 1

Defining and Understanding Complex Trauma and Complex Traumatic Stress Disorders

Julian D. Ford
Christine A. Courtois

As the research and clinical knowledge base relevant to the treatment of clients with complex trauma histories continues to evolve, we expect that the exact features characterizing complex traumatic stress disorders and the relevant assessment and treatment protocols also will change dynamically. However, the core problems of affect dysregulation, structural dissociation, somatic dysregulation, impaired self-development, and disorganized attachment patterns are likely to remain the foundation for clinicians working with survivors of complex trauma, regardless of the specific diagnoses or assessment and treatment methodologies in use. Thus, the approaches to conceptualizing, assessing, and treating clients with complex trauma histories, and the guidelines for professional practice management and self-care presented in this book can provide a lasting foundation for clinicians and researchers well into the future.

We define *complex psychological trauma* as resulting from exposure to severe stressors that (1) are repetitive or prolonged, (2) involve harm or abandonment by caregivers or other ostensibly responsible adults, and (3) occur at developmentally vulnerable times in the victim's life, such as early childhood or adolescence (when critical periods of brain development are rapidly occurring or being consolidated; see Ford, Chapter 2, this volume). *Complex posttraumatic sequelae* are the changes in mind, emotions, body, and relationships experienced following complex psychological trauma, including severe problems with dissociation, emotion dysregulation, somatic distress, or relational or spiritual alienation, hereafter referred to as *complex traumatic stress disorders*.

Complex psychological trauma represents extreme forms of traumatic stressors due to their nature and timing: In addition to often being life-threatening or physically violating, terrifying, or horrifying, these experiences are typically chronic rather than one-time or limited, and they compromise the individual's personality development and basic trust in primary relationships. Therefore, complex traumatic stress disorders go well beyond the classic clinical definition of what is traumatic, and beyond the triad of criteria (intrusive reexperiencing of traumatic memories, avoidance of reminders of traumatic memories and emotional numbing, and hyperarousal) that make up the diagnosis of posttraumatic stress disorder (PTSD) in the text revision of the fourth edition of the *Diagnostic and Statistical Manual of Mental Disorders* (DSM-IV-TR; American Psychiatric Association, 2000). Complex traumatic stress disorders often include a combination of other DSM-IV-TR Axis I and Axis II (personality) disorders and symptoms, Axis III physical health problems, and severe Axis V psychosocial impairments. As a result of the complex traumatic antecedents, and the traumatic stress symptoms and impairments that are involved, complex traumatic stress disorders tend to be difficult to diagnose accurately and treat effectively.

DEFINING COMPLEX TRAUMA

The word *trauma* has multiple meanings, referring alternatively to medical/physical injury or psychological injury, as well as to the events that cause this injury. Physical and psychological trauma often co-occur, but we follow the tradition of the field of traumatic stress in focusing on the latter, psychological trauma. Of note, it is often difficult to find a clear definition of psychological trauma, even in books on the topic. According to Weathers and Keane (2007):

> Achieving a consensus definition of trauma is essential for progress in the field of traumatic stress. However, creating an all-purpose, general definition has proven remarkably difficult. Stressors vary along a number of dimensions, including magnitude (which itself varies on a·number of dimensions, e.g., life threat, threat of harm, interpersonal loss ...), complexity, frequency, duration, predictability, and controllability. At the extremes, i.e., catastrophes versus minor hassles, different stressors may seem discrete and qualitatively distinct, but there is a continuum of stressor severity and there are no crisp boundaries demarcating ordinary stressors from traumatic stressors. Further, perception of an event as stressful depends on subjective appraisal, making it difficult to define stressors objectively, and independent of personal meaning making. (p. 108)

The English word *trauma* originates from the ancient Greek word for "injury" or "wound." It originally "connotes a physical injury and parallels the psychic wounding that can potentially follow a traumatic episode" (Dass-Brailsford, 2007, p. 3). *Trauma* is often used interchangeably (and confusingly) to refer to (1) the *traumatic stressor event(s)* including *the individual's experience during exposure to the stressor(s)*, or (2) the individual's *response*, whether *peritraumatic* (occurring during *or in the immediate aftermath of* the experience) or *posttraumatic* (occurring weeks, months, or years afterwards) (McFarlane & de Girolamo, 1996; Weathers & Keane, 2007). We refer to the stressor event(s) as *psychological or psychic trauma*, the *traumatic stressor*, or *complex trauma*, and to the response or aftermath as *posttraumatic reactions and disorders* or *complex traumatic stress disorders*.

Psychological trauma was originally considered to be an abnormal experience (i.e., "outside the range of normal human experience" in DSM-III (American Psychological Association, 1980), but as epidemiological evidence accumulated to demonstrate that a majority of adults (e.g., Kessler, Sonnega, Bromet, Hughes, & Nelson, 1995) and a substantial minority of children (e.g., Costello, Erklani, Fairbank, & Angold, 2002) are exposed to traumatic events, there has been a shift to defining psychological trauma without any qualifications about its normality or abnormality. Generally, people who have not experienced traumatic events do not expect trauma to occur in their (or their families' or communities') lives, but once psychological trauma has occurred, he or she is both more likely *objectively* to experience subsequent traumatic events and more prone *subjectively* to expect trauma to be a possibility. With the increasing diffusion of virtually instantaneous information through the many forms of electronic and other media—not only in Westernized societies but also in socioeconomically underdeveloped countries—people's awareness of traumatic events has been greatly heightened, even if these events never happen to them or to anyone they know personally (e.g., the Silver, Holman, McIntosh, Pulin, & Gil-Rivas [2002] national U.S. survey on the effects of the September 11, 2001, terrorist incidents).

Traumatic events take many forms. Terr (1991) distinguished between "Type I" single-incident trauma (e.g., an event that is "out of the blue" and thus unexpected, such as a traumatic accident or a natural disaster, a terrorist attack, a single episode of abuse or assault, witnessing violence) and "Type II" complex or repetitive trauma (e.g., ongoing abuse, domestic violence, community violence, war, or genocide). Type II trauma is more prevalent than typically recognized (i.e., affecting as many as 1 in 7 to 1 in 10 children), more often occurs in combination or cumulatively (i.e., "polyvictimization"; Finkelhor, Ormrod, & Turner, 2007), and usually involves a fundamental betrayal of trust in primary relationships, because it is often perpetrated by someone known by or related to the victim. Complex or Type II trauma not only is associated with a much higher risk for the development of PTSD than is Type I trauma (e.g., 33–75+% risk vs. 10–20% risk, respectively; Copeland, Keeler, Angold, & Costello, 2007; Kessler et al., 1995) but it also may compromise or alter a person's psychobiological and socioemotional development when it occurs at critical developmental periods. Such "developmentally adverse interpersonal traumas" (Ford, 2005) are "complex" because they place the person at risk for not only recurrent anxiety (e.g., PTSD; other anxiety disorders) but also interruptions and breakdowns in the most fundamental outcomes of healthy psychobiological development: the integrity of the body; the development of a healthy identity and a coherent personality; and secure attachment, leading to the ability to have healthy and reciprocal relationships (Cook et al., 2005; van der Kolk, 2005).

Therefore, complex trauma is a subset of the full range of psychological trauma that has as its unique trademark a compromise of the individual's self-development. The timing of its occurrence—in critical windows of development during childhood, when self-definition and self-regulation are being formed and consolidated—and its very nature—the disruption or distortion of fundamental attachment security due to betrayal of the developing child's security and trust in core relationships—distinguish complex trauma from all other forms of psychological trauma. Thus, complex trauma involves not only the shock of fear but also, more fundamentally, a violation of and challenge to the fragile, immature, and newly emerging self. Complex trauma often leaves the child unable to self-regulate (i.e., to control his or her feelings, cognitions, beliefs, intentions, and actions), to achieve a sense of self-integrity (i.e., the feeling and belief that one is a unique, whole, coherent, and worthy individual), or to experience relationships as nurturing and reliable resources that support self-regulation and self-integrity.

As a result of compromising self-regulation, self-integrity, and attachment security, complex trauma constitutes objective threats not only to physical survival—but also to the development and survival of the self. The nature of the objective threat involved in complex traumas often encompasses features that go beyond obvious instances of a threat of death or violation of bodily integrity as currently defined in Criterion A1 of the PTSD diagnosis in the DSM-IV-TR (American Psychiatric Association, 2000). For example, emotional abuse by an adult caregiver that involves systematic attacks upon the psychological integrity and the very selfhood of a child may not be immediately life threatening and may involve no violent or sexual violations of the child's bodily integrity, but it may nevertheless lead to the long-standing severe problems with self-regulation that are associated with psychobiological stress dysregulation and reactivity (Teicher, Samson, Polcari, & McGreenery, 2006). Thus, the threat to self-integrity posed by developmentally adverse interpersonal stressors, particularly when interwoven into a developing child's primary family/caregiver relationships, may induce both long-term biological and psychosocial stress reactivity even in the absence of life threat or violation of bodily integrity (Ford, 2005). Consistent with these findings, a proposed *developmental trauma disorder* (DTD; van der Kolk, 2005) requires exposure to "developmentally adverse interpersonal trauma" (e.g., abuse, betrayal, abandonment, threats to bodily integrity) as its objective (A1) criterion.

Similarly, in complex trauma, the individual's subjective reactions during stressful experiences extend beyond those that define psychological trauma in

DSM-IV-TR PTSD Criterion A2 (i.e., extreme fear, helplessness, or horror). Complex PTSD (Herman, 1992) or disorders of extreme stress not otherwise specified (DESNOS; van der Kolk, Roth, Pelcovitz, Sunday, & Spinazzola, 2005) were proposed for DSM-IV. Although ultimately included as associated features of PTSD, DESNOS was empirically shown to be related to exposure to interpersonal psychological trauma in childhood (van der Kolk et al., 2005). The proposed DTD diagnosis for children with complex traumatic stress symptoms is even more specific in identifying "rage, betrayal, fear, resignation, defeat, and shame" as the subjective (A2) criterion for childhood complex traumatic stress disorders (van der Kolk, 2005, p. 405).

This description of the subjective components of complex trauma offers a more nuanced and phenomenologically specific elucidation of the global descriptors provided for Criterion A2 in traditional PTSD. For example, "resignation" and "defeat" might be cognates for helplessness, as might "rage" or "betrayal" be for horror. However, the DTD A2 criterion provides more than just a better detailed operationalization of the subjective sense of traumatization than that used in the traditional definition of PTSD. DTD's more complex subjective reactions articulate aspects of psychological shock that are not clearly implied by fear, helplessness, or horror. The inclusion of betrayal is derived from clinical and theoretical work on the distinct phenomenology and clinical sequelae of "betrayal trauma" (Freyd, DePrince, & Gleaves, 2007). Including shame also expands the clinician's focus from fear or anxiety to the sense of a damaged self (Feiring, Taska, & Lewis, 2002). Including rage is consistent with research suggesting that children exposed to traumatic victimization may be defiantly oppositional and victimizing toward others, as well as anxious (Ford et al., 2000).

Thus, identifying complex trauma as a distinct subset of psychological traumas provides the clinician and researcher with a basis for identifying individuals who have experienced not only the shock of extreme fear, helplessness, and horror but also disruption of the emergent capacity for psychobiological self-regulation and secure attachment. In addition to hyperarousal and hypervigilance in relation to *external* danger, complex trauma poses for the person the *internal* threat of being unable to self-regulate, self-organize, or draw upon relationships to regain self-integrity.

Cumulative adversities are faced by many persons, communities, ethnocultural minority groups, and societies that may lead to—as well as worsen the impact of—complex trauma (Vogt, King, & King, 2007):

- Economically impoverished inner city ethnoracial minority persons.
- Incarcerated individuals and their children and families.
- Homeless persons and their families.
- Sexually and physically revictimized children or adults.
- Victims of political repression, genocide, "ethnic cleansing," torture, or displacement.

- Developmentally, intellectually, or psychiatrically challenged individuals.
- Civilian workers and soldiers harassed and assaulted on the job or in the ranks.
- Emergency responders who are repeatedly exposed to grotesque death and suffering.

Another unfortunate reality concerning complex trauma is related to its interpersonal nature. The closer the relationship between perpetrator(s) and victim(s) and their group memberships (e.g., in a family, religion, gender, political party, institution, chain of command), the more likely they are to face conditions of divided loyalty. As a self-protective strategy, the group may coalesce around silencing, secrecy, and denial. As a result, victims *do not receive* the help they expect and need when the victimization is disclosed or otherwise exposed. This circumstance has been labeled the *second injury* (Symonds, 1975) or *betrayal trauma* (DePrince & Freyd, 2007). A lack of response or protection—or victim blaming—is betrayal of the victim's trust and the helper's responsibility that can severely exacerbate traumatic victimization. In the worst case scenario, a caregiver directly and repeatedly abuses a vulnerable child or does not respond or protect the child from abuse by others. Young children exposed to betrayal trauma by caregivers often develop a *disorganized/dissociative* attachment style in childhood and an adult attachment style described as *fearful/avoidant/dissociative* (Lyons-Ruth, Dutra, Schuder, & Bianchi, 2006). Children, more than adults, are prone to use dissociation to cope with such overwhelming circumstances (Putnam, 2003), and it is now hypothesized that this style transforms the personality, preventing the integration of the traumatization across all aspects of the child's and later the adult's self. The result is a person who maintains a "front" or an "as if" or "apparently normal" personality that seems functional but is numb to and even unaware of the trauma, and an "emotional" personality that is incapacitated psychosocially by the knowledge of the trauma (see Steele & van der Hart, Chapter 7, this volume).

CONCEPTUALIZING COMPLEX TRAUMATIC STRESS DISORDERS

Complex traumatic stress reactions are those that are most associated with histories of multiple traumatic *stressor exposures and experiences*, along with severe disturbances in primary caregiving relationships. PTSD alone is insufficient to describe the symptoms and impairments that follow exposure to complex trauma. The combination of PTSD with other DSM-IV-TR Axis I and II disorders and Axis III medical problems would be a more parsimonious solution to the dilemmas posed by complex trauma than to postulate an entirely new "complex traumatic stress disorders" diagnosis or syndrome. However, existing diagnoses, including PTSD, cannot fully account for or guide the treatment of the sequelae of complex trauma.

Complicated, Chronic, or Axis I Comorbid PTSD

PTSD was first codified in DSM-III as a formal diagnosis to identify individuals who had experienced extreme stressors (especially in combat) and were more than transiently (i.e., at least 1 month) troubled by anxiety associated with those stressor exposures. PTSD was designed to be distinct from another diagnosis attributable to exposure to stressors: *adjustment disorder*, which involves time-limited (i.e., less than 6 months) difficulties with distress or behavioral coping following adverse life events within "the normal range of human experience" (e.g., divorce, job loss, interpersonal conflict, financial problems, bereavement). Similar to adjustment disorders, PTSD involves not only symptoms of anxiety, dysphoria, and emotionally based behavioral problems (e.g., irritability, detachment from relationships) but also includes intrusive reexperiencing (unwanted memories and reminders, behavioral reenactments), avoidance (of unwanted memories or reminders of them), and hyperarousal (startle and jumpiness) and hypervigilance symptoms not included in adjustment disorders.

PTSD has been found to have variable expression and duration, ranging from relatively short-term acute responses to those that are chronic and do not remit, even with treatment. Some cases of PTSD also go dormant for periods of time, emerging episodically, usually in response to triggers of one sort or another that set off the psychobiological PTSD response that in turn cascades into physical and psychological symptoms. Noteworthy for our discussion is that the symptoms required for the diagnosis of PTSD, as it is currently defined, do not cover the full range of posttraumatic impairments. PTSD does not include emotion dysregulation (i.e., extremely intense or absent emotions other than anxiety or dysphoria, e.g., guilt, shame, sadness) and associated dysregulation of consciousness (e.g., dissociation), physical reactions and functioning (e.g., somatization), information processing (e.g., schemas or attention processes that are biased toward expecting to be assaulted, betrayed, exploited, or abandoned), and existential and spiritual adjustment (e.g., a fundamental sense of alienation from oneself, other people, and spiritual faith as a result of feeling permanently damaged) (Herman, 1992).

PTSD was designed to be distinct from (Summerfield, 2001) but potentially to occur comorbidly with other DSM Axis I disorders that involve chronic (episodic or continuous) problems with anxiety (e.g., phobias, generalized anxiety, panic, obsessions, or compulsions), mood (e.g., major depression or dysthymia, mania), or self-regulation (e.g., schizophrenia, dissociative disorders, eating disorders, substance use disorders). In addition, PTSD was designed to be distinct from childhood psychiatric disorders, including both "externalizing" disorders (e.g., attention-deficit/hyperactivity disorder [ADHD], conduct disorder) and "internalizing" anxiety and mood disorders. Epidemiological studies show that anxiety and mood disorders often are comorbid with PTSD among adults (Kessler et al., 1995; Kessler, Chiu, Demier, Merikangas, & Walters, 2005), and with childhood internalizing and externalizing disorders (Copeland et al., 2007). PTSD also has been shown to be comorbid with severe Axis I psychiatric disorders in as many as one-third to almost one-half of cases (e.g., bipolar disorder, major depression with psychotic features, schizophrenia spectrum disorders; see Mueser, Rosenberg, Goodman, & Trumbetta, 2002). Substance use disorders also often are comorbid with chronic PTSD (Kessler et al., 2005). *Psychoform* and *somatoform* (i.e., medically unexplained physical problems) dissociative disorders also are overrepresented among persons with PTSD (Sar, Aküyz, & Dogan, 2006).

PTSD and Comorbid Axis II Personality Disorders

Axis II personality disorders also are intended to be distinct from PTSD, but they frequently occur comorbidly (in 25–33% of PTSD cases, e.g., chronic PTSD and borderline personality disorder [BPD]), schizotypal disorder, and antisocial personality disorders; Yen et al., 2002). When PTSD is accompanied by Axis I or II disorders, the extent of biopsychosocial impairment exceeds that which is attributable to PTSD alone (Kessler et al., 1995). For example, in a study of a low-income community health care sample of women, major depression, dissociative disorders, and BPD were the most common comorbidities of PTSD, and when any of these disorders was comorbid with PTSD, the risk of major physical illness was significantly increased over the already high level of risk conferred by PTSD alone (Seng, Clark, McCarthy, & Ronis, 2006). Patients diagnosed with PTSD have been found to have more severe somatic problems and intrusive reexperiencing symptoms (Ford, 1999), and suicidality and impulsiveness (Zlotnick et al., 2003) when they have comorbid complex traumatic stress disorders or BPD, respectively.

Although Axis I and II disorders commonly co-occur with PTSD, reliance on them leads to a confusing plethora of comorbidity combinations that do not cohere as a syndrome. To the extent that this Babel of comorbidities reflects common underlying problems in posttraumatic self-dysregulation and attachment disorganization, reliance on PTSD plus comorbidities deprives the clinician of an efficient organizing system for assessment and treatment planning. Rather than addressing the core psychobiological adaptations that are sequelae of complex trauma, the clinician must instead focus assessment and treatment on the symptoms of multiple disorders. This may undermine clinical efficiency and effectiveness. It also burdens therapists with shifting their clinical protocols to address each new type of comorbidity.

PTSD can literally get lost in the shuffle, leading to a focus on "mental illness" (rather than on posttraumatic adaptation) that can be stigmatizing for clients. One of the core elements in the original rationale for a distinct diagnosis of complex PTSD was to reduce the stigma on clients (and families), and to increase the willingness and ability of clinicians to examine carefully the client's history and presentation to determine whether clinical impairments may constitute forms of trauma-related self-dysregulation (Herman, 1992). When symptoms (e.g., mood swings, internal voices, hallucinatory reexperiencing symptoms, dissociative reenactments) are assumed a priori to be due to other psychiatric disorders, the role of trauma-related adaptations in self-regulation, self-integrity, and attachment disorganization are likely to be ignored in treatment planning and outcome monitoring. Many complex traumatic stress disorder symptoms parallel or mimic those of other psychiatric diagnoses; thus, differential diagnosis is necessary in order not to assign causality falsely to an existing disorder, without consideration of the potential role of adaptation to complex trauma. This was a primary *raison d'être* for the development of the original PTSD diagnosis; therefore, it warrants careful consideration with complex trauma.

Although simply classifying impaired complex trauma survivors as PTSD plus comorbid BPD may seem to be a straightforward solution, the high likelihood of stigma faced by persons (especially women) diagnosed with BPD has led some clinicians and researchers to seek a way for clients diagnosed with PTSD and BPD to be "extricated from the diagnosis of borderline personality disorder and subsumed under that of complex PTSD" (MacLean & Gallop, 2003, p. 369). Effective treatments have been developed for BPD, but even the most efficacious ones (e.g., dialectical behavior therapy) primarily have shown evidence of enabling people to cope with the intense emotional and interpersonal distress and dysregulation associated with that disorder—but not of remediating traumatic stress symptoms (Wagner & Linehan, 2006).

PTSD and Comorbid Dissociative Disorders

Another possible solution to comorbidity is to treat the impaired complex trauma survivor as having comorbid PTSD and a dissociative disorder. When structural dissociation is a prominent problem (e.g., dissociative disorder not otherwise specified [DDNOS] and dissociative identity disorder), treatment modalities such as those described in this book (Steele & van der Hart, Chapter 7; Fosha, Paivio, Glesier, & Ford, Chapter 14; Schwartz, Schwartz, & Galperin, Chapter 17) provide means to address dissociative symptoms as posttraumatic adaptations. In addition, thorough assessment of dissociative symptoms is crucial when clients present with complex trauma histories (Courtois, Ford, & Cloitre, Chapter 4, this volume), in order not to overlook or misclassify (e.g., manic or psychotic symptoms) dissociative aspects of clinical cases involving complex trauma histories.

However, structural dissociation is not inevitably observed clinically as an impairment for clients with complex trauma histories. Dissociation is particularly likely to occur when complex trauma involves sexual abuse (Putnam, 2003), but complex trauma involving physical or emotional violence or victimization without sexual violation may be associated with extreme forms of affect/interpersonal dysregulation that do not always include structural dissociation. Relying solely on existing dissociative disorders might inadvertently lead to their overdiagnosis and to treatment that does not address the full range of complex, trauma-related impairments.

PTSD Subtypes

Another approach to the clinical/scientific conundrum of classifying and treating complex traumatic stress disorders has been to identify subtypes of PTSD. A rational approach based on research on the high level of persistence of PTSD that occurs for more than 6 months, particularly when it occurs over many years or decades, is to separate acute and chronic PTSD (not to be confused with acute stress disorder, which can last no longer than the shortest possible duration of PTSD, 30 days, and must begins within a month after a traumatic event).

Chronic PTSD is more persistent, refractory to treatment, and more impairing than acute PTSD (Norris & Slone, 2007). Even after years of intensive treatment, it is subject to what Wang, Wilson, and Mason (1996) termed *cyclical decompensation*. However, the comorbid psychopathology that typically accompanies chronic PTSD, rather than chronicity per se, may account for the exacerbated symptoms and impairments (e.g., Ford, 1999; Ford & Kidd, 1998).

An empirical approach to identifying PTSD subtypes has been undertaken by Miller, Kaloupek, Dillon, and Keane (2004), replicating a prior study by using Minnesota Multiphasic Personality Inventory—second edition (MMPI-2) data for over 700 military veterans with clinically diagnosed PTSD. Three subtypes were identified: (1) a "low pathology cluster," with MMPI-2 scores in the nonclinical range; (2) an "internalizing cluster," characterized by severe anxiety and negative affect, low levels of positive affect, and high rates of panic disorder and major depressive disorder; and (3) an "externalizing" problems cluster, characterized by high levels of impulsivity, aggression, anger and other negative emotions, antisocial personality traits, and alcohol use problems. Cases classified as externalizing subtype tended to have the most chronic PTSD, the most numerous and severe psychiatric comorbidities, and the most severe psychosocial impairment. Complex trauma histories were not reported in this study, but the externalizing PTSD subtype includes most of the major features associated with a history of complex trauma (with the possible exception of dissociation, which was not reported).

Thus, it is possible that complex traumatic stress disorders may be an externalizing subtype of PTSD. Yet this approach to classification may not be a good fit, because it requires the addition of many symptoms not currently included in the PTSD diagnosis, essentially comprising a new or expanded diagnostic classification rather than purely a subtype of PTSD. The question of how best to define the features of a hybrid form of severe, chronic externalizing PTSD would therefore remain no less an issue than if a complex traumatic stress disorder formulation were used.

Disorders of Extreme Stress Not Otherwise Specified

The first systematic conceptual/clinical model describing complex traumatic stress disorders was formulated by Herman (1992) and van der Kolk and colleagues (2005) as complex PTSD or disorders of extreme stress not otherwise specified. DESNOS has been assessed by structured interview (Pelcovitz et al., 1997) in college (Ford, Stockton, Kaltman, & Green, 2006) and in midlife and older adult community samples (van der Kolk et al., 2005); in inpatient (Ford, 1999; Ford & Kidd, 1998) and outpatient samples (van der Kolk et al., 2005); and in substance abusing (Ford & Smith, 2008), seriously mentally ill (Ford & Fournier, 2007), and incarcerated (Scoboria, Ford, Lin, & Frisman, in press) samples. DESNOS involves persistent alterations in seven aspects of self-regulation following exposure to traumatic stress: (1) affect and impulse regulation (i.e., persistent distress; risky behavior or self-harm); (2) biological self-regulation (i.e., somatization, e.g., pain or physical symptoms or impairments that cannot be fully medically explained); (3) attention or consciousness (i.e., dissociation); (4) perception of perpetrator(s) (e.g., idealization, preoccupation with revenge); (5) self-perception (e.g., self as damaged or ineffective, profound shame or guilt); (6) relationships (e.g., inability to trust, revictimization, avoidance of sexuality); and (7) systems of meaning or sustaining beliefs (e.g., hopelessness, loss of faith). PTSD is an anxiety disorder, but DESNOS involves a broader set of self-regulatory impairments that takes the form of profound and enduring problems with overwhelming emotional distress, dissociation, loss of relational trust and spiritual faith, and chronic unexplained health problems. In civilian clinical samples (Ford et al., 2006; Ford & Fournier, 2007; Ford & Smith, 2008; Roth, Newman, Pelcovitz, van der Kolk, & Mandel, 1997; van der Kolk et al., 2005) and military clinical samples (Ford, 1999), DESNOS has been shown to be most likely to occur following (1) trauma in *early childhood*, when many self-capacities are formed or malformed, and (2) *interpersonal violence or violation*.

Posttraumatic Personality Disorders

Other formulations of complex traumatic stress disorders include the "enduring personality change after catastrophic experience" diagnosis in the World Health Organization (WHO; 1992) *International Classification of Diseases* (ICD-10; Beltran & Silove, 1999), Parson's (1997) traumatic stress personality disorder (TrSPD), and posttraumatic personality disorder (PPD; Classen, Pain, Field, & Woods, 2006). The ICD diagnosis closely parallels DESNOS, differing primarily in defining dissociative features in greater detail. TrSPD is postulated to occur when PTSD becomes a chronic focus for the individual's life and involves (1) hypervigilance, (2) "self-preoccupation and social ambivalence or withdrawal," (3) "persistent fears or terror over the return of dissociated elements of the past," (4) "work inhibitions," (5) "existential reactions of despair, emptiness, and lack of meaning in life," and (6) chronic maladaptive inflexible

behavior patterns (Parson, 1997; p. 333). Thus, TrSPD includes some, but not all, of the features of PTSD and complex traumatic stress disorders. PPD is postulated to be a sequela of childhood abuse with two subtypes. The disorganized PPD subtype is similar to the abuse/attachment model of complex traumatic stress disorders described by D. Brown in Chapter 6, this volume. The organized type of PPD involves self-dysregulation similar to that of DESNOS, and social avoidance but no fundamental loss or fluctuations in trust and security in primary relationships. PPD's disorganized type includes more profound disturbance in core attachment working models, such that rage, pathological mourning, and self-harm are predominant features. PPD is distinguished from BPD, in that BPD often derives from significant attachment failures, without a severe history of psychological trauma such as childhood sexual abuse. BPD has more prominent features of emotion and relational dysregulation, and a lesser degree of dissociation than PPD.

Whereas both TrSPD and PPD offer clinicians an approach to conceptualize and assess chronic characterological problems associated with exposure to developmentally adverse interpersonal trauma, neither formulation specifies diagnostic criteria in the detail provided by DESNOS. The distinction between organized and disorganized PPD highlights the importance of identifying the effects of compromised attachment security in combination with traumatic experiences such as childhood abuse, as noted in several chapters in this book—and most specifically by Brown's (Chapter 6, this volume) conceptualization of attachment/trauma disorders. It also suggests the possibility that the contribution of self-dysregulation and attachment disorganization to complex traumatic stress disorders may be distinct even though they often co-occur. However, the utility of distinguishing PPD from BPD based on severity of abuse exposure is unclear given findings that DESNOS and BPD are commonly comorbid and difficult to distinguish in psychiatric samples (McLean & Gallop. 2003). PPD is defined as PTSD plus DESNOS (Classen et al., 2006), and DESNOS addresses the core features of BPD, while adding a focus on potentially alterable traumatic stress underpinnings. Therefore, DESNOS appears to be the most efficient and well-articulated approach to describing the sequelae of complex trauma as a single syndrome for adults.

Developmental Trauma Disorder

DESNOS has not been formally extended to describing complex traumatic stress disorders among children. However, the complex trauma work group of the National Child Traumatic Stress Network (NCTSN) has advanced a potential new diagnosis for complexly traumatized children to complement the existing childhood anxiety, affective, behavioral, and attachment disorders in the next (fifth) edition of the American Psychiatric Association's DSM. As noted earlier, DTD identifies developmentally adverse interpersonal trauma and subjective reactions that include not only fear but also self-related (e.g., shame) and defensive (e.g., rage) subjective reactions as a specific traumatic

stressor criterion. DTD was designed to enable clinicians and researchers to treat and study traumatized children who display symptoms similar to those that lead to diagnoses of (1) severe mental illnesses, such as bipolar disorder or schizoaffective disorder; (2) disruptive behavior disorder conditions, such as conduct disorder or oppositional defiant disorder; or (3) dissociative or reactive attachment disorders.

DTD includes two primary features. The first DTD feature is stressor-triggered dysregulation that occurs when trauma-related cues occur. Dysregulation may occur in one or more domains (Ford, Hartman, Hawke, & Chapman, 2008) including emotions (e.g., extreme lability or numbing), cognitions (e.g., dissociation, preoccupation with threats), somatic functioning (e.g., unexplained pain or medical problems), relationships (e.g., oppositionality, dependency), behavior (e.g., reenactments of traumatic experiences, self-injury), or self-attributions (e.g., self-hatred). The second DTD feature involves beliefs that are altered by persistent experiences with abandonment, betrayal, and other forms of victimization that potentially influence the child's personality development. These altered beliefs include an expectation of being victimized, unprotected, or denied justice, and a related sense of distrust of others and self-blame. Finally, DTD involves serious functional impairment in peer or family relationships, school or work, or legal (e.g., juvenile justice) domains.

DTD is similar to DESNOS in describing an organized and specific set of alterations in the person's ability to self-regulate when confronted with reminders of traumatic experiences (i.e., the emotion/impulse dysregulation, dissociation, and somatization features of DESNOS, and the dysregulation feature of DTD) and in fundamental guiding beliefs (i.e., traumatically distorted expectations concerning self and relationships). The specific forms of dysregulation identified in DTD include behavioral and relational problems that are more common in childhood than among adults (e.g., oppositional defiant behavior; extreme dependency). The domain of altered systems of meaning (e.g., loss of spiritual faith) described in DESNOS is not identified in DTD, because those existential changes are less evident (e.g., more likely to be expressed indirectly in behavior or in generalized distrust of self or others) in traumatized children than in adults. However, DTD and DESNOS together provide a potential lifespan framework for conceptualizing the sequelae of complex trauma as a unified clinical syndrome, complex traumatic stress disorders. The approaches described in this book for clinical assessment and psychotherapy with children or adults who have experienced complex trauma and have clinically significant psychosocial impairment address both PTSD and DESNOS (for adults) or DTD (for children).

The Challenge and the Opportunity Facing Us

In making a distinction between types of posttraumatic disorders, *we are in no way diminishing the complexity that is inherent in the criteria for "traditional" PTSD*. PTSD itself is a complex and dynamic biopsychosocial spectrum disorder with numerous personal and interpersonal manifestations and ramifications for those so diagnosed, and it may appear in different structural configurations at different times (Wilson, Friedman, & Lindy, 2002). PTSD has symptoms and impairments that overlap with those of other Axis I psychiatric disorders, but it has syndromal integrity (Elhai, Grubaugh, Kashdan, & Frueh, 2007). Careful attention to the diagnostic criteria for PTSD and other disorders therefore permits accurate differential diagnosis without overlooking or overdiagnosing PTSD. However, in the absence of a formal diagnosis for complex traumatic stress disorders, there is the potential mis- or overdiagnosis of severe disorders (e.g., bipolar or schizophrenia spectrum disorders, BPD, conduct disorder).

According to experts on complex traumatic stress disorders, a sophisticated trauma-based approach to conceptualizing and classifying these disorders is essential to prevent complexly traumatized clients from being burdened with stigmatizing diagnoses and to provide these clients with treatment that is informed by current scientific and clinical knowledge bases (Herman, 1992, and Foreword, this volume; van der Kolk, 2005, and Afterword, this volume; van der Kolk et al., 2005). Whether complex traumatic stress disorders should be consolidated into a single diagnosis (or two complementary diagnoses for adults and children, such as DESNOS and DTD) or be viewed as a set of distinct clinical features that do not necessarily have to co-occur in every unique case (e.g., emotion dysregulation, structural dissociation, somatic dysregulation, disorganized attachment working models; see Briere & Spinazzola, D. Brown, and Steele & van der Hart, Chapters 5–7, respectively) remains open to debate and empirical testing by clinicians, researchers, and theoreticians. The critical domains of complex traumatic stress disorders have been demarcated (i.e., the alterations in mind, emotion, body, and relationships that cut across every conceptual model of the sequelae of complex trauma). Now the critical challenge to clinicians and researchers is to understand each domain well enough to be able to do the following:

- *Accurately assess each core domain* (i.e., to recognize core forms of self-regulation and dysregulation when they are present, without being distracted, confused, or misled by diagnostic or conceptual presumptions, blinders, habits or biases).
- *Understand how dysregulation in each domain has resulted from complex trauma* (i.e., to grasp the person's way of being in the world well enough to see the whole person in context—specifically, to distinguish between the adaptive components of experience and personality from the pathological accommodations that traumatic disruptions of development and attachment have required the survivor to make).
- *Plan and carry out interventions that enable the person to develop capacities for self- regulation in each domain* (i.e., to utilize evidence-based or evidence-informed [American Psychological Association, 2006] ways of interacting therapeutically and approaches to modeling and teaching skills that replicate [*not* replace] developmental opportunities that the

person missed or that were altered as a result of having to survive and cope with complex trauma [Ford, Courtois, van der Hart, Nijenhuis, & Steele, 2005]).

Thus, in the psychotherapy (and pharmacotherapy; see Opler, Grennan, & Ford, Chapter 16, this volume) of complex traumatic stress disorders, there is no disjuncture between the therapeutic relationship/alliance and therapy "interventions," because each simply is a different lens for seeing and understanding a ubiquitous therapeutic process: the repair and restoration of the person's adaptive self-development (Wilson, 1989). This is not a fuzzy "feel good" endeavor; rather, it is a very delicate, deliberate, precise, and mindful intervention with a person whose life both figuratively and literally hangs in the balance. The opportunity to assist another human being in engaging in the most fundamental acts of learning and psychological growth, after that person has been denied that opportunity by fate and trauma, also is a sacred trust that requires the extraordinary mental, emotional, spiritual, and ethical dedication from both therapist and client. It is our hope that clinicians and trainees will find the guidance they need and deserve for this task in the subsequent chapters in this book.

REFERENCES

American Psychiatric Association. (1980). *Diagnostic and statistical manual of mental disorders* (3rd ed.). Washington, DC: Author.

American Psychiatric Association. (2000). *Diagnostic and statistical manual of mental disorders* (4th ed., text rev.). Washington, DC: Author.

American Psychological Association. (2006). *American Psychological Association Presidential Task Force on Evidence-Based Practice*. Washington, DC: Author.

Beltran, R., & Silove, D. (1999). Expert opinions about the ICD-10 category of enduring personality change after catastrophic experience. *Comprehensive Psychiatry, 40*, 396–403.

Classen, C., Pain, C., Field, N. P., & Woods, P. (2006). Posttraumatic personality disorder: A reformulation of complex posttraumatic stress disorder and borderline personality disorder. *Psychiatric Clinics of North America, 29*, 87–112.

Cook, A., Spinazzola, J., Ford, J. D., Lanktree, C., Blaustein, M., Cloitre, M., et al. (2005). Complex trauma in children and adolescents. *Psychiatric Annals, 35*, 390–398.

Copeland, W., Keeler, G., Angold, A., & Costello, E. J. (2007). Traumatic events and posttraumatic stress in childhood. *Archives of General Psychiatry, 64*, 577–584.

Costello, E. J., Erklani, A., Fairbank, J., & Angold, A. (2002). The prevalence of potentially traumatic events in childhood and adolescence. *Journal of Traumatic Stress, 15*, 99–112.

Dass-Brailsford, P. (2007). *A practical approach to trauma: Empowering interventions*. Los Angeles: Sage.

DePrince, A. P., & Freyd, J. J. (2007). Trauma-induced dissociation. In M. J. Friedman, T. M. Keane, & P. A. Resick (Eds.), *Handbook of PTSD: Science and practice* (pp. 135–150). New York: Guilford Press.

Elhai, J., Grubaugh, F., Kashdan, T., & Frueh, C. (2007). Empirical examination of a proposed refinement to posttraumatic stress disorder's symptom criteria using the National Comorbidity Survey Replication data. *Journal of Clinical Psychiatry, 68*, 1–6.

Feiring, C., Taska, L. S., & Lewis, M. (2002). Adjustment following sexual abuse discovery: The role of shame and attributional style. *Developmental Psychology, 38*, 79–92.

Finkelhor, D., Ormrod, R., & Turner, H. (2007). Poly-victimization: A neglected component in child victimization. *Child Abuse and Neglect, 31*, 7–26.

Ford, J. D. (1999). Disorders of extreme stress following war-zone military trauma. *Journal of Consulting and Clinical Psychology, 67*, 3–12.

Ford, J. D. (2005). Treatment implications of altered neurobiology, affect regulation and information processing following child maltreatment. *Psychiatric Annals, 35*, 410–419.

Ford, J. D., Courtois, C. A., van der Hart, O., Nijenhuis, E., & Steele, K. (2005). Treatment of complex post-traumatic self-dysregulation. *Journal of Traumatic Stress, 18*, 437–447.

Ford, J. D., & Fournier, D. (2007). Psychological trauma, post-traumatic stress disorder, and health-related functioning of low-income urban women receiving community mental health services for severe mental illness. *Journal of Psychiatric Intensive Care, 3*(1), 27–34.

Ford, J. D., Hartman, J. K., Hawke, J., & Chapman, J. (2008). Traumatic victimization, posttraumatic stress disorder, suicidal ideation, and substance abuse risk among juvenile justice-involved youths. *Journal of Child and Adolescent Trauma, 1*, 75–92.

Ford, J. D., & Kidd, P. (1998). Early childhood trauma and disorders of extreme stress as predictors of treatment outcome with chronic PTSD. *Journal of Traumatic Stress, 11*, 743–761.

Ford, J. D., Racusin, R., Ellis, C., Daviss, W. B., Reiser, J., Fleischer, A., et al. (2000). Child maltreatment, other trauma exposure, and posttraumatic symptomatology among children with oppositional defiant and attention deficit hyperactivity disorders. *Child Maltreatment, 5*, 205–217.

Ford, J. D., & Smith, S. F. (2008). Complex post-traumatic stress disorder (PTSD) in trauma-exposed adults receiving public sector outpatient substance abuse disorder treatment. *Addiction Research and Theory, 16*, 193–203.

Ford, J. D., Stockton, P., Kaltman, S., & Green, B. L. (2006). Disorders of extreme stress (DESNOS) symptoms are associated with interpersonal trauma exposure in a sample of healthy young women. *Journal of Interpersonal Violence, 21*, 1399–1416.

Freyd, J. J., DePrince, A. P., & Gleaves, D. H. (2007). The state of betrayal trauma theory. *Memory, 15*, 295–311.

Herman, J. L. (1992). *Trauma and recovery.* New York: Basic Books.

Kessler, R., Chiu, W., Demier, O., Merikangas, K., & Walters, E. (2005). Prevalence, severity, and comorbidity of 12-month DSM-IV disorders in the National Comorbidity Survey Replication. *Archives of General Psychiatry, 62*, 617–627.

Kessler, R. C., Sonnega, A., Bromet, E., Hughes, M., & Nelson, C. B. (1995). Posttraumatic stress disorder in the National Comorbidity Survey. *Archives of General Psychiatry, 52*, 1048–1060.

Lyons-Ruth, K., Dutra, L., Schuder, M., & Bianchi, I. (2006). From infant attachment disorganization to adult dissociation: Relational adaptations or traumatic experiences? *Psychiatric Clinics of North America, 29*, 63–86.

McFarlane, A. C., & de Girolamo, G. (1996). The nature of traumatic stressors and the epidemiology of posttraumatic reactions. In B. A. van der Kolk, A. C. McFarlane, & L. Weisaeth (Eds.), *Traumatic stress: The effects of overwhelming experience on mind, body, and society* (pp. 129–154). New York: Guilford Press.

McLean, L., & Gallop, R. (2003). Implications of childhood sexual abuse for adult borderline personality disorder and complex posttraumatic stress disorder. *American Journal of Psychiatry*, 160, 369–371.

Miller, M., Kaloupek, D., Dillon, A., & Keane, T. (2004). Externalizing and internalizing subtypes of combat-related PTSD. *Journal of Abnormal Psychology*, 113, 636–645.

Mueser, K. T., Rosenberg, S., Goodman, L. A., & Trumbetta, S. (2002). Trauma, PTSD and the course of severe mental illness. *Schizophrenia Research*, 53, 123–143.

Norris, F. H., & Slone, L. B. (2007). The epidemiology of trauma and PTSD. In M. J. Friedman, T. M. Keane, & P. A. Resick (Eds.), *Handbook of PTSD: Science and practice* (pp. 78–98). New York: Guilford Press.

Parson, E. R. (1997). Traumatic stress personality disorder (TrSPD): Intertheoretical therapy for the PTSD/PD dissociogenic organization. *Journal of Contemporary Psychotherapy*, 27, 323–367.

Pelcovitz, D., van der Kolk, B., Roth, S., Mandel, F., Kaplan, S., & Resick, P. (1997). Development of a criteria set and a structured interview for disorders of extreme stress (DESNOS). *Journal of Traumatic Stress*, 10, 3–16.

Putnam, F. (2003). Ten year research update review: Child sexual abuse. *Journal of the American Academy of Child and Adolescent Psychiatry*, 42, 269–278.

Roth, S., Newman, E., Pelcovitz, D., van der Kolk, B., & Mandel, F. (1997). DESNOS in victims exposed to sexual/physical abuse. *Journal of Traumatic Stress*, 10, 539–555.

Sar, V., Akyüz, G., & Dogan, O. (2006). Prevalence of dissociative disorders among women in the general population. *Psychiatry Research*, 149, 169–176.

Scoboria, A., Ford, J. D., Lin, H., & Frisman, L. J. (in press). Exploratory and confirmatory factor analyses of the Structured Interview for Disorders of Extreme Stress. *Assessment*.

Seng, J., Clark, M. K., McCarthy, A., & Ronis, D. (2006). PTSD and physical comorbidity among women receiving Medicaid: Results from service-use data. *Journal of Traumatic Stress*, 19, 45–56.

Silver, R., Holman, A., McIntosh, D., Poulin, M., & Gil-Rivas, P. (2002). Nationwide longitudinal study of psychological responses to September 11. *Journal of the American Medical Association*, 288, 1235–1244.

Summerfield, D. (2001). The invention of posttraumatic stress disorder and the social usefulness of a psychiatric category. *British Medical Journal*, 322, 95–98.

Symonds, M. (1975). Victims of violence: Psychological effects and after-effects. *American Journal of Psychoanalysis*, 35, 19–26.

Terr, L. (1991). Childhood traumas. *American Journal of Psychiatry*, 148, 10–20.

Teicher, M., Samson, J., Polcari, A., & McGreenery, C. (2006). Sticks, stones, and hurtful words: Relative effects of various forms of childhood maltreatment. *American Journal of Psychiatry*, 163, 993–1000.

van der Kolk, B. A. (2005). Developmental trauma disorder. *Psychiatric Annals*, 35, 401–408.

van der Kolk, B. A., Roth, S., Pelcovitz, D., Sunday, S., & Spinazzola, J. (2005). Disorders of extreme stress: The empirical foundation of a complex adaptation to trauma. *Journal of Traumatic Stress*, 18, 389–399.

Vogt, D. S., King, D. W., & King, L. A. (2007). Risk pathways for PTSD: Making sense of the literature. In M. J. Friedman, T. M. Keane, & P. A. Resick (Eds.), *Handbook of PTSD: Science and practice* (pp. 99–115). New York: Guilford Press.

Wagner, A. W., & Linehan, M. M. (2006). Applications of dialectical behavior therapy to posttraumatic stress disorder and related problems. In V. M. Follette & J. I. Ruzek (Eds.), *Cognitive-behavioral therapies for trauma* (2nd ed., pp. 117–138). New York: Guilford Press.

Wang, S., Wilson, J. P., & Mason, J. W. (1996). Stages of decompensation in combat-related posttraumatic stress disorder: A new conceptual model. *Integrative Physiological and Behavioral Science, 31,* 237–253.

Weathers, F., & Keane, T. (2007). The Criterion A problem revisited. *Journal of Traumatic Stress, 20,* 107–121.

Wilson, J. P. (1989). *Trauma, transformation, and healing.* New York: Brunner/Mazel.

Wilson, J. P., Friedman, M. J., & Lindy, J. D. (2002). Treatment goals for PTSD. In J. P. Wilson, M. J. Friedman, & J. D. Lindy (Eds.), *Treating psychological trauma and PTSD* (pp. 3–27). New York: Guilford Press.

World Health Organization. (1992). *ICD-10 classification of mental and behavioural disorders.* Geneva: Author.

Yen, S., Shea, M. T., Battle, C. L., Johnson, D. M., Zlotnick, C., Dolan-Sewell, R., et al. (2002). Traumatic exposure and posttraumatic stress disorder in borderline, schizotypal, avoidant, and obsessive–compulsive personality disorders. *Journal of Nervous and Mental Disease, 190,* 510–518.

Zlotnick, C., Johnson, D., Yen, S., Battle, C., Sanislow, G., Skodol, A., et al. (2003). Clinical features and impairment in women with borderline personality disorder (BPD) with posttraumatic stress disorder (PTSD), BPD without PTSD, and other personality disorders with PTSD. *Journal of Nervous and Mental Disease, 191,* 706–713.

CHAPTER 2

Neurobiological and Developmental Research

Clinical Implications

Julian D. Ford

Developmentally adverse interpersonal traumas in early childhood (or *developmental trauma*) include sexual, physical, and emotional abuse, abandonment by caregiver(s), chronic and severe neglect, domestic violence, or death or gruesome injuries as a result of community violence, terrorism, or war (Ford, 2005). Psychological traumas are developmentally adverse if they block or interrupt the normal progression of psychological development in periods when a child (usually in infancy and early childhood) is acquiring the fundamental psychological and biological foundations necessary for all subsequent development: (1) attention and learning; (2) working (short-term), declarative (verbal), and narrative (autobiographical) memory; (3) emotion regulation; (4) personality formation and integration; and (5) relationships (attachment). This chapter provides an overview for the clinician and clinical researcher of the current knowledge base concerning the biological and psychological underpinnings of healthy child development and the potentially adverse impact of traumatic stressors and stress reactions. Self-regulation serves as the organizing framework for this overview and discussion of the implications for the assessment and treatment of complex traumatic stress disorders (see also Koenen, 2006).

IMPACT OF PSYCHOLOGICAL TRAUMA ON EARLY CHILDHOOD DEVELOPMENT: THE SURVIVAL BRAIN

In essence, when psychological trauma interferes with or derails normal psychobiological development, particularly in infancy and early childhood, there is a shift from a brain (and body) focused on *learning* to a brain (and body) focused on *survival*. The *learning brain* is engaged in exploration (i.e., the acquisition of new knowledge and neuronal/synaptic connections) driven and reinforced by a search for an optimal balance between novelty and familiarity. The *survival brain* seeks to anticipate, prevent, or protect against the damage caused by potential or actual dangers, driven and reinforced by a search to identify threats, and an attempt to mobilize and conserve bodily resources in the service of this vigilance and defensive adjustments to maintain bodily functioning. The learning brain and the survival brain are the same brain, with the same capability and core processes (i.e., neural networks and pathways), but their orientations to the environment and their utilization of core processes are critically different. The survival brain relies on rapid automatic processes that involve primitive portions of the brain (e.g., brainstem, midbrain, parts of the limbic system, such as the amygdala), while largely bypassing areas of the brain involved in more complex adaptations to the environment (learning, e.g., anterior cingulate, insula, prefrontal cortex, other parts of the limbic system, such as the hippocampus; see below).

The organizing brain–body system for survival responding is the *stress response system*, which involves the brain areas noted earlier (Neumeister, Henry, & Krystal, 2007) and operates automatically to maintain the inner balance of all body systems (*homeostasis*) by adjusting these systems' activity. The stress response system includes the autonomic nervous system, which controls the body's arousal levels to achieve a balance of mobilization and restoration of bodily energy and organ activity. The sympathetic branch of the autonomic nervous system and the neurotransmitter noradrenaline (also known as norepinephrine, NE) are responsible for increasing arousal in many body systems (e.g., cardiovascular, pulmonary, gastrointestinal), as well as in the brain. The parasympathetic branch of the autonomic nervous system operates via the vagus nerve and functions as a brake on arousal, enabling the body to conserve energy.

The stress response system directly influences immune system activity, generally reducing its level of activity and potentially compromising its ability to detect and fight off pathogens, and promote tissue and organ healing, as well as increasing autoimmune responses that can damage bodily integrity (Kendall-Tackett, 2007). The stress response system also tends to override and reduce the functionality of brain systems that are necessary for learning, including brain systems that promote seeking rewards (involving the neurotransmitter dopamine), managing distress (involving the neurotransmitter serotonin), and making conscious judgments and plans (i.e., *executive* functions involving emotion and information processing, which involve the prefrontal cortex). Thus, a survival brain operates automatically to defend against external threats, but in so doing it diverts crucial resources from brain–body systems that are essential to prevent the body from succumbing to exhaustion, injury, or illness (*allostasis*; Friedman & McEwen, 2004) and to promote learning (e.g., reward seeking, distress tolerance, emotion awareness, problem solving, episodic/narrative memory). Thus, the dominance of the *survival brain* over the *learning brain* represents a biological trade-off between dealing with danger and facilitating growth, healing, rejuvenation, learning, and self-development.

THE DEVELOPING (LEARNING) BRAIN

As the brain develops in early childhood with the birth, death, and shaping ("pruning") of neurons and the pathways that interconnect them, the child's personality forms as a result of both inborn (genetically based) characteristics (e.g., temperament) and formative experiences that combine to shape the brain's neural networks (Lewis, 2005). The emerging brain is a self-organizing set of elements (e.g., neurons, brain areas) and systems (e.g., cortices, limbic and paralimbic systems, brainstem) in which "real-time processes" (i.e., new experiences, changes in the external and bodily environment) "give rise to developmental trajectories, and developmental trajectories constrain the activities of [brain and body systems] in real time" (Lewis, 2005, p. 254). *Developmental trajectories* are the changes in the body and personality that evolve as a person grows and both copes with and learns from experiences. To understand and treat traumatic stress disorders that begin in early life, it is important to be aware of—thus, able to therapeutically utilize—the psychobiological mechanisms that shape these trajectories.

First, current experiences and bodily changes "lay down traces" that "permanently alter the structure of the system" (Lewis, 2005, p. 254): These traces are changes in the activity of neurons or the pathways interconnecting them, in which they become increasingly ("long-term potentiation") or decreasingly ("long-term depression") sensitized; therefore, they are more or less likely to respond to environmental circumstances or changes. Second, there is a "consolidation of structure over development" (p. 254), such that the pathways and networks linking brain neurons are selectively strengthened and increasingly fixed (i.e., they become the biological and psychological "structure" that defines the individual's identity and way of approaching life experiences). Third, as psychobiological structures become consolidated, "cascading constraints" (p. 255) emerge, and new structures (pathways, networks) are less and less likely to develop. These three processes of brain development tend to limit the brain's (and the child's) ability to acquire new trajectories, causing a loss of "degrees of freedom" (p. 255) that limits the child's potential but results in the development of a consistent, integrated self.

The fourth principle of brain development provides a counterbalancing increase in degrees of freedom and is based on periods of unusually rapid neuronal or neural network change that are evident as "developmental transitions" or critical periods (Lewis, 2005, p. 255). A classic transition period is the emergence of verbal language and individuation in the second year of life, a time when neuronal growth and shaping occur at a rapid pace in brain systems associated with those psychological functions, such as the prefrontal cortices and the (para)limbic system (e.g., anterior cingulate, hippocampus, amygdala) (Lewis, 2005). Another transitional period occurs late in preadolescence and in early adolescence, when neuronal growth and shaping is not accelerated; instead, the protective covering for neural connections (the myelin sheath) is put into place rapidly in brain areas involved in higher-order symbolic thought and memory (e.g., hippocampus) (Benes, Turtle, Khan, & Farol, 1994). At the transitional periods of accelerated brain development, "behaviors become unmoored from their entrenched habits, a variety of new forms proliferate for a while ... then some subset of these forms stabilizes, providing new habits for the next stage of development" (Lewis, 2005, pp. 255–256).

IMPACT OF PSYCHOLOGICAL TRAUMA IN EARLY LIFE: COMPLEX TRAUMATIC STRESS DISORDERS

Although change in neural pathways is possible throughout the lifespan, the aphorism about teaching old dogs new tricks aptly captures the increasing difficulty of changing personality after early childhood, or changing behavior, thinking, and emotion patterns after adolescence. If psychological trauma occurs during these transitional periods, the lasting traces (most of which are not in the person's conscious memory) and fixed structures (i.e., relatively automatic habit patterns and fixed beliefs/expectations) can be extremely difficult to alter; hence, psychological trauma in those periods is likely to be *complex* in its effects, precisely because it occurs in a one-time-only period of developmental growth (in childhood) or consolidation (in adolescence). Experience can shape the brain or alter neural networks at any time in life, but never as much as in early childhood and adolescence. These also are developmental periods when experiences with other human beings—such as models, helpers, guides, comforters, competitors, and sources of validation and security—appear to be particularly catalytic for brain and self-development. Therefore, psychological trauma in these periods is likely to involve interpersonal experiences that, whether on purpose or by accident, have an adverse effect on a brain that is particularly malleable.

Thus, the most complex occurrences of psychological trauma tend to involve interactions with people who teach the child or adolescent to focus on danger and survival rather than on trust and learning during transitional periods in which lasting changes in the personality and self occur. If traumatic events push the brain's trajectory of development away from creative exploration and learning toward defensive states geared to promote survival, the child's biological and psychological flexibility and ability to change may be diminished or largely lost. Neural networks in the brain will be correspondingly fixed and difficult to change as a result of experience-driven but biologically entrenched expectations of danger that lead to preoccupation with detecting and defending against threats in all walks of life. The "learning brain's" pathways become excessively and prematurely consolidated into a structure geared mainly toward survival.

TWO DEFINING CHARACTERISTICS OF THE POSTTRAUMATIC SURVIVAL BRAIN

In early childhood brain development, if traumatic stressors lead neural networks to be shaped to operate preferentially based on automatic processes organized by the stress response system, there is a corresponding preference for one of the fundamental personality orientations, *harm avoidance* (e.g., anxiety, anger, introversion, selective bias toward familiar rather than novel information and experiences) rather than another, equally fundamental orientation, *openness to experience* (e.g., interest, curiosity, pleasure, novelty seeking, extraversion). If a further preference in neural network development emerges toward avoidance of, and detachment from, relationships due to adverse relational (attachment) experiences (D. Brown, Chapter 6, this volume; Schore, 2001; Siegel, 2001), personality capacities that enable meaningful and beneficial involvement in relationships (e.g., sociability, responsibility) are likely to be underdeveloped as well. Thus, psychosocial impairments involved in complex traumatic stress disorders can be traced back to early life alterations in neural network development (Lewis, 2005) involving a shift, due to environmental adversity, from a learning brain to a survival brain. The shift involves lasting—but not necessarily irreversible—changes in key brain areas' function (i.e., neural/neurochemical activity within and between key brain areas) and structure (i.e., size and integrity of key brain areas). The survival brain is fixated on automatic, nonconscious scanning for and escape from threats, which fundamentally alters two core psychological processes (Ford, 2005).

Emotion Dysregulation

Areas within the brain that develop primarily prenatally and in infancy and toddlerhood account for the core components of experiencing, expressing, and modulating emotion (Lewis, 2005, pp. 258–259). *Experiencing* core emotion states (e.g., anger, fear, sadness, joy, love, interest) involves brainstem (medulla, pons, midbrain, locus coeruleus) (Bracha, 2008) areas that activate the body neurally by producing neurotransmitters (dopamine, NE). *Expressing* emotions in mood states and action (e.g., aggression, reward seeking, mating) involves striatal (putamen, caudate, nucleus accumbens) brain areas that are activated by input (afferents) from the cortex and selectively alter sensory perception (via the thalamus) and intentional behavior, as well as by the hypothalamus (Heim & Nemeroff, 2001), which modulates body states by producing or triggering production of neuropeptides (e.g., stress hormones, oxytocin, vasopressin) and engaging the autonomic nervous system. *Modulation* of emotions involves the limbic system, which focuses sustained attention and triggers automatic (via the brainstem and hypothalamus) and conscious (via the cortex) responses based on the emotional significance of perceptual and memory information (i.e., the amygdala) (Milad et al., 2007), and coordinates these responses based on the overall context, including past experiences (episodic memory) and current circumstances (i.e., the hippocampus) (Bremner, 2008).

Emotion regulation is the use of "biologically vital sources of information processing" (Schulkin, Thompson, & Rosen, 2003) to monitor and maintain the integrity of internal bodily states either automatically (e.g., visceral [bodily] thermoregulation—internal bodily adjustments to maintain healthy body temperature) or self-reflectively (i.e., by cognitively identifying discrepancies between actual and ideal body states and environmental conditions, and purposefully interacting with the external sociophysical environment to reduce the discrepancy). For example, an individual who feels overheated might automatically alter body temperature or adjust the room temperature. Or, in a social context, the person might respond to a feeling of anger with not only an automatic increase in vagal tone but also by reflectively considering how to handle a problematic relationship by talking with a trusted friend or therapist. The central nervous system (CNS) areas most involved in these forms of affect regulation constitute the *limbic* system, which extends from the brainstem and midbrain reticular activation system (i.e., locus coeruleus, raphe nuclei, ventral tegmentum, striatum, pallidum, and periaqueductal gray matter) to the thalamus, hypothalamus, amygdala, bed nucleus of the stria terminalis, hippocampus, and septum, and ultimately to the anterior cingulate cortex (ACC) and orbital prefrontal cortex (PFC) (Ressler, 2004, p. 29).

Beyond these innate affect regulation processes, self-directed emotion regulation involves higher-order functions and CNS cortical areas. The ACC appears to monitor potential problems with positive or negative outcomes (e.g., conflict, errors), signaling the PFC to become engaged when a discrepancy between intended and actual outcomes requires conscious evaluation and effortful correction of behavior (Eisenberger, Lieberman, & Williams, 2003, p. 291). Neural pathways from the orbital PFC reduce reactivity by inhibiting neural activation in the locus coeruleus (Bracha, 2008), amygdala (Amaral, 2002), and hippocampus (Anderson et al., 2004; Bremner, 2008). The dorsolateral PFC seems to exert *preemptive* control (i.e., reining in reactive responding; Matsumoto, Suzuki, & Tanaka, 2003), whereas the orbital PFC is implicated in self-awareness of connections between emotions, goals, and behavioral options.

Emotion regulation begins initially in infancy, with relatively automatic reactions to distress (crying) and pleasure (visual attention, smiling) (Cicchetti, Toth, & Lynch, 1995; Kagan, 2001). Infancy is a "stress hypo-responsive period" (Andersen, 2003, p. 7) with limited stress hormone release and quiescent hypothalamus–pituitary–adrenal (HPA) axis reactivity, and infants relentlessly explore the physical and social world (Kagan, 2001), consistent with early development of dopamine chemical messenger systems (Rogeness & McClure,

1996). Between ages 6 and 12 months, evolving neural pathways from the PFC to the amygdala and hippocampus lead to the ability to discriminate unfamiliar and familiar persons or objects, and fear of the unfamiliar emerges (e.g., the face of a stranger; Kagan, 2001). If the infant has repeated success in coping with mild, brief episodes of fear, self-regulation is enhanced. However, if abuse prolongs, exacerbates, or prevents the learning of ways behaviorally and biologically to modulate fear of the unfamiliar, novelty may become a lasting source of unmanageable distress, not because fear or novelty itself is toxic, but *because of the infant's failure to learn how to regulate the body when experiencing fear of the unfamiliar.*

As infants become toddlers in the second and third years of life, continued rapid growth in the orbital PFC (Matsuzawa et al., 2001) and experience-dependent refinement (Andersen, 2003) in connectivity between the nucleus accumbens (Nacc), hippocampus, thalamus, ACC, and the PFC (Nair, Berndt, Barrett, & Gonzalez-Lima, 2001) provide the brain infrastructure for awareness of self and others as separate individuals with distinct goals, expectations, and emotions (Adolphs, 2002; Frith & Frith, 1999). Several distinct emotions arise in this epoch (Kagan, 2001), ranging from shame (e.g., embarrassment when experiencing or anticipating disapproval), anxiety (e.g., despair when uncertain whether an absent caregiver will return), and moral anger (e.g., protest when perceiving others as being unfair) to empathy (e.g., interest in what other people think or feel) and pride (e.g., feeling a rewarding sense of self-worth upon completing a task). With modeling and guidance, toddlers experience and express emotions symbolically (e.g., verbally labeling distinct emotions), and use cognitive representations of emotion states and of their caregivers to reduce unpleasant and increase pleasant affect states (Cicchetti et al., 1995, p. 550).

If these systems' development in the first 2 to 3 years of life is altered by significant survival threats posed by traumatic events and compromised caregiving, their neural and neurochemical circuits are likely to become organized by stress reactivity (i.e., identifying and avoiding distress rather than exploring, learning, and engaging in relationships). Persistent neglect or maltreatment in toddlerhood can lead to persistent states of extreme emotional distress (e.g., paralyzing shame, absence of empathy, anger expressed in aggressive behavior) and impairment in the ability to express or modulate these affects (Cicchetti et al., 1995).

As a result, not only emotions but also bodily feelings tend to be experienced as signals of danger or, in and of themselves, as actual threats leading to (1) persistent affective states of anxiety, anger, sadness, and depression; (2) bodily (somatic) discomfort, pain, preoccupation, and loss of physical function (e.g., "hysterical" symptoms, such as paralysis or pseudoseizures); and (3) associated deficits in basic self-regulation (e.g., feeding, sleep–wake cycles, self-soothing) and behavioral disinhibition (e.g., impulsivity, risk taking, aggression, addictive behaviors) that can result in severe and persistent behavioral and physical health problems.

Dysregulated Information Processing

Although information-processing centers in the brain's outer layers (the cortex) develop somewhat later than do lower brain areas, their most rapid period of development (due to the birth of new neurons [*neurogenesis*], the shaping of neurons [*pruning* and *sculpting*], and the death of infrequently activated neurons [*apoptosis*]) takes place from infancy through early childhood. The brain's cortices coordinate information processing

> through a matrix of associations, comparisons, synthesis across modalities, planning, reflection, and sometimes, but not always, conscious control. These operations take time, and emotions maintain a coherent orientation to the world during that period of time. For example, deliberate action is guided by attention to alternative plans and anticipatory attention is constrained by emotions concerning the pursuit of particular goals ... and a continuously refined model of the world achieved by selecting, comparing, and pursuing particular plans while integrating the information fed back by the world. (Lewis, 2005, p. 259)

The entire brain is involved in perception, emotion, thought, and action. However, two cortical areas toward the front of the brain, which are highly interconnected with one another and also closely linked to the limbic system (and are therefore called "paralimbic"), appear to be critical to synthesizing all of this information with self-awareness. To be self-aware is more than just being aware of one's thoughts, feelings, or behavior. Self-awareness also requires *self-reflection*, the ability to step back and observe one's own *processes* of thinking and feeling, as well as the resultant thoughts, feelings, and behavior. Reflective self-awareness is necessary if we are not only to feel, think, and act but also to be *consciously aware of and able to modulate* emotional and bodily feelings, thoughts, and actions. The middle (medial) and underside (ventral) portions of the frontal cortex (orbital frontal cortex [OFC]) and the connecting area between the PFC and the limbic system (ACC), appear to be crucial to reflective self-awareness, facilitating conscious recognition of both implicit (i.e., "intuitive") and explicit (i.e., self-selected and self-defining) emotions and intentions (goals and choices). These ventromedial areas in the PFC enable us not only to think, feel, know, decide, and act on purpose but also, more importantly, to be able to observe and change our information processing.

During the first 2 years of life, children develop the capacity for narrative knowledge (i.e., "a temporally and spatially unified 'movie-in-the-brain' ... [when] the brain makes neural patterns in its neural circuits and turns those neural patterns into explicitly mental patterns of the whole range of possible sensory images, which stand for any object, any relationship, concrete or abstract, any word or any sign") and autobiographical self-awareness (i.e., "in parallel with creating mental patterns for an object, the brain also creates a sense of self in the act of knowing") (Parvizi & Damasio, 2001, p. 137). Before the metaphorical "movie-in-the-brain" can become a true autobiographical narrative, the child must evolve from an initial "proto-self," who has "word-less knowledge (a coherent collection of neural patterns which map, moment by moment, the state of the physical structure of the organism" [p. 138]), to being a "core self" (i.e., awareness of a "me" who observes, knows, and acts [pp. 139–140]).

The proto-self develops in the first year of life (Parvizi & Damasio, 2001) via maturation and differentiation of brain areas necessary for sustained men-tal attention and integration of internal and external sensory inputs into coher-ent perceptions (e.g., locus coeruleus and raphe nucleus neural pathways to the thalamus and somatosensory cortices; Berger-Sweeney & Hohman, 1997). Operation of the proto-self is based on a "comprehensive and continually changing map of the organism state" and how this "state is being changed as a result of an interaction with" the external environment (Parvizi & Damasio, 2001, pp. 152–153). Newborns actively categorize perceptions based on the egocentric functions of objects (e.g., providing food when hungry), but in the second half of the first year of life (with the onset of crawling) they shift toward using a more objective approach (e.g., based on perceptual similarities and differences) that is fully evident as early as 18 months (Johnson & Mareschal, 2001). The transition from egocentricity to self-awareness involves language: By 8 months of age, the infant recognizes words and their component syllables, and can store them in long-term memory (Johnson & Mareschal, 2001).

By about age 2 years, the core self emerges (Parvizi & Damasio, 2001), with psychological capacities that are made possible by fully functional neural projections from the brainstem and midbrain (Berger-Sweeney & Hohman, 1997; Mayes, Swain, & Leckman, 2005) to the amygdala (for self-protection), hippocampus (for conscious memory consolidation), and PFC (for goal-directed behavior), and neural projections to the somatosensory cortices (for conscious spatial perception). The medial/orbital/dorsolateral PFC also experiences rapid neurogenesis (Matsuzawa et al., 2001; Nair et al., 2001), and descending neu-ral projections from the PFC modulate subcortical brain activity (Mayes, 2000; Parvizi & Damasio, 2001). Self-awareness is thought to emerge from this neu-ral network: a "remapping of the changing organism state" that is "the basis for the experience of knowing, the core of consciousness and self" (Parvizi & Damasio, 2001, pp. 152–153) and "mentalizing" (i.e., forming and using men-tal representations; Fonagy, 2003, p. 226) with "functional awareness" (i.e., recognition of one's own and others' mental states and emotions as distinct, and using knowledge of those psychological phenomena to achieve not only behavioral goals but also desired body states; Fonagy, 2003, p. 227).

In the third year of life, children develop an *autobiographical self* (Parvizi & Damasio, 2001)—the capacity to elaborate mental representations of self and other selves in an organized chronological narrative that has continu-ity (e.g., consistent traits, goals, relationships) extending from the past into the present and future (Kagan, 2001). This quantum leap includes achieving "reflective awareness" (Fonagy, 2003, p. 227), the capacity to create, elaborate, and hold mental representations without necessarily acting upon them (e.g., to recognize emotions and intentions as distinct from impulses or behavior). By age 4 years, children's psychological capacities for working (Gathercole, Pickering, Ambridge, & Wearing, 2004) and autobiographical (Howe, Courage, & Edison, 2003) memory can "integrate past with present and ... anticipate future events by reflecting on retrieved schemata and semantic representations" (Kagan, 2001, p. 977).

In early and middle childhood, inhibitory chemical messenger systems develop rapidly (Rogeness & McClure, 1996). From childhood into adolescence, CNS somatosensory cortices appear to shrink and become more efficient (Sowell, Thompson, Tessner, & Toga, 2001), whereas CNS areas activated by reward (e.g., medial/orbital PFC; May et al., 2004) appear to grow and become complex (Giedd et al., 1999; Kanemura, Aihara, Aoki, Araki, & Nakazawa, 2003; Sowell et al., 2001). These brain changes are consistent with the shift in childhood away from impulsiveness and self-protectiveness toward "ego control" or "inhibition control" (Eisenberg et al., 1995). Emotions that emerge in this epoch involve learning to balance exploration with restraint and self-correction, and include guilt (e.g., regret following impulsive behavior), self-doubt and envy (e.g., evaluating oneself as falling short of an ideal), and vicarious pride or shame (i.e., embarrassment at being seen with family members by peers) (Kagan, 2001). The development of information-processing capacities in childhood is facilitated by guided experiences that are likely to activate and require coordination among brain areas ranging from the brainstem to the PFC (e.g., modeling and coaching in selecting goals and activities that focus motivation and attention on attaining rewards based on self-control and self-initiated learning).

When traumatic stressors or absent or problematic caregiving occur early in life, the ventral and medial areas of the PFC do not show signs of structural damage (De Bellis, 2002), but they are likely to be underutilized as a result of competing demands on the more primal brain areas required for survival and stress management. This may lead to underdevelopment of the neural capacities and pathways required for reflective self-awareness, thus leading to an imbalance between *self-augmenting* (i.e., new learning via changes in the synapses that link neurons) and *self-stabilizing* (i.e., consolidation of learning in memory via conservation of existing synaptic linkages) in the brain (Lewis, 2005). Consistent with this hypothesis, research studies with animals and humans have shown that the ventral/medial PFC is crucial to changing from fear-based responding to that based on a sense of safety and seeking novelty and reward.

Thus, exposure to traumatic stressors in early childhood may reduce the brain's ability to create neural networks to support reflective self-awareness (what we are calling the "learning brain"), because the neural networks that enable the child to prepare for and survive danger become overdeveloped (the "survival brain"). Without the capacity to observe one's own thought processes, it is not possible for one to seek or to create new knowledge (i.e., "experience-dependent" learning; Lewis, 2005), only to react to experiences with relatively automatic, chaotic, and fixated perceptions, thoughts, and actions (i.e., "experience-expectant" reactivity; Lewis, 2005).

Complex Traumatic Stress Disorder: Dysregulated Emotion and Information Processing

Exposure to traumatic stressors in early childhood may lead to neural networks in the brain that operate without the person's awareness to focus his or her attention on preparing for and avoiding danger and reduce the person's ability to become aware of these survival-based patterns of thinking and feeling. As a result, rather than seeking and being guided by reflective self-awareness, the person focuses on anticipating and reacting to threats. In the brain, this may take the form of what Lewis (2005, p. 262) describes as "sudden changes in global neural patterning, causing a rapid switch in appraisals." Such instability is consistent with cardinal symptoms of posttraumatic stress disorder (PTSD): unwanted memories (intrusive reexperiencing) and attempts to avoid them, difficulty sustaining mental concentration, and frequent shifts from positive or neutral appraisals of events and people to fearful or angry appraisals (irritability, anxiety, hypervigilance).

In toddlerhood, these impairments take the form of stress reactivity, mood instability, difficulty delaying gratification, problems in maintaining attention and completing activities, irritability and oppositionality, and withdrawal from or overbearing relationships with peers and adults (Manly, Kim, Rogosch, & Cicchetti, 2001). In the school years and in preadolescence, posttraumatically dysregulated affect and impulses can lead children to display behavioral problems consistent with internalizing (e.g., depression, agoraphobia/panic, social anxiety, phobias, dissociative disorders), externalizing (e.g., oppositional defiant or conduct disorder, attentional or impulse control disorders, mania/bipolar disorder), and psychosomatic (e.g., eating disorders, sexual and gender identity disorders, sleep disorders) diagnoses (Cook et al., 2005). Impaired affect and impulse regulation in adolescence may involve exacerbated forms of these psychiatric disorders, as well as substance use or personality disorders, and serious problems in the legal, school, family, and community domains (e.g., incarceration, truancy, teen pregnancy, gang involvement, suicidality) (Ford, Hartman, Hawke, & Chapman, 2008).

At the root of these complex traumatic stress disorders are survival-based neural patterns resulting in "emotional responses [that] lead to global stabilization, causing appraisals to become entrenched," without the person being able to shift to "some [other] activity (either physical or mental) [that] intervenes and reduces emotional activation" (Lewis 2005, p. 262). Thus, what begin as neural and behavioral responses to traumatic experiences may become "stabilized" in the form of chronic biological, emotional, and mental hyperarousal, and "entrenched" beliefs that survival is in jeopardy, from which the person is unable to disengage. Thus, complex traumatic stress disorders may be understood as occurring when the child (and subsequently, the adult) is trapped by and literally helpless to understand or change survival-based neural network patterns that result in extreme states of emotional emptiness or distress (*emotion dysregulation*), mental disorientation and confusion (*dissociation*), bodily hyperarousal and exhaustion, and an associated sense of hopelessness and defeat. To the extent that the child was able to develop the neural networks that support a "learning brain" prior to exposure to traumatic stressors, or that the person is able to reengage or augment these neural networks later in childhood, adolescence, or adulthood, we may hypothesize that PTSD and complex traumatic stress disorder impairments are less likely to occur and less severe if they do occur, and that the person is more likely to recover from them.

In contrast to reflective self-regulation, automatic responses to fear or pain involve reflexive or habitual adjustments that maintain a fairly stable (homeostatic) equilibrium. When stressors require complex adaptations that exceed the body's innate capabilities, the body appears to activate a "neurochemical switch" (Mayes, 2000) to engage more extensive and widespread brain activation—particularly in the PFC—that not only enables the individual to use long-term and working memory to develop flexible adjustments in the body and behavior, but also rapidly depletes body resources (i.e., *allostatic load*; Charney, 2004). Survival responses are preconscious. Within milliseconds of receiving sensory input from the external environment or the body that signals a *threat*, chemical messengers activate fast-acting neural receptors (Riedel, Platt, & Micheau, 2003) in the thalamus and orbital/medial PFC (Moghaddam, 2002). Although the PFC can inhibit amygdala activation and reduce stress reactivity, feed forward from the PFC to the midbrain ventral tegmental area also can trigger the release of neural messengers in the striatum and amygdala, leading to fear-related mental disorganization (Moghaddam, 2002) and encoding (by fast-acting neural receptors in the amygdala) of fear memories (Riedel et al., 2003).

A second, slower self-protective process occurs within several seconds to minutes and lasts up to several hours following a threat (Moghaddam, 2002). This process includes the encoding of fear in long-term memory (Moghaddam, 2002), and reconsolidation and retention of reactivated fear memories (Riedel et al., 2003). Key areas involved include the hypothalamus (to mediate the body's arousal level), the hippocampus (to imprint and access memories of contextual fear and passive avoidance), and the amygdala (for memories of fear of specific stimuli, smells, or tastes) (Riedel et al., 2003). Slow-acting hippocampal receptor activity also may impair active self-regulation by blocking learning and memory of *active* escape behaviors.

"The sensory information contained in a fear or anxiety-inducing stimulus is transmitted from peripheral receptor cells to the dorsal thalamus" (Neumeister et al., 2007, p. 152), except for olfactory (smell) data, which are relayed directly to the amygdala or entorhinal cortex. From the thalamus, sensory information is relayed to the insula, then to the visual, auditory, and somatosensory association cortices, which in turn transmit the information to the amygdala (emotional/fear memories), entorhinal cortex (and through this to the hippocampus [contextual declarative/narrative memories]), orbital PFC, and ACC (emotion regulation). From these cortical and limbic structures, efferent (brain-to-body) signals are transmitted to the amygdala and the brainstem's locus coeruleus (which stimulates glucocorticoid stress hormone release by the paraventricular nuclueus of the hypothalamus, and sympathetic nervous system activation via the lateral nucleus of the hypothalamus), the periaqueductal gray region of the basal ganglia, and the striatum (Neumeister et al., 2007). Amygdala, locus coeruleus, and hypothalamus efferents signal the vagus nerve to activate the parasympathetic nervous system, which conserves bodily resources but may lead to gastrointestinal and genitourinary distress.

Amygdala activation is associated with learning of both fear and extinction (i.e., the learning of when to be afraid and when not to; Milad et al., 2007). When exposed to a conditioned fear stimulus following extinction training, successful recall of extinction (measured by a reduced level of a conditioned response, e.g., skin conductance) has been shown to be associated in humans with activation of both the hippocampus (hypothesized to be the basis for memory of the extinction context, and known to inhibit glutamate-related neuropeptides by the hypothalamus and associated brain and body glands, which indirectly reduce amygdala activation) and the ventral/medial PFC when extinction recall begins, and when the persistence of extinction is most uncertain (which is hypothesized to be the basis for recalling that a threat cue no longer signals danger), and with functional connectivity between these brain areas (Milad et al., 2007).

Consistent with these findings concerning how the brain responds to stressors, research has shown (Neumeister et al., 2007) that persons with PTSD have altered structure and function in most of these brain areas. PTSD is associated with smaller hippocampal volume (which may be a genetic predisposition or a by-product of untreated major depression; increased right amygdala activation secondary to traumatic imagery or pictures, and left amygdala activation secondary to trauma related sounds; reduced ACC and ventral/medial PFC activation secondary to trauma memory or negative emotion provocation (hypothesized to lead to reduced inhibition of amygdala activation). Similarly, PTSD is associated with altered levels and function of brain neurotransmitters and neuropeptides that are involved in these brain areas' responses to stressors (Southwick et al., 2007). Glutamate is the primary excitatory neurotransmitter and gamma-aminobutyric acid (GABA) is the primary inhibitory neurotransmitter, the latter operating on an ongoing basis in the thalamus and amygdala to enable the filtration of extraneous sensory inputs.

Low plasma levels of GABA may be a vulnerability factor for PTSD, based on a study of accident victims. Serotonin may stimulate GABA interneurons, which inhibit glutamatergic (glutamate-related) activity and increase the threshold for amygdala firing, as well as inhibiting locus coeruleus activity. In PTSD there is evidence of decreased platelet serotonin uptake and positive clinical response to selective serotonin reuptake inhibitors (which enhance medial/ orbital/frontal cortex activity). Norepinephrine (NE) is elevated systemically in PTSD, with reduced alpha-2 receptors (which enhance executive functioning and inhibit sensory cortex and limbic activity, and which are activated by moderate but not high levels of NE) and exaggerated NE response to trauma reminders, which may be associated with increased cardiovascular reactivity and increased adrenergic "alpha-1" receptor activity, which effectively takes the PFC "offline" (Arnsten, 1998).

Neuropeptide Y (NPY) may be a particularly important neuromodulator when stressors occur, and is associated with reduced anxiety in both animals and humans (Southwick et al., 2007). NPY is coreleased with NE in the amygdala, hippocampus, basal ganglia periaqueductal gray region, locus coeruleus, and PFC during intense stressors. NPY's anxiolytic effects may be due to enhancing the effects of NE and (through a metabolite) inhibiting further release of NE and the locus coeruleus firing rate. NPY levels, which are reduced when animals or humans are chronically exposed to stressors, may be similarly reduced when PTSD occurs.

When emotions and information processing become dysregulated, somatic states also tend to become dysregulated. Rapid bodily reactions are triggered by pain or preoccupation, with diffuse body distress or discomfort (or fear of the body breaking down), and these are coordinated by chemical messengers (opioids) that reduce pain awareness by (1) inhibiting activation of excitatory (Benedetti & Amanzio, 1997) and pain-amplifying (Rosen, Zhang, Lund, Lundeberg, & Yu, 2004) chemical messengers in the midbrain "pain center" (the periaqueductal gray area); (2) increasing attention and motivation, by cueing the release of chemical messengers in the dorsal (upper) portion of the striatum and brainstem (i.e., dopamine in the ventral tegmentum) (Rainville, 2002); (3) reducing alarm reactions by activating opioid receptors in the brainstem and thalamus (Behbehani, 1995); and (4) activating the ACC and insula to reduce the noxious quality of anticipated pain (Rainville, 2002). Thus, brain areas responsible for experiencing and coping with pain are generally the same as—or are closely connected to—brain areas (e.g., amygdala) that become hyperactive when traumatic stressors occur. Consistent with these research findings, preoccupation with somatic pain often is a key symptom of complex traumatic stress disorders.

DISORGANIZED ATTACHMENT: SEQUELA OF, AND CONTRIBUTOR TO, COMPLEX TRAUMATIC STRESS DISORDERS

When emotion/bodily dysregulation and survival-based information processing become entrenched in early childhood, formative relationships often are disrupted. A preoccupation with survival is fundamentally incompatible with the child's development of dependable emotional bonds with caregivers. These bonds, and the sense of security that they provide, have been described as the capacity for relational "attachment" (Lyons-Ruth, Dutra, Schuder, & Bianchi,

2006). A secure sense of attachment not only provides a sense of comfort and nurturance to the developing child but also is necessary if the child is to acquire the ability be reflectively self-aware. Newborn humans have several essential, innate bodily self-regulation systems (e.g., "sucking, swallowing, breathing, thermoregulating, vocalizing") (Doussard-Roosevelt, Porges, Scanlon, Alemi, & Scanlon, 1997, p. 174). Innate self-regulation processes depend on the brainstem areas to send and receive feedback along the vagus nerve to bodily organs (e.g., heart, lungs, esophagus), enabling the body to adapt constantly to the changing environment. Innate self-regulation processes are the foundation for more complex self-regulatory functions (e.g., sustained and selective attention, social affiliation) (Doussard-Roosevelt et al., 1997) that predict self-regulation in toddlerhood (e.g., problem solving, gross motor skills, impulse control, social skills) (Doussard-Roosevelt et al., 1997). Facilitative relationships with caregivers, described by Bowlby as "goal-directed partnerships" (Fonagy, 2003, p. 225), are essential to the development of self-regulation in infancy and, moreover, to acquiring the ability purposively to adjust bodily, affective, and mental processes later in life to have conscious control of self-regulation.

Newborns are alert, attending selectively to change in the sensory environment, and assimilating *schemas* (i.e., distinctly remembered sensory patterns that evoke a pleasurable response, such as smiling in response to a caregiver's gaze) (Kagan, 2001). Tactile contact with caregivers is vital, enhancing motor control, pain/distress tolerance, parasympathetic autonomic nervous system (ANS) arousal modulation, and activity–rest and sleep–wake rhythms (Weller & Feldman, 2003). Neonates also actively explore the world visually and preferentially attend to face-like stimuli based on subcortical neural paths (Johnson & Mareschal, 2001). By 6 months of age, they have distinct rapid responses in the occipital and temporal lobes when viewing familiar faces or objects (Gauthier & Nelson, 2001). By age 12 months, they attend to, learn from, and imitate others, particularly after responsive interactions (Johnson & Mareschal, 2001).

Across sensory modalities, infants seem primed to develop *affective synchrony* through a "highly organized dialogue of visual and auditory signals," in which infant and caregiver match cyclically alternating "states of attention and inattention" and "simultaneously adjust their social attention, stimulation, and accelerating arousal" in "mutually attuned synchronized interactions" that result in a "psychophysiological state similar to the partner's" (Schore, 2001, pp. 18–19). Bioaffective synchrony (Harrist & Waugh, 2002; Niebur, Hsiao, & Johnson, 2002) enables the infant not only to gain control over bodily states by tuning her or his body to that of a caregiver (i.e., coregulation) (Schore, 2001, p. 26), but also to see in the caregiver's behavior a mirror of him- or herself that becomes the "scaffold" (Schore, 2001) for subsequent development later in toddlerhood and childhood of the ability to observe his or her own thoughts and intentions, and to use those mental processes purposefully to modulate bodily, emotion, and mental states (i.e., reflective self-awareness).

The presence of the mother, even without tactile contact, reduces cortisol elevations when young primates experience separation or the presence of strangers (see Gunnar & Donzella [2002, p. 206] for review). Beyond mere presence or physical contact, caregiver *responsive verbal and nonverbal attention* facilitates infant coping with separation and other stressors without biological (Gunnar & Donzella, 2002) or affective/behavioral (Stanley, Murray, & Stein, 2004) dysregulation, and subsequent developmental attainments later in childhood (e.g., self-efficacy, language, cognitive skills) (Stanley et al., 2004). Infants seem innately motivated to acquire responses from caregivers that provide them with a mirror of their own bioaffective state: When a caregiver is present but fails to show any interest or affect facially (the "still-face" paradigm), 3-month-old infants react with "impressive behavioral organization, showing a clear motivation to keep in emotional contact with their mother … without becoming disengaged or disorganized," even if their mother is depressed and usually not positively responsive (Stanley et al., 2004, p. 14). In addition, when caregivers resume normal interaction (the "reunion" phase in the still-face procedure), infants show increased engagement and positive affect regardless of maternal depression or responsivity (Stanley et al., 2004). However, older infants (e.g., age 6 months) whose parents are not positively responsive become *dys*regulated during the still-face reunion (i.e., more negative affect, elevated heart rate) (Haley & Stansbury, 2004), consistent with the hypothesis that impaired caregiver responsivity may not only lead to insecurity but also to persistent problems with stress reactivity and relational engagement (Stanley et al., 2004).

Caregiving and social affiliation are facilitated but not sustained alone by a complex interaction of chemical messengers operating in the brainstem/midbrain (locus coeruleus, ventral tegmentum), limbic system (septum), and its connector to the striatum (the bed nucleus of the stria terminalis), and cortex (orbital PFC) (Bartels & Zeki, 2004; Eisenberger et al., 2003; Leckman & Herman, 2002; Lorberbaum et al., 2002; Young, 2002). Two peptides released in the hypothalamus appear to trigger a cascade of neural activity throughout the brain that enhances affiliation. *Oxytocin* (see Carter, 1998, for review) contributes to birth and lactation, and facilitates infant bonding with caregivers (e.g., preference for maternal odors), female bonding as an infant caregiver, nesting (place preference), and reduced stress reactivity, as well as to adult pair-bonds (Carter, 1998; Young, 2002), social memory (Young, 2002), and sexual receptivity (Young, 2002). *Vasopressin* enhances defensive activities (e.g., mate guarding, territoriality; Carter, 1998), and attention and learning (Carter, 1998). Both oxytocin and vasopressin also contribute to body-state awareness (Carter, 1998). Thus, oxytocin and vasopressin facilitate not only social contact and caregiving but also emotion and somatic self-regulation and information processing. The benefits of social affiliation and secure attachment may extend to *future generations*: Infant rodents receiving maternal care have enhanced oxytocin (for females) and vasopression (for males) activity as adults, and females reliably provide high levels of maternal care to their offspring or to foster pups (Francis, Young, Meaney, & Insel, 2002). In humans, parental nurturing also may be transmitted across generations (Miller, Kramer, Warner, Wickramaratne, & Weissman, 1997).

However, exposure to persistent survival-threatening stressors can fundamentally disrupt the development of these crucial attachment bonds. For example, when adult animals are stressed by unreliable access to food supplies, they and their offspring experience increased hypothalamic production of stress hormones (Leckman & Herman, 2002). Under those circumstances, or when caregivers experience threat-related amygdala activation due to their children's stress reactions (e.g., in animal studies, due to novel smells from infant offspring that trigger olfactory input to the amygdala) (Leckman & Herman, 2002), infant animals show signs of hypothalamic-mediated stress reactivity until security is reinstated and other bodily changes occur that signal safety (e.g., increased oxytocin and vasopressin levels in both the infant and the caregiver) (Carter, 1998). These stress-related changes in brain activity lead to infant animals' behavior that is remarkably similar to disorganized attachment in human children (Maunder & Hunter, 2001).

Disorganized attachment in human children is characterized by a chaotic mix of excessive help seeking and dependency, social isolation and disengagement, impulsiveness and inhibition, and submissiveness and aggression (Lyons-Ruth et al., 2006). Neurobiological studies have reported elevated brain excitatory chemical messenger levels proportionate to the duration of PTSD in maltreated children and altered sleep–wake cycles of stress hormones, as well as either hyper- (if abuse is ongoing, or if the child is depressed) or hypo- (if abuse is in the past) production of stress hormones (De Bellis, 2002; Kaufman, Plotsky, Nemeroff, & Charney, 2000). Maltreated children also may have impaired neural development in the corpus callosum, ACC, and frontal cortex (particularly in males) (De Bellis et al., 2002; Teicher et al., 2003), and reduced maturation of the brain's left hemisphere (Teicher et al., 2003). Child neglect (e.g., impoverished orphanage or foster home placements) also is associated with disorganized attachment (Gunnar & Donzella, 2002; Rutter, O'Connor, & the English and Romanian Adoptees Study Team, 2004).

In preclinical studies, rats separated from caregivers repeatedly for prolonged periods in early life show behavioral and biological signs of anxiety, reactivity to relatively mild stressors or reexposure to stressor-related contexts, and reduced exploratory behavior in adulthood (Meaney, Brake, & Gratton, 2002). In animal studies, such stress reactivity in adulthood after prolonged early life maternal separation is associated with chronic depletion or down-regulation of the hypothalamus and associated brain (e.g., pituitary gland) and body (e.g., adrenal gland) areas responsible for producing stress hormones. These alterations appear to be a compensatory reaction to the excess production of stress hormones (Friedman & McEwen, 2004), and lead to inadequate inhibition of subsequent production of stress hormones by the hippocampus, ACC, and PFC when minor stressors are encountered (Francis, Diorio, Plotsky, & Meaney, 2002; Ladd, Huot, Thrivikraman, Nemeroff, & Plotsky, 2004;

Vazquez, Eskandari, Zimmer, Levine, & Lopez, 2002). Neither simulated maternal contact (Zhang et al., 2002) nor medication (Vazquez et al., 2002) prevents this sensitization of the stress response system, although serotonin-based medication in adulthood may partially—but not fully—reverse it (Vermetten, Vythilingam, Southwick, Charney, & Bremner, 2002).

Byrne and Suomi (2002) provided a template for the development of disorganized attachment by mapping the longitudinal course of disrupted self-regulation in anxious young primates as follows: (1) early withdrawal from caregivers, (2) little autonomous play or exploration during childhood, (3) seeking caregivers and avoiding peers later in childhood (i.e., regression to coregulation and social withdrawal), and (4) increasing stress reactivity throughout childhood. When attachment relationships are disrupted or lost in infancy or toddlerhood, the coregulation, modeling, and guidance that is necessary for children to learn how to recognize, label, and modulate the behavioral expression of emotions and impulses may be severely compromised (Lyons-Ruth et al., 2006). When psychological trauma further burdens the young child with a need to focus on survival and anxiety management, erratic patterns of behavior may develop with caregivers, and in play and activities with peers and adults that suggest that the child's body feelings, emotions, thinking, and relationships have become disorganized and unmanageable (i.e., "disorganized" attachment) (Lyons-Ruth et al., 2006; Scheeringa & Zeanah, 2001).

Human infants with clinically depressed mothers are at risk for stress hormone and cortical dysregulation as preschoolers (Essex, Klein, Cho, & Kalin, 2002) and adolescents (Halligan, Herbert, Goodyer, & Murray, 2004), and for mental health problems as first graders (Essex et al., 2002). However, it is not depression per se, but *impaired maternal responsivity* (Gunnar & Donzella, 2002) or exposure to *potentially traumatic events* (Carpenter et al., 2004), or both, that seems to account for the adverse sequelae of maternal depression. Consistent with this view, secure attachment, functional family relationships, and affective (i.e., low anger) and somatic self-regulation were found to protect against adverse effects of parental problem drinking and depression in 6- to 12-year-old children (El-Sheikh, 2001).

Consistent with findings that neural networks are rapidly consolidated in adolescence, there is evidence from animal studies that adolescence may be a special window of opportunity to reverse some of the negative effects of early life exposure to traumatic stressors. Young adults who grew up in families and communities vulnerable to traumatic stressors and other forms of socioeconomic adversity have been found to be most likely to make a positive adjustment in psychological and sociovocational/educational functioning, if as preadolescents they had secure and supportive relationships with an adult caregiver or mentor and peers (Bifulco, 2008). Similarly, providing pre- or early postpubertal rodents with an "enriched" environment (i.e., opportunities to interact with peers and explore novel stimuli) (1) stimulates neuron growth and activity in the visual cortex and hippocampus (Torasdotter, Metsis, Henriksson, Winblad, & Mohammed, 1998), and (2) reverses many separation-related impairments in hypothalamic modulation of arousal levels in adulthood (Francis, Diorio, et al., 2002).

IMPLICATIONS FOR ASSESSMENT AND TREATMENT OF COMPLEX TRAUMATIC STRESS DISORDERS

Traumatic stress interventions cannot ameliorate all of the problems associated with the adaptive—but ultimately problematic—shift from a learning brain to a survival brain. However, a focus on enhancing clients' core abilities to engage in reflective self-awareness in the service of consciously regulating emotions and processing information could provide a framework to guide clinical conceptualization, engagement, and education of clients; treatment planning; and monitoring of therapeutic progress and outcomes for clients experiencing complex traumatic stress reactivity. Implications are discussed using the three-phase model of treatment that is the current standard of practice for posttraumatic psychotherapy (see Ford & Cloitre, Chapter 3, and Courtois, Ford, & Cloitre, Chapter 4, this volume).

Phase 1: Safety and Stabilization

The shift from an innate ("experience-expectant") orientation toward learning to the survival brain's posttraumatic ("experience-dependent") preoccupation with detecting and surviving threats may begin in childhood, but it persists in the course of living every day thereafter. A first implication for assessment and treatment is that the client and clinician together need to identify how survival concerns have altered the client's emotion and information processing. This means that the significance of assessing the client's memories of past traumatic experiences and difficulties with PTSD (e.g., avoidance and hypervigilance related to reminders or memories of past traumatic experiences) or other symptoms of traumatic stress conditions (e.g., dissociation) is *not primarily archeological* (i.e., unearthing the past) but is instead based on learning how current survival-based alterations in emotion regulation and information processing are interfering with functioning. For example, if dissociative blackouts occurred contemporaneously and the client recalls having felt initially confused, then diffusely distressed, emotionally numb, and ultimately psychologically absent and detached while experiencing sexual abuse as a child, then this can enable the client and therapist to understand the client's current symptoms as the result of an expectable self-protective (and potentially reversible) progression from feeling safe and engaged in life (learning brain) to feeling overwhelmed and coping automatically by disengaging (survival brain).

This perspective has implications for defining what it means for clients with complex traumatic stress disorders to feel (as well as to actually be) safe and stabilized in their current lives (and in treatment). *Safety* usually is interpreted as meaning an absence of objective danger from self or others, and the presence of supportive and protective relationships that can be called upon should harm occur or become imminent. Although this is always a crucial foundation, it is not sufficient to ensure that the person can prevent, attenuate, or recover from future harm. The key to a more complete and enduring sense of safety may be the knowledge that one can exert a meaningful degree of control over one's own survival responses, which, although automatic, are nevertheless modifiable when the person is able to regulate emotion and information processing. Thus, helping the client to recognize, enhance, and build capacities for self-reflective emotion and information processing may be the best way to promote not only objective survival but also the ability to retain or reinstate the learning brain when stressors activate the survival brain. For example, when clients engage in dangerous or risky behavior when dissociated, their safety is best ensured by developing the self-regulatory capacities to prevent or manage dissociation.

Similarly, *stabilization* typically is defined based on freedom from crises or significant emotional, behavioral, or relational upheavals. The bottom line for therapeutic stabilization is that the client is able to think sufficiently proactively and clearly to make safe, healthy choices. From this perspective, self-aware emotion and information processing are the cornerstones of therapeutic stabilization. Although emotion and information processing involve a complex array of psychobiological adaptations (Ford, 2005), they can be bootstrapped or scaffolded from the very first therapeutic encounter if the clinician uses them as a focus for engagement and therapy.

Preliminary research findings suggest that psychotropic (Neumeister et al., 2007) and psychotherapeutic (Resick, Monson, & Gutner, 2007; Welch & Rothbaum, 2007) treatments for PTSD or associated disorders can stimulate changes in brain neural activity (and are associated with increased hippocampal volume) in adults. However, the extant treatments do not directly reduce the dysregulation of emotion or information processing. Pharmacotherapy may enhance mood or cognitive capacity, but it has not been shown to initiate or increase the self-reflective monitoring of emotion or cognitive (let alone somatic) *processing* that seems fundamental to psychobiological development, and that appears to be compromised by complex trauma. The PTSD psychotherapy for which there is the strongest evidence base, cognitive-behavioral therapy (CBT), may reduce PTSD-related avoidance and symptom severity, and increase positive affect and optimistic, self-affirming cognitive appraisals, but they do not directly target and have not been shown to enhance self-reflective emotion and information processing. However, adaptations of CBT for complex traumatic stress disorders explicitly aim to enhance reflective self-awareness as a foundation for changing cognitions and behavior (see Gold, Chapter 11, and Jackson, Nissenson, & Cloitre, Chapter 12, this volume).

A clinical note of caution is indicated when utilizing any therapeutic intervention to increase the client's degrees of freedom neurobiologically or psychologically. As Lewis (2005) describes, this also leaves behaviors and habits "unmoored," thus potentially increasing the client's biologically based, as well as psychological, predispositions to anxiety, confusion, or difficulties in managing personal safety and daily life. This is the inevitable trade-off of growth (including therapeutic efforts to enable clients with posttraumatic conditions to resume a stance of "learning" rather than being mired in survival defenses) versus symptomatic stasis.

Phase 2: Memory Reconstruction

Constructing memories is an everyday prerequisite to achieving both integration and continuity in one's sense of self and a distinct meaningful personal narrative or life story (Harvey, 1996). Episodic or narrative memory is largely based in engaging self-reflectively in activities of daily living (including but not limited to therapy), which involves observation of one's own processes of feeling and thinking, and experimenting with a conscious (versus automatical) focus on acquiring new information, and elaborating and integrating familiar information (i.e., learning). If the goal of therapy is to provide clients with carefully guided opportunities to experience the self-control and integrated self-awareness that is normal when in "learning" rather than "survival" mode, the therapeutic process must be based on self-reflection and not merely on facilitation of remembering, enhanced coping, or any other essentially nonreflective (survival-based) responses. The learning brain responds to stressors based on reflective self-awareness rather than on purely non-self-aware automatic survival responses. No matter how useful it is, or has been, to be able to respond rapidly and automatically when (dis)stressed, treatment cannot rely on teaching or strengthening automatic or rote approaches to feeling, thinking, remembering, or pursuing goals, even if those approaches are intuitively appealing as ways of reducing anxiety. The crucial problem is that survival-based avoidance increases automaticity and reduces self-reflective autonomy. Consistent with this view, reducing automaticity and enhancing reflective self-awareness is the primary focus in psychotherapy for complex traumatic stress disorders. This may involve increased attunement to thoughts (e.g., CBT; Chapters 11 and 12, this volume), emotions (e.g., experiential and emotion-focused therapies: Fosha, Paivio, Gleiser, & Ford, Chapter 14, and Schwartz, Schwartz, & Galperin, Chapter 17, this volume), body states (e.g., sensorimotor psychotherapy: Fisher & Ogden, Chapter 15, this volume; pharmacotherapy: Opler, Grennan, & Ford, Chapter 16, this volume), self-states (e.g., structural dissociation therapy: Steele & van der Hart, Chapter 7, this volume; contextual internal family systems therapy: Schwartz et al., Chapter 17, this volume), or self-defining roles and involvement in relationships (e.g., family systems therapy: Ford & Saltzman, Chapter 19, this volume; group therapy: Ford, Fallot, & Harris, Chapter 20, this volume).

This paradigm shift does not in any way invalidate therapeutic approaches that are grounded in reducing posttraumatic avoidance of memories or reminders of past traumatic experiences (e.g., exposure-based CBT). Instead, it suggests that these and other treatment modalities for complex traumatic stress disorders are most effective if the clinician focuses on using them as a vehicle for enhancing self-reflective processing of emotion and information (i.e., bodily sensations, perceptions, thoughts, intentions, plans, appraisals) rather than simply limiting the focus to overcoming avoidance of traumatic memories. With enhanced emotion and information processing comes a corresponding increase in the capacity to choose not to avoid but instead to confront, to recall fully, and to reconstruct distressing current experiences and past memories. The true antithesis to intrusive reexperiencing is not freedom from trauma memories or trauma-related distress, but the capacity to choose whether, when, and how to recall and make sense of (i.e., emotionally and cognitively finding meaning in) those memories. This presupposes sophisticated emotion and information-processing abilities that are precisely the mode of the "learning" brain that is overridden by posttraumatic stress-related survival reactions. Thus, authority over one's own memory (Harvey, 1996) may best be construed as the ability to choose whether, when, and how to recall memories (i.e., specific emotion and information processing skills) rather than purely reducing avoidance of traumatic memories.

Phase 3: Integration of Learning and Increased Adaptive Living

What is learned and must be integrated and applied in daily living as a result of therapy depends on the clinician's metamodel and goals for treatment. In the PTSD field, this tends to be phrased in terms of reducing anxiety by reducing avoidance of traumatic memories and associated fears or beliefs (e.g., "I'll fall apart if I think about that experience"). From the viewpoint of regaining access to the learning brain in daily living, the goal might instead be defined as reducing the dominance of threat-based, survival-oriented emotional responding and information processing by promoting self-reflective examination of how one experiences and makes sense of emotions (including associated bodily sensations and thoughts), and how one derives coherent meaning from memories (including but not limited to recollection of traumatic experiences). For example, the ability to be aware when traumatic stress-related bodily and affective feelings stimulate anxious or hopeless thoughts, and to observe and reflect on this as an understandable (but not currently adaptive) survival-based attempt to anticipate and cope with future traumatic threats, could have the effect of engaging orbital PFC, ACC, and hippocampal activation, and dampening amygdala and associated adrenergic and stress hormone reactivity. Although this hypothesis remains to be tested, it is consistent with extant neuroimaging findings regarding PTSD (Neumeister et al., 2007), and it focuses the client and clinician on using self-reflective awareness as a vehicle for integrating and adaptively utilizing emotion and information-processing skills in daily life.

From this perspective, posttraumatic dissociation and somatization are fundamental impediments to achieving an integration of learning and increased adaptive living—but both forms of complex traumatic stress symptoms derive from, and can be addressed by altering, stress-related emotion and information processing. PTSD symptoms, such as avoidance of trauma-related cues or hyperarousal/hypervigilance, require substantial cognitive and somatic resources, unless they occur automatically (i.e., without conscious awareness or control). When survival is fundamentally threatened, as is the case with developmentally adverse interpersonal traumas (particularly in early childhood), PTSD symptoms originate or rapidly become largely automatic, because the child either does not have or cannot mobilize conscious self-protective defenses. The result is psychoform or somatoform dissociative fragmentations of consciousness (i.e., compartmentalized, disconnected parts of the self, each of which is defined by a distinct dominant motivation or set of motivations; see Steele & van der Hart, Chapter 7, this volume). What begin as attempts to mobilize brain and bodily systems to survive traumatic stressors in developmentally sensitive periods can become a chronic biological predisposition to dissociate psychologically or physiologically, or both. The resultant fragmented bodily sensations, perceptions, emotions, and thoughts require careful examination—not only by the therapist but also by the client and therapist together, to engage in reflective self-awareness (i.e., to observe one's own automatic acts of mental and somatic dissociation and thereby place those acts under increased conscious control).

REFERENCES

Adolphs, R. (2002). Neural systems for recognizing emotion. *Current Opinion in Neurobiology, 12,* 169–177.

Amaral, D. (2002). The primate amygdala and the neurobiology of social behavior. *Biological Psychiatry, 51,* 11–17.

Andersen, S. (2003). Trajectories of brain development. *Neuroscience and Biobehavioral Reviews, 27,* 3–18.

Anderson, M., Ochsner, K., Kuhl, B., Coper, J., Robertson, E., Gabrieli, S., et al. (2004). Neural systems underlying the suppression of unwanted memories. *Science, 303,* 232–235.

Arnsten, A. F. T. (1998). The biology of being frazzled. *Science, 280,* 1711–1712.

Bartels, A., & Zeki, S. (2004). The neural correlates of maternal and romantic love. *NeuroImage, 21,* 1155–1166.

Behbehani, M. (1995). Functional characteristics of the midbrain periaqueductal gray. *Progress in Neurobiology, 46,* 575–605.

Benedetti, F., & Amanzio, M. (1997). The neurobiology of placebo analgesia: From endogenous opioids to cholecystokinin. *Progress in Neurobiology, 52,* 109–125.

Benes, F. M., Turtle, M., Khan, Y., & Farol, P. (1994). Myelination of a key relay zone in the hippocampal formation occurs in the human brain during childhood, adolescence, and adulthood. *Archives of General Psychiatry, 51,* 477–484.

Berger-Sweeney, J., & Hohman, C. F. (1997). Behavioral consequences of abnormal cortical development. *Behavioural Brain Research, 86,* 121–142.

Bifulco, A. (2008). Risk and resilience in young Londoners. In D. Brom, R. Pat-Horenczyk, & J. D. Ford (Eds.), *Treating traumatized children: Risk, resilience, and recovery* (pp. 117–130). London: Routledge.

Bracha, S. (2008). Locus coeruleus. In G. Reyes, J. D. Elhai, & J. D. Ford (Eds.), *Encyclopedia of psychological trauma* (pp. 396–397). Hoboken, NJ: Wiley.

Bremner, J. D. (2008). Hippocampus. In G. Reyes, J. D. Elhai, & J. D. Ford (Eds.), *Encyclopedia of psychological trauma* (pp. 313–315). Hoboken, NJ: Wiley.

Byrne, G., & Suomi, S. (2002). Cortisol reactivity and its relation to homecage behavior and personality ratings in tufted capuchin juveniles from birth to six years of age. *Psychoneuroendocrinology, 27,* 139–154.

Carpenter, L., Tyrka, A., McDougle, C., Malison, R., Owens, M., Nemeroff, C., et al. (2004). Cerebrospinal fluid corticotrophin-releasing factor and perceived early-life stress in depressed patients and healthy control subjects. *Neuropsychopharmacology, 29,* 777–784.

Carter, C. S. (1998). Neuroendocrine perspectives on social attachment and love. *Psychoneuroendocrinology, 23,* 779–818.

Charney, D. S. (2004). Psychobiological mechanisms of resilience and vulnerability. *American Journal of Psychiatry, 161,* 195–216.

Cicchetti, D., Toth, S., & Lynch, M. (1995). Bowlby's dream comes full circle. In T. Ollendick & R. Prinz (Eds.), *Advances in child clinical psychology* (Vol. 17, pp. 1–75). New York: Plenum Press.

Cook, A., Spinazzola, J., Ford, J. D., Lanktree, C., Blaustein, M., Cloitre, M., et al. (2005). Complex trauma in children and adolescents. *Psychiatric Annals, 35,* 390–398.

De Bellis, M. D. (2002). Developmental traumatology. *Psychoneuroendocrinology, 27,* 155–170.

De Bellis, M. D., Keshavan, M., Shiflett, H., Iyengar, S., Beers, S., Hall, J., et al. (2002). Brain structures in pediatric maltreatment-related PTSD. *Biological Psychiatry, 52,* 1066–1078.

Doussard-Roosevelt, J., Porges, S., Scanlon, J., Alemi, B., & Scanlon, K. (1997). Vagal regulation of heart rate in the prediction of developmental outcome for very low birth weight preterm infants. *Child Development, 68,* 173–186.

Eisenberg, N., Fabes, R. A., Murphy, B., Maszk, P., Smith, M., & Karbon, M. (1995). The role of emotionality and regulation in children's social functioning: A longitudinal study. *Child Development, 66,* 1360–1384.

Eisenberger, N. I., Lieberman, M. D., & Williams, K. D. (2003). Does rejection hurt?: An FMRI study of social exclusion. *Science, 302,* 290–292.

El-Sheikh, M. (2001). Parental drinking problems and children's adjustment: Vagal regulation and emotional reactivity as pathways and moderators of risk. *Journal of Abnormal Psychology, 110,* 499–515.

Essex, M., Klein, M., Cho, E., & Kalin, N. (2002). Maternal stress beginning in infancy may sensitize children to later stress exposure: Effects on cortisol and behavior. *Biological Psychiatry, 52,* 776–784.

Fonagy, P. (2003). The development of psychopathology from infancy to adulthood: The mysterious unfolding of disturbance in time. *Infant Mental Health Journal, 24,* 212–239.

Ford, J. D. (2005). Treatment implications of altered neurobiology, affect regulation and information processing following child maltreatment. *Psychiatric Annals, 35,* 410–419.

Ford, J. D., Hartman, J. K., Hawke, J., & Chapman, J. (2008). Traumatic victimization, posttraumatic stress disorder, suicidal ideation, and substance abuse risk among juvenile justice-involved youths. *Journal of Child and Adolescent Trauma, 1,* 75–92.

Francis, D., Diorio, J., Plotsky, P., & Meaney, M. (2002). Environmental enrichment reverses effects of maternal separation on stress reactivity. *Journal of Neuroscience, 22,* 7840–7843.

Francis, D., Young, L., Meaney, M., & Insel, T. (2002). Naturally occurring differences in maternal care are associated with the expression of oxytocin and vasopressin (V1a) receptors. *Journal of Neuroendocrinology, 14,* 349–353.

Friedman, M. J., & McEwen, B. (2004). Posttraumatic stress disorder, allostatic load, and medical illness. In P. Schnurr & B. L. Green (Eds.), *Physical health consequences of exposure to extreme stress* (pp. 157–188). Washington, DC: American Psychological Association.

Frith, C., & Frith, U. (1999). Interacting minds—a biological basis. *Science, 286,* 1692–1695.

Gathercole, S., Pickering, S., Ambridge, B., & Wearing, H. (2004). The structure of working memory from 4 to 15 years of age. *Developmental Psychology, 40,* 177–190.

Gauthier, I., & Nelson, C. (2001). The development of face expertise. *Current Opinion in Neurobiology, 11,* 219–224.

Giedd, J., Blumenthal, J., Jeffries, N., Castellanos, F., Liu, H., Zijdenbos, A., et al. (1999). Brain development during childhood and adolescence: A longitudinal MRI study. *Nature Neuroscience, 2,* 861–863.

Gunnar, M. R., & Donzella, B. (2002). Social regulation of cortisol levels in early human development. *Psychoneuroendocrinology, 27,* 199–220.

Haley, D., & Stansbury, K. (2004). Infant stress and parent responsiveness. *Child Development, 74,* 1534–1546.

Halligan, S., Herbert, J., Goodyer, I., & Murray, L. (2004). Exposure to postnatal depression predicts elevated cortisol in adolescent offspring. *Biological Psychiatry, 55,* 376–381.

Harrist, A., & Waugh, R. (2002). Dyadic synchrony. *Developmental Review, 22,* 555–592.

Harvey, M. (1996). An ecological view of psychological trauma and trauma recovery. *Journal of Traumatic Stress, 9,* 3–23.

Heim, C., & Nemeroff, C. (2001). The role of childhood trauma in the neurobiology of mood and anxiety disorders. *Biological Psychiatry, 49,* 1023–1039.

Howe, M. L., Courage, M. L., & Edison, S. C. (2003). When autobiographical memory begins. *Developmental Review, 23,* 471–494.

Johnson, M., & Mareschal, D. (2001). Cognitive and perceptual development during infancy. *Current Opinion in Neurobiology, 11,* 213–218.

Kagan, J. (2001). Emotional development and psychiatry. *Biological Psychiatry, 49,* 973–979.

Kanemura, H., Aihara, M., Aoki, S., Araki, T., & Nakazawa, S. (2003). Development of the prefrontal lobe in infants and children. *Brain and Development, 25,* 195–199.

Kaufman, J., Plotsky, P., Nemeroff, C., & Charney, D. (2000). Effects of early adverse experiences on brain structure and function. *Biological Psychiatry, 48,* 778–790.

Kendall-Tackett, K. (2007). Inflammation, cardiovascular disease, and metabolic syndrome as sequelae of violence against women. *Trauma, Violence and Abuse, 8,* 117–126.

Koenen, K. (2006). Developmental epidemiology of PTSD: Self-regulation as a core mechanism. *Annals of the New York Academy of Sciences, 1071,* 255–266.

Ladd, C., Huot, R., Thrivikraman, K., Nemeroff, C., & Plotsky, P. (2004). Long-term adaptations in glucocorticoid receptor and mineralocorticoid receptor mRNA and negative feedback in the HPA axis following neonatal separation. *Biological Psychiatry, 55*, 367–375.

Leckman, J., & Herman, A. (2002). Maternal behavior and developmental psychopathology. *Biological Psychiatry, 51*, 27–43.

Lewis, M. D. (2005). Self-organizing individual differences in brain development. *Developmental Review, 25*, 252–277.

Lorberbaum, J., Newman, J., Horwitz, A., Dubno, J., Lydiard, R., Hamner, M., et al. (2002). A potential role for thalamocingulate circuitry in human maternal behavior. *Biological Psychiatry, 51*, 431–445.

Lyons-Ruth, K., Dutra, L., Schuder, M., & Bianchi, I. (2006). From infant attachment disorganization to adult dissociation: Relational adaptations or traumatic experiences? *Psychiatric Clinics of North America, 29*, 63–86.

Manly, J., Kim, J., Rogosch, F., & Cicchetti, D. (2001). Dimensions of child maltreatment and children's adjustment: Contributions of developmental timing and subtype. *Development and Psychopathology, 13*, 759–782.

Matsumoto, K., Suzuki, W., & Tanaka, K. (2003). Neuronal correlates of goal-based motor selection in the prefrontal cortex. *Science, 301*, 229–232.

Matsuzawa, J., Matsui, M., Konishi, T., Noguchi, K., Gur, R., Bilker, W., et al. (2001). Age-related volumetric changes of brain gray and white matter in healthy infants and children. *Cerebral Cortex, 11*, 335–342.

Maunder, R., & Hunter, J. (2001). Attachment and psychosomatic medicine: Developmental contributions to stress and disease. *Psychosomatic Medicine, 63*, 556–567.

May, J. C., Delgado, M., Dahl, R., Stenger, A., Ryan, N., Fiez, J., et al. (2004). Event-related magnetic resonance imaging of reward-related brain circuitry in children and adolescents. *Biological Psychiatry, 55*, 359–366.

Mayes, L. (2000). A developmental perspective on the regulation of arousal states. *Seminars in Perinatology, 24*, 267–279.

Mayes, L., Swain, J., & Leckman, J. (2005). Parental attachment systems. *Clinical Neuroscience Research, 4*, 301–313.

Meaney, M., Brake, W., & Gratton, A. (2002). Environmental regulation of the development of mesolimbic dopamine systems. *Psychoneuroendocrinology, 27*, 127–138.

Milad, M., Wright, C., Orr, S., Pitman, R., Quirk, G., & Rauch, S. (2007). Recall of fear extinction in humans activates the ventromedial prefrontal cortex and hippocampus in concert. *Biological Psychiatry, 62*, 446–454.

Miller, L., Kramer, R., Warner, V., Wickramaratne, P., & Weissman, M. (1997). Intergenerational transmission of parental bonding among women. *Journal of the American Academy of Child and Adolescent Psychiatry, 36*, 1134–1139.

Moghaddam, B. (2002). Stress activation of glutamate neurotransmission in the prefrontal cortex. *Biological Psychiatry, 51*, 775–787.

Nair, H., Berndt, J., Barrett, D., & Gonzalez-Lima, F. (2001). Maturation of extinction behavior in infant rats. *Journal of Neuroscience, 21*, 4400–4407.

Neumeister, A., Henry, S., & Krystal, J. H. (2007). Neurocircuitry and neuroplasticity in PTSD. In M. J. Friedman, T. M. Keane, & P. A. Resick (Eds.), *Handbook of PTSD: Science and practice* (pp. 151–165). New York: Guilford Press.

Niebur, E., Hsiao, S., & Johnson, K. (2002). Synchrony. *Current Opinion in Neurobiology, 12*, 190–194.

Parvizi, J., & Damasio, A. (2001). Consciousness and the brainstem. *Cognition*, *79*, 135–159.

Rainville, P. (2002). Brain mechanisms of pain affect and pain modulation. *Current Opinion in Neurobiology*, *12*, 195–204.

Resick, P. A., Monson, C. M., & Gutner, C. (2007). Psychosocial treatments for PTSD. In M. J. Friedman, T. M. Keane, & P. A. Resick (Eds.), *Handbook of PTSD: Science and practice* (pp. 330–358). New York: Guilford Press.

Ressler, N. (2004). Rewards and punishments, goal-directed behavior and consciousness. *Neurosience and Biobehavioral Reviews*, *28*, 27–39.

Riedel, G., Platt, B., & Micheau, J. (2003). Glutamate receptor function in learning and memory. *Behavioural Brain Research*, *140*, 1–47.

Rogeness, G. A., & McClure, E. B. (1996). Development and neurotransmitter–environmental interactions. *Development and Psychopathology*, *8*, 183–199.

Rosen, A., Zhang, Y., Lund, I., Lundeberg, T., & Yu, L. (2004). Substance P microinjected into the periaqueductal gray matter induces antinociception and is released following morphine administration. *Brain Research*, *1001*, 87–94.

Rutter, M., O'Connor, T., & the English and Romanian Adoptees (ERA) Study Team. (2004). Are there biological programming effects for psychological development? *Developmental Psychology*, *46*, 81–94.

Scheeringa, M., & Zeanah, C. (2001). A relational perspective on PTSD in early childhood. *Journal of Traumatic Stress*, *14*, 799–816.

Schore, A. (2001). Effects of a secure attachment relationship on right brain development, affect regulation, and infant mental health. *Infant Mental Health Journal*, *22*, 7–66.

Schulkin, J., Thompson, B., & Rosen, J. (2003). Demythologizing the emotions. *Brain and Cognition*, *52*, 15–23.

Siegel, D. (2001). Toward an interpersonal neurobiology of the developing mind. *Infant Mental Health Journal*, *22*, 67–94.

Southwick, S. M., Davis, L. L., Aikins, D. E., Rasmusson, A., Barron, J., & Morgan, C. A., III. (2007). Neurobiological alterations associated with PTSD. In M. J. Friedman, T. M. Keane, & P. A. Resick (Eds.), *Handbook of PTSD: Science and practice* (pp. 166–189). New York: Guilford Press.

Sowell, E., Thompson, P., Tessner, K., & Toga, A. (2001). Mapping continued brain growth and gray matter density reduction in dorsal frontal cortex. *Journal of Neuroscience*, *21*, 8819–8829.

Stanley, C., Murray, L., & Stein, A. (2004). The effect of postnatal depression on mother–infant response to the still-face perturbation, and performance on an Instrumental Learning task. *Development and Psychopathology*, *16*, 1–18.

Teicher, M., Andersen, S., Polcari, A., Anderson, C., Navalta, C., & Kim, D. (2003). Neurobiological consequences of early stress and childhood maltreatment. *Neuroscience and Biobehavioral Reviews*, *27*, 33–44.

Torasdotter, M., Metsis, M., Henriksson, B., Winblad, B., & Mohammed, A. (1998). Environmental enrichment results in higher levels of nerve growth factor mRNA in the rat visual cortex and hippocampus. *Behavioural Brain Research*, *93*, 83–90.

Vazquez, D., Eskandari, R., Zimmer, C., Levine, S., & Lopez, J. (2002). Brain 5-HT receptor system in the stressed infant rat. *Psychoneuroendocrinology*, *27*, 245–272.

Vermetten, E., Vythilingam, M., Southwick, S., Charney, D., & Bremner, J. D. (2002). Long-term treatment with paroxetine increases verbal declarative memory and hippocampal volume in posttraumatic stress disorder. *Biological Psychiatry, 54,* 693–702.

Welch, S. S., & Rothbaum, B. O. (2007). Emerging treatments for PTSD. In M. J. Friedman, T. M. Keane, & P. A. Resick (Eds.), *Handbook of PTSD: Science and practice* (pp. 469–496). New York: Guilford Press.

Weller, A., & Feldman, R. (2003). Emotion regulation and touch in infants: The role of cholecystokinin and opioids. *Peptides, 24,* 779–788.

Young, L. (2002). The neurobiology of social recognition, approach, and avoidance. *Biological Psychiatry, 51,* 18–26.

Zhang, L., Levine, S., Dent, G., Zhan, Y., Xing, G., Okimoto, D., et al. (2002). Maternal deprivation increases cell death in the infant rat brain. *Developmental Brain Research, 133,* 1–11.

CHAPTER 3

Best Practices in Psychotherapy for Children and Adolescents

Julian D. Ford
Marylene Cloitre

Practice parameters for the assessment and treatment of children and adolescents with posttraumatic stress disorder (PTSD) were first developed by an expert panel convened a decade ago by the American Academy of Child and Adolescent Psychiatry (AACAP; 1998). Since the release of that seminal set of practice guidelines, substantial additional validation has been provided in scientific studies of the most robustly evidence-based treatment model, trauma-focused cognitive-behavioral therapy (TF-CBT; Cohen, Mannarino, & Deblinger, 2006). Other cognitive-behavioral therapy (CBT) interventions that were either developed originally for adults (e.g., eye movement desensitization and reprocessing [EMDR]) (Jabergharderi, Greewald, Rubin, Dolatabadim, & Zand, 2004) or modified for child-specific settings and clinical populations (e.g., cognitive-behavioral intervention for traumatized students [CBITS]) (Kataoka et al., 2003; Stein et al., 2003) have been adapted and tested in children with PTSD. Members of the National Child Traumatic Stress Network's (NCTSN) Complex Trauma Work Group (Cook et al., 2005) have developed and conducted randomized clinical trials (Van Horn & Lieberman, 2008) or scientifically rigorous but preliminary (Blaustein & Kinniburgh, 2007; Cloitre, Cohen, & Koenen, 2006; DeRosa & Pelcovitz, 2008; Ford & Russo, 2006; Kagan, 2008) tests of interventions for children and adolescents with complex traumatic stress disorders.

No new practice guidelines have been published for the treatment of children with PTSD in the past decade. Studies of the best-validated treatments for children with PTSD have not systematically assessed symptoms of complex traumatic stress disorders, such as dissociation, emotion dysregulation, and somatization, and toxic self-perceptions have not been systematically assessed (Saxe, MacDonald, & Ellis, 2007; Vickerman & Margolin, 2007). Thus, the utility of PTSD psychotherapies for children with complex traumatic stress disorders is uncertain. This chapter, therefore, provides an overview of preliminary practice guidelines for the treatment of children with complex traumatic stress disorders, building on the work of the NCTSN Complex Trauma Work Group (Cook et al., 2005; Spinazzola, Blaustein, & van der Kolk, 2005) and Systems Work Group (Ko et al., in press), as well as guidelines for the treatment of adults with complex traumatic stress disorders (Ford, Courtois, van der Hart, Nijenhuis, & Steele, 2005; Courtois, Ford, & Cloitre, Chapter 4, this volume).

Although empirically supported therapies are essential as a basis for effective treatment of children with psychological disorders, the American Psychological Association Presidential Task Force on Evidence-Based Practice (2006) also identified the experience of skilled clinicians and of ethnoculturally diverse children and families as being necessary to establish a psychotherapy as "evidence based." Therefore, in addition to describing empirically supported and empirically based psychotherapy models, we describe clinicians' observations and key features of children and families that may be relevant to the assessment and psychotherapy of toddlers, children, adolescents, and families with complex traumatic stress disorders.

GOALS OF PSYCHOTHERAPY FOR CHILDREN WITH COMPLEX TRAUMATIC STRESS DISORDERS

The proposed new diagnosis of developmental trauma disorder (DTD; van der Kolk, 2005) and empirically based conceptualizations of the core features of childhood complex traumatic stress disorders (Cloitre et al., 2006; Cook et al., 2005; Ford, 2005; Van Horn & Lieberman, 2008) provide frameworks for delineating the goals of psychotherapy for children with complex traumatic stress disorders. DTD requires a history of exposure to early life, developmentally adverse interpersonal trauma (Ford, 2005), such as sexual or physical abuse, violence, traumatic losses, or other significant disruption or betrayal (Freyd, 1994) of the child's relationships with primary caregivers (Schore, 2001), which has been postulated as an etiological basis for complex traumatic stress disorders (Herman, 1992; Roth, Newman, Pelcovitz, van der Kolk, & Mandel, 1997; van der Kolk, Roth, Pelcovitz, Sunday, & Spinazzola, 2005). Serious and lasting alterations in the neurobiological substrates of emotion, information processing, bodily self-regulation, consciousness and motivation, and attachment often occur following complex trauma in early childhood (Browne & Winkelman, 2007; Dumont, Widom, & Czaja, 2007; Finkelhor, Ormrod, & Turner, 2007).

Increasing Affect Regulation and Impulse Control

To manage distress, think clearly, and make and act on choices that optimize the social and academic consequences, children need to be able to recognize, label, and modulate the behavioral expression of emotions and impulses. A primary goal of psychotherapy with children with complex trauma is to enable them (and their caregivers) to experience emotions and motivational states as tolerable, helpful, and practically manageable. Acquiring the capacities for emotion regulation requires safe, facilitated opportunities for playing, exploring, learning, and developing relationships with adults and peers in which other persons model mindful ways to recognize and verbalize emotions and goals (wishes, hopes, intentions). In psychotherapy, traumatized children can acquire the capacities necessary for recognizing, expressing, and modulating (i.e., restoring a tolerable and balanced level of affective and physiological arousal) a range of emotions. Helping children (and caregivers) enhance their abilities to regulate emotions and impulses may increase the child's (and the caregiver's) self-control, thereby reducing the risk or severity of the myriad dilemmas that occur when emotions and impulses are dysregulated.

Altered Information Processing (Attention, Memory, and Executive Functions)

Children who have been maltreated or exposed to pervasive domestic violence or profound traumatic loss often present clinically with problems in sustaining and focusing attention, in remembering both immediate and remote experiences and events, in thinking clearly when making decisions and planning courses of action, and in following through in pursuit of their plans and goals. Although these difficulties in information processing may be due, at least in part, to purely physiological causes (e.g., traumatic brain injury, neurological disease) or genetically based conditions (e.g., attention-deficit/hyperactivity disorder [ADHD], learning disabilities), the impact of prolonged severe stressors on the developing nervous system includes alterations in brain chemistry, structure, and function that may impair attentional focusing, memory, and executive decision making and goal-directed behavior (De Bellis, 2001).

Dissociation (Dysregulation of Motivation and Consciousness)

If emotions and impulses are poorly regulated and information processing is compromised by stress reactivity, then the child is likely to have difficulty in accessing and sustaining a clear and consistent motivation other than avoidance and hypervigilant self-protection. Avoidance and hypervigilance require a great deal of cognitive capacity and neurobiological resources, except when done automatically (i.e., without conscious awareness or control). As they become automatic, avoidance and hypervigilance shift from conscious avoidance and self-protection to dissociative detachment and fragmentation of consciousness into compartmentalized, disconnected parts of the self, each of which is defined by a distinct dominant motivation or set of motivations (Steele & van der Hart, Chapter 7, this volume). What begins as an attempt to survive and to cope with traumatic stress may devolve into dissociation: detached and fragmented emotions, thoughts, perceptions, and self-awareness outside of conscious awareness or control. The optimal alternative to dissociative fragmentation is a mindful, self-aware, emotionally attuned, and cognitively planful approach to each step in ordinary day-to-day activities.

Somatization (Dysregulation of Bodily Functioning)

Traumatized children, particularly if the psychological traumas involved pervasive violence, neglect, or abuse by persons whom the child otherwise would have reason to trust—and most especially when those persons are the children's primary caregivers and role models—often report persistent chronic or episodic physical discomfort, distress, and illness symptoms (Cook et al., 2005; van der Kolk, 2005). Posttraumatic somatic complaints may be the product of several, often interrelated etiological factors, including (1) medically diagnosed illnesses, conditions, or injuries that are exacerbated by traumatic stress reactions (e.g., orthopedic conditions, asthma, congenital cardiovascular or neurological syndromes) or for which persistent stress reactions (e.g., irritable bowel syndrome) or health risk behaviors associated with traumatic stress reactions (e.g., obesity secondary to overeating, bronchitis secondary to cigarette smoking) may play a partial causal role; and (2) medically unexplained physical symptoms that are associated with emotion dysregulation (e.g., gastrointestinal or sexual organ pain, or conversion disorders related to alexithymia) or severe dissociation (e.g., tics, pseudoseizures, paralysis, or pain related to somatoform dissociation). The common therapeutic goal for all of the many complex forms of somatic dysregulation is to enable the children (and caregivers) to be able to recognize, label (in terms of discrete ordinary bodily sensations and physical/affective feelings), and utilize input from their bodies as a guide to managing their emotions, drawing on their cognitive competencies, and making purposeful consequence-sensitive behavioral choices that help their bodies to feel and be healthy.

Disorganized Attachment (Relational Dysregulation)

Children with complex traumatic stress disorders commonly present with disorganized patterns of engagement and withdrawal in relationships (Lyons-Ruth, Dutra, Schuder, & Bianchi, 2006). Disorganized attachment involves a constellation of forms of relational dysregulation, including generalized expectancies ("working models"; Bowlby, 1969) based on profound distrust, alienation, and devaluation (van der Kolk, 2005), and patterns of interpersonal interaction characterized by all of the hallmarks of complex traumatic stress disorders: emotion dysregulation, fragmented information processing, impulsive/avoidant behavioral self-management, dissociation, and somatization (Ford, 2005).

Summary

The goals of psychotherapy for children with complex trauma involve all domains of biopsychosocial functioning. The challenge to the clinician is to observe recursively, conceptualize, and intervene, with a simultaneous focus on all of these domains, while maintaining an awareness of the child as a whole person (not simply as a collection of emotions, bodily reactions, thought processes, and behavior). In practice, this involves ongoing reflective questioning by the clinician: What is this child aware of feeling and thinking, and of which bodily and emotional feelings and thoughts is the child unaware? What are the disconnects between what this child (or caregiver) wants and feels able to tolerate versus what he or she is actually experiencing? How can I communicate an understanding of this child's (or caregiver's) state of mind and body that will be meaningful and validating, while also moving him or her gradually toward greater integration, self-awareness, and self-control across all aspects of experiencing? Although these questions may seem obvious to experienced clinicians, they have therapeutic utility as a guide for the clinician's actual ongoing, moment-to-moment therapeutic interaction with children and caregivers. By asking these questions of him- or herself repeatedly in the course of therapeutic interactions, the clinician is engaging in the precise internal self-regulatory activities that are being taught to the client(s), and he or she is not just teaching but serving as a role model and coregulator (Schore, 2001) for the client(s).

EVIDENCE-BASED AND EMPIRICALLY INFORMED ASSESSMENT TOOLS AND PSYCHOTHERAPY MODELS

The observation and conceptualization components of psychotherapy with traumatized children and caregivers begin with the clinical assessment process. Assessment includes both semistructured interaction (e.g., psychosocial interview, observing spontaneous caregiver–child interactions) and the administration of formal psychometric measures (Pelcovitz et al., 1997). Assessment continues throughout all phases of treatment to monitor the therapy process and outcomes (and, as necessary, to revise the plan, goals, or interventions). The optimal sequencing and combination of assessment modalities differ for each individual child and caregiver, with a goal of maximizing engagement and therapeutic alliance, as well as giving the clinician an accurate and complete understanding of the clients' history, problems, strengths, resources, and goals. With children and adolescents, it is particularly crucial to obtain input and records (with appropriate consent from the guardian and assent from the child) from all accessible sources (e.g., current and past health care providers, therapists, schools, legal or child protection agencies or representatives). Although the assessment measures described below are completed in standard self-report and interview procedures, it also is important that these procedures be embedded in developmentally appropriate and caregiver- and child-friendly activities that enhance client buy-in and provide actual behavior samples.

Assessment Measures

Although there are a number of psychometrically robust measures for the assessment of adults' complex traumatic stress disorder symptoms and impairments, far fewer rigorously validated measures assess children with complex traumatic stress disorders (Briere & Spinazzola, Chapter 5, this volume). In addition to questionnaire and structured interview measures for childhood PTSD, and complex posttraumatic sequelae described in Chapter 5, this volume, clinicians may wish to consider the selective use of other psychometric measures to assess dysregulation and resilience in the domains of emotion, information processing and impulse regulation, bodily health, and relationships, as well as the social-environmental contexts that influence children's development or problems with these capacities (Nader, 2008). In addition to parent/caregiver rating measures, direct observation in the home or clinical settings of parent–toddler/preschooler interaction can provide valuable information about the caregiver's and the child's strengths and difficulties in self-regulation and relatedness. For school-age and preadolescent children (and also preschoolers and adolescents), self-report questionnaires assessing externalizing (aggression, attention problems, conduct problems, hyperactivity, learning problems) and internalizing (anxiety, atypicality [psychosis], depression, somatization, withdrawal) problems, and several domains of self-regulation and social competence (daily activities, adaptability, functional communication, leadership, social skills, study skills) are an important addition to the perspective of the parent or caregiver and the teacher. For preadolescents and adolescents, it is important to assess key risks (e.g., self harm, substance use problems) and competencies (e.g., impulse control, consideration for others and responsibility, emotion regulation, self-efficacy, and optimism).

In special settings, such as psychiatric inpatient, residential, or day treatment programs, special education classrooms or programs, or the juvenile justice system, assessment measures should be either specifically developed or adapted, normed, and validated for the children in those distinct subpopulations (Ko et al., in press). For example, the juvenile justice system has custodial, school, treatment, and rehabilitative programs in which screening for complex trauma histories and related biopsychosocial impairments is crucial (Ford, Chapman, Hawke, & Albert, 2007). Across all age groups, thorough assessment of the family system (Josephson & the AACAP Work Group on Quality Issues, 2007) and the school environment and peer group is essential for understanding and building into the treatment plan the primary context for children's behavioral and emotional problems and competencies in context. Specific measures may be useful in identifying parents who—due to emotional rigidity; lack of pleasure in parenting and childrearing; low self-efficacy as caregivers; limited or inaccurate knowledge of children's developmental milestones and pathways, and parenting roles and responsibilities; or high levels of parenting stress—may have difficulty facilitating secure attachment and healthy, safe growth.

Psychotherapy Models

As noted earlier, the best-validated psychotherapy approach for sexually or physically abused or traumatically bereaved children with PTSD is TF-CBT (Cohen et al., 2006). CBITS has been rigorously evaluated in a quasi-experimental study with primarily ethnoculturally minority group children (Kataoka et al., 2003) and a randomized clinical trial study with an ethnoculturally diverse urban sample of children (Stein et al., 2003), most of whom reported accident, disaster, loss, or community violence traumas rather than abuse or family violence traumas. Therefore, it is important to consider TF-CBT as a first treatment option for children with complex traumatic stress problems if they meet the generally accepted inclusion–exclusion criteria for this treatment (see below), and to consider CBITS for children who can be treated in groups in their school setting. However, if child clients do not have a clear, specific memory of traumatic incidents that serve as the focus for TF-CBT, or if their behavioral or psychosocial problems are sufficiently acute or severe, or their family/caregiver support systems are sufficiently unstable or fragmented (e.g., due to severe parental psychopathology or multiple out-of-home placements) to require being addressed prior to group or individual PTSD education and trauma memory work, then other psychotherapy models may warrant consideration as an approach to stabilization prior to implementing TF-CBT or as an alternative approach to enhance traumatic stress–impaired self-regulatory capacities.

For traumatized toddlers and preschoolers, adaptations of TF-CBT have shown promise and provide evidence that trauma memory work (exposure) and relaxation skills training are feasible as long as the protocol is developmentally appropriate and the parent is able to bind his or her anxiety sufficiently to be able to help the child with each step of the process (Scheeringa et al., 2007)—although to date this has been tested only with survivors of disasters or motor vehicle accidents. Van Horn and Lieberman (2008) describe a well-validated parent–child dyadic model (child–parent psychotherapy, CPP) for a traumatized infant/toddler and a parent/caregiver, in which the therapist educates and guides the parent in understanding how traumatic stress is affecting the child and developing skills to respond to and nurture the child during play and tasks of daily living with sensitivity to the traumatic stress impact. CPP's relationally and psychodynamically informed therapeutic model, validated by two independent research teams, has been found to reduce children's PTSD symptoms and problem behaviors; moreover, it is unique in that it has been shown to enhance their attachment security. Other approaches to dyadic family psychotherapy with traumatized young children and their parent(s) include a more behavioral approach that has shown promise in field trials, including trials with formerly abusive parents (parent–child interaction therapy; Ford & Gurwitch, 2008), a psychodynamic model that helps parents develop a practical theory of their child's emotions and motivations (Watch, Wait, and Wonder; N. Cohen et al., 1999), and a psychoeducational model in which the parents view videotapes of interactions with their child, using their observations to develop ways of interacting that elicit prosocial behavior (interaction guidance; McDonough, 2000).

With traumatized school-age and preadolescent children, Kagan (2008) has developed and field-tested the Real Life Heroes psychoeducation protocol. In the intervention, children who are receiving intensive residential or outpatient mental health services participate in nine group lessons, in which they identify their heroes, recognize how they have the same or similar qualities and skills as their heroes, and utilize this sense of "the hero within" to revisit and organize important memories (including both positive and distressing events) and plan for future goals and challenges. In the field trial study, the Real Life Heroes model was found to be associated with both immediate and longer-term (1 year after beginning the program) reductions in traumatic stress symptoms and problem behaviors according to children and caregivers, and an increased sense of security in participating children's relationships with caregivers.

For traumatized preadolescent and adolescent youth, psychotherapy models have shown promise in open clinical trial evaluations in school (DeRosa & Pelcovitz, 2008), community clinic (Cloitre et al., 2006; DeRosa & Pelcovitz, 2008; Najavits, Gallop, & Weiss, 2006), and juvenile justice (Ford et al., 2007) settings and populations. Structured psychotherapy for adolescents responding to chronic stress (SPARCS; DeRosa & Pelcovitz, 2008) is a psychoeducational group therapy that teaches skills adapted from cognitive therapy, dialectical behavior therapy, and Trauma Affect Regulation: Guidelines for Education and Therapy (TARGET; Ford & Russo, 2006) for self-regulation of anger, anxiety, dysphoria, and impulsivity. SPARCS has been widely disseminated through the NCTSN.

The Life Skills/Life Story model was adapted for adolescents by Cloitre and colleagues (2006) from their efficacious PTSD treatment model for women survivors of childhood sexual abuse, Skills Training in Affect and Interpersonal Regulation with Prolonged Exposure (STAIR-PE). This individual psychotherapy model begins with sessions devoted to teaching and guided practice in using skills for emotion regulation and interpersonal effectiveness and, with this as a base, continues into sessions in which youth review their lives and develop a narrative "story" that acknowledges the impact of psychological trauma, while encouraging awareness of personal and relational strengths and resilience. Thus, in the adaptation for youth, the behavioral technique of prolonged exposure is replaced by personal narrative construction (incorporating but not focusing primarily on traumatic experiences). Life Skills/Life Story is being evaluated with girls who are receiving services in several mental health systems nationally.

Seeking Safety (Najavits et al., 2006) is a 25-session, structured psycho-educational model that addressed cognitive, behavioral, interpersonal, and case management issues in the treatment of co-occurring substance use dis-orders (SUDs) and PTSD. The adaptation for girls provides for greater use of oral (versus written) presentations than the original adult version, in a format designed to reduce the client's sense of personal stigma and to engage parents (if the girl consents). In a randomized controlled trial, 33 primarily European American girls who reported multiple traumatic exposures (88% sexual abuse, 82% disaster/accident, 73% physical abuse) and met criteria for PTSD and one or more SUD, attended Seeking Safety for approximately half of the sched-uled sessions, with greater improvements than with treatment as usual (TAU) in self-reported SUD problems and somatization (the latter maintained at a 3-month follow-up).

The Trauma Affect Regulation: Guide for Education and Therapy (TAR-GET; Ford & Russo, 2006; Ford et al., 2007) intervention was adapted for youth after being developed and validated with traumatized men and women in substance abuse treatment, and with low-income women with PTSD who were parenting young children (see *www.nrepp.org*). TARGET is manual-ized for individual or group therapy with traumatized girls or boys and their families, providing psychoeducation about the impact of psychological trauma on the brain, a skills set organized into seven sequential, self-regulation steps by the acronym FREEDOM: Focusing to interrupt stress-related reactivity or impulsivity, Recognizing stress/trauma triggers, Emotion recognition, Evalu-ating the thinking process, Defining personal goals, choosing incremental Options to achieve goals, and Making a contribution in others' lives. Woven into the skills-based education is a "lifeline" process in which youth create a multimedia creative arts representation of their lives, identifying how they used the FREEDOM skills to cope with past psychological traumas and challenges, and how they planfully use the skills in the future.

PROVISIONAL PRACTICE PRINCIPLES FOR TREATING CHILDREN WITH COMPLEX TRAUMATIC STRESS DISORDERS

To select, adapt, and successfully deploy available evidence-based or promising (evidence-informed) assessment and intervention protocols clinically in chil-dren with complex traumatic stress disorders, several practical, therapeutic, and ethical considerations are essential.

1. *Identifying and addressing threats to the child's or family's safety and stability comprise the first priority.* The ethical principles of *primum non noc-ere* (first do no harm) and *parens patriae* (temporary guardianship) are cru-

cial in the assessment and treatment of victimized or traumatized children, as well as with their often secondarily (or directly) traumatized families. Potential threats to safety include (a) self-harm and suicidality; (b) ongoing family violence, abuse, neglect, substance abuse, or psychopathology; or (c) behavior that places the child or youth at risk for sexual victimization, community violence (e.g., physical assault, gang conflicts), abduction or kidnapping, life-threatening accidents, life-threatening illness (e.g., sexually or needle-transmitted diseases), or legal problems and incarceration. When threats to safety are ongoing or imminent, assessment should concentrate on delineating their acuteness and severity, and monitoring change in these key indicators as services are delivered; treatment should focus on accessing external resources (e.g., child protective services, legal representation in the form of a guardian *ad litem* and legal protections, such as restraining orders or supervised visitation, alternative respite, foster care, or residential or inpatient treatment placements) and internal resources (i.e., drawing on and enhancing self-regulation and problem-solving competencies of the child and caregivers) (Faust & Katchen, 2004). Addressing substance use concurrently with PTSD is a safety priority (Najavits et al., 2006).

The goal of accessing and strengthening internal resources often is overlooked in the press to modify or protect against the external conditions that cause threats to safety. An optimal scenario combines externally focused interventions with systematic identification and reinforcement of the child's and the caregiver's internal competencies, resulting in a greater likelihood that child and caregiver will attribute improvements in safety to their own actions (and thereby internalize an increased sense of self-efficacy and personal responsibility; i.e., an internal locus of control) rather than viewing themselves as helpless and dependent upon powerful others to protect and rescue them (i.e., an external locus of control).

2. *A relational bridge must be developed to engage, retain, and maximally benefit the child and caregiver(s).* Although the importance of a therapeutic relationship and working alliance between therapist and client is widely recognized as crucial to effective psychotherapy (Kinsler, Courtois, & Frankel, Chapter 9, this volume), these concepts require elaboration to be adapted fully to psychotherapy with traumatized children and their caregivers. The crucial relational consideration with regard to traumatized children is that they are still young enough to be developing what Bowlby (1969) described as their "working models" of secure, responsive, helpful, and trustworthy primary relationships. This is particularly true with infants, toddlers, and preschoolers, who are in the developmentally critical period for the formation of attachment working models; when psychological trauma occurs in those early years, particularly developmentally adverse interpersonal trauma (Ford, 2005), children's working models (and associated capabilities for self-regulation of emotion, consciousness, impulses, and bodily functioning) may remain in flux and become chronically disorganized for the rest of childhood and adolescence (Miltenburg & Singer, 1999), and into adulthood (Liotti, 2004; Lyons-Ruth et

al., 2006). The child's caregivers, often traumatized in their own lives (as well as secondarily or vicariously due to their child's traumatization), may have difficulty in establishing and maintaining a secure and responsive relationship with their child and with the therapist (Cohen, 2008). Thus, the therapeutic relationship with children with complex traumatic stress disorders should be viewed as triadic rather than dyadic: as a bridge linking the child, caregiver, and therapist affectively to each other, such that the therapist provides coregulation for the child and caregiver, and empowering the caregiver to assume this role with the child while securely within the therapist's unconditional, nonintrusive, noncompetitive empathy and guidance. The therapist's role as coarchitect and cobuilder of these affective bridges with and between the child and caregiver is most evident in dyadic parent–child psychotherapies with young children (Van Horn & Lieberman, 2008). (Re)creating and maintaining the triadic affective bridge is equally important with traumatized children and their primary attachment figures (who may be peers or mentors rather than the more obvious caregivers as the child grows into (pre)adolescence) at all ages.

3. *Diagnosis, treatment planning, and outcome monitoring are always relational.* The child's and parent's immediate needs and resources, and long-term dreams and goals, must not only be the therapist's map for treatment planning but must also be constantly reaffirmed by the therapist as the organizing principle for all assessment and therapeutic interventions. The tendency to pathologize is an inherent risk in all medicalized and other hierarchical (i.e., authority/expert-based) professional encounters, particularly when clients are still maturing and present with the kinds of intense distress and dysregulation characteristic of complex traumatic stress disorders. There is a parallel tendency to focus on long-term goals, such as achieving full remission, or short-term goals, such as increasing superficial compliance with parental commands or teachers' instructions, to avoid disappointment in the face of what may seem to be intractable problems. Formal diagnoses and diagnostic criteria, by providing a reassuringly straightforward list of the problems that require correction to achieve remission from a psychiatric disorder such as PTSD, may inadvertently reinforce these disconnections between treatment goals and clients' hopes and strivings.

The challenge for clinicians is to shift from an emphasis on overcoming pathology or deficits as the goal of treatment to focus on validating the child's (and the caregiver's) wishes, hopes, and strivings by creating a treatment plan and rationale that makes sense to the child and caregiver as a way to link reducing symptomatic responses to achieving those personal goals (Ford & Russo, 2006). For example, rather than assuming that a child and his or her caregiver will automatically agree that reducing avoidance of reminders of past traumatic experiences is a desirable treatment goal, their engagement and buy-in to therapy is likely to be stronger if the therapist links reducing avoidance to the child's desire to be able to engage in a prosocial recreational activity (e.g., sports, theater, dance, arts, auto mechanics) and the caregiver's hope that the child will be more involved with peers who ascribe to the prosocial values represented by that activity. Although this reframing may seem intuitively obvious, it is easily forgotten when clinicians face stressful challenges and demands of treating children with complex traumatic stress disorders.

4. *Diagnosis, treatment planning, and outcome monitoring are always strengths-based.* Existing or former strengths, resources, and resilience are the best predictors of children's recovery from complex traumatic stress disorders and socioeconomic adversity. It can be very difficult to discern meaningful strengths or competencies in children or youth who seem to be severely impulsive, withdrawn, oppositional, despondent, terrified, regressed, dissociative, or detached. Similarly, their parents or caregivers often seem to be reactive, dejected, resigned, confused, and easily narcissistically wounded, although this may be an understandable outcome of experiencing frustration, loss, isolation, and helplessness secondary to their child's past victimization and ongoing complex traumatic stress reactions. The proposed DTD conceptualization (van der Kolk, 2005) offers not only an expanded range of options for describing children's post-traumatic impairment (beyond existing DSM-IV-TR diagnoses, e.g., PTSD or other internalizing or externalizing childhood disorders) but also a careful review of self-regulation capacities and generalized expectancies (akin to Bowlby's [1969] "working models") that may reveal the child's strengths and internal resources, as well as problems or deficits.

The therapist's own experience of vicarious traumatization and counter-transference (see Pearlman & Caringi, Chapter 10, this volume) may make it difficult to recognize child and caregiver strengths and competencies. However, these pressures may be offset by a rigorous and disciplined focus on identifying and building on the capabilities that have made it possible for the child and caregiver(s) to continue to seek help (even if they seem to be rejecting or sabotaging that very help) and to pursue their personal goals (even if the goals primarily seem to be dysfunctional), beginning from the first therapeutic encounter and continuing in each subsequent assessment and treatment session. Interventions that explicitly orient therapist and clients toward identifying the functional aspects of clients' goals and behavioral choices (e.g., TARGET's distinction between "reactive" and "main" personal goals and behaviors; the emphasis in Real Life Heroes on finding the inner hero; Life Skills/Life Story's provisions for helping youth express their achievements, as well as disappointments, in a personal life story) may help therapists maintain a consistent strengths-based approach.

5. *All phases of treatment should aim to enhance self-regulation competencies.* To fundamentally change a child's perspective from the posttraumatic "survival orientation" that characterizes PTSD and complex traumatic stress disorders to attaining a sense of trust and confidence in self and others, every phase of treatment must be designed to strengthen the child's (and the caregiver's) self-regulation competencies. Self-regulation requires the traumatized child (and the child's caregivers and role models) to shift from affect dysregulation to modulated emotional awareness and expression; from dissociation to planful and mindful, goal-directed behavior; from bodily dysregulation to

awareness and utilization of bodily cues as a guide to self-care and healthy growth; and from disorganized relational engagement and working models to responsive, responsible, and empathic engagement in relationships.

5a. *Emotion regulation.* In toddlerhood, emotion regulation may be enhanced in psychotherapy by assisting the child and caregiver in play and in preparing for and rehearsing daily activities (e.g., meals, bedtime, self-care, problem solving), while labeling their emotions and describing their thoughts, intentions, and choices (Van Horn & Lieberman, 2008). Reducing young children's emotion dysregulation is an important element in secondary or tertiary prevention of self-regulatory and reactive attachment disorders of infancy and early childhood. Psychotherapy addresses emotion regulation in school-age and preadolescent children by assisting children to develop a balance of autonomy, relatedness, and impulse control; adult caregivers (e.g., parents, teachers) often require assistance in learning and effectively using skills that enable them to be primary sources of modeling, encouragement, and rule adherence (Vickerman & Margolin, 2007). At this developmental epoch, peer interactions (e.g., educational or therapeutic groups) also are an important avenue for learning and applying emotional regulation skills—hence, the potential benefit of structured group approaches such as Real Life Heroes (Kagan, 2008), SPARCS (DeRosa & Pelcovitz, 2008), and TARGET (Ford & Russo, 2006). With school-age and preadolescent children, addressing emotion regulation also is crucial to early intervention for or prevention of internalizing and externalizing disorders.

In adolescence, emotion dysregulation may take the form of more severe and potentially chronic internalizing, externalizing, and psychosomatic disorders (e.g., eating disorders, conduct disorder, sexual and gender identity disorders, substance dependence, suicidality, and self-injurious behaviors) that may subsequently lead to personality disorders and serious problems in the legal, school, family, and community domains (e.g., incarceration, truancy, teen pregnancy, gang involvement, suicidality) (Ford, Hartman, Hawke, & Chapman, 2008). Individual, group (Ford, Fallot, & Harris, Chapter 20, this volume), and family (Ford & Saltzman, Chapter 19, this volume) therapies designed or adapted for adolescents can help them to acquire or resume the use of skills for emotion regulation by teaching them ways to deal proactively with unexamined feelings (Fosha, Paivio, Gleiser, & Ford, Chapter 14, this volume), unchallenged beliefs (Gold, Chapter 11, and Jackson, Nissenson, & Cloitre, Chapter 12, this volume), and bodily arousal (Fisher & Ogden, Chapter 15, this volume).

5b. *Attention, memory, decision making (information processing).* Traumatic stress interventions for children cannot singlehandedly remediate significant information processing deficits; therefore, the clinician should always consider using or referring to colleagues with expertise in neuropsychologically informed approaches to cognitive rehabilitation and psychopharmacological treatment. However, to the extent that a child's difficulties in information processing are an adaptation developed to survive and cope with psychological trauma, traumatic stress interventions can address some of the potentially overlooked sources of cognitive impairment facing the child. For example, traumatic stress interventions help children to develop skills for mental "focusing" (Ford & Russo, 2006), mindfulness (DeRosa & Pelcovitz, 2008), cognitive restructuring (Cohen, Mannarino, & Deblinger, 2006), and narrative processing of memories (Cloitre et al., 2006; Ford & Russo, 2006; Kagan, 2008). Each of these models offers specific interventions designed to enhance the traumatized child's ability purposefully to modulate arousal and invoke the controlled (vs. automatic) forms of information processing that involve self-directed attention, memory, logical analysis, and reflective *mentalizing* (i.e., observation of one's own thought processes) (Fonagy, 2003). Cognitive skills also are important in addressing learning problems and enhancing the child's chance of success in school, which is a key to recovery from PTSD (Faust & Katchen, 2004).

5c. *Self-regulation of consciousness and motivation.* Posttraumatic dissociation in children is very challenging to treat directly, because in most children, at least until adolescence, dissociation interferes with the requisite degree of reflective self-awareness necessary to recognize distinct ego states or dissociated "part-selves" (D. Brown, Chapter 6, and Steele & van der Hart, Chapter 7, this volume) and also is beyond their normal developmental capacities. However, the same approaches used in other complex traumatic stress disorder interventions to enhance affect, impulse regulation, and information processing may enable children to reduce the affective and cognitive overload that contribute to and sustain dissociation, and to think mindfully in ways that elicit conscious self-awareness. Caregivers who participate actively in treatment can be assisted in recognizing, understanding, accepting, and validating their children's fragmented experiences of self and others, while they also help their children to experience different states of mind and part-selves as collaborative, and to reconcile their full range of feelings, thoughts, and action potentials. Therapists and group facilitators serve as models for both child and caregiver(s) for how to accept the child's fluctuating states of mind and emotion, while always explicitly making the child's core self the focus for all interactions. Interventions that enhance traumatized children's capacities for emotion, impulse regulation, and information processing are likely to have additional value if they address dissociation as well. For example, labeling specific emotions and role modeling (e.g., by "thinking out loud") a mindful or focused approach defines immediate goals and behaviors that increase the child's access to euthymic feelings and reduces the intensity of negative affect. These approaches not only enhance emotion regulation and information processing but also they are key interventions for dissociative states.

5d. *Bodily self-regulation.* Somatic conditions require a systemic approach to treatment, which includes collaboration among medical (e.g., pediatric, family practice, emergency medicine), psychiatric/psychopharmacology, social work, education, and psychotherapy professionals (Saxe, Ellis, & Kaplow, 2007). In the psychotherapeutic component of treatment, somatic dysregulation may be addressed by explicit mind–body interventions (e.g., mindfulness and distress tolerance skills in dialectic behavior therapy: DeRosa & Pelcovitz, 2008; sensorimotor psychotherapy: Fisher & Ogden, Chapter 15, this volume), as well as indirectly through emotion regulation and information-processing interventions that reduce dissociation and enhance assertive self-determination (Cloitre et al., 2006; DeRosa & Pelcovitz, 2008; Ford & Russo, 2006), and TF-CBT interventions (Cohen et al., 2006) that enable the child and caregivers carefully to reconstruct somatic, as well as behavioral, affective, and cognitive, elements in narrative memories of traumatic experiences.

5e. *Relational self-regulation.* In psychotherapy, both the dyadic therapeutic relationship and relationships with peers and adult caregivers, mentors, and authorities are crucial areas in which role modeling and incremental practice of the self-regulation skills described earlier are necessary to enable the child or adolescent (and often key adults in their lives) to reclaim relatedness (Cloitre, Cohen, & Koenen, 2006). Developmentally, secure attachment appears to be an essential prerequisite for the acquisition of all self-regulation competencies (Farrar, Fasig, & Welch-Ross, 1997). However, in child psychotherapy for complex traumatic stress disorders, the two must be acquired concurrently in a "scaffolding" process that alternately uses gains in one domain to strengthen capacities in the other domain. To experience security and engagement in relationships, traumatized children not only need to have responsive, caring, and facilitative caregivers (and psychotherapists) (Faust & Katchen, 2004) but also to develop the self-regulation skills to be able to tolerate the concurrent post-traumatic reactivity and distress associated with being genuinely cared for, valued, and helped.

6. *Determining with whom, when, and how to address traumatic memories.* The core goal for the treatment of children with complex traumatic stress disorders is to enable them (and their caregivers) to attain what Harvey (1996) described as mastery or "authority" in relation to their own memories—including but not limited to memories of traumatic events (Vickerman & Margolin, 2007). As children develop or regain self-regulation competencies that they need to modulate bodily arousal, recognize and utilize their emotions, think and remember clearly, and maintain a continuous sense of a unified self in secure and healthy relationships, they may spontaneously gain a sense of being able to tolerate and understand traumatic memories. However, memories that remain unprocessed and avoided are likely both to undermine their overall functioning and interfere with or prevent self-regulation. Thus, the answer to the first question—"With whom should traumatic memories be addressed in psychotherapy?"—clearly is, with *every* child (and when possible, with the caregiver) who is impaired as a result of PTSD or complex traumatic stress disorders (Cohen et al., 2006; Saxe, Ellis, & Kaplow, 2007).

The answer to the second question—"When?"—depends on the answer to the third question—"How?" There are really three answers to the latter question: (a) The therapist recognizes the cues and reactions that indicate a child is probably experiencing, or about to experience, traumatic stress reactions and associated self-dysregulation, and he or she guides the child and caregiver in anticipating, preparing for, and, without avoidant coping with these post-traumatic sequelae in the course of therapeutic and daily activities; (b) the therapist teaches the child and caregiver to recognize traumatic stress reactions as ways that they adaptively coped with past traumatic events, and helps them to use self-regulation skills to choose mindfully how to modify unnecessary or unhelpful aspects of those reactions, while preserving and intentionally utilizing the currently ego-syntonic and psychosocially adaptive aspects of those reactions (i.e., to keep the baby but not the bathwater); and (c) the therapist guides the child and caregiver in story-building activities that enable the child to recall purposively and gain a sense of mastery in relation to memories of specific past, troubling traumatic events.

Option *a*, sensitive psychotherapeutic management of clients' triggered distress, is at the core of all psychotherapies for children (and adults). This approach is the hallmark of clinically sensitive and effective therapeutic assessment, therapeutic alliance building, and treatment planning; therefore, it begins in the first client–therapist encounter and continues throughout treatment. This approach involves more than "supportive" psychotherapy, because the clinician specifically guides the client(s) toward more adaptive ways of recognizing and self-regulating when experiencing traumatic stress reactions. It also typically includes more than client-centered empathy and validation (i.e., psychoeducation about stress reactions or signals the client can use to recognize distress), but it does not involve psychoeducation about (nor a detailed assessment of) traumatic stress experiences or reactions. This approach is the appropriate default modality when first beginning child/adolescent or child–parent treatment, unless prior information (e.g., previous evaluations or specific referral requests) confirms that an explicit therapeutic focus on traumatic events and posttraumatic reactions is indicated.

Option *b*, psychoeducation and self-regulation skills training to enhance clients' understanding of and ability to manage trauma-related stress reactions and self-dysregulation, is indicated when a history of exposure to specific psychologically traumatic event(s) has been confirmed or is probable based on credible (preferably multiple, independent) sources, including archival (e.g., child protective services, legal, school) or clinical records, and child and caregiver self-reports on structured trauma history instruments (e.g., Ford et al., 2007); and the child's living arrangements and social support network are sufficiently stable to enable him or her regularly to attend therapeutic sessions frequently enough to learn and recall educational information, and to practice self-regulation skills in emotionally and physically safe, relatively predictable, and validating relationships. The outer boundary for these inclusion criteria includes the child who does not have an intact family system or permanent residence but has at least a temporarily stable residence and relationship with a meaningful caregiver (e.g., living with a single parent and siblings in a homeless shelter or a transitional living or substance abuse rehabilitation setting, or living in an inpatient or residential treatment program, a juvenile detention or incarceration facility, or a group or foster home). In these cases, there is sufficient instability in the predictability or continuity of meaningful caregiver involvement and residential placement to contraindicate more direct traumatic memory work, but the child may benefit from learning about traumatic stress reactions and skills for increasing his or her sense of personal control despite the future uncertainties.

Option *c*, direct reconstruction of traumatic memories, is typically undertaken with a young child and caregiver(s) conjointly, in spontaneous nonverbal activities (Van Horn & Lieberman, 2008). With older children (Cohen et al., 2006) and adolescents (Cloitre et al., 2006), traumatic memory reconstruction more often is done separately with the youth, as a project in which the therapist assists the youth in repeatedly confronting a troubling memory (i.e., *exposure therapy*), with the goal of enabling the youth to think of the memory as a past experience that is over and done, and that can be recalled as fully (i.e., including self-validating as well as upsetting aspects) as other memories and placed within the youth's larger personal story of her or his life (i.e., *narrative reconstruction*). With older children and adolescents, if possible, separate sessions are conducted to prepare caregivers for their child's disclosures, and to help them address their own traumatic memories or stress reactions, followed by a conjoint closure session(s) in which the child shares the reconstructed memory with the caregiver.

Given these parameters, criteria for undertaking trauma memory exposure/reconstruction work should include a stable, physically and psychologically available, permanent primary caregiver who is willing and able to help the child work through traumatic memories; a child with adequate core self-regulation capacities and environmental supports (in daily life settings and via a therapeutic safety net) to be able to manage episodically intense distress and stress reactions, without becoming sufficiently affectively, dissociatively, or behaviorally destabilized to pose an immediate or chronic threat to the child's psychological health or safety (e.g., suicidality; psychotic or dissociative identity decompensation; severe self-injury, substance dependence, or reactive aggression); and a therapist with expertise in conducting traumatic memory reconstruction intervention with children of this age and developmental epoch who have significant complex traumatic stress disorder impairments, and who has access to sufficient psychiatric and crisis backup (e.g., pharmacotherapy, acute crisis evaluation and hospitalization, case management wraparound resources, pediatric care) to be able to identify, prevent, or rapidly resolve treatment-related or -unrelated crises.

The overall approach involves an initial linear progression from option *a* to option *c*, with each successive approach utilized only if traumatic stress or potentially traumatic stress-related symptoms and impairments are present and not sufficiently resolved or managed, and the necessary resources and competencies are in place to move to the next level. In practice, the progression from trauma-informed psychotherapy (option *a*) to traumatic memory re-construction (option *c*) might occur as rapidly as within a single intake evaluation or initial treatment session (e.g., a child referred following or during a course of psychotherapy and pharmacotherapy in which the child and caregiver were stably and productively involved, but the child nevertheless was persistently troubled or impaired by PTSD or complex traumatic stress symptoms associated with well-documented traumatic experience(s) and the therapist did not feel qualified to conduct trauma memory reconstruction interventions). Alternatively, therapy might progress from the trauma-informed to the trauma-focused (option *b*) approach following a few, or several, sessions of initial assessment and therapeutic engagement, then continue at that level while completing a self-regulation–based intervention for PTSD and complex traumatic stress disorders, such as the life skills portion of Life Skills/Life Story (Cloitre et al., 2006), Real Life Heroes (Kagan, 2008), SPARCS (DeRosa & Pelcovitz, 2008), or TARGET (Ford & Russo, 2006). During or after trauma-focused treatment, the approach might be shifted back to trauma-informed treatment (e.g., if addressing traumatic past experiences as a source of current stress reactions or dysregulation is poorly tolerated by the child or caregiver or, in positive contrast, is sufficient to achieve full or substantial remission and to warrant either maintenance therapy or a focus on closure) or moved to trauma memory reconstruction (if sufficient remission has not been accomplished).

7. *Preventing and managing relational discontinuities and psychosocial crises.* Children with complex traumatic stress disorders typically have had to cope with chronic and often unpredictable discontinuities in their primary relationships and social support systems: losses due to deaths, out-of-home placements, institutionalization, family abandonment, and serial treatment providers (Faust & Katchen, 2004); neglect and abuse due to parental and familial psychopathology, substance use disorders, violent or antisocial lifestyles, or severe socioeconomic adversities. They often have come to view caring and facilitative adults or prosocial and accepting peers or peer-group activities (e.g., school, recreational, or social) as transient and likely to lead to disappointment or rejection; thus, even apparently positive events (e.g., birthday, holidays, field trips, family visits, recognition for accomplishments in school, sports, or arts, graduation ceremonies, new residence or school) may elicit stress-related dysregulation. This may be misinterpreted in pathologizing terms as self-sabotage; oppositional defiance or incorrigibility; an inability to tolerate delay of gratification or any deviation from the familiar; dependency; immaturity; or relational "splitting" consistent with borderline personality disorder. The corollary result is increased restrictiveness and intensity of supervision, and treatment emphasizing crisis deescalation or, alternatively, a determination that the child cannot tolerate (or even benefit from) therapeutic placement or services.

From a complex traumatic stress disorder or developmental trauma perspective, distress and dysregulation are predictable when traumatic memories are elicited by and reenacted in response to repetitions of relational discontinuities. Most such instances occur outside of the child's conscious awareness rather than as explicit declarative narrative memories, both due to developmental (Ford & Courtois, Chapter 1, this volume) and dissociative (Steele &

van der Hart, Chapter 7, this volume) factors. Therefore, the best approach to preventing or managing relational discontinuity–related crises or deterioration is to assist the child and caregiver (including health care, educational, judicial/legal, and mental health professionals and social/human service program staff) in anticipating and addressing the predictable dysregulation. This involves understanding the adaptive components (e.g., the child's attempt to protect against additional distress and demoralization, and to communicate to responsible adults the importance of relational continuity) and collaboratively (i.e., both the adults and the child) using self-regulation skills to increase or restore relational continuity. For example, rather than relying on medication, psychotherapy, and psychoeducation primarily to decrease symptom severity in preparation for the transition from an intensive residential treatment program to a group or foster home, treatment for a child with complex traumatic stress impairments would focus on helping the child to use affect regulation and relational skills to strengthen the internalized "working model" of important adults and peers as still caring, supportive, and accessible, despite a greater degree of physical separation.

When crises cannot be prevented, a similar approach that focuses on restoring a sense of relational continuity and self-regulation provides a framework for helping to deescalate distress and stabilize the traumatized child or adolescent. This is an adaptation or special case of generic models of crisis intervention, which prescribe activating two palliative factors: (a) social support to reduce extreme spikes in the intensity of anxiety, dysphoria, anger, confusion, or detachment; and (b) active problem solving to increase the sense of control, efficacy, and optimism. The primary threat to both objective and subjective social support for children with complex traumatic stress disorders is the loss of core relational (attachment) security, which the child experiences as a breakdown not only in relationships but also in self-regulation of the body, emotions, impulse control, memory and thinking, and consciousness (dissociation). Thus, beyond the generic approaches to providing reassurance, immediate safety, structure and limits (e.g., verbal deescalation tactics, timeout), crisis deescalation with traumatized children requires the use of several focal interventions: "grounding" strategies to counteract detachment, dissociation, and impulsivity (e.g., Cloitre et al., 2006; DeRosa & Pelcovitz, 2008; Ford & Russo, 2006); affective engagement strategies to reestablish an immediate sense of emotional connection with self and others (Fosha et al., Chapter 14, this volume); and sensorimotor strategies to increase bodily awareness and arousal modulation (Fisher & Ogden, Chapter 15, this volume). In the aftermath of crises, if therapeutic processing includes discussion of how these self-regulation skills were used by the child to restabilize, the result may be more than a generic review of the "lessons learned" and reaffirmation of the child's commitment to responsible behavior and self-care. Every crisis is an opportunity to highlight and enhance the traumatized child's competence and sense of efficacy in her or his self-regulation skills and trust in relational continuity.

CONCLUSION

Important innovations have been developed for the psychosocial treatment for children and adolescents with complex traumatic stress disorders (see also Resick, Monson, & Gutner, 2007; Welch & Rothbaum, 2007). Approaches to assessment and treatment of pediatric PTSD provide a strong foundation for this work. Two overarching conceptual models have been developed to guide clinicians in treating pediatric PTSD (trauma systems therapy [TST]; Saxe, Ellis, & Kaplow, 2007) and complex traumatic stress disorders (attachment, self-regulation, and competency [ARC]; Kinniburgh, Blaustein, Spinazzola, & van der Kolk, 2005). Each of these models has developed detailed, manualized guidelines for clinicians, extensive worksheets and exercises for children and families, and fidelity monitoring protocols. Clinical application of these models and the other interventions described in this chapter requires a focus on child and caregiver developmental attainments and limitations for self-regulation and relational involvement (Amaya-Jackson & DeRosa, 2007). The clinician also has a responsibility to serve as a role model, coregulator, and guide by using self-regulation skills not only to "talk the talk" but also to "walk the walk" with the child and caregivers. Until definitive guidelines are developed, the provisional principles and suggested strategies provided in this chapter are intended as a starting point for clinicians and clinical researchers.

REFERENCES

Amaya-Jackson, L., & DeRosa, R. (2007). Treatment considerations for clinicians in applying evidence-based practice to complex presentations in child trauma. *Journal of Traumatic Stress, 20,* 379–390.

American Psychological Association Presidential Task Force on Evidence-Based Practice. (2006). Evidence-based practice in psychology. *American Psychologist, 61,* 271–285.

Blaustein, M., & Kinniburgh, K. (2007). Intervention beyond the child: The intertwining nature of attachment and trauma. *British Psychological Society, Briefing Paper, 26,* 48–53.

Bowlby, J. (1969). *Attachment and loss* (Vol. 1). New York: Basic Books.

Browne, C., & Winkelman, C. (2007). The effect of childhood trauma on later psychological adjustment. *Journal of Interpersonal Violence, 22,* 684–697.

Cloitre, M., Cohen, L. R., & Koenen, K. C. (2006). *Treating survivors of childhood abuse: Psychotherapy for the interrupted life.* New York: Guilford Press.

Cohen, E. (2008). Parenting in the throes of traumatic events: Risks and protection. In D. Brom, R. Pat-Horenczyk, & J. D. Ford (Eds.), *Treating traumatized children: Risk, resilience, and recovery* (pp. 72–84). London: Routledge.

Cohen, J. A., Mannarino, A. P., & Deblinger, E. (2006). *Treating trauma and traumatic grief in children and adolescents.* New York: Guilford Press.

Cohen, N. J., Muir, E., Lojkasek, M., Muir, R., Parker, C. J., Barwick, M., et al. (1999). Watch, wait, and wonder. *Infant Mental Health Journal, 20,* 429–451.

Cook, A., Spinazzola, J., Ford, J. D., Lanktree, C., Blaustein, M., Cloitre, M., et al.

(2005). Complex trauma in children and adolescents. *Psychiatric Annals, 35,* 390–398.

De Bellis, M. D. (2001). Developmental traumatology. *Psychoneuroendocrinology, 27,* 155–170.

DeRosa, R., & Pelcovitz, D. (2008). Group treatment for chronically traumatized adolescents: Igniting SPARCS of change. In D. Brom, R. Pat-Horenczyk, & J. D. Ford (Eds.), *Treating traumatized children: Risk, resilience, and recovery* (pp. 225–239). London: Routledge.

Dumont, K., Widom, C. S., & Czaja, S. (2007). Predictors of resilience in abused and neglected children grown-up. *Child Abuse and Neglect, 31,* 255–274.

Farrar, M. J., Fasig, L. G., & Welch-Ross, M. (1997). Attachment and emotion in autobiographical memory development. *Journal of Experimental Child Psychology, 67,* 389–408.

Faust, J., & Katchen, L. B. (2004). Treatment of children with complicated posttraumatic stress reactions. *Psychotherapy: Theory, Research, Practice and Training, 41,* 426–437.

Finkelhor, D., Ormrod, R., & Turner, H. (2007). Poly-victimization: A neglected component in child victimization. *Child Abuse and Neglect, 31,* 7–26.

Fonagy, P. (2003). The development of psychopathology from infancy to adulthood: The mysterious unfolding of disturbance in time. *Infant Mental Health Journal, 24,* 212–239.

Ford, J. D. (2005). Treatment implications of altered neurobiology, affect regulation and information processing following child maltreatment: *Psychiatric Annals, 35,* 410–419.

Ford, J. D., Chapman, J. F., Hawke, J., & Albert, D. (2007). *Trauma among youth in the juvenile justice system.* Delmar, NY: National Center for Mental Health and Juvenile Justice.

Ford, J. D., Chapman, J. F., Pearson, G., Borum, R., Hawke, J., & Wolpaw, J. M. (2008). MAYSI-2 factor structure, reliability, and predictive validity in juvenile detention. *Journal of Psychopathology and Behavioral Assessment, 30,* 87–99.

Ford, J. D., Courtois, C., van der Hart, O., Nijenhuis, E., & Steele, K. (2005). Treatment of complex post-traumatic self-dysregulation. *Journal of Traumatic Stress, 18,* 437–447.

Ford, J. D., & Gurwitch, R. (2008). Parent–child intervention. In G. Reyes, J. D. Elhai, & J. D. Ford (Eds.), *Encyclopedia of psychological trauma* (pp. 457–463). Hoboken, NJ: Wiley.

Ford, J. D., Hartman, J. K., Hawke, J., & Chapman, J. (2008). Traumatic victimization, posttraumatic stress disorder, suicidal ideation, and substance abuse risk among juvenile justice-involved youths. *Journal of Child and Adolescent Trauma, 1,* 75–92.

Ford, J. D., & Russo, E. (2006). A trauma-focused, present-centered, emotional self-regulation approach to integrated treatment for post-traumatic stress and addiction. *American Journal of Psychotherapy, 60,* 335–355.

Freyd, J. (1994). Betrayal trauma. *Ethics and Behavior, 4,* 307–329.

Harvey, M. (1996). An ecological view of psychological trauma and trauma recovery. *Journal of Traumatic Stress, 9,* 3–23.

Herman, J. L. (1992). Complex PTSD. *Journal of Traumatic Stress, 5,* 377–391.

Jaberghaderi, N., Greenwald, R., Rubin, A., Dolatabadim, S., & Zand, S. O. (2004). A comparison of CBT and EMDR for sexually abused Iranian girls. *Psychology and Psychotherapy, 11,* 358–368.

Josephson, A., & the AACAP Work Group on Quality Issues. (2007). Practice parameter for the assessment of the family. *Journal of the American Academy of Child and Adolescent Psychiatry, 46*, 922–937.

Kagan, R. (2008). Transforming troubled children into tomorrow's heroes. In D. Brom, R. Pat-Horenczyk, & J. D. Ford (Eds.), *Treating traumatized children: Risk, resilience, and recovery* (pp. 255–268). London: Routledge.

Kataoka, S., Stein, B. D., Jaycox, L., Wong, M., Escudero, P., Tu, W., et al. (2003). A school-based mental health program for traumatized Latino immigrant children. *Journal of the American Academy of Child and Adolescent Psychiatry, 42*, 311–318.

Kinniburgh, K., Blaustein, M., Spinazzola, J., & van der Kolk, B. (2005). Attachment, self-regulation, and competency. *Psychiatric Annals, 35*, 424–430.

Ko, S., Ford, J. D., Kassam-Adams, N., Berkowitz, S., Saunders, B., Smith, D., et al. (in press). Creating trauma-informed child-serving systems. *Professional Psychology.*

Liotti, G. (2004). Trauma, dissociation and disorganized attachment: Three strands of a single braid. *Psychotherapy: Theory, Research, Practice, and Training, 41*, 472–484.

Lyons-Ruth, K., Dutra, L., Schuder, M., & Bianchi, I. (2006). From infant attachment disorganization to adult dissociation: Relational adaptations or traumatic experiences? *Psychiatric Clinics of North America, 29*, 63–86.

McDonough, S. (2000). Interaction guidance. In C. H. Zeanah, Jr. (Ed.), *Handbook of infant mental health* (2d ed., pp. 485–493). New York: Guilford Press.

Miltenburg, R., & Singer, E. (1999). Culturally mediated learning and the development of self-regulation by survivors of child abuse. *Human Development, 42*, 1–17.

Nadar, K. (2008). *Understanding and assessing trauma in children and adolescents.* New York: Routledge.

Najavits, L. M., Gallop, R. J., & Weiss, R. D. (2006). Seeking Safety therapy for adolescent girls with PTSD and substance use disorder: A randomized trial. *Journal of Behavioral Health Services and Research, 33*, 453–463.

Pelcovitz, D., van der Kolk, B., Roth, S., Mandel, F., Kaplan, S., & Resick, P. (1997). Development of a criteria set and a structured interview for disorders of extreme stress (DESNOS). *Journal of Traumatic Stress, 10*, 3–16.

Resick, P. A., Monson, C. M., & Gutner, C. (2007). Psychosocial treatments for PTSD. In M. J. Friedman, T. M. Keane, & P. A. Resick (Eds.), *Handbook of PTSD: Science and practice* (pp. 330–358). New York: Guilford Press.

Roth, S., Newman, E., Pelcovitz, D., van der Kolk, B., & Mandel, F. (1997). Complex PTSD in victims exposed to sexual and physical abuse. *Journal of Traumatic Stress, 10*, 539–555.

Saxe, G. N., Ellis, B. H., & Kaplow, J. B. (2007). *Collaborative treatment of traumatized children and teens: The trauma systems therapy approach.* New York: Guilford Press.

Saxe, G. N., MacDonald, H. Z., & Ellis, B. H. (2007). Psychosocial approaches for children with PTSD. In M. J. Friedman, T. M. Keane, & P. A. Resick (Eds.), *Handbook of PTSD: Science and practice* (pp. 359–375). New York: Guilford Press.

Scheeringa, M. S., Salloum, A., Armberger, R., Weems, C., Amaya-Jackson, L., & Cohen, J. (2007). Feasibility and effectiveness of cognitive-behavioral therapy for posttraumatic stress disorder in preschool children: Two case reports. *Journal of Traumatic Stress, 20*, 631–636.

Schore, A. (2001). The effects of early relational trauma on right brain development, affect regulation, and infant mental health. *Infant Mental Health Journal, 22,* 201–269.

Spinazzola, J., Blaustein, M., & van der Kolk, B. (2005). Posttraumatic stress disorder treatment outcome research. *Journal of Traumatic Stress, 18,* 425–436.

Stein, B. D., Jaycox, L. H., Kataoka, S. H., Wong, M., Tu, W., Elliott, M. N., et al. (2003). A mental health intervention for schoolchildren exposed to violence: A randomized controlled trial. *Journal of the American Medical Association, 290,* 603–611.

van der Kolk, B. (2005). Developmental trauma disorder. *Psychiatric Annals, 35,* 439–448.

van der Kolk, B., Roth, S., Pelcovitz, D., Sunday, S., & Spinazzola, J. (2005). Disorders of extreme stress. *Journal of Traumatic Stress, 18,* 389–399.

Van Horn, P., & Lieberman, A. (2008). Using dyadic therapies to treat traumatized children. In D. Brom, R. Pat-Horenczyk, & J. D. Ford (Eds.), *Treating traumatized children: Risk, resilience, and recovery* (pp. 210–224). London: Routledge.

Vickerman, K., & Margolin, G. (2007). Posttraumatic stress in children and adolescents exposed to family violence: II. Treatment. *Professional Psychology, 38,* 620–628.

Welch, S. S., & Rothbaum, B. O. (2007). Emerging treatments for PTSD. In M. J. Friedman, T. M. Keane, & P. A. Resick (Eds.), *Handbook of PTSD: Science and practice* (pp. 469–496). New York: Guilford Press.

CHAPTER 4

Best Practices
in Psychotherapy for Adults

Christine A. Courtois
Julian D. Ford
Marylene Cloitre

In recent years, numerous professional organizations have sought to improve and to standardize treatment of medical and mental disorders by publishing treatment guidelines. Although the intention was to draw from the scientific evidence base for these guidelines, expert opinion and consensus often have contributed heavily, because the more formalized research base on treatment efficacy and outcome was slim for some disorders. Such was initially the case with posttraumatic stress disorder (PTSD) and dissociative disorders. The first treatment guideline, published in 1994 on the treatment of what was then called multiple personality disorder, subsequently has been revised twice for the renamed dissociative identity disorder (International Society for the Study of Dissociation, 2005). The initial treatment guideline specifically for PTSD was published in 1999 (Foa, Davidson, & Frances, 1999). Since then, a number of PTSD treatment guidelines have been published, mostly for adults, although two have been directed specifically toward the treatment of children and adolescents (Ford & Cloitre, Chapter 3, this volume).

In the past decade, a number of other guidelines for treating adult PTSD have been produced. Each has made recommendations based on the evaluation of the quality of the aggregate research database and on expert opinion. PTSD treatment guidelines published to date include a definitive set by the International Society for Traumatic Stress Studies (ISTSS), based on reviews assessing the strength of the available evidence for a range of psychological and psychiatric treatments for PTSD (Foa, Keane, & Friedman, 2000); the U.S. Department of Veterans Affairs (VA; 2004); the Clinical Resource Efficiency

Support Team, part of the Northern Ireland Health Service (CREST; 2003); the American Psychiatric Association (2004); the British National Institute for Clinical Excellence (NICE; 2005); the Institute of Medicine of the National Academies (IOM; 2006); and the Australian Centre for Posttraumatic Mental Health at the University of Melbourne (ACPMH; 2007) (see *www.trauma-pages.com/s/tx_guides.php*).

Development of these PTSD treatment guidelines is based on the established diagnostic criteria for PTSD in the fourth text revised edition of the *Diagnostic and Statistical Manual of Mental Disorders* (DSM-IV-TR; American Psychological Association, 2000), criteria that do not formally include the symptom constellations associated with more complex repeated and cumulative interpersonal and attachment trauma. The PTSD criteria from DSM-IV-TR identify several of these symptoms (e.g., affect dysregulation, dissociation) as "associated features" of PTSD but do not include them in the diagnostic algorithm for PTSD. This limited focus has been challenged, and the applicability of recommendations contained in the currently available PTSD treatment guidelines has been called into question (van der Kolk & Courtois, 2005), because treatment outcome research has focused almost exclusively on PTSD symptomatology. Posttraumatic problems not captured in the PTSD criteria, including affective, anxiety, dissociative, somatoform, and obsessive–compulsive disorders, as well as substance abuse, often are referred to as *comorbid conditions*. Yet many patients with the most severe "comorbidities" drop out of (McDonagh-Coyle et al., 2005) or are screened out of (Spinazzola, Blaustein, & van der Kolk, 2005) PTSD treatment studies.

Despite this critique, the currently available treatment guidelines for PTSD definitely have applicability to complex traumatic stress disorders, especially explicit PTSD symptoms. Ford and Kidd (1998) reported that a percentage of the individuals they studied met criteria for "stand-alone" complex PTSD/ disorders of extreme stress not otherwise specified (DESNOS) but others met criteria for DESNOS *and* PTSD. The treatment guidelines for the dissociative disorders are highly applicable, because they address a significant subpopulation of individuals whose complex trauma reactions include considerable dissociation. For more than two decades (Kluft, 1985; Putnam, 1989), dissociation has been an underrecognized feature of complex traumatic stress exposure (see Steele & van der Hart, Chapter 7, this volume). Developmental studies have offered theoretical and research evidence to suggest how dissociation is an intergenerational process in many abusive families, related in part to unresolved trauma and loss at the parental level. Dissociation becomes a physiologically and emotionally mediated symptom and interactional process for many complex trauma survivors. The available guidelines also include much useful information in organizing and managing treatment, such as the establishment of treatment assessment strategies and instruments, goals of treatment, and techniques that have empirical support.

Since the publication of the van der Kolk and Courtois (2005) editorial, although more research has been undertaken and outcome data have been made available for the treatment of complex posttraumatic stress disorders, the empirical base remains limited, and no formal treatment guidelines for complex trauma have yet been published. However, a number of theory-based books, chapters, and summaries from a variety of theoretical orientations (some of which also include research substantiation) have been published by clinicians who have been treating complex traumatic stress disorders; these document some of the lessons learned over past 25 years and provide treatment recommendations and guidance drawn from that experience (Briere, 2002; Bromberg, 1998; Brown & Fromm, 1986; Chu, 1998; Cloitre, Cohen, & Koenen, 2006; Courtois, 1999, 2004; Davies & Frawley, 1994; Ford, Courtois, van der Hart, Nijenhuis, & Steele, 2005; Herman, 1992; Kluft, 1999; McCann & Pearlman, 1990; Solomon & Siegel, 2003). To date, these works, along with the current development of integrative (or hybrid) treatment models and outcome testing (see Chapters 11–20, this volume) are an *evolving evidence base* for *preliminary treatment recommendations and provisional best practices* for complex traumatic stress disorders.

The purpose of this chapter is to present preliminary best-practice guidelines based on this growing evidence base that, per the American Psychological Association Presidential Task Force on Evidence-Based Practice (2006), comprises not only research findings but also clinicians' real-world observations and client values and preferences. The guidelines are based on "the judicious, explicit, and conscientious use of the evidence base to guide one's clinical practice" (Sackett, Rosenberg, Gray, Haynes, & Richardson, 1996, quoted in Amaya-Jackson & DeRosa, 2007, p. 379).

COMPLEX TRAUMA, COMPLEX REACTIONS, COMPLEX TREATMENT

Complex Trauma

Complex psychological trauma refers to experiences that (1) involve repetitive or prolonged exposure to, or experiencing of multiple traumatic stressors, most often of an interpersonal design in a variety of milieus and roles; (2) involve harm or abandonment by caregivers or ostensibly responsible adults; and (3) occur at developmentally vulnerable times in the person's life, especially over the course of childhood, and become intertwined with and incorporated within the child's biopsychosocial development.

Complex Reactions

The psychological, emotional, and social consequences of these experiences are viewed as being based in and shaped by developmental processes and are further understood to be efforts that follow adaptation to highly adverse and aversive events rather than a disease process. The consequences of such adaptation can lead to a reduction in the growth of normative emotional and social capacities that would otherwise have developed, the stunting of self-development, and impairment in routine functions of day-to-day life. Symptoms are viewed as the result of adaptive efforts that have gone awry, in which the individual does not have sufficient resources to respond to the traumatic stressor or additional nontraumatic environmental demands, or to renew adaptive processes when environmental circumstances change.

Moreover, effective responses to traumatic stressors lead to emphasis in particular responses, particularly those related to heightened arousal, narrowing of attentional resources, and constriction of emotional and bodily experience to fight, flee, avoid, or defend against the trauma. Over time, particularly during the developmental years, such responses can become relatively crystallized, leading to limitations in flexibility and strength in the full range of responses available within each of these domains of human capacity. This is reflected in what is termed *self-dysregulation*, or impairment in modulation of arousal, attention, cognition, and relational behaviors. In addition, *self-dysregulation* refers to difficulty in integrating all of these capacities such that emotion, cognition, and bodily experience are unified in a single experience and can lead to self-directed and purposeful behavior. Self-regulation and a sense of identity, core beliefs, and relationships are major foci of treatment goals. The following seven criteria proposed for complex PTSD/DESNOS (Herman, 1992) include attention to the central role of dysregulation. These criteria, along with attachment disturbances, are foci of the treatment of complex traumatic stress disorders.

1. *Alterations in the regulation of affective impulses*, including difficulty with modulation of anger and self-destructiveness. This category has come to include all methods used for emotional regulation and self-soothing, including addictions and self-harming behaviors that, paradoxically, are often life saving.

2. *Alterations in attention and consciousness*, leading to amnesias and dissociative episodes and depersonalization. This category includes emphasis on dissociative responses other than those found in the DSM criteria for PTSD.

3. *Alterations in self-perception*, such as a chronic sense of guilt and responsibility, and ongoing feelings of intense shame. Chronically abused individuals often incorporate the "lessons of abuse" into their identities and self-worth: They often feel bad, evil, malignantly special, and not worthy of attention from others.

4. *Alterations in perception of the perpetrator*, including taking on the perpetrator's views or feeling a sympathetic bond with the perpetrator following repetitive and premeditated abuse, which may exacerbate problems with ambivalent, avoidant, or disorganized attachment.

5. *Alterations in relationship to others* due to insecure or disorganized attachment inner working models (e.g., pervasive distrust or not being able to feel intimate with others).

6. *Somatization and/or medical problems* that relate directly to the type of abuse suffered and resultant physical damage, or that diffusely involve all body systems.

7. *Alterations in systems of meaning*, including hopelessness about finding anyone who can help or understand one's suffering, and despair of being able to recover.

Complex Treatment

Philosophical Foundations

The treatment of complex traumatic stress disorders is explicitly founded on professionalism and a scientific attitude, including the standards of practice and codes of ethical conduct that have been developed over the years by the mental health professions to guide the responsible practice of psychotherapy. The following are additional philosophical foundations upon which this treatment is built.

RECOGNIZING THE UNIQUENESS OF THE INDIVIDUAL

The model is organized around recognition of the primacy and uniqueness of the individual, and the maintenance of his or her welfare. Treatment is not one size fits all; rather, each client is assessed, and treatment is planned differentially according to the specific needs of the individual: This is a phenomenological approach; see Briere & Spinazzola, Chapter 5, this volume). A "whole person" philosophy prevails: Although symptoms, deficits, and distress are reasons for seeking treatment and generally become the targets for intervention, the individual's strengths, resources, resilience, personalized needs, values, and contexts are identified and reinforced.

PERSONAL EMPOWERMENT

A strengths- and resilience-based philosophy of personal empowerment and self-determination encourages the therapist to seek to understand the individual's unique phenomenological experience and its specific meaning and relationship to symptoms, distress, and treatment goals. The individual has authority over the meaning and interpretation of his or her personal life history, current needs and preferences, and goals for the future. The therapist functions as an active, empathic, and responsive listener and guide to enable the client to voice openly, examine, and therapeutically work through feelings of confusion, shame, or other emotions that have been suppressed or forbidden. The therapist seeks to create relational conditions in which the client is emotionally validated and is "seen" and appreciated, to counter the invalidation experiences typically associated with attachment trauma and subsequent victimization, and to encourage emotional expression and development.

The therapist strives within the treatment to create conditions that are as egalitarian as possible and that encourage collaboration with and empowerment of the client; however, the responsibilities and inherent power differences in the treatment relationship are explicitly acknowledged. The therapist seeks to use power effectively on the individual's behalf, while encouraging the client's development and autonomy. Importantly, the therapist conveys an openness to the client's questioning of authority (including that of the therapist) and supports the client's ultimate authority over his or her life, memories, and therapeutic engagement and progress. Moreover, the therapist is careful to maintain appropriate boundaries and limitations, and is responsible for avoiding dual relationships and situations in which the client might be subject to intentional or inadvertent pressure, coercion, or exploitation by the therapist. *Treatment should be based in a systematic (not* laissez-faire*) shared plan that utilizes effective treatment practices, and is organized around a careful assessment and a hierarchically ordered, planned sequence of interventions* (see below).

Professional Training and Ongoing Supervision and Consultation

The treatment relies on the therapist's foundation of professional training, suitable qualifications, emotional maturity, and competence. Unfortunately, issues of interpersonal violence and traumatization continue to be omitted from most curricula in the mental health professions. Training or supervision in the treatment of posttraumatic conditions, especially as it concerns complex stress disorders, has been difficult to find (Courtois, 2001). In addition to an appropriate knowledge and skills base, therapists must have sufficient emotional maturity to deal with affectively charged disclosures and relational dynamics associated with complex trauma histories and symptoms, as well as the often comorbid problems with addiction, serious mental illness, and client histories of marginally effective or ineffective treatment. Therapists who have not had training and supervision to anticipate these issues may have great difficulty managing transference, countertransference, and vicarious trauma reactions, leading to therapeutic errors they might otherwise not have made (Dalenberg, 2000). Without this preparation, therapists may become very frustrated and distressed in ways that may add to the client's sense of stigma and reactivate or intensify client distress rather than assist therapeutically in the resolution of these issues.

Assessment

PRINCIPLES AND STRATEGIES

Strategies and instruments for the assessment of traumatized individuals are relatively recent developments in clinical practice. A variety of specialized instruments are now available for both posttraumatic and dissociative conditions and disorders (Briere & Spinazzola, Chapter 5, this volume). Yet the assessment of standard forms of PTSD using instruments developed for DSM-IV criteria may not cover the complexity of these patients, including developmental aspects of the trauma history, functional and self-regulatory impairment, personal resources and resilience, and patterns of revictimization (D. Brown, Chapter 6, this volume).

1. *Embed assessment of trauma within a standard psychosocial assessment.* From the point of intake, the clinician should include questions having to do with attachment, various types of trauma and victimization in the individual's past and/or current life, and posttraumatic and/or dissociative symptomatology. The rationale for this recommendation is that a large number of individuals seeking mental health treatment do so because of the direct or indirect consequences of past traumatization and attachment problems (Briere & Spinazzola, Chapter 5, this volume), and individuals who meet diagnostic criteria for PTSD and for dissociative disorders often use substantial amounts of mental health services.

2. *Inquiry about attachment problems, trauma or victimization history, or trauma/dissociative symptoms do not automatically result in disclosure.* Some individuals are unwilling or unable to disclose much about themselves, especially early in the assessment or treatment process.

3. *The individual must be approached with respect and with the understanding that being asked about and/or disclosing trauma/victimization/attachment problems can lead to dysregulated emotions.* The therapist must convey an attitude of openness and sensitivity, and ask questions from a position of interested and supportive neutrality.

4. *Inquiry about and discussion of trauma details can cause the spontaneous emergence of symptoms.* The therapist should be aware of this possibility and be prepared to respond in a preventive way. Being sensitive to this range of possible responses conveys several important messages to the client, namely, that the emotional content associated with traumatization can be overwhelming, and that the therapist recognizes this and gives precedence to the individual's safety and welfare.

5. *Specialized assessment might need to be repeated at different points in treatment, because trauma history and posttraumatic and dissociative symptoms may emerge gradually as safety and stabilization are achieved, some precursor issues have been addressed, or the individual's PTSD symptoms have been triggered in some way.* Although some symptoms are blatant and highly evident, others are very subtle, and their function is to maintain secrecy and safety. Unfortunately, most clinicians are not trained to recognize flashbacks and other posttraumatic symptoms, or numbing, state switching, and other dissociative symptoms, so they might miss their emergence or misunderstand/misdiagnose them.

INSTRUMENTS AND STRATEGIES

1. *Traditional and standard psychological assessment instruments do not adequately tap posttraumatic or dissociative symptoms.* When utilizing psychological questionnaires or interviews in the initial assessment (e.g., Minnesota Multiphasic Personality Inventory or Millon Multiaxial Clinical Inventory; Structured Clinical Interview for DSM-IV), the assessor should be aware that although the measures may identify many symptom and function domains, they likely will not adequately tap domains associated with posttraumatic and dissociative symptomatology, or with attachment style. Therefore, the recommendation is to supplement standardized tests with methodologically sound screening instruments, symptom inventories, and clinical interviews designed for those domains (Briere & Spinazzola, Chapter 5, this volume).

2. *Assessment begins in a general way and becomes more specialized according to the symptoms and needs of the individual.* The recommended strategy is to start with a general biopsychosocial assessment and move toward trauma-focused screenings, tests, and interviews, as indicated. Clinical indications of potential PTSD or dissociative symptoms should be carefully examined, followed by a detailed specialized assessment. Because comorbid medical and psychological conditions and symptoms (e.g., problems with eating, sexuality, dysphoria, addiction, physical illness) are common among clients with complex trauma histories, specialized instruments are used as needed. In some cases, outside consultations or specialized corollary assessments (e.g., sleep monitoring, neuropsychological or neuroimaging testing; hormonal testing) might be in order.

Treatment Goals for PTSD Symptoms

Obviously, treatment goals are linked to the integrated assessment findings and to the client's identified needs. A number of specifically designed goals for the treatment of the major symptoms of PTSD have been identified (Wilson, Friedman, & Lindy, 2001) and are applied alone or in combination as needed. They include increased physical and psychological safety and stability; enhanced self-esteem and trust; reduced severity of PTSD symptoms; reestablishment of normal stress response; deconditioning of anxiety/fear; processing of emotions and traumatic memories; recovery from comorbid problems; maintained or improved adaptive functioning and social relationships; reengagement in life; enhanced social support; and development of a relapse prevention plan.

Additional Treatment Goals for Complex Traumatic Stress Disorders

As a group, clients with complex trauma disorders have developmental/attachment deficits that require additional treatment focus. Thus, treatment goals are more extensive than those directed at PTSD symptoms alone and are geared to work with developmental deficits and the seven symptom categories of DESNOS/complex PTSD, as noted earlier. The goals include the following: overcoming developmental deficits; acquiring skills for emotion experiencing, expression, and self-regulation; restoring or developing a capacity for secure, organized relational attachments; enhancing personality integration and recovery of dissociated emotion and knowledge; restoring or acquiring personal authority over the remembering process; and restoring or enhancing physical health.

Several therapeutic foci must be addressed to achieve these goals:

- Bodily as well as mental functioning, including both sensorimotor integration and neurochemical and psychophysiological integrity.
- The capacity not just to tolerate but to actively modulate emotional distress.
- Restoration or acquisition of internal working models of attachment security and the capacity to selectively engage with and trust others.
- Skills for inhibiting risky or ineffective behaviors, and activating and consistently utilizing effective problem-solving and life management tactics.
- Identification of dissociative processes and dissociative sequestering of emotions, thoughts, perceptions, and memories, while encouraging personality integration and the integration of emotions and knowledge that have been dissociated.
- A sense of self as whole, integrated, worthy, and efficacious, while coming to understand the origins and falsity of a view of self as defective, failing, incompetent, dependent, or irreversibly damaged.
- Prevention of reenactments of the trauma and revictimization of self and others.
- Overcoming the dynamics of betrayal-trauma and ambivalent attachment to abusive and nonprotective caregivers.
- Restoration or acquisition of an existential sense of life as worth living and a sense of spiritual connection and meaning.

Goals may also be developed for highly individualized concerns raised by the client (e.g., specific sexual problems; safe visits with abusive family members; lack of parenting skills; conflict resolution in the family or at work; confrontation of addictive denial). These goals may change according to the phase and focus of treatment, and to the emergence of crisis circumstances and requirements (e.g., suicide attempt, self-harm, addiction relapse). The therapist should not be surprised that the achievement of a goal and/or the resolution of an issue might lead to the emergence of other concerns that were previously dormant or not in evidence. For example, sobriety might lead to the emergence of intrusive memories of abuse that the client did not find troubling previously. Smoking cessation might lead to increased dissociation or problems with anger. Death of a trauma perpetrator might lead to the emergence of clients' previously unacknowledged feelings and memories.

Phases and Guiding Principles of Treatment

The metamodel most widely used in contemporary treatment of complex traumatic stress disorders involves three stages or phases of treatment organized to address specific issues sequentially and skills in a relatively hierarchical order (Herman, 1992; Janet, 1889). Careful sequencing of therapeutic activities and tasks is called for, with initial emphasis placed on safety and emotion regulation. Functionality may be reduced temporarily at critical junctures in therapy (e.g., at the outset, when disclosing trauma memories, as completion approaches). It is therefore important that the therapist carefully monitor signs of such functional decline and, when it is identified, work collaboratively to help the client modulate the intensity of emotional reactions and enhance sources of support and relational security outside therapy.

PHASE I. SAFETY AND STABILIZATION: PRINCIPLES AND TASKS

Phase 1 is usually the longest stage of the treatment and the most important to its success. It includes pretreatment issues, such as the development of motivation for treatment, informed consent, and education about what psychotherapy is about and how to participate most successfully. It begins the development of the treatment relationship in a way that allows a collaborative alliance over time. It is now recognized that good foundational work in this phase is likely to improve the client's life substantially (Pearlman & Caringi, Chapter 10, this volume). Some clients do so well in this phase that they may either have no need to complete the other two phases of treatment or choose not to do so. Others never move beyond or complete this phase, and instead use it as life maintenance and a source of needed support.

1. *Personal and interpersonal safety is an essential condition for successful treatment and may take time to develop.* As noted earlier, complex trauma survivors often live in conditions of relational and life chaos and lack basic forms of safety in relation to others (e.g., domestic or community violence) and themselves (e.g., self-harm, suicidality, addictions, risk taking). Therefore, a first order of treatment is to establish conditions of safety to the fullest extent possible. The client cannot progress if a relative degree of safety is not available or attainable: Lack of safety means that the client must continue to engage in defensive and protective strategies, without which he or she will be emotionally overwhelmed and more vulnerable to further victimization. When the client continues to be in an unsafe situation (ongoing domestic violence, incest, sexual harassment, political repression, etc.), the therapist should focus almost entirely on providing education and support, and developing safety plans, and should not move beyond the initial stage of treatment. This prin-

ciple also relates to the treatment relationship, which must provide conditions of interpersonal safety and security.

2. *Treatment must enhance the client's ability to manage extreme arousal states.* Treatment assists the client in identifying arousal states, clarifying perceptions and thoughts, labeling emotions, and carrying through decisions that result in actions to prevent or manage the extremes of hyperarousal (e.g., panic, impulsive risk taking, rage, dissociation) or hypoarousal (e.g., emotional numbing, relational detachment, exhaustion, paralysis, hopelessness) associated with complex traumatic stress disorders. Thus, clients learn to self-modulate their states of arousal, often through specific skills training interventions, rather than remaining reactive or dissociated.

3. *Treatment must enhance the client's ability to approach and master rather than avoid internal bodily/affective states and external events that trigger intrusive reexperiencing, emotional numbing or dissociation, and hyper- or hypoarousal.* Avoidance is a hallmark of traumatic stress disorders, and resolving avoidance is a benchmark for successful treatment (Foa et al., 1999); however, avoidance that may have been driven by a healthy motivation to survive overwhelming experiences may have become problematic when it became automatic. Reversing avoidance and developing ways of actively engaging with both positive and negative experiences and memories requires growth in the form of a shift from automaticity and reactivity to conscious approach and self-regulation. A fundamental challenge beginning in Phase 1 and continuing in all treatment phases is to enhance awareness of subtle, as well as obvious, forms of avoidance of anticipated danger or distress, and of the safety signals that may be used as focal points to modulate anxiety to lead to more effective active coping tactics.

4. *Client education is also an integral component of Phase 1 and optimally begins immediately.* Education can demystify psychotherapy, a process that might be terrifying to the client. Education about trauma and its impact is important and may effectively help clients understand their reactions and develop increased self-compassion. Education is also the foundation for the subsequent teaching of specific skills.

5. *The first phase of treatment should introduce awareness about and enhance the client's sense of self and of relational capacities.* Developmentally adverse interpersonal trauma fundamentally interferes with the acquisition of a sense of positive identity, personal control, and self-efficacy (Ford & Courtois, Chapter 1, this volume). Particular attention needs to be paid to assisting clients in identity development and in recognizing ways that they are (or can be) personally and interpersonally capable, without being overwhelmed by negative emotions. This process is a collaborative analysis by client and therapist of the client's self-perceptions, values, and emotions, current and past relational capacities and interpersonal problems, and personal resources. Based on this assessment, the therapist can provide education about how early life experiences with caregivers and subsequent psychological trauma shape

the individual's "working model" of attachment, and how this develops into *schemas* or templates for a sense of self, and current and future relationships.

Building relations with others and support networks is a crucial part of this phase. Mistrust is a major interpersonal hallmark of many complex trauma clients due to their experience with exploitive and nonprotective caregivers. Clients are assisted in recognizing and understanding the origins of their insecure and disorganized attachment patterns, while experiencing a secure relational base through interaction with the therapist and the role modeling of interpersonal skills by the therapist.

6. *Although Phase 1 does not specifically focus on trauma memory processing and resolution, much of the work described earlier either directly or indirectly relates to traumatic antecedents.* The major difference between this phase and the next is that in Phase 1, the impact of past traumatic experiences is addressed primarily by teaching the client how posttraumatic stress and developmental problems are expectable and adaptive reactions to traumatic experiences in childhood. The client's ongoing symptoms become the basis for determining whether more directed work with trauma memories is required. If the client continues to have PTSD, as well as other symptoms, and is willing to work more directly on trauma memories, treatment proceeds to Phase 2. At times, the shift into Phase 2 is explicitly initiated by the clinician, based on an evaluation of the client's readiness. At other times, it proceeds rather seamlessly from some of the cognitive work to a discussion of feelings associated with the cognitive process. Clients might also move back and forth between phases, especially in times of crisis and/or when they need to refresh skills or apply, or reformulate, their safety plan.

PHASE 2. THE PROCESSING OF TRAUMATIC MEMORIES: PRINCIPLES AND TASKS

1. *Safe self-reflective disclosure of traumatic memories and associated reactions in the form of progressively elaborated and coherent autobiographical narrative is the primary tasks of this phase.* Narrative reconstruction of memories must be timed and structured to support the client's ability not only to tolerate trauma memories and emotions but also to gain a sense of self-efficacy and a coherent life story that encompasses personal success and growth, as well as psychological trauma and decline. In this phase, clients are encouraged to feel the emotions associated with the traumatic experiences and relationships, in other words, to associate or reassociate rather than to dissociate reactions. Thus, they feel, rather than detach from, the impact of trauma as they are helped to understand and to accept their trauma-related emotions. In complex traumatic stress disorder treatment, the focal emotions are not limited to anxiety (as is the case in PTSD treatment, in which other emotions are considered secondary). Grief and mourning often are foci, as are shame and rage. Additionally, the client may undertake specific actions to resolve

relationships with abusers or others, for example, through disclosures and discussions, boundary development, separation or reconnection from a position of increased awareness, understanding, and interpersonal and self-regulatory skills.

In light of the arousal and distress management difficulties experienced by clients with complex traumatic stress disorders, revisiting traumatic memories is a particularly sensitive endeavor. Some treatment models specifically do not prescribe recall of traumatic memories, focusing instead on enhancing clients' capacities for self-regulation in their current lives (e.g., McDonagh-Coyle et al.'s, 2005, present-centered therapy) or on strengthening clients' abilities to examine reflectively the full range of past and recent memories, without focusing on traumatic experiences per se (e.g., Courtois, 1999; Ford & Russo, 2006; Pearlman & Caringi, Chapter 10, and Follette, Iverson, & Ford, Chapter 13, this volume). These therapies explicitly link the client's processing of current stressful or emotionally evocative experiences to the resolution of the sense of distress and helplessness that can lead to avoidance of traumatic memories. Thus, they approach memory work with an emphasis on helping the client to reconstruct and process memories and associated emotions when and if he or she chooses, thus countering the posttraumatic avoidance of feared or overwhelming memories by building self-regulation capacities for memory processing rather than prescribing memory recall as a required or even recommended component of treatment. Those self-regulation capacities can then be called upon by client and therapist if and when traumatic memories are a source of concern for the client, or if the client wishes to tell his or her story in the therapy.

Other treatment models utilize a similar "narrative reconstruction" approach to assist clients in gaining a sense of mastery or authority over their memories, first in relation to the full range of life experiences, as a preparation for systematically revisiting and reconstructing traumatic memories in narrative form (e.g., Cloitre et al.'s, 2006, Life Skills/Life Story model). These approaches also include the strengthening of a range of skills for emotion and interpersonal self-regulation prior to engaging the client in the narrative reconstruction of traumatic memories. The goal of narrative reconstruction is to restore both the client's sense of authority over his or her own memories (Harvey, 1996) and the actual ability to recall traumatic memories using episodic/declarative memory operations (which may be impaired by complex trauma; Ford & Courtois, Chapter 1, this volume).

An alternative approach to memory reconstruction is the cognitive-behavioral therapy method of exposure therapy. Whether using a desensitization (i.e., graduated exposure), flooding (i.e., prolonged exposure), or hybrid (e.g., eye movement desensitization and reprocessing [EMDR]; cognitive processing therapy [CPT] method, exposure therapy involves the client recalling a specific traumatic memory as vividly as possible in first-person mode (i.e., as if it were happening in the present moment). Exposure therapy seeks to directly counter anxiety-based avoidance of traumatic recollection and to give the client a sense of self-determination and hardiness in recalling traumatic memories (in contrast to feeling that these memories intrude in an unwanted and overwhelming manner).

No approach to memory reconstruction work has been definitively validated for clients with complex traumatic stress disorders, although Resick, Nishith, and Griffin (2003) showed that CPT was well tolerated and effective with women who had PTSD secondary to childhood abuse, and Cloitre, Koenen, Cohen, and Han (2002) showed that an early variant of Life Skills/Life Story, which included eight sessions of prolonged exposure, was well tolerated and effective with a sample from that population. There is suggestive evidence in another study, McDonagh and colleagues' (2005) randomized clinical trial of prolonged exposure versus present-centered therapy, that exposure may be associated with high dropout levels (>40%) with this population, particularly at the beginning of exposure sessions and at a midsession review. Therefore, memory reconstruction using exposure-based approaches should be considered but carefully adapted and titrated to meet the needs and capacities of the individual client. The self-regulation and narrative reconstruction approaches warrant consideration in addition to (or as an alternative or preparation for) exposure-based traumatic memory work.

2. *Throughout the treatment, but particularly during emotional processing work, the client must be assisted in maintaining an adequate level of functioning, consistent with past and current lifestyle and circumstances.* At no point should therapy substitute for living life, or be a direct precipitant of—or tacit collusion with—a view of the client as permanently damaged. Empathizing with the client's struggle with altered self-control facilitates growth rather than a sense of disability. Helping the client to experience and work through painful emotions, traumatic memories, and altered beliefs about self, others, and life meaning bolsters the client's positive self-esteem and internal and external resources.

PHASE 3. REINTEGRATION

Although Phase 3 may be seen as the culmination of the previous work and as an exciting time of growth, it may also be fraught with difficulty for clients who have never had the opportunity for a life that is in the range of normal. Phase 3 might be a time when clients specifically realize the dysfunction and pathology of the past as they continue to attempt to move beyond its influence. Phase 3 frequently involves work on unresolved developmental deficits and fixations, and on fine-tuning self-regulatory skills. Commonly encountered challenges include the continued development of trustworthy relationships and intimacy; sexual functioning; parenting; career and other life decisions; ongoing discussions or confrontations with abusive or neglectful others; determining courses of action for ongoing self-protection; and so on. In this phase, as in the others, the clinician continues to provide the secure base for self-exploration.

Additional Treatment Considerations and Issues

1. *Treatment, like complex traumatic stress symptoms, is complex and multimodal.* As noted earlier, the range of symptoms and comorbidities involved may require a number of treatment goals and a variety of treatment approaches. Thus, treatment should incorporate a variety of theoretical perspectives and clinical modalities in an integrative rather than a unimodal or fragmented manner. Treatment is also individualized to the needs and capacities of the client, and is modified as needed.

2. *Therapists must be aware of and effectively manage clients' transferential reactions and their own vicarious traumatization and countertransference.* Transference, vicarious traumatization, and countertransference can be understood as related to past experiences enacted within or projected onto the therapeutic relationship. Self-dysregulation can complicate or alter the specific themes that arise in transference or countertransference, requiring the therapist to consciously model and utilize self-regulatory skills to manage her or his own secondary or vicarious trauma reactions and provide a secure emotional presence and reliable therapeutic boundaries. Therapist self-care and professional development are crucial to being able to recognize and address transference, vicarious traumatization, and countertransference reactions and dynamics in a constructive, therapeutic manner.

3. *The client's development of an outside support system must be encouraged.* In a related vein, the development of a personal support network outside of treatment, and apart from the therapist, is encouraged. The client may start from the position that no one is to be trusted, because trusting others results in hurt or harm. The therapist must, over time, counter these beliefs (while respecting their origin), model and teach social skills when necessary, and encourage outside engagement with others in a range of settings.

DURATION OF TREATMENT

On average, this treatment is longer-term than that for less complex clinical presentations. For some clients, treatment may last for decades, whether provided continuously or episodically. For others, treatment may be quite delimited, but it rarely can be meaningful if completed in less than 10–20 sessions. Even therapeutic modalities that are designed to be completed within 20–30 sessions may require more sessions or repetitions of "cycles," or episodes, of the intervention. Obviously, goals and duration of treatment should be geared to the client's ability, motivation, and resources. When they are limited, interventions are directed toward safety, support, education, specific skills and, in some cases, psychosocial rehabilitation and case management.

FREQUENCY OF AND TYPE OF SESSIONS

Most therapy occurs on a once- or twice-weekly basis (50- to 75-minute individual sessions; 75- to 120-minute group sessions); however, when multiple modalities are required (i.e., group and individual; substance abuse treatment in addition to psychotherapy; couple and/or family work plus individual therapy; partial hospitalization in addition to or instead of individual therapy) more sessions per week are obviously needed. Therapy should exceed the usual standard of frequency only when symptom and impairment severity are sufficient to warrant the additional costs to the client, family, and payor(s), unless more intensive treatment is mandated by the therapeutic orientation (i.e., psychoanalysis three to four times per week), and/or in the event of an ongoing emergency. More frequent or prolonged sessions, especially if oriented toward memory processing, without a strong foundation of emotional regulation skills, often destabilize clients; furthermore, they may cause an unhealthy dependency to develop.

TREATMENT FRAME

Therapists must carefully set and maintain boundaries that are ultimately protective of the treatment and its continuance. Sharing a written document with the client at the outset of treatment that spells out mutual rights and responsibilities as the foundation of informed consent is recommended. Standard issues, such as scheduling, availability and methods of contact, therapist responsibilities and limitations, treatment planning and monitoring, confidentiality (including state laws for mandated reporting, as applicable), electronic transmission of information, and fee and payment expectations are also spelled out in such a document. Templates that therapists can individualize to their practice specifications are available from most professional organizations, and one tailored for use with this population is available in Courtois (1999). It is advisable for treatment to begin with tighter boundaries and limitations that can be loosened as treatment progresses. While maintaining a consistent treatment frame, therapists should always be flexible and take client needs and preferences into consideration.

CONTINUITY OF CARE

Given the likelihood of clients having had neglectful and/or traumatic personal (and possibly treatment) histories of abandonment and betrayal, therapists and clients benefit from the availability of backup therapists or programs during times when the primary therapist is unavailable. Backup resources provide some security against feelings of rejection and abandonment that often accompany separations, because these often serve as reminders of past neglect. When treatment must end due to exigencies in the client's or the therapist's life (e.g., geographic or career changes, illness), the ending process is a critical opportunity to support and sustain the client's gains in relational, emotional, and behavioral self-regulation. Incorporating strategies for the client to preserve a sense of psychic connection to and continuity with the therapist (e.g., developing tangible and symbolic transitional objects that represent the therapist's continued interest and caring, despite the reduced or terminated physical availability) can be very helpful. Integrating these transitional interventions with the client's gradual and self-paced (if possible) engagement with a new therapist or treatment system/provider serves to extend therapy's benefits in terms of self-regulation, self-integration and efficacy, and trust in and ability to rely on caregiving resources.

TREATMENT TRAJECTORIES

Therapists must be aware of differences in clients' capacities to engage in therapy and to resolve their symptoms and distress. There are as many degrees of self- and relational impairment as there are of healing capacities and resources, resulting in different degrees and types of resolution and recovery. All clients do not heal the same way or to the same degree of completeness or health. What might objectively be a partial success for one client might meet another's full capacity (or that of the same client at a different stage of treatment and recovery). For example, some clients never progress beyond life stabilization and/or sobriety, and this is a sufficient and valuable attainment if it is meaningful for them, a genuine victory, and a profound change of life even if no further change is undertaken.

SERVICE SETTINGS

Most psychotherapeutic treatment for clients with complex traumatic stress disorders occur in outpatient settings, whether a mental health center, a clinic, or a private practice. At times, clients require specialized services and settings, including inpatient, partial hospital or day treatment, residential rehabilitation or supportive housing, or intensive outpatient programs (e.g., for substance abuse, eating disorders, sexual addiction, or compulsive and dangerous self-harm). These settings often provide, in addition to increased monitoring and stabilization resources, intensive skills-building programs; psychopharmacology services for medication evaluation and management; peer support programs (e.g., 12-step groups such as Alcoholics Anonymous [AA], Narcotics Anonymous [NA], Al-Anon, Debtors Anonymous, day treatment, "clubhouse"); and case management and specialized consultants to address vocational, educational, residential, financial, and legal needs.

There is limited evidence on the efficacy of inpatient and partial hospitalization for clients with complex traumatic stress disorders (Courtois & Bloom, 2000). Most hospitalizations are of short duration (1 week or less) due to managed care restrictions. Longer lengths of stay, although infrequent, may be necessitated by ongoing and severe suicidality or homicidality, or for severely dissociated or decompensated clients (some of whom may have experienced additional present-day trauma). Day treatment or residential rehabilitation programs that offer an alternative to, as well as a "step down" from or a "step up" into, in-patient programs may supplement individual treatment and provide a bridge between outpatient and inpatient treatment.

Unfortunately, in some cases, inpatient care may cause the client additional distress, such as when he or she is housed with actively manic and/or psychotic patients who are disruptive and physically/emotionally intrusive, or when a unit is understaffed and/or staff members who do not recognize posttraumatic distress misunderstand and stigmatize the client and his or her symptoms. Outpatient therapists should be aware of the quality, or the lack thereof, of the particular inpatient unit in which they hospitalize clients. Optimally, they have attending privileges or other professional contacts with inpatient or partial hospital providers.

Whatever treatment setting is the best fit or is clinically determined to be necessary, it is advisable for the outpatient therapist to communicate with and coordinate treatment with other, involved treatment professionals for optimal continuity of care. Splitting between caregivers can complicate what may be an already complicated treatment, and it may also be a very habitual mode of functioning for clients with complex trauma, who may have learned this survival skill in their family and between their parents. Collaboration has the dual benefit of stopping the process of splitting and introducing clients to another mode of interaction between themselves and authority figures. The decision to undertake intensive psychiatric, addiction recovery, and/or traumatic stress or dissociative disorder treatment should always be made collaboratively with the client and (as necessary and appropriate) with spouse/partner, guardians, caregiver(s), or significant others.

PSYCHOPHARMACOLOGY

Several psychotropic medications (e.g., antidepressants, anxiolytics, adrenergic blockers, mood stabilizers, and antipsychotics) have shown promise in treating some PTSD symptoms (Opler, Grennan, & Ford, Chapter 16, this volume). Clients with complex traumatic stress disorder may benefit from these medications, but they may also need more complex medication regimens (but not necessarily larger numbers or amounts of medications; see Chapter 16). Finding the right medication, combined medications, and dosage and titration may be a prolonged and complicated process that requires careful, empathic therapeutic management (Chapter 16). The risk of suicide and substance abuse (in addition to the client's degree of adherence, trustworthiness, and motivation in relation to medication) requires careful consideration. Medication tends to be used in combination with psychotherapy in treatment of complex traumatic stress disorders (Chapter 16).

INTEGRATIVE TREATMENT MODELS

Rather than relying on a single treatment model, integrative treatment models that combine techniques and skills spanning the range of biopsychosocial modalities are available to clinicians treating clients with complex traumatic stress disorders. As described in Parts II and III of this volume, these integrative models not only address the range of complex traumatic stress symptoms and impairments (e.g., DESNOS), but also have been tailored for subpopulations, such as clients diagnosed with borderline personality disorder or chronic addictive or psychiatric disorders, women survivors of psychological trauma, and survivors of childhood sexual abuse.

INTEGRATION OF THERAPEUTIC GAINS IN DAILY LIFE

Throughout treatment, clients are encouraged to apply adaptive skills to daily life in order to enhance their current functioning.

ENDING THE TREATMENT

At its best, ending treatment is part of the entire process and is related to the completion of stated goals and thus can be a cause for satisfaction and even celebration. At whatever point treatment comes to an end, it poses special issues and often stirs up clients' feelings of abandonment, grief, fear, and loss of security as well as satisfaction. However or whenever it occurs, the ending of treatment is best n as a collaborative process with a clearly demarcated ending. It should be anticipated, prepared for, and not come as a surprise to the client. In the event that a therapist is only available for a set period of time or must leave practice for some reason (unless it is an emergency situation and leave taking), the client should be informed of the situation and be given adequate time to process the change and plan for the future. In any event, *it is incumbent on the therapist not to abandon the client.* This is especially the case with clients who have been relationally challenging on an ongoing basis and whom the therapist might act out against by "dumping" them without warning or preparation. When a therapist chooses to discontinue a treatment, professional ethics require that he or she take care to communicate reasons to the client and provide treatment referrals.

It is also helpful to have an agreement in place that the client not abruptly discontinue treatment without a last session, to prevent a premature ending that might be based on miscommunication or miscontrual. Even if limited to a single final session, this can be a beneficial way for the therapist to help the client experience the therapist as validating his or her achievements and self-determination.

Posttreatment contacts should be a point of discussion and agreement between the client and therapist. Different therapists have different perspectives on how they manage such contacts or communications. It is recommended that no dual or outside relationships be developed posttermination that would impede a return to and resumption of treatment, if needed. As part of the ending process, clients should be prepared for the possibility of the need for additional therapeutic contact (whether for a "check-in," a "booster," or the resumption of treatment) and realize that this is not considered treatment failure.

CONCLUSION

Psychotherapy for adults with complex traumatic stress disorders is widely practiced but still in the early phases of scientific and clinical validation. While awaiting the results of systematic clinical research, therapists can nevertheless benefit from the application of the practice principles and evolving treatment interventions developed specifically for complex traumatic stress disorders and the dissociative disorders.

Guidelines and models for the treatment of PTSD are applicable to clients with complex traumatic stress disorders, but they cannot be assumed fully or even effectively to ameliorate or resolve the complex self-regulation problems and dissociation that originate when developmentally adverse interpersonal traumas derail or impair the growing child's ability to function adaptively (Spinazzola et al., 2005). The extant clinical knowledge base suggests that safety-focused, strengths-based, self-defining, self-regulation enhancing, self-integrating, avoidance challenging, individualized approaches to treatment, delivered by emotionally healthy and professionally responsible therapists who have specialized training and professional resources to support this very demanding work, make an important difference in the lives of clients who have had substantial life adversity.

REFERENCES

Amaya-Jackson, L., & DeRosa, R. (2007). Treatment considerations for clinicians in applying evidence-based practice to complex presentations in child trauma. *Journal of Traumatic Stress, 20,* 379–390.

American Psychiatric Association. (2000). *Diagnostic and statistical manual of mental disorders* (4th, ed., text rev.). Washington, DC: Author.

American Psychiatric Association. (2004). *Practice guideline for the treatment of patients with acute stress disorder and posttraumatic stress disorder.* Washington, DC: Author.

American Psychological Association Presidential Task Force on Evidence-Based Practice. (2006). Evidence-based practice in psychology. *American Psychologist, 61,* 271–285.

Australian Centre for Posttraumatic Mental Health. (2007). *Australian guidelines for the treatment of adults with acute stress disorder and posttraumatic stress disorder.* Melbourne: Author.

Briere, J. (2002). Treating adult survivors of severe childhood abuse and neglect: Further development of an integrative model. In J. E. B. Myers, L. Berliner, J. Briere, C. T. Hendrix, T. Reid, & C. Jenny (Eds.), *The APSAC handbook on child maltreatment* (2nd ed., pp. 175–202). Newbury Park, CA: Sage.

Bromberg, P. M. (1998). *Standing in the spaces.* Hillsdale, NJ: Analytic Press.

Brown, D. P., & Fromm, E. (1986). *Hypnotherapy and hypnoanalysis.* Hillsdale, NJ: Erlbaum.

Chu, J. A. (1998). *Rebuilding shattered lives: The responsible treatment of complex post-traumatic and dissociative disorders.* New York: Wiley.

Clinical Resource Efficiency Support Team (CREST). (2003). *The management of post traumatic stress disorder in adults.* Belfast: Author.

Cloitre, M., Koenen, K., & Cohen, L. (2006). *Treating survivors of childhood abuse: Psychotherapy for the interrupted life.* New York: Guilford Press.

Cloitre, M., Koenen, K., Cohen, L., & Han, H. (2002). Skills training in affective and interpersonal regulation followed by exposure. *Journal of Consulting and Clinical Psychology, 70,* 1067–1074.

Courtois, C. A. (1999). *Recollections of sexual abuse: Treatment principles and guidelines.* New York: Norton.

Courtois, C. A. (2001). Traumatic stress studies: The need for curricula inclusion. *Journal of Trauma Practice, 1*(1), 33–58

Courtois, C. A. (2004). Complex trauma, complex reactions: Assessment and treatment. *Psychotherapy: Theory, Research, Practice and Training, 41,* 412–426.

Courtois, C. A., & Bloom, S. L. (2000). Inpatient treatment. In E. B. Foa, T. M. Keane, & M. J. Friedman (Eds.), *Effective treatments for PTSD: Practice guidelines from the International Society for Traumatic Stress Studies* (pp. 199–223). New York: Guilford Press.

Dalenberg, C. J. (2000). *Countertransference and the treatment of trauma.* Washington, DC: American Psychological Association.

Davies, J. M., & Frawley, M. G. (1994). *The psychoanalytic treatment of adult survivors of childhood sexual abuse.* New York: Basic Books.

Foa, E. B., Davidson, J. R. T., & Frances, A. (Eds.). (1999). Treatment of posttraumatic stress disorder. *Journal of Clinical Psychiatry, 60*(Suppl. 16).

Foa, E. B., Keane, T. M., & Friedman, M. J. (Eds.). (2000). *Effective treatments for PTSD: Practice guidelines from the International Society for Traumatic Stress Studies.* New York: Guilford Press.

Ford, J. D., Courtois, C. A., van der Hart, O., Nijenhuis, E., & Steele, K. (2005). Treatment of complex post-traumatic self-dysregulation. *Journal of Traumatic Stress, 18,* 437–447.

Ford, J. D., & Kidd, P. (1998). Early childhood trauma and disorders of extreme stress as predictors of treatment outcome with chronic PTSD. *Journal of Traumatic Stress, 18,* 743–761.

Ford, J. D., & Russo, E. (2006). A trauma-focused, present-centered, emotional self-regulation approach to integrated treatment for post-traumatic stress and addiction: TARGET. *American Journal of Psychotherapy, 60,* 335–355.

Harvey, M. (1996). An ecological view of psychological trauma and trauma recovery. *Journal of Traumatic Stress, 9,* 3–23.

Herman, J. L. (1992). *Trauma and recovery.* New York: Basic Books.

Institute of Medicine of the National Academies. (2006). *Posttraumatic stress disorder: Diagnosis and assessment.* Washington, DC: Author.

International Society for the Study of Dissociation. (2005). Guidelines for treating dissociative identity disorder in adults. *Journal of Trauma and Dissociation, 6*(4), 69–149.

Janet, P. (1889). *Psychological healing.* New York: Macmillan.

Kluft, R. P. (1985). *Childhood antecedents of multiple personality disorder.* Washington, DC: American Psychiatric Press.

Kluft, R. P. (1999). An overview of the psychotherapy of dissociative identity disorder. *American Journal of Psychotherapy, 53,* 289–319.

McCann, I. L., & Pearlman, L. A. (1990). *Psychological trauma and the adult survivor: Theory, therapy, and transformation.* New York: Brunner/Mazel.

McDonagh-Coyle, A., Friedman, M., McHugo, G., Ford, J., Sengupta, A., Mueser, K., et al. (2005). Randomized trial of cognitive-behavioral therapy for chronic posttraumatic stress disorder in adult female survivors of childhood sexual abuse. *Journal of Consulting and Clinical Psychology, 73*, 515–524.

National Institute for Clinical Excellence (NICE). (2005). *Posttraumatic stress disorder (PTSD): The management of PTSD in adults and children in primary and secondary care.* London: Author.

Putnam, F. W. (1989). *Diagnosis and treatment of multiple personality disorder.* New York: Guilford Press.

Resick, P., Nishith, P., & Griffin, M. (2003). How well does cognitive-behavioral therapy treat symptoms of complex PTSD? *CNS Spectrums, 8*, 340–342, 351–355.

Sackett, D. L., Rosenberg, W. M., Gray, J. A., Haynes, R. B., & Richardson, W. S. (1996). Evidence-based medicine: What it is and what it isn't. *British Medical Journal, 312*, 71–72.

Solomon, M., & Siegel, D. J. (2003). *Healing trauma.* New York: Norton.

Spinazzola, J., Blaustein, M., & van der Kolk, B. A. (2005). Posttraumatic stress disorder treatment outcome research. *Journal of Traumatic Stress, 18*, 425–436.

U.S. Department of Veterans Affairs. (2003). *Management of posttraumatic stress.* Washington, DC: Author.

van der Kolk, B. A., & Courtois, C. A. (2005). Editorial: Complex developmental trauma. *Journal of Traumatic Stress, 18*(5), 385–388.

van der Kolk, B. A., McFarlane, A. C., & van der Hart, O. (1996). A general approach to treatment of posttraumatic stress disorder. In B. A. van der Kolk, A. C. McFarlane, & L. Weisaeth (Eds.), *Traumatic stress: The effects of overwhelming experience on mind, body, and society.* New York: Guilford Press.

Wilson, J. P., Friedman, M. J., & Lindy, J. D. (Eds.). (2002). *Treating psychological trauma and PTSD.* New York: Guilford Press.

CHAPTER 5

Assessment of the Sequelae of Complex Trauma

Evidence-Based Measures

John Briere
Joseph Spinazzola

Until recently, clinical understanding of trauma exposure and subsequent symptomatology tended to emphasize relatively straightforward psychological reactions to a single, relatively circumscribed traumatic event. Typically, such reactions are thought to involve posttraumatic stress, various forms of anxiety, and depression. The most cited of these, posttraumatic stress disorder (PTSD) (American Psychiatric Association, 2000), has been linked to a variety of specific traumatic events, including combat, rape, physical assault, motor vehicle accidents, and natural disasters (Breslau, Davis, Andreski, & Peterson, 1991; Briere, 2004; Davidson & Fairbank, 1993; Green & Solomon, 1995). Although the effects of single traumas are well established, many individuals have experienced more than one major traumatic event in their lives (Breslau, Chilcoat, Kessler, Peterson, & Lucia, 1999; Classen, Palesh, & Aggarwal, 2005). When multiple traumas accumulate over time, they may be associated with more severe and complex psychological reactions (Banyard, Williams, & Siegel, 2001; Briere, Kaltman, & Green, 2008; Follette, Polusny, Bechtle, & Naugle, 1996; Kubiak, 2005; van der Kolk, Roth, Pelcovitz, Sunday, & Spinazzola, 2005). In addition, many survivors of multiple traumas have a history of extended childhood abuse and/or neglect (Cook et al., 2005; Courtois, 2004). Such experiences not only can produce long-term sequelae themselves, but they are also risk factors for revictimization in the future (e.g., Classen et al., 2005) and for responding to later traumas with more extreme symptomatology (e.g., Bremner, Southwick, Johnson, Yehuda, & Charney, 1993).

Other variables may further complicate the clinical picture. For example, more severe and complex posttraumatic outcomes frequently are associated with preexisting nervous system hyperreactivity (Perry & Pollard, 1998; Yehuda, 1997); the presence of other anxiety, depressive, or personality-level disorders (Breslau et al., 1991); excessive use of drugs or alcohol (Acierno, Resnick, Kilpatrick, Saunders, & Best, 1999); a generally avoidant response style (Briere, 2004); and, early in life, an insecure (especially disorganized) parent–child attachment relationship (Cook et al., 2005; Pearlman & Courtois, 2005)—all of which both mediate the effects of trauma exposure and may themselves arise from previous trauma (Felitti et al., 1998; McCauley et al., 1997).

Trauma symptomatology also may be intensified by environmental variables, such as inadequate social support (Steketee & Foa, 1987) and stigmatization associated with certain traumas (e.g., Lebowitz & Roth, 1994), and may vary according to whatever idioms of distress are most acceptable within a given culture (Marsella, Friedman, Gerrity, & Scurfield, 1996). Social marginalization and oppression are also likely to exacerbate or complicate psychological symptoms (Carter, 2007; Kubiak, 2005).

COMPLEX POSTTRAUMATIC OUTCOMES

When the symptoms associated with repeated trauma (and, in many cases, the mediating or exacerbating factors described earlier) are especially pervasive and varied, and occur in late adolescence or adulthood, they are sometimes characterized as *complex PTSD* (Herman, 1992) or *disorders of extreme stress not otherwise specified* (DESNOS) (van der Kolk et al., 2005). These constructs refer to a relatively broad range of symptom clusters experienced simultaneously by the same individual, typically involving some combination of affect dysregulation, relational problems, cognitive distortions, dissociation, tension reduction behaviors, and somatization (Pelcovitz et al., 1997). Less research has been conducted on complex trauma symptoms in children (see Cook et al. [2005] for a review of available studies), although a diagnosis similar to DESNOS, developmental trauma disorder (DTD), has been suggested (van der Kolk, 2005).

Despite the attraction of models such as DESNOS, complex PTSD, or DTD, however, the psychological effects of accumulated trauma may not easily fit into any single diagnostic framework or syndrome. Instead, such symptomatology may involve different levels of complexity according to the nature, number, and timing of the specific traumas a given individual has experienced, as well as the presence of relevant biological, social, and psychological phenomena. In light of the problems inherent in defining a unitary complex trauma diagnosis, this chapter emphasizes a more deconstructed, phenomenologically based framework to guide assessment of the many psychological responses associated with exposure to complex traumatic stressors.

Symptoms Associated with Trauma Exposure

Because complex trauma outcomes vary widely, psychological assessment in this area must potentially address a wide range of symptoms. For the sake of discussion, these can be viewed in terms of a number of intrinsically overlapping categories, including, but extending beyond, those described for complex PTSD or DESNOS. Such trauma-related responses include the following:

- *Posttraumatic stress*, as outlined earlier
- *Cognitive disturbance*, such as low self-esteem, self-blame, hopelessness, expectations of rejection, and preoccupation with danger (e.g., Briere, 2000a; Foa, Ehlers, Clark, Tolin, & Orsillo, 1999; Janoff-Bulman, 1992; Vondra, Barnett, & Cicchetti, 1990)
- *Mood disturbance*, such as anxiety (including panic and phobias), depression, and anger or aggression (e.g., Gilboa-Schechtman & Foa, 2001; Heim & Nemeroff, 2001; Putnam, 2003)
- *Somatization* (e.g., Dietrich, 2003; Loewenstein, 1990)
- *Identity disturbance* (e.g., Briere & Rickards, 2007; Cole & Putnam, 1992)
- *Difficulties in emotional (affect) regulation* (e.g., van der Kolk et al., 1996; Zlotnick, Donaldson, Spirito, & Pearlstein, 1997)
- *Chronic interpersonal difficulties* (e.g., Cole & Putnam, 1992; Cook et al., 2005)
- *Dissociation* (e.g., Chu, Frey, Ganzel, & Matthews, 1999; Putnam, 1997)
- *Substance abuse* (e.g., Ouimette & Brown, 2003; Najavits, 2002)
- *Tension reduction activities*, such as compulsive sexual behavior, binge–purge eating, impulsive aggression, suicidality, and self-mutilation (e.g., Brennan & Shaver, 1995; Herpertz et al., 1997; Zlotnick et al., 1997)

A number of these outcomes can be viewed as symptoms (or associated features) of borderline personality disorder (American Psychiatric Association, 2000), which also has been linked to childhood trauma in a number of studies (e.g., Herman, Perry, & van der Kolk, 1989; Ogata, Silk, Goodrich, Lohr, Westen, & Hill, 1990).

Given the broad range of potential posttraumatic outcomes, it is unlikely that the psychological assessment of traumatized individuals can be accomplished through the mere administration of a test for PTSD. Instead, once it has been determined that trauma exposure is part of the clinical picture, the number of possible assessment targets proliferate. The remainder of this chapter concerns the technical aspects of this expanded assessment process.

THE ROLE OF ASSESSMENT IN TRAUMA TREATMENT: ASSESSMENT-BASED TREATMENT

Other than in forensic contexts, the primary function of psychological assessment is to inform treatment. This may be especially true for complex posttraumatic presentations, where the variety of potential symptoms for any given client may be significant. Without structured assessment, the clinician may inadvertently miss important intervention targets (e.g., fail to detect depression or sexual issues in a person with PTSD, or miss dissociative or anxious symptoms in a person with a "borderline" presentation), leading to inadequate or incomplete treatment. Accurate specification of initial treatment targets is especially critical for what may be called a *components* approach to complex trauma (Briere & Scott, 2006). This general model suggests that clinical intervention be customized for any given client, because each individual will necessarily vary in terms of what symptoms or problems he or she experiences, thus requiring different treatment components or modalities according to his or her specific issues. In this context, a battery of psychometrically valid psychological tests is necessarily the first step in the development of a treatment plan.

When repeated over time, psychological testing also can signal the need to change or augment the focus of treatment (Briere, 2001b). For example, ongoing assessment may suggest a shift in approach when posttraumatic stress symptoms begin to respond to treatment but other symptoms (e.g., eating disturbance or tension reduction behaviors) continue relatively unabated or even increase (Courtois, 2004). Repeated administration of measures also can increase accountability and quality control, and add to the clinical knowledge base regarding the effectiveness of various trauma-related psychotherapies.

PSYCHOMETRIC ISSUES

As is true of psychological tests in general, those evaluating the effects of complex trauma must have adequate reliability and validity, and should be standardized on demographically representative samples of the general population. Such tests also should have good sensitivity and specificity if they are offered as diagnostic instruments. For example, a measure intended to identify PTSD should be able to predict with reasonable accuracy both true cases of PTSD (sensitivity) and those cases in which no PTSD is present (specificity).

Unfortunately, because of the relative recency of the understanding of posttraumatic conditions, a number of currently used trauma-specific instruments were developed in research contexts and do not meet current standards for clinical psychological tests. Although many of these tests are internally consistent, and vary as a function of relevant trauma variables, their actual clinical applicability and utility are often unknown. Equally problematic, some trauma impact measures have not been normed on the general population. Without normative data, clinicians are unable to compare a given score on a measure with "normal" individuals' scores on that measure; thus, they cannot determine the extent to which said score represents dysfunction or disorder. In the case of solely diagnostic screening instruments, the absence of normative data is generally not a problem, because the only issue is whether a given set of symptoms is—or is not—present. For these reasons, the clinician is advised to avoid, whenever possible, nonstandardized measures in the assessment of trauma effects, complex or otherwise. In fact, for the reasons outlined earlier, a majority of the measures recommended in this chapter are *evidence-based* (i.e., they have been fully normed on the general population or, in the case of diagnostic measures, they have been shown to have adequate sensitivity and specificity in well-controlled research).

APPROACH TO ASSESSING COMPLEX TRAUMA

Because complex posttraumatic outcomes vary widely, the initial approach to assessment is critically important. In a sense, the clinician must make an educated guess as to the likely relevant areas of distress or dysfunction for a given client, even though he or she has yet to determine them psychometrically. In most cases, this determination is made during the initial interview, when presenting complaints and trauma history are elicited and the client's overall clinical presentation is considered. This process may be assisted by the early use of broad-spectrum screening instruments that assess a number of different areas of symptomatology simultaneously. These include generic measures that tap phenomena such as anxiety, depression, or psychosis, as well as broadband instruments that evaluate a range of posttraumatic outcomes.

MEASURES FOR CHILDREN AND ADOLESCENTS

Assessment approaches to complex posttraumatic responses in children and adolescents are less developed than they are for adults, because complex trauma has been less investigated in children and there are fewer measures available for assessing posttraumatic outcomes. Although a number of measures are reviewed below, other tests—although not trauma-focused—also evaluate symptoms and problems highly relevant to complex posttraumatic outcomes in children and adolescents. These include the Behavioral Assessment System for Children–2 (BASC-2; Reynolds & Kamphaus, 2006), the Children's Depression Inventory (CDI; Kovacs, 1992), the Conners Rating Scales (1989), and the Personality Inventory for Children (PIC; Lachar, 1982).

Child Behavior Checklist

The Child Behavior Checklist (CBCL; Achenbach, 1991) is one of the most widely used clinical instruments for the assessment of general psychological distress in children, and often is used to evaluate those who have experienced childhood abuse (Friedrich, 2002). A revised version of the CBCL can be found in the Achenbach System of Empirically Based Assessment (ASEBA; Achenbach, 2002), and it appears to be an improvement over the previous instrument(s), with new norms, more items and scales, and specific reference to DSM-IV disorders. Unfortunately, the age ranges for each normative group remain quite broad. The most popular form of the CBCL is completed by a caretaker or teacher, although there also is a self-administered Youth Self-Report version for children ages 11–18, and a new Young Adult Self-Report for individuals ages 18–30. The CBCL measures a range of problems that may arise from abuse or other traumas, such as withdrawal, somatic complaints, thought problems, and delinquent behavior, and examines competencies that may modify or reduce these problems.

Trauma Symptom Checklist for Children

The Trauma Symptom Checklist for Children (TSCC; Briere, 1996) evaluates self-reported trauma symptoms in children ages 8–16, with minor normative adjustments for 17-year-olds. It has two validity scales (Underresponse and Hyperresponse) and six clinical scales: Anxiety, Depression, Anger, Posttraumatic Stress, Sexual Concerns (with two subscales), and Dissociation (with two subscales). An alternate form (the TSCC-A) does not include any sexual items. The TSCC was normed on over 3,000 children and demonstrates good reliability and validity. It has been used in a range of settings, including clinical, school-based, general population, and forensic (Lanktree et al., 2008; Singer, Anglin, Song, & Lunghofer, 1995; Wolpaw, Ford, Newman, Davis, & Briere, 2005). Because it examines both trauma symptoms and common comorbidities, the TSCC can be a helpful review of more complex trauma outcomes.

Trauma Symptom Checklist for Young Children

The Trauma Symptom Checklist for Young Children (TSCYC; Briere, 2005) is a caretaker report instrument developed for the assessment of a range of trauma-related symptoms in children ages 3–12. There are two caretaker report validity scales, Response Level (RL) and Atypical Response (ATR), as well as a norm-referenced item evaluating how many hours a week the caretaker spends with the child. The TSCYC contains nine clinical scales: Posttraumatic Stress–Intrusion, Posttraumatic Stress–Avoidance, Posttraumatic Stress–Arousal, Posttraumatic Stress–Total, Sexual Concerns, Anxiety, Depression, Dissociation, and Anger/Aggression. TSCYC scales are reliable and sensitive to a range of traumas, including childhood physical and sexual abuse, community violence, and witnessing domestic violence (e.g., Briere et al., 2001; Finkelhor, Hamby, Ormrod, & Turner, 2005; Gilbert, 2004).

Child Sexual Behavior Inventory

The Child Sexual Behavior Inventory (CSBI; Friedrich, 1998) is a reliable and valid measure that evaluates the sexual behaviors observed in children ages 2–12, during the prior 6 months. Nine domains frequently associated with childhood sexual abuse are tapped by this instrument: boundary problems, exhibitionism, gender role behavior, self-stimulation, sexual anxiety, sexual interest, sexual intrusiveness, sexual knowledge, and voyeuristic behavior. The CSBI yields a total score and two scale scores: Developmentally Related Sexual Behavior, which reflects the level of age and gender-appropriate sexual behavior; and Sexual Abuse–Specific Items, which comprises items that have been empirically related to a history of sexual abuse. Normative data for the CSBI were collected on over 1,000 children.

Trauma Symptom Inventory

Described in detail under adult self-report measures, the Trauma Symptom Inventory (TSI; Briere, 1995) is often used for older adolescents (i.e., ages 18–21). Certain aspects of the TSI, such as its focus on anger/aggression, dysfunctional sexual behavior, identity disturbance, and affect dysregulation, are especially relevant to traumatized adolescents who tend to externalize or "act out" their distress.

Recommendation

Because the number of standardized tests available to evaluate complex trauma effects in children is small, options for the evaluator are relatively limited. Evaluation of preadolescent children would ideally include administration of the parent- and self-report versions of the CBCL, the TSCYC and TSCC, and, if there is a possibility of sexual victimization, the CSBI. Additional tests might be added to this battery as needed, including, for example, the Conners Rating Scales or the Revised Children's Manifest Anxiety Scale (RCMAS). Unfortunately, other than the BASC-2, PIC, and the CBCL, which address some of these issues tangentially, there are few standardized tests available to assess children's impaired self-capacities, such as identity disturbance, affect dysregulation, or relational problems. Assessment of complex trauma in adolescents might include the youth/young adult- and parent-report versions of the CBCL, as well as some combination of the BASC-2, the Minnesota Multiphasic Personality Inventory—Adolescents (MMPI-A) (Butcher et al., 1992), the TSCC, and/or the TSI. Clinicians trained in the use of the Rorschach (Rorschach, 1981) might also consider using this measure for older adolescents.

ADULT SELF-REPORT MEASURES

Psychological tests of complex trauma effects in adults can be divided into two groups: instruments that tap a wide range of generic (i.e., non-trauma-specific) psychological symptoms, and tests that directly assess various forms of posttraumatic disturbance.

Generic Measures

A variety of psychological tests are available for the assessment of non-trauma-specific symptoms in complex trauma survivors. Several evaluate syndromes relevant to Axis I of DSM-IV (e.g., the Millon Clinical Multiaxial Inventory–III [MCMI-III; Millon, 1994], Minnesota Multiphasic Personality Inventory, Second Edition [MMPI-2; Butcher, Dahlstrom, Graham, Tellegen, & Kaemmer, 1989], Personality Assessment Inventory [PAI; Morey, 1991], and the Symptom Checklist-90—Revised [SCL-90-R; Derogatis, 1983]). Of these, the PAI, MMPI-2, and MCMI-III also yield detailed information on Axis II and self-capacity difficulties frequently associated with complex posttraumatic outcomes, and include PTSD scales of moderate sensitivity and specificity (Carlson, 1997). The majority of these instruments also include validity scales, developed to detect under- or overreporting of symptoms. It should be noted that although validity scales can be helpful, traumatized individuals—perhaps by virtue of the unusual quality of some posttraumatic symptoms—tend to score higher than others on negative impression scales, even when not attempting to malinger (Jordan, Nunley, & Cook, 1992).

Posttraumatic Stress Measures

Tests of posttraumatic stress can be divided into those that tap symptoms without reference to a specific trauma, thus yielding scores that represent the overall "amount" of posttraumatic symptoms experienced by an individual in a variety of different areas, and those that examine responses to a specific traumatic event and typically provide a provisional diagnosis of PTSD. Among standardized tests for adults, only one is available for the evaluation of overall posttraumatic stress, whereas several may be used to determine a possible diagnosis of trauma-specific PTSD.

Trauma Symptom Inventory

The TSI taps the overall level of posttraumatic symptomatology experienced by an individual in the prior 6 months. It has three validity scales (Response Level, Atypical Response, and Inconsistent Response) and 10 clinical scales (Anxious Arousal, Depression, Anger/Irritability, Intrusive Experiences, Defensive Avoidance, Dissociation, Sexual Concerns, Dysfunctional Sexual Behavior, Impaired Self-Reference, and Tension Reduction Behavior). Various studies indicate that the TSI is reliable, demonstrating various forms of validity in a range of contexts (e.g., McDevitt-Murphy, Weathers, & Adkins, 2005), and because of its range of scales, it may serve as an omnibus measure of complex posttraumatic outcomes (e.g., Briere et al., 2008; Resick, Nishith, & Griffin, 2003).

Posttraumatic Stress Diagnostic Scale

The Posttraumatic Stress Diagnostic Scale (PDS; Foa, 1995) evaluates four domains: exposure to potentially traumatic events, characteristics of the most traumatic event, 17 symptoms corresponding to DSM-IV PTSD criteria, and extent of symptom interference in the individual's daily life. The PDS demonstrates good sensitivity and specificity with respect to a PTSD diagnosis (.82 and .77, respectively) and fair diagnostic efficiency (kappa = .59). The PDS has not been normed on the general population; thus, it does not yield standardized T-scores. Instead, PTSD symptom severity estimates are based on qualitative extrapolation from a clinical sample of 248 individuals.

Detailed Assessment of Posttraumatic Stress

The Detailed Assessment of Posttraumatic Stress (DAPS; Briere, 2001b) has two validity scales and 10 scales that evaluate lifetime exposure to traumatic events, immediate cognitive, emotional, and dissociative responses to a specified trauma, the subsequent symptoms of PTSD and acute stress disorder (ASD), and three associated features of posttraumatic stress: trauma-specific dissociation, suicidality, and substance abuse. The DAPS was normed on general population individuals with a history of exposure to at least one DSM-IV Criterion A traumatic event. This measure has good sensitivity (.88) and specificity (.86) with respect to a Clinician-Administered PTSD Scale (CAPS) PTSD diagnosis.

Self-Capacity Measures

As noted earlier, complex posttraumatic outcomes often include difficulties in identity and boundary awareness, affect regulation, and interpersonal relationships. As a result, an accurate evaluation of complex trauma effects usually includes tests of the self-domain.

Several tests have scales or subscales that tap one or more aspects of impaired self-capacities, including the Borderline Features subscales of the PAI, the Impaired Self-Reference scale of the TSI, and various personality scales of the MCMI-III. In addition to the Rorschach (described later in this chapter), there are also two stand-alone standardized tests available to assess psychological functioning in this area.

Bell Object Relations and Reality Testing Inventory

The only standardized test of what is generally referred to as object relations, the Bell Object Relations and Reality Testing Inventory (BORRTI; Bell, 1995) has scales that yield data on four constructs: Alienation, Insecure Attachment, Egocentricity, and Social Incompetence. These scales have been shown by the test author to predict and potentially to explain relational dysfunction in individuals thought to have some form of personality disorder. Because the scales are linked to object relations theory, the results of this measure are most directly applicable to clinicians who endorse that perspective.

Inventory of Altered Self-Capacities

The Inventory of Altered Self-Capacities (IASC; Briere, 2000b) is a standardized test of difficulties in the areas of relatedness, identity, and affect regulation. The scales of the IASC assess the following domains: Interpersonal Conflicts, Idealization–Disillusionment, Abandonment Concerns, Identity Impairment, Susceptibility to Influence, Affect Dysregulation, and Tension Reduction Activities. In contrast to the BORRTI, this measure is not linked to any specific treatment model. Elevated scores on the IASC have been shown to predict adult attachment style, childhood trauma history, interpersonal problems, suicidality, and substance abuse history in various samples (e.g., Briere & Rickards, 2007; Briere & Runtz, 2002).

Cognitive Disturbance Measures

As noted in the Introduction of this volume, complex traumas often produce relatively chronic cognitive symptoms. Fortunately, a number of available measures tap cognitive distortions and negative relational schemas. Three of these scales, especially helpful in the assessment of complex trauma, are presented below.

Tennessee Self-Concept Scale

The Tennessee Self-Concept Scale (TSCS; Roid & Fitts, 1994) is the most frequently used and widely accepted self-esteem measure available to clinicians (Byrne, 1996). It includes a variety of subscales that tap physical, moral, personal, family, and social self-concept. Although not widely included in trauma-impact test batteries, clinical experience indicates that the TSCS is relatively sensitive to the effects of childhood maltreatment on subsequent (i.e., adolescent and adult) psychological functioning.

Cognitive Distortions Scale

The Cognitive Distortions Scale (CDS; Briere, 2000a) is a 40-item test of dysfunctional cognitions that evaluates a range of distortions in a relatively rapid manner. The scales of the CDS assess five types of cognitive distortion: Self-Criticism, Helplessness, Hopelessness, Self-Blame, and Preoccupation with Danger. CDS scales are reliable and predict past exposure to interpersonal violence, as well as suicidality, depression, and posttraumatic stress.

Trauma and Attachment Belief Scale

The Trauma and Attachment Belief Scale (TABS; Pearlman, 2003; formerly the Traumatic Stress Institute Belief Scale) measures disrupted cognitive schemas and need states associated with complex trauma exposure. It evaluates disturbance in five areas: Safety, Trust, Esteem, Intimacy, and Control. There are reliable subscales for each of these domains, rated both for "self" and "other." In contrast to more symptom-based tests, the TABS measures the self-reported needs and expectations of trauma survivors as they predict self in relation to others. As a result, the TABS is likely to be helpful in understanding important assumptions that the client carries in his or her relationships to others, including the therapist.

Dissociation Measures

The term *dissociation* refers to a defensive alteration in consciousness or awareness, usually invoked to reduce the distress associated with psychologically traumatic events. Unfortunately, despite the potential importance of dissociation in complex posttraumatic stress, there are few standardized or validated measures of this construct available to the clinician.

Dissociative Experiences Scale

The Dissociative Experiences Scale (DES; Bernstein & Putnam, 1986) is the most widely used questionnaire measure of dissociation. It has good psychometric characteristics, and a wide variety of studies indicate that traumatized individuals have elevated scores on this measure (Carlson & Putnam, 1993). More importantly for clinicians, a cutoff of 30 has been shown to discriminate the presence versus absence of a dissociative disorder with reasonable sensitivity and specificity (Carlson et al., 1993). The DES is not normed on the general population, however; thus, a specific score on this measure is not easily interpreted in terms of its relative extremity from "normal" dissociative response (Armstrong, 1995). Despite this problem, the availability of a cutoff score, and its especially wide use in clinical and research settings, supports the inclusion of the DES as an evidence-based assessment instrument.

Multiscale Dissociation Inventory

The Multiscale Dissociation Inventory (MDI; Briere, 2002) is a freestanding, standardized, and normed questionnaire measure of dissociative responses. Based on the conclusion that dissociation is a multidimensional phenomenon

(Briere, Weathers, & Runtz, 2005), the MDI comprises six scales (Disengagement, Depersonalization, Derealization, Memory Disturbance, Emotional Constriction, and Identity Dissociation) that together form an overall "dissociation profile." The MDI is reliable and correlates as expected with victimization history, PTSD, and other measures of dissociation, including the DES (e.g., Briere, 2002; Dietrich, 2003). Analyses in a sample of over 1,000 clinical and nonclinical individuals indicates that the MDI has substantial factorial validity (Briere et al., 2005). In the standardization study, the Identity Dissociation scale had a specificity of .92 and a sensitivity of .93 with respect to a dissociative identity disorder (DID) diagnosis (Briere, 2002).

Measures of Dysfunctional Behavior

As noted earlier in this chapter, many individuals with complex traumatic stress disorders (perhaps especially those with affect regulation problems) engage in externalization or other tension reduction behaviors when confronted with trauma-related memories and affects. In addition to the Tension Reduction Behavior (TRB) scale of the TSI, and the Tension Reduction Activities (TRA) scale of the IASC, various measures can be used to assess specific dysfunctional behaviors common to complex posttraumatic distress. These include the Dysfunctional Sexual Behavior (DSB) scale of the TSI, the Suicidality scale of the DAPS (as well as freestanding suicide measures, such as the Adult Suicidal Ideation Questionnaire [ASIQ; Reynolds, 1991] and the Suicide Intent Scale [Beck, Morris, & Beck, 1974]), the Eating Disorder Inventory–3 (EDI-3; Garner, 2004), and the Substance Abuse scale of the DAPS.

Rorschach

The Rorschach differs from the other instruments described in this chapter in that it is a projective test rather than a self-report or interview measure. This test can yield meaningful information about various constructs relevant to complex posttraumatic symptoms, such as psychological defenses, ego strength, reality testing, self-capacities, aggression, and bodily concerns (Exner, 1986), as well as posttraumatic stress and dissociation (Armstrong, 1995; Luxenberg & Levin, 2004). When interpreted by those without specific training in assessment of patients with complex posttraumatic clinical presentations, however, some trauma-related outcomes may be misrepresented as impaired reality testing or personality disorder on the Rorschach (Luxenberg & Levin, 2004).

ADULT INTERVIEW-BASED MEASURES

Clinician-Administered PTSD Scale

The Clinician-Administered PTSD Scale (CAPS; Blake et al., 1995) is a structured diagnostic interview that generates both dichotomous and continuous scores for current and lifetime PTSD. This interview also briefly examines phenomena relevant to complex posttraumatic disturbance, such as dissociation, guilt, homicidality, disillusionment with authority, hopelessness, memory impairment, depression, and feelings of being overwhelmed. Although well validated for the assessment of PTSD, the CAPS items assessing complex posttraumatic outcomes have not been validated.

Structured Interview for Disorders of Extreme Stress

The Structured Interview for Disorders of Extreme Stress (SIDES; Pelcovitz et al., 1997) was developed as a companion to existing interview-based rating scales for PTSD. The 45 items of the SIDES measure the current and lifetime presence of the DESNOS criteria set, both for the total construct and for each of six symptom clusters: Affect Dysregulation, Somatization, Alterations in Attention or Consciousness, Self-Perception, Relationships with Others, and Systems of Meaning. Item descriptors contain concrete behavioral anchors to facilitate clinician ratings. The SIDES interview has good interrater reliability (kappa = .81), internal consistency (alpha = .96), predictive validity (Ford & Kidd, 1998), and construct validity across a variety of clinical populations (Pelcovitz et al., 1997; Zlotnick & Pearlstein, 1997) and cultures (De Jong et al., 2005).

Structured Clinical Interview for DSM-IV Dissociative Disorders

The Structured Clinical Interview for DSM-IV Dissociative Disorders (SCID-D; Steinberg, 1994) evaluates the existence and severity of five dissociative symptoms: amnesia, depersonalization, derealization, identity confusion, and identity alteration. This interview provides diagnoses for the five major DSM-IV dissociative disorders, along with ASD. Also evaluated by the SCID-D are "intrainterview dissociative cues," such as alterations in demeanor, spontaneous age regression, and trance-like appearance.

RECOMMENDATIONS

Several recommendations can be made for the assessment of adult complex trauma effects. First, in most cases, at least two broadband screening instruments should be administered: one for general psychological symptomatology (e.g., the PAI or MMPI) and at least one for general trauma-related disturbance (e.g., the TSI or SIDES). In addition, those trained in projective testing should consider using the Rorschach when indicated, and when time permits. If, based on these tests and/or the general clinical interview, PTSD is suspected, a diagnostic test or interview such as the PDS, DAPS, or CAPS may be used. When additional trauma-related outcomes are possible, the interviewer should administer whatever tests or interviews seem most relevant, including those tapping dissociation (e.g., the SCID-D or MDI), cognitive distortions (e.g., the TSCS or CDI), self–other disturbance (e.g., the TABS), or disturbed self-capacities (e.g., the IASC or BORRTI). When suicidality, substance abuse, or dysfunctional sexual behavior are particular concerns, trauma-specific tests with relevant scales may be helpful, as well as non-trauma-specific tests.

CONCLUSIONS

Complex posttraumatic responses reflect the wide variety of potential adverse experiences in the world and the many biological, social, cultural, and psychological variables that moderate the impact of these experiences. As a result, these outcomes are quite variable and cover many domains, and the notion of a one-size-fits-all diagnosis often is untenable. Instead, the clinician should consider the entire range of posttraumatic responses potentially attributable to a given client's history and risk factors. In many cases, this may require the administration of a wide range of psychological tests, both generic and more trauma-specific, followed by, or concurrent with, other tests relevant to the individual's specific clinical presentation.

Focused psychological assessment of complex posttraumatic responses not only informs diagnosis but also can assist in treatment. Evaluation approaches that examine the full range of trauma-related outcomes may highlight treatment targets that might otherwise be overlooked, both in terms of identifying trauma symptoms within more generic syndromes and generic symptoms within a stress disorder. Assessment of complex traumatic stress sequelae also may identify phenomena that interfere with effective treatment. For example, information that a client in traumatic stress disorder therapy has a significant drug abuse history or affect regulation difficulties may lead the clinician to use an empirically supported intervention strategy that increases affect regulation capacities, focuses more on cognitive phenomena, or more directly addresses substance abuse issues, either prior to or in lieu of a prolonged exposure approach to the client's posttraumatic stress symptoms.

The last decade has witnessed the rapid development of a number of standardized and psychometrically validated psychological tests that can be used to evaluate the wide range of symptoms and disorders associated with trauma exposure. Partially as a result of this improved instrumentation, and partially arising from a general increase in scientific interest in traumatic stress effects beyond solely PTSD, the fields of psychology and psychiatry are becoming increasingly aware of complex traumatic disturbance as a meaningful construct and focus for clinical assessment. The results of this burgeoning attention are already leading to new ways of understanding and treating multiply traumatized clients who present with complex posttraumatic psychological difficulties.

REFERENCES

Achenbach, T. M. (1991). *Manual for the Child Behavior Checklist/4-18 and 1991 Profile*. Burlington: University of Vermont, Department of Psychiatry.

Achenbach, T. M. (2002). *Achenbach System of Empirically Based Assessment (ASEBA)*. Burlington, VT: Research Center for Children, Youth, and Families.

Acierno, R., Resnick, H. S., Kilpatrick, D. G., Saunders, B. E., & Best, C. L. (1999). Risk factors for rape, physical assault, and posttraumatic stress disorder in women: Examination of differential multivariate relationships. *Journal of Anxiety Disorders, 13*, 541–563.

American Psychiatric Association. (2000). *Diagnostic and statistical manual of mental disorders* (4th ed., text rev.). Washington, DC: Author.

Armstrong, J. (1995). Psychological assessment. In J. L. Spira (Ed.), *Treating dissociative identity disorder* (pp. 3–37). San Francisco: Jossey-Bass.

Banyard, V. L., Williams, L. M., & Siegel, J. A. (2001). The long-term mental health consequences of childhood sexual abuse: An exploratory study of the impact of multiple traumas in a sample of women. *Journal of Traumatic Stress, 14*, 697–715.

Beck, R. W., Morris, J. B., & Beck, A. T. (1974). Cross-validation of the Suicidal Intent Scale. *Psychological Reports, 34*, 445–446.

Bell, M. D. (1995). *Bell Object Relations and Reality Testing Inventory*. Los Angeles: Western Psychological Services.

Bernstein, E. M., & Putnam, F. W. (1986). Development, reliability, and validity of a dissociation scale. *Journal of Nervous and Mental Disease, 174*, 727–734.

Blake, D. D., Weathers, F. W., Nagy, L. M., Kaloupek, D. G., Gusman, F. D., Charney, D. S., et al. (1995). The development of a clinician-administered PTSD scale. *Journal of Traumatic Stress, 8*, 75–90.

Bremner, J. D., Southwick, S. M., Johnson, D. R., Yehuda, R., & Charney, D. S. (1993). Childhood physical abuse and combat-related PTSD in Vietnam veterans. *American Journal of Psychiatry, 150*, 235–239.

Brennan, K. A., & Shaver, P. R. (1995). Dimensions of adult attachment, affect regulation, and romantic relationship functioning. *Personality and Social Psychology Bulletin, 21*, 267–283.

Breslau, N., Chilcoat, H. D., Kessler, R. C., Peterson, E. L., & Lucia, V. C. (1999). Vulnerability to assaultive violence: Further specification of the sex difference in post-traumatic stress disorder. *Psychological Medicine, 29*, 813–821.

Breslau, N., Davis, G. C., Andreski, P., & Peterson, E. (1991). Traumatic events and post-traumatic stress disorder in an urban population of young adults. *Archives of General Psychiatry, 48*, 216–222.

Briere, J. (1995). *Trauma Symptom Inventory (TSI)*. Odessa, FL: Psychological Assessment Resources.

Briere, J. (1996). *Trauma Symptom Checklist for Children (TSCC)*. Odessa, FL: Psychological Assessment Resources.

Briere, J. (2000a). *Cognitive Distortions Scale (CDS)*. Odessa, FL: Psychological Assessment Resources.

Briere, J. (2000b). *Inventory of Altered Self-Capacities (IASC)*. Odessa, FL: Psychological Assessment Resources.

Briere, J. (2001a). *Detailed Assessment of Posttraumatic Stress (DAPS)*. Odessa, FL: Psychological Assessment Resources.

Briere, J. (2001b). Evaluating treatment outcome. In M. Winterstein & S. R. Scribner (Eds.), *Mental health care for child crime victims: Standards of care task force guidelines*. Sacramento: California Victims Compensation and Government Claims Board, Victims of Crime Program, State of California.

Briere, J. (2002). *Multiscale Dissociation Inventory*. Odessa, FL: Psychological Assessment Resources.

Briere, J. (2004). *Psychological assessment of adult posttraumatic states: Phenomenology, diagnosis, and measurement* (2nd ed.). Washington, DC: American Psychological Association.

Briere, J. (2005). *Trauma Symptom Checklist for Young Children*. Odessa, FL: Psychological Assessment Resources.

Briere, J., Johnson, K., Bissada, A., Damon, L., Crouch, J., Gil, E., et al. (2001). The Trauma Symptom Checklist for Young Children (TSCYC): Reliability and association with abuse exposure in a multi-site study. *Child Abuse and Neglect, 25*, 1001–1014.

Briere, J., Kaltman, S., & Green, B. L. (2008). Accumulated childhood trauma and symptom complexity. *Journal of Traumatic Stress, 21*, 223–226.

Briere, J., & Rickards, S. (2007). Self-awareness, affect regulation, and relatedness: Differential sequelae of childhood versus adult victimization experiences. *Journal of Nervous and Mental Disease, 195*, 497–503.

Briere, J., & Scott, C. (2006). *Principles of trauma therapy: A guide to symptoms, evaluation, and treatment*. Thousand Oaks, CA: Sage.

Briere, J., Weathers, F. W., & Runtz, M. (2005). Is dissociation a multidimensional construct?: Data from the Multiscale Dissociation Inventory. *Journal of Traumatic Stress, 18*, 221–231.

Butcher, J. N., Dahlstrom, W. G., Graham, J. R., Tellegen, A., & Kaemmer, B. (1989). *Minnesota Multiphasic Personality Inventory (MMPI-2): Manual for administration and scoring*. Minneapolis: University of Minnesota Press.

Butcher, J. N., Williams, C. L., Graham, J. R., Archer, R. P., Tellegen, A., Ben-Porath, Y. S., et al. (1992). *Minnesota Multiphasic Personality Inventory—Adolescents (MMPI-A): Manual for administration, scoring, and interpretation*. Minneapolis: University of Minnesota Press.

Byrne, B. M. (1996). *Measuring self-concept across the lifespan: Issues and instrumentation*. Washington, DC: American Psychological Association.

Carlson, E. B. (1997). *Trauma assessments: A clinician's guide*. New York: Guilford Press.

Carlson, E. B., & Putnam, F. W. (1993). An update on the Dissociative Experiences Scale. *Dissociation, 6*, 16–27.

Carlson, E. B., Putnam, F. W., Ross, C. A., Torem, M., Coons, P. M., Dill, D., et al. (1993). Validity of the Dissociative Experiences Scale in screening for multiple personality disorder: A multicenter study. *American Journal of Psychiatry, 150*, 1030–1036.

Carter, R. T. (2007). Racism and psychological and emotional injury: Recognizing and assessing race-based traumatic stress. *Counseling Psychologist, 35*, 257–266.

Chu, J. A., Frey, L. M., Ganzel, B. L., & Matthews, J. A. (1999). Memories of childhood abuse: Dissociation, amnesia, and corroboration. *American Journal of Psychiatry, 156*, 749–755.

Classen, C. C., Palesh, O. G., & Aggarwal, R. (2005). Sexual revictimization: A review of the empirical literature. *Trauma, Violence and Abuse, 6*, 103–129.

Cole, P. M., & Putnam, F. W. (1992). Effect of incest on self and social functioning: A developmental psychopathology perspective. *Journal of Consulting and Clinical Psychology, 60*, 174–184.

Conners, C. K. (1989). *Conners Rating Scales manual: Instruments for use with children and adolescents*. New York: Multi-Health Systems.

Cook, A., Spinazzola, J., Ford, J. D., Lanktree, C., Blaustein, M., Cloitre, M., et al. (2005). Complex trauma in children and adolescents. *Psychiatric Annals, 35*, 390–398.

Courtois, C. A. (2004). Complex trauma, complex reactions: Assessment and treatment. *Psychotherapy: Theory, Research, Practice and Training, 41*, 412–425.

Davidson, J. R. T., & Fairbank, J. A. (1993). The epidemiology of posttraumatic stress disorder. In J. R. T Davidson & E. B. Foa (Eds.), *Posttraumatic stress disorder: DSM-IV and beyond* (pp. 147–169). Washington, DC: American Psychiatric Press.

de Jong, J. T., Komproe, I. H., Spinazzola, J., van der Kolk, B. A., & Van Ommeren, M. H. (2005). DESNOS in three post-conflict settings: Assessing cross-cultural construct equivalence. *Journal of Traumatic Stress, 18*, 13–21.

Derogatis, L. R. (1983). *SCL-90-R administration, scoring, and procedures manual II for the revised version* (2nd ed.). Towson, MD: Clinical Psychometrics Research.

Dietrich, A. M. (2003). Characteristics of child maltreatment, psychological dissociation, and somatoform dissociation of Canadian inmates. *Journal of Trauma and Dissociation, 4*, 81–100.

Exner, J. E. (1986). *The Rorschach: A comprehensive system* (2nd ed.). New York: Wiley.

Felitti, V. J., Anda, R. F., Nordenberg, D., Williamson, D. F., Spitz, A. M., Edwards, V., et al. (1998). Relationship of childhood abuse and household dysfunction to many of the leading causes of death in adults: The Adverse Childhood Experiences (ACE) study. *American Journal of Preventative Medicine, 14*(4), 245–258.

Finkelhor, D., Hamby, S. L., Ormrod, R., & Turner, H. (2005). Measuring poly-victimization using the Juvenile Victimization Questionnaire. *Child Abuse and Neglect, 29*, 1297–1312.

Foa, E. B. (1995). *Posttraumatic Stress Diagnostic Scale*. Minneapolis: National Computer Systems.

Foa, E. B., Ehlers, A., Clark, D. M., Tolin, D. F., & Orsillo, S. M. (1999). The Posttraumatic Cognitions Inventory (PTCI): Development and validation. *Psychological Assessment, 11*, 303–314.

Follette, V. M., Polusny, M. A., Bechtle, A. E., & Naugle, A. E. (1996). Cumulative trauma: The impact of child sexual abuse, adult sexual assault, and spouse abuse. *Journal of Traumatic Stress, 9*, 25–35.

Ford, J. D., & Kidd, P. (1998). Early childhood trauma and disorders of extreme stress as predictors of treatment outcome with chronic posttraumatic stress disorder. *Journal of Traumatic Stress, 11*, 743–761.

Friedrich, W. N. (1998). *The Child Sexual Behavior Inventory professional manual*. Odessa, FL: Psychological Assessment Resources.

Friedrich, W. N. (2002). *Psychological assessment of sexually abused children and their families*. Thousand Oaks, CA: Sage.

Garner, D. M. (2004). *Eating Disorder Inventory–3 professional manual*. Odessa, FL: Psychological Assessment Resources.

Gilbert, A. M. (2004). *Psychometric properties of the Trauma Symptom Checklist for Young Children*. Unpublished doctoral dissertation, Alliant University, San Diego, CA.

Gilboa-Schechtman, E., & Foa, E. B. (2001). Patterns of recovery from trauma: The use of intra-individual analysis. *Journal of Abnormal Psychology, 110*, 392–400.

Green, B. L., & Solomon, S. D. (1995). The mental health impact of natural and technological disasters. In J. R. Freedy & S. E. Hobfoll (Eds.), *Traumatic stress: From theory to practice* (pp. 163–180). New York: Plenum Press.

Heim, C., & Nemeroff, C. B. (2001). The role of childhood trauma in the neurobiology of mood and anxiety disorders: Preclinical and clinical studies. *Biological Psychiatry, 49*, 1023–1039.

Herman, J., Perry, J., & van der Kolk, B. A. (1989). Childhood trauma in borderline personality disorder. *American Journal of Psychiatry, 146*, 490–495.

Herman, J. L. (1992). Complex PTSD: A syndrome in survivors of prolonged and repeated trauma. *Journal of Traumatic Stress, 5*, 377–391.

Herpertz, S., Gretzer, A., Steinmeyer, E. M., Muehlbauer, V., Schuerkens, A., & Sass, H. (1997). Affective instability and impulsivity in personality disorder: Results of an experimental study. *Journal of Affective Disorders, 44*, 31–37.

Janoff-Bulman, R. (1992). *Shattered assumptions: Towards a new psychology of trauma*. New York: Free Press.

Jordan, R. G., Nunley, T. V., & Cook, R. R. (1992). Symptom exaggeration in a PTSD inpatient population: Response set or claim for compensation? *Journal of Traumatic Stress, 5*, 633–642.

Kovacs, M. (1992). *Children's Depression Inventory (CDI) manual*. Toronto: Multi-Health Systems.

Kubiak, S. P. (2005). Trauma and cumulative adversity in women of a disadvantaged social location. *American Journal of Orthopsychiatry, 75*, 451–465.

Lachar, D. (1982). *Personality Inventory for Children (PIC) revised format manual supplement*. Los Angeles: Western Psychological Services.

Lanktree, C. B., Gilbert, A. M., Briere, J., Taylor, N., Chen, K., Maida, C. A., et al. (2008). Multi-informant assessment of maltreated children: Convergent and discriminant validity of the TSCC and TSCYC. *Child Abuse and Neglect, 32*, 621–625.

Loewenstein, R. L. (1990). Somatoform disorders in victims of incest and child abuse. In R. P. Kluft (Ed.), *Incest-related syndromes of adult psychopathology* (pp. 75–111). Washington, DC: American Psychiatric Press.

Luxenberg, T., & Levin, P. (2004). The role of the Rorschach in the assessment and treatment of trauma. In J. P. Wilson & T. M. Keane (Eds.), *Assessing psychological trauma and PTSD* (2nd ed., pp. 190–225). New York: Guilford Press.

Marsella, A. J., Friedman, M. J., Gerrity, E. T., & Scurfield, R. M. (Eds.). (1996). *Ethnocultural aspects of posttraumatic stress disorder: Issues, research, and clinical applications*. Washington DC: American Psychological Association.

McCauley, J., Kern, D. E., Kolodner, K., Dill, L., Schroeder, A. F., DeChant, J. K., et al. (1997). Clinical characteristics of women with a history of childhood abuse. *Journal of the American Medical Association, 277*, 1362–1368.

McDevitt-Murphy, M. E., Weathers, F. W., & Adkins, J. W. (2005). The use of the Trauma Symptom Inventory in the assessment of PTSD symptoms. *Journal of Traumatic Stress, 18*, 63–67.

Millon, T. (1994). *Millon Clinical Multiaxial Inventory–III: Manual for the MCMI-III*. Minneapolis: National Computer Systems.

Morey, L. C. (1991). *Personality Assessment Inventory professional manual*. Odessa, FL: Psychological Assessment Resources.

Najavits, L. M. (2002). *Seeking Safety: A treatment manual for PTSD and substance abuse*. New York: Guilford Press.

Ogata, S., Silk, K., Goodrich, S., Lohr, N., Westen, D., & Hill, E. M. (1990). Childhood sexual and physical abuse in adult patients with borderline personality disorder. *American Journal of Psychiatry, 147,* 1008–1013.

Ouimette, P., & Brown, P. J. (2003). *Trauma and substance abuse: Causes, consequences, and treatment of comorbid disorders.* Washington, DC: American Psychological Association.

Pearlman, L. A. (2003). *Trauma and Attachment Belief Scale.* Los Angeles: Western Psychological Services.

Pearlman, L. A., & Courtois, C. A. (2005). Clinical applications of the attachment framework: Relational treatment of complex trauma. *Journal of Traumatic Stress, 18,* 449–459.

Pelcovitz, D., van der Kolk, B. A., Roth, S., Mandel, F., Kaplan, S., & Resick, P. (1997). Development of a criteria set and a structured interview for disorders of extreme stress (SIDES). *Journal of Traumatic Stress, 10,* 3–16.

Perry, B. D., & Pollard, R. (1998). Homeostasis, stress, trauma, and adaptation: A neurodevelopmental view of childhood trauma. *Child and Adolescent Psychiatric Clinics of North America, 7,* 33–51.

Putnam, F. W. (1997). *Dissociation in children and adolescents: A developmental perspective.* New York: Guilford Press.

Putnam, F. W. (2003). Ten-year research update review: Child sexual abuse. *Journal of the American Academy of Child and Adolescent Psychiatry, 43,* 269–278.

Resick, P. A. Nishith, P., & Griffin, M. G. (2003). How well does cognitive-behavioral therapy treat symptoms of complex PTSD? *CNS Spectrums, 8,* 340–342, 351–355.

Reynolds, C. R., & Kamphaus, R. W. (2006). *Behavior Assessment System for Children* (2nd ed.). New York: Pearson.

Reynolds, W. M. (1991). Psychometric characteristics of the Adult Suicidal Ideation Questionnaire in college students. *Journal of Personality Assessment, 56,* 289–307.

Roid, G. H., & Fitts, W. H. (1994). *Tennessee Self-Concept Scale* [Rev. manual]. Los Angeles: Western Psychological Services.

Rorschach, H. (1981). *Psychodiagnostics: A diagnostic test based upon perception* (P. Lemkau & B. Kronemberg, Eds. & Trans., 9th ed.). New York: Grune & Stratton.

Singer, M. I., Anglin, T. M., Song, L. Y., & Lunghofer, L. (1995). Adolescents' exposure to violence and associated symptoms of psychological trauma. *Journal of the American Medical Association, 273,* 477–482.

Steinberg, M. (1994). *Structured Clinical Interview for DSM-IV Dissociative Disorders—Revised (SCID-D-R).* Washington, DC: American Psychiatric Press.

Steketee, G., & Foa, E. B. (1987). Rape victims: Post-traumatic stress responses and their treatment: A review of the literature. *Journal of Anxiety Disorders, 1,* 69–86.

van der Kolk, B. A. (2005). Developmental trauma disorder: Toward a rational diagnosis for children with complex trauma histories. *Psychiatric Annals, 35*(5), 401–408.

van der Kolk, B. A., Pelcovitz, D., Roth, S. H., Mandel, F., McFarlane, A. C., & Herman, J. L. (1996). The complexity of adaptation to trauma. *American Journal of Psychiatry, 153*(Suppl.), 83–93.

van der Kolk, B. A., Roth, S. H., Pelcovitz, D., Sunday, S., & Spinazzola, J. (2005). Disorders of extreme stress. *Journal of Traumatic Stress, 18,* 389–399.

Vondra, J. I., Barnett, D., & Cicchetti, D. (1990). Self-concept, motivation, and competence among preschoolers from maltreating and comparison families. *Child Abuse and Neglect, 14,* 525–540.

Wolpaw, J. M., Ford, J. D., Newman, E., Davis, J. L., & Briere, J. (2005). Trauma Symptom Checklist for Children. In T. Grisso, G. Vincent, & D. Seagrave (Eds.), *Mental health screening and assessment in juvenile justice* (pp. 152–165). New York: Guilford Press.

Yehuda, R. (1997). Sensitization of the hypothalamic–pituitary–adrenal axis in posttraumatic stress disorder. *Annals of the New York Academy of Sciences, 821,* 57–75.

Zlotnick, C., Donaldson, D., Spirito, A., & Pearlstein, T. (1997). Affect regulation and suicide attempts in adolescent inpatients. *Journal of the American Academy of Child and Adolescent Psychiatry, 36,* 793–798.

Zlotnick, C., & Pearlstein, T. (1997). Validation of the Structured Interview for Disorders of Extreme Stress. *Comprehensive Psychiatry, 38,* 243–247.

CHAPTER 6

Assessment of Attachment and Abuse History, and Adult Attachment Style

Daniel Brown

Complex posttraumatic stress disorder (PTSD), "disorders of extreme distress not otherwise specified" (DESNOS; van der Kolk, Roth, Pelcovitz, Sunday, & Spinazzola, 2005), has been defined by Herman (1992) as a "spectrum of conditions rather than a single entity" that includes "personality changes, alterations in affect regulation and meaning systems, consciousness, self-perception, and relations with others" (p. 125). She hypothesized that complex PTSD had its origins in "a history of childhood trauma" (p. 125). DESNOS was defined as a constellation of 27 symptoms across seven distinct symptoms categories (Pelcovitz et al., 1997). The complex PTSD or DESNOS syndrome has been seen as an alternative to subsuming these often-observed problems of affect regulation, self-regulation, and interpersonal difficulties under the borderline personality disorder diagnosis (van der Kolk et al., 2005). However, the DESNOS literature is unclear in its definition of what constitutes *extreme stress*. The original field trials associated DESNOS with chronic, early-onset child abuse and specifically with *interpersonal childhood trauma* (Roth, Newman, Pelcovitz, van der Kolk, & Mandel, 1997). Zlotnik and colleagues (1996) defined *early trauma* as sexual abuse prior to age 16. They found that a history of childhood sexual abuse compared to no history of abuse significantly predicted DESNOS symptoms. Roth and colleagues (1997) defined *early onset* as child sexual abuse prior to age 13. Even when veterans with combat exposure histories were assessed, *developmentally adverse interpersonal traumas*, such as physical abuse, sexual abuse, or witnessing domestic violence, were associated with DESNOS (Ford, 1999). More recent studies have delineated "early life psychological trauma" more clearly. For example, individuals in the DSM-IV Field Trial with a history of childhood sexual abuse prior to age 14 were significantly more likely to develop DESNOS than those with a history of sexual abuse after age 14 (van der Kolk et al., 2005). Another study found that a history of childhood abuse was most strongly associated with DESNOS symptoms among college women, with other types of interpersonal trauma in childhood or adolescence less strongly related to DESNOS symptoms, and noninterpersonal traumas associated with PTSD rather than DESNOS (Ford, Stockton, Kaltman, & Green, 2006).

A problem with the DESNOS definition of *early interpersonal trauma* is that it fails to account for the differential effects of early dysfunction in the infant–caregiver attachment system and the effects of specific abusive events, such as sexual and/or physical abuse in later childhood. There has been a trend in the more recent literature on DESNOS to expand the definition of *early childhood trauma* to include "trauma early in the life cycle" (van der Kolk et al., 2005, p. 389) or "developmentally adverse interpersonal trauma" (Ford, 2005, p. 410), but these attempts to push back the age of traumatization do not alter the fundamental assumption, namely, that complex PTSD is a result of early childhood trauma per se. According to Roth and colleagues (1997), for example, complex PTSD is "specific to trauma" (p. 541). This formulation obscures the extent to which early attachment pathology may account for DESNOS and/or multiple comorbidities, independent of or in combination with frank abuse. However, van der Kolk and Courtois (2005) have used the term *developmental trauma* (p. 385), which includes both "nonresponsive and abusive caregivers" (p. 386), thereby opening the door to a reconsideration of the relative contribution of early attachment failure, in addition to, or instead of, psychological trauma per se in the etiology of complex PTSD.

THE CONTRIBUTION OF ATTACHMENT STATUS TO ADULT PSYCHOPATHOLOGY

An exception to the focus on traumatic events rather than on the disruption of attachment relationships in the complex PTSD literature is research by Alexander (1993) with women who have survived childhood sexual abuse. Childhood sexual abuse was correlated with PTSD and other Axis I conditions, but a personality disorder diagnosis was significantly correlated with early childhood attachment status. Attachment research also challenges the "trauma per se" view. Although the long-term effects of sexual abuse per se have been well documented (Putnam, 2003), longitudinal studies also have shown that childhood disorganized or resistant–insecure attachment status is a risk factor for the development of personality disorders (Barone, 2003; Fonagy, 2007), anxiety disorders (Bosquet & Egeland, 2006), and addictions in adulthood (Widom, Ireland, & Glynn, 1995). The combination of disorganized attachment status and later childhood abuse is a risk factor for the development of dissociative disorders in adulthood (Lyons-Ruth, Dutra, Schuder, & Bianchi, 2006; Sroufe, Egeland, Carlson, & Collins, 2005). Insecure attachment status, notably, preoccupied attachment, also predicts which survivors of childhood sexual abuse are more likely to have unresolved status with respect to the abuse (Stalker & Davies, 1995). Furthermore, early attachment disorganization predicts frequency and range of dissociative experiences in childhood and adolescence (Main & Morgan, 1996); dissociation predicts the emergence of multiple comorbid psychiatric disorders in adulthood (Brown, 2001; Putnam, 2003).

The Minnesota Longitudinal Study (Sroufe et al., 2005) is the "gold standard" in prospective studies of neglect and abuse. High-risk mothers (some very young, others involved in domestic abuse, drugs, or prostitution) and their infants were studied for more than 30 years with multimethod assessment instruments at every phase of development from infancy. The Minnesota study also assessed attachment status with the Strange Situation paradigm twice, at 12 and at 18 months, and again with the Adult Attachment Interview (AAI) in early adulthood (Sroufe et al., 2005). Because many of these high-risk children were physically and/or sexually abused in childhood, the study allowed for an assessment of the relative contribution of both early attachment disruption and later specific abusive incidents to the overall risk and type of psychopathology emerging in early adulthood. Study findings indicated that a combination of disorganized attachment aggravated by later childhood abuse at the time and later predicted the development of dissociative disorders in adulthood (Carlson, 1998; Ogawa, Sroufe, Weinfield, Carlson, & Egeland, 1997). Specifically, children who were found to have disorganized attachment at 12 or 18 months showed a wide range of dissociative experiences throughout childhood and adolescence that tended to decline in adulthood. However, if the child with disorganized attachment was physically and/or sexually abused at any time in childhood, he or she tended primarily to use a dissociative coping style to deal with the abuse. The combination of a dissociative coping style and abuse was associated with an increased risk of developing pathological dissociation characterized by rigid compartmentalization of perceptions and self-states (see Steele & van der Hart, Chapter 7, this volume). This is consistent with evidence from other studies that sexually abused children, compared to demographically matched, nonabused children, are more likely to use a dissociative coping style and to develop a range of psychiatric conditions in adulthood (Putnam, 2003). Thus, the combination of early disorganized attachment and later childhood abuse places the child at risk for clinically significant dissociative disorders in adulthood.

Retrospective studies with adults diagnosed with borderline personality disorder indirectly support the hypothesis that long-standing problems with attachment are associated with complex PTSD. Studies in which the AAI was administered to patients diagnosed with borderline personality disorder consistently have shown a propensity toward anxious/preoccupied attachment and disorganized attachment (Barone, 2003). These studies also assessed whether trauma or loss histories in these patients were resolved or remained unresolved according to AAI criteria. Unresolved status with respect to loss or abuse ranged from 60 to 89%. Considering all of the evidence together, simple PTSD appears to be best predicted by single or cumulative specific trauma events, whereas complex PTSD appears to be best predicted by insecure, especially disorganized attachment aggravated by childhood abuse. Preexisting insecure attachment status also increases the likelihood that the childhood physical and/ or sexual abuse remains unresolved (Stalker & Davies, 1995), defined in terms of ongoing disoriented states of mind and lapses in reasoning and discourse with respect to the abuse (Main, Kaplan, & Cassidy, 1985). An implication of these findings is that adults presenting with symptoms and impairments consistent with complex PTSD should be assessed for current disorganized attachment and a history of early childhood attachment failure, as well as for abuse and trauma history in childhood (Allen, 2001). The utility of such broadband clinical assessment is illustrated with the findings of an ongoing study.

AN ASSESSMENT STUDY OF MEN WITH ABUSE HISTORIES

As part of my forensic evaluation as an expert witness for the plaintiffs in civil lawsuits alleging damages from childhood sexual abuse, 24 men recruited into the study were administered the battery of tests described below. Each case involved repeated sexual abuse in the elementary school years, often along with severe physical abuse, while living in an orphanage or group residential home for boys. This sample can be divided into two broad categories: (1) *secure but disrupted family life*: men from essentially loving homes who had a secure attachment status but were eventually sent to an orphanage or a group home because of severe financial difficulties, and/or the death of a family member that resulted in dissolution of the family; and (2) *extremely disorganized and abusive family life*: men from high-risk families characterized by drug or alcohol dependent and domestically violent parents, and mothers who engaged in prostitution or had forfeited parental right as a result of neglect.

Thus, the sample provides a naturalistic comparison of men with different attachment histories and very similar types of later sexual and physical abuse in similar residential facilities. Each man was administered between 16 and 20 hours of face-to-face psychological assessment interviews and instruments as part of the lawsuit. Very detailed medical, school, and work records were reviewed and compared to psychological testing results *after* completion of all testing to minimize testing bias. The hypothesis was that men with insecure attachment status who were later abused would be significantly more likely to present with symptoms and impairments consistent with complex PTSD than would men with secure attachment status who were later abused. Although these data represent initial findings from an ongoing clinical study without a control group, they provide preliminary data on the relative contribution of attachment disruption to complex PTSD.

Standardized structured clinical interviews have a distinct advantage over open-ended interviews in achieving better reliability and validity, because they are more comprehensive, and they reduce diagnostic disagreement, interviewer bias, and criterion variance (Rogers, 1995). Self-report inventories, with established norms and empirically derived cut scores, allow the assessor to compare the responses and scores of the individual being tested to scores from a range of criterion groups, and to calculate the probability of correctly classifying each case for each disorder (Brown, 2004). The evolving standard in psychological assessment is a multimethod assessment battery, using several different types of tests for each area of testing, along with a comparison of test results to the patient's history and medical record (see Courtois, Ford, & Cloitre, Chapter 4, this volume; Brown, 2004; Meyer et al., 2001). The use of multiple test strategies and multiple sources of evidence reduces the error rate and adds to the incremental validity of the overall findings (Garb, 1984). *Incremental validity* means that if the evidence drawn from psychological tests and patient history or previous medical records is consistent, or if the findings derived from a number of different test strategies are similar, then the overall validity of multimethod conclusions is somewhat higher than the validity derived from a single source of evidence.

Structured Clinical Interviews

The Structured Clinical Interview for DSM-IV Disorders (SCID) consists of standardized questions, branch questions, and probe questions, and standardized scoring rules, with portions of the SCID that closely mirror most DSM-IV (American Psychiatric Association, 1994) diagnostic categories. The SCID-I thoroughly covers many Axis I disorders, such as affective disorders, anxiety disorders, and drug abuse, but is weaker on PTSD and somatoform disorders (First, Spitzer, Gibbon, & Williams, 1997). The Structured Clinical Interview for DSM-IV Axis II Disorders Personality Questionnaire (SCID-II-PQ) is a quick screening/quick scoring self-report that covers each of the 11 DSM personality disorders. If an individual meets, or comes close to meeting, the cut number of criteria for a given personality disorder on the SCID-II-PQ, the assessor can then administer the relevant sections of the SCID-II to determine whether the subject meets the more stringent SCID-II criteria of pervasiveness and persistence in a cluster of maladaptive personality traits required for a diagnosis of a personality disorder (First, Gibbon, Spitzer, Williams, & Benjamin, 1997).The SCID-D covers all five types of major dissociative disorders (Steinberg, 1993).

Because the Clinician-Administered PTSD Scale (CAPS) follows all of the *DSM* PTSD criteria carefully, it allows for assessment of both past and current PTSD, and of both the frequency and severity of PTSD symptoms (Weathers et al., 2004).

Given the extent to which early attachment status predicts a significant portion of the variance of adult psychopathology, independent of or in combination with traumatic events, it is imperative to measure attachment status as part of a comprehensive assessment of complex trauma. The Adult Attachment Inventory (AAI), an effective inventory for measuring attachment status in adolescents and adults (Main, Goldwyn & Hesse, 2002), is a standardized, semistructured interview about attachment themes (e.g., perception of early childhood relationship with parents, separations, traumatic experiences, and significant losses). Scoring of attachment status is based on the nature of discourse used to describe attachment themes. The underlying principles are that secure attachment discourse is collaborative and coherent. It is collaborative in the sense that the interviewee keeps track of the questions and selects relevant information from personal life experiences that directly address the questions. It is coherent in the sense that the narrative is succinct, relevant, and fresh. Insecure attachment discourse shows low coherence, in that the description of attachment themes may contain many contradictions, may be under- or overinclusive, may contain numerous irrelevancies, and may contain numerous examples of passive or canned speech as a way of distancing from the topic of attachment. Attachment status as assessed by the AAI is relatively stable over the life course (Sroufe et al., 2005). Following Ainsworth, Blehar, Waters, and Wall (1978) and then Main and Hesse (1990) most experts use a four-way classification of attachment status: secure (F), avoidant (dismissing [Ds]), resistant (anxious/preoccupied [E]), and disorganized (cannot classify [CC]); parentheses refer to terminology used for adult attachment status. One advantage of the AAI is its arrangement of attachment subtypes along a continuum, with F3 representing the prototype of secure attachment, with F2, F1, Ds4 … Ds1 representing gradations in the direction greater dismissing attachment, and with F4, F5, E1 … E3 representing gradations in the direction of greater preoccupied attachment. A second advantage of the AAI is its rating system for the degree to which loss and/or trauma is unresolved, based on significant lapses in interviewee reasoning and/or discourse about major losses, trauma, and abuse. A third advantage is that an AAI supplemental scoring manual assesses the degree of metacognitive reflection on mental states, *mentalization*—an important component of recovery (Bateman & Fonagy, 2004; Fonagy, Target, Steele, & Steele, 1998).

Standardized Face-Valid Self-Report Inventories of PTSD

Selected inventories were (1) generally accepted (i.e., widely used in published outcomes research); (2) had acceptable reliability and validity, including the capacity to detect correctly a given psychiatric condition (*sensitivity*) and to discriminate correctly between that and other conditions (*specificity*); (3) had established norms by which to compare a given subject's score to that of various comparison groups; (4) had empirically derived cut scores that specify the probability of correctly classifying the individual as having a given condition, say, for example, a 95% chance of correctly classifying this individual as having PTSD, above a certain cutoff score; and (5) controlled for response style (see

Courtois et al., Chapter 4, this volume). The Impact of Event Scale—Revised (IES-R; Sundin & Horowitz, 2002), the Davidson Trauma Scale (DTS; Davidson et al., 1997), and the Trauma Symptom Inventory (TSI; Briere, Elliott, Harris, & Cotman, 1995) were used. The Ways of Coping Checklist (WCC; Lazarus, 1966) was used to assess ways of coping with trauma, along with the Defensive Avoidance and Dissociation scales of the TSI.

Actuarial Self-Report Inventories

Generally, it is advisable to use two very different types of self-report inventories, those in which the items are obviously about the condition in questions (e.g., "Do you have unwanted memories about the trauma?"; face-valid inventories), and those in which the items are not obviously about the condition in question (actuarial inventories). For example, Minnesota Multiphasic Personality Inventory—Second Edition (MMPI-2) (Hathaway & McKinley, 1989) questions such as "I find it hard to keep my mind on a task or job" or "Most any time I would rather sit and daydream than do anything else" are obviously not about PTSD. However, administering the MMPI-2 independently to subjects suspected of having PTSD yields from the total pool of 567 MMPI-2 items a stable set of items characteristically endorsed with relatively high frequency by persons with PTSD. These items constitute an actuarial PTSD scale, even though the contents of the items do not seem to be about PTSD symptoms. It is harder to fake actuarial PTSD scales, because to do so would require a patient to respond in the right way to number of specific questions, none of which are directly about PTSD, scattered throughout the instrument. Conclusions drawn from a combination of face-valid and actuarial strategies have incremental validity, provided that the findings across both types of self-report inventories are similar and not contradictory. In addition to the MMPI-2, the Millon Clinical Multiaxial Inventory–II (MCMI-II; Millon, 1987) and the Malingering Probability Scale (MPS; Silverton & Gruber, 1998) were used as actuarial assessments.

Psychophysiological Testing of Physiological Reactivity in PTSD

Because PTSD entails hyperarousal, it is useful to measure physiological response (e.g., heart rate, frontalis electromyograph [EMG], and skin conductance during exposure to brief, audio-recorded scripts of neutral events, negative life events, and events associated with emotionally evocative or and trauma-specific stimuli) (Orr & Kaloupek, 1997). Such an assessment is especially useful in (1) determining which traumatic event(s) are currently associated with physiological reactivity in a given individual with a history of multiple traumatic events; (2) identifying highly dissociated trauma patients who show attenuated physiological reactivity across all scripts; and (3) collecting evidence beyond self-report when there is a question of simulated PTSD.

Ancillary Testing with Self-Report Inventories

A variety of well-validated self-report inventories were used for a more detailed assessment of dissociation, including the Dissociative Experiences Scale (DES; Bernstein-Carlson & Putnam, 1986), the Somatoform Dissociation Questionnaire (SDQ; Nijenhuis et al., 1996), the MPS, and the Peritraumatic Dissociative Experience Questionnaire (PDEQ; Marmar, Weiss, & Metzler, 1998). Anxiety symptoms were assessed with the Body Sensations Questionnaire (BSQ; Chambless, Caputo, Bright, & Gallagher, 1984), the Penn State Worry Questionnaire (PSWQ; Brown, Antony, & Barlow, 1992; Meyer, Miller, Metzger, & Borkovec, 1990), the Fear of Negative Evaluation (FNE; Watson & Friend, 1969), and the Social Avoidance and Distress Scale (SADS; Watson & Friend, 1969). Affective symptoms were assessed with the Beck Depression Inventory–2 (BDI-2; Beck, Steer, & Garbin, 1988), the Automatic Thoughts Questionnaire (ATQ; Hollon & Kendall, 1980), the Dysfunctional Attitude Scale (DAS; Weissman, 1979), and the Index of Self-Esteem (ISE; Hudson, 1997). Addictive behaviors were assessed with the Michigan Alcohol Screening Test (MAST; Selzer, 1971), the Eating Attitudes Test (EAT; Gardner & Garfinkel, 1979), and the Revised Bulimia Test (BULIT-R; Thelen, Farmer, Wonderlich, & Smith, 1991). Sexual disorders were assessed with the Multidimensional Sexuality Questionnaire (MSQ; Snell, Fisher, & Walters, 1993), the Sexual Arousal Inventory (SArI; Chambless & Lifshitz, 1984), the Sexual Anxiety Inventory (SAnI; Janda, 1980), and the Wilson Sexual Fantasy Questionnaire (WSFQ; Wilson, 1978). Interpersonal functioning was assessed with the Relationship Questionnaire (Bartholomew & Horowitz, 1991), Experiences in Close Relationships (ECR; Brennan, Clark, & Shaver, 1998), the Interpersonal Dependency Inventory (IDI; Hirschfield et al., 1977), and the Interpersonal Competency Scale (ICS; Burhmester, Furman, Wittenberg, & Reis, 1988). Memory distortion was assessed with the Gudjonsson Suggestibility Scale (GSS; Gudjonsson, 1984) and the Inventory of Childhood Memories and Imaginings (ICMI; Wilson & Barber, 1983), as well as the Bizarre Mentation (BM) scale on the MMPI-2 and the Thought Disorder and Delusional Disorder scales on the MPS. Malingering was assessed with the Structured Interview of Reported Symptoms (SIRS; Rogers, Bagby, & Dickens, 1992), the Structured Inventory of Malingered Symptomatology (SIMS; Widows & Smith, 2005), and the MPS (Silverton & Gruber, 1998). In addition to the AAI, attachment style was assessed using the Trauma and Attachment Belief Scale (TABS; Pearlman, 2003), an instrument that assesses attachment disruption and/or trauma related to five basic needs (safety, trust, intimacy, esteem, and control), and the Young Schema Questionnaire–3 (YSQ-3; Young & Brown, 2001).

Results

Table 6.1 summarizes the relationships among attachment history, adult attachment classification, and SCID-II and MCMI-2 findings regarding personality

TABLE 6.1. Attachment Status in Forensically Evaluated Men

Attachment status	Any PD	BPO	Mixed PD	OCPD, AVPD	MDD	S	ED
F 9 (37.5)	2 (8.3)	0	0	2 (8.3)	0	8 (66.6)	0
Ds 2 (8.3)	2 (8.3)	0	2 (8.3)	0	1 (41.6)	1 (4.2)	1 (4.2)
CC 13 (54)	12 (50)	4 (33.3)	8 (66.6)	0	11 (45.8)	1 (4.2)	11 (45.8)
Ud 13 (54)	8 (66.6)	3 (25)	4 (33.3)	2 (8.3)	9 (37.5)	3 (25)	10 (41.6)

Note. PD, personality disorder; BPO, borderline personality organization; OCPD, obsessive–compulsive personality disorder; AVPD, avoidant personality disorder; DD, dissociative disorder; S, secure, but disrupted family life; ED, extremely disorganized, disrupted family life; F, secure; Ds, dismissing; CC, disorganized; Ud, unresolved/disorganized. Percentage of subjects in parentheses.

disorder, and SCID-D evidence regarding major dissociative disorders, such as dissociatve identity disorder (DID) or dissociative disorder not otherwise specified (DDNOS). Consistent with research findings to date, most of the men in the secure but disrupted family environment group were classified as secure (F) on the AAI ($N = 9$), and most in the extremely disorganized/abusive family environment group were classified as disorganized (CC; $N = 13$) or dismissing (Ds; $N = 2$). No participant received a purely preoccupied (E) attachment status, although many men classified as disorganized (CC) had preoccupied as the first best-fit classification. Because all of the men were victims of comparable sexual and physical abuse in the same orphanage or group home settings, the main difference between these two groups is attachment status, not abuse background. None of the men classified as secure met criteria for borderline personality disorder. Two met the criteria for avoidant personality disorder and another two for obsessive–compulsive personality disorder. In contrast, 12 of the 13 men with disorganized attachment had a personality disorder diagnosis, with four men meeting criteria for borderline personality disorder, and another eight meeting the criteria for mixed personality disorder. Two men with a dismissing attachment style also had a mixed personality disorder diagnosis. These results suggest a strong relationship between disorganized attachment and the presence of a personality disorder.

None of the men classified as having secure attachment had a major dissociative disorder; Nine of the 13 men classified as disorganized attachment had a major dissociative disorder characterized by identity alteration. One met full criteria for the diagnosis of DID, and eight met criteria for DDNOS. Two of these men had high levels of identity confusion. Combining the identity confusion and identity alteration data, 11 of 13 men in the disorganized attachment group showed clinically significant dissociated self-states in one form or another. Using the AAI unresolved/disoriented (Ud) state-of-mind categorization with respect to loss or trauma, 13 of the 24 men had unresolved status on the AAI, 10 from the disorganized attachment group, and three from the secure attachment group. Two of the three securely attached men with unresolved status had obsessive–compulsive personality disorder (OCPD), but no major dissociative disorder, whereas the third man had no personality disorder but demonstrated identity confusion. Seven of the 10 men with a combination of unresolved trauma/loss status and disorganized attachment had both a personality disorder and a major dissociative disorder; the other three men had either a personality disorder or major dissociative disorder, but not both. The six men classified as resolved and securely attached were completely free of a personality disorder or any major dissociative disorder.

Overall, these findings suggest that disorganized attachment is correlated with adult personality disorders and major dissociative disorders, and that secure attachment rarely is associated with personality disorders or major dissociative disorders (except OCPD), even among men who experienced severe and recurrent childhood abuse. Based on these data, it does not appear that child abuse per se, in the absence of attachment disorganization, manifests as a personality disorder or major dissociative disorder in adulthood. The combination of attachment disorganization and abuse in later childhood appears to be the main correlate of complex traumatic stress impairment in adulthood.

CASE ILLUSTRATIONS OF SIMPLE AND COMPLEX PTSD

Case M: Simple PTSD

M's parents got divorced shortly after he was born. His father left, and he never knew him. He and his brother were raised by their mother, who in the early years lovingly raised both boys. When M was around 6 years old, his mother sent him to an orphanage, because "there was no one to take care of us while my mother worked." Early on into his stay, a male staff member came into his bed one night and kissed and fondled him; shortly thereafter, a female staff member did the same. The pattern of sexual abuse progressed over time and included the female staff member frequently removing him from the classroom to hold and fondle him, the male staff member requiring him to perform oral sex on him and to participate in group sexual encounters with other orphanage boys, and to submit to anal penetration. The male staff member gave M "special privileges" in exchange for sex. However, the physical abuse by other staff continued. His physical punishment at the orphanage included being locked in a closet for several days, having his hand and arm burned on a radiator, and frequent beatings.

During his adolescent years M was able to leave the orphanage to resume living with his mother, who, by then, unfortunately had become an active alcoholic. He quit school, took a job, and became "the responsible one," supporting his family while his mother became increasingly "irresponsible" and "unable to take care of us" because of her drinking. In late adolescence, M joined the military and served active duty in Vietnam. M was exposed to several life-threatening mortar attacks on his bunker, but otherwise he was not in active combat. He held a responsible position in the military and was honorably discharged. After returning home, he had a long-lasting, stable job and a stable, intimate relationship over the next several decades. From early adolescence, M had completely forgotten the orphanage abuse, only recovering the abuse memories in recent years, after watching a news program about priest abuse.

On the AAI, M showed clear evidence of a secure attachment style—F4. On the Relationship Questionnaire, his self-report of relational style was also secure. The F4 pattern is characterized by "strong expressed valuing of relationships, accompanied by some manifestations of preoccupation with attachment figures, or past trauma" (Main et al., 2002, p. 158). His ability as an adult to have a stable, intimate partner for nearly three decades is consistent with a secure attachment style. His testing showed no evidence of a personality disorder. His scores fell well below the cutoff point of clinical significance both on the SCID-II Personality Questionnaire and on the full SCID-II. On the MCMI-II actuarial assessment of personality disorder, no scale score reached a level of significance (base rate score [BR] > 85). On the YSQ, he showed no very high or high scores that would be indicative of a personality disorder. Taken together, the assessment evidence consistently ruled out a personality disorder. Furthermore, no data provided evidence of a major DD, but suggested a normal dissociative coping style. His scores on the DES and the SDS were both very low, as was the score on the Dissociation scale of the MPS (T = 44). On the full SCID-D, he scored positive for dissociative amnesia but showed no evidence for depersonalization, derealization, identity confusion, or identity alteration. However, his high score on the PDES, along with significant elevations on the Dissociation and Defensive Avoidance scales of the TSI showed consistent usage of a dissociative coping style, predictive of dissociative amnesia for traumatic experiences. M had a 1-year period of alcohol abuse while in Vietnam, in full remission since returning home. He drank for about a week after first recovering his childhood abuse memories, but stopped, because he did not want to drink like his mother.

According to the psychological testing results for M, the pattern of psychological damage related to the orphanage physical and sexual abuse is quite specific: He met criteria for PTSD. On the CAPS, M met all of the criteria for past and current PTSD. The content of current unwanted memories, dreams, flashbacks, emotional distress, and physical reactions is specific to the orphanage physical and sexual abuse, and not to other traumas in his life, such as combat exposure, exposure to natural disasters, parental divorce, separation from his family during his orphanage years, and his mother's later alcoholism. Likewise, psychophysiological measurement during exposure to relaxation, negative life event, and trauma scripts showed significant elevations across all physiological indices (heart rate, frontalis EMG, and skin conductance) specifically in response to three orphanage sexual abuse scripts (fondled by female staff member, anal rape by male staff member, group sex with male staff member and other boys), and one physical punishment script (being locked in a closet). There was no significant physiological elevation in response to scripts about combat exposure, his mother's alcoholism, his mother's death, or witnessing physical abuse. The TSI showed a clinically significant elevation on the Intrusive Experience scale ($T = 79$), and also on the Defensive Avoidance and Dissociation scales, but not on any other scale. He showed a moderate elevation on the Mistrust-Abuse scale of YSQ.

M experienced panic attacks for the first time in his life upon recall of the orphanage abuse memories. His fears were specific to the orphanage abuse, namely, a phobia of unwanted sexual contact and a phobia of unfamiliar places. Scores on general self-report inventories for anxiety conditions were not clinically significant, nor were the depression scores significant across a number of inventories and structured interviews.

On a variety of self-report inventories regarding sexual functioning, M showed clear evidence of a sexual desire disorder, which took the form of mildly compulsive sexuality in adolescence, with the progressive development of inhibited sexual desire in adulthood.

On a variety of self-report and actuarial inventories of interpersonal functioning, M consistently showed evidence of being outgoing and sociable with peers, sustaining close intimate relationships, and having a long-standing mistrust of authority figures.

The overall pattern of findings is highly consistent across all testing with respect to PTSD. M's defensive avoidant and dissociative coping style caused him to develop dissociative amnesia for the orphanage abuse for decades, until he was exposed to priest abuse stories in the news media. Following that, he began having intrusive experiencing symptoms, whose content and the physiological reactivity to which were specific to the orphanage abuse and not to other negative or traumatic life events. M's case of simple or classic PTSD illustrates very specific, circumscribed damage that is causally related to the orphanage abuse: the presence of dissociative amnesia, PTSD, panic, inhibited sexual desire, trauma-related phobias, and a specific mistrust of authority figures in an otherwise psychologically healthy individual who shows no major interpersonal damage, and no evidence of a personality disorder or a major DD.

Case X: Complex Trauma-Related Disorder

X grew up in a large family of nine children. Both his mother and his father worked. His mother was an active alcoholic who was "around and then not around" for the children during X's early years, and was often out of the home at the bar. His father was authoritarian and physically abusive. The children more or less took care of each other. His older brothers stole food to feed everyone. Quite suddenly, around age 5, X was sent to an orphanage. After some time, there he was told that his mother had died of cancer. During his stay at the orphanage, X was beaten on a regular basis. He was forced to have anal sex with a male staff member, oral sex with another staff member, as well as unwanted oral sex with several other orphanage boys. After leaving the orphanage around age 12, X returned to live with his father. There he began drinking, doing drugs, and stealing. He was sentenced to a juvenile detention center for a year, after which he lived on the street, drinking heavily, and stealing to get food. In his mid-20s he got a girl pregnant. X took several jobs to support his family but continued to drink and do drugs. Eventually he was arrested for drug possession and "straightened up" after that.

According to the psychological testing, the pattern of psychological damage related to the orphanage physical and sexual abuse was nested within a broader pattern of psychological consequences from early attachment disruption. On the AAI X showed clear evidence of a disorganized/insecure attachment style (Ud/CC//E2, Ds2), with evidence for "contradictory insecure discourse strategies" (Main et al., 2002), namely, strongly dismissing idealization and lack of memory with respect to inquiry about his early childhood relationships with his mother, and strongly angry preoccupation with respect to inquiry about his early childhood relationship to his father and also to the orphanage staff. Similarly, on the Relationship Questionnaire, he endorsed a dismissing/insecure style of relating.

On the SCID-II Personality Questionnaire, X self-reported a wide variety of maladaptive personality traits that were above the cutoff scores for avoidant, obsessive–compulsive, passive–aggressive, dependent, paranoid, narcissistic, and borderline personality disorders. On the more detailed SCID-II Structured Interview, X met all nine diagnostic criteria (cut score of 5 or more) for borderline personality disorder, with additional avoidant, depressive, paranoid, obsessive, and passive–aggressive features. Similarly, the MCMI-II actuarial assessment showed strong evidence of a personality disorder, with clinically significant BR elevations on the avoidant (BR = 105), narcissistic (BR = 85), antisocial (BR = 110), aggressive (BR = 110), passive–aggressive (BR = 110), self-defeating (BR = 105), schizotypal (BR = 99), borderline (BR = 99), and paranoid (BR = 83) features. The evidence from both the SCID-II structured interview and the actuarial MCMI-II concur that X has a severe mixed personality disorder. On the YSQ, X showed very high elevations on four schema domains (emotional deprivation, abandonment, mistrust-abuse, and social isolation), and high elevation on five schema domains (defectiveness, failure, self-sacrifice, emotional inhibition, and insufficient self-control). This pattern of scores is consistent with a personality disorder diagnosis (six or more very high or high scale scores). Elevated scores on the TSI Tension-Reducing Behavior scale and the YSQ Insufficient Control scale suggests problems with affect dysregulation, consistent with a borderline personality disorder diagnosis.

On the self-report inventories of dissociative symptoms, X scored very low. His score on the DES was 2.5 and on the SDQ, 20. However, on the full SCID-D structured interview, X met the criteria for four of five dissociative disorders, namely, dissociative amnesia, derealization, identity confusion, and identity alteration. With respect to the dissociative amnesia diagnosis, X had no memories for the orphanage abuse for over three decades, until he saw a report about it in the news, in which a man spoke of his physical and sexual abuse at the same orphanage. X immediately remembered the man as another boy he lived with at the orphanage; shortly thereafter, his memories "came back in full force." The SCID-D data show that X meets full criteria for identity confusion, and suggest that he lacks a stable, integrated self-representation. He has a number of self-states or self-described "sides" of himself, including a serious side, a child-like playful side, a sexually domineering side, and an angry side. These self-states involved partial amnesia when state changes occurred, with no resultant loss of executive control (except for the anger). SCID-D findings confirmed that X has a major dissociative disorder, DDNOS.

X showed evidence of alcohol dependency and polysubstance abuse, currently in remission. On the MAST he scored 19, with a cut score of 5 or higher predicting alcoholism risk. Likewise, on the actuarial-based MMPI-2, he showed a significant elevation of the Addiction Admission scale, indicating actual drug involvement. On the SCID-I structured interview, X met the diagnostic criteria for alcohol and polysubstance dependency spanning 12 years before he became sober.

On the SCID-I and self-report inventories, X met the diagnostic criteria for both episodic panic attacks and continuous generalized anxiety. On the SCID-I, he also met the diagnostic criteria for Type I bipolar disorder (manic–depressive illness), characterized by extended periods of intensely irritable states (up to 2 weeks at a time), an inflated sense of self, a decreased need for sleep, pressured speech, flight of ideas, and occasional psychotic signs, such as ideas of reference and auditory, visual, and tactile hallucinations. He had a long history of episodic dyscontrol, characterized by numerous physical fights and verbally abusive behaviors (*Note. T* = 82 on the MMPI-2 Anger Content scale). He also had a long history of dysthymia, starting when he was 5 years old, and several major depressive episodes.

X's responses to three self-report and four actuarial measures of PTSD consistently met criteria for the diagnosis. On the TSI, he showed clinically significant *T*-score elevations on three scales—Depression (T = 78), Anger/Irritability (T = 79), and Tension-Reducing Behavior (T = 65), with subclinical elevations on Intrusive Experiencing (T = 63), Defensive Avoidance (T = 63), and Dissociation (T = 62). On the CAPS, he met diagnostic criteria for past and current PTSD. The content of unwanted memories, dreams, flashbacks, emotional states, and physiological reactions mainly pertained to the orphanage abuse, but also to a serious motor vehicle accident that resulted in death of a family member and physical injury to X. In response to relaxation, neutral, stressful life, and trauma scripts, he showed significant elevation across all three physiological indices (heart rate, frontalis EMG, and skin conductance) on the two orphanage sexual abuse and the orphanage physical abuse scripts, and also on a script about his own heavy drinking and neglect of his child (but not on the motor vehicle accident script, an early neglect script, his father's physical abuse script, or various loss scripts). He did not show a pattern of trauma-related failed habituation to any script. On the self-report inventories of sexuality, X showed consistent evidence of a sexual desire disorder (compulsive type), characterized by fantasy preoccupation with sex, along with themes of control, dominance, and being dominated.

In summary, X showed evidence of multiple comorbid psychiatric conditions: PTSD; borderline personality disorder; dissociative disorders, including dissociative amnesia, derealization, identity confusion, and identity alteration, meeting criteria for DDNOS; a major affective disorder (bipolar Type I, with sustained states of irritability and also of depression); alcohol dependency (in remission); polysubstance dependency (in remission); generalized anxiety disorder; panic attacks; and sexual desire disorder (compulsive type). He showed evidence of developmental deficits along the three lines: relational (disorganized attachment), self (identity confusion); and affective (general affect dysregulation), with episodic dyscontrol, managed in adolescence and early adulthood through the use of alcohol and street drugs.

This complex picture of psychopathology is clearly not related solely to the physical or sexual abuse at the orphanage. Although there is a genetic contribution in his diagnosed bipolar condition, trauma-related intrusive experiences of unwanted memories and nightmares may aggravate a bipolar condition and, in X's case, serve as a potential for aggravating his overall affective condition. Some of his conditions are more clearly linked to the early childhood attachment disruption. Some areas of his overall psychopathology are more clearly related to the orphanage abuse per se, namely, the PTSD (although the motor vehicle accident also contributes to his overall PTSD symptoms) and the sexual desire disorder. His vulnerability to multiple addictions is also related to the early disorganized attachment and its association with general affect dysregulation, subsequently aggravated by the orphanage abuse, in the sense that the intense conflict about the abuse caused X to use alcohol and drugs, along with a dissociative coping style, to block from his awareness the abuse-related memories and feelings during adolescent and early adult years.

CLINICAL IMPLICATIONS

The clinical implications of this case series challenge application of the trauma-processing approach to the treatment of complex traumatic stress impairments. The phase-oriented trauma-processing model has been the dominant treatment model for PTSD since the 1980s (Brown, Scheflin, & Hammond, 1999). However, data from studies on the contribution of attachment disorganization to the development of complex trauma-related conditions suggest that perhaps developmentally informed treatment designed to remap attachment representations (Liotti, 2004), foster self-development (Bateman & Fonagy, 2004; Fonagy, 2007), and facilitate affective development (Ablon, Brown, Khantzian, & Mack, 1993; Follette, Iverson, & Ford, Chapter 13, this volume) plays a more important role in recovery from complex trauma than trauma processing per se. Furthermore, a primary focus on processing *traumatic events per se, with-*

out attention to developmental deficits, may lead to increased disorganization of states of mind (Brown et al., 1999; Chu, 1998; Liotti, 2004), especially in patients with major dissociative disorders and borderline personality disorder. Therefore, currently effective treatment of patients with complex trauma, with personality disorder and dissociative disorders, emphasize interventions that foster the development of stable, positive internal attachment representations (Liotti, 2004); increased organization or coherence of mind, and relatedness and collaboration in therapy (Liotti, 2004); transformation of maladaptive schemas through limited reparenting (Giesen-Bloo et al., 2006); development of a stable, integrated sense of self (Stevenson & Meares, 1992); development of tolerance for and transformation of core affects (Follette et al., Chapter 13, this volume; Schore, 2003); development of a general capacity to mentalize or reflect on mental states (Allen & Fonagy, 2006; Bateman & Fonagy, 1999, 2001) and/or condition-specific metacognitive skills, such as mindfulness of internal states, differentiation of internal states and behaviors, the capacity to assess the relative degree of disorganization of mind at any given moment, and the capacity to reflect in a way that leads to increased control over states of mind (Liotti, 2004; Semerari et al., 2003). For such patients, developmental repair takes priority over trauma processing. Behavioral interventions may reduce therapy-interfering behaviors and self-destructiveness, but there is little evidence that behavioral interventions alone lead to coherence of mind and developmental repair (Linehan et al., 2006).

Patients diagnosed with DID or DDNOS and/or personality disorders may have difficulty tolerating or benefiting from trauma processing or prolonged exposure interventions (van der hart, Nijenhuis, & Steele, 2005). The development of stable internal secure attachment representations, healthy self- and self-esteem structures, affective regulatory structures, and metacognitive abilities are the key ingredients of successful treatment of major dissociative disorders (Steele & van der Hart, Chapter 7, this volume), and the assessment study findings in this chapter suggest that these treatment foci are likely to be important for adults with complex PTSD, whether specific traumatic events are or are not processed in treatment.

Addressing the structural pathology of mind associated with attachment insecurity or disorganization—mental disorganization and lack of metacognition—warrants careful attention in treatment to prepare patients therapeutically to address traumatic memories. Attachment-based treatment leads directly to increased organization of mind, the development of affect regulatory structures, and metacognitive abilities, whereas trauma processing presupposes the presence of an organized mind, a healthy self, and secure attachment representations.

Another implication of developmentally based research is that measuring PTSD alone may be ineffective as an outcome measure in detecting major therapeutic changes when treating complex trauma-related disorders. Measures of treatment outcome with complex PTSD should address (1) the relative degree of organization or disorganization, as illustrated by narrative coherence of personal memories and schemas, and coherence of mind, as measured by the AAI; (2) the degree to which the patient becomes securely attached and collaborative in treatment measured by the AAI; (3) the degree to which the patient manifests core affective states (Follette et al., Chapter 13, this volume); (4) the development of healthy self-representation and healthy esteem (Stevenson & Meares, 1992, this volume); (5) the relative absence of maladaptive schemas (Young & Brown, 2001), as measured by the YSQ; and (6) development of a general capacity to reflect on experience (Fonagy et al., 1998) and/or the development of specific metacognitive abilities (Semerari et al., 2003), as measured by the Reflective Function Scale (Fonagy et al., 1998) and the Metacognitive Assessment Scale (Semerari et al., 2003).

REFERENCES

Ablon, S., Brown, D., Khantzian, E., & Mack, J. (1993). *Human feelings: Explorations in affect development and meaning.* Hillsdale, NJ: Erlbaum.

Ainsworth, M. D. S., Blehar, M., Waters, E., & Wall, S. (1978). *Patterns of attachment: A psychological study of the Strange Situation.* Hillsdale, NJ: Erlbaum.

Alexander, P. C. (1993). The differential effects of abuse characteristics and attachment in the prediction of the long-term effects of sexual abuse. *Journal of Interpersonal Violence, 8,* 346–362.

Allen, J. G. (2001). *Interpersonal trauma and serious mental disorders.* Chichester, UK: Wiley.

Allen, J. G., & Fonagy, P. (Eds.). (2006). *Handbook of mentalizing-based treatment.* New York: Wiley.

American Psychiatric Association. (1994). *Diagnostic and statistical manual of mental disorders* (4th ed.). Washington, DC: Author.

Barone, L. (2003). Developmental protective and risk factors in borderline personality disorder. *Attachment and Human Development, 5,* 64–77.

Bartholomew, K., & Horowitz, L. M. (1991). Attachment styles among young adults: A test of a four-category model. *Journal of Personality and Social Psychology, 61,* 226–244.

Bateman, M. A., & Fonagy, P. (1999). Effectiveness of partial hospitalization in the treatment of borderline personality disorder: A randomized controlled trial. *American Journal of Psychiatry, 156,* 1563–1569.

Bateman, M. A., & Fonagy, P. (2001). Treatment of borderline personality disorder with psychoanalytically oriented partial hospitalization: An 18-month follow-up. *American Journal of Psychiatry, 158,* 36–42.

Bateman, M. A., & Fonagy, P. (2004). *Psychotherapy for borderline personality disorder: Mentalization-based treatment.* New York: Oxford University Press.

Beck, A. T., Steer, R. A., & Garbin, M. G. (1988). Psychometric properties of the Beck Depression Inventory. *Clinical Psychology Review, 8,* 77–100.

Bernstein-Carlson, E. B., & Putnam, F. W. (1986). Development, reliability, and validity of a dissociation scale. *Journal of Nervous and Mental Disease, 174,* 727–735.

Bosquet, M., & Egeland, B. (2006). The development and maintenance of anxiety symptoms from infancy through adolescence in a longitudinal sample. *Development and Psychopathology, 18,* 517–550.

Brennan, K. A., Clark, C. L., & Shaver, P. R. (1998). Self-report measurement of adult attachment: An integrative overview. In J. A. Simpson & W. S. Rholes (Eds.), *Attachment theory and close relationships* (pp. 46–76). New York: Guilford Press.

Briere, J., Elliott, D. M., Harris, K., & Cotman, A. (1995). Trauma Symptom Inventory: Psychometrics and association with childhood and adult victimization in clinical samples. *Journal of Interpersonal Violence, 10,* 387–401.

Brown, D. (2001). (Mis)representations of the long-term effects of childhood sexual abuse in the courts. *Journal of Child Sexual Abuse, 9,* 79–107.

Brown, D. (2004). The evolving standard in forensic psychological testing. In R. I. Simon & L. H. Gold (Eds.), *American Psychiatric Publishing textbook of forensic psychiatry* (pp. 525–555). Washington, DC: American Psychiatric Association.

Brown, D., Scheflin, A. W., & Hammond, D. C. (1999). *Memory, trauma treatment, and the law.* New York: Norton.

Brown, T. A., Antony, A. A., & Barlow, D. H. (1999). Psychometric properties of the Penn State Worry Questionnaire in a clinical anxiety disorders sample. *Behavior Research and Therapy, 30,* 33–37.

Burhmester, D., Furman, W., Wittenberg, M. T., & Reis, H. T. (1988). Five domains of interpersonal competence in peer relationships. *Journal of Personality and Social Psychology, 55,* 995–1008.

Carlson, E. A. (1998). A prospective longitudinal study of disorganized/disoriented attachment. *Child Development, 69,* 1970–1979.

Chambless, D. L., Caputo, G. C., Bright, P., & Gallagher, R. (1984). Assessment of fear in agoraphobics. *Journal of Consulting and Clinical Psychology, 52,* 1090–1097.

Chambless, D. L., & Lifshitz, J. L. (1984). Self-reported sexual anxiety and arousal: The expanded Sexual Arousability Inventory. *Journal of Sex Research, 20,* 241–254.

Chu, J. A. (1998). *Rebuilding shattered lives.* New York: Wiley.

Davidson, J. R. T., Book, S. W., Colket, L. A., Tupler, L. A., Roth, S., Hertzberg, M., et al. (1997). Assessment of a new self-rating scale for post-traumatic stress disorder. *Psychological Medicine, 27,* 153–160.

First, M. B., Gibbon, M., Spitzer, R. L., Williams, J. B. W., & Benjamin, L. S. (1997). *Structured Clinical Interview for DSM-IV Axis II Personality Disorders (SCID-II) Personality Questionnaire: SCID-II scoring booklet.* Washington, DC: American Psychiatric Press.

First, M. B., Spitzer, R. L., Gibbon, M., & Williams, J. B. W. (1997). *User's guide for the Structured Clinical Interview for DSM-IV Axis I Disorders: Clinician Version.* New York: American Psychiatric Press.

Fonagy, P. (2007). Attachment, the development of the self, and its pathology in personality disorders. Available at *www.psychomedia.it.*

Fonagy, P., Gergely, G., Jurist, E. L., & Target, M. (2002). *Affect regulation, mentalization, and the development of the self.* New York: Other Press.

Fonagy, P., Target, M., Steele, H., & Steele, M. (1998). *Reflective function manual—version 5.* Unpublished manuscript, University College, London.

Ford, J. D. (1999). PTSD and disorders of extreme stress following warzone military trauma. *Journal of Consulting and Clinical Psychology, 67,* 3–12.

Ford, J. D. (2005). Treatment implications of altered neurobiology, affect regulation and information processing following child maltreatment. *Psychiatric Annals, 35,* 410–419.

Ford, J. D., Stockton, P., Kaltman, S., & Green, B. L. (2006). Disorders of extreme stress (DESNOS) symptoms are associated with interpersonal trauma exposure in a sample of healthy young women. *Journal of Interpersonal Violence, 21,* 1399–1416.

Garb, H. N. (1984). The incremental validity of information used in personality assessment. *Clinical Psychology Review, 4,* 641–655.

Gardner, D., & Garfinkel, P. (1979). The Eating Attitudes Test. *Psychological Medicine, 9,* 273–279.

Giesen-Bloo, J., van Dyck, R., Spinhoven, P., van Tilburg, W., Dirksen, C., van Asselt, T., et al. (2006). Outpatient psychotherapy for borderline personality disorder. *Archives of General Psychiatry, 63,* 649–658.

Gudjonsson, G. (1984). A new scale of interrogative suggestibility. *Personality and Individual Differences, 5,* 303–314.

Hathaway, S. R., & McKinley, J. C. (1989). *MMPI-2: Minnesota Multiphasic Personality Inventory–2.* Minneapolis: University of Minnesota Press.

Herman, J. L. (1992). *Trauma and recovery.* New York: Basic Books.

Hirschfield, R., Klerman, G. L., Gough, H. G., Barrett, J., Korchin, S. J., & Chodoff, P. (1977). A measure of interpersonal dependency. *Journal of Personality Assessment, 41,* 610–618.

Hollon, S. D., & Kendall, P. K. (1980). Cognitive self-statements in depression: Development of an automatic thoughts questionnaire. *Cognitive Therapy and Research, 4,* 383–395.

Hudson, W. W. (1997). *The WALMYR Assessment Scales scoring manual.* Tallahassee, FL: WALMYR.

Janda, L. H. (1980). Development of a sex anxiety inventory. *Journal of Consulting and Clinical Psychology, 48,* 169–175.

Lazarus, R. S. (1966). *Psychological stress and the coping process.* New York: McGraw-Hill.

Linehan, M. M., Comtois, K. A., Murray, A. M., Brown, M. Z., Gallop, H. L., Korslund, K. E., et al. (2006). Two-year randomized controlled trial and follow-up of dialectical behavior therapy vs. therapy by experts for suicidal behaviors and borderline personality disorder. *Archives of General Psychiatry, 63,* 757–766.

Liotti, G. (2004). The inner schema of borderline states and its correction during psychotherapy: A cognitive–evolutionary approach. In P. Gilbert (Ed.), *Evolutionary theory and cognitive psychotherapy* (pp. 137–160). New York: Springer.

Lyons-Ruth, K., Dutra, L., Schuder, M. R., & Bianci, I. (2006). From infant attachment disorganization to adult dissociation. *Psychiatric Clinics of North America, 29,* 63–86.

Main, M., Goldwyn, R., & Hesse, E. (2002). *Adult attachment scoring and classification systems.* Unpublished manuscript, University of California, Berkeley.

Main, M., & Hesse, E. (1990). Parents' unresolved traumatic experiences are related to infant disorganized attachment status: Is frightened and/or frightening parental behavior the linking mechanism? In M. Greenberg, D. Cicchetti, & E. Cummings (Eds.), *Attachment in the preschool years* (pp. 161–180). Chicago: University of Chicago Press.

Main, M., Kaplan, N., & Cassidy, J. (1985). Security in infancy, childhood, and adulthood: A move to the level of representations. In I. Bretherton & E. Waters (Eds.), Growing points in attachment theory and research. *Monographs of the Society of Research in Child Development, 50*(1–2, Serial No. 209), 66–106.

Main, M., & Morgan, H. (1996). Disorganization and disorientation in infant Strange Situation behavior: Phenotypic resemblance to dissociative states. In L. K. Michelson & W. J. Ray (Eds.), *Handbook of dissociation: Theoretical, empirical, and clinical perspectives* (pp. 107–138). New York: Plenum Press.

Marmar, C. R., Weiss, D. S., & Metzler, T. J. (1998). Peritraumatic dissociation and posttraumatic stress disorder. In J. D. Bremner & C. R. Marmar (Eds.), *Trauma, memory, and dissociation* (pp. 229–252). Washington, DC: American Psychiatric Press.

Meyer, G. J., Finn, S. E., Eyde, L. D., Kay, G. G., Moreland, K. L., Dies, R. R., et al. (2001). Psychological testing and psychological assessment: A review of evidence and issues. *American Psychologist, 56*, 128–165.

Meyer, T. J., Miller, M. L., Metzger, R. L., & Borkovec, T. (1990). Development and validation of the Penn State Worry Questionnaire. *Behaviour Research and Therapy, 28*, 487–495.

Millon, T. (1987). *Millon Clinical Multiaxial Inventory–2*. Minneapolis: National Computer Systems.

Nijenhuis, E. R. S., Spinhoven, P., van Dyck, R., van der Hart, O., & Vanderlinden, J. (1996). The development and psychometric characteristics of the Somatoform Dissociation Questionnaire (SDQ-20). *Journal of Nervous and Mental Disease, 184*, 688–694.

Ogawa, J. R., Sroufe, L. A., Weinfeld, N. S., Carlson, E. A., & Egeland, B. (1997). Development and the fragmented self: Longitudinal study of dissociative symptomatology in a nonclinical sample. *Development and Psychopathology, 9*, 855–880.

Orr, S. P., & Kaloupek, D. G. (1997). Psychophysiological assessment of posttraumatic stress disorder. In J. P. Wilson & T. M. Keane (Eds.), *Assessing psychological trauma and PTSD* (pp. 69–97). New York: Guilford Press.

Pearlman, L. A. (2003). *Trauma and Attachment Belief Scale: Manual*. Los Angeles: Western Psychological Services.

Pelcovitz, D., van der Kolk, B. A., Roth, S., Mandel, F., Kaplan, S., & Resick, P. (1997). Development of a criteria set and a structured interview for disorders of extreme stress (SIDES). *Journal of Traumatic Stress, 10*(1), 3–16.

Putnam, F. W. (2003). Ten-year research update review: Child sexual abuse. *Journal of the American Academy of Child and Adolescent Psychiatry, 42*, 269–278.

Rogers, R. (1995). *Diagnostic and structured interviewing: A handbook for psychologists*. Odessa, FL: Psychological Assessment Resources.

Rogers, R., Bagby, R. M., & Dickens, S. E. (1992). *Structured Interview of Reported Symptoms: Professional manual*. Lutz, FL: Psychological Assessment Resources.

Roth, S., Newman, E., Pelcovitz, D., van der Kolk, B. A., & Mandel, F. S. (1997). Complex PTSD in victims exposed to sexual and physical abuse: Results from the DSM-IV Field Trial for Posttraumatic Stress Disorder. *Journal of Traumatic Stress, 10*(4), 539–555.

Schore, A. N. (2003). *Affect-regulation and the repair of the self*. New York: Norton.

Selzer, M. L. (1971). The Michigan Alcoholism Screening Test: The quest for a new diagnostic instrument. *American Journal of Psychiatry, 127*, 89–94.

Semerari, A., Carcione, A., Dimaggio, G., Falcone, M., Nicolo, G., Procacci, M., et al. (2003). How to evaluate metacognitive functioning in psychotherapy? *Clinical Psychology and Psychotherapy, 10*, 238–261.

Silverton, L., & Gruber, C. (1998). *Malingering Probability Scale (MPS) manual*. Los Angeles: Western Psychological Services.

Snell, W. E., Fisher, T. D., & Walters, A. S. (1993). The Multidimensional Sexuality Questionnaire. *Annals of Sexual Research, 6,* 27–55.

Sroufe, L. A., Egeland, B., Carlson, E. A., & Collins, W. A. (2005). *The development of the person: The Minnesota Study of Risk and Adaptation from Birth to Adulthood.* New York: Guilford Press.

Stalker, C. A., & Davies, F. (1995). Attachment organization and adaptation in sexually abused women. *Canadian Journal of Psychiatry, 40,* 234–240.

Steinberg, M. (1993). *Structured Clinical Interview for DSM-IV Dissociative Disorders—Revised (SCID-D).* Washington, DC: American Psychiatric Press.

Stevenson, J., & Meares, R. (1992). An outcome study of psychotherapy for patients with borderline personality disorder. *American Journal of Psychiatry, 149,* 358–362.

Sundin, E. C., & Horowitz, M. J. (2002). Impact of Event Scale. *Journal of Consulting and Clinical Psychology, 50,* 407–414.

Thelen, M. M., Farmer, J., Wonderlich, S., & Smith, M. (1991). A revision of the bulimia test: The BULIT-R. *Psychological Assessment, 3,* 119–124.

van der Hart, O., Nijenhuis, E. R. S., & Steele, K. (2005). Dissociation: Recognized major feature of complex posttraumatic stress disorder. *Journal of Traumatic Stress, 18*(5), 413–423.

van der Kolk, B. A., & Courtois, C. A. (2005). Editorial comments: Complex developmental trauma. *Journal of Traumatic Stress, 18,* 385–388.

van der Kolk, B. A., Roth, S., Pelcovitz, D., Sunday, S., & Spinazzola, J. (2005). Disorders of extreme stress. *Journal of Traumatic Stress, 18,* 389–399.

Watson, D., & Friend, R. (1969). Measurement of social-evaluative anxiety. *Journal of Consulting and Clinical Psychology, 33,* 448–457.

Weathers, F. W., Newman, E., Blake, D. D., Nagy, L. M., Schnutt, P., Kaloupek, D., et al. (2004). *Clinician-Administered PTSD Scale (CAPS).* Los Angeles: Western Psychological Services.

Weissman, A. N. (1979). *The Dysfunctional Attitude Scale: A validation study.* Unpublished doctoral dissertation, University of Pennsylvania, Philadelphia.

Widom, C. S., Ireland, T. O., & Glynn, P. G. (1995). Alcohol abuse and neglected children followed-up: Are they at increased risk? *Journal of the Study of Alcohol, 56,* 207–217.

Widows, M. R., & Smith, G. P. (2005). *Structured Inventory of Malingered Symptomatology.* Lutz, FL: Psychological Assessment Resources.

Wilson, G. D. (1978). *The secrets of sexual fantasy.* London: Dent & Sons.

Wilson, S. C., & Barber, T. X. (1983). The fantasy-prone personality. In A. A. Sheikh (Ed.), *Imagery: Current theory, research, and application* (pp. 340–387). New York: Wiley.

Young, J. E., & Brown, G. (2001). *Young Schema Questionnaire.* New York: Schema Therapy Institute.

Zlotnick, C., Zakriski, A. L., Shea, M. T., Costello, E., Begin, A., Pearlstein, T., et al. (1996). The long-term sequelae of sexual abuse. *Journal of Traumatic Stress, 9,* 195–205.

CHAPTER 7

Treating Dissociation

Kathy Steele
Onno van der Hart

Individuals with dissociative identity disorder (DID) and dissociative disorder not otherwise specified, subtype 1 (DDNOS), have multiple symptoms and comorbid diagnoses that typically exclude them from treatment efficacy studies (Spinazzola, Blaustein, & van der Kolk, 2005) and give them a reputation of being difficult to treat. Yet experienced clinicians find that a consistent and predictable phase-oriented approach can be successful with many such patients, a claim supported by several outcome studies (e.g., Coons & Bowman, 2001; Ellason & Ross, 1997). Phase-oriented treatment of trauma-related disorders, first proposed by Pierre Janet (cf. van der Hart, Brown, & van der Kolk, 1989), has been incorporated in major contemporary approaches and is considered the current standard of treatment for these disorders (e.g., Brown, Scheflin, & Hammond, 1998; Courtois, 2004; Herman, 1992; International Society for the Study of Dissociation [ISSD], 2005; Kluft & Fine, 1993; Steele, van der Hart, & Nijenhuis, 2005; van der Hart, Nijenhuis, & Steele, 2006).

Evidence-based treatments, such as those comprising cognitive-behavioral therapy (CBT), especially prolonged exposure (PE) and eye movement desensitization and reprocessing (EMDR), have been utilized in the successful treatment of posttraumatic stress disorder (PTSD; e.g., Foa, Keane, & Friedman, 2000; Follette & Ruzek, 2007), and in the alleviation of specific PTSD symptoms and psychosocial skills deficits in some patients with a more complicated course (e.g., Cloitre, Cohen, & Koenen, 2006; Kimble, Riggs, & Keane, 1998). Although these treatments have been helpful to some chronically traumatized individuals, their efficacy in addressing the major and enduring difficulties that result from complex structural dissociation has not been tested. We define *structural dissociation* as a division of the personality as a biopsychosocial system into two or more subsystems of personality that should normally be integrated (which we call *dissociative parts of the personality*). These subsystems involve at least a rudimentary self-awareness, and related mental and behavioral actions.

Complex structural dissociation involves an extensive range of phobias that exacerbate and maintain dissociation and impede functional adaptation. They include the phobia of (1) mental actions (i.e., an individual's inner experience of emotions, thoughts body sensations, needs, wishes); (2) dissociative parts of the personality; (3) attachment and attachment loss; (4) traumatic memory; and (5) change and healthy risk taking (van der Hart et al., 2006). These trauma-related phobias are major manifestations of underlying integrative, regulatory, and skills deficits; thus, they are the central focus of treatment in this chapter.

THEORETICAL MODELS USED IN THE TREATMENT OF DISSOCIATIVE DISORDERS

Numerous theories have been utilized to understand dissociation in clinical populations. These include affective neuroscience, affect, attachment, cognitive, ego state, evolutionary psychology, Janetian, learning, neurodevelopmental, psychoanalytic, psychodynamic and self psychology, and systems theories (cf. ISSD, 2005; van der Hart et al., 2006). The mainstream treatment of complex dissociative disorders has long relied on an eclectic mix of interventions that draws from most, if not all, of these theories (ISSD, 2005), and from other approaches, such as hypnosis (e.g., Kluft, 1992; Phillips & Frederick, 1995), and most recently, from skills training (e.g., Gold, 2000) and EMDR (e.g., Gelinas, 2003; Twombly, 2005).

ESSENTIAL CONCEPTS IN THE TREATMENT OF DISSOCIATION

Several concepts are essential to understanding treatment of dissociative disorders: *integration, mental level, dissociation,* and *dissociative parts of the personality.* We take our definitions of these concepts from the theory of structural dissociation, a theory that has integrated Janetian, affective neuroscience, evolutionary psychology, learning, and attachment theories (van der Hart et al., 2006). This model provides a conceptual umbrella that embraces and transcends specific theoretical orientations, and under which guiding principles and goals are formulated.

Integration: Synthesis and Realization

Complex dissociation involves a fragmentation or "disintegration" of the person's sensory–perceptual awareness, thoughts, feelings, memories, and sense of self such that these are no longer adequately cohesive and coordinated. There-fore, *integration* is a major treatment goal with dissociative patients whenever possible (e.g., Kluft & Fine, 1993; Ross, 2001). Integration is much more than eventual "fusion" of dissociative parts of the individual into a more cohesive and coherent personality. An *integrated personality* includes a unified sense of self (e.g., Kluft & Fine, 1993; Ross, 2001), as well as ongoing integrative actions that support functioning in everyday life, including regulatory and reflective skills. Integration is an adaptive process involving mental and behav-ioral actions that help to assimilate experiences and sense of self over time and contexts. Well-integrated individuals have a consistent sense of who they are, realizing they can grow and change, while remaining the same person. Such a person experiences him- or herself as "me," regardless of what he or she is thinking, feeling, or doing, and remains grounded in the present when remem-bering traumatizing events, and experiences the recall as an autobiographical narrative memory rather than a reliving of the past. Moreover, the person typi-cally is able to recognize and accept reality for what it is, including his or her history and present circumstances, acting adaptively based on present circum-stances rather than reacting with habituated dysfunctional patterns.

Basic levels of integration involve *synthesis*, through which experiences, such as sensory perceptions, movements, thoughts, affects, memories, and a sense of self, are bound together (linked) *and* differentiated (distinguished). For example, an integrated experience of reminders of traumatic experiences might be expressed as follows: "That man has a mustache like the man who abused me [binding], but he is not dangerous" [differentiation]; "I am the same person who was abused as a child [binding], but I am also different as an adult, and am not being abused now" [differentiation]. Survivors typically overgeneralize their traumatic experiences and are often unable to differentiate the past and present.

At higher levels, integration involves *realization*, which is defined as devel-oping personal awareness of reality as it is, accepting it, then reflectively and creatively adapting to it. The awareness and acceptance of experience as one's own is defined as *personification* (Janet, 1929; van der Hart et al., 2006): "That happened to *me* and I am aware of how it helped shape who I am"; "These are *my* feelings and *my* actions." Individuals who dissociate do not sufficiently own or *personify* their inner and outer experiences. Full realization is achieved not only through personal ownership but also through *presentification* (Janet, 1928; van der Hart et al., 2006), defined as being in the present with a synthe-sis of all one's experiences—past, present, and anticipated future—at the ready to support reflective decision making and adaptive action.

An individual's capacity for integration and adaptive action has been called the *mental level*. A chronically insufficient mental level results in dysregulation, and maladaptive mental and behavioral actions. Patients who dissociate often have varying mental levels, depending on the extent to which they are experi-encing lower or higher levels of integration.

Dissociation is maintained by a series of trauma-related phobias that are reinforced by strong conditioning effects, inadequate social and emotional support, and lack of regulatory skills and reflective functioning (van der Hart et al., 2006). For example, patients often fear or are ashamed of and unable to understand their own feelings. Thus, their dissociation is maintained by ongoing avoidance of having or expressing particular feelings. Treating these trauma-related phobias in sequence allows patients progressively to reach more adaptive levels of integration, thereby gradually developing a *capacity to engage in adaptive mental and behavioral actions.*

Dissociation and Dissociative Parts of the Personality

From the standpoint of the structural theory, dissociation involves the coexistence and alternation of psychobiological subsystems within an individual's personality that lack adequate cohesions and coherence (*dissociative parts of the personality*; e.g., van der Hart et al., 2006). Many other labels exist for these parts, such as alternate personalities (alters, identities, ego states, dissociative states, disaggregate self-states, dissociative self-states, self-aspects, and part-selves). Regardless of the term and theory used to describe and explain what is dissociated, there is consensus among experts in the dissociative disorders field that these are *not* separate entities or personalities within the same person, nor are they mere role playing; rather, they are *manifestations of significant and chronic breaches in the coherence and cohesiveness of a single personality across time and contexts.* Thus, a systemic approach that considers dissociative parts as interrelated psychobiological subsystems of the individual's larger personality system should be the fundamental foundation for all therapeutic interventions. Pierre Janet originally referred to the concept of dissociation as "the dissociation and emancipation of systems of ideas and functions" (1907, p. 332). In dissociation, these "systems" are disconnected from each other to an extent, are autonomous to varying degrees, are characterized by at least a rudimentary sense of self, and exhibit relatively rigid psychobiological patterns of response (e.g., Nijenhuis & Den Boer, 2007).

Dissociation ranges from the extreme of obviously alternating "identities" in DID that take over the executive functioning of the individual, to much less overt manifestations that appear, for example, as intrusive ego-dystonic feelings or somatic sensations, or persistent patterns of relational conflict. Yet even minor dissociative phenomena experienced by the patient as "not me," such as intrusive affect or sensations, still include at least a rudimentary sense of self (e.g., "*I* feel," "*I* think," "*I* have pain"). In fact, modern neuroscientists have proposed that a single mental action (e.g., an emotion of sadness or a thought or sensation) does not exist in the mind by itself, nor is it dissociated alone; it instead remains synergistically connected within a particular cycle of related attention, perceptions, beliefs, behaviors, physiology, *and* sense of self (van der Hart et al., 2006). For example, although a feeling of sadness may be the most prominent and observable portion of the cycle to the therapist and patient, the feeling still remains associated, at minimum, with certain body movements and sensations, facial expressions, physiological states, cognitions, and the experience of self that accompanies that particular emotion. For this reason, we prefer the term *dissociative parts of the personality* whether dissociative symptoms are major or minor.

Action Systems and Dissociation

Dissociative parts of an individual are likely mediated by innate psychobiological or motivational systems. From the standpoint of evolutionary psychology, these are probably the most basic "fault lines" along which an individual's personality may dissociate and divide, and they are called *action systems* (van der Hart et al., 2006). Action systems involve distinct neural networks that organize and regulate attention, emotion, physiology and, behavior (Panksepp. 1998; van der Hart et al., 2006). At the most basic level of mammalian functioning are two major categories of action systems: those that guide functioning in daily life, and those that guide defense (Panksepp. 1998; Porges, 2003; van der Hart et al., 2006). Daily life action systems include social engagement, attachment, caregiving, exploration, play, sexuality, and energy management (Panksepp. 1998; Porges, 2003; van der Hart et al., 2006). Defense action systems include several subsystems: attachment or separation cry, hypervigilance, flight, fight, tonic immobility (freeze), and flaccid immobility (collapse).

In trauma-related dissociative disorders, at least one dissociative part of the individual becomes fixated in tendencies of defense during traumatic experiences, while another becomes fixated in tendencies mediated by daily life action systems, avoiding traumatic reminders in an effort to go on with normal life. The rigid persistence and inappropriate intrusion of these defenses into daily life has long been recognized in patients with PTSD, and in more complex dissociative disorders (e.g., Foa, Zinbarg, & Rothbaum, 1992; Nijenhuis, Spinhoven, & Vanderlinden, 1998; Rivers, 1920). It is essential for clinicians to understand whether a dissociative part is primarily mediated by daily life action systems or by defense-oriented ones, because treatment interventions differ by type. To distinguish these major prototypes, we adapted the original language of Charles Myers (1940), who observed dissociation in "shell-shocked" World War I combat soldiers. Dissociative parts of the individual that are mediated by daily life action systems, and that thereby need to avoid reminders of the trauma, are called the *Apparently Normal Parts of the Personality* (ANPs). Parts fixated in defensive action tendencies are called the *Emotional Parts of the Personality* (EPs), because survivors typically experience overwhelming and maladaptive or *vehement emotions*, in that psychobiological condition (Janet, 1909; van der Hart et al., 2006). When patients experience *vehement* emotion (as opposed to intense adaptive emotion), they typically lose connection to the present, often engage in impulsive and destructive behaviors to stop the feeling (e.g., self-injury or drinking, aggression toward others, risk taking), and cannot reflect on or learn from what they are experiencing. The expression of vehement emotion rarely leads to adaptive change or integration; thus, the survivor as EP must be supported in learning to regulate and integrate these overwhelming experiences, to relegate them to their proper place in his or her life history (Janet, 1928).

ANPs and EPs exist in various combinations that we believe correspond to current trauma-related diagnoses. *Primary structural dissociation* involves one major part focused on daily life (i.e., the ANP), and the other (i.e., the EP) fixated in defenses and reliving traumatic memories. This type of dissociation is often seen in PTSD and other, more straightforward trauma-related disorders as currently defined by DSM-IV. In primary structural dissociation, the EP is typically less elaborated and autonomous, generally involves only a rudimentary sense of self, and is not in control of the majority of the individual's daily functioning.

Case Vignette

Carol, age 37, was raped once at age 10 by a drunken neighbor, and had a diagnosis of PTSD. She was a highly functional executive who led a relatively normal life but she avoided intimate contact with men and complained of nighttime episodes of choking sensations, vaginal pain, and intense panic and fear. She would awaken screaming and huddled in her closet, making gestures with her hands as though to push someone away. From the ANP perspective, Carol knew she had been raped but felt like it had happened to someone else (lack of personification). From the EP perspective, Carol reexperienced the rape as though it were happening again. Carol did not think of herself as a different person, but she did feel that her nighttime experiences were "not me," and during those times Carol seemed unaware that she was an adult in the present.

Secondary structural dissociation is common when traumatization is more repetitive, severe, and prolonged, especially during childhood. Whereas a single major part of the individual's personality remains focused on daily life (ANP), multiple parts are fixated in defense (EPs), increasing the survivor's risk for being destabilized by EP intrusions that are reactivated by trauma-related triggers. This level of dissociation likely characterizes complex PTSD, DDNOS, and trauma-related borderline personality disorder (BPD).

Case Vignette

Melvin, diagnosed with complex PTSD and BPD, started unprovoked fights with his girlfriend and had amnesia for the mean things he shouted at her. He had frequent intrusions of unexplained back pain, feelings of panic and despair, and memories of physical abuse by his mother's boyfriend. He heard punitive voices, as well as the sounds of a child crying internally. The therapist was able to distinguish three dissociative parts in addition to ANP: an angry adolescent protector-type EP, a child EP that reexperienced beatings, and a persecutor EP that internally reenacted the role of the mother's abusive boyfriend.

The most complex form of dissociation is DID, which we propose involves *tertiary structural dissociation*. In such cases, more than one ANP evolves, in addition to multiple EPs. Thus, more than one dissociative part is functioning routinely in daily life. For example, if Melvin experienced amnesia for daily life activities or insisted "I don't go to work; someone else does," then this division of his personality into several ANPs (in addition to several distinct EPs) might warrant a DID diagnosis.

At secondary and tertiary levels of dissociation, EPs may, but need not be more differentiated and autonomous than those involved in primary structural dissociation. In any given individual, various parts may be more or less elaborated, ranging from parts that, for example, only manifest as intrusive fear and pain related to a traumatic event, to parts that take over executive control of daily life functioning and may have different names, ages, and functions. In many patients, the majority of "self-aspects" do not operate directly in daily life but do influence the patient internally. For example, Martha often heard internal voices commenting or criticizing her actions, which made her change her behavior, and she sometimes felt that she was compelled to say or do things that she did not intend.

PHASE-ORIENTED TREATMENT

Phase-oriented approaches to complex posttraumatic dissociative disorders have been described in various ways but involve the following components:

Phase 1: Safety, stabilization, symptom reduction, skills building, and development of the treatment alliance.
Phase 2: Integration of traumatic memories.
Phase 3: Personality (re)integration and (re)habilitation.

These treatment phases are not linear, but are recursive over time, with the periodic need to return to an earlier phase, or the occasional short excursion into the next phase (Courtois, 2004; Steele et al., 2005).

Phase-oriented treatment stresses the need for careful pacing and regulation of exposure to traumatic memory, including its attendant psychobiological (hyper- or hypo-) arousal, because patients with dissociative disorders are especially prone to regulatory difficulties (e.g., D. Brown, Chapter 6, this volume; Ford, Courtois, Steele, van der Hart, & Nijenhuis, 2005). Due to severe integrative deficits found in these patients, interventions involving early and direct confrontation with traumatic memories can be acutely destabilizing, sometimes leading to decompensation and posttraumatic decline. Treatment for complex dissociative disorders is distinguished from treatment for standard PTSD, in which direct exposure to traumatic memories has been found to be effective (Foa et al., 2000). Patients must first learn skills to identify and to tolerate their mental actions, such as emotions, thoughts, and sensations, rather than to avoid them. This, the sine qua non of trauma therapy, must precede integration of traumatic memories and dissociative parts. As patients gradually increase their mental level with therapeutic support, they learn to confront and to overcome these phobias in small steps. Each small step, in turn, further raises their integrative capacity.

Goals of Treatment

The overarching goal of treatment for all trauma-related disorders is to raise patients' integrative capacity, so they can better manage and integrate inner and outer experiences and function adaptively to the best of their abilities. *Thus, the therapist recognizes the unique issues related to dissociation of the personality (i.e., abrupt shifts and discontinuities in sense of self, experience, consciousness, time, and memory) and works directly and indirectly with dissociative parts of the individual, and with their major and minor manifestations, neither ignoring nor reifying them, using a systemic perspective to foster increasing integration* (e.g., Chu, 1998; ISSD, 2005; Kluft, 2006; Ross, 2001; van der Hart et al., 2006). First and foremost, the therapist should be aware that he or she is dealing with a whole person, and direct interventions to the individual as a whole regardless of the dissociative part(s) that are in executive control or the focus at that point in therapy. Simultaneously, the therapist recognizes the patient's persistent subjective experience of "not me" regarding dissociative parts of his or her personality. When it is not feasible to make a systemic intervention at the level of the whole personality, the therapist intervenes directly with groups of subsystems (i.e., dissociative parts) or with a single part (van der Hart et al., 2006). For example, all parts of the patient can be supported in working together; several parts may be encouraged to cooperate in accomplishing a task in which other parts are not yet able to participate (e.g., soothing other parts, maintaining safety); or the therapist may work with a single part to help orient the patient to the present and to make beginning connections as a whole. Regardless of the level of systemic intervention, the goal is always that of supporting integration of the personality and eliminating the reasons and need for ongoing dissociation. Internal empathy, cooperation, and negotiation among all dissociative parts of the individual are key to successful integration and often must be actively taught and developed (e.g., Fine, 1999; Kluft, 2006; Krakauer, 2001).

Principles of Treatment

In addition, therapy of complex dissociative disorders is guided by principles that apply to the psychotherapy of all trauma-related disorders:

1. *The therapist conducts therapy and manages the therapeutic relationship such that social engagement and secure attachment are maximized, while*

activation of defense in both therapist and patient is minimized. A secure therapy frame and clear but flexible boundaries are essential in maintaining the relational environment necessary for treatment success. The therapist will find it helpful to maintain a high degree of personal reflective functioning and self-regulation in the face of the patient's intense emotions and behaviors. In this way, the therapist provides relational regulation, while modeling the very skills the patient needs to learn (Schore, 2003).

2. *The therapist supports the patient in maintaining psychophysiological arousal within a window of tolerance according to the patient's mental level, both in sessions and in daily life.* A patient must first learn to identify, accept, and tolerate inner and outer experiences within his or her limited window of tolerance, then learn to expand the tolerance level.

3. *The therapist helps the patient develop and maintain external and internal safety.* Therapy cannot progress if the patient is not safe externally (i.e., continues to be victimized or engages in self-harm) or internally (i.e., has critical or punitive dissociative parts of the personality that act to influence his or her beliefs and behaviors "behind the scenes" as an "inner critic," "saboteur" or even an internal "persecutor" that engages in self-harm).

4. *The therapist supports the patient in maintaining and improving functioning in daily life.* Therapy is geared to the maintenance and improvement of functioning, and the reduction of symptoms that interfere with quality of life. Education about trauma, PTSD, dissociation, therapy, and other topics helps the patient to gain an understanding of symptoms and fosters functional improvement and stabilization (e.g., van der Hart et al., 2006), in keeping with current PTSD practice guidelines. Psychotropic medication may also be needed to remediate specific symptoms, as specified in PTSD practice guidelines.

5. *The therapist supports patients in transforming maladaptive behaviors into adaptive ones.* Patients often engage in less than adaptive patterns of thinking, feeling, perceiving, predicting, and behaving. Therapy helps patients to identify and to build adaptive coping capacities and self-regulation skills in a stepwise fashion over the course of treatment (e.g., Chu, 1998; Gold, 2000; Ross, 2001; van der Hart et al., 2006).

6. *The therapist helps the patient reduce and eliminate trauma-related conditioned responses, while preventing further avoidance and dissociation.* Interventions that enable the patient to integrate traumatic memories with relapse prevention (often over extended periods of time) are extremely helpful in overcoming various trauma-related phobias that maintain dissociation (van der Hart et al., 2006). Such "graduated exposure" is not only a conventional behavioral treatment intervention, but it also occurs naturally as a result of repetition, careful pacing, dyadic regulation, and empathic confrontation in the context of most theoretical frameworks. The therapist supports the patient in maintaining modulated arousal, while he or she recalls (in tolerable increments) and works through traumatic memories.

Phase 1: Symptom Reduction, Stabilization, and Skills Building

Phase 1 is oriented toward raising the mental level of dissociative parts that operate in daily life (ANPs) and dominant defensive parts (EPs), thereby allowing for more effective functioning. Strategies involve education on a wide variety of topics, including establishment of safety; management of daily life (e.g., scheduling, working, shopping, cooking, relaxing, paying bills) and self-care (e.g., sobriety, nutrition, exercise, disease prevention, balance of life activities); development of routine patterns of sleep, meals, work, and recreation; improvement of current and development of healthy new relationships; and information about therapy, trauma, and dissociation. Skills building especially for awareness and acceptance of present experience (mindfulness), reflective functioning, and for self- and interactive regulation is essential in the first phase of therapy. Numerous structured skills building approaches are now available (for an overview, see Ford et al., 2005). During sessions, the therapist attends not only to the patient's narrative discourse but also to physical sensations and tendencies, because they are a rich source of information about the patient's dissociative experience that may not be available to conscious awareness or that he or she may not be able to verbalize (Fosha, Paivio, Gleiser, & Ford, Chapter 14, this volume). In this (often) lengthy phase of treatment, the therapist helps the patient begin to address several major phobias: of attachment and attachment loss, of mental actions (i.e., inner experiences), and of dissociative parts.

Treatment of Phobia of Attachment and Attachment Loss

Patients with dissociative disorders exhibit disorganized/disoriented patterns of attachment involving abrupt and confusing alternations between relational approach and avoidance (Liotti, 2006). The phobias of attachment and attachment loss evoke different action systems (e.g., proximity seeking, attachment cry, flight, fight, freeze, submission), thus evoking different dissociative parts of the personality. In fact, dissociative parts with phobias of attachment and attachment loss form the core of multiple and contradictory transference phenomena (e.g., Kluft, 2000; Ross, 2001; van der Hart et al., 2006), manifesting in the "I hate you—don't leave me" conflict so common in individuals traumatized as children.

In the initial phase of treatment, the phobias of attachment and attachment loss are addressed within the therapeutic relationship in the establishment of initial contact with the therapist, then in the development of the relationship and alliance, and later, as a more intense transference (and countertransference) becomes apparent. Relational interventions are first geared towards the ANPs, the parts of survivors that most often interact(s) directly with the therapist, and later toward the various EPs. The therapist provides a "holding environment" for the patient through personal and professional reliability, and by maintaining predictable (although not constant) availability. Patients need to be exposed time and again to "good enough" therapeutic interactions to relinquish long-standing defensive reactions and cognitive distortions, such as overgeneralization.

Treatment of Phobia of Trauma-Related Mental Actions

Some of the most difficult work in therapy is helping patients to recognize, accept, and personify their own mental actions that they have so strenuously avoided (i.e., emotions, thoughts, body sensations, fantasies, needs, and memories). Specific, sustained training and practice in regulatory and relational skills are usually necessary in Phase 1 to overcome the phobia of mental actions. Hypnosis, and/or EMDR for bolstering ego resources, and somatosensory and expressive therapy approaches may be useful in moderating and containing overwhelming affect and sensations (Gelinas, 2003; Kluft, 1992; Phillips & Frederick, 1995; Twombly, 2005; Fosha et al., Chapter 14, this volume).

Survivors need not only to learn that mental actions, such as feelings and thoughts, provide important and helpful information, but also not to make judgments about them. The patient is routinely encouraged to be aware of and to explore his or her *present experience* (i.e., to be mindful, and to act reflectively). Then, cognitive errors that maintain avoidance of mental actions can be challenged and corrected (e.g., "If I am needy, that means I am weak"; "If I am angry, I will be like my abusive father").

Case Vignette

Susan, diagnosed with DDNOS, was extremely panicked whenever she became aware of her feelings or other inner experiences. She attempted to avoid feelings and constantly heard a berating internal voice. Paradoxically, breathing exercises increased her panic, because she became too aware of her body sensations. The therapist began with psychoeducation about the phobia of mental actions, helping Susan understand why she was so avoidant of them, and challenged some of her anxiety- and shame-based beliefs (e.g., "I am crazy"; "Feelings are bad"). Susan and her therapist focused a portion of each session on noticing Susan's reactions to her inner experiences rather than on the experiences themselves. Very gradually she learned to control her freezing and panic reactions, and she was better able to tolerate her emotions and body sensations.

Treatment of Phobias of Dissociative Parts

The therapist begins treatment of phobias of dissociative parts and their many manifestations with the presenting part(s) of the patient, typically the ANP(s). Early psychoeducation about the nature of dissociation and the function of various dissociative parts is helpful to reassure patients they are not "crazy" because they hear voices, lose time, and/or feel influenced by mysterious forces beyond their control.

ANPs are first strengthened through the teaching of grounding, regulation, and reflective functioning skills, with the goal of improvement of daily functioning. When more than one ANP has developed, the therapist supports some positive form of communication and cooperation among these parts that function in daily life, always with the goal of helping the patient function in a more integrated fashion. Such inner communication is one technique that supports the patient as a unitary individual, whose subjective experience is one of internal separation, in gradual acceptance and improved coordination and cohesion of his or her personality as a whole system.

The therapist firmly encourages and insists on the responsible participation of the patient in recognizing and accepting various parts, particularly parts that tend to be most avoided: those that are angry, acting out, terrified, hurt, or otherwise overwhelmed and stuck in past trauma. However, premature attempts to focus on the EPs in therapy, before the patient as ANP is ready to tolerate them, can result in increased dissociation, decompensation, or flight from therapy. When possible, the therapist "talks through" the ANP to various other parts rather than encouraging switching between them, thus working with the personality system as a whole. When this is not feasible, the therapist encourages the patient as ANP to "watch and listen," while other dissociative parts emerge (e.g., Kluft, 2006). In stepwise fashion, the patient as ANP becomes consciously aware of other dissociative parts, first to diminish avoidance reactions, orient to the present, and foster understanding and empathy for their various roles; next to facilitate cooperation in daily life functioning; and only then to share traumatic material (van der Hart et al., 2006).

Protector or persecutor EPs often emerge in situations that are perceived to lead to danger or difficult emotions, such as fear, shame, humiliation, or rejection; their purpose is to protect patients from such experiences, paradoxically, by hurting or berating them.

Case Vignette

Anne had a panic attack as she attempted to register for college, because she heard an inner voice shouting, "You are stupid and incompetent!" This part of Anne tried to prevent her from going back to school, because the part was convinced that Anne would fail and be shamed. Another patient, Rae, heard a screaming voice—"Shut up and put up, slut!"—when she tried to talk to her therapist about being raped as a child. This screaming part was desperate for Rae not to tell the secret, because the perpetrator had threatened to hurt her if she ever told. This underlying protective function is crucial for both therapist and patient to understand (Kluft, 2006; Ross, 2001; van der Hart et al., 2006). As Anne and Rae were able to become aware of and understand these parts of themselves, they were able consciously to experience and manage the intense feelings, without being controlled by the fixed defensive strategies in these EPs. Over time, they stopped experiencing those feelings or defenses as internal threats and instead came to understand them as self-protective mechanisms that were no longer needed.

Survivors can become destabilized if both they and their therapists are not aware of such EPs and how they act internally "behind the scenes." However, if consciously accessed, understood, and engaged in constructive ways by therapist and patient as ANP, even the most primitive EPs eventually can be integrated. The therapist models empathic responses, reframing the actions of these parts' original protective intent, without condoning destructive tendencies. The therapist offers help in enabling these parts to function in constructive and cooperative ways (see Schwartz, Schwartz, & Galperin [Chapter 17, this volume] for a similar approach to working with dissociative parts of the personality).

Case Vignette

A vicious part of Karen would angrily slash her arms and face with a dull knife, repetitively screaming "Shut up! I'm going to kill you!" in response to hearing other child-like parts crying in pain when they internally reexperienced physical abuse. The therapist empathized with how hard it must be to hear that sort of crying without being able to stop it (an indirect empathic statement about the patient's helplessness in the face of the abuse as a child), and suggested that perhaps if they helped those crying parts be more in the present and feel safer, then they would stop crying. The therapist worked directly with Karen's ANP, encouraging her in taking care of the crying EPs lost in their abusive past. They were reassured that the abuse had ended and of their safety in present-day time. Karen used imagery of a cabin by a lake, in which each of these "child" parts had its own safe room, while she watched over them. This considerably reduced her sense of ongoing danger and desperation that had resulted in self-harm, and supported greater trust in the therapist's ability to help. Karen began to understand that the anger of the protector EP was a way to defend against the overwhelming experiences and needs contained in the "child" EPs. She also began to use the lake house as a metaphor: Karen was the house, and she could make room for each of the EPs within herself and keep them safe. As she did this, Karen felt less divided internally and more that her feelings belonged to her and were not alien intruders that she could not tolerate or accept.

As patients resolve phobias of mental actions and dissociative parts, and become more secure in therapy and in other primary relationships, integration among parts may begin to occur rather naturalistically in Phase I, at least in some patients. When the patient's mental level has been raised such that he or she is able to maintain a more stable awareness of ANP(s) and key EPs in the present and in the therapeutic relationship, as well as to tolerate and regulate mental actions, and experience a degree of internal empathy and cooperation, Phase 2 treatment is initiated.

Phase 2: Integrating Traumatic Memories

Exposure to traumatic memories, with simultaneous prevention of maladaptive reactions, is considered a fundamental intervention in trauma-related disorders. Although exposure proponents in the field of PTSD have noted that therapists are often more hesitant than is warranted to employ exposure techniques for fear of overwhelming the patient (Cahill, Foa, Hembree, Marshall, & Nacash, 2006), therapists in the dissociative disorders field have painfully learned that premature and prolonged exposure without the capacity to modulate arousal can be disastrous in patients with dissociation. They have genuine integrative deficits underlying their vigorous avoidance of realizing painful memories. Intense exposure, without the capacity to manage arousal, is usually destabilizing.

Phase 1 is designed to address many trauma-related issues and self-management deficits prior to focus on specific traumatic memories. Initiation of Phase 2 interventions directed toward exposure to and processing of traumatic memories comes with several caveats. First, the therapist needs to understand that not all dissociative parts have access to a given traumatic memory. Second, exposure does not automatically occur across all dissociative parts without additional specialized interventions. Third, the patient's mental level typically varies among dissociative parts, so exposure that seems tolerable to one dissociative part may not be to another. Fourth, when arousal is too high, as in standard exposure techniques, an individual with dissociative disorder may respond with further dissociation in an effort to self-regulate, and become either excessively hypo- or hyperaroused.

Major contraindications to Phase 2 work include lack of adequate motivation or resources, especially an insufficient mental level achieved by the patient. These issues may be enduring and related to poor prognosis (e.g., Boon, 1997), or temporary, due to transient crises or the need to give full attention to other issues. The major phobia addressed in Phase 2 is that of traumatic memories. However, disorganized attachment to abusive and neglectful family members must also be addressed, because these unresolved relational experiences, often sequestered in various EPs outside conscious awareness of the patient, may interfere with the integration of traumatic memories by promoting ongoing avoidance and dissociation.

Treatment of Insecure Attachment to the Perpetrator

The inner conflict between attachment to and defense against perpetrators becomes heightened when traumatic memories are reactivated, hindering integration. Some patients may be enmeshed with their families in the present, unable to set healthy boundaries and limits. Simultaneously, other dissociative parts of individuals may hold strong feelings of hatred, anger, shame, neediness, or terror toward family perpetrators and others (Steele, van der Hart,

& Nijenhuis, 2001). The therapist must empathically explore *all* the patient's conflicted feelings and beliefs related to perpetrators and not scapegoat them, remembering that one part of the patient may hold one view of the perpetrator (e.g., "I hate my mother! Every time I'm around her I want to kill myself!"), while another espouses a completely different view ("I love my mom! She always bakes my favorite cookies when I visit!"). The patient must be strongly encouraged to set appropriate boundaries that ensure both emotional and physical safety despite these contradictory feelings.

Treatment of the Phobia of Traumatic Memory

The phobia of traumatic memory is one of the most difficult to overcome, requiring high and sustained integrative capacity. The intensity and duration of exposure must be matched to the patient's overall mental level. Particular dissociative parts may be especially reluctant to realize these memories, in spite of growing recognition and awareness among other parts of the personality. For example, one part may continue to have a "golden fantasy" of having perfectly loving parents, even as other parts become more aware of and accepting of past abuse. Thus, the individual, as a whole, continues to lack sufficient personification and presentification. Sadness and grief over past and current losses must be supported to encourage growing realization.

Exposure, or what we have termed *guided synthesis*, requires several steps to ensure full realization of traumatic memories in patients with dissociative disorders (van der Hart, Steele, Boon, & Brown, 1993; van der Hart et al., 2006). First, therapist and patient plan collaboratively, deciding on a specific memory or group of memories to address, and whether all parts or only some will participate. Some patients with dissociative disorder have sufficient integrative capacity to tolerate sharing a traumatic experience throughout the entire personality at once. Other times, it may be necessary to work with smaller groups of parts in a graduated manner (e.g., van der Hart et al., 2006). Containment in the form of an inner safe space can be used temporarily for parts with mental levels too low to be included in a given session.

Guided synthesis involves the sharing of traumatic memories that have been (fully or partially) dissociated up until that time. The dissociative disorder literature includes numerous specialized approaches (e.g., Kluft, 2000; Ross, 2001; Twombly, 2005; van der Hart et al., 1993, 2006). Certainly, not every detail of every memory or every memory of trauma need be processed; rather, it is essential for the patient to realize his or her reactions surrounding the event, the most threatening aspects of the memory, and/or the maladaptive core beliefs and behavior that evolved from the memory. Synthesis is the necessary beginning of a difficult and longer course of realization that involves accepting, owning, and adapting to what was and what is (i.e., personification and presentification). Realization continues throughout Phase 2, and long into Phase 3.

Case Vignette

Eddie, a high-functioning patient with DDNOS, had established excellent cooperation and communication among the majority of his dissociative parts, using his own spiritual concepts of wholeness and unity as a paradigm for empathically restructuring his inner world. After 18 months of stabilization, Eddie felt ready to approach a very painful and shameful memory of sexual abuse by an aunt, during which they were discovered and he was blamed. He imagined all parts of himself sitting in the therapy room. In this image, he gave each part a stone to hold, as a reminder of being in the present, then each part shared its portion of the memory with all the others. A 0- to 10-point Subjective Units of Distress Scale (SUDS) was utilized throughout the session, so that any part of Eddie could rate his level of distress, allowing therapist and patient collaboratively to help maintain his arousal level within an acceptable window of tolerance among all parts. During the synthesis, Eddie had intense feelings and sensations, but not beyond what any part of him could tolerate. At the end of the session all parts had come to recognize, "It happened to me, and it wasn't my fault, despite being blamed!"

Melanie, who has DID, underwent sadistic abuse as a child and had little empathy and cooperation among parts. Phase 1 was prolonged and rocky. For this patient, synthesis took place in much smaller, graded steps than was the case for Eddie. After years of work to build an alliance with a major persecutor EP, which she called "Buddy," Melanie felt ready to deal with a particular traumatic memory associated with Buddy, but she felt it would overwhelm her. The therapist then supported Melanie to touch her right and left index fingers together, a previously used symbol in therapy of connection and caring among parts. This allowed Melanie to view herself as working together with "Buddy" and the therapist. Melanie recalled the traumatic experience from the perspective of "Buddy," which enabled her consciously to make sense of the experience rather than simply to experience diffuse physical pain when reminded of it. She and "Buddy" intensely cried together but remained grounded in the present. Afterward, Melanie said she felt closer than ever to "Buddy" ("He really has been my 'buddy' all along!") and now realized why she had had so much physical pain. She also was aware that, as "Buddy," she felt "lighter" and, in a strange way, more like herself, indicating a gradual integrative process. The therapist supported Melanie in planning how she would share the memory with other parts of herself in due time.

Phase 3: Integration of the Personality and Rehabilitation

Though begun from the start of treatment, ongoing resolution of the phobia of healthy risk taking and change become a more intense focus in Phase 3. As patients make efforts to be more involved in present life over the course of this phase, they increasingly experience the conflict between the desire to change and intense fears of doing so. In fact, adaptive change in this phase of treatment requires some of the most difficult integrative work yet: painful grieving that paves the way for deepening realization; relinquishing habituated maladaptive beliefs and behaviors; learning to live with a (more) unified personality; and ongoing struggles to engage in the world in unfamiliar ways, and with new coping skills that demand a higher mental level. In large part, as in Phase 2, Phase 3 involves grieving as the patient increasingly realizes the cumulative losses suffered as a result of being traumatized and the fact that life at times can continue to be very difficult and painful (van der Hart et al., 1993, 2006). Yet this integrative grief work can eventually support the patient in making adaptive changes that bring greater meaning, pleasure, and balance to current life. Patients often have the fantasy that all will be well when they have reconciled with their histories. In fact, although Phase 3 may indeed include pleasure, relief, and newfound enthusiasm for life, it also involves the ongoing need to reconcile with serious losses of the past, present, and future. The therapist has an obligation to educate the patient regarding this painful dichotomy and to support healthy grieving.

Phase 3 also requires a return to the phobias of attachment and attachment loss in the form of developing new and healthy relationships, and risking intimacy. Patients who cannot successfully complete Phase 3 often continue to have difficulty with normal life, despite significant relief from traumatic intrusions. However, it is also common for additional traumatic memories and dissociative parts to emerge in Phase 3, in response to patients' growing capacity to integrate. During such times, Phase 1 and Phase 2 issues need to be revisited.

Essential interventions during this phase include imaginal rehearsal; practice; graduated exercises, such as successive approximation; increased realization through reinforcement of safe and positive changes that have occurred in therapy; and ongoing support to tolerate the ambivalence and uncertainty that are normal companions of change. Over the course of Phase 3, patients experience incremental gains in the ability to experience themselves as whole, unified individuals. As personal ownership broadens, dissociative parts become successively merged or integrated into a more coherent and cohesive personality. This process mostly occurs in a gradual fashion as the reasons for ongoing dissociation are eliminated, although some integration of parts occurs quite spontaneously. Through this integrative process, patients are increasingly able to experience more *presentification* (Janet, 1928; van der Hart et al., 2006); that is, they are able to be present and to act adaptively as a whole person, no longer doomed to react in fixed ways to internal and external triggers, no longer suffering from lack of awareness and voluntary control over mental and behavioral actions, and no longer phobic or avoidant of their experiences.

The process of termination should be carefully planned, because it often needs to be undertaken gradually over time and includes an invitation to return to therapy, if needed. Termination can be very emotional, because it involves change and loss due to separation from the therapist, who has become a central attachment figure for the patient. Follow-up is considered essential to monitor full integration (i.e., fusion) of the patient's personality.

DISCUSSION

Complex dissociative disorders can now be diagnosed with increasing accuracy and be distinguished from other disorders (Dell, 2006). Yet many myths, misconceptions, and prejudices about them remain. Part of the problem is that clinical training often does not include attention to trauma and especially to dissociation; thus, therapists have little or no awareness about these disorders and their presentations. In addition, it is difficult to grasp the idea that, for dissociative patients, a subjective experience of inner separateness is more than mere metaphor: It is their lived experience, which has both psychological and physiological underpinnings; therefore, it should be a central focus of treatment. After all, integration is not a task achieved by the self (or personality); rather, a stable yet dynamic self (or personality) is the result of ongoing integration (i.e., integrative actions) (Loevinger, 1976). A proper therapeutic focus on dissociative experiences should no more promote a sense of separateness than an appropriate focus on self-harm or suicidality increases those behaviors. Yet mental health professionals were for decades encouraged to ignore self-harm or suicidal ideations for fear that patients would increase these behaviors out of suggestibility and secondary gain, rather than to help them overcome the reasons for the behaviors.

Clinicians and researchers need to be more open and communicate with each other regarding dissociative disorders and their treatment, and become familiar with the large body of clinical literature now available (see ISSD, 2005, for a brief overview). Those who specialize in the treatment of classic PTSD have a responsibility to become familiar with assessment and treatment of cases involving more attachment and developmental complexity. The parameters and symptoms of dissociation need further clarification, along with consensus building among researchers and clinicians regarding a standardized definition. We propose that the definition of dissociation presented in this chapter is taken as a point of departure.

Clearly, the traumatic stress field needs more concerted efforts to study systematically the effectiveness of the principles and interventions of phase-oriented treatment of complex posttraumatic dissociative disorders, as exemplified in the treatment guidelines for DID (ISSD, 2005; see Ford & Cloitre, Chapter 3, this volume, for a discussion of best practices). Indeed, major outcome studies are currently in progress. In the meantime, decades of accumulated clinical wisdom and experience among a wide range of clinicians around the world support the effectiveness of phase-oriented treatment in many patients who, at best, are difficult to treat. Regardless of theoretical orientation and specific techniques, it is essential for therapists to be aware of and support resolution of trauma-related phobias that maintain and strengthen dissociation, which is primarily an integrative deficit and only secondarily a defense (cf. Liotti, 2006; van der Hart et al., 2006). Consistent clinical observation suggests that many chronically traumatized patients generally achieve resolution of chronic dissociation through long-term, phasic treatment with specialized interventions.

REFERENCES

Boon, S. (1997). The treatment of traumatic memories in DID. *Dissociation, 10*, 65–79.

Brown, D., Scheflin, A. W., & Hammond, D. C. (1998). *Memory, trauma treatment, and the law.* New York: Norton.

Cahill, S. P., Foa, E. B., Hembree, E. A., Marshall, R. D., & Nacash, N. (2006). Dissemination of exposure therapy in the treatment of posttraumatic stress disorder. *Journal of Traumatic Stress, 19*, 597–610.

Chu, J. A. (1998). *Rebuilding shattered lives.* New York: Wiley.

Cloitre, M., Cohen, L. R., & Koenen, K. C. (2006). *Treating survivors of childhood abuse: Psychotherapy for the interrupted life.* New York: Guilford Press.

Coons, P. M., & Bowman, E. S. (2001). Ten-year follow up study of patients with dissociative identity disorder. *Journal of Trauma and Dissociation, 2*, 73–89.

Courtois, C. A. (2004). Complex trauma, complex reactions: Assessment and treatment. *Psychotherapy: Theory, Research, Practice and Training, 41*, 412–425.

Dell, P. F. (2006). A new model of dissociative identity disorder. *Psychiatric Clinics of North America, 29*(1), 1–26.

Ellason, J., & Ross, C. (1997). Two-year follow-up of inpatients with dissociative identity disorder. *American Journal of Psychiatry, 154*(6), 832–863.

Fine, C. G. (1999). The tactical-integration model for the treatment of dissociative identity disorder and allied dissociative disorders. *American Journal of Psychotherapy, 53*, 361–376.

Foa, E. B., Keane, T. M., & Friedman, M. J. (Eds.). (2000). *Effective treatments for PTSD: Practice guidelines from the International Society for Traumatic Stress Studies.* New York: Guilford Press.

Foa, E. B., Zinbarg, R., & Rothbaum, B. O. (1992). Uncontrollability and unpredictability in post-traumatic stress disorder. *Psychological Bulletin, 112*, 218–238.

Follette, V. M., & Ruzek, J. I. (Eds.). (2007). *Cognitive-behavioral therapies for trauma* (2nd ed.). New York: Guilford Press.

Ford, J. D., Courtois, C. A., Steele, K., van der Hart, O., & Nijenhuis, E. (2005). Treatment of complex posttraumatic self-dysregulation. *Journal of Traumatic Stress, 18*, 437–448.

Gelinas, D. J. (2003). Integrating EMDR into phase-oriented treatment for trauma. *Journal of Trauma and Dissociation, 4*(3), 91–135.

Gold, S. N. (2000). *Not trauma alone.* Philadelphia: Brunner/Routledge.

Herman, J. L. (1992). *Trauma and recovery.* New York: Basic Books.

International Society for the Study of Dissociation (ISSD). (2005). Guidelines for treating dissociative identity disorder in adults. *Journal of Trauma and Dissociation, 6*(4), 69–149.

Janet, P. (1907). *Major symptoms of hysteria.* New York: Macmillan.

Janet, P. (1909). Problèmes psychologiques de l'émotion [Psychological problems and emotion]. *Revue Neurologique, 17,* 1551–1687.

Janet, P. (1928). *L'évolution de la mémoire et de la notion du temps* [The evolution of memory and the notion of time]. Paris: Chahine.

Janet, P. (1929). *L'évolution psychologique de personnalité* [The psychological evolution of the personality]. Paris: Chahine.

Kimble, M. O., Riggs, D. S., & Keane, T. M. (1998). Cognitive behavioural treatment for complicated cases of post-traumatic stress disorder. In N. Tarrier, A. Wells, & G. Haddock (Eds.), *Treating complex cases* (pp. 105–130). Chichester, UK: Wiley.

Kluft, R. P. (1992). Hypnosis with multiple personality disorder. *American Journal of Preventive Psychiatry and Neurology, 3,* 19–27.

Kluft, R. P. (2000). The psychoanalytic psychotherapy of dissociative identity disorder in the context of trauma therapy. *Psychoanalytic Inquiry, 20,* 259–286.

Kluft, R. P. (2006). Dealing with alters: A pragmatic clinical perspective. *Psychiatric Clinics of North America, 29,* 281–304.

Kluft, R. P., & Fine, C. G. (Eds.). (1993). *Clinical perspectives on multiple personality disorder.* Washington, DC: American Psychiatric Press.

Krakauer, S. Y. (2001). *Treating dissociative identity disorder.* Philadelphia: Brunner/Routledge.

Liotti, G. (2006). A model of dissociation based on attachment theory and research. *Journal of Trauma and Dissociation, 7*(4), 55–74.

Loevinger, J. (1976). *Ego development.* San Francisco: Jossey-Bass.

Myers, C. S. (1940). *Shell shock in France, 1914–1918.* Cambridge, UK: Cambridge University Press.

Nijenhuis, E. R. S., & Den Boer, H. (2007). Psychobiology of traumatization and trauma-related structural dissociation of the personality. In E. Vermetten, M. Dorahy, & D. Spiegel (Eds.), *Traumatic dissociation* (pp. 219–236). Washington, DC: American Psychiatric Press.

Nijenhuis, E. R. S., Spinhoven, P., & Vanderlinden, J. (1998). Animal defensive reactions as a model for dissociative reactions. *Journal of Traumatic Stress, 11,* 243–260.

Panksepp, J. (1998). *Affective neuroscience.* New York: Oxford University Press.

Phillips, M., & Frederick, C. (1995). *Healing the divided self.* New York: Norton.

Porges, S. W. (2003). The polyvagal theory: Phylogenetic contributions to social behavior. *Physiology and Behavior, 79,* 503–513.

Rivers, W. H. R. (1920). *Instinct and the unconscious.* Cambridge, UK: Cambridge University Press.

Ross, C. A. (2001). *Dissociative identity disorder* (2nd ed.). New York: Wiley.

Schore, A. N. (2003). *Affect regulation and the repair of the self.* New York: Norton.

Spinazzola, J., Blaustein, M., & van der Kolk, B. A. (2005). Posttraumatic stress disorder treatment outcome research. *Journal of Traumatic Stress, 18,* 425–436.

Steele, K., van der Hart, O., & Nijenhuis, E. R. S. (2001). Dependency in the treatment of complex posttraumatic stress disorder and dissociative disorders. *Journal of Trauma and Dissociation, 2*(4), 79–116.

Steele, K., van der Hart, O., & Nijenhuis, E. R. S. (2005). Phase-oriented treatment of structural dissociation in complex traumatization. *Journal of Trauma and Dissociation, 6*(3), 11–53.

Twombly, J. H. (2005). EMDR for clients with dissociative identity disorder, DDNOS, and ego states. In R. Shapiro (Ed.), *EMDR solutions: Pathways to healing* (pp. 86–120). New York: Norton.

van der Hart, O., Brown, P., & van der Kolk, B. A. (1989). Pierre Janet's treatment of post-traumatic stress. *Journal of Traumatic Stress, 2,* 379–396.

van der Hart, O., Nijenhuis, E. R. S., & Steele, K. (2006). *The haunted self: Structural dissociation and the treatment of chronic traumatization.* New York: Norton.

van der Hart, O., Steele, K., Boon, S., & Brown, P. (1993). The treatment of traumatic memories: Synthesis, realization and integration. *Dissociation, 6,* 162–180.

CHAPTER 8

Cultural Competence

Laura S. Brown

Complex trauma occurs within the psychosocial framework of external cultural realities, and the internal, intrapsychic representations of those realities. A child who is being repeatedly abused and neglected, an adult trapped in painful and apparently inescapable intimate violence or held captive and tortured, is not a generic human being experiencing these traumata. He or she is always a person who is unique, and perhaps uniquely targeted for traumatic experiences, because of the various and multiple strands of her or his identity. He or she then experiences the distress of the trauma, and attempts to cope with that distress, in the psychosocial realities of a particular time, place, and location in the social and political world. Finally, the psychotherapist working with the complex trauma survivor is also the product of this process of identity development in the context of cultural and social realities, and represents meanings to trauma survivors that may assist, or undermine, the development of a therapeutic alliance and the conduct of psychotherapy itself.

Responding effectively to these realities in clinical work requires the development of cultural competence by all psychotherapists working with complex trauma survivors. This goal has often seemed daunting, largely because of how cultural competence has most commonly been defined, and has led many therapists to distance themselves from work with individuals whom they perceive as different in some way that might preclude competent practice. This stance is not unique to those working with complex trauma; such distancing, often accompanied by feelings of guilt, shame, and inadequacy, is as normative among many clinicians when issues of difference become foreground as distancing from trauma survivors has been for those psychotherapists to whom posttrauma presentations seemed alien or overpowering. *A goal of this chapter is both to disrupt the common narrative of how a therapist develops cultural competence, and to engage those working with survivors of complex trauma in the project of becoming culturally competent in their work.*

In contrast to the rest of this volume, this chapter focuses on an overarching stance about cultural competence that can, and should, be woven into the fabric of specific treatment models for working with complex trauma. The theoretical frameworks presented here focus on creating heightened awareness of personal, inevitable biases and distortions, and on developing overarching epistemologies of difference rather than algorithms for working with so-called "special populations" and models of multiple identities as they affect both the experience of complex trauma and the later development of both distress and dysfunction, and resilience, hopefulness, and posttraumatic growth.

Why should a clinician working with complex trauma survivors be centrally concerned with becoming culturally competent? Why not simply take the stance of referring the survivor who is a member of group *X* to the specialist in that group, and maintain competence and ethical practice by means of limiting the populations with whom one works? Or see all clients as simply human and take a stance of "color-blindness"? The first reason is that, more than any other form of psychic distress, the very nature of complex trauma is inherently concerned with culture, context, politics, and identity. All complex trauma is interpersonal in nature, and each person comes to the experience of trauma, whether as perpetrator or target, as a human with identities and social realities that, if denied, can silence the survivor just as surely as denying the trauma itself. Complex trauma is a trauma of intimacy, of shared physical and social realities, and frequently of shared or overlapping cultures and meanings. In consequence, the violations of body, mind, and spirit at the core of complex traumatic stress disorders are each flavored and shaped by those psychosocial, contextual, political, and cultural milieus in which that trauma occurs. Herman (1992) directly recognized and addressed these social and political realities when she first proposed this construct, but others have not always followed her lead, because the bulk of subsequent clinical and research discussions of complex trauma has shifted to the specifics of symptom pictures and treatment strategies. Ironically, within a subject matter that itself voices previously silenced realities, culture, identity, and social context have largely been the invisible components of conceptualizations of working with complex trauma survivors. "If you pretend not to see my color, then you do not see me, and for sure you do not see how I see you," says my Native American client to me, her European American therapist.

The second reason is that, for readers who do not live in large metropolitan areas, replete with specialists in working with every possible population, the option of making a referral to such as specialist is not an option. Furthermore, as I explore later in this chapter, this strategy is itself a means of emotional distancing from difference, disguised as maintaining the boundaries of competence, a methodology that is likely to have continuing problematic results for the psyche of the clinician. Finally, this strategy reflects an epistemology of difference that, although revolutionary and highly valuable in its day, is no longer a tenable stance for understanding human difference, nor a foundation for culturally competent practice. It ghettoizes the experiences of those who differ from the dominant cultural norm. Ultimately, developing cultural competence is but one brick in the foundation of general competencies that clinicians working with survivors of complex trauma should bring to their work. As I discuss later in this chapter, all of us have every single marker of identity present in ourselves, and to routinely decline to work with people who do not appear to share our identity markers reduces our capacities to examine those markers thoughtfully and critically in ourselves, and in clients who appear to resemble us.

A FEW WORDS ABOUT LANGUAGE

Mental health course work and textbooks on working with difference have commonly used the term *minority group* to refer to those populations defined as "other" than that of the author. This terminology is not used in this contribution, because it is both numerically inaccurate in many instances and it carries a metamessage experienced by many "minorities" as pejorative. Instead, the terms *target* and *dominant* groups are used. *Target groups* are defined as those groups in a given cultural and political setting that have been historically, and/or currently are the targets of systemic discrimination, violence, and/or prejudice. *Dominant groups* are defined as those groups in a particular cultural and political setting that represent the norm and possess power within that setting's hierarchy and institutions. Most individuals' identities contain some mixture of dominant and target experiences. These group memberships, although they may be founded on biological variables such as sex or phenotype, are socially constructed and differ from context to context. They are then given meaning and value by the specific cultural, social, political, and existential realities in which a person exists; as such, these meanings and values may change as the narrative themes of those settings transform. Trauma survivors comprise one large, diverse target group, marginalized by a dominant culture that wishes to obscure the realities of human capacities for cruelty.

DEFINING CULTURAL COMPETENCE:
ETIC VERSUS EMIC EPISTEMOLOGIES

Beginning in the 1960s, emergent literatures in the various mental health disciplines noted that the science and scholarship of those fields were distorted through the lenses of dominant cultures, with almost everything written about human beings reflecting, in reality, only the experience of human who were male, European American, and middle class—members of the cultural dominant groups of the United States, in other words. The decades of the 1970s and 1980s were marked by an explosion of scholarship on the psychological experiences and needs of target groups, with volumes dedicated to women, African Americans, lesbians and gay men, older adults, people with disabilities, and other, similar specific target groups.

This sort of scholarship that focuses on within-group similarities, as well as differences between target and dominant groups, is referred to as an *etic* epistemology. Etic strategies for knowledge are those emphasizing allegedly objective collections of information about a group based on categories of analysis developed outside of the group. In the instance of this "Handbook of psychotherapy with Bajorans" period of scholarship, the etic knowledge offered about members of target groups referred to how they did or did not fit into the dominant culture's diagnostic categories, and how they did or did not respond to conventional, dominant cultural approaches to psychotherapy. (Bajorans are an ethnic group from the television series *Star Trek: Deep Space Nine*. Like many of Earth's target groups, they have a history of colonization, oppression, and resistance, making them an excellent fictive placeholder for actual target groups. Their colonizers and oppressors, the Cardassians, serve as the fictive placeholder for dominant groups.)

Cultural competence within this etic epistemology of difference required clinicians to acquire large amounts of information about specific groups, developing sets of clinical rules and algorithms for working with clients who were group members. Etic epistemologies, and the scholarship arising from them, tended to downplay within-group differences, emphasize the homogeneity of groups, and highlight the differences between target and dominant groups. Implicit assumptions in this scholarship were that group membership is always a core and foreground component of an individual's identity, and target group memberships are relatively fixed, rather than fluid, categories of experience. Thus, a culturally competent practitioner in this model would have specific limits to his or her competence, for instance, being able to work well with Bajorans but not with Klingons.

Etic models of cultural competence were important and necessary correctives to the state of the mental health disciplines in an era when all behavioral norms were defined unquestioningly through those of the dominant group. They were a valuable and irreplaceable initial step in moving these disciplines and their practitioners toward the capacity to work with people from the full range of human experience, punctuating as they did the varieties of human experience and the diversity of expressions of psychological distress and behavioral dysfunction.

But these etic models were also problematic in some ways. Problems included the tendency to enhance the clinician's sense of self as expert via the acquisition of specific knowledge, and as a credible source of authority about cultural variables present in a client's problems. The clinician, having read "the Handbook," presumed to know something about a Bajoran client, and in fact, perhaps more than would the Bajoran client, him- or herself. Also problematic were unquestioned assumptions about the value of dominant cultural diagnostic categories and practices. Etic models simply demonstrated, for the most part, how they applied poorly to members of some target groups, rather than raising fundamental questions about the inherent value of diagnoses or thera- peutic strategies that might have had implications for work with all clients. A conceptual ghetto was created in which a "diverse populations" literature flourished but had little impact on the dominant culture of the mental health disciplines. One was culturally competent to treat Bajorans only if one were interested in working with Bajorans; *cultural competence* itself became defined as a type of special focus in the work of a clinician.

Etic models also have had another extremely unfortunate set of unintended consequences. By creating a standard for competence based on the acquisition of specific knowledge, many clinicians defined themselves as not competent to work with members of most target groups and, in an attempt to practice ethically, withdrew from working with such individuals, feeling uncomfortable and in some instances ashamed of not knowing the correct information. As I discuss later in this chapter, actual and emotional withdrawal, and feelings of shame about difference in members of dominant groups, frequently fuel nonconscious biases that themselves render the development of cultural com- petence more daunting.

For these reasons, and because of changes in how the study of difference has been approached since the late 20th century, *emic* epistemologies of differ- ence and human diversity have emerged in the mental health disciplines as a new paradigm for culturally competent practice. Emic models do not assume an invariant human behavioral norm or standardized categories of understanding and analyzing human experiences. Nor do they place authority in the hands of the external expert. Rather, they are more qualitative and phenomenological in nature, assuming the presence of within-group differences that are meaning- ful to people in those groups, even if they are not easily apparent to outside observers. These models invite the development of categories of analysis of experience from within a group, disclaiming the existence of the objective or universal. Emic models create an epistemic framework in which members of target groups are themselves the experts on the realities and meanings of their experiences, and in which the experience of multiple strands of identity is nor- mative and assumed.

Additionally, within the mental health disciplines, these models have emphasized the importance of clinicians' understanding and examining the meaning of their own identities and biases, as well as the implications of those variables for the accurate observation of the distress of others, and the design and implementation of healing strategies. Thus, emic models are not simply about understanding Bajorans; they are also about understanding humanness, and about apprehending for all parties the intersubjective meanings of being a human psychotherapist working with a Bajoran client. In emic models, both parties are observers, and both parties co-construct the meanings of experi- ences.

Emic models assume, not a stance of expertise on the part of the clinician, but a stance of curiosity and ignorance, an important foundation for culturally competent practice. The culturally competent therapist knows and embraces the reality that she or he is indeed ignorant, lacking in sufficient knowledge of the person of the client; she or he embraces the ambiguity of psychotherapeutic situation and creates space in which to experience compassionately, and without judgment, how she or he may fail to understand her or his client, because the client is both apparently different and apparently similar. Ironically, such a stance of high tolerance for ambiguity is generally considered necessary for the effective practice of psychotherapy and the development of therapeutic relationships. Embracing ambiguity about cultural phenomena and knowing that one truly does not know what it means that the client is biologically female, has darker-toned skin, and has parents who were born in Cape Verde, are the core of cultural competence in work with that individual. Embracing the same ambiguity with the complex trauma survivor who is European American, sports straight blonde hair, and comes from the sixth generation of her family to inhabit a small, Midwestern U.S. town is equally a core issue in cultural competence in that person's therapy process.

However, the affects of guilt and shame that frequently distort dynamics in relationships between target and dominant groups seem to disconnect otherwise emotionally competent psychotherapists from their willingness to be uncertain and tentative with clients who represent the cultural other. Because of the problematic narrative of etic competence, psychotherapists frequently experience themselves as more different, more deficient, and less competent to consider engaging with clients who visibly differ from them. In work with survivors of complex trauma, where the psychotherapist's own emotional responses will be captured, read, and interpreted by clients whose interpersonal realities have been dangerous and confusing, the presence of such distortions, and the performance anxieties placed upon themselves by therapists to emit evidence of etic knowledge, can lead to serious, difficult-to-repair ruptures in the therapeutic alliance. Consequently, a step toward the development of emic cultural competence for psychotherapists is the direct confrontation and acceptance of the realities of personal bias.

BIAS: YOURS, MINE, ALL OF OURS

As people of goodwill, psychotherapists tend to see themselves as nonjudgmental and lacking in malignant bias. They are, in many instances, trained to become aware of their judgments and to let them go, and cautioned to maintain neutral, objective stances in relationship to clients. This narrative of the unbiased, nonjudgmental therapist is deadly to the development of cultural competence, because it presumes a way of being that is difficult, if not possible, for most human beings to achieve.

Evolutionary biology and psychology indicate that humans are coded to notice difference. Their limbic systems, also implicated in the trauma response, light up and become active when data become available that another human differs in some way. Their limbic systems are what Data, the android character from the *Star Trek* series, referred to as the "subroutine for emotions," the component of human brains that runs in parallel with the cognitions of the prefrontal cortex, and that, as any trauma therapist knows only too well, can overpower that thinking brain, firing more quickly and with more impact. The notion that a therapist can be unbiased presumes the absence of limbic system input, as well as of any personal life history that has ascribed meaning to difference, either positive or otherwise. No psychotherapist matches these criteria.

By the time that the first Bajoran survivor of complex trauma seeks treatment, the average psychotherapist will have had multiple experiences of classically conditioned associations with the visual, auditory, kinesthetic, and other sensory cues presented by that individual. The psychotherapist will have bias simply by virtue of being human. Acknowledging this reality is akin to acknowledging any sort of affect evoked by clients. As noted by Pope and Tabachnick (1993), it is normal for psychotherapists to experience disgust, hate, fear, or sexual feelings in response to their clients. Dalenberg (2000), and Pearlman and Saakvitne (1995), have similarly noted that work with survivors of complex trauma is particularly likely to elicit in psychotherapists these kinds of painful and confusing emotional responses.

Yet when the client is identified as a member of a target group, and the therapist's identity is largely that of dominant group status, the awareness of the normative nature of therapist bias and negative affects in therapy that have been well-developed by many psychotherapists working with survivors of complex trauma, are often overshadowed by therapists' feelings of guilt and shame for experiencing those emotions toward the client whose group has been targeted. These affects are components of a larger phenomenon known as *aversive* or *modern* bias (Gaertner & Dovidio, 1986, 2005), an understanding of which is another core aspect of developing cultural competence.

AVERSIVE BIAS

Aversive bias refers to nonconscious biases held by individuals who consciously eschew overt expressions of bias. It developed during the latter half of the 20th century, as the holding of overt bias became socially stigmatized and unacceptable; a split developed in many individuals between their expressed, conscious beliefs that were not biased and emphasized the value of fairness, and their well-conditioned, nonconscious, now ego-dystonic biases that were consciously aversive to them. Social-psychological research suggested that around 85% of European American individuals hold aversive bias toward persons of color, even though their consciously held attitudes and behaviors are devoid of overt bias.

The presence of aversive bias in an individual has observable impact on her or his interactions with others; thus, rather than being simply a private affair, it is an intersubjective phenomenon with specific effects on the interpersonal field. Given the sensitivity of complex trauma survivors to a therapist's own unexplored or denied feelings, it stands to reason that aversive bias can play a large part in undermining the therapeutic relationship, thus reducing treatment effectiveness.

Aversive bias is supported by denial and undoing, and leads to shame, discomfort, and distancing of dominant group members from target group members. Members of target groups, who, like trauma survivors, are often highly attuned to cues about bias emanating from members of dominant groups, commonly experience their interactions with such dominant group persons as crazy making and fraught with inauthenticity. Similarly, the psychotherapy client encountering a therapist who claims to have no angry feelings, while emitting cues of angry affect, is likely to feel discounted and be made crazy. Therapists who are unaware of her or his aversive bias may emit interpersonal cues that undermine her or his conscious intentions to do well. Given the heightened importance of the therapeutic alliance for clients who have anxious or ambivalent attachment styles, which is true for many survivors of complex trauma (Norcross & Lambert, 2005), the presence of such nonconscious and disowned bias in psychotherapists may be particularly toxic to the alliance in psychotherapy with this population.

Cultural competence does not rest solely in knowing, in theory, about personal aversive bias, however. It requires a willingness to acknowledge this fact compassionately, without shaming or inducing guilt, as a step toward greater congruence and authenticity. As noted earlier, humans are biologically wired to respond to difference, and psychosocially conditioned to associate difference with negative ascriptions that are inescapable in the familial and cultural contexts in which each psychotherapist has been raised. Because virtually all humans have bias, acknowledging that reality enhances therapists' capacity to work with clients from target groups.

Shame about bias, however, undermines effectiveness. Nathanson (1992) has argued that humans have four predictable responses to shame: withdrawing or distancing from the source of the shame, attacking the self for being shameful, attacking the source of the shame, or denial. Each of these inter- and intrapersonal strategies is counter to psychotherapeutic effectiveness; ironically, the strategy of withdrawal (e.g., "I'm not trained to work with Bajorans") has been one accepted mode of behaving in a culturally competent manner within the framework of etic models. Compassionate acceptance of the reality of psychotherapist bias allows for approach and relationship between dominant and target group members, an interpersonal style more consistent with the development of a therapeutic alliance with the survivor of complex trauma. If I am able to accept the reality of my biases and make them conscious, I enact them less and distance less from clients who evoke these biases, because I am experiencing less shame about my own responses. Then I am more willing to be confronted by a client without responding defensively. Cultural competence creates therapeutic competence.

UNDERSTANDING PRIVILEGE

When the psychotherapist embraces the reality of personal bias without shame, then he or she is free to take the next step toward cultural competence, the acknowledgment of cultural privilege and disadvantage. Neither privilege nor disadvantage is earned or deserved; like the acquisition of bias, these experiences accrue to the individual because of the circumstances and realities of life, few of which, until adulthood, occur in response to personal desires or actions.

What is *privilege*? Peggy McIntosh (1998) described it as an "invisible backpack" of safety and positive experiences that is carried by each member of a dominant group. It cannot usually be taken off, and it is rarely noticed by the person who carries it. Rather, for most dominant group individuals, privilege is simply how life is, the description of "normal." In many dominant cultures, the absence of privilege in the lives of target group members is explained as deriving from some real or imagined deficiencies in the target group, thus justifying the denial of privilege, and implying that privilege might be earned, when such is never the case. Privilege and its opposite, disadvantage, have known effects on mental health and functioning, expressed in the form of risk and resiliency factors (e.g., childhood poverty as a risk factor, good health as a resiliency factor) in the pathways to psychological and somatic distress and dysfunction.

Some examples of dominant group privilege include the following:

- While driving your car, you are unlikely to be stopped by the police so long as you obey traffic laws.
- You can marry the person you love no matter where you live and have access to her or him in the emergency room if she or he is in an accident.
- You can walk into any store wearing anything you want, pretty well assured that you will not be followed or harassed by store security.
- Your culture's holidays are always days off from work or school.
- You can be imperfect, and few people will generalize from your imperfections to those of everyone in your group.
- If your day, week, or year is going badly, you need not ask of each negative episode or situation whether it has overtones of bias, or whether you're being paranoid; thus, no excess emotional energy needs to be spent parsing the meanings of a situation, and when you do not like what is happening, it is rare that you will be accused of overreacting or being paranoid.

Most individuals have some mixture of privilege and disadvantage due to the mingling of dominant and target group status in their identities. Invidious comparisons between experiences of disadvantage (e.g., is racism worse than homophobia?) frequently have the effect of creating divisions between target groups, while obscuring the psychological reality that for every person who experiences privilege or its absence, there are psychosocial effects. Privilege creates ease, safety, and a sense of clarity (whether false or real) about what is happening in the interpersonal field. Privilege can create resilience or give access to resources that speed the healing process.

Acknowledging privilege, like acknowledging one's aversive bias, is a process that often initially induces shame and guilt. Like aversive bias, privilege should be an occasion for neither; being born with pale skin or a penis in a culture that values these characteristics and gives privilege to those who have them is an accident of fate. Just as therapists working with the survivors of complex trauma convey that the terrible things done to clients were not their fault, so, too, a culturally competent therapist must acknowledge that whatever privilege she or he has accrued by accident of birth is not her or his fault.

Shame or guilt over privilege, similar to shame about aversive bias, can undermine both effective assessment and psychotherapy. Most centrally, empathic relating may be undermined when the powerful and sometimes insidious effects of the absence of privilege on well-being and psychological robustness are denied or downplayed, leading to overpathologizing of a survivor's behaviors by the therapist, who operates from unexamined assumptions of privilege. A therapist who denies privilege can also become numb to how the absence of privilege shapes life's realities. To call oneself color-blind is an excellent example of privilege at work; only if the shade of my skin has not systemically disadvantaged me can I act as if this variable matters little.

REPRESENTATION: TRANSFERENCE, PLUS

A therapist who has been able to unflinchingly observe her or his bias and privilege is better equipped to comprehend the complex phenomenon of *representation*. The 19th-century African American suffrage activist Anna Julia Cooper said, "When and where I enter, then and there the whole race enters with me" (quoted in Giddings, 1996, p. 14). Cooper's statement is true for each therapist and for each client. When and where therapy occurs, into the room enter personal and cultural histories, privileges, and biases. Therapists represent things to their clients, who represent things in return. These phenomena are more than simply transference or countertransference, because the things represented (i.e., ethnicity, gender, social class, and others, to be discussed later in this chapter) are currently active in the social environment rather than in past experiences that are symbolically or unconsciously evoked or transferred into the therapeutic environment. The dynamics of representation, even when symbolic, are not merely nonconscious representations of personal history; they are the interpersonal and political realities in which therapy takes place.

Culturally competent practice, with trauma survivors or with others, requires a heightened awareness of what is represented by both parties. This is especially the case when one or the other represents a component of personal or historical trauma to the other. For cultural competence to be infused into the work, therapists must consider how both visible and invisible aspects of identities may carry meanings to which clients are not insensitive. Therapists may attempt to deny social realities by telling themselves (and sometimes their clients) that they are inattentive to clients' phenotype, sex, size, or accent; such statements, reflecting experiences of privilege, are experienced as invalidating to clients from target groups, who rarely are not perceived, and treated, within the framework of those various markers of identity.

Privilege, ironically, confers a lack of awareness, because an aspect of privilege is that one member is not expected to represent the entire group: The divorcing heterosexual individual, for example, is not seen as evidence of the failure of that sexual orientation but simply as a person having a bad relationship experience, nor is the European American child who performs poorly in math seen as evidence that math capacities are lacking in that ethnic group. Thus, for psychotherapists whose primary identities are as members of dominant groups, and who are most likely to be affected by the nonconscious assumptions of privilege, heightened attention to how and what one represents is essential for culturally competent practice. This interrogation of personal identities may also deepen empathy as dominant-group therapists begin dimly to apprehend what it means to live as a visible, audible, or palpable symbol of something—good, bad, or indifferent. A basic assumption of culturally competent practice is never to assume that we have the trust of our clients. This dovetails with what is known about working with complex trauma. Trauma is itself destructive to trust; survivors of interpersonal trauma may take years to believe that their therapists will not become one of their perpetrators. When therapists overtly represent difference in a way that, consciously or not, conveys a message of threat, or if the client evokes that reaction in the therapist, the willingness to bring these dynamics of difference and representation into shared awareness not only increases cultural competence but also takes steps toward the deepening of empathy.

When therapists represent current or historical trauma to clients and are aware of it, however, they increase the possibility of earning trust when they tell the truths about accepting the role as representatives of their culture. Acknowledging and validating the presence of dynamics arising from such representations in the therapy office can communicate to clients a willingness to tell truths that are uncomfortable for therapists, not simply to invite clients to experience the rapists' own discomfort. Power becomes more balanced when therapists eschew the anonymity of privilege, and bring to the foreground their own identities, as their target group clients must do often in their daily lives.

Thus, simply saying, "I'm wondering what it means for our work together that I'm apparently able-bodied and you're a person with a visible disability," communicates a psychotherapist's cultural competence in several ways. First, the dominant-group therapist is being honest about privilege, and about the power dynamics engendered by that privilege. Second, the therapist is placing the burden of opening the discussion, which is usually more uncomfortable (because it is potentially a source of guilt and/or shame) for that dominant group member, withdrawing from neither the topic nor the client's realities. Finally, the therapist is acknowledging the awareness that he or she, a member of a dominant group, represents. These, and similar interventions, are not the be all and end all of cultural competence; they are, however, examples of very important components of culturally competent practice with complex trauma survivors, who may feel a modicum more safe knowing that they are not alone, and that there is a heightened awareness of the meaning of difference in the room.

DIVERSITY IS ABOUT EVERYONE: THE ADDRESSING MODEL

Finally, culturally competent practice stands on a foundation of belief that each human being represents the range of aspects of diversity, and that being culturally competent requires that the therapist be aware of her or his own identities and social locations, as well as those of clients. Human diversity is not about "special populations," but about the nature of being human. Challenging oppressive norms is something we do not only altruistically, on behalf of traumatized survivors, but also from enlightened self-interest, with the assumption that each person is in some manner harmed by current social structures of hierarchies of value. This further moves the definitions of cultural competence away from the "Handbook of psychotherapy with Bajorans" model to one that positions dominant group members of goodwill as allies to members of the target group, in part by disrupting the narrative of "normal" and "other," with a discourse of multiple identities across social locations that are present in most people. Using epistemologies of difference that invite the psychotherapist to consider how to think about and analyze experiences of identity supports cultural competence, because the therapist need not acquire discrete data bits about Bajorans; rather, the therapist learns how to think about what it might mean to be this particular Bajoran.

Experts on the development of cultural competence in psychotherapy have proposed a variety of epistemologies of difference; the one I discuss here is Pamela Hays's ADDRESSING model (2001, 2007). The acronym stands for a nonexhaustive but relatively complete list of social locations, each of which exists to some degree in all persons, and any of which can become central strands in the development of identities for all individuals:

A: Age-related factors, including chronological age and age cohort.
DD: Disability–ability, developmental and acquired, visible and invisible.
R: Religion and spirituality.
E: Ethnic origins, race/phenotype, and culture.
S: Social class, current and former.
S: Sexual orientation—lesbian, gay, bisexual, heterosexual, questioning.

I: Indigenous heritage/colonization, history/colonizer history.

N: National origin/immigration status/refugee/offspring of immigrants.

G: Gender/biological sex (male, female, intersex)/gender identity (masculine, feminine, transgender).

This model makes explicit that all humans have multiple identities; although one aspect may become central phenomenologically or assume the foreground interpersonally, each individual is the unique intersection of some combination of these social locations. Identity emerges in the dialectical struggle between individual experiences and temperament, and group and collectives experiences and norms. Not all of these variables have the same effect in any two persons; they are additive, multiplicative, or variable, depending on the situation.

TRAUMA: ANOTHER SOCIAL LOCATION

Trauma is another component of identity; this is as true for some therapists (Pope & Feldman-Summers, 1992) as for their clients. Many clients with complex trauma are children of trauma survivors, living with legacies of intergenerational transmission of trauma experiences (Danieli, 1998). Still others identify with cultures that have been so immersed in trauma, such as Native American, African American, Jewish, Khmer, Native Hawaian, or Armenian, that historical trauma has been woven into other aspects of identity by the centrality of historical trauma to that social location (Comas-Díaz & Jacobsen, 2001; Pole, Gone, & Kulkarni, 2008).

Perpetration is another facet of many people's identities, a variable that fuels some of the shame that leads to denial of bias. The descendants of slaveholders, of soldiers who shot women and children in this country's genocidal wars against its indigenous people, of those who imprisoned or tortured others in the countries from which they came are among the survivors of complex trauma. They or their ancestors suffered what Shay (1995) calls the "moral injury" of being trauma perpetrators. Both therapists and clients are the inheritors of moral injury that was often traumatic to the family cultures that it created. For some individuals of mixed heritage, the inner conflict between victim and oppressor is yet another component of identity flavoring the experiences of complex trauma.

Each social location in the ADDRESSING model can be linked to the experience of trauma in some manner; this may be due to direct targeting, as is the case for hate crimes or gender-based violations, or it may have occurred more indirectly (e.g., with poverty being a risk factor for exposure to violence). A complete discussion of this topic far exceeds the parameters of this chapter; readers are referred to Brown (2008) for a book-length discussion and review of pertinent literature on specific relationships between ADDRESSING variables and trauma exposure. Individuals may also, accurately or not, attribute their experiences of victimization to some component of their identities, and struggle with their hatred of an inescapable fact about themselves that they believe has rendered them vulnerable.

For example, the survivor of complex trauma who hates herself for having been a vulnerable child, unable to protect herself against abuse or soothe herself in the face of neglect, may have developed an intolerance of anything youthful or child-like in herself. In the extreme, this may lead to structural dissociation, in which inner "children" are punished by other parts for being young, thus representing the supposed cause of the experience of victimization. A man who is sexually assaulted as a child because of his supposed effeminacy may develop a hypermasculine style as an adult, expressing hatred of effeminate men or of women.

Because perpetrators of complex trauma are so frequently those with whom a survivor was or is emotionally intimate, the survivor's identities may overlap with those of her or his perpetrators, creating understandable confusion and difficulties when defenses of splitting are engaged, as is so frequently the case in the aftermath of overwhelming abuse or neglect. "I hate the white person in me," cries the mixed-race survivor of incest at the hands of her European American father. Struggles with identity, which are commonplace among survivors of complex trauma, may be intensified by the ways in which identification with or loyalty to a group has become contaminated by shared membership with the ones who did harm. Cultural competence can be enhanced by a psychotherapist's ability to embrace, and to invite clients to embrace, these painful contradictions and experiences of betrayal, and to see identity development as reflecting multiple social locations, and as being fluid rather than fixed.

TRAUMA AND IDENTITY DEVELOPMENT

Root, an identity theorist who has used the experiences of people of mixed phenotype (aka *racially mixed*) to develop her models (1998, 2000, 2004), has argued that several factors need to be present to develop an identity theory for persons of mixed social locations. First, this model needs to account for within-group bias and oppression, the sort of expression of internalized oppression or horizontal hostility that can occur when target group membership is present. Second, such a model must see as positive the experience of multiple identities. Root's model, a useful paradigm for cultural competence in understanding the identity experiences of trauma survivors, construes mixed identities as potentially mentally healthy. Her model next notes the importance of changes in social and political contexts, and social reference groups that are available to persons and affect their own understanding of identity. Finally, the model must acknowledge the interaction of experiences in people's social ecology, including family environment, history, and biological heritage. Root portrays her model graphically as a series of nested, interactive, overlapping boxes in which these various factors are in constant interplay, and in which identity is in a continuous process of development rather than moving toward a fixed and apparently stable state (see *www.drmariaroot.com*).

Cultural competence in trauma practice is enhanced by this or similar models of identity formation, because it allows the clinician to conceptualize the client's identity as a continuously transforming matrix of multiple social locations that does not require a fixed and stable state to be functional. Many survivors of trauma exist in a liminal identity state, one in which transition is a constant. What is less obvious but equally important for the culturally competent trauma psychotherapist to take into account is the degree to which liminal identities emerge as a function of a posttraumatic healing process, in which identity as a trauma survivor becomes integrated in a positive fashion into other aspects of identity.

Culturally competent practice takes clients' and psychotherapists' multiple identities into account in making sense of what occurs in the interpersonal field of the therapy process: The poverty-class European American woman client who has risen into middle management, and the upper-middle-class European American woman therapist who struggles to support herself in an independent practice, may need to interrogate one another regarding the centrality of social class to their respective identities to discover how their relationship has been plagued by disconnects. In this example, the hidden social location may have had important effects on identity for both women in ways that are obscured by their current apparent similarities. Because, as Root notes, one way to have a multiple identity is to refuse to accept the identity assigned to oneself by the interpersonal context, cultural competence in psychotherapy can be enhanced by thoughtful consideration of all potential aspects of identity, and embrace each person's strategy for weaving those aspects into a coherent whole.

THERAPY IN THE REAL WORLD

Finally, each aspect of identity, each social location informing that identity, and each of the ways that those variables have become embedded in the experiences of trauma and recovery are affected by the social and political realities of the world. Cultural competence requires therapists to remain attuned to the ways external events, which may seem distal to the therapy process, are proximal in their capacities to evoke affect, intensify bias, or change the meaning of the relationships between people in that process.

This does not mean that the culturally competent therapist must constantly be scanning the news for evidence of some emerging danger. Rather, it means a consideration that shifts in the therapy, steps back and to the side, and intensifications of painful affects and feelings of hopelessness or despair need not only represent the transit of intrapsychic processes, but may also reflect encounters with meaningful external realities. Root's (1992) concept of "insidious trauma" is a useful construct for considering how this might be the case. She describes how exposure to what Essed (1991) refers to as "everyday" bias operates as a continuous stream of small traumatizations that may appear to have no effect, but that can have a cumulative effect when the latest, equally seemingly small event occurs. Exacerbation of symptoms may not require news of a hate crime against members of one's own group; it can occur in response to the latest exposure to everyday bias, discrimination, or invisibility, which is itself a form of psychic violence. Culturally competent therapists explore how triggering life events are not simply Criterion B reminders of a trauma, but representations of threat to some aspect of identity, including some that might have remained in the background of the therapy process.

CONCLUSION

Becoming culturally competent as a psychotherapist is a process with no clear conclusion. As one grows in cultural competence, one grows in ignorance and in the awareness of how one might stretch one's intellectual, experiential, and emotional edges to better develop empathy for the persons with whom one works. Deepening cultural competence leads the therapist, paradoxically, to make more errors of commission at first, in place of the errors of omission and avoidance that are more common when the "refer to the Bajoran specialist" strategy is engaged. This trend should be familiar to therapists: Deepening of intimacy and relationship, whether in psychotherapy or elsewhere in life, allows sufficient contact that errors can be made. Aversive biases express themselves behaviorally, countertransferences evoked by representation are acted out, and willingness to acknowledge error and listen to distress is called upon repeatedly. Cultural competence requires ongoing consultation and training, in addition to continuing acquisition of specific knowledge; the therapist never achieves cultural competence but is always moving toward it. The parallel processes and skills inherent in working with complex trauma serve psychotherapists well on the journey to cultural competence; deepening cultural competence, in turn, sharpens the skills of the psychotherapist entering the world of complex trauma.

REFERENCES

Brown, L. S. (2008). *Cultural competence in trauma therapy: Beyond the flashback.* Washington, DC: American Psychological Association.

Comas-Díaz, L., & Jacobsen, F. (2001). Ethnocultural allodynia. *Journal of Psychotherapy Practice and Research, 10,* 246–252.

Dalenberg, C. I. (2000). *Countertransference and the treatment of trauma.* Washington, DC: American Psychological Association.

Danieli, Y. (Ed.). (1998). *International handbook of multigenerational legacies of trauma.* New York: Plenum Press.

Essed, P. (1991). *Everyday racism: Reports from women of two cultures.* New York: Hunter House.

Gaertner, S., & Dovidio, J. (1986). The aversive form of racism. In J. Dovidio & S. Gaertner (Eds.), *Prejudice, discrimination and racism* (pp. 61–89). Orlando, FL: Academic Press.

Gaertner, S., & Dovidio, J. (2005). Understanding and addressing contemporary racism: From aversive racism to the common in-group identity model. *Journal of Social Issues, 61,* 615–639.

Giddings, P. (1996). *When and where I enter: The impact of race and sex on black women's lives.* New York: Amistad.

Hays, P. A. (2001). *Addressing cultural complexities in practice: A framework for clinicians and counselors.* Washington, DC: American Psychological Association.

Hays, P. A. (2007). *Addressing cultural complexities in practice: Assessment, diagnosis, and therapy.* Washington, DC: American Psychological Association.

Herman, J. L. (1992). *Trauma and recovery.* New York: Basic Books.

McIntosh, P. (1998). White privilege: Unpacking the invisible knapsack. In M. McGoldrick (Ed.), *Re-visioning family therapy: Race, culture, and gender in clinical practice* (pp. 147–152). New York: Guilford Press.

Nathanson, D. (1992). *Shame and pride: Affect, sex, and the birth of the self.* New York: Norton.

Norcross, J. C., & Lambert, M. J. (2005). The therapy relationship. In J. C. Norcross, L. E. Beutler, & R. F. Levant, (Eds.), *Evidence-based practice in mental health: Debate and dialogue on the fundamental questions* (pp. 208–217). Washington, DC: American Psychological Association.

Pearlman, L. A., & Saakvitne, K. W. (1995). *Trauma and the therapist: Countertransference and vicarious traumatization in psychotherapy with incest survivors.* New York: Norton.

Pole, N., Gone, J., & Kulkarni, M. (2008). Posttraumatic stress disorder among ethnoracial minorities in the United States. *Clinical Psychology: Science and Practice, 15,* 35–61.

Pope, K. S., & Feldman-Summers, S. (1992). National survey of psychologists' sexual and physical abuse history and their evaluation of training and competence in these areas. *Professional Psychology: Research and Practice, 23,* 353–361.

Pope, K. S., & Tabachnick, B. G. (1993). Therapists' anger, hate, fear, and sexual feelings. *Professional Psychology: Research and Practice, 23,* 142–152.

Root, M. P. P. (1992). Reconstructing the impact of trauma on personality. In L. S. Brown & M. Ballou (Eds.), *Personality and psychopathology: Feminist reappraisals* (pp. 229–265). New York: Guilford Press.

Root, M. P. P. (1998). Preliminary findings from the biracial sibling project. *Cultural Diversity and Mental Health, 4,* 237–247.

Root, M. P. P. (2000). Rethinking racial identity development: An ecological framework. In P. Spickard & J. Burroughs (Eds.), *We are a people.* Philadelphia: Temple University Press.

Root, M. P. P. (2004). From exotic to a dime a dozen. *Women and Therapy, 27,* 19–32.

Shay, J. (1995). *Achilles in Vietnam: Combat trauma and the undoing of character.* New York: Simon & Schuster.

CHAPTER 9

Therapeutic Alliance and Risk Management

Philip J. Kinsler
Christine A. Courtois
A. Steven Frankel

Child abuse and attachment failures are relational events and experiences, occurring most often within families, between parents and children. The consequences profoundly affect the child's physiological/biological and psychological development, and ability to form close and trusting relationships. Victimized children are *hurt in relationships*, yet, paradoxically, *relationships can be the core component of healing from these injuries*. At times, special relationships, such as close friendships, mentorships, marriages, partnerships and, in some cases, parenting of one's own children, can be restorative when they provide the attachment security the individual needs to learn new ways of relating and trusting others. Psychotherapy may also provide the needed "safe haven" within which to modify old relational patterns that were built on insecurity and exploitation. Stated simply, whether it occurs within or outside of psychotherapy, healing of complex and chronic trauma associated with abuse (especially when there is a foundation of attachment trauma) occurs in safe, dependable, kind, and bounded relationships.

Therefore, in this chapter, we briefly review the psychological circumstances that bring about complex traumatic stress outcomes and disorders, and define some major parameters of psychotherapy that promote relational healing of traumatized persons. The client's relational history and the "lessons of abuse" he or she has learned are brought to the treatment relationship, often creating barriers to the development of a collaborative working alliance. They may also create tumultuous and challenging relationships that test client and therapist alike. Chu (1988) wrote of the treatment traps (including intense relational demands, extreme mistrust coupled with neediness, and dysregulated emotions) facing therapists in the course of their work with traumatized individuals. In a later article, he characterized the treatment of previously abused adults as "the therapeutic rollercoaster" due to its intensity and instability at times. Chu exhorted therapists to be mindful of the many relational challenges that attend treatment with this population, and the risks that they can pose for client and therapist (Chu, 1992). Many of these issues have also been discussed in Dalenberg (2000), Pearlman and Courtois (2005), and Pearlman and Saakvitne (1995). Therefore, in this chapter we also review management of risks inherent in providing this type of therapy.

THE RELATIONAL HISTORIES OF PERSONS WITH COMPLEX TRAUMA

The histories of patients with complex trauma include a variety of abusive experiences across the life cycle, beginning in family contexts that make processing and resolving these experiences extremely difficult. Patients with complex trauma do not typically grow up in a benign context, then suffer an act of abuse. Rather, they typically live in chronically abusive environments that *combine* varied types of abuses. Children often experience combinations of emotional, physical, and sexual abuse; parental substance abuse; domestic violence; a parent or parents with mental illness; and/or the criminal incarceration of a parent. There is a dose–response relationship between the number of types of abuse suffered and later effects (Dube et al., 2001, 2007; Edwards, Holden, Felitti, & Anda, 2003).

Multiple-category childhood victimization has important consequences for how children view themselves and their worlds, especially influencing their later relationships with others. In overwhelming circumstances of violence and exploitation perpetrated by other human beings, there is a major attempt to make meaning, to understand (Frankl, 1946). When abuse starts early and continues over much of a child's life, and especially when it is perpetrated by a parent/caregiver and there is no escape and no help from others, how does the child understand and make sense of it? Chronic abuse impacts the entire meaning of life—what McCann and Pearlman (1990) termed the individual's overall *frame of reference*. In general, persons who experience severe abuse *come to believe, at a very deep level, that the world is unsafe, that other people are not trustworthy.* By virtue of their repeated experiences of abuse and neglect, they come to "know," *in the deepest sense of internal knowing, that they are somehow to blame and deserving of the abuse.* They feel "in their bones" that they are bad, that it is fruitless to hope, that they will never be safe, and that they must keep their pain a secret from others. They may look to others for help, but simultaneously they often expect to be beyond help and to be betrayed by the person(s) to whom they turn. Erik Erikson (1950) called this *basic mistrust.*

In recent years, findings from developmental psychology have expanded understanding of the relational circumstances that usually precede frank physical, emotional, and/or sexual abuse in a family. Adverse childhood events and experiences occur within and interact with difficulties in early attachment patterns between infants and primary caregivers. Numerous researchers investigating the quality of early attachment experiences between primary caregivers (usually parents) and young children (before age 2) have found that seriously disrupted attachment, without repair or intervention for the child can, in and of itself, be traumatic (labeled *attachment trauma* by Allen [2001], and Schore [2003a, 2003b]). British psychiatrist John Bowlby (1969, 1980) pioneered the study of attachment between caregiver and young child, and its significance to human development. He noted that children need a stable caregiver who is affectively attuned, offers protection from overstimulation and threat, and teaches social interaction skills. Four primary attachment styles in childhood have been identified, each of which has a corresponding style in adulthood: (1) *secure*; (2) *insecure–ambivalent (resistant)*; (3) *insecure–fearful/avoidant*; and (4) *insecure–disorganized/disoriented*. These patterns have been found to be relatively stable over the lifespan but are subject to modification according to individual factors, such as the child's temperament and perceptual style; and contextual factors, such as idiosyncratic life events and experiences, including other primary and influential relationships.

Accumulated evidence now strongly suggests that the majority of chronically abused individuals develop an insecure and/or disorganized/dissociative attachment style (Lyons-Ruth & Jacobovitz, 1999) that impacts their view of others and their sense of self, both within and apart from relationships. Beliefs such as "No one is trustworthy," "It's a dog-eat-dog world," "To feel safe, I need to be in control," "I feel disconnected from other people," "I am bad," and "I deserve to be treated badly by others" influence the quality of individuals' interactions and relationships. When interactions are disappointing in some way, these beliefs get reinforced. These convictions often have enormous resilience, even in the face of contradictory data. They arise from the child's needs to protect him- or herself in the crucial relationship with the primary caregiver. Children use these nonconscious beliefs, full of self-blame, to maintain the crucial illusion that the world could be safe "if only they were better" (Janoff-Bulman, 1992).

Attachment theory posits that these early experiences are organized internally and implicitly as the template for adult personality and all interpersonal relationships (Shorey & Snyder, 2006). Bowlby (1969) introduced the concept of *inner working model* (IWM) to describe cognitive and emotional representations of self and others that typically operate automatically and unconsciously to monitor attachment-related experiences, and that form the basis for behavior. These IWMs are comparable to schemas about self and others proposed by other theorists (e.g., McCann & Pearlman, 1990; Young, Klosko, & Weishaar, 2003). Importantly, these IWMs are flexible enough to be updated through the provision of new relational experiences. It is on this basis that we posit the importance of the relationship in the treatment of clients with complex trauma.

TECHNIQUE OR RELATIONSHIP?: A "BOTH–AND"

Recent years have seen an enormous push for "empirically validated treatments." Research in psychotherapy effectiveness has focused on treatment provided according to manual-based protocols (Binder, 2004), designed in part to eliminate variations between therapists. In contrast, however, a long line of therapeutic outcome research suggests that it is *precisely these individual therapeutic relational differences*, a part of each treatment relationship, that contribute to and predict outcome (Hubble, Duncan, & Miller, 1999). Client factors account for approximately 40% of therapeutic change; the therapeutic relationship, for 30%; expectancy effects, for 15%; and specific therapeutic techniques, for only 15% (Hubble et al., 1999).

The consensus among therapists treating the severely traumatized is that *both technique and relationship* are important influences on outcome. Researchers are now studying this very issue as it pertains to the treatment of survivors. Cloitre, Stovall-McClough, Miranda, and Chemtob (2004) reported that "in the treatment of childhood abuse-related PTSD, the therapeutic alliance and the mediating influence of emotion regulation capacity appear to have significant roles in successful outcome" (p. 411). They also noted that two specific areas of technique are important in treating complex traumatic stress disorders: (1) teaching of stabilization/emotional regulation/self-soothing and (2) processing of traumatic experiences. Each area requires specialized training, approaches, and interventions; therefore, therapists must be skilled and comfortable working in both of these areas. Clients who report a history of pervasive childhood abuse and neglect, especially one that occurs in the context of insecure attachment, have emotional regulation deficits that may in turn cause reliance on a variety of problematic behaviors (i.e., addictions, compulsions, self-injury, chronic suicidality) in the interest of self-soothing leading to emotion and self-regulation. Thus, therapists need a repertoire of skills and approaches to help the client approach rather than avoid emotion, and to learn to tolerate and modulate a variety of emotional states through more adaptive self-soothing strategies. Therapists also must be able to tolerate the personal feelings they experience in working with these maladaptive coping strategies, that often are based on self-harm and self-invalidation. A variety of available workbooks now provide specific information, guidance, and a series of exercises and worksheets on these various topics (Allen, 2005; Cloitre, Cohen, & Koenen, 1996; Conterio & Lader, 1998; Copeland & Harris, 2000; Jobes, 2006; Linehan, 1993; Miller; 1994; Najavits, 2002; Vermilyea, 2000).

In addition to these important interventions geared toward client self-regulation, the authors' experience, in concordance with the findings of many other clinicians and clinical researchers, strongly supports the view that *the therapy relationship is itself the vehicle of change*. Optimally, it models secure attachment and provides containment of the patient's anxiety, the opportunity for expression of other core emotions, a context within which to work out relational issues, and a basic *valuing of or validation* that the patient may never have had. As expressed by a patient of Kinsler at the end of treatment, "I was always OK with you. You saw me *and let me be me*."

A healing therapy relationship handles relational distress, including mistrust, hypervigilance, and mistakes made by each member of the dyad, without retaliation or defensiveness on the part of the therapist. As such, it becomes a model for what can be. As attachment becomes more secure over the course of treatment, emotions become more accessible and less onerous, the client's self-regard increases, and relationship skills develop. As a result, the client has a new template for relationships and new abilities to apply in his or her interpersonal world.

The remainder of this chapter covers some aspects of what we have learned in attempting to create this type of relationship with clients through our own direct clinical experience, reading of expert literature, peer consultation, supervision, personal reflection, and professional training. Guidance is offered on how to approach the treatment relationship, as well as manage the risks inherent in it, because the relationship itself tends to elicit strong feelings and reactions of both client and therapist. Without forethought and preparation, treatment mistakes, including misalliances and misadventures, can develop, an unfortunately common occurrence in the treatment of those with complex traumatic stress (and dissociative) disorders.

A "WORKING ALLIANCE"

Virtually all schools or orientations to psychotherapy discuss helpful qualities in the clinician–patient relationship. *The quality of the therapeutic relationship is of central concern*. The central features for most schools and writers include a sense that both clinician and patient are working hard, with shared goals, a common language (and, for that matter, a mutual acceptance of situations for which there is no adequate language; see Dalenberg, 2000, p. 59), and a mutual respect for what is shared and learned over the course of treatment. The therapist is open to the client and provides acceptance for his or her emotions, thereby countering the invalidation of the past. The client can learn self-respect, self-calming, and effective interpersonal negotiation—central goals of treatment with this population. The therapist also strives to be "interpersonally transparent" to counter the client's lack of information about relationship dynamics and to bolster the client's trust and security. Thus, the relationship becomes both context and container for interpersonal experimentation and learning.

COMPONENTS OF A WORKING ALLIANCE
WITH COMPLEX TRAUMA CLIENTS

Working alliances with trauma survivors are characterized primarily by the growth toward safety within the relationship (Herman, 1992). As a starting point, therapists must work from the principle of "Do no *more* harm" (Courtois, 1999) and constantly strive to be accessible, yet with clear boundaries. We list below some of the most central components of establishing safe treatment for this population, as presented and discussed by Frankel (2002) in his Presidential address to the International Society for the Study of Dissociation.

1. *Trust and testing*: The clinician cannot and should not expect automatic trust on the part of the patient, especially at the outset of treatment. If trust occurs, it develops *within the context of relational testing*. Trauma survivors, having been schooled in ways of betrayal and violation of personal boundaries, know little of trust. Few warning signs are more powerful to a trauma survivor than a clinician who asks or expects to be trusted, and/or who takes the client's mistrust personally rather than using it as a mechanism to understand the client's schema about self and others. Trust that arises in the therapy relationship is hard-earned and long in coming. Tests of trustworthiness are, at best, not failed, rather than passed. A client who claims to "trust you" early in therapy is likely to be placating you as a dangerous potential betrayer.

2. *Blame and behavior*: Safety grows when therapists do not blame clients for their troubles, problems, lifestyles, "choices," failings, symptoms, and behaviors that appear to be (or actually are) manipulative. These behaviors developed as protective strategies (survivor skills) and resulted from what the client learned and/or did not learn in formative relationships. Adult survivors of childhood trauma are used to being blamed for all bad things in their lives. They perfectly illustrate the admonition that if blaming someone for their problems would help, then they would have fully recovered years ago. This requires therapeutic steadiness and the ability to contain rather than react to client behavior.

3. *Shame and symptoms*: Therapists must not shame clients for their troubles, failings, symptoms, and behavioral repertoires. Trauma survivors, who already are shamed by how they have been treated, may engage in behaviors that reenact their shame. They require helpers who can be *sensitive to their shame* and help them to explore their negative self-worth and sense of being apart from/less than other humans, without adding to their shame.

4. *Consistency and connection*: The clinician must provide consistency with regard to his or her personal style and behavior, appointment times (start and finish), punctuality, and availability between sessions. Consistency applies to connection, to the therapist's willingness to engage in a close connection with the patient. Connection and support are essential elements of healing from trauma of any sort. In interpersonal trauma, real connection with others often takes a long time and much testing to develop.

5. *Humility*: The clinician must learn humility—the quality of not taking oneself too seriously. Competent clinicians acknowledge errors, blunders, and imperfections; are not afraid to express sorrow and regret; and work to repair damage to the therapeutic relationship when it occurs. Trauma survivors are not used to relationships with people who admit errors and foibles, which makes repair of therapeutic mistakes both difficult and incredibly helpful. Schore (2003b) comments on *relational repair as a core strategy in the development of secure relationships*. Competent clinicians maintain clear and firm boundaries, and reveal only a modicum of information about their personal lives (and then only when there is a clear therapeutic rationale for such disclosure), but they judiciously use and disclose their feelings and reactions within the treatment to be more transparent to the client, as a means of modeling collaborative problem-solving approaches and of negotiating relational impasses.

Dalenberg (2000) studied individuals who had completed trauma treatment. As patients, they felt they would have benefited had their therapists been more transparent with them regarding therapist feelings "in the moment." Without this, they were left wondering about how their therapist felt and were anxious as a result. This was especially the case with therapist anger. Clients reported that if a therapist did not acknowledge his or her anger, the anger tended to get acted out, either passively or more directly, in ways that damaged rather than strengthened the relationship. This client feedback offers therapists important information about one of the most difficult emotions for trauma survivors. Therapist disclosure of personal history pales in significance to the therapist's ability to be present and mindful in the relationship, and to engage with honesty and directness.

6. *Demeanor*: Safety grows when the clinician's demeanor is warm, kind, calm, gentle, interested, and empathically attuned. Calm demeanor and empathic attunement contribute to a "holding environment" (Winnicott, 1965) within which the client is respected and validated as a unique individual. It contrasts with the ways abuse survivors are accustomed to being treated by others. Being treated with respect and attunement may initially be uncomfortable, and the client might even try to reject it; however, when accepted and internalized by the client, it provides conditions for personal growth and change.

7. *Awareness*: Safety grows as the clinician is aware (mindful) of his or her own emotional states, life stresses, and countertransference reactions, and is willing to talk with patients about these "awarenesses," when it is appropriate to do so. Therapist mindfulness is being promoted across all major treatment orientations, from psychoanalysis to cognitive-behavioral, to somatosensory treatment as a necessary component for client development (Fonagy, 1997; Linehan, 1993; Ogden, Pain, & Minton, 2006; Siegel, 2007; see also chapters in Parts II and III, this volume). Psychophysiological synchrony and relational attunement contribute directly to the client's well-being. In response to research findings that such attunement on the part of a significant other can lead to development of new neural pathways in the brain that, in turn, can lead

to changed behavior and a more secure attachment style, Schore (2003b) and Siegel (2007) have labeled the process *interpersonal neurobiology*.

8. *Professionalism*: Safety grows when therapist behaviors reflect professionalism. This includes articulated practice policies; defined and defensible billing practices; maintenance of a confidential setting and confidentiality of session content; open discussion of boundary crossings and their effects; records that the client can read and come away feeling respected; meeting the client within the established structure unless there is a well-planned and discussed reason for other arrangements. In these ways, a professional frame increases a client's sense of safety. A dissociative client once transferred care to Kinsler because the prior therapist had moved and reconstructed her office four times in 1 year of treatment. The client asked, "Who in that relationship was really unstable?"

In summary, *the essential therapist task is to provide relational conditions that encourage the safety of the attachment between client and therapist*. It is through provision of such conditions that the therapy work can lead to a change in the client's attachment style. The client can move to what is termed an *earned secure* style within the therapy that then extends to extratherapeutic relationships (Valory, 2007).

Importantly, *relational attunement increases client self-regulation and self-development*. It includes the process of attending closely and reflecting upon the relational meaning of therapeutic events and reactions. Perhaps the most important question for the therapist to ask repeatedly is "How will this (considered) statement/intervention increase the client's *reflection on self-in-relationship*?" A safe relationship in which to explore self in relationship to others is the goal of the treatment process rather than insight or correct interpretation. Relational safety supports the client in learning new skills, especially new ways of coping. As the possibility of the safety and trustworthiness of others in the world is incorporated by the client, there is less need for dissociation and other defensive operations to self-regulate. The client's feelings and experiences are acceptable to the therapist and do not require exclusion from awareness, allowing an increase in personal coherence/personal narrative. There is less need for compartmentalization; rather than being overwhelmed by emotional reactions, the client begins to feel secure enough just to notice and experience emotions as they happen (labeled as increased capacity for self-reflection, reflective awareness, or mindfulness) (see Siegel, 2007). A clinical example serves to illustrate.

A client began therapy exceedingly sensitive to whether the therapist "cared." Any change in the established appointment times due to personal or professional obligations was personalized by the client and taken to signify that the therapist was indifferent to her. "You don't care. I'm just a marker in your book ... another hour to fill ... another paying customer. I'm always bad, wrong, the one no one gives a damn about!" The therapist had to work against feeling attacked or becoming defensive or reactive, instead responding with comments such as the following: "It's hard to believe anyone cares if something that matters to you changes." Of particular importance were times when the treating therapist acknowledged his own mistakes in relationship management: "You're right. It was inconsiderate of me to wait too long to tell you I was going to be away. I apologize" or "I agree, I could have handled that better." This stance of nonretaliation toward the client's blame and attack was crucial. The client began to realize that she was important enough that the therapist took her position seriously and offered an apology. Making a mistake with her *mattered* to the therapist. Relational repairs of this sort became major therapeutic change points for the client.

Another, more paradoxical change point came when the therapist expressed his irritation after the client made a series of repeated quasi-emergency and increasingly dependent calls in a short time period, straining the therapist's patience. After considering that the client had (he hoped) become strong enough to hear it, the therapist commented, "This is the third time you've called in 2 hours. You know, I'm *not* the endless source of peace and comfort!" By this time, the relationship was strong enough for the client to take this in, not as personal rejection or an indication that the therapist did not care but as an honest acknowledgment of the therapist's humanity and limitations. After acknowledging her initial hurt, she told the therapist in the subsequent session, "Sure I was taken aback, but it was good for me to realize you're human too. Sometimes you run out of patience, sometimes you get overwhelmed, just like I do." These comments communicated a marked increase in the patient's ability to obtain personal control over her initial emotional reactions, based in large measure on the long-term safety and holding environment of the relationship. A further example follows.

As the therapy moved toward the end, the client was able to incorporate the relational lessons she learned in the laboratory of therapy into important life relationships. She became capable of mutual, collaborative, give-and-take relationships with her children. She became able to set limits on and avoid exploitive relationships with men. She no longer "deserved" to be exploited. She asserted herself gently but firmly in her romantic relationships. For the first time in many years, she lived an organized, nonchaotic life. There was an increase in her ability to relate to others in healthy ways in all types of relationships: intimate, parenting, friendship, and colleagueship. These changes were enormously satisfying for client and therapist alike.

In summary, *changing the entire self-in-the-world schema, of how relationships and people work, is the goal of this therapy.*

AREAS OF RISK AND THEIR MANAGEMENT

Listed below is a series of the common relational "demands" often made by these clients, whether explicitly or implicitly, that often challenges therapists, along with considerations of how to manage them ethically in ways that simultaneously attend to the risk that mismanagement can create.

1. *"Re-parent/rescue me."* Perhaps the most common mistake in this therapy is trying to become the good parent the client never had, by rescuing and attempting to meet all his or her unmet dependency needs. Such a strategy, instead of emphasizing the client's responsibility for self- and personal growth within and outside the therapy, often leads to increased demands and an entitled stance toward the therapist (e.g., needing more time, multiple crisis calls), and the therapist trying to do more in response. Therapists who do not communicate or address limitations can become entrapped in an impossible level of patient responsiveness and care. Examples include cards and phone calls while on vacation; nightly phone calls to assuage loneliness and to prove the therapist's caring; extended and extra sessions on an ongoing basis; and continuous crisis management, including suicidal crises and emergency hospitalizations. Therapists who engage in this way usually end up losing patience and tolerance, and taking such reactions out on the client—usually in a way that is blaming or hostile. Therapists learn that rescuing can boomerang as client demands and needs increase to the point that they become impossible to meet. Instead, the therapeutic task is to help the client learn self-responsibility and practice give and take with others. Therapists who maintain appropriate boundaries and limitations provide appropriate modeling. Clients learn that therapy does not exist "outside of the bounds of other human relationships," and that *their losses are not compensable by their therapist* and instead need to be grieved (Calof, cited in Courtois, 1999).

2. *"Promise you won't ever leave or hurt me."* Clients who were seriously neglected in childhood understandably yearn for constancy and reassurance that they will not be abandoned or hurt by the therapist. They may test this out through hypervigilance, hypersensitivity, and/or acting-out behavior. The therapist must be empathic about the seriousness of these issues and help clients understand how they developed in the context of unpredictable, unresponsive, and chaotic relationships. Concurrently, the therapist must openly address this issue by not offering false reassurances and promises (i.e., "I will never leave you") and by assuring the client of his or her intention to remain available as long as the relationship is working, the treatment is progressing, and other life circumstances do not interfere. All relationships are conditional, and therapists cannot guarantee what they themselves are unable to control (e.g., their own health, the health and needs of members of their families, the stability of their practice, change in life circumstance or life plans, or that they will never make a mistake).

3. *"You will neglect me, or you have abused me."* In a similar vein, it is inevitable that therapists will disappoint their clients by having other priorities and life vicissitudes. At times, they may be late, distracted, or overworked; the pager may go off; they may need to deal with an emergency or make a patient wait; and so forth. Therapists have their own life struggles that limit how much they can give. Therapeutic mistakes and limitations are "teachable moments" in which the lesson is "Yes, I am really tired today and maybe I have not been as present as we both wish—but I can and do still care about you.

This does not mean that I am going to abandon you." These moments teach the relational middle ground: Every letdown is *not* a prelude to neglect, abuse, or abandonment.

What has been identified as *traumatic transference* occurs when the survivor client, expecting that the therapist will be yet another abuser, is ever vigilant to that likelihood. This can be a very difficult projection for therapists to understand, because they entered their profession to be helpers, not abusers. Therapists must work to not take this transference expectation personally, while helping clients to explore and understand its origin. They must also understand a relational paradox of betrayal-trauma and attachment insecurity (especially disorganized attachment) that is based on past abuse within relationships with others known to the client (e.g., family members, acquaintances, clergy, teachers). Often, the relationship was the context and conduit for grooming of the child victim, and role relationships and responsibilities were perverted: It was when the relationship became close that the abuse occurred. Thus, when the therapeutic relationship deepens, the client may become most fearful and vigilant, surprising the therapist who, in fact, may be feeling more connected. When therapists do not behave in abusive, exploitive, or retaliatory ways, and when they help clients to understand their fears as legitimate and as projections of past experiences, they provide a different model for relationships in which that abuse/exploitation is not the inevitable outcomes. Other people can be trustworthy.

4. *"How dare you have faults?"* A client once noted that Kinsler had a vanity license plate, and became so enraged at the "narcissism" of this that he left a nasty note under the therapist's windshield, and was extremely critical for several therapy sessions. The vanity plate was interpreted as an example of the therapist's personal aggrandizement, a belief that undercut the client's belief that to be helpful the therapist should be without flaws. Everyone wishes for a perfect father, mother, therapist, and so forth. The therapist's job is to help clients have more realistic expectations, and to grieve the faults of those who were self-centered, abusive, or neglectful in the past. As they let go of the wish, they are freer to accept what therapists *do have* to give, namely, themselves in relationship—imperfections, pettiness, and all. With this stance, therapists also model that the client need not be perfect to be acceptable, a belief held by many survivor clients (i.e., "I can be helpful to you even if I am imperfect, and will care even when you are").

5. *"Your boundaries are killing me. Make me special/get involved in my life (including sexual involvement in some cases)."* Clients raised with abusive/ exploitive caregivers in the context of insecure–disorganized attachment experience a variety of boundary failures in these relationships. These may include stringent boundaries without flexibility on the one hand, lack of boundaries on the other, or boundaries that are ever-shifting and unpredictable. The fluidity of boundaries enables the development of dual relationships in childhood, and clients may be used to such relationships and try to establish them with the therapist. Understandably, abused and neglected clients yearn for the

"special-ness" they never had with their primary caregivers. Stable and predictable boundaries within the therapy work against the development of dual relationships and teach consistency, reliability, and trustworthiness. Although the client might experience boundaries as rejection, the therapist must make clear that a sexual or other dual relationship would not be in the client's best interests and would instead be unethical and retraumatizing: "Having a sexual relationship would not reassure you that you are special, but it would violate our relationship in many of the same ways your abusers did."

6. *"You solve this chaos/you make it all go away."* Some clients have the expectation that it is the therapist's responsibility to "fix it." The therapist who takes on this expectation is likely inadvertently telling clients that they are incapable and not in charge of life decisions. Often, such a stance invites oppositional behavior on clients' parts. No one really wants to be taken over. Additionally, clients' resiliency and strength need to be supported and applauded, and built upon: "I know you wish I could just fix it. No one can do that. You have a number of strengths and things going for you. Let's find ways to help you build on those and learn some new skills as well."

7. *"You find my memories for me."* Many clients enter therapy with the hope or expectation that the therapist will find their abuse memories for them (e.g., "My boyfriend/girlfriend was reading this checklist in a magazine and said I can't sleep and don't like sex because I was probably sexually abused. I want you to tell me if I was"). Without evidence, corroboration, or the client's autobiographical memory, no one can say for sure whether a person was or was not abused. There is no specific symptom that *proves* abuse (sexual or otherwise) or that arises *only* from sexual abuse. The therapist must start *with the patient's memories (if any are available) and symptoms as they are presented* (Courtois, 1999). Since it is not unusual for clients to want to "export the authority for memories to the therapist," rather than having to struggle with uncertainty and the possibility of real abuse and neglect in their backgrounds (Calof, in Courtois, 1999, p. 270), the therapist should not set him- or herself up as the arbiter of the patient's reality. Instead, the therapist can work to resolve presenting problems and provide an interpersonal context in which the client can explore the possibility of abuse without suggestion or suppression on the part of the therapist: "Without your remembering and without evidence, I have no way of knowing whether you may have been abused. You have mentioned problems in your upbringing that are worth exploring as to their personal meaning, and their possible influence on your sleep problems and sexual functioning. Let's see if we can work on these and help you manage these current problems."

8. *"Money: What am I worth to you?"* It is not unusual for severely abused clients to have poor financial management skills that leave some in dire financial straits. At the opposite end of the spectrum, others are scrupulous about money management, having vowed as children to become independent and never to have to rely on anyone for anything. Money can symbolize many

things for survivor clients. For the self-sufficient and untrusting client who views every relationship as a give-and-take transaction, each and every session might be paid for at the start of the sessions, "cash on the barrelhead." The therapist is promptly paid for services, and either party is then free to walk away *without owing anything*. For others, the therapy fee is yet another way they must "pay for" or be encumbered in the present by their past abuse. These clients are understandably resentful of the cost to them (financially and in other ways) and may resist paying for services, or may suggest that they are merely paychecks for the therapist. Still others may use money as a yardstick by which to measure the therapist's caring: If the therapist cares enough and the client is special enough, then he or she will not charge or will lower the standard fee in accommodation. To resist these treatment traps, and in keeping with professional standards, the therapist should have consistent fee setting and payment collection policies, and should not allow clients to build large back balances. We recommend carefully examining the relational meaning when a client fails to pay, falls seriously behind, and so forth. Often the latent meaning is a desire to be specially nurtured, a way to sabotage treatment, or a way to express anger or other emotions indirectly—issues that need to be made explicit and to be negotiated.

9. *"Emergencies: On call or on tap?"* In a population in which chaotic life and interpersonal revictimization might be the norm, at least toward the beginning of treatment, it is important to set clear standards regarding personal safety and how emergencies are defined and handled. It is optimal to have these detailed in the Informed Consent to Treatment Agreement given to the client at intake. Additionally, it is generally advisable to spend a certain amount of time toward the beginning of treatment conducting a risk and safety assessment and, for those clients in clear danger to themselves or others, to develop a plan of action (i.e., safety planning) that the client agrees to put into place in an ongoing manner, but especially in the event of an emergency. A wide variety of self-soothing and emotion regulation techniques should be taught to and implemented by the client in the initial stabilization portion of treatment. These form the foundation of self-management, and the therapist serves as a backup resource on an as-needed basis and when a given situation escalates. When clients do reach out for contact in dire circumstances, and in accordance with the agreements spelled out in the safety plan, the therapist must respond positively and in ways that reinforce honoring the plan before taking action. In Linehan's (1993) words, the therapist is then "reinforcing the right thing."

ADDITIONAL RISK MANAGEMENT TOOLS

We authors also recommend the following tools to aid in the management of risk, in what can sometimes be a challenging population.

Record Keeping

Treatment notes concerning the content of each session are generally required by professional ethics codes and can be used as an important risk management strategy. Many notes follow a format that resembles the following: (1) session content/topics/disclosures; (2) interventions; (3) client comments and behaviors; and (4) homework. This format is helpful in addressing two fundamental areas of compromise that many adult survivors of childhood trauma have undergone: self-reflexivity ("observing ego functions") and continuous memory. Both areas are addressed when the client is shown these notes, in the context of a treatment session covering topics that have been discussed on prior occasions. Review of the notes helps to reinforce memory. The "client comments and behaviors" section, which is primarily a record of things said/done by the patient, often clarifies the meaning to the client of material discussed, teaches, and reinforces an observing ego. Furthermore, this section can be extraordinarily helpful for documenting "boundary pushes" and how these are handled (e.g., a client may ask to be touched or held after a session in which an exposure treatment for flashbacks was done). The therapist makes a verbatim record of what the client said and the therapist's response. By documenting pushes and responses, the client (and, in the event of the need for any legal or regulatory body, reviewing personnel) knows that the therapist is aware of boundary issues and addresses them in ways consistent with the standards of care.

When Content Speaks Indirectly about Process

Process comments—comments by clinicians about what is transpiring in the therapeutic interaction—are a typical part of psychotherapy. A research finding in the treatment of trauma (e.g., see Dalenberg, 2000) is that adult survivors often have repeated experiences of disappointment, mistreatment, and victimization over the course of their lives, and also experience a range of feelings similar to those that occur in therapy—often ranging from disappointment and hurt to outright betrayal. At times, when clients are complaining about myriad episodes of mistreatment in their lives, it is a useful strategy to ask whether any of those complaints are applicable to their therapy. As noted earlier, it takes courage and commitment for clinicians to request this kind of feedback. There may be times when therapists may be surprised by something they said, or when something they did had a negative impact on a client, with intensity varying from mild to very strong. Making therapy safe enough for clients to disclose all feelings, including those of being misunderstood, let down, or betrayed, communicates respect and validation of the client's perspective.

Discussions of the Future

It can be very helpful to talk about the future in general and as it relates to the therapy relationship. In addition to avoiding impossible commitments (e.g.,

"I'll be your therapist for as long as you need me") these conversations open discussion about issues such as "How will I know I'm done with treatment?", "Will you tell me that it's time to stop?", "Will I be having flashbacks like this forever?", and so forth. These discussions address not only the therapist's view of the client's recovery but also his or her view of the client.

Management of the Therapeutic Impasse

Occasions arise in treatment of adult trauma survivors when an impasse is reached. One of the most helpful ways to manage an impasse is to acknowledge it and try to discuss what events or feelings have contributed to it. If a sense of goodwill remains between clinician and client (of course, this depends on the seriousness and intensity of the impasse), albeit with the feeling of being "stuck," it may be helpful to seek out the services of a consultant with expertise in the treatment of childhood trauma survivors and the negotiation of impasses. Depending on the consultant's standard of practice and assessment of the situation, the therapist–client dyad may meet together with the consultant, or there may be individual meetings to discuss each point of view, followed by conjoint meetings. The clinician's best approach to impasse consultation involves openness to understanding and appreciating all factors that may be at work, willingness to avoid blame or shame, and working toward a resolution that moves treatment either forward or toward a decision (gently, the therapist hopes) to terminate the treatment and make referrals as needed.

As an alternative to a consultant, some dyads may decide to begin recording sessions—either audio- or videotapes—so that perceptions of the process may be measured against the "reality" offered by the recording. Again, the willingness to avoid a stance of blame or shame and to work toward a resolution of the stalemate is essential.

Ending the Relationship on a Positive Note

Powerful connections develop in relationship-based therapy. The end of treatment may activate or recapitulate feelings associated with past abandonment or other losses. Termination needs to be handled carefully, because inattentive management can undo some of the gains of "earned-security." Generally, termination should be discussed as the client naturally begins to reconnect to the outside community and to reestablish a life that is less encumbered by the effects of the past trauma. The client may begin to cancel appointments to attend other activities, change appointment times, reduce frequency of sessions, and ask for telephone check-ins as opposed to in-person sessions. As therapy winds down, enough time should be given for discussion of the impact and the feelings that leave taking elicits. The relational lesson is "I and our work will always be with you as you move on." For some clients, we have discussed this as being analogous to the time a child is ready to go off to college, with the same hopes for the future and feelings of sadness and loss.

Sometimes, the client cannot take leaving this way, and he or she manufactures a reason to storm out and slam the door. Our experience has been that such clients often continue to function much better in their lives, and that they are ending a significant relationship in the best way they can manage. Therapists may need to cope with being left in an incomplete or less than optimal way, just as parents cope when an adolescent distances in terms of achieving independence. Leaving home—or a safe haven—is difficult. As with other issues in relational treatment, it is best if the issue is discussed, mutually decided, and undertaken with preparation, but that is not always the way it happens. The question of termination, of course, raises the question of what the outline may be for a posttherapy relationship, if any.

Posttherapy Contacts

Therapists have different values and policies regarding posttherapy contact. Some accept phone calls, e-mails, and visits, possibly even a meeting for coffee or lunch, as an extension of their ongoing concern for the now ex-client. Others are uncomfortable with maintaining any form of contact: They may endorse a therapeutic orientation that such contact is invariably infantilizing and calls up transference feelings. Whatever the therapist's stance, it should be based on a careful assessment with the former client about whether it is in the individual's best interest, whether it will be manageable, and whether it will interfere with the ending itself and the client's newly developed independence. An extratherapeutic relationship may make a needed return to therapy for additional treatment difficult, if not impossible, so the situation calls for caution and informed consent.

Although some professional ethics codes allow the establishment of romantic or sexual relationship with past clients several years posttherapy (American Psychological Association, 2002), others strictly forbid such a relationship. Due to the potential for retraumatization that characterizes this treatment population, and due to the power dynamics involved in the relationship between therapist and client, the development of a romantic/sexual relationship is fraught with the potential to damage the ex-client. For this reason, such a relationship with complex trauma survivor clients is inadvisable under any circumstance and patently unethical in some instances.

The Outcome

When this therapy works, changes can be dramatic. A client can move from a life completely centered on trauma, flashbacks, fear of abandonment, self-harm, and tolerance of exploitation to relative stability, coherence, safety, warmth, and human connection. Kinsler had the challenge and privilege to work for years with a woman who had previously spent a quarter of a million dollars on psychiatric hospitalizations. Multiple prior therapies had failed. In establishing therapy goals at the beginning, the client was quite frustrated and blurted out, "I just want to have *normal person problems.*" Years later, the client had not been in hospital for 5 years. The chronically dysfunctional relationship with her husband had become a working partnership. Two children with previously chaotic lives had become honor students. Therapist and client noticed that they had spent three or four sessions discussing where one child was applying to college, whether another would get into a prep school, and whether the client's (formerly chronically unemployed) husband would get a promotion. Therapist and client looked at each other in recognition and mutually realized that the client had achieved "normal person problems." They proceeded to a smooth, kind, and warm ending. This kind of therapy can achieve profound and long-lasting changes.

In this chapter, we have discussed the relational "teachings" that can occur for clients with multiple traumatizations in childhood, and have presented a therapy method based on the relational healing of such relational injuries, along with the parameters for conducting such a therapy, and for managing the risks of this deeply interconnected therapy method.

REFERENCES

Allen, J. G. (2001). *Traumatic relationships and serious mental disorders.* Chichester, UK: Wiley.

Allen, J. G. (2005). *Coping with trauma: Hope through understanding* (2nd ed.). Washington, DC: American Psychiatric Press.

American Psychological Association. (2002). *Ethical principles of psychologists and code of conduct.* Washington, DC: Author.

Binder, J. L. (2004). *Key competencies in brief dynamic psychotherapy: Clinical practice beyond the manual.* New York: Guilford Press.

Bowlby, J. (1969). *Attachment and loss: Vol. 1: Attachment.* New York: Basic Books.

Bowlby, J. (1980). *Attachment and loss: Vol. 3: Loss.* New York: Basic Books.

Chu, J. (1988). Ten traps for therapists in the treatment of trauma survivors. *Dissociation, 1*(4), 24–32.

Chu, J. (1992). The therapeutic roller coaster: Dilemmas in the treatment of childhood abuse survivors. *Journal of Psychotherapy: Practice and Research, 1,* 351–370.

Cloitre, M., Cohen, L. R., & Koenen, K. C. (2006). *Treating survivors of childhood abuse: Psychotherapy for the interrupted life.* New York: Guilford Press.

Cloitre, M., Stovall-McClough, C., Miranda, K., & Chemtob, C. M. (2004). Therapeutic alliance, negative mood regulation, and treatment outcome in child abuse-related posttraumatic stress disorder. *Journal of Consulting and Clinical Psychology, 72*(3), 411–416.

Conterio, K., & Lader, W. (1998). *Bodily self-harm: The breakthrough healing program for self-injurers.* New York: Hyperion.

Copeland, M. E., & Harris, M. (2000). *Healing the trauma of abuse: A women's workbook.* Oakland, CA: New Harbinger.

Courtois, C. A. (1999). *Recollections of sexual abuse: Treatment principles and guidelines.* New York: Norton.

Dalenberg, C. (2000).*Countertransference and the treatment of trauma*. Washington, DC: American Psychological Association.

Dube, S., Anda, R., Felitti, V., Chapman, D., Williamson, D., & Giles, W. (2001). Childhood abuse, household dysfunction, and the risk of attempted suicide throughout the life span. *Journal of the American Medical Association, 286*, 3089–3095.

Dube, S., Felitti, V., Dong, M., Chapman, D., Giles, W., & Anda, R. (2007). Childhood abuse, neglect and household dysfunction and the risk of illicit drug use. *Pediatrics, 111*, 564–572.

Edwards, V., Holden, G., Felitti, V., & Anda, R. (2003). Relationship between multiple forms of childhood maltreatment and adult mental health in community respondents. *American Journal of Psychiatry, 160*(8), 1453–1460.

Erikson, E. H. (1950). *Childhood and society*. New York: Norton.

Fonagy, P. (1997). Attachment and theory of mind: Overlapping constructs? *Association for Child Psychology and Psychiatry Occasional Papers, 14*, 31–40.

Frankel, A. S. (2002). *What I have learned*. Presidential Plenary Lecture, 19th Annual Fall Conference of the International Society for the Study of Dissociation, Baltimore.

Frankl, V. (1963). *Man's search for meaning: An introduction to logotherapy*. Oxford, UK: Washington Square Press.

Herman, J. L. (1992). *Trauma and recovery*. New York: Basic Books.

Hubble, M., Duncan, B., & Miller, S. (1999). *The heart and soul of change: What works in psychotherapy*. Washington, DC: American Psychological Association.

Janoff-Bulman, R. (1992). *Shattered assumptions: Towards a new psychology of trauma*. New York: Free Press.

Jobes, D. A. (2006). *Managing suicidal risk: A collaborative approach*. New York: Guilford Press.

Linehan, M. M. (1993). *Cognitive-behavioral treatment of borderline personality disorder*. New York: Guilford Press.

Lyons-Ruth, K., & Jacobovitz, D. (1999). Attachment disorganization unresolved loss, relational violence, and lapses in behavioral and attentional strategies. In J. Cassidy & P. R. Shaver (Eds.), *Handbook of attachment: Theory, research, and clinical applications* (pp. 520–554). New York: Guilford Press.

McCann, I. L., & Pearlman, L. A. (1990). *Psychological trauma and the adult survivor*. New York: Brunner/Mazel.

Miller, D. (1994). *Women who hurt themselves*. New York: Basic Books.

Najavits, L. (2002). *A women's addiction workbook*. Oakland, CA: New Harbinger.

Ogden, P., Pain, C., & Minton, K. (2006). *Trauma and the body*. New York: Norton.

Pearlman, L. A., & Courtois, C. A. (2005). Clinical applications of the attachment framework: Relational treatment of complex trauma. *Journal of Traumatic Stress, 18*(5), 449–459.

Pearlman, L. A., & Saakvitne, K. W. (1995). *Trauma and the therapist: Countertransference and vicarious traumatization in psychotherapy with incest survivors*. New York: Norton.

Schore, A. N. (2003a). *Affect dysregulation and disorders of the self*. New York: Norton.

Schore, A. N. (2003b). *Affect dysregulation and the repair of the self*. New York: Norton.

Shorey, H., & Snyder, C. (2006). The role of adult attachment styles in psychopathology and psychotherapy outcomes. *Review of General Psychology, 10*(1), 1–20.

Siegel, D. (2007). *The mindful brain: Reflection and attunement in the cultivation of well-being*. New York: Norton.

Valory, M. (2007). Earning a secure attachment style: A narrative of personality change in adulthood. In R. Josselson, A. Lieblich, & D. P. McAdams (Eds.), *The meaning of others* (pp. 93–116). Washington, DC: American Psychological Association.

Vermilyea, E. (2000). *Growing beyond survival: A self-help toolkit for managing traumatic stress*. Baltimore: Sidran Press.

Winnicott, D. W. (1965). *The maturational process and the facilitating environment: Studies in the theory of emotional development*. New York: International Universities Press.

Young, J. E., Klosko, J. S., & Weishaar, M. E. (2003). *Schema therapy: A practitioner's guide*. New York: Guilford Press.

CHAPTER 10

Living and Working Self-Reflectively to Address Vicarious Trauma

Laurie Anne Pearlman
James Caringi

Supporting the recovery of people who have been affected by severe, pro-longed, or early violence, neglect, or abuse is an honor and a challenge. It is an honor because it requires earning the trust of those whose trust has been compromised in other relationships. It is a challenge because it requires the therapist to maintain self-awareness and attention to emotional reactions and behaviors, while remaining attuned to the client's needs. The empathic engagement necessary for truly therapeutic relationships with this population often has transformative negative personal repercussions for the therapist, a process that has been labeled vicarious traumatization (VT; McCann & Pearlman, 1990b; Pearlman & Saakvitne, 1995). In this chapter, we describe VT as it is experienced by helpers working with complex trauma survivors, discuss both a possible mechanism for and particular client factors that contribute to VT, suggest ways helpers can address it, and provide some research and policy suggestions. *The primary goal is to support helpers (psychotherapists, domestic violence advocates, and social services providers; humanitarian assistance workers; crisis center, shelter, and hotline staff; clergy; health care workers; law enforcement and justice system personnel; and mental health and rehabilitation staff) in protecting themselves in ways that enable them to provide better services to persons with complex psychological trauma.*

DEFINITION

VT is the negative transformation in the helper that results from empathic engagement with trauma survivors and their trauma material, combined with a commitment or responsibility to help them. Its hallmark is disrupted spirituality, just as with direct psychological trauma, in which the signature loss is that of meaning and hope. The VT construct emerged primarily from observations of the effects of working with complex trauma survivors who experienced multiple forms of childhood abuse and neglect (McCann & Pearlman, 1990b). Although the VT literature does not explicitly differentiate between those who work with persons with complex trauma ("Type II") and other kinds of trauma ("Type I") (Terr, 1989), the theoretical literature largely refers to, and the research literature has primarily studied, helpers who work with complex trauma. It does, however, apply to helpers working with all forms of traumatization. The study of VT focuses on the self and well-being of the helper. Although psychoanalytic theory has long been interested in the self of the therapist as a technical factor, the focus on the helper's well-being is a newer area of study. We draw here from some of the relevant therapist well-being literature but focus very specifically on VT, its risk factors, mechanism of development, and antidotes as they apply to helpers working with complex trauma.

Constructivist self development theory (CSDT; McCann & Pearlman, 1990b), the foundation for the VT construct, suggests that helpers' unique VT responses arise from an interaction between the helper and the situation (McCann & Pearlman, 1990a). Recent research with trauma therapists has indeed found "different patterns of reactions to trauma work" (Wilson & Thomas, 2004, p. 171). These are responses that parallel victims' and survivors' adaptations, including common posttraumatic signs, symptoms, and relational patterns. Several researchers have addressed symptoms of VT and related concepts that correspond to those of complex trauma. Disturbances in cognitive schemas; symptoms of posttraumatic stress, such as avoidance, hyperarousal, and numbing; relational adaptations, such as aggression, reenactments, and difficulty with boundary management; as well as general psychological stress have been identified (Arvay & Uhlemann, 1996; Bober, Regehr, & Zhou, 2006; Brady, Guy, Poelstra, & Brokaw, 1999; Cunningham, 1999; Ghahramanlou & Brodbeck, 2000; Schauben & Frazier, 1995). Anecdotal accounts from complex trauma clinicians include reports of dissociation and depersonalization during sessions, intimacy and sexual difficulties, somatization, social isolation, and loss of meaning and hope. Wilson and Thomas (2004) reported results of the Clinicians' Trauma Reaction Survey, a study of 345 therapists. Using Wilson and Lindy's (1994b) conceptual framework of empathic strain, Pearlman and colleagues' conceptual work on vicarious trauma (McCann & Pearlman, 1990b; Pearlman & Saakvitne, 1995), and Figley's (1995) work on compassion fatigue, these researchers documented five factors of professionals' reactions to trauma work: (1) unmodulated affect in response to clients' trauma narratives; (2) somatic complaints; (3) posttraumatic stress disorder (PTSD) symptoms; (4) impact on personal frame of reference; and (5) symptoms associated with PTSD, such as acute traumatic stress disorder, depression, and anxiety (Wilson & Thomas, 2004, p. 154). These categories are concordant with the adaptations of survivors with complex trauma.

VT can be differentiated from the related constructs of countertransference, burnout, and compassion fatigue. *Vicarious trauma* refers to the negative changes that can take place in trauma workers across time, whereas *countertransference* (Freud, 1912) describes the therapist's responses to a single client, whether trauma is involved or not (see Pearlman & Saakvitne, 1995, for a discussion of this distinction). Countertransference focuses primarily on the therapist's role in that process, whereas *burnout* focuses on the situation, the gap between what the helper is expected to do and what he or she is able to do. In contrast to *burnout* (Freudenberger, 1974) and *compassion fatigue* (formerly known as secondary traumatic stress disorder; Figley, 1995), which focuses on the parallel trauma symptoms that helpers may develop in working with traumatized clients, VT is not an endpoint, nor is it best understood by its symptoms.

Wilson and Thomas (2004) conceptualize therapist responses of compassion fatigue, VT, and secondary traumatic stress syndrome as "traumatoid states," a sort of "occupationally related stress response syndrome" (p. 143). Whereas gathering these responses into one syndrome can be useful in calling attention to therapist responses, that process may gloss over important nuances in each construct. The value in gathering is simplicity and parsimony; the cost is loss of the richness of specific ways for helpers to understand their own contributing factors and to design their own management and treatment strategies.

The unique value of the VT construct is in its theoretical base, CSDT (McCann & Pearlman, 1990a; Pearlman & Saakvitne, 1995). With any clinical issue, a theoretical framework guides treatment. It allows for connections among observations (signs, symptoms, adaptations), as well as suggests etiology and treatment possibilities. CSDT frames symptoms as adaptations rather than pathologizing normal responses to abnormal events. It identifies areas of the self that are affected by both direct and indirect trauma, providing a basis for understanding myriad individual symptoms (e.g., social withdrawal, dissociation, self-injury) that may arise from negative effects on one area of self-functioning (e.g., affect tolerance). Thus, the theory base of the VT construct allows for a valuable depth and complexity of comprehension and avenues for intervention. In addition to signs and symptoms, the theory describes what contributes to vicarious trauma and how helpers can ameliorate it. The theory base supports helpers in addressing their VT, so that it is less likely to curtail their effectiveness and their work-related satisfaction. Vicarious trauma is an experience that parallels that of direct trauma, with similar, if less intense, characteristic responses; however, if left unaddressed, it can escalate in severity until it meets criteria for a psychiatric diagnosis such as PTSD, other anxiety disorders, mood disorders, and substance abuse disorders. The alterations in meaning, relationships, and overall life satisfaction can resemble those of complex trauma survivor clients, although one would expect the helper's work-related difficulties to be less intense than those related to clients' direct traumatic experiences.

It is not yet known whether VT is inevitable in trauma treatment. Research findings, as well as anecdotal evidence from experienced clinicians, suggest that most, if not all, helpers experience some negative transformation of their personal frame of reference (spirituality, worldview, and identity), relationships, ability to self-regulate emotional states, judgment or decision-making abilities, and/or bodily experiences. Left unaddressed, VT can have deleterious effects on helpers and on those they assist. It is important to emphasize that *neither clients nor negligent helpers are responsible for VT*. Rather, it is an occupational hazard, a cost of doing the work. Helpers must respond through recognizing and managing it.

A HYPOTHESIZED MECHANISM UNDERLYING VT

The hypothesized mechanism for the development of VT is the helper's *empathic engagement with the client* (Pearlman & Saakvitne, 1995). Specifically, when helpers enter empathically into the world of trauma clients and their responses are not adequately processed, VT can result. The many contributing factors (discussed below) identified in both the clinical and research literature can increase the risks to helpers. When the helper opens him- or herself to another's pain, he or she may experience personal distress or empathy. Personal distress arises when one imagines *personally experiencing* the traumatic event, resulting in negative feelings. Empathy arises from imagining *what the client experienced* and results in compassion for the other and prosocial behavior (Batson, Fultz, & Schoenrade, 1987). The empathy research literature suggests that responding, whether with personal distress or empathy, is determined by both personality and situation characteristics. Batson and colleagues (1987) define *emotional empathy* as "other-focused feelings evoked by perceiving another person in need" (p. 19). They distinguish "two distinct types of congruent emotional responses to perceiving another in need: feelings of personal distress (e.g., alarmed, upset, worried, disturbed, distressed, troubled, etc.) and feelings of empathy (e.g., sympathetic, moved, compassionate, tender, warm, softhearted, etc.)" (p. 19). If unprocessed, both empathic responses and personal distress can lead to VT.

Dalenberg (2000) has documented the harmful effects reported by clients concerning therapists' unprocessed trauma-related countertransference. *We propose here that helpers' personal distress and empathic responses, if processed adequately, can result in growth for both client and helper.* We elaborate here the contribution of unprocessed countertransference responses, and the possibilities for growth in the section on coping with and transforming vicarious trauma.

Other authors have also proposed empathy as the mechanism that creates the opening for countertransference responses (Wilson & Lindy, 1994b), compassion fatigue (Figley, 1995), and vicarious trauma (Pearlman & Saakvitne, 1995) in work with trauma survivors. Empathy in the treatment of trauma survivors was the topic of research by Thomas (1998), reported by Wilson and Thomas (2004), who define *empathic attunement* as "the capacity to resonate efficiently and accurately to another's state of being; to match self–other understanding; to have knowledge of the internal psychological ego-states of another who has suffered a trauma; and to understand the unique internal working model/schema of their trauma experience" (p. 7).

In a research study of 183 psychotherapists, Moosman (2002) examined the relation between empathy and vicarious trauma. Although she did not find a relationship between general emotional empathy and VT (as measured by the Traumatic Stress Institute [TSI] Belief Scale; Pearlman, 1996, 2003), she did find that those who were "highly emotionally reactive" in their empathic engagement with clients were more likely to experience vicarious trauma. Moosman's (2002) study is consistent with the research on personal distress, as distinct from empathy (Batson et al., 1987). Within this framework, Moosman's findings can be interpreted as making a link between personal distress (or emotional reactivity) and changed cognitions (as measured by the TSI Belief Scale), one aspect of vicarious trauma.

Rodrigo (2005) proposes traumatic contagion as a possible mechanism for developing VT. *Contagion* may represent an "unconscious exchange of traumatic material (thoughts, feelings, and imagery)" (p. 157). In this sense, contagion is consistent with the process of empathic engagement, which is necessary in the treatment of complex trauma and, indeed, in any successful psychotherapy relationship.

In *Help for the Helper*, Babette Rothschild (2006) offers support from the psychophysiology literature for empathy as the mechanism in the development of VT. She presents the neurophysiology of empathy in a readily comprehensible style. Building on the work of clinical neuroscience researchers, Rothschild suggests that mirror neurons are the physical tool that allows the helper to tune in to the client's experience, with potential for both positive and negative effects on the helper. The negative effects, sometimes in the form of VT, occur when the helper takes on the affect states of the client through the empathy process. Lamm, Batson, and Decety (2007) found that instructions to research participants about taking the perspective of pain to self or to other altered participants' neural responses to the observed pain, which Lamm and colleagues connected to the distinction between personal distress and empathy.

CONTRIBUTING FACTORS TO VT IN THE TREATMENT OF COMPLEX PSYCHOLOGICAL TRAUMA

Possible interacting contributors to VT can be grouped as follows: (1) aspects of the work (situation variables, which include things such as relational dynamics, horrific experiences that many complex trauma survivors disclose and discuss, interaction between the dynamics and the stories on the one hand, and the confidentiality demands of the work on the other, amount of trauma work or exposure); (2) aspects of the helper (person variables, such as personal history, coping style, current life stressors, attachment style); and (3) sociocultural context (including social realities such as racism, sexism, poverty, and injustice, which often are elements of complex trauma clients' traumatic experiences and recovery environments). We discuss only particular aspects of work with complex trauma survivors that are not addressed extensively elsewhere (Pearlman & Saakvitne, 1995; Saakvitne, Gamble, Pearlman, & Lev, 2000; Saakvitne, Pearlman, & the Staff of the Traumatic Stress Institute, 1996).

CONTRIBUTING FACTORS: ASPECTS OF THE WORK

Although there are differences in what affects helpers as individuals and in how they respond to each potential contributing factor, there also are effects of working with survivors of complex psychological trauma that increase the likelihood of VT in any helper. In this section, we focus first on complex trauma survivors' adaptations, then on the traumatic experiences that can give rise to complex trauma as a potential situational contributing factor.

Adaptations

The adaptations that characterize the population of complex trauma survivors can provide ongoing challenges in treatment relationships. Many adult survivors of childhood neglect and abuse exhibit insecure or disorganized attachment. (See Pearlman & Courtois, 2005, for further discussion.) These attachment styles give rise to certain developmental problems, or disrupted areas of the self and relationships (elaborated below). These disruptions are reflected in symptoms that affect life functioning, including relationship and life satisfaction concerns that often propel people to psychotherapy.

CSDT posits four realms of self development to be affected by early or severe violence or neglect: self capacities, psychological needs, frame of reference, and the memory system (McCann & Pearlman, 1990a; Pearlman & Saakvitne, 1995; Saakvitne et al., 2000). In addition, we briefly discuss a fifth realm, survivors' bodily responses to early or severe violence, neglect, or abuse, as they may contribute to helpers' vicarious trauma.

Disrupted Self Capacities

Underdeveloped self capacities include affect tolerance, self-worth, and lack of an internalized benign other (Brock, Pearlman, & Varra, 2006; Pearlman, 1998). Diminished self capacities are reflected in the emotional dysregulation that is apparent in intense and rapidly changing affect states, dissociation (Briere, 2006), aggression toward others, and self-injurious acts (Connors, 2000; Deiter, Nicholls, & Pearlman, 2000), among many other behaviors. These affect states give rise to very intense and challenging transference and countertransference responses, and pose significant challenges to helpers, who must manage their own affect, while providing a calm, compassionate, therapeutic presence.

The intensity of affect that is common early in the recovery process of these clients is a major contributor to countertransference responses, as is the tendency to enact rather than talk about strong feelings and dysregulated affect. When the helper is the object of a negative transference, the client may view him or her not simply as a fallible parent or other important figure from the past but as a persecutor, abuser, torturer, and/or abandoner. When a client finds it difficult to trust or respect the helper due to past traumatic experiences, he or she may enact these feelings in the helping relationship, sometimes without obvious reference in the present. The helper who does not expect or understand the transference process and attachment style, and is not cognizant of his or her own countertransference, may react with equally intense feelings toward the client. Over time, if the helper is not able to process these responses, then he or she cannot use them productively, and they can accumulate and contribute to VT.

Dissociation is another feature of complex traumatic stress disorders (Steele & van der Hart, Chapter 7, this volume). CSDT conceptualizes dissociation as a cognitive disruption (McCann & Pearlman, 1990b) resulting from inadequately developed self capacities (Pearlman, 1998; Saakvitne et al., 2000). Dissociation may lead clients to be disconnected from helpers or the helping relationship in ways that interfere with the recovery process. A client may "leave" the relationship, or demonstrate an inability to make a connection. When the client dissociates and/or is incoherent in his or her presentation of self, the helper may feel lost, abandoned, confused, frustrated, or de-skilled (Pearlman & Saakvitne, 1995). The work is interrupted, and the helper may feel frustrated about the lack of continuity in the relationship and treatment. The helper may also become the repository of feelings the client has dissociated. For example, a client with a horrific trauma history was in the process of recounting an episode of abuse to her therapist when she dissociated and regressed, talking as if she were a young child, conveying her intense fear to the therapist. The therapist was surprised at this unexpected behavior, disoriented, and challenged by the demand to respond quickly to the client's fear—all with only 10 minutes left in the session. Even less dramatic episodes of dissociation can wreak havoc with the helper's internal state, and as this havoc accumulates over time it can contribute to VT.

Clients with complex trauma also may direct aggressive behaviors toward themselves or others, in the form of substance abuse, chronic suicidality, or other types of self-injury, including cutting, biting, burning, and so forth (Connors, 2000; Deiter et al., 2000). Unfortunately, it is not uncommon for childhood abuse survivors to become involved in adult relationships in which they are again being victimized (Messman-Moore & Long, 2003). When helpers witness these behaviors across clients and feel helpless to intervene effectively, they may experience VT. The helper's lack of control echoes the victim's experiences during the traumatic events.

Disrupted Psychological Needs

People who have endured terrible victimization experience disruptions in central psychological needs such as safety, trust, esteem, intimacy, and control (Pearlman, 2003); they generally bring these disruptions to the helping relationship, either directly or indirectly. When clients chronically mistrust and feel the need to control helpers, express lack of security in their presence, are unable or unwilling to open up over time, treat helpers disrespectfully without apparent reason, and expect to be exploited by helpers in some way, they challenge helpers' identities and functions. In addition, these disrupted needs may lead to chronic social isolation of the client. For the helper whose work is based in a desire to be helpful and to see clients' lives improve, ongoing client relationship difficulties (including with the helper) can contribute to VT, challenging the helper's values, effectiveness, and identity. Finally, it seems possible that disrupted needs for trust, safety, and control might be at the core of behaviors such as the tendency "to test, manipulate, and control the therapist, and not infrequently ... [to behave] abusively toward him or her" (Kluft, 1994, p. 126). These behaviors and related countertransference responses, if unprocessed, can further contribute to VT.

Disrupted Frame of Reference

Perhaps most profoundly, severe and prolonged traumatization affects survivors' ability to remain connected to personal meaning making, hope, and something that transcends self and relationships with others (although Tokayer, 2002, found that for some survivors, traumatic experiences ignite a search for meaning). Disrupted "systems of meaning" (van der Kolk et al., 1996) reflect limitations in the development of the self and impede the development of satisfying interpersonal relationships. Disrupted spirituality is a hallmark of both direct and indirect trauma, and rampant cynicism or despair in clients with complex trauma can challenge the helper's sense of meaning and hope, resulting in "passion depletion" (McKay, personal communication, March 25, 2008). The loss of innocence that some helpers experience as their worldviews shift may induce grief, another dimension of VT (Cunningham, 1999).

Disrupted Memory System

Reenactments of victim–perpetrator–bystander dynamics, not uncommon among complex trauma survivors, can be unnerving and leave the helper feeling "de-skilled" and hopeless (Putnam, 1989; for valuable discussions of this pattern, see Davies & Frawley, 1994; Miller, 1994). CSDT conceptualizes enactments and reenactments as arising from disrupted memory systems; that is, rather than remembering in words and images, traumatized people implicitly remember what happened to them through current behaviors or actions that are a repetition of the past. Reenactments may serve to support a fragmented identity through the reliving of familiar patterns. They also may reflect disrupted affect regulation (self-soothing through familiar behavior patterns), memory integration (remembering by reliving), and psychological needs (for safety and control, with attempted reassertion through reenactments). Becoming entangled in reenactments or witnessing clients' revictimization can contribute to VT. The helper's identity as a "protective presence" (Miller, 1994) or "active bystander" (Staub, 2003) is challenged, as are the helper's worldview (including a comprehension of relationships as reflecting one's presence) and the helper's own needs for control, esteem, and trust.

Bodily Responses

Researchers and clinicians increasingly understand and are documenting the extra burden of chronically aroused physiology and related physical health problems among complex trauma survivors (Dube, Felitti, Dong, Giles, & Anda, 2003; Kendall-Tackett, 2004; Schnurr & Green, 2004). In addition, *somatization*, meaning either the physical representation of psychological problems or medically unexplained symptoms, is also common in this population (van der Kolk et al., 1996). When helpers witness the excessive physical health problems, coupled with the difficulty many survivors have in finding appropriate medical care, they may feel like helpless witnesses. This experience of helplessness repeats the client's original traumatic situation, reviving the victim–perpetrator–bystander dynamic. Furthermore, when a client reacts to the therapy process with body pain or illness and is alexithymic, the helper may experience guilt, frustration, or anger at the client's inability to put feelings into words.

Traumatic Events

Pearlman and Saakvitne (1995) have written about vicarious trauma that arises in response to the specifics of clients' traumatic experiences. Danieli (1981) used the term *event countertransference* to describe the therapist's reactions to the realities of specific traumatic events. Along these lines, Danieli described therapists' affective reactions to and defenses against the realities of the Holocaust. Haley (1974), Herman (1992), and Wilson and Lindy (1994b) have also described countertransference responses to the event itself. Unless addressed, such responses can be harmful to clients. The helper must choose between taking in the horrors of people's capacity to harm one another, which assaults the helper's spirituality and worldview, and denying survivors' realities, thus abandoning one's clients and one's own identity as helping professional. Such choices can contribute to helpers' VT.

CONTRIBUTING FACTORS: ASPECTS OF THE HELPER

Many aspects of helpers as individuals (e.g., personality and temperament, ego resources, coping styles, personal history, support system) and as professionals (e.g., level of training and experience, theoretical orientation, and the way one works) may contribute to or protect against experiencing vicarious trauma. In this section, we discuss two aspects of the helper that are especially salient to work with complex trauma clients: personal trauma history and an avoidant interpersonal style.

Personal Trauma History

Research examining the role of the helper's personal trauma history in the development of VT has produced mixed findings, at least in part because of the varied ways both personal trauma history and VT are assessed (see Bride, 2004, for a review of the literature addressing personal trauma history related to VT). It is now apparent that helpers with trauma histories (sometimes referred to as "wounded healers") may bring both special gifts and unique responses to the work. Having "walked the path" can bring a depth of understanding that might otherwise be less available. The ability to identify seems to increase when the helper and the client share similar experiences. In Wilson and Thomas's (2004) study of 345 trauma therapists, most therapists with their own trauma history were working with clients who had experienced a similar type of trauma. For example, Wilson and Thomas found that 81% of their sample with a history of adult sexual assault reported treating clients with the same kind of experience; 100% of therapists who were war veterans were treating other veterans; other types of concordant traumatic experiences ranged between 81 and 100% (pp. 158–163). The researchers did not note whether these were the only or the primary survivor groups their respondents treated. But this finding does suggest the importance of self-awareness for survivor therapists who may overidentify, then respond to clients' experiences in ways that are countertherapeutic and potentially hazardous for them.

Thayer (personal communication, February 8, 2007) has suggested that the role of the helper's trauma history in motivation to do the work may also be key in determining whether he or she experiences more VT than someone without a trauma history or for whom that history is not a motivating factor; that is, the therapist who is seeking personal healing through the work *instead of* through his or her own growth and change processes may be more susceptible to VT as his or her own history is awakened and the ability to help the client or him- or herself is impeded. In a similar vein, Pearlman and Mac Ian (1995) explored the role of personal trauma history in their study of 188 trauma therapists. Those therapists with a personal trauma history who had the most disrupted cognitive schemas were less likely to be receiving clinical supervision than those with fewer disruptions, and the former were addressing the effects of their work in their personal psychotherapies. Clearly, this population of therapists would very much benefit from ongoing consultation and/or supervision (and personal therapy, as needed).

Helper Avoidance

Another factor contributing to VT is the chronic or persistent *avoidance* of clients' pain, described by Wilson, Lindy, and Raphael (1994) as a "Type I" countertransference response. They group avoidant, counterphobic, and detachment responses together, and contrast them to "Type II" responses, which include overidentification, enmeshment, and rescuer responses. It is likely that the persistent avoidance or detachment from clients that serves a defensive purpose (managing the helper's anxiety) does not actually protect the helper from either the negative impact of the complex trauma survivors' stories of violation and pain or the negative experience of being drawn into a victim–perpetrator–bystander enactment. When helpers respond persistently with avoidance, they are less able to process the pain, fear, sorrow, frustration, anger, and resentment that may build over time across these treatment relationships. This cumulative unprocessed countertransference can contribute to VT.

One final dimension deserves mention here: the helper's attachment style. Marmaras and Lee (2006) reported results of a study of the impact of attachment styles on VT in female trauma therapists. Those with an insecure attachment style who treated trauma survivors reported more symptoms of VT than did secure therapists. Significant relationships were found among the attachment styles of the therapists (secure vs. insecure), their cognitive schemas, and their symptoms of avoidance, intrusion, and hyperarousal, which they considered to be VT symptoms. The authors stated:

> The findings of the present study with respect to attachment and vicarious traumatization may provide a theoretical framework to understand the effect of vicarious traumatization from a developmental perspective. The implication of these findings may be that therapists with insecure attachment style who as a result may have experienced negative self-worth and/or negative view of others, interpersonal difficulties in close relationships, and discomfort with intense emotions, may hinder the therapeutic process and provide a disservice to trauma survivors. (pp. 18–19)

This perspective also suggests implications for training of trauma therapists, for self-care (as discussed below), and for ongoing consultation and supervision.

CONTRIBUTING FACTORS: ASPECTS OF THE SOCIAL–CULTURAL CONTEXT

An important aspect of the context that may contribute to VT (see Pearlman & Saakvitne, 1995, for others) is the *lack of support that agencies generally provide for client services and for staff* working with complex trauma (Pryce, Shackelford, & Pryce, 2007). These clients are often the most marginalized members of society because of both the stigma of their traumatic experiences and their complex psychological, interpersonal, physical, social, economic, and spiritual problems. One practical consequence is that many survivors do not have means for private treatment; thus, they receive treatment in public systems that are notoriously underresourced. Complex humanitarian emergencies, such as those stimulated by Hurricane Katrina or the genocides in Darfur and Rwanda, often take the greatest toll on people who started out with very little. The combination of multifaceted needs and inadequate resources, including staff support, can contribute to helpers' frustration, helplessness, hopelessness, and VT, particularly when clients' or beneficiaries' traumatic experiences continue into the present and may be ongoing (e.g., homelessness, disrupted communities, domestic violence, sexual harassment, and other forms of revictimization). In failing in their intention and commitment to assist, helpers may experience guilt and challenges to their worldview, identity, and their own experience of meaning and hope. The notion of staff care as essential to helper and client well-being in these settings has only recently emerged (Fawcett, 2003; McKay, 2004; Pearlman & McKay, 2008; Pryce et al., 2007; Saakvitne et al., 2000).

Other problems related to specific aspects of a sociocultural context may also affect psychotherapists working with complex trauma clients. For example, in private practice and clinic settings, managed care and other insurance restrictions, as well as clinic policies and procedures, may limit treatment duration. Yet chronic problems of self-worth and meaning often require longer-rather than shorter-term treatment. These clients often require a long time to develop enough trust in the therapist to allow them to then reveal their innermost feelings, thoughts, and struggles.

Other clients with complex trauma, such as domestic violence survivors with childhood trauma histories, may return repeatedly to harmful situations, while they are in the process of developing alternatives. During this long-term treatment process, both public and private insurers may require frequent updates, sometimes challenging the need for continuing treatment. Although it is certainly important to develop goals, assess progress in treatment, and spend public monies judiciously, it is also essential to convey to survivors that they are equal citizens, entitled to remediation. Continuous struggles for payment leave helpers and clients feeling frustrated, questioning the value of their work, and often at odds with one another. These feelings can contribute to VT when helpers experience the helplessness that parallels that of clients and again find themselves in the role of passive bystander to others' suffering.

Public mental health, child welfare, and substance abuse treatment are generally underfunded, and there is often an understandable, if shortsighted, attitude that all resources must be directed toward client care, and that staff care is a luxury or boondoggle. Research and clinical experience increasingly support the essential role staff care plays in these settings.

COPING WITH AND TRANSFORMING VT:
SELF-CARE AND BEYOND

The theoretical and clinical literatures offer suggestions for addressing VT (Figley, 2002a, 2002b; Saakvitne et al., 1996, 2000; Stamm, 1999). We highlight four aspects of self-care: social support, professional consultation, spiritual renewal, and "radical self-care."

Social Support

The literature indicates that *social support* is one of the most robust correlates of well-being and recovery from traumatic stress. Indeed, it may be thought of as an extension of healthy attachment behavior. Trauma helpers may find their lives and jobs more fulfilling, and may be less likely to develop VT if they create personal and professional networks and communities (Catherall, 1995; Munroe et al., 1995; Rosenbloom, Pratt, & Pearlman, 1995). Social support may be a source of both emotional and instrumental assistance. Each helper gains some inoculation to the corrosive effects of trauma work by deliberately defining and creating one or more meaningful and supportive communities that serve to broaden identity beyond that of "trauma helper," and that promote personal well-being through interpersonal connection.

Consultation

Helpers in various settings often work without the benefit of professional consultation. Pearlman and her colleagues have written about the importance of ongoing trauma-informed consultation for this work (Pearlman & Courtois, 2005; Pearlman & Saakvitne, 1995). The intensity and complexity of transference–countertransference dynamics in complex trauma relationships are such that working without clinical consultation, at any level of helper experience, can pose great hazards for both clients and therapists. Consultation allows helpers to acknowledge and reflect upon their reactions to complex trauma clients' often intense feelings and sometimes extreme behaviors. Examining personal responses in a supportive, confidential, trauma-informed, professional consulting relationship can be a powerful source of support in identifying and managing VT. Consultation provides a forum for processing empathic responses, as well as personal distress.

Spiritual Renewal

Perhaps most important in ameliorating VT responses, especially despair and hopelessness, is the development of a *spiritual life*. Given the posited central role of spirituality, or meaning systems, to trauma, of course, it is essential to attend to the development of whatever is self-nourishing. There are many paths to spirituality. For some it involves engaging in traditional practices such as prayer and organized religion. For others, it means creating or finding community, being useful to others, enjoying nature, or seeking awe, joy, beauty, and wonder in relationships and in nature. We encourage helpers to find or to create their own meaningful spiritual practices to counter the dispiriting challenges that accompany work with complex trauma.

Positive psychology suggests some dimensions that may be relevant to the transformation of VT. Peterson and Seligman (2004) have suggested that aligning your life to your "signature" strengths, using those strengths to contribute to others, and experiencing gratitude can contribute to personal happiness and fulfillment. These processes seem spiritual in nature, because they connect the helper with his or her authentic self, allowing and supporting self-transcendence. They may also contribute to spiritual renewal to mitigate VT.

One of the best antidotes to VT is to be transformed positively by the work, a process that might be termed *vicarious transformation*. Opening the self to the darker aspects of human experience can contribute to personal and professional perspective and growth. Developing a frame of reference that includes some way of making sense of the human capacity for cruelty and evil allows the helper to approach the work with more equanimity. Understanding why such horrors occur is not the same as accepting their inevitability or forgiving harmdoers. Indeed, trauma helpers may be moved to social activism, another strategy that might help to transform VT. Hernandez, Gangsei, and Engstrom (2007) have researched the positive effects reported by psychotherapists who work with victims of political torture. They coined the term *vicarious resilience* to describe the "complex array of elements contributing to the empowerment of therapists through interaction with clients' stories of resilience" (p. 238). They grouped the effects, based on interviews with 12 therapists, as follows:

> witnessing and reflecting on human beings' immense capacity to heal; reassessing the significance of the therapists' own problems; incorporating spirituality as a valuable dimension in treatment; developing hope and commitment; articulating personal and professional positions regarding political violence; articulating frameworks for healing; developing tolerance to frustration; developing time, setting, and intervention boundaries that fit therapeutic intervention in context; using community interventions; and developing the use of self in therapy. (p. 238)

Many of these same elements are reported by helpers who work with all forms of traumatic stress.

Self-Care

All trauma helpers must understand self-care not as an indulgence or afterthought but rather as essential to their physical and mental health, and to the constructive treatment of their clients (Norcross & Guy, 2007; Wicks, 2008). We particularly encourage those who engage with the traumatized to practice what may be termed *committed* or *radical self-care*. This means *intentionally and frequently* creating opportunities for respite and replenishment (i.e., to engage in activities that offer distraction and/or personal growth; to exercise, have fun, rest, relax, and connect with one's body; and to develop and maintain sustaining intimate, family, and other interpersonal relationships). It also means, wherever possible, to disengage from activities and relationships that are depleting and to replace them with those that are sustaining. *Such self-care is an ethical imperative for all therapists, but especially for those working with complex trauma.*

Working Protectively: Perspective

We next address ways of thinking about the work (perspective) and of engaging in it (practice) that may prove valuable to the management of vicarious trauma.[1] We first emphasize *the development of a theoretical basis* that guides the use of countertransference responses, because, as noted earlier, accumulated unprocessed countertransference responses can contribute to VT. A theoretical framework is the map that gives therapy direction and provides guideposts to the therapist. For example, theory offers possible reasons for complex trauma clients' ways of interacting and coping, and a rational basis for responding to them constructively.

Staying connected to personal experience, being aware of personal emotions while sitting with clients, helps to maximize empathic attunement. At the same time, helpers need to *remain aware of the present moment and the treatment frame* (the fact that they are the responsible party in a therapy relationship; that they have a fiduciary duty to the client; that the relationship is bounded by time constraints, ethical and legal rules, professional roles; etc.). It is easy to be caught up in the intensity of complex trauma clients' needs and feelings, and to lose perspective. It is the helper's job to think before responding, to put clients' immediate needs into a larger therapeutic context, and to respond in a way that conveys respect, collaboration, empowerment, and sound professional judgment.

Accepting the inevitably of vicarious trauma can perhaps paradoxically be helpful, as can *accepting personal and professional limitations*. Realizing that psychotherapy, although a powerful process, cannot accomplish miracles, that it can neither undo the past nor protect clients from all future harm, and that it will not go on forever keeps the therapist connected to the realities of human relationships. This in turn can lessen wishful thinking, a strategy that Norcross and Guy (2007) identify as ineffective in their discussion of empirically proven self-care strategies for psychotherapists. Wishing things were different impedes accepting what is. Acceptance frees the helper to change what

---

[1] Laurie Anne Pearlman would like to thank the many workshop participants who contributed suggestions for this section from their own clinical experience.

can be changed, reinforcing agency and countering the helplessness of direct and indirect trauma.

Clinicians also recognize the value of *focusing on process rather than on outcomes*. This strategy is well-known in the behavior change literature. For many trauma survivors, especially those with complex trauma adaptations, healing is a long, slow process. A focus on doing what needs to be done rather than on the client's ability to live differently will likely result in less frustration for both therapist and client. Similarly, *focusing on the positive, reinforcing desired behaviors and outcomes rather than highlighting shortcomings and disappointments*, can also enhance the therapeutic relationship and provide encouragement and support for both parties.

Working Protectively: Practice

In addition to promoting restorative relationships with complex trauma survivors, managing boundaries appropriately helps to limit VT. *Appropriate boundary management* means many things; it includes remembering the therapist's role and mandate, treating the client with respect, leaving work at the office (Norcross & Guy, 2007), and participating authentically, while keeping the goals of the treatment and the client's needs in focus. Boundaries are particularly salient with clients who have been subjected to violations, exploitations, and dual relationships. These clients often enter treatment without a well-formed ability to negotiate or manage boundaries in relationships, and often expect harm or abuse rather than care and protection. For example, after 2 years of therapy, a survivor of childhood sexual abuse by multiple perpetrators told her therapist she felt that everyone who had ever been kind to her had wanted something from her. When the therapist asked, "Has that happened in here?", the client replied, "Not yet."

Some therapeutic relationships have more built-in boundaries than others. At one end of the spectrum are those that are highly structured (i.e., the 50-minute therapy session, payment for professional services, and client privacy statutes) and at the other are those with less structure and fewer boundaries (i.e., a clergy or therapist visit to bedridden clients in their homes or care facilities, field work with war-affected refugee children, residential care, foreign language translation for psychotherapies). Yet even those more boundaried relationships are often unsupervised, confidential, and behind closed doors. Professional boundaries support the specialized nature of the relationship, and invite self-awareness and regulation on the part of the therapist.

To understand adequately and attune to the client, helpers must *listen with respect and an open mind and heart*. This implies entering the client's world, imagining his or her experience both during the traumatic events of the past and while recounting and reliving it in the present relationship. It means feeling the pain of the victim, and the fear and confusion of the survivor; such an intense process can induce VT when clients' experiences are quite horrific, including, for example, torture, violence, or, prolonged abuse or neglect. It is not only possible but also essential both to *engage with clients empathically and to respect boundaries*. That means that the helper lets the client know through words and actions that he or she cares deeply about the harm the client has experienced and about the struggle to recover. And it means collaborating with the client to establish a frame (including helper availability, fees, consultation arrangements, third-party involvement, frequency and purpose of meetings, etc.) with which both parties can live throughout the duration of the helping relationship. Empathy allows the development of healing connections. Boundaries help to ensure that the relationship is therapeutic and not exploitive, and that the client's needs come first.

Writing a progress note at the end of each session or meeting according to professional ethics and record-keeping guidelines documents the helping process. It can also help the therapist to decompress and gain perspective on the session and the overall process of therapy. In addition, personal journal writing allows helpers to document and explore their responses to the various challenges they face. *Processing clinical material in professional consultation relationships* also allows helpers to explore and to integrate their own feelings more effectively, rather than to be overwhelmed by them or to discharge them inappropriately (either with the client or more personally). Helpers may also find it useful to *do something very different between meetings with clients*. Activities that encourage the helper's physical engagement may provide an antidote to ongoing bodily tension and may further counter the sedentary nature of the therapeutic setting. Physical activities might take forms such as meditating, deep breathing, stretching, taking a walk, exercising, having lunch alone or with colleagues, and so forth. Some helpers find it useful to engage in brief creative activities, such as making a quick sketch or drawing, after particularly challenging sessions, or to take the opportunity to debrief with a colleague.

Rothschild (2006) suggests that the therapist *attend to his or her bodily responses and experiences* while working with traumatized clients as a way to address the vicariously traumatizing effects of empathic attunement and resonance (also see Fisher & Ogden, Chapter 15, this volume). Awareness of and adjustments to bodily states that help the helper to remain grounded and emotionally contained may protect him or her from the effects of VT. *Using countertransference responses to promote the client's growth* is a powerful antidote to the lack of choice and control that helpers (as well as clients) often feel in the trauma recovery process. Helplessness or lack of control is a central dynamic of traumatic experiences. The process of using feelings and the information they provide about clients' experiences to move the helping relationship forward counters the powerlessness that helpers often feel as they bear witness to the horrific experiences and their painful aftermath. Personal reactions can contribute to understanding clients and to feeling more empathy and compassion for them (Pearlman & Saakvitne, 1995). Sorting out those feelings might require (and certainly may be enhanced by) professional consultation.

POLICY IMPLICATIONS

Helpers providing trauma services do not operate in a vacuum. Whatever the setting in which they work, helpers are impacted by policies regarding the services they render. Research is beginning to show the impact that agency, state, and federal policies and procedures can have on VT levels (Bell, Kulkarni, & Dalton, 2003; Hormann & Vivian, 2005). In some settings, it is the unfortunate fact that the least experienced, novice professionals or paraprofessional helpers often provide care to the most traumatized individuals. This is not to say that grassroots workers or paraprofessionals are ineffective, or that they do not provide valuable and therapeutic services; rather, it is often the case that undertrained and/or newly degreed helpers are "thrown into the deep end of the pool," with little or no attention to whether they can "swim," often without adequate training, consultation, and/or supervision. Such a scenario is a recipe for burnout , VT, and more. It may also result in serious misjudgments, including boundary crossings and violations. Therefore, it is essential to take policy into account when examining the causes, prevention, and treatment of VT, particularly in settings where helpers have inadequate training and/or support.

The "ABC" (awareness, balance, and connection) model of preventing and mitigating VT for individuals (Saakvitne et al., 1996) offers a way to frame how agency, state, and federal policy may be formulated and implemented to support helpers in treating complex trauma. Recent research offers preliminary evidence that awareness at the policy level may help to prevent VT (Caringi, 2007). At the most basic level, that of *awareness*, policy offers an avenue for helpers in agencies to know that their leaders understand the difficult nature of trauma work and the potential impact of VT. *Training that addresses the impact of trauma work and VT is essential, not optional.* Trainings for this purpose exist in experiential, workbook, and online formats (Pearlman & McKay, 2008; Pryce et al., 2007; Saakvitne et al., 1996, 2000); yet state and agency policies frequently neither address these issues nor make such training available (Caringi, 2007; Pryce et al., 2007).

Policy at the agency level can impact how helpers are able to achieve *balance* in their work and personal lives. Two of the most basic and important ways that organizations can help to balance the challenges of working with complex trauma clients relate to caseload size and composition, and clinical consultation. Agency policy often dictates a hierarchical top-down management style, with little communication up or down; too much work, due to short staffing; too much paperwork; and little or no clinical supervision. In social service agencies, these realities often result from managed care restrictions in which services can be driven by time-limiting, cost-cutting strategies. "Top-down" leadership style, in which managers question and sometimes invalidate helpers' practice knowledge and self-care attempts, can be particularly disruptive. For example, policies that inhibit helpers' abilities to take breaks, work flexible schedules, and even access vacation time impact the balance needed to work in a service setting. Policies that allow flexible work schedules and mandate that staff use compensatory and annual leave in a timely manner provide opportunities to rest and to process and integrate the effects of the work.

Connection both inside and outside the workplace is necessary. Peer support teams within agencies can offer a first line of defense in dealing with VT (Caringi, 2007). Such teams require administrative support or a mandate in the form of policy. Two states, Massachusetts and New York, currently pilot a "teaming" method of casework in an attempt to break the isolation that often exists in difficult, trauma-involved child welfare cases. Research with humanitarian staff also suggests the central importance of the team to helpers' well-being (Fawcett, 2003). Such policies have great potential and require research on their effectiveness.

RESEARCH DIRECTIONS

Although the literature on VT in helpers who work with complex trauma survivors is substantial and growing, VT is still a relatively new concept. As with any new line of inquiry, there has been substantial debate regarding the causes, contributing factors, and even existence of VT. The critics of VT research raise three common themes, addressed very briefly here. First, some researchers question whether the concept of VT is needed, suggesting that PTSD offers a sufficient construct (Sabin-Farrell & Turpin, 2003). The mechanisms, theoretical underpinnings, and manifestations of VT are related yet distinctly different from PTSD. The fact that the construct is theory-based and not symptom-focused clearly differentiates it from PTSD. PTSD does not include the alterations in meaning, affect tolerance, and relationships that characterize VT. Second, researchers have questioned the validity or existence of VT (Jenkins & Baird, 2002; Kadambi & Ennis, 2004). Although the phenomenon clearly needs more exploration, VT has been defined, operationalized, described, or measured in a variety of populations, differentiated from burnout, and correlated with other theoretically related phenomena (e.g., empathy; Moosman, 2002). Third, as with many new concepts, the necessary exploratory research design to explain the phenomenon has been criticized (Jenkins & Baird, 2002; Kadambi & Ennis, 2004; Sabin-Farrell & Turpin, 2003). Based on these exploratory studies, it is possible to generate hypotheses that experimental and other, more rigorous research designs can examine while addressing sampling and methodological issues more vigorously. Such inquiries might help to clarify prevention and treatment approaches, perhaps the most important aspects of why we must continue research on VT.

Policy, research, and practice are necessarily intertwined. A continuing issue in the helping professions is the divide between researchers and those helpers working directly with clients. Research can and must be demystified to be useful to helpers. This can be achieved with participatory action research methods that value "practice knowledge" and involve helpers. This empowerment is crucial to understanding VT, while simultaneously preventing and treating it.

CONCLUSION

Supporting the recovery of survivors with complex trauma requires much skill, patience, and awareness. Our detailed examination of the manifestations, mechanisms, and contributing factors related to vicarious trauma may assist in increasing helpers' awareness of VT, and their ability to address it. This in turn may increase the likelihood of providing effective and ethical treatment for this population, and sustaining helpers in this challenging work.

REFERENCES

Arvay, M. J., & Uhlemann, M. R. (1996). Counsellor stress in the field of trauma: A preliminary study. *Canadian Journal of Counselling, 30*, 193–210.

Batson, C. D., Fultz, J., & Schoenrade, P. A. (1987). Distress and empathy. *Journal of Personality, 55*, 19–39.

Bell, H., Kulkarni, S., & Dalton, L. (2003). Organizational prevention of vicarious trauma. *Families in Society: The Journal of Contemporary Social Services, 84*, 463–473.

Bober, T., Regehr, C., & Zhou, Y. R. (2006). Development of the Coping Strategies Inventory for trauma counsellors. *Journal of Loss and Trauma, 11*(1), 71–83.

Brady, J., Guy, J., Poelstra, P., & Brokaw, B. (1999). Vicarious traumatization, spirituality, and the treatment of sexual abuse survivors. *Professional Psychology, 30*, 386–393.

Bride, B. (2004). The impact of providing psychosocial services to traumatized populations. *Trauma and Crisis, 7*, 29–46.

Briere, J. (2006). Dissociative symptoms and trauma exposure: Specificity, affect dysregulation, and posttraumatic stress. *Journal of Nervous and Mental Disease, 194*(2), 78–82.

Brock, K. J., Pearlman, L. A., & Varra, E. M. (2006). Child maltreatment, self capacities, and trauma symptoms. *Journal of Emotional Abuse, 6*, 103–125.

Caringi, J. (2007). *Secondary traumatic stress in New York State child welfare workers.* Doctoral dissertation, State University of New York at Albany.

Catherall, D. R. (1995). Coping with secondary traumatic stress: The importance of the therapist's peer group. In B. H. Stamm (Ed.), *Secondary traumatic stress: Self-care for clinicians, educators and researchers* (pp. 80–92). Lutherville, MD: Sidran Press.

Connors, R. E. (2000). *Self-injury.* Northvale, NJ: Jason Aronson.

Cunningham, M. (1999). The impact of sexual abuse treatment on the sexual abuse clinician. *Child and Adolescent Social Work Journal, 16*, 277–290.

Dalenberg, C. J. (2000). *Countertransference and the treatment of trauma.* Washington, DC: American Psychological Association.

Danieli, Y. (1981). Therapists' difficulties in treating survivors of the Nazi Holocaust and their children. Doctoral dissertation. *University Microfilms International*, No. 949-904.

Davies, J. M., & Frawley, M. G. (1994). *Treating the adult survivor of childhood sexual abuse: A psychoanalytic perspective.* New York: Basic Books.

Deiter, P. J., Nicholls, S. S., & Pearlman, L. A. (2000). Self-injury and self capacities: Assisting an individual in crisis. *Journal of Clinical Psychology, 56*(9), 1173–1191.

Dube, S. R., Felitti, V. J., Dong, M., Giles, W. H., & Anda, R. F. (2003). The impact of adverse childhood experiences on health problems. *Preventive Medicine, 37*(3), 268–277.

Fawcett, J. (Ed.). (2003). *Stress and trauma handbook.* Monrovia, CA: World Vision International.

Figley, C. R. (Ed.). (1995). *Compassion fatigue.* New York: Brunner/Mazel.

Figley, C. R. (2002a). Compassion fatigue. *Journal of Clinical Psychology, 58,* 1433–1441.

Figley, C. R. (Ed.). (2002b). *Treating compassion fatigue.* New York: Brunner-Routledge.

Freud, S. (1910). The future prospects of psychoanalytic therapy. In J. Strachey (Ed. & Trans.), *The standard edition of the complete psychological works of Sigmund Freud* (Vol. 7, pp. 3–122). New York: Norton.

Freudenberger, H. R. (1974). Staff burnout. *Journal of Social Issues, 30*(1), 159–165.

Ghahramanlou, M., & Brodbeck, C. (2000). Predictors of secondary trauma in sexual assault trauma counselors. *International Journal of Emergency Mental Health, 2,* 229–240.

Haley, S. (1974). When the patient reports atrocities: Specific treatment considerations of the Vietnam veteran. *American Journal of Psychiatry, 30,* 191–196.

Herman, J. L. (1992). *Trauma and recovery.* New York: Basic Books.

Hernandez, P., Gangsei, D., & Engstrom, D. (2007). Vicarious resilience. *Family Process, 46,* 229–241.

Hormann, S., & Vivian, P. (2005). Toward an understanding of traumatized organizations and how to intervene in them. *Traumatology, 11*(3), 159–169.

Jenkins, S. R., & Baird, S. (2002). Secondary traumatic stress and vicarious trauma: A validation study. *Journal of Traumatic Stress, 15*(5), 423–432.

Kadambi, M., & Ennis, L. (2004). Reconsidering vicarious trauma: A review of the literature and its limitations. *Journal of Trauma Practice, 3*(2), 1–22.

Kendall-Tackett, K. A. (2004). *Health consequences of abuse in the family: A clinical guide for evidence-based practice.* Washington, DC: American Psychological Association.

Kluft, R. P. (1994). Countertransference in the treatment of multiple personality disorder. In J. P. Wilson & J. D. Lindy (Eds.), *Countertransference in the treatment of PTSD* (pp. 122–150). New York: Guilford Press.

Lamm, C., Batson, C. D., & Decety, J. (2007). The neural substrate of human empathy. *Journal of Cognitive Neuroscience, 19*(1), 42–58.

McCann, I. L., & Pearlman, L. A. (1990a). *Psychological trauma and the adult survivor: Theory, therapy, and transformation.* New York: Brunner/Mazel.

McCann, I. L., & Pearlman, L. A. (1990b). Vicarious traumatization: A framework for understanding the psychological effects of working with victims. *Journal of Traumatic Stress, 3*(1), 131–149.

McKay, L. (2004). *Helping the helpers: Understanding, assessing, and treating humanitarian workers experiencing acute stress reactions.* Pasadena, CA: Headington Institute. Retrieved May 21, 2007, from *www.headington-institute.org/Default.aspx?tabid=1335*

Marmaras, E., & Lee, S. S. (2006, March/April). Impact of attachment styles on vicarious traumatization in female trauma therapists. *Maryland Psychologist*, pp. 14–15, 18–19.

Messman-Moore, T. L., & Long, P. J. (2003). The role of childhood sexual abuse sequelae in the sexual revictimization of women. *Clinical Psychology Review, 23*, 537–571.

Miller, D. (1994). *Women who hurt themselves.* New York: Basic Books.

Moosman, J. (2002). *Vicarious traumatization.* Doctoral dissertation, George Mason University, Fairfax, VA.

Munroe, J. F., Shay, J., Fisher, L., Makary, C., Rapperport, K., & Zimering, R. (1995). Preventing compassion fatigue: A team treatment model. In C. R. Figley (Ed.), *Compassion fatigue: Coping with secondary traumatic stress disorder in those who treat the traumatized* (pp. 209–231). New York: Brunner/Mazel.

Norcross, J. C., & Guy, J. D. (2007). *Leaving it at the office: A guide to psychotherapist self-care.* New York: Guilford Press.

Pearlman, L. A. (1996). Review of the TSI Belief Scale. In B.H. Stamm (Ed.), *Measurement of stress, trauma, and adaptation* (pp. 415–417). Lutherville, MD: Sidran Press.

Pearlman, L. A. (1998). Trauma and the self. *Journal of Emotional Abuse, 1*, 7–25.

Pearlman, L. A. (2002). Treatment of persons with complex PTSD and other trauma-related disruptions of the self. In J. P. Wilson, M. J. Friedman, & J. D. Lindy (Eds.), *Treating psychological trauma and PTSD* (pp. 205–236). New York: Guilford Press.

Pearlman, L. A. (2003). *Trauma and attachment belief scale manual.* Los Angeles: Western Psychological Services.

Pearlman, L. A., & Courtois, C. A. (2005). Clinical applications of the attachment framework: Relational treatment of complex trauma. *Journal of Traumatic Stress, 18*, 449–460.

Pearlman, L. A., & Mac Ian, P. (1995). Vicarious traumatization: An empirical study of the effects of trauma work on trauma therapists. *Professional Psychology: Research and Practice, 26*, 558–565.

Pearlman, L. A., & McKay, L. (2008). *Understanding and coping with vicarious trauma: On-line training module.* Pasadena, CA: Headington Institute. Manuscript in preparation.

Pearlman, L. A., & Saakvitne, K. W. (1995). *Trauma and the therapist: Countertransference and vicarious traumatization in psychotherapy with incest survivors.* New York: Norton.

Peterson, C., & Seligman, M. E. P. (2004). *Character strengths and virtues: A handbook and classification.* Oxford, UK: Oxford University Press.

Pryce, J. G., Shackelford, K. K., & Pryce, D. H. (2007). *Secondary traumatic stress and the child welfare professional.* Chicago: Lyceum Books.

Putnam, F. W. (1989). *Diagnosis and treatment of multiple personality disorder.* New York: Guilford Press.

Rodrigo, W. D. (2005). *Conceptual dimensions of compassion fatigue and vicarious trauma.* Master's thesis, Simon Fraser University, Vancouver, British Columbia.

Rosenbloom, D. J., Pratt, A. C., & Pearlman, L. A. (1995). Helpers' responses to trauma work: Understanding and intervening in an organization. In B. H. Stamm (Ed.), *Secondary traumatic stress: Self-care issues for clinicians, researchers, and educators* (pp. 65–79). Lutherville, MD: Sidran Press.

Rothschild, B. (2006). *Help for the helper.* New York: Norton.

Saakvitne, K. W., Gamble, S., Pearlman, L., & Lev, B. (2000). *Risking connection: A training curriculum for working with survivors of childhood abuse.* Lutherville, MD: Sidran Press.

Saakvitne, K. W., Pearlman, L. A., & the Staff of the Traumatic Stress Institute. (1996). *Transforming the pain: A workbook on vicarious traumatization.* New York: Norton.

Sabin-Farrell, R., & Turpin, G. (2003). Vicarious traumatization: Implications for the mental health of health workers? *Clinical Psychology Review, 23*(3), 449–480.

Schauben, L. J., & Frazier, P. A. (1995). Vicarious trauma: The effects on female counselors of working with sexual violence survivors. *Psychology of Women Quarterly, 19,* 49–64.

Schnurr, P. P., & Green, B. L. (2004). *Trauma and health: Physical health consequences of exposure to extreme stress.* Washington, DC: American Psychological Association.

Stamm, B. H. (Ed.). (1999). *Secondary traumatic stress* (2nd ed.). Lutherville, MD: Sidran Press.

Staub, E. (2003). *The psychology of good and evil.* Cambridge, UK: Cambridge University Press.

Terr, L. C. (1989). Treating psychic trauma in children: A preliminary discussion. *Journal of Traumatic Stress, 2*(1), 3–20.

Thomas, R. B. (1998). *An investigation of empathic stress reactions among mental health professionals working with PTSD.* Doctoral dissertation, Union Institute, Cincinnati, OH.

Tokayer, N. (2002). *Spirituality and the psychological and physical symptoms of trauma.* Doctoral dissertation, University of Hartford, Hartford, CT.

van der Kolk, B. A., Pelcovitz, D., Roth, S., Mandel, F., McFarlane, A. C., & Herman, J. L. (1996). Dissociation, somatization and affect dysregulation. *American Journal of Psychiatry, 153*(Suppl.), 83–93.

Wicks, R. J. J. (2007). *The resilient clinician.* New York: Oxford University Press.

Wilson, J. P., & Lindy, J. D. (Eds.). (1994a). *Countertransference in the treatment of PTSD.* New York: Guilford Press.

Wilson, J. P., & Lindy, J. D. (1994b). Empathic strain and countertransference. In J. P. Wilson & J. D. Lindy (Eds.), *Countertransference in the treatment of PTSD* (pp. 5–30). New York: Guilford Press.

Wilson, J. P., Lindy, J. D., & Raphael, B. (1994). Empathic strain and therapist defense: Type I and II CTRs. In J. P. Wilson & J. D. Lindy (Eds.), *Countertransference in the treatment of PTSD* (pp. 31–61). New York: Guilford Press.

Wilson, J. P., & Thomas, R. B. (2004). *Empathy in the treatment of trauma and PTSD.* New York: Brunner/Routledge.

INDIVIDUAL TREATMENT
APPROACHES
AND STRATEGIES

Attention in Part II focuses on selected psychotherapy models that have been developed to treat adults experiencing complex traumatic stress disorders. The first three chapters (11–13) describe models designed to facilitate a shift in the context from helplessness, self-blame, and alienation to personal effectiveness, worth, and trust. Chapter 11 describes a relational model of contextual change, whereas Chapters 12 and 13 describe adaptations of behavior therapy for complex traumatic stress disorders. Chapters 14 and 15 introduce psychotherapy perspectives that focus on enhancing self-regulation of emotion and body state, respectively. Chapter 16 describes the use of psychotropic medications in pharmacotherapy for complex traumatic stress disorders.

In each chapter, the authors, many of whom are researchers and educators as well as clinicians, first describe their model and its theoretical foundation, then summarize empirical support to date. The authors then go on to illustrate their models' clinical application in a simulated client interaction and transcript.

CHAPTER 11

Contextual Therapy

Steven N. Gold

Contextual therapy was specifically designed as a treatment for adult survivors of prolonged child abuse (PCA). Although certainly not the only form of trauma that can lead to complex posttraumatic stress disorder (PTSD), PCA is the prime exemplar of complex trauma and the main impetus for the development of the construct. This observation is clearly delineated by Judith Herman (1992a) in the article in which she first introduced the concept of complex PTSD:

> The pathological environment of prolonged abuse fosters the development of a prodigious array of psychiatric symptoms. A history of abuse, particularly in childhood, appears to be one of the major factors predisposing a person to become a psychiatric patient. While only a minority of survivors of chronic childhood abuse become psychiatric patients, a large proportion (40–70%) of adult psychiatric patients are survivors of abuse. (p. 379)

Herman (1992b) appears to have had several aims in formulating the complex PTSD construct. One was to alert practitioners that a wide range of psychological difficulties—most notably, borderline personality disorder, somatization disorder, and multiple personality disorder (now referred to as dissociative identity disorder)—are often related to a history of PCA but rarely have been recognized as being trauma-related disorders. A closely related goal was to destigmatize this spectrum of psychological problems, one that has often elicited denigrating attitudes from mental health professionals. Individuals manifesting these conditions—especially women—were seen as "temperamental, manipulative, and provocative." Their symptoms were difficult to fit within traditional psychiatric diagnoses and often were perceived as being feigned or purposely exaggerated. However, as Herman explained, when viewed as manifestations of a history of ongoing childhood abuse trauma, this constellation of problems became comprehensible. Yet another objective was to sensitize practitioners to how commonly trauma contributed to the difficulties that brought clients to therapy, and to make them aware that trauma-related difficulties take many forms that extend well beyond those that comprise PTSD as currently conceptualized and delineated in the DSM-IV-TR (American Psychiatric Association, 2000).

THE CONCEPTUAL AND EMPIRICAL BASIS FOR THE DEVELOPMENT OF CONTEXTUAL THERAPY

Despite the considerably broader range of difficulties that comprise complex PTSD, it has often been assumed that the same strategies of uncovering, exposure, and processing of traumatic material that are the cornerstone of therapy for PTSD would be effective with complex PTSD. If the consequences of single-event trauma resolved in response to these approaches, certainly the same interventions would be effective for the sequelae of repeated or ongoing developmentally adverse interpersonal traumas.

The Clinical Evidence

The experience at the Trauma Resolution and Integration Program (TRIP), a university-based outpatient treatment program founded in 1990, suggested otherwise. Although TRIP currently treats adult survivors of all types of trauma, in its early years it exclusively served adult survivors of childhood sexual abuse, the vast majority of whom reported histories of severe PCA and met criteria for complex PTSD. Program staff quickly found that standard trauma treatments focused on addressing traumatic material not only failed to lead to improvement but also often led to rapidly escalating distress and exacerbation of problem behaviors. It was not uncommon for TRIP clients to report that previous treatment using these approaches had had similar consequences.

In the absence of existing models to address the needs of this population, TRIP staff turned to what to us appeared to be the best remaining source— the clients themselves. When clients were allowed to guide staff to what was important to *them*, explicit incidences of abuse, as dramatic and compelling as they seemed, were rarely their primary focus. Instead, they attended to the unremittingly bleak tenor of their everyday lives growing up. Whether or not clients had been abused by a family member, they described formative years that were bereft of the conditions that many would like to believe are universally present for children: consistently loving and supportive parents; predictable routine and structure; and sufficient supervision and guidance. Additionally, features in their backgrounds made them especially vulnerable to abuse. In the absence of reliable nurturance and affection, they were eager for attention and caring. Having adapted to capricious and constantly shifting "rules," they had also learned that the overarching rule was to obey immediately and without questioning.

The salience of this *context* of their abuse—having been reared in an ineffective, unpredictable, and largely nonresponsive family environment—became clear. It seemed that these factors contributed as much or more to problems with functioning than the trauma of abuse itself. Growing up with emotionally distant, disinterested, or unpredictable family members prevented the development of secure attachment. Inadequate familial structure and guidance led to a wide range of deficits in social learning, resulting in relational styles that were dismissive, overly pleasing and caretaking of others, or disorganized and inconsistent. Familial modeling of counterproductive methods of dealing with problems (e.g., substance abuse, interpersonal aggression, and compulsive behaviors) fostered the adoption of maladaptive coping strategies. Independent of the adverse impact of abuse, the resulting gaps and warps in development left survivor clients inadequately prepared for adult living.

The Empirical Evidence

Although this initial conceptual framework was constructed on the basis of client feedback and clinical experience, there is a substantial but little-recognized body of empirical literature that supports the premises underlying the contextual model. Studies have repeatedly and consistently found that PCA survivors' families of origin manifest a configuration of characteristics that render them appreciably different from normative families (Alexander & Lupfer, 1987; Harter, Alexander, & Neimeyer, 1988; Justice & Calvert, 1990; Long & Jackson, 1994; Ray, Jackson, & Townsley, 1991; Williamson, Borduin, & Howe, 1991; Yama, Tovey, & Fogas, 1993). This research has been bolstered by studies of attachment and child maltreatment (Karen, 1994). The research indicated that families of abuse survivors tend to be low in adaptation, suggesting that they are poorly equipped to model and to teach adaptive living skills to their younger members. They also often are rated by survivors as low in both cohesion and emotional expressivity, so that they provide little sense of belonging, connectedness, and secure attachment to members. Despite their failure to offer a secure sense of kinship, several studies have also found that abuse survivors rate their families of origin as low in encouraging independence of their members and instead are highly controlling and demanding of loyalty. Together, this conglomeration of family characteristics closely conforms to the descriptions given by clients and depicts an interpersonal atmosphere that fails to promote, and in many respect hampers, the development of emotion regulation, autonomous decision making, and interpersonal relatedness and security.

It is of particular importance to distinguish here between the families of survivors of child abuse and abusive families. What the research demonstrates is that the family pattern I have described is not exclusive to families that are abusive to their children; essentially the same constellation of family-of-origin characteristics is reported by survivors who were abused by perpetrators outside the family (Alexander & Lupfer, 1987; Gold, Hyman, & Andres, 2004; Ray et al., 1991; Yama et al., 1993). What this finding suggests is that families failing to provide the conditions needed for normal development—such as security, reliability, consistent affection, emotional validation and support, guidance, direction, and the promotion of autonomy—render their offspring particularly vulnerable to abuse, whether by family members or by persons outside the family. It also is possible that some of these families functioned more effectively before being traumatically impacted by the abuse of a child, or that some adults who experienced abuse as a child selectively recalled or attributed abuse-related issues to their families. In any case, the question is not one of blame—for the family or the survivor—but how to help the survivor acquire a life context in the present that supports the development of healthier patterns of interactions and relationships.

Even more pertinent to the contextual treatment model is a wide-ranging collection of studies that found family environment to be related to long-term psychological problems, over and above the contribution made by abuse (Fassler, Amodeo, Griffin, Clay, & Ellis, 2005; Higgins & McCabe, 2000, 2003; Nash, Hulsey, Sexton, Harralson, & Lambert, 1993; Ray & Jackson, 1997; Yama et al., 1993). *This is the crucial observation that guides contextual intervention.* Difficulties that are attributable to the family-of-origin environment and to resultant gaps in development and learning cannot reasonably be expected to be addressed effectively by trauma-focused intervention. Resolving the impact of traumatic experiences per se may not help survivors acquire relational stability, knowledge, skills, and capacities that, rather than having been disrupted by trauma, were never attained. Helping complex trauma survivors remediate these breaches in learning and development is an essential component of therapy, one that forms an indispensable foundation for and prerequisite to confronting particulars of past trauma productively.

The Empirical Base

The first empirical research study investigating the effectiveness of contextual therapy is now being conducted. However, a series of three individual case studies with pre- and posttreatment standardized measures has been published (Gold et al., 2001). Although as case studies they are preliminary, the findings suggest that further controlled investigation of this approach is warranted. These cases were notable on several counts. All three clients met criteria for dissociative identity disorder (DID), a challenging syndrome to treat effectively, which manifests several comorbid conditions. In all three instances the therapy was conducted by doctoral trainees, most of whom had only 1 year of previous supervised clinical experience. Due to the constraints of receiving treatment in a training setting to which therapists were assigned for only 1 year, each client had to adapt to switching therapists during the course of therapy. Despite these challenges, all three clients showed not only appreciable symptom reduction but also attained important lifestyle improvements, such as becoming employed and financially independent, and forming a more extensive and reliable social network.

KEY FEATURES OF CONTEXTUAL TREATMENT

In addition to delineating complex PTSD, Herman (1992b) articulated a three-phase model of trauma psychotherapy that is now widely disseminated. This framework emphasizes the importance of an initial phase of helping trauma survivors firmly establish conditions of safety and a sense of interpersonal security *before* proceeding to direct trauma work in the second phase of therapy, followed by a third phase of integration and reconnection.

From the perspective of contextual therapy, Phases 1 and 3 are not merely bookends to the trauma processing that constitutes Phase 2. After repeatedly hearing accounts from PCA survivors indicating that they had experienced an upbringing that never adequately prepared them to cope effectively with life in general, as well as its daily stressors, it seemed obvious that the extraordinary stressor of intensive trauma work was bound to be destabilizing in the absence of extensive preparation. In contrast, one way to understand the contextual treatment approach formulated for PCA survivors is that instead of Phase 2 trauma work being the centerpiece of treatment, the elements that comprised Herman's first and third phases were elevated into a position of prominence.

An additional major difference was that Herman described the capacities attained in Phases 1 and 3—safety, and a sense of security, integration, and connection—as being ones that the client *re*gains or *re*claims through treatment. The contextual treatment model conceives of these capacities as being ones that, rather than being *re*established, need to be developed by most PCA survivors *for the first time*. This shift in perspective translates into a crucial difference in intervention strategies: One goes about acquiring a capacity that never existed in a very different fashion than how one would access a resource that has been blocked or hampered by adversity.

As the treatment model initially developed, trauma work was seen as one phase of intervention that occurred relatively late in the course of therapy (e.g., see Gold, 2000). In these earlier formulations the contextual therapy model conceived of trauma processing for PCA survivors as being a phase of treatment which, if retained at all, would only be attempted after a protracted period of treating gaps in development, interpersonal security in the treatment relationship, and adaptive living skills. This perspective grew out of the concern that encouraging clients with complex PTSD to confront the detailed narrative of their traumatic experiences prematurely would lead to personal decline due to intense exacerbation of their difficulties.

However, what this approach failed to acknowledge adequately is that much of trauma work consists not of processing the traumatic events themselves, but of addressing the distorted perceptions and beliefs engendered by trauma. The cognitive aspect of trauma work does not carry the same destabilizing risk as does confronting the explicit trauma narrative and emotions. Even survivors of complex trauma can usually benefit from the cognitive aspect of trauma work beginning relatively early in treatment, without appreciable danger of decompensation, a perspective that has received the empirical support of cognitive-behavioral therapists (Follette & Ruzek, 2006), as well as other clinician researchers who have studied incest and other sexual abuse survivors (Jehu, 1988; McCann & Pearlman, 1990; Roth & Batson, 1997). Consequently, the contextual perspective has increasingly included interventions that target the cognitive components of trauma to be interwoven throughout the course of treatment rather than held in abeyance, until later phases of therapy. Refraining from extensive intervention focused on the detailed narrative of traumatic experiences, until a solid foundation of cognitive skills and adaptive coping has been established, remains a cornerstone of contextual philosophy and treatment.

Three Major Areas of Intervention

Partly in response to the intricate web of difficulties that most survivors of complex trauma bring to treatment, contextual therapy stresses the importance of a clear and straightforward conceptual formulation to guide intervention. An explicit theoretical framework keeps the intervention process as simple as possible, makes it easy to explain, and encourages collaboration between therapist and client. The goals of therapy are conceptually divided into three main areas: interpersonal, practical, and conceptual.

The Interpersonal Area

A nearly universally agreed-upon premise in clinical work is that the effectiveness of any form of therapy depends on the establishment of a strong and resilient therapeutic relationship (a "secure base"). An important advantage is that the contextual model calls attention to the gaps in learning and development commonly manifested by survivors of complex trauma. This perspective helps practitioners be sensitive to the likelihood that many of these clients lack many of the abilities required to engage in a productive therapeutic alliance.

Many survivors of complex trauma not only have experienced repeated hurt and exploitation at the hands of others but also have had little or no experience that would teach them that cooperative interpersonal relationships exist, let alone how to participate in them. Consequently, the contextually oriented practitioner is alert from the outset of treatment to recognize and remediate deficits in the client's capacity to interact collaboratively. This awareness enables the therapist to help the client learn how to develop the type of therapeutic interaction essential to progress. Just as importantly, it assists the clinician in attenuating his or her own reactions to what on the surface may appear to be provocative or contentious behavior. By remembering that what may actually be operating is the client's lack of models for collaborative interpersonal relating and the hyper- or hypoactivation of attachment-related behaviors, which is the legacy of a history of insecure attachment with primary caregivers, the therapist is assisted in noticing gaps in the client's interpersonal repertoire, and teaching the principles and abilities needed to establish a collaborative rapport.

The Practical Area

The information, skills, and capacities that may be lacking due to having grown up in an ineffective family of origin can vary widely. They can range from very concrete matters, such as how to open and manage a checking account, to highly abstract abilities, such as how to initiate and maintain a friendship. In the contextual approach, the clinician is aware of these areas of deficiency and of the client's need to remediate them (or learn them from scratch). Although the particular skills that each client needs to master in treatment may vary, certain abilities are so commonly lacking and so essential for overcoming the adverse impact of trauma that they form a standard component of contextual therapy for most clients. These latter capacities are usually addressed in a particular sequence based on their importance and beneficial impact, and are referred to as *prioritized treatment goals*.

The highest priority goal is to teach the client how to self-soothe. A core aspect of trauma-related difficulties is chronic arousal. Unlike survivors of single-event or circumscribed trauma whose pretrauma adjustment was good, those whose trauma was repetitive and occurred during crucial developmental epochs are likely never to have learned how to moderate distress in ways that do not have destructive consequences. Between being faced with constant, lifelong emotional distress and never having learned productive ways to self-soothe through the sufficient caregiving of others, these individuals almost universally resort to reliance on addictive and compulsive behaviors for relief. Although these behaviors are harmful, at least in the long run, they carry the extremely attractive benefit of providing immediate, albeit often short-lived, relief. Teaching the client strategies for reducing distress as early in treatment as possible is crucial, because when one is in the throes of emotional upheaval, it is next to impossible to focus or to concentrate sufficiently on much else. Moreover, a successful decrease in levels of baseline arousal makes the client less disposed to rely as heavily on addictive and compulsive behaviors, reduces other difficulties (e.g., insomnia, flashbacks, and depression), and bolsters the hope that change is possible.

A second common area of difficulty for survivors of complex developmental trauma that can substantially impede therapeutic progress is dissociation. Flashbacks, spacing out, amnesic episodes, depersonalization, and general difficulty staying focused on and attentive to the here and now greatly interfere with the client's capacity to benefit from therapy. All of these experiences are much more likely to occur when distress levels are high, necessitating instruction on how first to reduce baseline distress. Once progress is made in that area, the next priority is to teach the client how to sustain attention in the present.

Until gains have been made in reducing arousal and increasing the client's capacity to stay focused (mindfulness), there is little point in attempting much in the way of cognitive intervention. Distress and dissociation are major obstacles to productive cognitive processing and learning. Therefore, once progress has been made in reducing anxiety and dissociative distractibility, the survivor is helped to establish the cognitive capacity for exercising the logical, evidence-based reasoning, judgment, and decision making that was unlikely to have been previously taught or developed.

With distress and dissociation attenuated, and the capacity for productive cognitive processing augmented, the client is now better equipped to work on relinquishing addictive and compulsive behaviors. Contextual therapy employs a modified version of functional behavioral analysis as an intervention to overcome gradually the pull toward addictive and compulsive behavior patterns (Gold, 2000; Gold & Seifer, 2002). Armed with the ability to self-soothe, to stay focused in the present, to think things through rationally, and to resist the pull toward addictive and compulsive behaviors as self-soothing, the client is now prepared to process traumatic stress reactions and troubling memories of traumatic experiences effectively in a sustained, detailed, and systematic way. These capacities greatly increase the probability that trauma processing will be productive rather than debilitating. With this foundation in place, what previously would have been destabilizing can now be safely accomplished.

Coming to terms with traumatic events is not the final accomplishment in the process of trauma resolution. For survivors of circumscribed trauma, there remains the challenge of how to return to the routine of daily living after having faced the disruption of catastrophic unanticipated events. Survivors of complex trauma face the appreciably greater challenge of establishing a pattern of stable and effective adult living that they have never attained. Not only do these clients lack many of the capacities necessary for this complex task, but also the invalidation, denigration, and pervasive criticism from the past has in all probability left them with a deeply felt conviction that they do not *deserve* a happy and gratifying life. Therefore, this final and extensive prioritized treatment goal encompasses not only the transmission of various broad and specific abilities needed to establish a stable and satisfying life but also extensive cognitive work to help these clients overcome the core belief that this achievement is forbidden to them.

The Conceptual Area

The survivor of complex trauma is unlikely to have mastered how to apply evidence-based logic to reasoning, judgment, and decision making. Although this is one of the skills areas within the practical area, it is sufficiently broad to be considered one of the three major areas of contextual treatment as well. The role of the therapist in this enterprise is to guide the client through the *process* of thinking something through to a conclusion, while leaving the *outcome* or actual conclusion in the hands of the client. The standard cognitive-behavioral procedure of Socratic interviewing (Hoyt, 1996; Overholser, 1993) is the main approach to reasoning in contextual therapy. The key to effective application of this intervention strategy is to deviate substantially from the approach taken by Socrates: The therapist must avoid assuming that he or she knows the correct answer in advance. The therapist's role is not to lead the client to a particular conclusion, but to walk the client step by step through the *process* by which a logical, evidence-based conclusion can be reached.

To accomplish this goal, therapists must consider when it is reasonable for survivor clients (with the therapist's assistance) to arrive at conclusions on their own, and when it would be best simply to provide them with answers. As a general rule, matters *about the client* are best left to the client to tackle. Matters such as the motives and reasons behind behavior and what the client feels, wants, believes, and so forth, are also best addressed by the client. Although this may sound too obvious to mention, a long tradition of interpretation in psychotherapy fosters a habit in many practitioners to "explain the client to the client." This interpretive psychoanalytic/psychodynamic approach has recently shifted as relational psychoanalysis has emphasized the significance of the client's making his or her own meaning within the intersubjective context of the therapy relationship (Wallin, 2007).

On the other hand, clients cannot reasonably be expected to "figure out" the answers to questions regarding facts or procedures with which they may be unfamiliar (e.g., how to set up a filing system for their personal financial records) or social conventions to which they may never have been exposed (e.g., where the salad fork goes in a table setting). Explicitly distinguishing concrete information and social convention from subjective experience can make it clear to clients when it is reasonable to come to conclusions on their own and when it is best to turn to others for answers.

SIMULATED TRANSCRIPT OF CONTEXTUAL THERAPY

The tone and direction of a particular session of contextual therapy can vary considerably depending on its focus. For example, work on the interpersonal area to facilitate a collaborative therapeutic alliance entails encouraging an active give-and-take on the part of both therapist and client. When the conceptual area is emphasized, the therapist encourages the client to take the lead in self-exploration and in discussing personal issues, values, and preferences. In contrast, when the focus is on the transmission of practical skills, the clinician takes the lead and directly teaches skills and reasoning. The session that follows takes place fairly early in treatment, when the therapeutic alliance is still being established and the client is orienting to the parameters of treatment. However, the transcript intentionally incorporates elements of the conceptual and practical areas as well.

CLIENT: I can't believe you're not more supportive. When I called you after last session and asked you to leave a message reassuring me that everything would be all right, you didn't do it.

THERAPIST: I don't understand. Didn't you get my message? I left one.

CLIENT: Oh, I got your message all right. And it wasn't very reassuring. I asked you to just say that everything would be all right. But you couldn't just leave it at that. You had to impose conditions and say that everything would work out fine *if* we were able to work cooperatively together.

THERAPIST: I'm not following. How is that not supportive?

CLIENT: It just would have been nice to hear that things would be fine *without* the "if" ... even if you didn't mean it.

THERAPIST: You're pretty sharp at picking up on where people are coming from. Don't you think you'd be able to tell if I was being insincere?

CLIENT: I just didn't like hearing the "if," that's all. Why was it so important to put that in?

THERAPIST: Because I don't want to mislead you. You've been telling me that you've been having horrible flashbacks, you've hardly slept for weeks now, you're exhausted from overwork, and the thought of suicide is actually comforting. Is that all still happening?

CLIENT: Yes, of course. That's exactly why I wanted you to call and leave me that message. I'm at the end of my rope. I need reassurance.

THERAPIST: And do you think if I called and simply said that everything would be all right, then all those things would go away?

CLIENT: (*softly*) No. I guess not.

THERAPIST: I agree. And in the same way, those things are not just going to stop because we meet.

CLIENT: (*in a desperate, pleading tone*) So those things are never going to go away?

THERAPIST: Absolutely not. They're just not going to get better simply because you and I meet periodically and talk.

CLIENT: Then how in the world will things get better?

THERAPIST: It's going to take follow-through on the things I've been teaching you about how to bring your distress level down and finding ways to distract yourself from the flashbacks. And to lead you to believe that I'll keep meeting with you whether you start doing them or not would be misleading and unfair. I'm not willing to do that.

CLIENT: So you're going to give up on me? I can't believe you're saying that!

THERAPIST: I'm not saying that. What I'm saying is that my willingness to keep meeting with you depends on your demonstration that you will do your best to make use of the solutions we come up with here in session.

CLIENT: And what if it still doesn't work?

THERAPIST: Then you and I *together* will figure out another way to approach things until we find a way that *does* work ... as long as I see that you're making an honest effort to put into practice what we come up with.

CLIENT: You just don't understand. It's not that easy to do the things you suggest.

THERAPIST: I do understand that it's not easy. It takes a lot of repetition and commitment.

CLIENT: That's not it. You know how hard I work at my job. But this is different.

THERAPIST: Different how?

CLIENT: (*long pause*) I guess it's different because at work I feel I *have* to do things.

THERAPIST: How so?

CLIENT: Because it's what other people need from me.

THERAPIST: And what about what *you* need?

CLIENT: (*after a long pause*; *softly*) That's just it. I'm not supposed to need anything.

THERAPIST: I don't understand. Everybody needs things. Do you know anyone else at work who doesn't need things?

CLIENT: No. But I'm different.

THERAPIST: Different from everyone else?

CLIENT: *Yes.*

THERAPIST: In what way are you different from everyone else? You don't need or want things?

CLIENT: Well, whether I need them or not, it doesn't matter. I'm not supposed to need them.

THERAPIST: You just lost me again.

CLIENT: (*yelling*) Don't you get it? Damn, you're dense! I'm not allowed to *do* things for *me*! I can do everything in the world for everyone else, but I can't do things for *me*!

THERAPIST: Really? Says who?

CLIENT: *What?*

THERAPIST: (*softly*) I said, "Says who?"

CLIENT: (*long pause*; *gently sobbing*) Damn you!

THERAPIST: Well there must be a reason for it. Let's try to figure it out together.

CLIENT: It's just always been that way. It just doesn't feel right. I don't deserve it.

THERAPIST: OK. I'm afraid you've lost me again ... the reason you don't deserve to be taken care of?

CLIENT: If I do the sort of things you're asking me to do, things might get better. And the whole idea of that is very scary.

THERAPIST: Not being constantly terrified by flashbacks or suffering from sleeplessness is scary?

CLIENT: I'm sure that if things go well, then as soon as I let myself think everything is all right something terrible will happen and take it all away.

THERAPIST: Wow. I guess we're up against a lot then, huh?

CLIENT: What? What do you mean?

THERAPIST: Well, I was thinking that the whole reason we're here is to make things better for you ... to stop the terror and the flashbacks and for you to be able to get some restful sleep.

CLIENT: I don't see your point.

THERAPIST: You just told me that that's not allowed. That if things get better somehow, then you will be punished.

CLIENT: (*long pause*) Oh. I see what you're saying. There's no point. No wonder you're trying to get rid of me. You think I'm hopeless.

THERAPIST: No. That's not what I'm saying at all.

CLIENT: Then what are you saying?

THERAPIST: I'm saying that unless we stay alert to the fact that progress is going to be uncomfortable for you, we're not likely to get very far.

CLIENT: So what do we do?

THERAPIST: We make sure to move ahead *very slowly* ... just one little step at a time.

CLIENT: Brilliant. How the hell do we move ahead *s-l-o-w-l-y*?

THERAPIST: Well, for example, take getting your level of terror down.

CLIENT: Yes. What about it?

THERAPIST: I've asked you to practice that exercise for 5 minutes three times a day to help get your terror level down.

CLIENT: Right.

THERAPIST: Have you done it?

CLIENT: No.

THERAPIST: Right. And why not?

CLIENT: It feels self-indulgent to do something to make me feel better.

THERAPIST: Right. So I'm not going to ask you to do that.

CLIENT: So you *are* giving up!

THERAPIST: No, I'm not giving up. *We're* going to slow things down. I'm going to ask you to do the exercise just once a day. For no more than 1 minute. Will you do that?

CLIENT: (*long pause*) Well ... I guess so. But I don't see the point. It probably won't do much good.

THERAPIST: That's OK. We can't afford to do too much too quickly, because that would be scary.

CLIENT: Are you making fun of me?

THERAPIST: Not at all. I'm completely serious. So, are you willing to do the exercise just once a day, and not for one second more?

CLIENT: Sure. But I told you. I can't see where that will do much good.

THERAPIST: We'll just have to wait and see whether it does any good. For now, I'm just asking for your commitment to practice it *just* once a day for *no more* than a minute.

CLIENT: OK, but. I just don't see where it will do much of anything.

THERAPIST: And I told you I wasn't going to insist to you that it does do much of anything. I just want your word that you will follow through.

CLIENT: OK, OK. You have it.

THERAPIST: I mean it. I'm going to check in with you next time and see if you followed through.

CLIENT: I told you I'd do it. I'll do it.

SUMMARY OF KEY POINTS

This transcript encapsulates many of the central points of contextual therapy. The main thrust at the beginning of therapy is helping the complex trauma survivor—who, in all probability, has little or no experience with collaborating—learn how to enter into a cooperative relationship with the therapist. Like much that is accomplished in therapy, this objective rarely occurs in a direct, straightforward way. In the course of identifying—with the indispensable help of the client—what is getting in the way of therapeutic progress, the foundation for a collaborative relationship begins to form. Many clients, like this hypothetical one, harbor a deep and strongly rooted conviction that they do not deserve to have good things to happen to them. And if, by chance, they do, then they fear they will quickly and inevitably lose the good things and/or pay dearly for them. Consequently, a constant, underlying push–pull in the relationship style is often exhibited by these clients, especially early in treatment. For example, at the same time this client is asking for support, she is behaving in a way that is likely to disincline the therapist to be supportive by putting him or her in a double bind. On some level, the client genuinely wants support. At the same time, she feels that she does not deserve to be treated well, that she would become confused and anxious if this were to happen, and she does not trust the therapist's motives.

The therapist is able to remain supportive by understanding the client's dilemma and attachment style, and by titrating distance and closeness to her. In this instance, the therapist does this in part by engaging with her in a way that she might perceive as "sparring." For some clients, this back-and-forth wrangling is familiar and reassuring. It creates enough of a sense of distance and the appearance of conflict that the client is unlikely to worry that the relationship is getting too close. This therapeutic stance is similar to that taken in dialectical behavior therapy (Linehan, 1993), designed to keep the client's attention and to open space for other possibilities by deliberately engaging in a mildly upending verbal give-and-take.

Another basic principle illustrated here is that of breaking tasks down into very small, manageable components. Due to her fear of things going too well, the client is not willing to risk practicing the distress reduction exercise she was taught previously. The risk that it might actually work, and that she would have to "face" the prospect of succeeding, works against her low self-esteem and her defensive belief that she does not deserve good things. Like many PCA survivors, she is concerned that if things do improve, then someone or something will destroy it or take it away. Better not to have it at all than to be disappointed again.

Underlying all of this is the therapist's understanding that the repeating pattern of dysfunctional interactions the client experienced growing up, and the resultant conviction that people are unsafe and hurtful, play a role in her difficulties Recognizing the role that family environment played in the evolution of her current interpersonal patterns helps the therapist understand that the client has no clear template for collaboration. The task of the therapist, then, is not only to help the client overcome her fear of becoming aligned with him but also to guide her gradually in learning patterns of cooperation, as well as other skills she was never taught while growing up. The goal of the therapy is to develop a relational context that does not "make up for" what was missing in the client's childhood experience and family, but that provides the scaffolding that enables the client to develop independence, trust, and efficacy in the present.

REFERENCES

Alexander, P. C., & Lupfer, S. L. (1987). Family characteristics and long-term consequences associated with sexual abuse. *Archives of Sexual Behavior, 16*, 235–245.

American Psychiatric Association. (2000). *Diagnostic and statistical manual of mental disorders* (4th ed., text rev.). Washington, DC: Author.

Fassler, I. R., Amodeo, M., Griffin, M. L., Clay, C. M., & Ellis, M. A. (2005). Predicting long-term outcomes for women sexually abused in childhood: Contribution of abuse severity versus family environment. *Child Abuse and Neglect*, 29(3), 269–284.

Follette, V. M., & Ruzek, J. I. (Eds.). (2006). *Cognitive-behavioral therapies for trauma* (2nd ed.). New York: Guilford Press.

Gold, S. N. (2000). *Not trauma alone: Therapy for child abuse survivors in family and social context*. Philadelphia: Routledge.

Gold, S. N., Elhai, J. D., Rea, B. D., Weiss, D., Masino, T., Morris, S. L., et al. (2001). Contextual treatment of dissociative identity disorder: Three case studies. *Journal of Trauma and Dissociation*, 2, 5–36.

Gold, S. N., Hyman, S. M., & Andres, R. A. (2004). Family of origin environments in two clinical samples of survivors of intra-familial, extra-familial, and both types of sexual abuse. *Child Abuse and Neglect*, 28(11), 1199–1212.

Gold, S. N., & Seifer, R. E. (2002). Dissociation and sexual addiction/compulsivity: A contextual approach to conceptualization and treatment. *Journal of Trauma and Dissociation*, 3(4), 59–82.

Harter, S., Alexander, P. C., & Neimeyer, R. A. (1988). Long-term effects of incestuous abuse in college women: Social adjustment, social cognition, and family characteristics. *Journal of Consulting and Clinical Psychology*, 56, 5–8.

Herman, J. L. (1992a). Complex PTSD: A syndrome in survivors of prolonged and repeated trauma. *Journal of Traumatic Stress*, 5(3), 377–391.

Herman, J. L. (1992b). *Trauma and recovery: The aftermath of violence—from domestic abuse to political terror*. New York: Basic Books.

Higgins, D. J., & McCabe, M. P. (2000). Multi-type maltreatment and the long-term maladjustment of adults. *Child Abuse Review*, 9, 6–18.

Higgins, D. J., & McCabe, M. P. (2003). Maltreatment and family dysfunction in childhood and the subsequent adjustment of children and adults. *Journal of Family Violence*, 18(1), 107–120.

Hoyt, M. F. (1996). Cognitive-behavioral treatment of posttraumatic stress disorder from a narrative constructivist perspective: A conversation with Donald Meichenbaum. In M. F. Hoyt (Ed.), *Constructive therapies* (Vol. 2, pp. 124–147). New York: Guilford Press.

Jehu, D. (1988). *Beyond sexual abuse: Therapy with women who were childhood victims*. Chichester, UK: Wiley.

Justice, B., & Calvert, A. (1990). Family environment factors associated with child abuse. *American Journal of Orthopsychiatry*, 66, 458.

Karen, R. (1994). *Becoming attached: First relationships and how they shape our capacity to love*. New York: Oxford University Press.

Linehan, M. M. (1993). *Cognitive-behavioral treatment of borderline personality disorder*. New York: Guilford Press.

Long, P. J., & Jackson, J. L. (1994). Childhood sexual abuse: An examination of family functioning. *Journal of Interpersonal Violence*, 9, 270–277.

McCann, I. L., & Pearlman, L. A. (1990). *Psychological trauma and the adult survivor: Theory, therapy, and transformation*. New York: Brunner/Mazel.

Nash, M. R., Hulsey, T. L., Sexton, M. C., Harralson, T. L., & Lambert, W. (1993). Long-term sequelae of childhood sexual abuse: Perceived family environment, psychopathology, and dissociation. *Journal of Consulting and Clinical Psychology*, 61, 276–283.

Overholser, J. C. (1993). Elements of the Socratic method: I. Systematic questioning. *Psychotherapy: Theory, Research, Practice and Training*, 30(1), 67–74.

Ray, K. C., & Jackson, J. L. (1997). Family environment and childhood sexual vic-timization: A test of the buffering hypothesis. *Journal of Interpersonal Violence*, *12*(1), 3–17.

Ray, K. C., Jackson, J. L., & Townsley, R. M. (1991). Family environments of victims of intrafamilial and extrafamilial child sexual abuse. *Journal of Family Violence*, *6*, 365–374.

Roth, S., & Batson, R. (1997). *Naming the shadows: A new approach to individual and group psychotherapy for adult survivors of childhood incest*. New York: Free Press.

Wallin, D. J. (2007). *Attachment in psychotherapy*. New York: Guilford Press.

Williamson, J. M., Borduin, C. M., & Howe, B. A. (1991). The ecology of adoles-cent maltreatment: A multilevel examination of adolescent physical abuse, sexual abuse, and neglect. *Journal of Consulting and Clinical Psychology*, *59*, 449–457.

Yama, M. F., Tovey, S. L., & Fogas, B. S. (1993). Childhood family environment and sexual abuse as predictors of anxiety and depression in adult women. *American Journal of Orthopsychiatry*, *63*, 136–141.

CHAPTER 12

Cognitive-Behavioral Therapy

Christie Jackson
Kore Nissenson
Marylene Cloitre

Cognitive-behavioral therapy (CBT) seeks to improve functioning and emotional well-being by identifying the beliefs, feelings, and behaviors associated with psychological disturbance, and revising them through critical analysis and experiential exploration to be consistent with desired outcomes and positive life goals (e.g., Dobson & Dozois, 2001). This approach to psychotherapy is in distinct contrast to the traditions that came before it, and expresses an optimistic philosophy about human nature that is consistent with the American pragmatism from which it emerged: that new ways of thinking, behaving, and feeling are possible, and that the client can effect change.

Advances in CBT research have traditionally emphasized symptom reduction or resolution, yet the evolution of CBT for complex traumatic stress disorder has also focused on the dynamics of the therapeutic relationship, and we highlight such approaches in this chapter (see also Gold, Chapter 11, this volume). Interpersonal expectations and relational dynamics are inextricably woven into psychotherapeutic work, and this is particularly salient in the treatment of patients with complex traumatic stress disorder, because the "injury" for which they seek treatment is essentially an interpersonal one (i.e., experiencing abuse, neglect, or violence in critically important relationships). Effective CBTs for complex traumatic stress disorders include an approach that maintains the traditional view in which interventions provide guidance and instruction to improve functioning (e.g., skills development, more adaptive cognitive appraisals of current conflicts). However, the interventions also provide a means for clients to shift their inner experience of themselves and their sense of interpersonal relatedness.

Some CBTs explicitly articulate the goals and process of therapy as enhancement of self-regulation and secure attachment, as in Skills Training in Affective and Interpersonal Regulation/Modified Prolonged Exposure (STAIR-MPE; Cloitre, Cohen, & Koenen, 2006). Dialectical behavior therapy (DBT), a well-established CBT, emphasizes the client's experience of self as "authentic," a critical part of the process of acceptance and change (Linehan, 1997), through the therapist's validation of the client's difficulties in self-regulation as derived from an "invalidating" relational environment.

CBT therapists incorporate psychoeducation about the etiology of clients' symptoms, as well as the mechanisms of change. Identification of symptoms as resulting from adverse or traumatic events rather than from perceived character flaws can liberate the client from a burdensome and potentially paralyzing sense of shame. This point of view can engender a sense of hope and empowerment. In addition, psychoeducation about the mechanisms of change, such as explaining the rationale and behavioral principles involved in skills training or exposure exercises, can increase clients' sense of control and mastery over their symptoms and their lives. Playing an active role in their own recovery can be especially important for individuals with complex trauma histories, because their symptoms can reduce individual autonomy and self-direction. The use of between-session or "homework" assignments, including *in vivo* exposure exercises and practice of skills outside of session to promote treatment generalizability, encourages the adoption of an active stance on the part of the client.

CBT is based on collaborative empiricism, whereby client and therapist act as "coinvestigators" to identify explicitly the goals for therapy, and the means by which they reach these goals. They explore the logic and experiential basis for the client's assumptions, beliefs, and behaviors. The therapist often prompts the client to identify ways in which thoughts limit flexible and healthy functioning, and together they develop potential alternatives. Behavioral exploration or tests of these proposed changes are implemented in a graduated (incremental) fashion, documented, and corrected to lead to the desired change. Repeated practice and elaboration of alternative thoughts, feelings, and behaviors promote the acquisition and consolidation of new skills and thinking strategies, as well as flexibility in their application.

Finally, the fact that CBT is a relatively short-term therapy focused on the acquisition of skills may itself provide some benefit. The structured nature of the sessions and interventions seems to reduce clients' anxiety about working with their feelings, and facilitates a sense of "containment of affect" and increased ability to tolerate often intense emotions, which is particularly beneficial for complex trauma survivors who have difficulties with inter- and intrapersonal boundaries. A structured approach to therapy models for clients how experiences, including feelings, can have finite beginnings and endings. In addition, explicitly shaping the parameters of therapy, setting goals, and outlining session agendas gives clients a clear idea of what to expect from the therapy.

REVIEW OF RESEARCH ON CBT WITH COMPLEX TRAUMATIC STRESS DISORDERS

CBTs for complex traumatic stress disorders (see Foa, Keane, & Friedman, 2000) have been largely adapted from cognitive-behavioral interventions for PTSD, including prolonged exposure (PE), cognitive processing therapy (CPT), eye movement desensitization and reprocessing (EMDR), and stress inoculation therapy (SIT). These adaptations have involved the importation of interventions into a complex trauma therapeutic framework (e.g., Herman, 1992) and the integration of CBT interventions related to other disorders, including those from DBT. CBTs have consistently demonstrated efficacy for reducing PTSD symptoms (Bradley, Greene, Russ, Dutra, & Westen, 2005). Six randomized controlled trials (RCTs) evaluated the efficacy of CBT and specifically targeted or assessed complex trauma symptoms (Chard, 2005; Cloitre, Koenen, Cohen, & Han, 2002; Edmond, Rubin, & Wambach, 1999; McDonagh-Coyle et al., 2005; Resick, Nishith, & Griffin, 2003; Zlotnick et al., 1997). CPT, STAIR-MPE, EMDR, and group and individual CBT were each found to be superior to a wait-list control in reducing PTSD symptoms. The studies variably assessed and were found to produce reductions in complex trauma symptoms, such as dissociation (Chard, 2005; Cloitre et al., 2002; McDonagh-Coyle et al., 2005; Resick et al., 2003; Zlotnick et al., 1997), negative mood regulation (Cloitre et al., 2002), interpersonal problems and negative interpersonal beliefs (Cloitre et al., 2002; Edmond et al., 1999), and impaired self-reference (e.g., identity diffusion) (Resick et al., 2003).

Twenty additional CBT outcome studies were identified, in which the majority of participants endorsed a history of childhood trauma and symptoms of complex traumatic stress symptoms (e.g., dissociation, self-injurious behaviors, substance abuse) were treated and assessed. An affect management group treatment for women with PTSD related to childhood sexual abuse (Zlotnick et al., 1997) and a Seeking Safety intervention for women with PTSD related to childhood trauma and comorbid substance use disorders (Najavits, Weiss, Shaw, & Muenz, 1998) were associated with a range of improvements, although there was no control group. DBT was associated with improvements in women with borderline personality disorder (BPD), most of whom reported histories of childhood psychological trauma (Koons et al., 2001).

CLINICAL APPLICATION OF CBT TO COMPLEX TRAUMATIC STRESS DISORDERS

Emotion Dysregulation and Dissociation

Skills training in affect regulation is integral to CBT models such as STAIR-MPE (Cloitre et al., 2002), DBT (Linehan, Armstrong, Suarez, Allmon, & Heard, 1991), CPT (Resick et al., 2003), and Seeking Safety (Najavits et al., 1998). *Emotion regulation* refers to a broad range of abilities, including awareness of emotional states; identifying, differentiating, and describing feelings; self-soothing, tolerating negative states; and pursuing and heightening positive emotional states. CBT emotion regulation strategies include exposure to emotion-eliciting situations, while being aware of both feelings and the situation, focused breathing, practiced naming and verbalization of feelings, and building of client self-efficacy in the ability to experience, manage, and even enjoy feelings.

Acceptance and exploration of frightening feelings is a core task of trauma-focused CBT and is viewed as a prerequisite to self-coherence and self-identity. Several CBTs extend emotion and interpersonal regulation strategies to address dissociation and to enhance a sense of positive self-identity. Feelings that are viewed as unacceptable or overwhelming, such as rage, shame, envy, fear, and sadness, may be avoided or defended against through radical means, such as the "splitting off" of the feelings and the events that prompted them. This process takes place in the contexts of various interventions, such as the processing of traumatic memories, direct exploration of feelings and beliefs about the self, and exposure to difficult emotions, such as shame. EMDR, another CBT model that has proven efficacious for PTSD, includes a study that specifically assessed complex traumatic stress symptoms (Edmond et al., 1999) and one that includes adults with complex trauma histories (e.g., van der Kolk et al., 2007).

Insecure–Disorganized Attachment and Related Relationship Problems

Most CBT approaches for complex traumatic stress disorders recognize the potential role of disturbed attachment in the early life of many clients, although treatments vary in the ways they address this problem. STAIR-MPE, for example, explicitly introduces the concept of attachment to the client (psychoeducation), systematically explores the nature of the client's caretaker relationships using Bowlby's (1988) *working models*, and identifies templates for interpersonal relating based on early life experiences. STAIR-MPE uses the cognitive-behavioral construct of the *interpersonal schema* to provide a frame for articulating specific expectations that the individual holds regarding relationships. Schema work involves the examination of current interpersonal interactions with respect to basic beliefs about trust, intimacy, and fairness to evaluate and enhance these beliefs and the person's flexibility in engaging in relationships. STAIR-MPE, Seeking Safety, and DBT also include interpersonal skills interventions to help the client develop assertiveness, focus on personal needs, and cope with imbalances of power, authority, and distrust (see also Follette, Iverson, & Ford, Chapter 13, this volume). Role playing also may be used to test and to integrate more adaptive self–other schemas with changes in behavior (e.g., body language, verbal tone), and emotional attitude and expression.

Somatic Symptoms

STAIR-MPE uses focused breathing as the central intervention (i.e., practiced every session) to help patients be present and calm in their bodies. In addition, fearful or negative appraisals of bodily sensations are explored and tested in an experiential fashion. Anxiety management training interventions use relaxation training for this purpose. Mindfulness is a core component of DBT that helps clients focus in the present moment purposefully and nonjudgmentally, and includes attention to bodily feelings. Emotion regulation skills in DBT, STAIR-MPE, and Seeking Safety aid clients in experiencing emotions, while being fully present in their bodies. Strategies from cognitive-behavioral interventions for chronic fatigue and other somatic disorders incorporate activity scheduling (see Bazelmans, Prins, & Bleijenberg, 2006). CBT paradigms often utilize scheduling of pleasant activities to provide distraction from somatic symptoms. Imagery rehearsal therapy (IRT; Krakow et al., 2001) focuses on improving sleep quality and decreasing nightmares or distressing dreams.

CBT TREATMENT OF COMPLEX TRAUMATIC STRESS DISORDERS: CASE STUDY EXAMPLE

CBT treatment for complex traumatic stress disorders begins with an evaluation of the client's symptoms, particularly any threats to client safety, such as self-harm or substance use. In addition to identifying all symptoms and problematic behaviors, clear identification of strengths, including coping skills, are critical at the outset of CBT.

Phase 1: Safety/Stabilization, Emotion Regulation, and Interpersonal Self-Regulation

Early sessions of CBT focus on psychoeducation and normalization about maladaptive coping behaviors, such as drinking, cutting oneself, or dissociating. Clients are taught to identify and to stop the spiral of reinforcement following these behaviors. These behaviors are understood as efforts intended to be adaptive (e.g., to reduce distress or to regain feelings). The therapeutic goal is to replace them with strategies that promote health and have fewer negative consequences.

At this stage of therapy, it is of critical importance that the clinician work with the client to establish a safety plan. This should include a thorough assessment of any self-harm behaviors in which the client may engage and a plan for alternate, safe behaviors that may be utilized during times of distress. Together, client and therapist should determine what the client should do in emergency situations (call 911, go to the nearest emergency room, page the therapist if available, etc.). During this process, the therapist should determine his or her own limits of on-call availability and comfort level with various types of harmful behavior. Clients should commit to not acting on suicidal or homicidal urges and to trying their best to avoid other destructive behaviors. For example, the client may commit to not killing herself during the course of therapy and to trying to replace bingeing–purging with distress tolerance skills. Work on reconstructing memories of traumatic experiences and other potentially distressing therapeutic tasks should be implemented only after the client has attained a sufficient period of stabilization and acquired emotion regulation skills.

Another important task in the early stages of CBT is to begin building the therapeutic alliance. In CBT, the alliance is based on not only the therapist's genuine concern for and willingness to work with the client toward achieving the client's goals but also describing clearly how the therapy process will enable the client to know that he or she is successful in accomplishing these goals. The therapist helps the client to formulate specific behavioral changes that operationalize the client's goals, and describes how experimenting with new ways of thinking and new behavioral choices may be undertaken in the therapy. Demonstrating that change is possible and offering clients a projected time frame for the course of therapy is an extremely effective way for therapists to instill hope. Moreover, the strength of the early therapeutic alliance in CBT is associated with clients' improved capacity to regulate negative mood states during the trauma memory reconstruction phase of therapy, and this enhances the overall success of treatment for clients with complex traumatic stress disorders (Cloitre, Stovall-McClough, Miranda, & Chemtob, 2004).

Session Sample on Establishing Client Safety

THERAPIST: So, your history includes pretty regular drinking, cutting yourself, and dissociative behaviors.

CLIENT: Yeah, I feel really ashamed about that. It makes me feel really bad about myself, and then I end up doing even more of it!

THERAPIST: Believe it or not, that is not so unusual. Many clients with a history like yours engage in these behaviors as an effort to adapt and survive. So, for example, people who cut may do it in order to feel, or to feel a release from stress. People might engage in these behaviors to bring themselves into an emotional comfort zone that feels manageable. Cutting and drinking can be used to tamp down feelings that seem unacceptable and overwhelming, and maybe even scary. Our goal in this therapy is for you to get into an emotional comfort zone that you can live in and function in, without using strategies that have so many negative consequences. Another way for you to think about this is that you're trying to use rules that applied under extreme situations from the past in situations that now are very different. It's like you are applying rules from an arctic survival guide to get through your daily life in a warm climate!

CLIENT: Hmm, I never thought about it that way. That would be great, but how can it really happen?

THERAPIST: Well, you already have some real strengths, including some healthy coping strategies. I'm here to help you increase the use of these and ultimately let go of the need for the others. The first priority in this treatment is always going to be your safety. So we need to figure out how to keep you safe, which means not engaging in dangerous drinking, cutting, or dissociative behaviors while you go through this treatment. Now let's develop a plan that we can both commit to. So, for example, do you think you can replace cutting and drinking with more adaptive behaviors, like talking with people whom you trust when you need help?

CLIENT: I can call my friend Cathy—I can rely on her. Sometimes writing in my diary helps, too. And instead of binge drinking, I can binge clean!

THERAPIST: And don't forget about how you feel better after going for a walk or working out. I will also be teaching you focused breathing, a basic form of meditation to help you feel "centered" and remain in the present. It is also a basic building block to various other emotion regulation strategies we will work on later.

Enhancing capacities for emotion regulation and interpersonal efficacy begins shortly after stabilization. It incorporates continued efforts to help clients recognize triggers for urges to self-harm and other maladaptive behaviors, and to replace safety-interfering behaviors with more effective coping skills. This phase of treatment also explores the bases for habitual emotion regulation strategies and interpersonal tendencies in the context of early life experiences. It also provides an opportunity for clients to expand on and enhance important life skills, with an emphasis on healthy emotional and interpersonal functioning. Finally, this phase of treatment is intended to provide clients with sufficient security in their emotional experience and in their working relationship with the therapist to develop a sense of competence and confidence to confront and explore traumatic memories in later phases of treatment. Examples of introducing and applying interventions to enhance emotion and interpersonal regulation skills follow.

Sample Session on Emotion Regulation

In this session, the client works with her therapist to identify the kinds of feelings she has, what she thinks about them, and how she manages them. Her emotion regulation strategies are understood in the context of her family history. This facilitates better understanding of her patterns of emotional reaction and emotion-driven behaviors. It also helps reduce feelings of shame and opens up curiosity about how feelings might be managed differently.

THERAPIST: How were emotions expressed in your family while you were growing up, and what kind of strategies did you learn? A lot of people manage their feelings based on strategies emerging from their family. Some families scream out their feelings. Other families sweep them under the rug. How was it in your family?

CLIENT: It was never safe for me to have emotions. I would get hit. You never knew what type of mood my father was in when he walked in the door. He was a rage-aholic. And it terrified me! I learned to be as invisible as I could. I've learned to keep my feelings to myself.

THERAPIST: So you learned that feelings were explosive and dangerous.

CLIENT: Yeah, I avoid them, because I was at the other end of the stick. I don't want to go there now.

THERAPIST: It makes sense that you would feel this way given the damage that you saw caused by your father's rage. But you're paying the price by cutting, drinking, and dissociating, because you do have feelings, and they are very important. Feelings, both good and bad, give you information about a situation. For example, fear can help you know it's time to protect yourself. And feeling happiness reminds you that life is worth living. Feelings don't need to be so extreme or overwhelming. Feelings can exist at different levels of intensity. The first step at managing your emotions involves awareness of your emotions, including body sensations and thoughts and urges. This allows you to intervene sooner, so that your feelings can be more manageable and help you stay in that comfort zone we have been talking about. I'd like to ask you to keep track of your feelings over the next week. Here is a self-monitoring form. Let's do an example now. Can you think of a time in the past when you had an especially strong emotional reaction?

CLIENT: OK, yesterday, I had to confront my roommate about not paying her share of the rent.

THERAPIST: OK, so let's put this down at the prompting event. What thoughts went through your mind when you had to confront her?

CLIENT: Umm, she's going to yell at me. She will hate me. She'll say why am I bothering her. And umm, I also feel like I should pay her half of the rent for her, because she's going through a tough time now financially.

THERAPIST: OK, good. What were you feeling in your body at the time?

CLIENT: What do you mean exactly?

THERAPIST: Well, what was your heart doing? Was it pounding or beating regularly?

CLIENT: Well, now that you mention it, my heart was racing. It was hard for me to breathe. I felt kind of nauseous.

THERAPIST: OK, very good. Let's put that down, too. And so, now, what emotion do you think you were feeling? Here is a list of feelings to help you identify yours. Sometimes it's hard to put a name to your emotions. Like anything else, it's going to take some practice.

CLIENT: I felt afraid.

THERAPIST: Anything else?

CLIENT: Oh, yeah, I think I was feeling ashamed, too.

THERAPIST: And how did you cope with those feelings?

CLIENT: I avoided my roommate. I closed my door and had three glasses of wine. Then I sent her an e-mail.

THERAPIST: OK, so that's very important to note. We'll come back to this later. We'll be talking about other ways to cope with these feelings next session. Let's end today by planning some specific ways you can practice identifying your feelings and associated thoughts during the next week. This will help us decide when and how you can apply some coping strategies that we'll discuss in our next session. What this will enable you to do is learn to tolerate and accept feelings, rather than avoiding them by drinking or dissociating.

Sample Session on Dissociation and Its Relationship to Emotion Regulation

In this session, dissociation is viewed as resulting from the client feeling overwhelmed by intense anger. Therapy focuses on helping the client resolve her fear of her own anger and in order to accept her feelings (previously associated with danger) instead of dissociating.

THERAPIST: How did the self-monitoring forms go for you this past week?

CLIENT: Well, I didn't do it every day like you asked me to, but I have a few of them for you.

THERAPIST: OK, good, you managed to do it several times. Let's look over the ones you do have. I see it was your birthday. You wrote that you felt sad and empty on that day. Your thoughts were that you aren't worthy of other people's attention.

CLIENT: Yeah, if they really liked me, then they would have planned a surprise party for me.

THERAPIST: So let's talk about how you coped with the feelings of sadness and emptiness. I see that you found yourself on the subway in your pajamas. That sounds very scary.

CLIENT: It was terrifying! I had no idea where I was or how I got there. Especially since this hasn't happened to me in a long time.

THERAPIST: Often when people experience feelings that are overwhelming, they disconnect. This was a survival strategy that you adopted during the traumatic experiences of your childhood. Actually, those strategies were essential for you; they helped keep you alive. Now, however, this kind of dissociative behavior can be really dangerous and, in fact, is typically more harmful than helpful. As we've been discussing, awareness of your feelings is very important. People dissociate because they are afraid that if they feel their emotions, then they will lose control. Ironically, dissociating strips you of control, because you are not able to have choice over your emotions and behaviors and respond appropriately. So let's talk about how you might cope without dissociating, and let's review what happened before the subway event, so we can identify experiences or situations that create a risk for you to dissociate. On the self-monitoring sheet you wrote that the prompting event was not having a surprise party on your birthday.

CLIENT: I was given gifts by my friends but really wanted a party. It just made me sad and angry, because I started thinking about all the things I didn't get as a kid.

THERAPIST: Your birthday elicited strong feelings, including anger. Feeling angry is incredibly scary for you, and it makes sense that you wouldn't want to feel anger and would try to avoid it. So we've learned that birthdays are emotionally risky for you and can lead to dissociation. Now that we're aware of this connection, what coping strategies could you use in the future to help regulate these feelings before they escalate?

CLIENT: Well, one thing I can do is engage in calming and self-soothing activities, like you showed me at the beginning of our work. Using the breathing on a regular basis really helps me to stay in the moment. Now that I know ahead of time how hard birthdays can be, I can use these skills to negotiate this really rough patch. I can tell myself it's a rough moment and won't last forever, I can rely on my friends, and I can write in my journal, which I did yesterday because I was still upset about my birthday.

THERAPIST: That sounds like a terrific plan. That includes strategies to deal with how your body is feeling, what you are thinking, and the presence of friends as a resource. And don't forget that you can share your feelings with your boyfriend, since that's something we've been working on as well. You may recall that old schemas, such as "I cannot trust others enough to ask for help," are often activated when you experience strong emotions.

Session on Interpersonal Skills

The concept of interpersonal schemas, expectations about ourselves and others in relationships, is introduced to identify ways in which feelings from past interactions can influence current functioning. Good emotion regulation includes the ability to distinguish the presence of a feeling from the past that interferes with current interpersonal goals. The therapist also works with the client to develop an alternative schema that is better suited to current circumstances and consistent with the client's goals of establishing more positive trusting and stable relationships with friends.

THERAPIST: Let's go back to your very disappointing birthday. Let's see if some of your reactions, particularly those of disappointment, may have arisen from negative and deep-seated beliefs about yourself and others. Your reaction may be explained as a schema about your expectations regarding what you deserve from others.

CLIENT: What's a schema?

THERAPIST: A *schema* is a way of viewing the world. People have schemas for how they see themselves and how they expect other people to react to them. This is called an *interpersonal schema.* These beliefs are based on early experiences in childhood with your primary caregivers. These schemas guide how we interact with other people and are "rules" for dealing with the world. Schemas are often triggered when there is high affect. But what made you so angry?

CLIENT: Well, at the time, I was thinking, "If I allow myself to expect certain things from my friends and they don't do it, then I feel rejected and invalidated."

THERAPIST: You noted that you sometimes think, "I don't deserve things. People don't feel like I'm worth it." I remember that you told me your father used to say this to you when you were growing up. Given this, it makes sense that you would have these thoughts about yourself—like echoes of your father's hurtful words, and not necessarily what *you* really think. It also explains why you would feel sad and angry. The problem is, you are applying this rule from childhood in your life now, and this may not be true anymore. Your friends remembered your birthday. They may have gotten the manner of celebration wrong, but, given everything you have said about them, the gifts and cards were intended to send the message "We appreciate you." Your expectation that others view you as "undeserving" may have colored your interpretation of your friends' actions. How might you think about this differently? Let's see if together we can find an alternative schema.

CLIENT: I can think they still care, and I can still reach out and communicate with them, even if I'm disappointed. I guess I can be pretty all-or-nothing, but I like this middle ground!

THERAPIST: That's perfect. So now, when you notice that you are feeling like "I don't deserve things—people don't feel like I'm worth it," remind yourself that this is a schema from the past. What you just came up with—"I can think they still care, and I can reach out"—is your new schema that matches with people in your present life.

CLIENT: You know, this sounds good but I can't really imagine doing anything to change how I deal with my friends. I can handle the idea that they intended well. But I can't imagine asking for what I really want, even if they were interested in hearing what I had to say.

THERAPIST: It's hard for you to believe that your friends would care about what you want. But that may be what they really feel. It may be hard for you to experience that, because you've had so little experience asking for what you wanted and getting a positive response. The action of "asking for something you want" has all but faded from your interpersonal repertoire. Why don't you just try finding the words and saying them out loud.

CLIENT: Just out loud?

THERAPIST: Yes. Imagine the situation. Pretend that I am your friend Barbara. Say out loud what you would want to communicate to her about your wish for a party.

CLIENT: Uhm, OK. How about: "Barbara, I am thinking about my birthday and would really love to have a party. We've had parties for Bill and Sandra, and well, I'm guessing I feel I think it's my turn, now."

THERAPIST: Good. You came out and said what you wanted. Congratulations, I know that was hard. But I do think I detected uncertainty in your tone of voice. Also, why bring Bill and Sandra into this? You have a right to your own desires, and your friends care for you and clearly want to find ways to celebrate your birthday. Just ask. Let it come from a place of your own desires, and your (developing) belief that your friends know you, enjoy you, and have a positive interest in and a desire to respond to your wants and wishes.

CLIENT: OK. Here goes: "Barbara. You know what I was thinking? I would very much love a birthday party this year. It would thrill me if you could consider putting something together like that rather than all the gifts and such. What do you think of that?"

THERAPIST: Congratulations. You got it out, straight from your heart's desire.

CLIENT: Just asking feels empowering. Saying what I am feeling and thinking out loud makes it all seem more real. And you know what? The here-and-now reality of my friendship with Barbara, not Barbara-as-my-father, is that she probably would say yes.

Phase 2: Emotional Processing of Traumatic Memories

In Phase 2, the goal is to reduce clients' PTSD symptoms, as well as put their trauma memories into perspective as part of their life story. Repeated exposure to traumatic memories through storytelling enables clients to confront fearful memories and develop a sense of control over them (Rothbaum & Foa, 1999). The process also creates awareness of a self that comprises a past, present, and potential future. The story is tape-recorded, and often, immediately following the first telling, client and therapist listen to the tape together. In this experience, the client is supported by the therapist as he or she listens to the tape for the first time. The therapist might make comments that facilitate this experience, such as "That *was* a terrible thing to have happened. But you are safe *now*."

Sense of self as part of, but distinct from, these events is furthered by two additional activities. After the client completes the narrative, he or she names the various feelings experienced as he or she told the story (anger, fear, shame, sadness). This reinforces the integration of feelings that belong in the story. It is also an important emotion regulation exercise. The client becomes aware that these feelings are alive in him or her, but that they do not have to be overwhelming. This further reinforces in an experiential way that the client is not quite the same person as the one in the story, who, understandably, was feeling overwhelmed in past traumatic experiences but can now look back at those experiences in a planful and effective manner.

Next, client and therapist identify the interpersonal schemas embedded in the narrative. These are often transparent variations of schemas that the client earlier identified as operating in current relationships. Often this realization is an important moment in the therapy. It provides the client with an explanation for ongoing behaviors that often seem mysterious, peculiar, or at odds with current circumstances. It also begins to liberate the client from the schemas, because the discovery highlights that some very negative schemas are rooted in relational circumstances that no longer exist and are not necessary or even helpful in the present. Identifying the link between past experience and current behavior validates the reality of the trauma and its enduring impact on the client.

However, the simultaneous observation that the present is in many ways very unlike the past is critical. The environmental contingencies that created chronic fear, absence of autonomy, and self-direction no longer exist. The interpersonal schemas that were once adaptive no longer apply. Disentangling the past from the present is a critical task for clients with complex traumatic stress disorder, because clients recognize that they have the opportunity to become active agents for change in their own behalf. This process contributes to the organization of an autobiographical memory and, from it, an evolving sense of self living in the present and imagining a future.

Therapist and client work together to decide on the amount of material (number of events and level of details) to cover, the pace at which the story is told, and the emotional intensity that they expect to arise in any single narration. Therapist and client also identify several favored emotion regulation strategies that the client will use to manage the emotions that arise while doing the memory recollection task. This includes beginning with reminders of the client's present safety, ending with preferred grounding exercises, and identifying emotion regulation strategies (e.g., breathing, self-talk) to implement as needed during the telling of the story. The story is told aloud by the client and tape-recorded to provide an enduring record of the event and sometimes as symbol of the process of "containing" the past. Once specifics of the task are agreed upon, the therapist guides the client through the process, gently lending structure and focus to the narrative work. The therapist also monitors the client's emotion state and offers encouragement. In this way, the therapist takes on the role of coregulator in the emotional experience that emerges from the creation of the narrative.

Plans for listening to the tape at home are developed by client and therapist, and include details relative to time and location to ensure uninterrupted and comfortable conditions for the task. The importance of self-care strategies after listening to the tape is emphasized. This includes identification of the amount of time the client will listen to the tape and a plan for putting the tape away and going on to other activities. Structuring the task in this way helps clients to understand that their traumatic memories should not prevent them from having a life beyond their traumatic past experiences.

Sample Trauma Memory Reconstruction Session

THERAPIST: As we discussed in our last session, today we will begin putting together some of the stories from your childhood. By telling what's happened to you, you have the opportunity to put together the pieces of the trauma—your thoughts, feelings, and sensations related to the experience—that now disturb you in your nightmares and in intrusive memories. Making the fragments of your memory whole will reduce your trauma-related symptoms. Although it may be painful and scary to confront your trauma memories, the reality is that you live with these experiences every day through reenactments, flashbacks, nightmares, and intrusive thoughts and images that are likely far more painful than the work we will do here. This is a safe place for you to do this work. I will be with you the entire time. We will go at your pace as we put together the memory. You will likely see that once we begin this work, you will be able to tolerate the feelings that these past events generate. And that will do something very important, which is to reduce your likelihood of dissociating. You will become confident in your ability to feel, stay present, and manage these emotions. You won't have to check out anymore—this won't be the only option when you are feeling these emotions.

CLIENT: This sounds good but hard to believe. How will this really change me?

THERAPIST: You will figure out more of who you are and more of who you can be in the future. And you will also realize that your trauma is in the past and can't hurt you anymore.

CLIENT: I've wanted to believe that for a long time, but the memories always seem to come back to haunt me. I can't seem to get them off my mind, especially when I really want to focus on something important like being close to someone or doing well at work. Replaying the memories seems like exactly the opposite of what I want to do, which is to get rid of them.

THERAPIST: It makes perfect sense that you want to put the memories out of your mind, and the truth is, the best way to put a memory away is to look at it carefully and not just try to avoid it. The harder you try to avoid a memory, the more it comes back and the more you want to check out. Does it make sense that dealing with a memory can put it to rest?

CLIENT: I guess so. I mean, it makes sense. I just don't know if I can do it.

THERAPIST: We'll do this very carefully, so that you can be sure you can handle it every step of the way. So we will be using the most distressing memory that you think you can *tolerate* from the hierarchy we put together last week. This would be the memory where your father is chasing you with a bat in the woods. We are going to audiotape your recollection of this memory for you to listen to at home. I will give you a recording log, so that you can note your levels of distress each time you listen. Let's begin by you closing your eyes. The tape recorder is on. (*pauses*) Now, using the present tense, tell me about your father chasing you in the woods.

CLIENT: I come home from working my afterschool job and I am already so very tired. I can hear Mom and Dad yelling as I walk up into the yard.

THERAPIST: What are you wearing?

CLIENT: I have on my blue work smock and my favorite jeans. I think I'm wearing my FRANKIE GOES TO HOLLYWOOD RELAX T-shirt.

THERAPIST: And what do you see and smell?

CLIENT: Well, I see the front of our mobile home. It has gray siding with blue trim. It has a wooden deck in the front, and there are two big windows. I think I can hear them yelling, because a window is open. Oh, and I smell a woodsy smell. I am crushing pine needles underfoot. And I smell something greasy—I think somebody was frying chicken.

THERAPIST: And what happens next?

CLIENT: I go toward the house and I'm already feeling apprehensive. I sense trouble brewing. I see an eviction notice on the front door and I begin to panic. Not again! We just moved in here. I walk inside, hearing the creak of the screen door. I take off my shoes and put them by the door like we always do. I put my head down and try to go in without being noticed. But then I decide to risk it and ask what we are going to do about the eviction notice. My Dad screams at me that it's none of my f---ing business. All I do is cause trouble, he says. I should have stayed at work! And I realize I should always keep my mouth shut. Why did I have to say anything!

THERAPIST: You're doing fine. What happens now?

CLIENT: I think about running into my bedroom, but my dad is blocking the doorway. And I know from experience that he can break the door down anyway. He is a very large man. Imposing shoulders. Booming voice. He's scowling at me. I can see his face so clearly. I just want to get out of there, just be invisible so he can't hurt me. (*Begins to cry.*)

THERAPIST: It's OK, take a breath and keep going.

CLIENT: I figure out that I'll never make it all the way to my bedroom. I just stand there for a second. "This is all your fault!" screams my dad. Both our eyes lock onto a wooden bat standing in the corner. I know what's coming next, so I take off, running out the door. I can hear my dad close behind. Luckily, he's been drinking, so he's kind of stumbling around. But I know I better run fast to avoid getting beat. There were so many times he did this to me. It is so unfair!

THERAPIST: You're absolutely right, you did *not* deserve to be treated this way. (*gently*) But now, I need you to stay focused and tell me the rest of what happens.

CLIENT: OK, well, I am running, running, running. I hide behind bushes and try to come out, but I'm afraid he's right there, so I just keep running and hiding. I think I ran for hours. I'm running so long I realize it has gotten dark. I am already so tired from school and work. And my stomach hurts because I'm hungry, but I'm afraid of being caught. So I'm just running and listening for him.

THERAPIST: And what are you feeling?

CLIENT: I am terrified! My heart is racing, I'm breathing fast, and my knees are aching. Wow, I didn't even realize that before.

THERAPIST: And what else are you feeling in your body?

CLIENT: Hmm, even though I'm hungry, I feel nauseous. Oh wow, and now I remember that I had no shoes on! My feet are bloody and cut up. I am so sweaty. Finally, I risk it and go back to the house. The door is wide open, and my father is not there. I race down the hall to my bedroom and lock the door. That's it.

THERAPIST: OK, now I want you to open your eyes. Look at me. Look around the room and out the window. See that you're here with me now, and you're safe. It's 2008. Feel yourself in the chair, safe in my office.

CLIENT: (*Sighs and looks around the room. Takes a deep breath.*)

THERAPIST: How do you see yourself in this story?

CLIENT: I should have known better than to come home then. My dad was usually getting off work about then, and I should have hung around at work longer. I was so stupid.

THERAPIST: So this is similar to the schema we were formulating several sessions ago: "If I don't plan ahead then bad things will happen."

CLIENT: Well, that's not exactly how I feel here. It's more like: "If I don't plan for my safety, I'll always be in danger from others." I constantly need to protect myself from how other people might hurt me both physically and emotionally.

THERAPIST: That's quite a principle to live by. It makes sense to plan for safety, and to choose how and with whom you associate, but does it have to be in the forefront "constantly"?

CLIENT: But that's how I live.

THERAPIST: That must take a lot of your time and energy. Wouldn't it be easier if you didn't always have to constantly be on red alert for danger? You mentioned before that you're always all or nothing, but that you really prefer the middle ground in between. Is there a middle ground here, where you can be aware of safety but not "constantly" on guard?

CLIENT: I don't know how to do that.

THERAPIST: Well, one thing with trauma storytelling is that it reminds you that this event is in the past. And that you are at a distance from these experiences. They are memories, and only memories. And the more you practice talking about them, the more you will feel you own them rather than them owning you. Also, one of the reasons we have been doing so many experiential exercises around positive experiences and self-soothing activities is to give you experiences to counter your belief that you are always in danger.

CLIENT: So, if I were to propose an alternative, so to speak, it would be "I can't always have a plan. There are ways of being safe other than predicting all the terrible things that can happen."

THERAPIST: Right, you've noticed that when you spend time talking with people and sharing your feelings, your view of the world changes, so you see that not everyone is dangerous and catastrophe isn't always around every corner. And that some people are good and kind. That sounds more like a livable middle ground. It requires you taking a risk though, which means reaching out and spending time with people, talking with them, and sharing your feelings. Depending on others is scary for you, of course, but so far in your adult life you've had experiences that tell you that others can be there for you.

CLIENT: It's funny. This memory of me running, running, running really contrasts with my other bad memory. The one where my father strapped me to a chair and was force-feeding me my birthday cake. There I couldn't move at all.

THERAPIST: It's so interesting that you can have these two very different and opposing bodily experiences—one where you are in flight and the other where you can't move. These are the two poles of the traumatized state. You have experienced both. Putting words to these experiences allows you to process the memory. In other words, creating this narrative enables you to make sense of these bodily experiences using words. Language helps you create a coherent story that then becomes less frightening. And just as your level of distress related to the birthday cake memory decreased significantly after the exposure exercises, your level of distress related to this memory with your father will also decrease.

Session Analyzing the Trauma Narrative and Discussing Its Implications

CLIENT: I listened to the tape every day this week, and I brought in some interpersonal schema sheets to review with you.

THERAPIST: Great. I can see from your distress record that your distress levels related to this memory decreased a great deal since we met last time.

CLIENT: Yes, I feel much better about this memory, and about the things I've been through in general. I am realizing that I couldn't control what happened back then, but now I have more choice over my life. Although it's still a little scary, I know I don't need to spend all my time warding off danger. It really does make me sad, though, that I didn't get the kind of care and concern that my boyfriend got from his parents. I see what a different person I could have been.

THERAPIST: You have every right to feel that way, and now you are creating the kind of life you should have had and want still to have. It sounds like you also might have a healthy feeling of pride and self-esteem—proud of yourself for working so hard at letting yourself be close to people you choose. It's impressive that you've been working to implement the belief that it's not always dangerous to become close to someone. There are some wonderful benefits when you allow yourself to experience intimacy in a healthy way. This is illustrated in one of the schema sheets you brought in, the one about your feelings with your boyfriend, and becoming closer to him.

CLIENT: It is so surprising that I can actually see myself settling down with him. If we have children, I know my parents won't be part of that; that still really hurts. But I'm learning to create my own family without them. I realize that there are some people, wonderful people, who care about me now. I am learning to be OK with who I am and what I have.

Summary of Case Sessions

As indicated in the previous dialogue, the narrative work attends to sensory perceptions, feelings, bodily sensations, beliefs, and behaviors. Consequently, the memory that emerges from this process integrates all aspects of experience. Clients often express their surprise, relief, pleasure, and pride in having accomplished this task. The telling of the story is a creative act and, as such, enhances a sense of autonomy, independence, and self-determination. The dynamic and repeated process of telling and then listening to the story facilitates a sense of a self in time. The ability of clients to recognize the psychic and physical injuries imposed on them, without being overwhelmed, derives in part from viewing these events from the safety of the present, and the safety of an emerging belief that the person listening to the story is not quite the same as the person about whom the story is being told. Clients note that doing the skills work gives them an inkling of their distance from these events, that they are not the same person as the person in the story.

Finally, the presence of the therapist creates a context in which the work can be successfully done, and in which a type of "secure attachment" is experienced. The therapist does not attempt to replace or substitute for other caregivers from the client's life. Rather, the therapist serves as a guide in the therapeutic task of the narrative work. This includes providing structure in the task of telling the story and functioning as a coregulator in the titration of the emotional intensity of the experience. The therapist gives comfort and encouragement at moments of both distress and success. In listening to the narrative, the therapist "sees" the client more completely than others might have in the past, both in the dark parts of the history and the client's success in emerging from those experiences. The therapist sustains engagement and interest in this task, often over several sessions, repeatedly providing guidance, support, and practical help, and in doing so, conveys belief in the client's worth and even admiration for the client's capacities for development. Providing comfort, recognition, and perception of worth to the client are all tasks of the therapeutic caregiver that engender a feeling of security in the client and model a template or interpersonal schema for future relationships.

CONCLUSION

CBT provides skills training that can address not only PTSD but also the emotion regulation and interpersonal disorganization characteristic of clients with complex trauma histories. Skills help clients prepare for and engage in trauma memory work, as well as promoting a sense of mastery in place of feeling "less than." CBT is an individualized assessment-guided approach (Wagner & Linehan, 2006), which facilitates objective assessment of treatment progress and clients' engagement in therapy. Another strength of CBT is its efficacy with psychiatric conditions that often involve complex trauma (e.g., schizophrenia [Turkington et al., 2008]; bipolar disorder [Miklowitz et al., 2007]; eating disorders [Fairburn, Jones, Peveler, Hope, & O'Connor, 1993]; BPD [Linehan et al., 2006]). CBT also can achieve positive outcomes with difficult disorders within a relatively short time period.

Finally, CBT recognizes the relation among thoughts, feelings, and behavior, and enables clients to modulate feelings by modifying thoughts and behavior. Thus, CBT models such as DBT, STAIR-MPE, CPT, EMDR, and Seeking Safety have great potential to help the clinician engage and successfully treat clients with complex traumatic stress disorders.

REFERENCES

Bazelmans, E., Prins, J., & Bleijenberg, G. (2006). Cognitive behavior therapy for relatively active and for passive chronic fatigue syndrome patients. *Cognitive and Behavioral Practice, 13*, 157–166.

Bowlby, J. (1988). *A secure base.* New York: Basic Books.

Bradley, R., Greene, J., Russ, E., Dutra, L., & Westen, D. (2005). A multidimensional meta-analysis of psychotherapy for PTSD. *American Journal of Psychiatry, 162*, 214–227.

Chard, K. M. (2005). An evaluation of cognitive processing therapy for the treatment of posttraumatic stress disorder related to childhood sexual abuse. *Journal of Consulting and Clinical Psychology, 73*, 965–971.

Cloitre, M., Cohen, L. R., & Koenen, K. C. (2006). *Treating survivors of childhood abuse: Psychotherapy for the interrupted life.* New York: Guilford Press.

Cloitre, M., Koenen, K. C., Cohen, L. R., & Han, H. (2002). Skills training in affective and interpersonal regulation followed by exposure. *Journal of Consulting and Clinical Psychology, 70*, 1067–1074.

Cloitre, M., Stovall-McClough, K. C., Miranda, R., & Chemtob, C. (2004). Therapeutic alliance, negative mood regulation, and treatment outcome in child abuse-related PTSD. *Journal of Consulting and Clinical Psychology, 72*, 411–416.

Dobson, K. S., & Dozois, D. J. A. (2001). Historical and philosophical bases of the cognitive-behavioral therapies. In K. S. Dobson (Ed.), *Handbook of cognitive-behavioral therapies* (2nd ed., pp. 3–39). New York: Guilford Press.

Edmond, T., Rubin, A., & Wambach, K. G. (1999). The effectiveness of EMDR with adult female survivors of childhood sexual abuse. *Social Work Research, 23*, 103–116.

Fairburn, C., Jones, R., Peveler, R., Hope, R., & O'Connor, M. (1993). Psychotherapy and bulimia nervosa. *Archives of General Psychiatry, 50*, 419–428.

Foa, E. B., Keane, T. M., & Friedman, M. J. (Eds.). (2000). *Effective treatments for PTSD: Practice guidelines from the International Society for Traumatic Stress Studies.* New York: Guilford Press.

Herman, J. L. (1992). *Trauma and recovery.* New York: Basic Books.

Koons, C. R., Robins, C. J., Tweed, J. L., Lynch, T. R., Gonzalez, A. M., Morse, J. Q., et al. (2001). Efficacy of dialectical behavior therapy in women veterans with borderline personality disorder. *Behavior Therapy, 32*, 371–390.

Krakow, B., Hollifield, M., Johnston, L., Koss, M., Schrader, R., Warner, T. D., et al. (2001). Imagery rehearsal therapy for chronic nightmares in sexual assault survivors with PTSD. *Journal of the American Medical Association, 286*, 537–545.

Linehan, M. M. (1997). Validation and psychotherapy. In A. C. Bohart & L. S. Greenberg (Eds.), *Empathy reconsidered* (pp. 353–392). Washington, DC: American Psychological Association.

Linehan, M. M., Armstrong, H. E., Suarez, A., Allmon, D., & Heard, H. L. (1991). Cognitive-behavioral treatment of chronically parasuicidal borderline patients. *Archives of General Psychiatry, 48*, 1060–1064.

Linehan, M. M., Comtois, K. A., Murray, A. M., Brown, M. Z., Gallop, R. J., Heard, H., et al. (2006). Two-year randomized controlled trial and follow-up of dialectical behavior therapy vs. therapy by experts for suicidal behaviors and borderline personality disorder. *Archives of General Psychiatry, 63*, 757–766.

McDonagh-Coyle, A., Friedman, M., McHugo, G., Ford, J., Sengupta, A., Mueser, K., et al. (2005). Randomized trial of cognitive-behavioral therapy for chronic posttraumatic stress disorder in adult female survivors of childhood sexual abuse. *Journal of Consulting and Clinical Psychology, 73*, 515–524.

Miklowitz, D. J., Otto, M. W., Frank, E., Reilly-Harrington, N. A., Wisniewski, S. R., Kogan, J. N., et al. (2007). Psychosocial treatments for bipolar depression: A 1-year randomized trial from the systematic treatment enhancement program. *Archives of General Psychiatry, 64*(4), 419–427.

Najavits, L. M., Weiss, R. D., Shaw, S. R., & Muenz, L. R. (1998). "Seeking safety": Outcome of a new cognitive-behavioral psychotherapy for women with posttraumatic stress disorder and substance dependence. *Journal of Traumatic Stress, 11*, 437–456.

Resick, P. A., Nishith, P., & Griffin, M. G. (2003). How well does cognitive-behavioral therapy treat symptoms of complex PTSD? *CNS Spectrums, 8*, 340–355.

Rothbaum, B. O., & Foa, E. B. (1999). *Reclaiming your life after rape*. New York: Oxford University Press.

Turkington, D., Sensky, T., Scott, J., Barnes, T. R. E., Nur, U., & Siddle, R., et al. (2008). A randomized controlled trial of cognitive-behavior therapy for persistent symptoms in schizophrenia. *Schizophrenia Research, 98*(1–3), 1–7.

van der Kolk, B. A., Spinazzola, J., Blaustein, M. E., Hopper, J. W., Korn, D. L., & Simpson, W. B (2007). A randomized clinical trial of EMDR, fluoxetine and pill placebo in the treatment of PTSD. *Journal of Clinical Psychiatry, 68*, 37–46.

Wagner, A. W., & Linehan, M. M. (2006). Applications of dialectical behavior therapy to posttraumatic stress disorder and related problems. In V. M. Follette & J. I. Ruzek (Eds.), *Cognitive-behavioral therapies for trauma* (2nd ed., pp. 117–145). New York: Guilford Press.

Zlotnick, C., Shea, M. T., Rosen, K., Simpson, E., Mulrenin, K., Begin, A., et al. (1997). An affect-management group for women with posttraumatic stress disorder and histories of childhood sexual abuse. *Journal of Traumatic Stress, 10*, 425–436.

CHAPTER 13

Contextual Behavior Trauma Therapy

Victoria M. Follette
Katherine M. Iverson
Julian D. Ford

The contextual behavioral therapy approach to conceptualizing and treating the effects of complex trauma focuses on experiential avoidance, which is assumed to be responsible for the maintenance of complex traumatic stress disorder symptoms and associated developmental deficits (Follette, Palm, & Rasmussen Hall, 2004; Pistorello, Follette, & Hayes, 2000). Contextual behavior trauma therapy (CBTT) represents a synthesis of third-generation behavior therapy, which evolved from both behavior-analytic and cognitive-behavioral traditions. Moving beyond those traditional approaches, "these treatments tend to seek the construction of broad, flexible and effective repertoires over an eliminative approach to narrowly defined programs" (Hayes, Follette, & Linehan, 2004, p. 6). With behavior analysis (Follette & Naugle, 2006) and acceptance and commitment therapy (Hayes & Strosahl, 2005) as a foundation, CBTT interventions identify and modify stimulus–response chains underlying traumatic stress disorder symptoms with a goal of enhancing mindfulness, acceptance, and the therapeutic relationship.

A CONTEXTUAL BEHAVIORAL CONCEPTUALIZATION OF COMPLEX TRAUMATIC STRESS DISORDERS

Mowrer's (1960) two-factor theory may be used to describe traumatic stress symptoms in terms of two primary learning processes: classical (respondent) and operant (instrumental) conditioning. The *classical conditioning* factor involves pairing previously neutral stimuli with a highly aversive event. As a result, fear, anxiety, or other distress or avoidance responses are triggered by the previously neutral stimuli. The *operant conditioning* factor involves an increase in the likelihood or frequency of behaviors that enable a person either to acquire desired outcomes ("reinforcers," e.g., help or validation from friends or family, an internal sense of hope, self-efficacy, or relief) or to avoid aversive outcomes (e.g., situations or interactions that are reminders of past traumas or are currently traumatic or distressing).

For instance, a woman who was sexually abused as a child by an adult male who used alcohol may find the smell of alcohol on the breath of her partner frightening. Automatic triggering of fear may lead her to avoid being close with her partner when she smells alcohol, even if there is no danger. From an operant conditioning perspective, avoidance is reinforced by the reduction of aversive internal experiences; for example, she may feel a sense of relief when she moves away from her partner after having smelled alcohol, although this avoidance may lead to conflict in their relationship. However, if she initiates a constructive dialogue with her partner to prevent his drinking from becoming a problem (sexually and in general) in the relationship, then this assertive behavior may be reinforced by changes in how she and her partner interact that might lead to a sense of increased trust and intimacy in the relationship.

This pattern of behavior can result in a cycle that not only can become more elaborated over time as generalization occurs but also interferes with new learning that would be more adaptive. For example, this woman may not learn that she can safely enjoy being with her partner when they are relaxing together. As her behavior becomes more rigid, or rule-governed, she has fewer opportunities to contact reinforcers that might enable her to overcome this automatic avoidance. In addition, stimuli that had set the occasion for her to engage in behavior based on her personal goals and preferences may come to elicit avoidance instead of these life-enhancing actions. Where she had previously sought opportunities to be close with and enjoy interacting with her partner, she may begin to avoid being with him. These are additional examples of the role of operant conditioning in posttraumatic avoidance: Stimuli that formerly were associated with behavior based on her goals and interests are now associated with avoidance behavior, and the avoidance behavior is reinforced by the sense of relief that accompanies a reduction in fear or anxiety. Unfortunately, avoidance can replace a wide range of life-affirming and relationally beneficial behaviors, leading the trauma survivor to relinquish many crucial reinforcers and opportunities that would be essential to living in line with her values and desires (e.g., developing intimate relationships, having children). Moreover, as this example illustrates, the arousal symptoms are likely to persist, because her avoidance of situations involving men does not allow her to develop a new learning history with males (i.e., that she can be safe from assault with them even if they have ingested alcohol). Finally, the avoidance behaviors prevent her from being able to develop more adaptive methods for dealing with her fear of men (or, more accurately, the fear of traumatic stress symptoms associated with "men").

As this scenario illustrates, a core psychological process that characterizes complex traumatic stress disorders is avoidance: attempts to avoid or to escape from trauma-related thoughts, emotions, memories, and bodily reactions. Hayes, Wilson, Gifford, Follette, and Strosahl (1996) conceptualize *experiential avoidance* as a functional dimension that underlies a variety of seemingly distinct forms of psychological impairment (e.g., addiction, self-injury, anxiety, depression, suicidality, and traumatic stress symptoms). A common denominator is the chronic, unsuccessful attempt to avoid experiencing intense psychological distress—hence the term *experiential* avoidance.

Researchers posit that experiential avoidance plays a central role in the long-term outcomes associated with a history of abuse (Follette et al., 2004). Survivors of repeated abuse may avoid negative private thoughts (e.g., "I hate myself") and emotions (e.g., fear, shame, guilt, or hopelessness), resulting in coping strategies, such as *dissociation, self-injury, numbing, substance use,* or *somatization,* that become increasingly ineffective when outside of the abuse context in which they may have functioned initially as effective means of coping and surviving (Polusny & Follette, 1995; Tull, Gratz, Salters, & Roemer, 2004; Wagner & Linehan, 2006). Such forms of avoidant coping provide short-term relief from distressing private events and are likely maintained by negative reinforcement (Hayes et al., 1996; Polusny & Follette, 1995). However, when trauma survivors rely on experiential avoidance as a primary coping mechanism, problems such as depression, substance abuse, anxiety disorders, and interpersonal difficulties often occur (Polusny & Follette, 1995). Experiential dysregulation and emotion avoidance also are associated with risk of parasuicidal and suicidal behavior (Follette et al., 2004; Wagner & Linehan, 2006).

To enhance emotion regulation, in CBTT the therapist works with the client to develop a sense of a *continuous self,* which is understood as a capacity to observe and label experiences, feelings, and thoughts from a unique personal perspective—what "I" observe, think, and feel—that often is undeveloped in individuals with extensive childhood histories of psychological trauma (Courtois, 2004). When an individual has difficulties identifying and labeling these private idiosyncratic experiences, especially when they are related to core values and goals, it is difficult to experience a stable sense of self or "self-acceptance." Without this experiential foundation, the person is likely to experience instability in knowing about personal preferences and values, depending instead on changes in the immediate environment and in body states.

At a basic level, therapeutic enhancement of the sense of self involves validation of the client's immediate experiences and acknowledgment of the client's life history (including psychological trauma). Skills are taught and experiential exercises are used to help the client become mindful and self-aware in noticing and labeling perceptions, feelings, and thoughts *in the moment* during therapy sessions to enhance the capacity for focused attention and increase the client's ability to recognize and reduce or manage episodes of self-detachment, such as dissociation and depersonalization. In CBTT the apparently paradoxical goal is to foster a sense of being connected to one's personal history and at the same time have a self that is not limited or irrevocably defined by that history (i.e., both self-integration and self-differentiation).

Enhancing the capacity for continuous sense of self is crucial to enabling abuse survivors to seek, select, and sustain healthier and safer (i.e., validating and responsive) relationships that reinforce their sense of self, self-worth, trust, and hope, particularly when complex trauma involves revictimization (Cloitre, Cohen, & Koenen, 2006). When abuse occurs, the child's thoughts, feelings, wants, and experiences are disregarded, trivialized, or negated. Such invalidating responses communicate rejection, misunderstanding, and criticism of the child's very selfhood, as well as his or her emotional expressions, thus promoting emotion dysregulation, experiential avoidance, dissociation, and a sense of detachment from or fragmentation of the self (Fruzzetti & Iverson, 2006; Wagner & Linehan, 2006). Disclosing and recovering from abuse involves being authentic and courageous; yet, not infrequently, it does not lead to help but instead to intensified verbal, physical, and even additional sexual abuse and ongoing invalidation that further corrodes trust in self, as well as others. CBTT addresses these corrosive dynamics.

CONTEXTUAL BEHAVIOR TRAUMA THERAPY

CBTT represents several components of what has been identified as the "third wave" of behavioral therapies that share the characteristics of being "empirical, principle-focused … and tend to emphasize contextual and experiential change strategies in addition to more direct and didactic ones" (Hayes et al., 2004, pp. 5–6). The term *contextual* indicates a focus on the function of behavior rather than simply its form. Understanding function requires a behavior analysis of antecedents and consequences of both problematic and adaptive behavior. Behavior-analytic therapies, developed to treat problems of fear and anxiety, have a strong base of empirical support (Follette & Ruzek, 2006). CBTT provides additional treatment benefits for clients with complex traumatic stress disorders, in that it addresses not only observable behaviors but also private events, such as thoughts, feelings, memories, and physiological sensations. CBTT also focuses on *radical acceptance* and *behavioral activation* as primary mechanisms for changing trauma-related patterns of classical and operant conditioned experiential avoidance, in addition to or instead of behavioral strategies such as exposure, extinction, and desensitization of fear responses and memories. The presenting problems of many clients with complex trauma histories range beyond intrusion and arousal symptoms most typically treated with behavioral/exposure methods. We discuss next the three distinct but related treatment approaches included in CBTT, which incorporate techniques from all three "waves" of cognitive-behavioral therapy (CBT) but particularly emphasize those of the third, namely, *radical acceptance* and *behavioral activation*. The CBTT treatment approaches are acceptance and commitment therapy, dialectical behavior therapy, and functional analytic psychotherapy.

Acceptance and commitment therapy (ACT; Hayes, Strosahl, & Wilson, 1999), a contextual behavioral therapy that has been found to be effective for the treatment of many forms of psychological distress (Hayes, Masuda, Bissett, Luoma, & Guerrero, 2004), was specifically designed as a treatment to counter experiential avoidance. ACT emphasizes the enhancement of acceptance, willingness, psychological flexibility, and "valued living" as means of challenging and reducing experiential avoidance. Clients are encouraged to examine their own valued life directions, to notice how their avoidance strategies have prevented them from living the life they want to live, and to commit themselves to meaningful behavioral change. ACT treats trauma-related problems by encouraging the acceptance of private experiences, including trauma-related intrusions and thoughts, as well as emotional states, such as fear, anxiety, shame or anger, to reduce avoidance of these inner experiences and traumatic memories and symptoms (Orsillo & Batten, 2005; Walser & Hayes, 2006). Clinical case study evidence suggests that ACT is an effective treatment for posttraumatic stress disorder (PTSD) (Batten & Hayes, 2005; Orsillo & Batten, 2005; Shipherd, 2006) and is promising for complex traumatic stress disorders (albeit in a more prolonged and graduated fashion in keeping with these clients' chronic self-regulation difficulties; Ford, Courtois, van der Hart, Nijenhuis, & Steele, 2005).

Dialectical behavior therapy (DBT; Robins & Chapman, 2004; Wagner & Linehan, 2006) was originally developed to treat the chronic emotion dysregulation problems associated with parasuicidality in clients diagnosed with borderline personality disorder (BPD). DBT combines the basic strategies of behavior therapy with mindfulness practices to form the central dialectic: Accept the client as he or she is, while concurrently pushing for change. The ultimate goal is to enhance emotional self-regulation and behavioral self-management through validation and teaching the skills of mindfulness, emotion identification, distress tolerance, and interpersonal effectiveness. DBT is conducted in stages. In Stage I, clients participate until they have reached personal and environmental safety and stabilization, then, in collaboration with their therapist, they decide whether to continue with more specific, trauma-focused work.

Stage II uses basic DBT techniques to focus specifically on symptoms associated with PTSD, building on basic skills and foundations that occurred in earlier treatment (see Wagner & Linehan, 2006). Two studies, one with female abuse survivors (Cloitre et al., 2006) and the other incarcerated women with PTSD (Bradley & Follingstad, 2003), utilized relatively brief (i.e., eight to nine sessions) initial preparation phases in their, respectively, individual and group therapy interventions, including skills training for affect regulation similar to that provided in DBT. Both studies reported improvements in affect regulation, interpersonal functioning, and PTSD symptoms following the complete treatment, which involved prolonged exposure (Cloitre et al., 2006) or written disclosure of traumatic memories (Bradley & Follingstad, 2003). Neither the full Stage I DBT intervention nor combined Stage I and Stage II DBT have been empirically evaluated with PTSD or complex traumatic stress disorders (Wagner & Linehan, 2006).

Functional analytic psychotherapy (FAP; Kohlenberg & Tsai, 1991) emphasizes *clinically relevant behaviors* (CRBs) that occur within the therapy relationship and session that functionally parallel problematic classes of behavior occurring outside of session. FAP appears similar to psychodynamic approaches that address transference reactions, in that the focus is on the client's reactions to the therapist. However, the therapist in FAP uses functional analysis to identify and shape CRBs, while also reinforcing improvements and accurate interpretations of behaviors both within and outside of session. The therapist uses the therapeutic relationship to model behavior and responds contingently to different client behaviors in ways that are similar to other relationally based strategies (see Steele & van der Hart [Chapter 7], Pearlman & Caringi [Chapter 10], Follette, Iverson, & Ford [Chapter 13], Schwartz, Schwartz, & Galperin [Chapter 17], Johnson & Courtois [Chapter 18], and Ford & Saltzman [Chapter 19], this volume). FAP uses intense interpersonal relationships as the vehicle for change and has demonstrated efficacy with forms of individual distress that either have significant interpersonal consequences or are mediated by interpersonal contingencies, such as depression and anxiety (Hayes et al., 2004).

FAP has particular relevance to the treatment of complex traumatic stress disorders, because it was developed and validated with patients whose clinical presentations are consistent with these disorders (Kohlenberg, Tsai, & Kohlenberg, 2006). In FAP, the therapist helps the client to identify and label private experiences, such as thoughts, feelings, and styles of interaction, and to build a trusting therapeutic relationship within which the client can become increasingly able to experience safely rather than avoid memories and reminders of traumatic experiences, and the feelings and thoughts associated with them.

CBTT Integration

CBTT integrates techniques from ACT, DBT, and FAP in working with clients with complex traumatic stress disorders. Such a strategy does not constitute a "one-size-fits-all-approach," because it utilizes a thorough *functional analysis* strategically to incorporate these three forms of CBTT, with fidelity to their unique concepts and technical procedures. In particular, it is crucial to provide a safe foundation, and to balance change and acceptance skills, a strategy that begins at the outset of therapy. The therapist clarifies treatment goals and strategies in a clear and collaborative manner. While working with the client to identify behavior patterns that have not been effective in enhancing the quality of his or her life, the therapist also validates the client as a person who has done the best that he or she could in surviving very difficult life events.

CBTT proceeds in stages that are consistent with the metamodel of treatment of complex traumatic stress disorders (Ford et al., 2005), with each stage involving interventions unique to CBTT.

Phase 1: Stability, Therapeutic Alliance, and Self-Awareness

The early phase of therapy (approximately five to six sessions, although more may be required in complex cases) has six primary goals: (1) orientation to treatment, (2) client commitment to treatment processes and goals, (3) functional analysis of current and past variables that may be impacting the client in the present, (4) psychoeducation regarding traumatic stress, (5) brief values exploration, and (6) development of an initial therapeutic relationship. Each of these goals is worked on in a collaborative manner, with therapist and client as equal partners in the endeavor. Although the therapist has specialized information and skills to impart, the relationship is treated as egalitarian rather than hierarchical. FAP approaches might be used to identify ways the client approaches the therapy relationship that are reminiscent of other significant hierarchical relationships and that are not consistent with the therapeutic context (i.e., CRBs). Many clients with complex traumatic stress disorder approach treatment and the therapist from a position of extreme mistrust as a result of their past experiences, and may be quite taxing and/or difficult to engage in a therapeutic relationship (see Steele & van der Hart [Chapter 7] and Kinsler, Courtois, & Frankel [Chapter 9], this volume). To create a safe therapeutic environment, the therapist uses strategies such as mindful listening and validation to develop rapport and begin to help the client modify thoughts and try behavioral changes outside of the treatment context. The therapist consistently attends to modeling and reinforcing positive change, while challenging the client to continue to modify behaviors that are maladaptive.

Functional Analysis

CBTT therapists utilize a *functional analysis* to help clients become more aware of the contingencies (or triggers) influencing their private experiences and overt behaviors. This strategy involves conducting a "chain" analysis that highlights the sequential connections (hence the term *chain*) that link (1) antecedents (i.e., events or changes in the external environment or in the client's internal bodily, affective, or cognitive experience); (2) behaviors, feelings, or thoughts that are either problematic or adaptive for the client; and (3) consequences (i.e., subsequent events or changes in the external environment or the client's internal experience that increase or decrease the likelihood of those behaviors, feelings, and thoughts stopping, continuing, or starting). For example, an antecedent of a sleepless night due to nightmares might be linked to feeling irritable and withdrawing from communication with a partner, which in turn may lead to an increase in PTSD symptoms (e.g., hypervigilance, anger, emotional numbing) for the client and feelings of worry, frustration, and hurt for the partner. This chain may continue and expand to include new problem behaviors, thoughts, and feelings, thus increasing problematic consequences in terms of worsening symptoms of PTSD and an increasingly compromised primary relationship. What began with a potentially correctable and manageable set of contingencies may become an apparently intractable disorder and an irreparably damaged intimate relationship or support system. A complex trauma survivor's behavioral chain might include more extreme dysregulation that could escalate into severe substance dependence, suicidality, self-harm, pathological dissociation, impulsive behaviors, or reactive aggression.

Even overwhelmingly large and complex chains of posttraumatic impairment, when broken down into small associative "links," can be carefully examined and incrementally modified to change from a cascade of escalating avoidance and dysregulation to the development and implementation of a step-by-step plan. For example, in a discussion in therapy about how traumatic experiences may lead to (classically conditioned) associations between sleep and being unsafe, the trauma survivor may be able to experience some improvements in sleep on some nights, then build on this initial change. Finding ways to alter crucial sleep antecedents to reduce the distress they elicit is a critical step in using the functional (chain) analysis to begin the shift from vicious cycles of distress and dysfunction to positive cycles of awareness, acceptance, and experimentation, with new outcomes that in turn elicit a sense of hope and reinforce changes. When improvement (e.g., a better night's sleep) occurs, functional analysis is used therapeutically to explore with the client what changed and to identify more adaptive behaviors, thoughts based on acceptance, self-efficacy, or hope, and feelings that are reinforcing rather than distressing. Chain analysis continues with examination of the consequences of those different behaviors, thoughts, and feelings that might, for example, include small steps toward effective intimacy-enhancing behavior with the partner as another reinforcer of change.

The key to understanding and clinically utilizing the functional (chain) analysis method is that no antecedent, behavior, experience (whether an observable or a private feeling, body sensation, or thought), or consequence is too small to be identified as a meaningful part of the "problem" and utilized as a therapeutic step toward solving even very severe and chronic problems. Functional analysis is an exercise in (and a role model for) mindfulness and acceptance, as well as a practical approach to helping clients develop adaptive new ways of coping and solving problems. Mindfulness requires attention to the present moment, without judgment and with keen observation of aspects of the environment and personal experience, and sensations that usually are overlooked in the press of daily life and the stress of posttraumatic impairment. When problems or symptoms are broken down into constituent parts with a functional analysis, therapist and client together mindfully attend to the client's experience. Acceptance involves taking things as they are and not becoming so wrapped up in trying to fix problems (or people) that obvious solutions are overlooked. To accept is not to be passively resigned or hopeless, but to be actively involved in understanding things as they are rather than as one wishes or demands they should be. Functional analysis is a means of accepting and being mindfully aware of the problems caused by traumatic stress, as well as changes that could lead to overcoming or living effectively with those problems. The components in a functional analysis are as follows:

1. Define problem behavior.
   - Behaviors may include substance abuse, dissociation, self-harm, suicidality, interpersonal problems, or PTSD-related problems, such as flashbacks and sleep disturbance.
2. Determine internal and external antecedents, or "links in the chain," including an assessment of physiological sensations, vulnerabilities, emotions, cognitions, and overt behaviors.
   - Antecedents may include feelings of fear, anxiety, shame and disappointment, critical self-judgments, and invalidation from significant others, friends, and colleagues.
   - Consequences may include the temporary "relief" provided by dissociation, substance abuse, compulsive sexual addiction, self-harm, anger, or isolation, followed by escalating problems and increasingly negative views of the self in a vicious cycle.
3. Identify internal and external barriers to resolution of the problem behavior in the future.
   - Internal barriers may include lack of awareness of and difficulty in regulating emotions (e.g., shame, rage, despair) and self-invalidating or self-defeating thoughts.
   - External factors may include conflictual and invalidating relationships.
4. Solution analysis includes generating behaviors that promote *acceptance* and *change*.
   - Acceptance solutions may include noticing emotional arousal and action urges before they are extreme (e.g., mindful noticing and labeling of emotions, thoughts, and urges).
   - Change solutions may include using distress tolerance skills to modulate arousal (e.g., self-soothing or relaxation activities) or stimulus control strategies, that is, changing the environmental conditions to enhance the probability of more effective responses.
5. Commitment to potential solutions involves agreeing to attempt the potential solutions.
6. Experimentation and evaluation involve actually enacting potential solutions and observing the outcomes of altering antecedents, behavior, and consequences.
7. Refinement of solutions involves modifying the potential solutions based on their outcomes in experimentation and developing further changes to the behavioral chain.

Skills Training

Complex trauma survivors may have difficulty engaging in therapeutic exposure without either fleeing emotionally or dropping out of treatment (McDonagh-Coyle et al., 2005). For these clients, a graduated and incremental approach to exposure therapy may be facilitated by skills training (Cloitre et al., 2006; Ford et al., 2005). CBTT assists clients in developing DBT-derived skills for mindfulness and emotion regulation.

Mindfulness skills comprise (1) emotional experiencing, including identification of the emotions and sensations being experienced and why (includes labeling/describing the emotion and recognizing its antecedents), (2) awareness of action urges in response to emotions (e.g., "I'm feeling disappointed because my friend did not call me back and I'm noticing the urge to shut down, or leave her a judgmental, angry, critical message"), (3) acknowledgment of long-term goals and values (e.g., "I value this friendship and my goal is to maintain the relationship while also doing something to address my disappointment"), and (4) validating or acknowledging the legitimacy of experience (e.g., "I was really looking forward to talking with my friend, so it makes sense I'm feeling disappointed"). Increased mindfulness, by means of skills development and validation from the therapist, helps the client to discriminate thoughts from feelings, with an emphasis on accurately labeling emotions and *defusion* ("mindful distancing") from the literality of thoughts (Hayes et al., 1999). Mindfulness skills have been found to increase clients' ability to experience painful memories, thoughts, and feelings, without using avoidance strategies or automatically engaging in a behavior to manage the feeling (Follette, Palm, & Pearson, 2006; Follette et al., 2004).

Skillful emotion regulation involves multiple components, beginning with mindful awareness of emotional experience, which includes noticing that one's own emotional arousal is rising or the "early warning signs" that are a prelude to feeling distressed. The behavior therapy-based Subjective Units of Distress Scale (SUDS) is useful within the therapy sessions and between sessions to help clients practice identifying their level of emotional distress. Mindfulness also can be facilitated by self-monitoring of specific crucial internal experiences, such as by using an Urge scale when substance abuse is a therapeutic issue, or a Connectedness scale when social detachment and support are key issues (Ford & Russo, 2006).

Emotion regulation also involves clients' toleration and acceptance of emotions through accurate labeling, experiencing, and validation of their emotional experiences. Self-validation and validation from the therapist can function as reinforcement of effective emotional experiencing, including the expression of emotions (Fruzzetti & Iverson, 2006). Clients learn to decrease their vulnerability to negative emotions by applying new consequences in response to emotional stimuli. This skill includes the recognition of earlier distress and engagement in acceptance (e.g., validation, radical acceptance) and/or change strategies (e.g., self-soothing or distracting) in the service of meeting treatment goals (Fruzzetti & Iverson, 2006).

Phase 2: Acceptance-Based Exposure to Traumatic Memories

CBTT expands traditional prolonged exposure treatments (Foa & Rothbaum, 1998; Resick & Schnicke, 1993) by approaching exposure in a graduated fashion, using mindfulness and acceptance strategies prior to and during exposure exercises. Acceptance-based exposure expands the *functional analysis* of both private and observable behaviors to *identify explicitly and label classes of private behavior that are most often avoided when recalling traumatic experiences*, including thoughts, feelings, physiological sensations, and memories and that appear to interfere with the client's goals and values (Hayes et al., 1999). The client and therapist engage in an in-depth discussion of these classes of behavior to help the client assess the utility of attempting to change or control aversive private experiences and to examine whether the client uses such avoidance strategies (Hayes et al., 2004). With the client's permission and informed consent, the therapist begins exposure treatment, focusing on the client's *identified classes of aversive private experiences and sensations*, while simultaneously supporting and coaching the client in *mindful acceptance*, without engaging in avoidance strategies (Follette et al., 2004). Client and therapist jointly engage in *values clarification* to assist the client in selecting and using effective behaviors in accord with identified goals and values rather than making decisions based on fear and avoidance (Hayes et al., 1999; Varra & Follette, 2005).

CLINICAL CASE EXAMPLE

Case Description

"Cathy" is a composite client who received CBTT over a span of approximately 6 months of individual hourly sessions. Cathy, a 41-year-old woman, sought treatment for PTSD symptoms related to childhood sexual abuse, as well as depression and relationship problems. She had been married to her second husband for 3 years, was the mother of two teenage sons, and had recently quit her job as a cook for a local day care center. Cathy had a few years of college course work but left school when she became pregnant with her first child. She reported having felt depressed on and off since adolescence and was currently in the midst of a severe depressive episode. Cathy also reported that she occasionally engaged in self-injurious behavior (e.g., hitting her body with her hand or fist) and that she had been experiencing hypersomnia, along with increasing nightmares and intrusive thoughts and memories relating to her childhood sexual abuse, and to the physical and emotional abuse in her first marriage. Although not currently suicidal, Cathy had attempted suicide when she was 17 years old, following a painful breakup with her boyfriend. Cathy had sought treatment two times previously. Cathy stopped each time, because she felt treatment was not progressing. Moreover, she had not revealed her history of childhood sexual abuse to either therapist.

Initial Appointment

The therapist began the intake interview by asking Cathy how she hoped therapy would be most helpful. Cathy responded that she wanted to "get over" the terrible memories of numerous episodes of sexual abuse (which Cathy later described in greater detail as including forced oral and vaginal intercourse by her mother's boyfriend when she was between ages 7 and 9) that bothered her "all the time." She spontaneously elaborated, saying that the perpetrator did not live with the family at that time but frequently spent days and nights at Cathy's house. Both her mother and the mother's boyfriend frequently drank to the point of intoxication that sometimes led to mutual violence, and her mother was generally emotionally unavailable to Cathy. Additionally, Cathy revealed that although her mother may have become suspicious that the boyfriend was abusing her daughter, she never asked about it. Cathy recalled that her mother got mad when she said she did not want the boyfriend around. Additionally, she reported that she currently had a hard time disclosing anything about the abuse to her husband, believing that he would leave her if she did so. Cathy described wanting to feel closer to her husband and two children, and to have close friends rather than just superficial acquaintances. She reported drinking alcohol on occasion and recently drinking more in the evenings to "take the edge off my bad mood" and to help her sleep.

Cathy was clearly uncomfortable discussing her history, as was evident in her shaky voice and limited eye contact. The therapist did not press for any specific, abuse-related details and was sensitive to Cathy's hesitancy to disclose abuse. The therapist used reflective comments and validation frequently, and conducted a brief safety assessment (Courtois, 1999). Cathy reported that although she had many thoughts about death, she only had occasional urges to end her life, no plan or means to do so, and was motivated to not kill herself because of the pain that her suicide would cause her sons. The therapist informed Cathy of her specialized knowledge in working with abuse issues, and of her success in the past helping other women with similar issues. Cathy expressed relief and agreed to begin treatment the following week.

Session 2 Transcript

THERAPIST: How does it feel to be here today?

CLIENT: I don't know. I guess I'm a little nervous. I'm not sure what I'm supposed to do. I just knew that I had to do something. So we'll see what happens.

THERAPIST: It's OK to feel nervous and even a little scared. A lot of people feel that way at the beginning of therapy—it's a big unknown and may feel scary. In today's session, I can tell you a bit more about what therapy will be like, and we can get to know each other better. Also, you will get to *choose* whether you want to do this therapy and whether you want to do this work with me. If you decide to go forward, you'll find that we will discuss your choices quite a bit. First, let's talk about how things have been going in your life and what led you to seek therapy.

CLIENT: Things haven't been so good, especially lately. I've been really edgy—I've been snapping at my kids, arguing with my husband, and sleeping during the day. I don't know what my problem is ... my life feels so overwhelming. ... I think there is something seriously wrong with me.

THERAPIST: Is that a familiar thought—something's "wrong" with you and you can't manage your life?

CLIENT: Yes, I feel like that all the time. I have a much harder time coping with everyday life than most other people. I feel like I was born different and I'll always have a horrible life.

THERAPIST: Tell me, exactly what kinds of things do you have difficulty coping with?

CLIENT: Well, work is a biggie. I was working at a day care for 2 years, but they basically fired me because I missed so much work. I would call in sick a lot. And when I did go to work, I would zone out and forget what I was doing. Sometimes I would have to hit myself to come back to reality. I hate telling you this—no one knows about it.

THERAPIST: I appreciate your openness. Hurting oneself to cope with painful feelings is not unusual when a person has experienced childhood trauma. How often do you slap yourself, or do you do anything else to intentionally hurt yourself, such as cut, scratch, burn, or hit yourself?

CLIENT: Well, I have been hitting myself maybe once every week or two, maybe even more lately, when I'm really hating myself. I haven't done anything else for over 10 years—I used to burn myself with cigarettes. Now I don't do anything that would leave a mark that my kids could see.

THERAPIST: It sounds like this has been a struggle for you for a long time, and my guess is that this has seemed like the only way you could keep functioning. I know it can be really uncomfortable to talk about when you hurt yourself, but it important to do so, and this behavior is definitely something that we can work on together. In order to really understand what is going on for you in moments when you hurt yourself, it will be important for us to talk carefully about what happens—what leads up to you hitting yourself and how you feel later. Would you be willing to take a deep breath and tell me what happened right before you hurt yourself and how you did it?

CLIENT: (*Takes a quick breath.*) After the last session, when I got home my husband asked me how it went and I snapped at him. He told me he was just trying to be supportive. I told him to leave me alone. I could tell I hurt his feelings. I was so mad at myself. I went into the bedroom, closed the door, sat on the bed. I thought I was going to explode. I punched my thigh three or four times.

THERAPIST: And how did you feel right after you did that?

CLIENT: A tiny bit calmer. It kind of took the edge off how bad I was feeling. Pretty stupid, huh?

THERAPIST: Well, given how upset you were feeling, my guess is that you felt like you *had* to do something to feel better or to at least not feel as bad. My guess is that hurting yourself, or drinking or sleeping during the day, may help you feel better in the short run but may not be working so well in the long run. Does that sound accurate to you?

CLIENT: Yes. I hate myself for doing that, but I don't know what else to do. I just want to run away ...

THERAPIST: As hard as it is, I can see that you have already gained some understanding of what has been going on for you. First, you stated that these things you do, such as hurting yourself or drinking, are not working for you. Second, you said that you'd like to run away. ... Is it possible you hit yourself, drink, sleep, stay home from work with headaches, push your husband away, all to run away or "escape" from your pain, even if it's just a temporary escape? Do you notice a pattern?

CLIENT: I guess I didn't think about it like that. It doesn't seem like I do any of these things on purpose, or that I even think about it before I do it. I just do it.

THERAPIST: Exactly. Sometimes these ways of coping work so well, at least in the sense that they may soothe or calm us down a little, that they can become automatic.

CLIENT: So you are saying that I do these things as a way of coping with stress?

THERAPIST: That may well be the case. We'll find out more about how these things work in your life as we go on. So here is one way to think about this that can be helpful. It is a little like you are a bubble going down your path and you come across another bubble blocking your way every time you move. So you can continue to go forward, with this bubble stuck to you—like bubbles do. You don't have to get rid of the bubble or burst it to move forward. You can just go forward with that feeling or bubble, without having to engage in old behaviors like hitting yourself to change the situation [Hayes et al., 1999]. I will help you learn to better identify, label, and express your emotions without the avoidance behaviors that actually hurt you. Once I help you get better at understanding and accepting your emotions, I can help you face and work through your abuse memories, so that they are less scary and distressing to you than they are now.

CLIENT: What do you mean? We aren't going to work on the sexual abuse now?

THERAPIST: That's a good question. We *will* be working on your abuse; however, before we talk about that in detail, we need to do some things to give you a safe foundation before we move on in therapy. How does that sound? Are you onboard with that plan?

CLIENT: Sure. You're the expert.

THERAPIST: Well, that doesn't sound like you are involved in deciding. How about allowing yourself some decision-making power and some personal expertise? This therapy is going to require a commitment on your part, some hard work, and you may even want to quit at times.

CLIENT: No, I can't quit this time! This has to work!

THERAPIST: I definitely think we can tackle these issues together, but I want you to be clear about the steps I'm proposing and about what you are committing to, and to know that you won't be alone in this. I know this work is difficult, and I'm committed to standing by you in this process.

CLIENT: Thanks. It scares me to be all alone with this, so I'm glad to hear you won't leave me.

THERAPIST: I'll be here to support you. But it's going to be hard work, maybe even painful at times. We need to consider steps you can take to cope and stay steady when it doesn't feel like the pain is behind you. Like when you're dealing with emotional pain and memories head on and stay with them.

CLIENT: I don't know. I guess you will have to keep pushing me.

THERAPIST: Do I have your permission to push you gently … to help you with your goals of resolving past issues, enhancing your marriage, being closer with your sons, and being who you want to be?

CLIENT: Yes, if it will get me through these horrible memories, I want you to push me!

THERAPIST: And I want you to tell me if I ever push you in a way that feels too hard or too much too fast. I will guide the process, but you are always the expert on what's right and OK for you.

Comment: Assessment/Building a Foundation for Therapy (Phase I)

The early phase of therapy drew on strategies from ACT, DBT, and FAP to help Cathy to (1) understand the course of treatment, (2) commit to treatment processes and goals, (3) begin to do a functional analysis of current and historical antecedents and consequences of behaviors that pose a risk to her or to engaging in therapy, (4) better understand PTSD, (5) begin values exploration, and (6) build trust in the therapist and a strong therapeutic relationship.

Session 6 (Midphase 1): Addressing Dissociation

THERAPIST: So, I see on your diary card that you "checked out" for several hours this week. Shall we work on helping you get more control over your tendency to dissociate today?

CLIENT: There's nothing I can do about it. It just happens all of the time, ever since I was a kid!

THERAPIST: Dissociation probably helped you in certain situations when you were being sexually abused or not noticed or responded to, or when you had strong, uncomfortable feelings. Many people learn to "leave their bodies" when in an overwhelming situation. Maybe dissociation helped you cope when you tried to tell your mother about what was going on and she didn't support and protect you. The thing is that nowadays you do it automatically, even when you are not really in danger and don't need it anymore. Now, it gets in your way.

CLIENT: If it is so automatic, then I don't think there is much I can do about it, is there?

THERAPIST: Actually there's a lot you can do. In a way, the process of learning to change it is somewhat similar to what happened when you would hurt yourself. If you know how you're feeling and what's happening before you begin to dissociate, you have more of a choice about when, if, and how you decide to "check out." Then it is *your* choice, not something out of your control.

CLIENT: How do we do that?

THERAPIST: Let's start with what happened before you dissociated on Friday.

CLIENT: OK, well, I got in a fight with my oldest son about his wanting to spend the night over at his girlfriend's house. I didn't want him to, because I worry about him. ... He told me that he doesn't have to listen to me and that he'd be home the next morning.

THERAPIST: OK, that sounds like it would be hard for any parent. How were you feeling then?

CLIENT: I was scared and worried about him, and I was yelling at him for not listening to me. When he left the house my SUDS rating was really high, maybe 8 out of 10.

THERAPIST: Yeah. I'd imagine that would be scary. Then maybe you were feeling pretty disregarded and hurt when he made those comments and left anyway?

CLIENT: Yeah, I guess I was probably feeling that way. Then, I was also thinking that he was right about what he was saying: Why should he listen to me? I haven't exactly been the perfect role model for him. I felt ashamed when he left.

THERAPIST: So you got pretty judgmental and ashamed of yourself? Tell me about when you judge yourself, and what that is like for you.

CLIENT: I think I just don't know what else to do when I feel like someone is not respecting me or taking me seriously. I start feeling small and invisible, and then I think that I deserve to feel bad.

THERAPIST: Do you feel "small" or judgmental of yourself right now?

CLIENT: A little bit.

THERAPIST: Are you willing to do some work on some of those judgments with me?

CLIENT: Yeah. What do you have in mind?

THERAPIST: Well, let's first take a look at where you are on your dissociation scale right now? So, if you think of 1 as being very aware of what is going on and in no danger of dissociation and 5 as feeling a little overwhelmed with emotions and in danger of losing awareness of the present moment … and 10 as being already dissociated and unaware of what is going on for you, where would you say you fall on that scale right now?

CLIENT: I would say that I'm about a 5 in terms of dissociation. I was maybe a little higher a few minutes ago, when we were talking about how I was feeling after my son left on Friday night.

THERAPIST: So maybe when we stop and give you a chance to figure out how your thoughts and feelings make sense, that might help you get off the negative self-judgment path and bring your dissociation level down? Hmm …

CLIENT: It was getting higher because I started having so many judgments about myself and feeling ashamed, similar to what you and I talked about last week when we analyzed how my thoughts can get stuck in a chain that reinforces depression and avoidance. But then I think I started focusing on you and what you were saying to me, and that helped me to sort of snap out of it.

THERAPIST: I'm glad that you were able to use mindfulness, and that you found that it helped. Actually, I think that it was being mindful—paying attention to what's happening right now and to what you think and feel in the moment, and how that makes sense—that made the difference. For now, I'm glad if I'm a helpful reminder to you to be mindful.

CLIENT: Yes, but it sure is easier to do when I'm with you and not caught up in all of it.

THERAPIST: That's probably true. But, if you are able to do it now, then you are capable of doing it at other times, even when it is hard, although it might take more attention on your part and practice. Let's try an exercise you can practice at home.

Comment: Addressing Experiential Avoidance in Current Life (Phase 1)

Phase 1 next moves into using functional analyses to address important problems or symptoms that are high priority because they impair the client's functioning or impede safety. As illustrated earlier, this is done by asking behaviorally specific questions about target behaviors and their potentially modifiable antecedents and consequences. A functional analysis provides opportunities for the therapist to model and coach the client in mindfulness, acceptance, and commitment to specific changes. This lays the groundwork for acceptance-based graduated exposure work on trauma memories.

Session 18 (Phase 2): Dealing with Intrusively Reexperienced Trauma Memories

CLIENT: I was making such good progress until I saw that movie, which reminded me of all the past abuse. It just seems like I don't deserve to be happy or to move forward in my life. I don't even know what that would mean. I don't want my family to suffer, but I don't know how to get over what happened to me. I feel so small, so ashamed of myself.

THERAPIST: You want a life where you're not thrown back into memories of the abuse and all the terrible feelings that go with those experiences. That's a clear statement. We can take some important steps in that direction now that you've done so much work to prepare yourself with mindfulness and acceptance skills. These unwanted memories are very tough to live with, and I know you don't want to just sweep them under the rug and avoid them—but you also don't want them to hijack your life and your feelings like what happened this week.

CLIENT: That's right. When the abuse feelings take over, I fall apart. I'm such a weak person. No ... I mean I *feel* so weak, but I want to feel and really *be* strong enough to deal with the memories. How does anyone get strong enough to stop these horrible memories from ruining their life?

THERAPIST: At the beginning of therapy, we talked about how there would come a time in this therapy when we could work on helping you deal with your memories of abuse. You've done the skills work to get ready for this, so let me explain briefly what we can do to support you in addressing your memories of abuse. The work involves first figuring out the feelings and thoughts that you have now that make these memories still seem too horrible to live with, like feeling small and terrified, and thinking that you can't protect yourself and make it stop. Then I'll work with you to accept and deal with those feelings and thoughts, while you talk through some specific memories that are troubling for you. Does it make sense to you that even memories of very bad experiences could be less horrible and maybe even manageable—the *memory*, not the past abuse itself—if you can face and deal with the feelings and thoughts that make memory overwhelming? We can't change past experiences, but we can change their impact on your life today. Thoughts and feelings connected to the abuse certainly are very painful, but by facing those thoughts and feelings, you can put the memories where they belong and move forward in your life.

CLIENT: I don't know. (*Pauses thoughtfully.*) Maybe. But it was so horrible when it happened, how could it not be that horrible to remember?

THERAPIST: That's a very good question, Cathy. This doesn't make the past abuse any less bad, but it's like what you've been doing in dealing with your feelings and thoughts that used to lead you to hurt yourself—the situation may still be very difficult, but when you stay in the present moment and handle the feelings or thoughts that are triggered, you can make different choices now and not fall back into the trap of hurting yourself.

CLIENT: Oh, I never thought about it that way. Like the memories don't have to overwhelm me if I know how to deal with my feelings. That sounds like a hard thing to do, but if you say its possible, then I really want to give it a try.

Comment: Acceptance-Based Exposure for Intrusive Trauma Memories

Phase 2 trauma memory work in CBTT shares many of the core parameters of prolonged exposure therapy for PTSD, which includes facilitating a shift from avoidance of traumatic memories to assertive confrontation of the memories, and frequently to desensitization to the associated thoughts, feelings, and sensations, especially fear and anxiety. Furthermore, acceptance-based exposure teaches and guides the client in confronting and gaining a sense of acceptance of the current feelings and thoughts that are elicited by traumatic memories. This approach shifts the client's focus from perseveration on the past events and avoidance of the associated reactions to a focus on the present moment, with an emphasis on safety in the present and effective life choices. This approach can help the client to accept the range of emotions, thoughts, and sensations connected to experiences of abuse and increase his or her sense of self-efficacy.

CONCLUSION

The CBTT treatment strategies outlined in this chapter provide a general guide to implementing CBTT with clients with complex traumatic stress disorders. In our experience, most clients with complex traumatic stress disorders desperately want to find or to reclaim the sense of confidence, hopefulness, and trust that make a "life worth living" (Hayes et al., 1999); at the same time, they feel ashamed, angry, and confused about their history of psychological trauma and terrified that they will never be able to overcome the distress they feel when they remember it. CBTT offers guiding principles and practical tools for therapists and clients to use in working together mindfully to accept and understand these dilemmas, and to enable the client to make and follow through with a commitment to take small steps toward managing feelings and thoughts, and changing behaviors and environmental contingencies.

As a coda, we have found that living these principles in our own lives is crucial to the process of becoming skillful in this work. As clinicians, mindfulness and a commitment to understand our own reactions to our clients and their life experiences (including, but not limited to, vicarious trauma reactions; Kinsler et al., Chapter 9, this volume) are crucial to being able to use the behavior-analytic approach with empathy and technical fidelity. Applying mindfulness, acceptance, and an awareness of the dynamics of behavior in our personal lives provides an authentic basis for teaching these skills to clients and an appreciation of the challenge that clients face in applying these skills to their own lives. In this sense, although it is essential to maintain a clear boundary between personal and professional aspects of our lives, we attempt not only to just "talk the talk" but also to "walk the walk" by applying mindfulness in our own lives.

REFERENCES

Batten, S., & Hayes, S. (2005). Acceptance and commitment therapy in treatment of comorbid substance abuse and post-traumatic stress disorder. *Clinical Case Studies, 4*, 246–262.

Bradley, R., & Follingstad, D. (2003). Group therapy for incarcerated women who experienced interpersonal violence. *Journal of Traumatic Stress, 16*, 337–340.

Cloitre, M., Cohen, M. R., & Koenen, K. C. (2006). *Treating survivors of childhood abuse: Psychotherapy for the interrupted life*. New York: Guilford Press.

Courtois, C. A. (1999). *Recollections of sexual abuse: Treatment principles and guidelines*. New York: Norton.

Courtois, C. A. (2004). Complex trauma, complex reactions: Assessment and treatment. *Psychotherapy: Theory, Research, Practice and Training, 41*, 412–425.

Foa, E. B., & Rothbaum, B. O. (1998). *Treating the trauma of rape: Cognitive-behavioral therapy for PTSD*. New York: Guilford Press.

Follette, V. M., Palm, K. M., & Pearson, A. (2006). Mindfulness and trauma: Implications for treatment. *Journal of Rational–Emotive and Cognitive-Behavior Therapy, 24*, 45–61.

Follette, V. M., Palm, K. M., & Rasmussen Hall, M .L. (2004). Acceptance, mindfulness, and trauma. In S. C. Hayes, V. M. Follette, & M. M. Linehan (Eds.), *Mindfulness and acceptance: Expanding the cognitive-behavioral tradition* (pp. 192–208). New York: Guilford Press.

Follette, W. C., & Naugle, A. E. (2006). A functional analytic clinical assessment in trauma treatment. In V. M. Follette & J. I. Ruzek (Eds.), *Cognitive-behavioral therapies for trauma* (2nd ed., pp. 17–33). New York: Guilford Press.

Follette, V. M., & Ruzek, J. I. (Eds.). (2006). *Cognitive-behavioral therapies for trauma* (2nd ed.). New York: Guilford Press.

Ford, J. D., Courtois, C., van der Hart, O., Nijenhuis, E., & Steele, K. (2005). Treatment of complex post-traumatic self-dysregulation. *Journal of Traumatic Stress*, *18*, 437–447.

Ford, J. D., & Russo, E. (2006). A trauma-focused, present-centered, emotional self-regulation approach to integrated treatment for post-traumatic stress and addiction. *American Journal of Psychotherapy*, *60*, 335–355.

Fruzzetti, A., & Iverson, K. (2006). Intervening with couples and families to treat emotion dysregulation and psychopathology. In D. Snyder, J. Simpson, & J. Hughes (Eds.), *Emotion regulation in families* (pp. 249–267). Washington, DC: American Psychological Association.

Hayes, S., Masuda, A., Bissett, R., Luoma, J., & Guerrero, L. (2004). DBT, FAP, and ACT. *Behavior Therapy*, *35*, 35–54.

Hayes, S., & Strosahl, K. (2005). *A practical guide to acceptance and commitment therapy*. New York: Springer Science and Business Media.

Hayes, S., Strosahl, K. D., & Wilson, K. G. (1999). *Acceptance and commitment therapy: An experiential approach to behavior change*. New York: Guilford Press.

Hayes, S., Wilson, K., Gifford, E., Follette, V., & Strosahl, K. (1996). Experiential avoidance and behavioral disorders. *Journal of Consulting and Clinical Psychology*, *64*, 1152–1168.

Hayes, S. C., Follette, V. M., & Linehan, M. M. (Eds.). (2004). *Mindfulness and acceptance: Expanding the cognitive-behavioral tradition*. New York: Guilford Press.

Kohlenberg, B. S., Tsai, M., & Kohlenberg, R. J. (2006). Functional analytic psychotherapy and the treatment of complex posttraumatic stress disorder. In V. M. Follette & J. I. Ruzek (Eds.), *Cognitive-behavioral therapies for trauma* (2nd ed., pp. 173–197). New York: Guilford Press.

Kohlenberg, R. J., & Tsai, M. (1991). *Functional analytic psychotherapy*. New York: Plenum Press.

McDonagh-Coyle, A., Friedman, M., McHugo, G., Ford, J., Sengupta, A., Mueser, K., et al. (2005). Randomized trial of cognitive-behavioral therapy for chronic posttraumatic stress disorder in adult female survivors of childhood sexual abuse. *Journal of Consulting and Clinical Psychology*, *73*, 515–524.

Mowrer, O. H. (1960). *Learning theory and behavior*. New York: Wiley.

Orsillo, S. M., & Batten, S. V. (2005). Acceptance and commitment therapy in the treatment of posttraumatic stress disorder. *Behavior Modification*, *29*, 95–129.

Pistorello, J., Follette, V., & Hayes, S. (2000). Long-term correlates of childhood sexual abuse. In M. Douger (Ed.), *Clinical behavior analysis* (pp. 75–98). Reno, NV: Context Press.

Polusny, M., & Follette, V. (1995). Long-term correlates of childhood sexual abuse: Theory and review of the empirical literature. *Applied and Preventive Psychology*, *4*, 143–166.

Resick, P., & Schnicke, M. (1993). *Cognitive processing therapy for rape victims: A treatment manual*. Thousand Oaks, CA: Sage.

Robins, C. J., & Chapman, A. L. (2004). Dialectical behavior therapy: Current status, recent developments, and future directions. *Journal of Personality Disorders*, *18*, 73–79.

Shipherd, J. C. (2006). Treatment of a case example with PTSD and chronic pain. *Cognitive and Behavioral Practice*, *13*, 24–32.

Tull, M. T., Gratz, K. L., Salters, K., & Roemer, L. (2004). The role of experiential avoidance in posttraumatic symptoms and symptoms of depression, anxiety, and somatization. *Journal of Nervous and Mental Disease*, *192*, 754–761.

Varra, A., & Follette, V. M. (2005). ACT with posttraumatic stress disorder. In S. Hayes & K. Strosahl (Eds.), *A practical guide to acceptance and commitment therapy* (pp. 133–152). New York: Springer Science and Business Media.

Wagner, A. W., & Linehan, M. M. (2006). Applications of dialectical behavior therapy to posttraumatic stress disorder and related problems. In V. M. Follette & J. I. Ruzek (Eds.), *Cognitive-behavioral therapies for trauma* (2nd ed., pp. 117–145). New York: Guilford Press.

Walser, R. D., & Hayes, S. C. (2006). Acceptance and commitment therapy in the treatment of posttraumatic stress disorder. In V. M. Follette & J. I. Ruzek (Eds.), *Cognitive-behavioral therapies for trauma* (2nd ed., pp. 146–172). New York: Guilford Press.

CHAPTER 14

Experiential and Emotion-Focused Therapy

Diana Fosha
Sandra C. Paivio
Kari Gleiser
Julian D. Ford

Living a life of vitality, resilience, and human connectedness in the face of adversity requires ready access to emotional experience. Access to basic emotions is necessary to be able to harness adaptive resources (e.g., assertiveness, self-protection, humor, conscientiousness, creativity, self-efficacy, trust), as well as rely on others to help bolster these coping resources. Experiential psychotherapies are designed to systematically assist people in enhancing the ability to access emotions and the psychosocial resources linked to emotions (Gleiser, Ford, & Fosha, 2008). In this chapter, we describe how experiential psychotherapies have been adapted to address the emotional and psychosocial dilemmas faced by those who are experiencing complex traumatic stress disorders.

RATIONALE FOR AN EXPERIENTIAL APPROACH TO THE TREATMENT OF COMPLEX TRAUMATIC STRESS DISORDERS

Psychological trauma fundamentally is a threat to self-integrity. Posttraumatic survival coping (Ford & Courtois, Chapter 1, this volume) is characterized by a consuming preoccupation with avoiding danger at all costs and is dedicated to avoiding trauma cues—which may include not only people, places, and activities but also thoughts and emotions associated with psychological trauma—through isolation from others and detachment from emotions. If this traumatically based shift in somatic response, emotional engagement, and consciousness occurs repeatedly during key periods of psychobiological development, survivors may suffer from not only recurrent fear (i.e., posttraumatic stress disorder [PTSD]) but also a lasting emotional disconnection from self and others. Therefore, therapy for complex traumatic stress disorders necessarily involves assisting clients to recover their core capacities for experiencing emotions and relatedness.

Although many psychotherapies for psychological trauma survivors now recognize emotion processing (e.g., cognitive-behavioral therapy [CBT]) or the resolution of emotional conflicts (e.g., psychodynamic therapy) as integral to effective treatment, accelerated experiential–dynamic psychotherapy (AEDP) and emotion-focused therapy for trauma (EFTT) expressly offer a systematic template for understanding and achieving renewed emotional experiencing in the wake of psychological trauma. These two experiential approaches conceptualize emotion and somatically felt subjective experience as the primary path to both biopsychosocial development and healing from psychological trauma. Drawing on the client-centered, existential, and Gestalt traditions, as well as CBT, short-term psychodynamic, and relational analytic traditions, AEDP and EFTT enhance clients' abilities to access and explore emotional experience within an affirming, empathy-based therapeutic relationship. Adaptive processing of intense emotions in the context of a safe relationship is a foundation for enlarging the trauma survivor's perspective from preoccupation with danger and damage to a fuller experiencing of oneself as alive and of one's life and relationships as having fundamental worth and meaning.

CLINICAL CASE VIGNETTE

A case vignette illustrates how AEDP and EFTT are actually practiced. Angela, a pseudonym for a composite client, is a 37-year-old European American woman who works as a paralegal for a criminal law firm. She grew up in a middle-class suburban family with two siblings. Teachers observed Angela, an average student, to be quiet and well behaved. She had no close friends and did not participate in extracurricular activities. However, Angela had an unwanted "secret life": Her parents sexually and physically molested her and other young children while filming child pornography. She recalled feeling confused as a young child because her parents were either angry with her or ignored her at home or in their group, but acted "normal" in public. They frequently punished her harshly (drugging, starving, and forcing her to witness and participate in terrifying and humiliating sexual and physical violations) for offenses that she did not understand. In response, Angela tried never to draw attention to herself, and she understandably came to believe that her parents hated her and wanted her dead.

To survive, Angela learned to empty her mind of all thoughts and erase all feelings; however, as a teenager, she increasingly could not hide feelings of rage and contempt. She escaped by setting fire to her family's house, whereupon she was placed in a juvenile correctional facility. At age 16, she became an emancipated minor and lived on the streets, where she survived by prostituting herself and selling drugs. Fortunately, Angela was "adopted" by and joined the stage "crew" of a touring musical band. Angela got a general equivalency degree (GED) and put herself through college, becoming a paralegal to "go after the bastards" who hurt innocent people. Despite achieving financial stability and feeling satisfaction in her work, Angela struggled with severe bouts of depression. Cutting herself and drinking or using drugs to the point of blackouts were her only means of relieving her depression. When promoted to oversee a paralegal office, she began—for the first time since childhood—to experience a deep sense of terror. Angela had increasing periods of "losing time" and was no longer able to regulate herself by cutting. She was too terrified to seek therapy, believing that she would be institutionalized, a threat made repeatedly by Angela's parents when she was a child. But after having a dissociative episode at work that led her boss to question her reliability, Angela decided that therapy might be her only way to forestall the complete breakdown she had always feared. She reluctantly made an appointment with a therapist, saying that she wanted therapy because she was depressed.

ACCELERATED EXPERIENTIAL– DYNAMIC PSYCHOTHERAPY

AEDP assumes that trauma survivors possess core bioaffective resources that can be activated therapeutically—in the right, safe, facilitating environment—right from the start of treatment. These dispositions exist as potentials that await facilitating conditions to become accessible to the person. AEDP views psychological healing not only as the eventual outcome of an effective therapy but also as an innate potential that therapists can seek to activate from the first moments of the first session and, then from that point, throughout the treatment. AEDP is based on a metatherapeutic paradigm that includes relational, experiential, and integrative techniques within a framework informed by *attachment research, emotion theory, affective neuroscience,* and *transformational studies* (Fosha, 2000, 2002, 2003, 2005, 2006; Fosha & Yeung, 2006; Russell & Fosha, 2008). With (1) the dyadic affect regulation of intense emotions in the context of an attachment-based therapeutic relationship as a cornerstone of its experiential work, and (2) its primary aim of having the client not be alone with intense emotional experience, AEDP directly addresses emotional dysregulation and social isolation, the cardinal features of complex traumatic stress disorders (Gleiser et al., 2008; Lamagna & Gleiser, 2007).

Relational Interventions in AEDP

The aim of the therapeutic relationship in AEDP is to be the secure base from which to undertake experiential explorations of deep, painful emotional experiences. This secure base is built through the therapist's active and explicit empathic, caring, emotionally engaged, affirming stance, as well as the moment-to-moment tracking of clients' receptive affective experiences (Fosha, 2000, 2006; Russell & Fosha, 2008), which refer to the client's subjective, bodily felt experience of the therapist, and whether and how the client feels seen, felt, helped, cared about, and understood. The therapist remains attuned to and respectful of a client's need for protection, his or her pacing and fears about intimacy, while holding and enacting the belief that the dyad can achieve a level of connection that both feels good to the client and can in fact be comforting and healing. Inevitable ruptures in the working alliance are promptly acknowledged and repaired, with the goal of strengthening faith in the resilience of the imperfect but real and honest relationship.

Affective engagement (i.e., communicating with explicit empathy and affirmation), *emotional transparency* (i.e., the therapist's willingness to see and to be deeply seen), and *an explicit willingness to help* are hallmarks of AEDP's relational stance. This therapeutic stance is modeled by the therapist, then nurtured in the client. As such, AEDP seeks to address the fear, anger, and loss experienced as a result of caregivers' chronic intentional or inadvertent abuse, neglect, betrayal, manipulation, misattunement, and/or rejection. AEDP does so by awakening and harnessing clients' natural healing tendencies that lie beneath fear, shame, and hopelessness (Winnicott, 1960/1965). AEDP therapists remain vigilant for glimmers of these strengths, articulating and amplifying them so that clients' appreciation for their own innate resilience, unique strengths, and inherent worth is highlighted in the treatment and can begin to flourish.

Experiential Emotion Processing

From this bedrock of relational connection and validation of the client's psychological resources and resilience, AEDP undertakes the painful experiential processing of heretofore avoided trauma-related emotions and memories by dealing with the self-at-worst from under the aegis of the self-at-best (Fosha, 2000). The AEDP experiential approach aligns with attachment theory's basic premise that security of attachment and felt safety not only are powerful antidotes to fear, but also promote an expanded range of exploration and curiosity. A primary aim of AEDP is to co-create new, positively valenced relational and emotional experiences in the here and now in therapy, as a foundation for forging new attachment and affective templates in the client's life outside of therapy.

Experiential processing of emotions is important, because many developmental trauma survivors experience intense emotions as retraumatizing: Emotions are associated historically and contemporarily with annihilation, tragic aloneness, helplessness, and being out of control. Trauma-related affects, such as anxiety, despair, or shame, are consciously perceived as things that must be—but paradoxically can never be—borne alone. AEDP restructures these associations through experiential interventions geared toward *dyadically* down-regulating floods of pathogenic, overwhelming affects, while focusing on dyadically regulating and gradually deepening *adaptive* core emotional experiences, such as fear, grief, and joy.

The dyadic regulation of affect occurs via moment-to-moment affective communication involving gaze, tone of voice, rhythm, touch, and other non-verbal processes that promote attuned and coordinated states between client and therapist. Moving in and out of what Fosha (2000, p. 82) has called "the unbearable states of aloneness," while always working to maximize awareness and modulation, builds clients' trust that they will not be left alone to flounder and drown in their own overwhelming emotions. AEDP therapists track emotional experiences via an ongoing, moment-to-moment dynamic assessment, carefully differentiating (1) *secondary, defensive, or pathogenic affects*, all of which require regulation, titration, and transformation, from (2) *adaptive emotions and core affective experiences*, which bear the seeds of healing and are inherently transformative when regulated and processed to completion (Fosha, 2003). AEDP's emotion-processing interventions gradually invite clients more fully into the realm of core affective experiencing through (1) somatic focusing, (2) explicit relational joining, (3) affective mirroring, and (4) deepening evocative portrayals.

Portrayals are one example of experiential interventions used by AEDP therapists to help clients process emotions. These interventions reflect the influence of and share features with Gestalt (e.g., Perls, Hefferline, & Goodman, 1951), short-term dynamic psychotherapy (e.g., Davanloo, 1995), ego-state (e.g., Watkins & Watkins, 1997) and internal family systems (Schwartz, Schwartz, & Galperin, Chapter 17, this volume) approaches, and are similar to EFTT's *imaginal confrontations* (see below). In addition to imaginal confrontations with perpetrators, AEDP portrayals also include imaginary dialogues with others or with parts of the self; completing incomplete emotion and action sequences; and reparative portrayals, with imagined fulfillment of unmet needs (Fosha, 2000). As portrayals restore clients' undefended yet regulated access to core affective experiences, they unlock adaptive action tendencies (e.g., anger that frees up self-protective urges and behaviors) and positive affects that underlie resilience (e.g., hope emerging from despair).

AEDP offers a heuristic model of emotional transformation that identifies the stages of processing emotional experiences to completion (see Figure 14.1). The preceding two paragraphs discussed the first state transformation, where the client moves from a state of defensive avoidance of emotion and relating—and where stress, distress, and symptom-driven functioning are in evidence (State 1)—to the second state, where adaptive emotions are accessed, deepened, and processed through to completion.

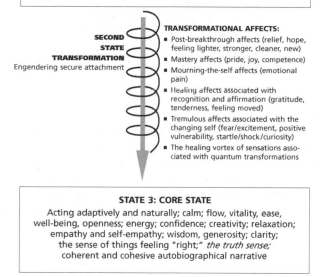

FIGURE 14.1. The structure of adaptive emotional experience processed to completion: The three states and two state transformations of AEDP.

Metatherapeutic Processing in AEDP

The second state transformation is effected through *metatherapeutic processing*, which involves focusing on and experientially exploring the corollaries of transformation itself. This processing involves helping the client to alternate experiential work, in which waves of emotion are experienced, with reflective observation and meaning making about the experience of emotional processing itself. This metaexamination of change occurring in therapy can unleash a cascade of transformations and transformational affects. These include post-breakthrough affects, such as relief, and feeling lighter, clearer, and/or stronger; mastery affects, such as pride and joy at having faced painful feelings; healing affects of gratitude and tenderness toward the other, and feeling deeply moved within the self in response to being deeply seen, known, and accepted (Fosha, 2005; Fosha & Yeung, 2006; Russell & Fosha, 2008); and the tremulous affects (i.e., the positive sense of vulnerability that arises in safe environments in the face of sudden unexpected positive transformational experiences).

The transformational affects are the hallmarks of the second state transformation and markers of the entry into the final stage of therapeutic processing: *core state* (Fosha, 2005; Fosha & Yeung, 2006; Russell & Fosha, 2008). Characterized by a wave of calm, clarity, and inner wisdom in the wake of a fully processed, deep emotional experience, core state is a place of integration and perspective, where affect and cognition come together and meaning is created (Fosha & Yeung, 2006). Core state involves the capacity for reflective observation, thought, and self-awareness that Fonagy, Gergely, Jurist, and Target (2002) call *mentalizing*. Clients talk about feeling open and having a sense of being grounded, solid, in flow, and at ease. They often say, "This feels like the true me." In core state, the client can now generate a coherent and cohesive autobiographical narrative, a capacity highly correlated with resilience and secure attachment. Core state is also characterized by clarity of purpose, agency, and confidence in one's capacity to act on behalf of the self. Core state is what has been lost (or never discovered) as a result of the shock and helplessness caused by complex psychological trauma. Core state emerges as a result of emotional processing within the context of a safe dyad. By facilitating the shift from defensive avoidance to core state, through regulating and processing to adaptive completion the emotion previously feared to be unbearable, and often doing so within one session, AEDP provides clients with an immediate experience of regaining the sense of secure self-awareness that is the hallmark of new learning and of recovery from PTSD and complex traumatic stress disorders.

A new variant of AEDP, called *intrarelational AEDP* (Lamagna & Gleiser, 2007), imports the relational and experiential interventions described earlier into the fragmented intrapsychic worlds of clients with dissociative symptomatology, including dissociative identity disorder (DID). The relational and affect regulating techniques used in AEDP to deepen the client–therapist relationship are brought into the internal world of the client in the form of experiential inner dialogues, and are used to enhance attunement, recognition, and empathy between previously dissociated and conflicting ego states (see also Steele & van der Hart [Chapter 7] and Schwartz et al. [Chapter 17], this volume).

In practice, AEDP follows a three-phase process involving *three states*—(1) defense (e.g., denial, projection), (2) core affective experiences (e.g., not only fear, grief, anger, and joy but also authentic self- and relational experiences), and (3) core state—and *two state transformations* (from defense to core affect, and from core affect to core state). As we see below in the case example, clients usually begin treatment in State 1, a state of *stress, distress, and symptom-driven functioning.*

AEDP APPLIED TO THE CASE EXAMPLE

Helping Angela to move from defensive avoidance, terror, and isolation to awareness, connection, and glimmers of core affective experience constitutes the first state transformation.

ANGELA: (*avoiding eye contact and speaking in a flat voice*) This incident at work has been so upsetting to me. My boss swears that she came into my office and found me huddled under my desk crying, but I don't remember any of that ever happening. I don't know why she would possibly lie to me about something like that, but ...

THERAPIST: (*in a soft, soothing voice*) That sounds very distressing on many levels. What's the worst part about it for you as you tell me right now? [empathy, specificity]

ANGELA: (*Breathing increases and voice becomes shaky.*) That she would see me in such a state. [shame and traumatic fear; hyperarousal]

THERAPIST: That brings up some strong feelings. [focus on immediate emotional experience]

ANGELA: No, I'm fine. [defense]

THERAPIST: You started to breathe faster just now and your voice trembled. It made me wonder if you weren't getting scared as you remembered it. [somatic focus, mirroring, empathy]

ANGELA: (*Says nothing; looks dazed, stares off into space.*)

THERAPIST: I get the sense that you have so many feelings inside right now that maybe they feel overwhelming. [anxiety/affect regulation]

ANGELA: I don't know. (*Looks panicked.*) [anxiety]

THERAPIST: (*very softly and gently*) Is there something scary about my seeing that in you? [empathic exploration of anxiety in the context of the relationship; note the therapist's directly exploring the anxiety in the context of the here and now of the therapeutic relationship]

ANGELA: (*whispering*) It's dangerous. [The client takes the risk of sharing her authentic experience: The process is moving forward; beginning of the first state transformation]

THERAPIST: Dangerous?

ANGELA: (*fragmented voice*) If people see, I'll get fired, or something terrible will happen.

THERAPIST: Angela, I see this profound terror in your face and hear it in your voice. I don't yet know what it's linked to—though I'm sure we'll get to that later, when it's safe to—but right now I'm so struck by your courage in coming here to talk to me even though you have all this fear inside of you. [going to the positive side of the fear: somatic mirroring in context of relationship; structuring; affirmation of courage]

ANGELA: (*Looks surprised, fleetingly smiles, wary, but glances at therapist.*) Really? [taking in the affirmation] I feel like such a spaz. I can barely talk. I don't know what's happening to me.

THERAPIST: Oh, you're anything but a spaz. This what it's like for anyone to be terrified. You freeze, you feel confused, your mind goes blank. [empathy, affirmation, psychoeducation, normalizing]

ANGELA: (*making brief, intermittent eye contact*) Well, I feel a little better knowing that. A little bit less like a freak. [decrease in anxiety and shame: first state transformation is proceeding]

THERAPIST: Quite the contrary. It takes a tremendous amount of strength to decide to start facing the terror of trauma and the other feelings that go along with it. [affirmative reframing]

ANGELA: (*soft, tremulous voice; tentative eye contact*) I don't feel very strong right now. [The client is taking the risk of allowing herself to feel vulnerable.]

THERAPIST: Well, I don't think anybody can when they're facing these things alone. It's too much. [empathic, supportive, explicit about things being too much when one is alone]

ANGELA: (*steadier voice, gazes down*) That's my life. One kind of hiding after another.

THERAPIST: Can I ask you something? I notice that you've been sneaking little peeks at me while we've been talking. What have you been seeing in me? What do you see in my eyes? [complex intervention: dyadic engagement, dyadic relational desensitization, facilitating new corrective experience; seeking to undo projection by inviting the client to track the therapist]

ANGELA: You look kind, like you want to help. But that's your job, right? And I've known a lot of people in my life who could go from Dr. Jekyll to Hyde in a split second.

THERAPIST: Wow, that must make it so hard to feel safe around anyone, like any minute they could turn on you. Must make it even harder for you to be here. [empathy]

ANGELA: Yeah, that's why I've gotten so good at hiding.

THERAPIST: And yet, despite all the terror and the betrayal, here you are, starting to find a way to let me be with you. [recognizing, affirming, and amplifying positive healthy glimmers of healing, self-reparative tendencies coming to the fore]

ANGELA: *(half-jokingly)* Hopefully, I won't find myself dead in an alleyway somewhere. But I can't go on living this way either. *(Starts to tear up.)* [increase in the client's motivation for therapeutic exploration: very important green light; beginning of State 2 work]

THERAPIST: What way?

At this early point in therapy, Angela has just begun to acknowledge and to touch upon the actual experience of her deeper emotions. With the therapist's consistent empathic and strength-based focus in the face of her dismissive and defensive stance, Angela is beginning to consider that the therapist might be genuinely respecting her competence rather than judging her deficits or pathology (based on Angela's abusive early life experiences and possible past encounters with trauma-insensitive professionals or systems). While the working alliance, the foundation for experiencing a secure attachment in therapy, is being formed, the therapist also is consistently tracking and mirroring Angela's moment-to-moment emotional experience, leading her closer to fuller, felt experience of her feelings.

Before Angela can relinquish the psychic defenses that paradoxically imprison her in a state of emotional detachment and powerlessness, she must first learn that it is safe and possible to recognize previously unacknowledged emotions, such as grief, shame, terror, love, anger, and joy. The *somatic microtracking interventions* provide the therapist a way to help Angela access and regulate core emotions. The next transcript section illustrates AEDP's use of *portrayal*, in this case, a dialogue between the client and one part of herself, to promote regulation and processing of the intense emotions associated with the trauma, thereby countering dissociation. Three interrelated affective experiences are illustrated: (1) the undoing of the client's experience of unbearable aloneness in the face of intense emotions; (2) the relational–affective experience between client and therapist, entraining right-brain to right-brain processing; and (3) processing the core emotion of emotional pain in such a way that feeling the emotion goes from feeling bad to feeling good in connection with the self and the therapist (Lamagna & Gleiser, 2007).

ANGELA: *(long pause)* I feel like I'm a little girl, curled up in a fetal position in some far, hidden corner of myself, crying silently so no one can find me. So far away from anyone. All alone and desperate. [vivid imagery; allowing access into internal world]

THERAPIST: *(with sadness and compassion in her voice)* What a devastating, heartbreaking way to stay safe—by needing to stay totally isolated. I wonder if there is any way we can start to get a little closer to this crying little part of you. Her distress seems unbearable. [empathy; leading edge of heightening corrective experience: intrarelational focus on interaction between dissociated parts of the self]

ANGELA: (*Looks up suddenly with suspicion.*)

THERAPIST: What just happened? [moment-to-moment tracking of experiential fluctuations]

ANGELA: How do I know you're not just another tormentor in disguise? [hypervigilance]

THERAPIST: That's such an important question. Is there any way you can tell? [validates client's concerns and affirms leading adaptive edge of acting on behalf of the self's safety]

ANGELA: (*Looks searchingly and long at therapist.*) You know, I never told anyone this before, but I could always tell when someone was a tormentor in disguise. They'd never look at me. Even when they were in public, putting on a show for everyone else, they never really looked at me, they never saw me. Like they knew their eyes would betray them. Even masks have holes for the eyes. [reflective processing is deepening]

THERAPIST: Very true and very wise. Thank you. So what do you see when you look in my eyes? [reciprocal interaction; therapist validates Angela and thanks her for the privilege of trust; relational processing in light of new affective experiences]

ANGELA: (*steady but searching gaze*) You're seeing me. [deepening relational engagement]

THERAPIST: I'm so glad you can see that.

ANGELA: Me too.

THERAPIST: Tell me what it's like to feel seen, because it is so new ... [metatherapeutic processing of new, positive, transformational experience]

ANGELA: It's weird 'cuz I'm not used to it. I don't know why, but I feel a bit more solid, I don't know, like there is an outline around my body. [transformational experience]

THERAPIST: Please tell me if this feels like it is going too fast and we don't have to go there, but I can't stop thinking about the part of you that feels like a little girl curled up in the fetal position inside. My heart goes out to her and I don't want her to be pushed aside. [With newly established shared affective experiences, therapist checks to see if another round of difficult work is possible.]

ANGELA: I don't know what to do with her ... it's too dangerous to let anyone else in.

THERAPIST: Despite the confusion, you've been doing your best to protect her. You must care very deeply for her. [affirming client; heightening adaptive, progressive aspects of experience]

ANGELA: I never thought of it that way before.

THERAPIST: Maybe you know more than you think you know about what she needs. [more affirmation; heightening client's awareness of her own resilience, resourcefulness, and goodness]

ANGELA: I don't know; there's so much pain ... (*starts to tear up slightly*) [core affective experience of emotional pain]

THERAPIST: Mmmm ... (*with sympathy and sadness*)

ANGELA: (*decisively, catching herself*). No. She has to stay hidden for now.

THERAPIST: That's fine, we can back off for now. [affirming client's choice as acting on her own behalf, and on behalf of keeping herself safe; validates client's regulation of her own safety] But it's important to acknowledge that you *do* see her, and that you feel sad for her pain. Not only that, but also that you let me see her, and now I, too, feel in me the very powerful impulse to help her, to reach out to her when she's ready. So she's not completely alone. Can she feel that? [consolidating transformation, connection, and forward movement that has already taken place]

ANGELA: She can feel it, but ... (*Stops, her gaze goes up, and her eyes fill up with tears.*) [healing affects associated with positive transformational experience]

THERAPIST: Go ahead, let yourself feel it. It's OK. I'm right here with you. [encouragement; explicit relational intervention of not letting client be alone with intense emotion]

As clients such as Angela become able to experience core emotions, they realize that they can do so without feeling overwhelmed or trapped; instead, they often feel a surprising sense of relief and buoyant yet grounded feelings of rejuvenation, resilience, and resourcefulness. This is the beginning of the second state transformation, the shift from core emotion to core state.

The second state transformation is completed by metaprocessing (i.e., discussing how it feels to be able to safely experience) a range of emotions, which accesses transformational affects (e.g., pride, mastery, gratitude) and culminates in core state (Fosha, 2000; Fosha & Yeung, 2006; Russell & Fosha, 2008). These metatherapeutic processes that lead to, and then characterize, core state as described by AEDP are akin to processes described in the language of mentalization by Fonagy (e.g., Fonagy et al., 2002) and of mindfulness by Siegel (2007). The turbulence of intense emotions defines State 2, but calm, clarity, confidence, centeredness, curiosity, compassion, courage, and creativity (Schwartz et al., Chapter 17, this volume) define the core state. Work with core state phenomena culminates in the assertion of personal truth and strengthening of the individual's core identity. Next we see the client fluctuating between State 2 core emotions, transformational affects, anxiety about this change, and State 3 core state phenomena.

ANGELA: ... she's too afraid to let herself hope. (*Cries harder.*) [grief for the self; healing affects associated with positive transformational experience; second state transformation]

THERAPIST: She's been so, so hurt, and so, so scared. [empathy]

ANGELA: (*Nods and continues to cry, sobbing now.*) [strong affects associated with corrective experience, a corrective experience in its own right]

THERAPIST: (*Waits until Angela's crying slows down.*) It's OK for her to be just where she's at right now. It's totally understandable given the fear. But can she let herself see your sadness and your tears? They are for her. [leading edge of exploring new experiences of intrarelational empathy and compassion for self: intrarelational State 2 work]

ANGELA: She sees, but she doesn't know what to do with it. [Client is able to tolerate a positive but very new experience, staying right on the edge of positive trepidation.]

THERAPIST: That's OK, she doesn't have to do anything. Just take it in, as much as she can. (*allows a moment of silence*). [relational intervention: helping, coaching, support, warmth] How are you feeling?

ANGELA: Calm. Less scared. Like I know I'm not going to be dragged out of my hiding place, but also maybe I'm not going to waste away there alone anymore. [postaffective breakthrough transformational affect of calm; increased capacity for coherent self-reflection; creation of safety and possibility of deeper connection; beginning of core state]

THERAPIST: I sense your calm, and the strength that you're accessing as you take the double risk of starting to let yourself feel some of this pain and aloneness, and letting me be here with you and share in it with you. [affirmation with affective self-disclosure of admiration] What's that like for you right now? [metatherapeutic processing of therapeutic experience]

ANGELA: Well, if you'd asked me, I'd have said I'd never let it happen! But it just kind of did. And, well, I don't know if this makes any sense, but it feels kind of comforting. And at the same time scary. [transformational affects: the tremulous affects]

THERAPIST: Tell me about both. [addressing both bad and good, dread and hope, old and new]

ANGELA: Scary because the comfort is so foreign. Comforting because you saw something in me that it's never been safe to let anyone see and, so far, I'm not hurt worse for it. But it's more than that. I actually feel better than I did before I came in here, and I never imagined that. It's like getting a balm for a very deep wound. It's not healed yet, but some of the sting is gone. Thank you for that. [hallmark of core state: capacity for coherent and cohesive self-reflection]

THERAPIST: You're very welcome. And thank you for taking the chance in letting me be a part of this. [Attachment is a two-way process—mutual, even if

asymmetrical—of affective communication, in which both dyadic partners are affected, have feelings, and are changed.]

As this vignette illustrates, in AEDP, safety is achieved *through* the dyadic
regulation and experiential processing of emotion and relatedness in *every*
phase of therapy. Building safety does not precede the experiential work; in
AEDP, the two go hand in hand. The transcript also illustrates why and how
positive *transformation* occurs in AEDP. Multiple transformative processes are
unfolding over the course of this single session. Tracking the various dimensions of change can help to illuminate further AEDP's integrative and "accelerated" nature. Angela arrived at her first session in a defensive state characterized by terror, shame, dissociation, and disconnection from self and others.
Her abuse history taught her that letting anyone see her distress or pain would
result in more pain and further abuse. AEDP therapeutic interventions begin
immediately with somatic microtracking of Angela's fear about being seen and
of her subsequent shutdown, thus transforming her experience from implicit,
forbidden, and unbearable to shared, accepted, and helped. Other specific types
of transformation that are illustrated, in addition to the two state transformations described earlier, include the following:

1. Affirmation of Angela's courage to transform her shame about her
   wounded self.
2. Tentative, step-by-step building of trust and intimacy in the therapeutic
   dyad to undo aloneness and isolation.
3. Gradual approach to Angela's own dissociated internal experience,
   using portrayal and intrarelational dynamics.
4. Reworking old belief that exposing pain and hurt leads to more rejection and abuse into new belief that processing pain and grief can lead
   to feelings of mastery and strength.

EMOTION-FOCUSED THERAPY
FOR INTERPERSONAL TRAUMA

EFTT is an integrative approach that applies the general theory of emotion-
focused therapy (Greenberg & Paivio, 1997) to the treatment of complex
traumatic stress disorders. EFTT is grounded in experiential therapy theory
and research (e.g., Greenberg & Paivio, 1997; Paivio & Greenberg, 1995) and
shares features with both CBT (e.g., Jackson, Nissenson, & Cloitre, Chapter 12, this volume) and other emotional/relational approaches (e.g., Fosha,
2000; Herman, 1992). EFTT, like all experiential approaches, is founded on
the premise that verbally symbolizing present moment subjective experience
(feelings and meanings) is the primary source of new information, psychological growth, and healing. When emotion is activated, the meaning system
influences current perceptions, motivation, and action (Damasio, 1999; Foa

& Kozak, 1986; LeDoux, 1996). Furthermore, basic emotions, such as fear, anger, and sadness, are associated with specific information that aids in adaptive functioning.

The multimodal associative network associated with traumatic experiences comprises complex feelings, images, somatic experiences, as well as thoughts and beliefs about self and others, and reality formed at the time of the trauma. Thus, experiences of maltreatment, betrayal, and neglect at the hands of caregivers can result in negative beliefs about self and intimate others that are colored by intensely negative, disjointed, poorly regulated, and misunderstood emotions. These internal working models (Bowlby, 1988) continue to influence current self-concept and close interpersonal relationships negatively. Therefore, emotional processing in EFTT is viewed as involving not only desensitization to painful feelings and memories but also the construction of new, affectively based meanings, that is, a new view of self, others, and traumatic experiences.

EFTT conceptualizes the adult disturbances associated with child abuse trauma as largely involving unresolved issues with attachment figures. Clients are not only disturbed by current symptoms and problems but also continue to be distressed by powerful unexpressed feelings, unmet needs, and disturbing memories. From an attachment perspective, they are unable to separate, let go of unmet needs, and move on, until feelings are expressed and processed, and past experiences are satisfactorily resolved (Greenberg & Paivio, 1997). Resolving issues with particular abusive and neglectful others, together with experiencing a positive relationship with the therapist, generalizes to other relationships and helps to restore the client's capacity for connectedness.

The posited mechanisms of change in EFTT are the *therapeutic relationship* and the *emotional processing of traumatic memories*. In these respects, EFTT is consistent with other models of therapy for complex traumatic stress disorders (e.g., Herman, 1992), including AEDP. Although EFTT includes attention to modifying maladaptive emotions, such as fear and shame, it also explicitly emphasizes accessing previously inhibited adaptive emotions, thus "changing emotion with emotion" (Greenberg & Paivio, 1997). For example, being able to feel anger at violation helps to counteract powerlessness, victimization, and self-blame. Similarly, the ability to feel sadness accesses compassion for self and self-soothing resources that aid in grieving losses.

Although EFTT utilizes standard emotion management strategies for severe affect dysregulation problems (e.g., attention to breathing, relaxation, present-centered awareness), the primary vehicle for promoting affect regulation in EFTT is empathic responding to client feelings and needs, similar to AEDP (Fosha, 2003) and other emotion-focused models of psychotherapy. Empathic responding fosters affect regulation capacities by first increasing clients' awareness of their emotions and helping them to label accurately and articulate the meaning of emotions (Paivio & Laurent, 2001). Understanding emotional experience also helps to reduce distress. Second, empathic responses help modulate emotional intensity by reducing feelings of isolation and distress, as well as increasing arousal, thereby activating inhibited or suppressed emotional experience. The associated information can thereby be integrated into current meaning systems. Third, empathic responses model appropriate emotional expression.

In the treatment of complex traumatic stress disorders, EFTT draws on principles of exposure and emotional processing, similar to those underlying CBTs (see Gold [Chapter 11] and Jackson et al. [Chapter 12], this volume). However, EFTT primarily draws on experiential/humanistic therapies' sophisticated technology for overcoming experiential avoidance, evoking affective experience, and promoting experiential awareness. Evocative empathy, experiential focusing, and Gestalt-derived procedures involve imagery and multimodal enactments that quickly evoke core processes to make them available for exploration, processing, and integration. Intervention principles and guidelines for conducting these techniques have been clearly delineated (e.g., Elliott, Watson, Goldman, & Greenberg, 2004; Gendlin, 1997; Greenberg & Paivio, 1997; Paivio & Laurent, 2001).

EFTT is a semistructured, manualized approach (Paivio & Pascual-Leone, in press). Therapy typically consists of 16–20 weekly, 1-hour sessions, although the exact length of therapy is based on individual client processes and treatment needs. Like all experiential approaches, EFTT is not a strictly linear model, but particular processes typically are dominant during particular phases of therapy. Initial sessions are devoted to cultivating a strong therapeutic bond and collaborating on the goals and plan for therapy. The second phase focuses on reducing fear, avoidance, shame, and self-blame. These self-related disturbances are blocks to resolving issues with perpetrators of harm. The second phase of therapy also includes a focus on improving affect management capacities. The third phase focuses on resolving issues with abusive/neglectful others and involves accessing adaptive anger and sadness, and associated meanings. The final phase focuses on integration of therapy experiences and closure.

To date, EFTT is the only evidence-based individual psychotherapy for both men and women who are dealing with different types (emotional, physical, sexual) of child abuse trauma (Paivio, Chagigiorgis, Hall, Jarry, & Ralston, 2007; Paivio & Nieuwenhuis, 2001). EFTT is based on an empirically verified model of the process of resolving "unfinished business" using imaginal confrontation (IC) (Greenberg & Malcolm, 2002). In IC, clients imagine perpetrators of abuse or neglect in an empty chair, attend to their current thoughts and feelings, and express these directly to the imagined other. Clients who benefited from IC differed from those who did not in being better able to express (1) adaptive emotion (anger and sadness) and associated needs; (2) entitlement to unmet needs; and (3) changed perceptions of self and others, with increased self-empowerment and self-esteem, a more differentiated view of abusive/neglectful others, and appropriately holding them (rather than self) accountable for harm.

EFTT specifically for child abuse-related disorders developed from intensive analyses of therapy sessions with clients dealing with these issues. An outcome study evaluating the efficacy of EFTT with IC found evidence of sustained improvements across a variety of functional domains (Paivio & Nieuwenhuis, 2001). A follow-up process–outcome study (Paivio, Hall, Holowaty, Jellis, & Tran, 2001) found that therapeutic alliance quality contributed to improved self-esteem and resolution of issues with specific abusive/neglectful others, whereas engagement in IC independently contributed to abuse resolution, and reduced symptom and interpersonal distress. Results of a randomized controlled trial study (Paivio et al., 2007) showed that EFTT, with either IC or an alternate empathic exploration (EE) procedure (see below), based on the same model of resolution and intervention principles as IC, were associated with statistically significant and sustained gains across gender and abuse type and severity.

EFTT intervention principles most frequently used throughout therapy include directing client attention to internal experience, evoking memories, establishing intentions and needs, and articulating the meaning of emotional experience. These principles can be implemented through a variety of therapist operations (e.g., empathic responses, questions, directives); however, empathic responding is the primary intervention used throughout therapy. The IC procedure typically is introduced at the beginning of the second phase of therapy. Therapist operations during IC are as follows: Promote psychological contact with the imagined abusive or neglectful other, evoke episodic memories associated with abuse, promote expression of feelings, explore and help clients overcome blocks to experiencing, differentiate feelings (e.g., anger, sadness) and associated meanings (including needs), promote entitlement to unmet needs (e.g., protection, love, justice), and explore evolving perceptions of self and imagined others. The therapist also maintains a balance between following the client's moment-by-moment experience and directing the process. IC is used judiciously throughout therapy according to individual client processes and treatment needs. Analyses of videotaped EFTT sessions (Paivio et al., 2007) indicated that two-thirds of clients substantially participated in IC over the course of therapy and that, on average, 5.4 sessions (SD = 1.6; range = 2–8) in a 16-session therapy contained substantial IC work. The length of IC ranged from a few statements to continuous dialogue lasting most of the session.

The alternative EE procedure was developed for clients who are unwilling or unable to engage in IC due to the evocative nature of the intervention, performance anxiety, or a preference for psychological contact with the therapist. EE is identical to IC except that clients vividly imagine abusive/neglectful others and traumatic events in their "mind's eye," and express their thoughts and feelings to the therapist rather than in dialogue with an imagined other. Process analyses indicated lower level of emotional arousal in EE compared to IC (Ralston, 2006), and EE was associated with lower dropout rates (7%) than IC (20%) (Paivio et al., 2007). These findings suggest that EE is a less evocative and thus a less stressful procedure than IC.

EFTT APPLIED TO THE CASE EXAMPLE

Angela's developmental trauma history is extreme. Therefore, EFTT with her likely will require more than 16–20 sessions, including a lengthy period to establish trust and a working alliance. It is also important to help Angela access resources beyond psychotherapy and increase her social support. EFTT focuses on helping her reduce maladaptive depression and shame, support healthy anger experience and associated desire for justice, and gradually approach and allow emotional pain, particularly grieving the profound losses she has endured.

During initial sessions, the real risk of danger from others (e.g., family members seeking retribution) is assessed, and adequate resources for ensuring safety need to be ensured. Safety and trust in therapy are fostered in several ways:

1. Validating her distrust and fear of disclosure ("Of course, you don't know me, so trust will take time. The things you've been though are very painful, so you want to be very careful about whom you share this with. My job is to understand how you see things and how you feel from your perspective, without judging you in any way").
2. Providing information about therapy processes and roles ("We are not going to hammer away at your traumatic experiences session after session. I am interested in you, Angela, as a whole person. You are in the driver's seat. We will explore both past and present concerns, whatever is most important to you. My job is to ensure your safety and to support and promote your growth. That will mean helping you get in touch with painful feelings, but only so that you can work them through here in this safe environment, when you're ready, and at a pace you can handle").
3. Communicating genuine compassion for her past and current suffering, and acknowledging and respecting her struggle to cope and to build a life for herself ("I understand that depression is a major challenge for you, that it's a big struggle at times just to keep going. You also have been through incredibly difficult and painful experiences, and you've struggled to cope with these alone and for a very long time. I don't want you to be alone with this stuff anymore. Together we can work on whatever experiences are troubling you, whatever you decide might be most helpful").

Angela might fear and resist therapist efforts to help her approach painful and vulnerable feelings. This resistance might include the conscious or unconscious use of secondary anger to push the therapist away. To avoid alliance ruptures, the therapist must first communicate understanding of Angela's fear of disclosure and her painful experience, then collaborate with her on how best to deal with these issues in therapy.

THERAPIST: I understand it must be very difficult to get close to those painful feelings ...

ANGELA: (*looking down*) I wish you would stop harping on my "painful feelings," it seems like your entire agenda is to make me cry and I don't want to cry.

THERAPIST: Oh, I see. I appreciate you bringing this up so directly; it's important. I don't want to push you into feelings you don't want to feel or don't feel ready for. If I understand, right now, you don't want to focus on things that could make you cry; you really don't want to go there.

ANGELA: Not now, not ever. I just don't want to get into all that past stuff. I need to forget it. I told you, my only goal is to stop being so depressed and stop spacing out, so I don't lose my job. In terms of the past, all I want is to make sure those "sickos" don't destroy any other kids' lives.

THERAPIST: We can focus on current difficulties, to help you with spacing out and depression. But we have to understand those experiences better to change them—the thoughts, feelings, and memories that contribute to depression and shutting down. If some of that is connected to your past, it's going to be pretty hard to avoid the past entirely. Does that make sense?

ANGELA: Yes, I know that.

THERAPIST: Plus many things that contribute to your current difficulties, I can only imagine, are extremely painful. It will take a lot of faith in yourself and your ability to handle it, as well as trust in me, in order to allow yourself to feel and open up about these things. But I think you know that continuing to push them away or keep them bottled up inside isn't working.

ANGELA: Yes, I know. I'm just scared. (*Eyes well up.*) I don't think I can take it much longer. No one really knows what I've been through. I don't know if I have the strength to tell.

THERAPIST: I understand you must be very scared and I respect your caution. You don't want to feel flooded by too many powerful feelings all at once. We can take all the time that you need to tell whatever you need to tell. But right now, I think you're saying some of these feelings have just gotten to be such a burden that you're not sure how to carry them anymore. There are ways I can help, if you decide you maybe can trust me enough to share what your feeling.

ANGELA: What could you understand? You don't know anything about my life really.

THERAPIST: I realize I know very little about your life yet, and it's always your choice what to share with me, but I'd like to understand and to know more about those deeper feelings and the experiences they come from. I also think it's good to focus not only on painful stuff but also on your legitimate anger and healthy desire for justice. These are very important.

Promoting affect regulation and reducing fear, avoidance, and depression are the work of the second phase of therapy. Difficulties with substance abuse and cutting behavior are understood as maladaptive strategies for coping with overwhelming affect. Results of a recent study indicated that difficulties identifying, labeling, and communicating feelings (alexithymia) mediated the relationship between a history of child abuse trauma and self-injurious behaviors (Paivio & McCullough, 2004). Thus, supporting healthy anger experience and expression, as well as a gradual process of helping Angela to articulate and explore painful feelings and memories in a safe environment, contributes to emotion regulation capacities. Verbal symbolization of meaning helps to create distance from these feelings, makes them comprehensible, and reduces distress and the need for avoidance (Greenberg & Paivio, 1997). Similarly, dissociation is understood as self-protective distancing from overwhelming feelings and memories. Work with dissociative processes additionally may include use of imaginary dialogues between the fearful and protective parts of self (see Steele & van der Hart, Chapter 7, this volume). The objective is to access self-soothing capacities to strengthen the fearful part of self and thereby reduce dissociation and foster self-integration. Explicit emotion management strategies from other models may be used (see Fosha, 2003; Lamagna & Gleiser, 2007; see also Chapters 11–13, this volume).

The primary source of fear and avoidance (including dissociation) is understood as the activation of a core insecure and vulnerable sense of self formed through childhood abuse experiences ("It's as if that scared helpless little kid gets activated, takes over, and you have no way of calming her"). Similarly, depression is viewed as the activation of a core sense of a self as weak, bad, and unlovable, formed through childhood experiences of powerlessness, isolation, and sexual exploitation. Therefore, a major focus of therapy involves exploring and changing this core sense of self. As current difficulties (e.g., Angela's fear that her employer will find out about her past) or memories of abuse are discussed in session, the therapist's interventions with Angela empathically affirm her vulnerability in approaching feelings, such as shame, and encourage her to stay with rather than run away from or immediately try to change these feelings. Therapeutic work with shame is particularly challenging, because the associated action tendency is to hide. EFTT involves accessing and exploring the complex of thoughts, feelings, somatic experiences, and behaviors that contribute to depression and shame. During this process, healthy resources may emerge spontaneously ("I can't keep it all bottled up inside anymore. All those dirty secrets are poisoning me!") or may be initiated by the therapist ("Can you get in touch with yourself at that time, hating what was happening to you, feeling trapped?").

An important dual focus and aim is to monitor and strengthen Angela's capacity to regulate her emotions, while encouraging her to gradually confront trauma-related emotions, thoughts, and memories. *Empathic exploration* (EE) of trauma feelings and memories exclusively in interaction with the therapist initially may be more tolerable for Angela than *imaginal confrontation* (IC) of abusive and neglectful others in an empty chair. Later in therapy, IC might be introduced occasionally at the emergence of assertiveness and other healthy resources. It also might be advisable initially to confront less threatening others, such as a minimally threatening but neglectful mother, rather than a cruel or sadistic other. For Angela it might be easier first to express fully and feel entitled to her anger at injustice and violation, before allowing herself to experience fully the vulnerability and emotional pain. Adaptive anger is associated with energy, vitality, protest, standing up for oneself, finding one's "backbone," and appropriately holding others, instead of the self, responsible for harm.

The goal of IC or EE initially is to help Angela shift from expressions of undifferentiated hurt and global distress to more differentiated expressions of adaptive anger and sadness. Upon the appearance of in-session indicators of unresolved feelings toward perpetrators ("He was such a disgusting pervert, I feel sick every time I think about him" or "It just eats away at me. How could she let him do that stuff?"), Angela is encouraged to imagine the relevant person either in an empty chair or in her "mind's eye," to attend to her thoughts and feelings ("What happens to you on the inside as you imagine him or her [there]?"), and to express them either directly to this imagined other or to the therapist ("That's very important. Try saying that to your father [*points to empty chair*]—'I don't want you near me'—and tell him why" or "Stay with that feeling. Tell me more. What do you find so repulsive?" or "Tell her what she should have done, what a good mother would do").

Some clients confuse imaginally confronting the other with behavioral rehearsal ("I could never say that to him or her. They wouldn't listen anyway"). It is important to clarify that this is not the purpose of the intervention ("It's not about them. We want you to say what you need to say, speak your truth, no holding back, not as practice for confronting in real life but for yourself, so you become clear and strong. Then you can decide what to do in real life"). In the early stages of therapy, Angela also might collapse in fear at imagining perpetrators. Interventions direct attention to this response ("Somehow you collapse. It's hard to stand up to him even in imagination"), and to Angela's implicit view of herself as a powerless victim, and of the other as powerful and dangerous ("He still has the power to shut you down, even in here"). Therapy then focuses on exploring and reducing this self-interruptive process. Confronting her father through IC can be resumed when Angela expresses a renewed sense of healthy assertiveness.

Another issue in terms of expressing anger to imagined others is that clients like Angela fear the intensity of their rage (being overwhelmed by it or hurting others) and are afraid of looking and behaving like abusive others. They have little or no experience of healthy anger. Therefore, interventions provide information about the role of adaptive anger, assurance that anger can be approached gradually, and model appropriate anger expression. *Two-chair dialogues* also may be used to access healthy resources (e.g., standing up for oneself, a desire for justice) to challenge maladaptive beliefs about anger. Criteria for appropriate anger expression (Paivio & Carriere, 2006) are as follows:

Anger is directed externally (rather than at the self) for specific harm done; anger is differentiated from global distress and other emotions (e.g., hurt, fear, sadness); arousal level is appropriate to the situation; expression is assertive (rather than passive or aggressive), with ownership of experience (e.g., use of "I" language); and expression includes some exploration of meaning. For example:

THERAPIST: I hear how much you hate him, despise him. Tell him, over there, what you hate, make him understand ...

ANGELA: Yes, I despise how you manipulated and corrupted innocent children for your own sick needs, and did it in the name of God! You perverted everything. I was innocent and you ruined my childhood, made sex disgusting, destroyed my trust in humanity and my faith in God. Damn you, I hope you rot in hell. ... Oh, I sound just like him. I can't stand this!

THERAPIST: But you're not him, Angela. You are justifiably angry and you want to see him punished for his despicable behavior, his crimes. Tell him.

ANGELA: Yes, I do want to see you punished. You deserve to be punished for all the harm you've done and I'm going to find a way to see that that happens. You are not going to get away with it. You fucked me up royally. My life has been such a mess because of you, but I refuse to let you ruin my life anymore. This whole thing is about your sickness not mine!

THERAPIST: How do you feel saying that?

ANGELA: It feels right. He was the adult, I was just a little kid. I deserved love and security, not that twisted life he imposed on me.

THERAPIST: How do you imagine your father over there would react, in his heart, if he knew how you really felt—defensive, remorseful, blaming, and angry?

ANGELA: Its funny, he used to seem so huge and powerful. Now I see a sick, pathetic old man. I don't think he's capable of understanding. But it doesn't matter anymore. I know the truth.

These interventions support Angela's anger and entitlement to justice, and, like a victim impact statement, help her begin to articulate the effects of the abuse and hold the perpetrator(s) accountable for harm. One goal is for clients to arrive at a more differentiated perspective, so that perpetrators are seen as more human and life size, and less powerful. An important step is to elicit the client's understanding of perpetrators' response to confrontation. Enacting or imagining the other also can elicit empathic resources. This can be particularly important in healing attachment relationships (if this is desirable for the client), for example, coming to understand that one or both parents were also victims or would regret their behavior.

Allowing the pain of rejection and the sadness of loss also are important aspects of resolution. Accomplishing this is a gradual and complex process that involves the many emotions associated with traumatic experiences. Angela needs to face the pain of not being loved by her parents, all the losses and things she has missed out on (e.g., friends, healthy sexuality, security, self-esteem), and how profoundly she has been victimized by years of loneliness, exploitation, cruelty, and abuse. Allowing herself fully to feel the pain of these experiences (even for a moment) requires confidence in her own ability to survive the pain, as well as in the therapist's supportive presence (e.g., soothing voice, touching her hand or knee), encouraging statements (e.g., "Let it come"), and help in symbolizing the meaning of the pain (e.g., "Put words to your tears"; "What's the worst part of it for you?"; "It's so devastating. Can you say more about what that meant to you?"). Accurate symbolization helps to create distance from the pain and to make Angela's experience more comprehensible. Facing the emotional pain of traumatic experiences also includes facing associated but previously avoided aspects of self. Facing the pain of her isolation as a child, for example, could include feeling the shame associated with sexual abuse, prostitution, and self-destructive behavior; rage at years of victimization, violation, and abuse; and deep sadness at all the disappointments, losses, and suffering.

Finally letting go and allowing the self to fully feel the pain of traumatic experiences typically is followed by a sense of relief, an increased sense of agency or control, and an implicit challenging of beliefs that perpetuated avoidance (e.g., "I *can* handle it. It won't destroy me"). Angela will be faced with a new view of herself and questions about herself ("How could I have done all those gross things?" or "What makes me think I could ever lead a normal life?"). This opens the door for Angela to acknowledge her sense of brokenness, to express the full range of feelings and anger at the persons responsible, and to acknowledge her own contributions (e.g., drug use, cutting, isolation) from a stance of compassion for herself rather than self-blame.

Feelings of primary sadness (as distinct from depression) emerge throughout therapy, but for clients like Angela, these typically are fleeting, quickly suppressed, or shift to anger. Fully experiencing and expressing sorrow requires surrender, letting go, and acknowledging the emptiness inside and the irrevocability of loss. This is likely to occur only after Angela feels fully entitled to her anger and stronger within herself. Expressing sadness to imagined abusive others in IC may not be advisable, because those persons often would not respond with compassion and comfort. However, disclosing vulnerability and sadness to the therapist elicits empathy and compassion for the client's sense of longing, disappointment or loss, or when her eyes well up in tears ("So lonely, dying inside," "Something about that touches you?"). Therapist responses also help the client acknowledge the losses and articulate their effects ("So many things you missed out on growing up—tell me what hurts the most," "Sounds like that would have meant so much. Can you say more about that?"). It might be a source of power for Angela to imagine herself as a child. This can elicit Angela's compassion for herself ("Imagine little Angela here [*moves the empty chair closer*] as a lonely, confused little girl. What do you want to say to her, want her to know?"). For clients like Angela, such an enactment would be very evocative and likely occur toward the end of therapy.

DISTINCT AND SHARED FEATURES OF AEDP AND EFTT

AEDP and EFTT are the two best-articulated approaches to helping trauma survivors with emotion processing in the context of an empathic, validating, and collaborative therapeutic relationship. They share a focus on increasing clients' abilities to (1) be aware of and utilize core adaptive emotions; (2) experience, modulate, and appropriately express the full range of emotional experience; and (3) experience healthy and intimate interpersonal relationships. Because emotions are viewed as vital guides to adaptive functioning, emotional competence must be enhanced for trauma recovery to occur. Both approaches emphasize client strengths, resilience, and internal resources rather than psychopathology.

There are several other specific commonalities. Both approaches view (1) the therapeutic relationship and (2) the emotional processing of trauma memories as fundamental change agents. In terms of memory work, both approaches incorporate principles of exposure and emotional processing, that is, trauma feelings and memories accessed in therapy are available for regulation, exploration, transformation, integration, and thus change (see also Gleiser et al., 2008; Paivio & Pascual-Leone, in press). Both approaches strongly emphasize accessing previously inhibited painful and threatening, but adaptive, emotions. These are viewed as healthy resources that aid in self-development and adaptive interpersonal functioning.

In terms of in-session processes, both approaches rely on the therapist's observation of somatic and affective markers to guide appropriate intervention. The primary task is to promote client emotional experiencing, awareness, and competence. Technically, both AEDP and EFTT balance *following* the client moment by moment, with *directing* the process. Both approaches rely on empathy, affirmation, and collaboration to reduce client isolation and distress, and to promote emotion regulation, awareness, and competence. Both incorporate a variety of experiential and Gestalt-derived imagery and emotion enactment procedures. Finally, both AEDP and EFTT recognize the importance of processing emotion to completion, and see as crucial the positive affects, emotional resources, and adaptive action tendencies that are released as a result.

In terms of differences, in AEDP, there is more explicit focus on and experiential processing of dyadic aspects of the relational experience: The therapist explicitly draws client attention to the positive qualities of the therapeutic relationship and attachment bond. This bond is the primary means of increasing client capacity for interpersonal connectedness. An original contribution of and feature unique to AEDP is the discovery that the metatherapeutic processing of the experience of transformation itself becomes a transformational change agent.

EFTT focuses more on the task of resolving issues with specific abusive and neglectful others. Resolution of these issues is seen as generalizing to other relationships. The process of therapy is guided by a specific, empirically verified model that identified steps in the process of resolving past attachment injuries. EFTT also is a scientifically based approach, with evidence directly supporting treatment efficacy and mechanisms of change. Therefore, EFTT typically follows a more formal sequence of manualized therapeutic interventions than does AEDP.

In summary, psychotherapy for complex traumatic stress disorders inevitably involves helping frightened or emotionally disorganized clients to gain (or regain) the ability to regulate and understand their emotions, and to harness the capacity for satisfying interpersonal relatedness. AEDP and EFTT assist traumatized individuals correspondingly in reclaiming mastery of their memories, their choices, their hopes and dreams, and in replacing the incoherence and alienation of trauma and traumatic stress with meaning, intimacy, and renewed connection to life and humanity.

REFERENCES

Bowlby, J. (1988). *A secure base*. New York: Basic Books.

Damasio, A. R. (1999). *The feeling of what happens*. New York: Harcourt.

Davanloo, H. (1995). *Unlocking the unconscious*. Oxford, UK: Wiley.

Elliott, R., Watson, J., Goldman, R., & Greenberg, L. S. (2004). *Learning emotion-focused therapy*. Washington, DC: American Psychological Association.

Foa, E. B., & Kozak, M. (1986). Emotional processing of fear. *Psychological Bulletin*, 99, 20–35.

Fonagy, P., Gergely, G., Jurist, E. L., & Target, M. (2002). *Affect regulation, mentalization, and the development of the self*. New York: Other Press.

Fosha, D. (2000). *The transforming power of affect*. New York: Basic Books.

Fosha, D. (2002). The activation of affective change processes in AEDP (accelerated experiential–dynamic psychotherapy). In J. J. Magnavita (Ed.), *Comprehensive handbook of psychotherapy: Vol. 1. Psychodynamic and object relations psychotherapies* (pp. 309–344). New York: Wiley.

Fosha, D. (2003). Dyadic regulation and experiential work with emotion and relatedness in trauma and disordered attachment. In D. J. Siegel & M. F. Solomon (Eds.), *Healing trauma: Attachment, trauma, the brain and the mind* (pp. 221–281). New York: Norton.

Fosha, D. (2005). Emotion, true self, true other, core state. *Psychoanalytic Review*, 92, 513–552.

Fosha, D. (2006). Quantum transformation in trauma and treatment: Traversing the crisis of healing change. *Journal of Clinical Psychology*, 62(5), 569–583.

Fosha, D., & Yeung, D. (2006). AEDP exemplifies the seamless integration of emotional transformation and dyadic relatedness at work. In G. Stricker & J. Gold

(Eds.), *A casebook of psychotherapy integration* (pp. 165–184). Washington, DC: American Psychological Association.

Gendlin, E. T. (1997). *Focusing-oriented psychotherapy: A manual of the experiential method.* New York: Guilford Press.

Gleiser, K., Ford, J. D., & Fosha, D. (2008). Contrasting exposure and experiential therapies for complex PTSD. *Psychotherapy: Theory, Research, Practice and Training, 45*(3), 340–360.

Greenberg, L. S., & Malcolm, W. (2002). Resolving unfinished business: Relating process to outcome. *Journal of Consulting and Clinical Psychology, 70*, 406–416.

Greenberg, L. S., & Paivio, S. C. (1997). *Working with emotions in psychotherapy.* New York: Guilford Press.

Herman, J. L. (1992). *Trauma and recovery.* New York: Basic Books.

Lamagna, J., & Gleiser, K. (2007). Building a secure internal attachment: An intra-relational approach to ego strengthening and emotional processing with chronically traumatized clients. *Journal of Trauma and Dissociation, 8*(1), 22–54.

LeDoux, J. (1996). *The emotional brain.* New York: Simon & Schuster.

Paivio, S. C., & Carriere, M. (2006). Contributions of emotion focused therapy to the understanding and treatment of anger and aggression. In T. A. Cavell & K. T. Malcolm (Eds.), *Anger, aggression, and interventions for interpersonal violence* (pp. 143–164). Mahwah, NJ: Erlbaum.

Paivio, S. C., Chagigiorgis, H., Hall, I., Jarry, J., & Ralston, M. (2007). *Comparative efficacy of two versions of emotion focused therapy for complex trauma.* Manuscript submitted for publication.

Paivio, S. C., & Greenberg, L. S. (1995). Resolving "unfinished business." *Journal of Consulting and Clinical Psychology, 63*, 419–425.

Paivio, S. C., Hall, I., Holowaty, K., Jellis, J., & Tran, N. (2001). Imaginal confrontation for resolving child abuse issues. *Psychotherapy Research, 11*, 433–453.

Paivio S. C., & Laurent, C. (2001). Empathy and emotion regulation. *Journal of Clinical Psychology, 57*, 213–226.

Paivio, S. C., & McCullough, C. R. (2004). Alexithymia as a mediator between childhood trauma and self-injurious behaviours. *Child Abuse and Neglect, 28*, 339–354.

Paivio, S. C., & Nieuwenhuis, J. A. (2001). Efficacy of emotion-focused therapy for adult survivors of childhood abuse. *Journal of Traumatic Stress, 14*, 115–134.

Paivio, S. C., & Pascual-Leone, A. (in press). *Emotion focused therapy for complex trauma: An integrative approach.* Washington, DC: American Psychological Association.

Perls, F. S., Hefferline, R., & Goodman, P. (1951). *Gestalt therapy.* New York: Dell.

Ralston, M. (2006). *Experiencing and emotional arousal in imaginal confrontation versus empathic exploration during emotion focused trauma therapy.* Unpublished doctoral dissertation, University of Windsor, ON, Canada.

Russell, E., & Fosha, D. (2008). Transformational affects and core state in AEDP: The emergence and consolidation of joy, hope, gratitude and confidence in the (solid goodness of the) self. *Journal of Psychotherapy Integration, 18*(2), 167–190.

Siegel, D. J. (2007). *The mindful brain.* New York: Norton.

Watkins, J. G., & Watkins, H. H. (1997). *Ego states: Theory and therapy.* New York: Norton.

Winnicott, D. W. (1960/1965). Ego distortion in terms of true and false self. In *The maturational processes and the facilitating environment* (pp. 140–152). New York: International Universities Press.

CHAPTER 15

Sensorimotor Psychotherapy

Janina Fisher
Pat Ogden

Psychological trauma affects not only the mind but also the body. When individuals experience overwhelming emotional or physical threat, prefrontal cortical activity in the brain is inhibited as mind and body prepare for the defensive operations of flight, fight, freeze, or submit (see Ford & Courtois, Chapter 1, this volume). Decades after the original traumatic experience(s), these automatic survival responses can persist in the form of symptoms of posttraumatic stress disorder (PTSD) and the more complex elaborations associated with complex traumatic stress disorders. The hallmark symptoms of PTSD (reexperiencing, emotional numbing, threat-related hyperarousal and, in some cases, aphasia or "speechless terror") and the symptom presentation associated with complex traumatic stress disorder (e.g., difficulties with affect regulation due to hypoarousal and/or alternating hyper- and hypoarousal, disorganized and insecure attachment patterns, somatoform and psychoform dissociation, disorders of the self, and relationship difficulties; Ford, Courtois, Steele, Hart, & Nijenhuis, 2005; van der Kolk, 2006) are characterized by both psychological and somatic components.

Most approaches to psychotherapy lack the tools and intervention methods to address posttraumatic physiological alterations directly. Cognitive-behavioral therapies may assist the client in learning relaxation skills to address states of hyperarousal, but they do not directly remediate the other complex physiological symptoms associated with these traumatic stress disorders. Experiential psychotherapies (see Fosha, Paivio, Gleiser, & Ford [Chapter 14] and Schwartz, Schwartz, & Galperin [Chapter 17], this volume) serve to help clients become more aware of the bodily changes associated with certain emotional states, but they do not facilitate the achievement of altered physiological responses. The absence of direct interventions to assist clients in regaining the ability to regulate bodily states that have been altered by traumatic stress disorders is a very significant omission. If these symptoms are not therapeutically addressed, the autonomic and physiological responses often maintain and exacerbate the psychological symptoms associated with both PTSD and complex traumatic stress disorders despite otherwise adequate treatment. To address body-based symptoms, in addition to the social–emotional and cognitive effects, a different approach to treatment may be helpful.

Traditional treatments of traumatic disorders are often complicated by the wide variety of disturbances in sensation, perception, and movement typically reported by individuals with traumatic stress disorders, symptoms that often prove baffling to clinicians and medical professionals and disorganizing for their patients (McFarlane, 1996). Among these disturbances are those that involve reliving/reexperiencing (e.g., pain and sensory distortions), unbidden movements, autonomic responses (e.g., rapid heart rate, constricted breathing, and muscle tension), and symptoms related to numbing and avoidance (e.g., anesthesia and analgesia), disconnection from one's body (depersonalization), and loss of pain perception (termed *somatoform dissociation*; Steele & van der Hart, Chapter 7, this volume), all of which can further aggravate the dysregulated emotions and distorted body and self-concepts typical of traumatic stress disorders.

In most available approaches to treating trauma-related disorders, the primary focus is the patient's verbalizations: however, when individuals describe traumatic events, the narrative retelling evokes associated nonverbal, implicit memory states: internal sensations, images, emotions, and autonomic dysregulation (van der Kolk & Fisler, 1995). In daily life, the same sensations and emotions can also become "situationally accessible" when activated by trauma-related stimuli or triggers, some of which are consciously identifiable by clients and others of which are not (Brewin, Dalgleish, & Joseph, 1996). Faced with fragmented event memories that reactivate traumatic stress symptoms in the form of altered bodily reactions, many individuals find the tasks of identifying traumatic memories and assimilating traumatic experiences within a life narrative challenging at best. In these cases, interventions that enable clients to become aware of somatic responses and their origins, appreciate their adaptive function, then modify them to become more appropriate to current reality may provide important avenues for therapeutic intervention and ultimately healing.

Within the context of an attuned therapeutic relationship that promotes collaboration and engagement, somatic interventions facilitate clients' growing ability to remain socially engaged, to maintain states of optimal autonomic arousal, and to take adaptive action even in the face of physical activation resulting from trauma-related stimuli. Body-centered interventions employed simply as rote physical exercises rather than emerging organically within an intersubjective relational context are anticipated to have minimal therapeutic benefit. Intersubjectivity from a somatic perspective emphasizes "right brain to right brain" attunement: The therapist, like the caregiver to an infant, uses his or her presence, voice tone, prosody, energy, and seriousness versus playful-ness to maximize pleasurable states and to minimize states of distress (Schore, 2003a, 2003b). The approach described here proposes that only within the context of a therapeutic dyad characterized by relational attunement and col-laboration can fears and phobias of trauma-related body experience be suc-cessfully overcome.

EVOLUTION OF SENSORIMOTOR PSYCHOTHERAPY FOR TRAUMA

Developed in the 1980s by Pat Ogden as a new model of body psychotherapy, sensorimotor psychotherapy has evolved into a comprehensive psychotherapy model, with interventions specifically designed to treat the effects of PTSD and complex traumatic stress disorders, as well as associated attachment and developmental disturbances (Ogden & Minton, 2000; Ogden, Minton, & Pain, 2006). By integrating theory and technique from the worlds of psycho-dynamic and cognitive-behavioral psychotherapy with somatic psychotherapy methods, as well as incorporating research from the fields of attachment, dis-sociation, and neuroscience, sensorimotor psychotherapy utilizes approaches derived from both research and practice. As a foundation for its therapeutic interventions and body orientation, sensorimotor psychotherapy has drawn heavily on the Hakomi method of body psychotherapy (Kurtz, 1990). The direct somatic interventions used in this work have been influenced by a number of physical disciplines, including yoga, dance, movement work, and structural integration (Rolf, 1977), all of which emphasize physical alignment, integrated posture, and movement. A diversity of other psychological influ-ences has also specifically shaped this method's interventions for trauma and attachment disturbance: the pioneering work of Janet (1925) at the beginning of this century and, more recently, the work of Nijenhuis (2006) and Steele and van der Hart (Chapter 7, this volume) on the dissociative and somatoform nature of trauma symptoms. These influences are reflected in sensorimotor psychotherapy elements such as the emphasis on the practice of new physical action patterns, focus on somatoform dissociation, completion of frozen and incomplete defensive responses, and attention to how the relational patterns stemming from disorganized attachment are related to and driven by bodily experience.

Allan Schore's (2003a, 2003b) groundbreaking work on the developmen-tal psychobiological underpinnings of affect regulation in human development has directly shaped the emphasis on attunement and interactive regulation in sensorimotor psychotherapy, as well as its emphasis on addressing disorganized attachment–related symptoms. Porges's (2001, 2003) elucidation of the auto-nomic nervous system's hierarchical response to safety, danger, and life threat has contributed to the focus on the social engagement system, modulation of autonomic arousal, and reorganization of self-protective active defenses, all of which are integral aspects of the sensorimotor method. In addition to Kurtz's (1990) focus on mindfulness as a tool for self-discovery, the research and writings of LeDoux (2002) and Siegel (1999, 2007), both of whom emphasize the role of mindfulness in restoring autonomic stability, have contributed to the understanding of mindfulness as a facilitator of integrative activity, reflected in the central role of mindfulness in sensorimotor interventions and treatment.

In addition, research has demonstrated that mindfulness meditation directly impacts brain functioning. Brain scans of mediators show increased activity in areas governing attentional processes (i.e., the frontal and parietal cortex and anterior cingulate) and arousal and autonomic control (i.e., amygdala and hypothalamus) (Creswell, Way, Eisenberger, & Lieberman, 2007; Davidson et al., 2003; Lazar et al., 2000). Because individuals with PTSD often demonstrate decreased activation in the medial prefrontal cortex (Lanius et al., 2002), the use of mindfulness as an intervention is intended to increase the activity in this part of the brain and to facilitate regulation of autonomic arousal and improved stimulus discrimination (i.e., the ability to differentiate a traumatic event from a stimulus that is reminiscent of that event). *Observing presence*, or the ability to self-witness one's experience mindfully, is thought to counteract "speechless terror" (van der Kolk & Fisler, 1995) and to offset the amygdala's sympathetic alarm activation in response to threat (LeDoux, 2002). According to LeDoux (2002), pathological fear may occur when the amygdala is unchecked by the prefrontal cortex, and treatment of pathological fear may require that the patient learn to increase activity in the prefrontal region, which can serve as a brake on amygdalar activation. Similarly, the works of Schore (2003a, 2003b) on attachment and self-regulation and Porges's (2001, 2003) polyvagal theory lead to the postulation that attunement and social engagement as deliberate strategies in the therapeutic relationship may also serve to regulate posttraumatic somatic dysregulation. Although there is currently little research that validates the use of movement as an intervention in traumatic stress disorders treatment, van der Kolk (2002) reports preliminary findings correlating participation in a yoga class with reduction in PTSD and complex traumatic stress disorder symptoms. Because yoga practice combines focused attention (mindfulness) and mastery of body movement, yoga as an intervention in the treatment of trauma may address two phenomena common to most traumatic experiences: loss of conscious witnessing and loss of control over the body and body movement.

Currently, no formal research has been conducted to attest to the efficacy of sensorimotor psychotherapy as a general treatment strategy or one that is specific to the treatment of traumatic stress, though a multisite research study is planned for 2008. As noted earlier, sensorimotor psychotherapy for the treatment of trauma has been developed entirely from clinical practice, guided by research findings and theoretical developments in the areas of attachment, trauma (developmental traumatology), and neuroscience that have been integrated with techniques derived from other, physically focused therapeutic methods. In single-case studies, subjects have reported satisfaction with the effectiveness of the sensorimotor techniques in resolving traumatic stress disorder symptoms and in increasing feelings of mastery and well-being, when used as either a "stand-alone" treatment or when incorporated into more traditional psychodynamic or cognitive-behavioral therapies. Clinical observations and experiences, as well as feedback from clients, have been utilized to develop and modify specific interventions. Until research studies are undertaken, however, the effectiveness of the sensorimotor psychotherapy method is unknown, as are the mechanisms underlying its principles and interventions.

MAJOR CLINICAL INTERVENTIONS OF SENSORIMOTOR PSYCHOTHERAPY FOR TRAUMA

Mindful Self-Awareness of Body Experience

In sensorimotor psychotherapy, *focus on both the body and the mind* is the central distinguishing feature: The body is utilized as both a source of information and an avenue for treatment intervention. Instead of emphasizing verbal/analytical skills, as is done in talking therapy, the client is asked to observe mindfully and describe the interactions of thoughts, feelings, inner body sensations, and movements as these occur in the present moment. The therapist not only carefully attunes to the client's words and physical reactions but also communicates empathy by closely mirroring the client's statements and movements. This co-attunement, with its encouragement for clients to pay close attention to reactions that are usually automatic and go noticed, is often inherently regulating and enables clients to begin to observe relationships between patterns of movement, physical response and reactivity, and posture, with accompanying thoughts, beliefs, and emotions. For example, when a self-attribution (e.g., "It was my fault") comes into awareness, the client is asked, "What happens inside when you have this thought?" and "How does that thought affect your body's sensations, posture, autonomic arousal, and movement?"

Through the therapist's repeatedly drawing the attention of clients to the relationship between thoughts or beliefs and body responses, clients may begin to discern that their posture can inadvertently reinforce beliefs about helplessness and hopelessness, that those same beliefs can affect body posture as the body responds to the thought, and that emotions are likely to affect both body experience and cognition, and to be affected by them. For example, the therapist may help a client to notice that his cognitive distortion "It's not safe to be seen" corresponds with a slump in his spine and eyes cast to the floor. After observing this and asking the client to be curious about it, the therapist may suggest exploring whether a physical intervention—such as sitting up rather than slumping, or lifting his gaze—might affect the strength of this belief or even offer the opportunity for changing the belief. Rather than studying the results of verbal interpretations, the client is encouraged to allow emotional meaning making to occur organically and "bottom up" through increased recognition of physical sensations and reactions, and their modification through experimentation and practice of new responses.

Clients with complex traumatic stress disorders typically have negative views of their bodies: They may be frightened of their own physical functions and somatic experiences, numb and disconnected, or perhaps even angry at their bodies for "betraying" them in some way. They may cope through ongoing depersonalization and disregard of their bodies to the point of extreme neglect, and even deliberate self-injury and risk taking. These clients often view the prospect of experiencing physical sensation as terrifying, foreign, repulsive, or simply not possible. Unprocessed and unassimilated traumatic experience that results in emotional (and accompanying physiological) arousal, which in turn leads to automatic and intense physical dysregulation, can confirm the client's worst fears, namely, that "going there" will be overwhelming and too much to bear. In sensorimotor psychotherapy, clients first learn how to put aside narrative content and emotional states to focus on their body responses and to be increasingly aware of their mind–body experience. Attention is always given on an ongoing basis to pacing the intensity of the work and to facilitating therapist–client attunement and collaboration, so that autonomic arousal can be modulated and maintained at a level that is tolerable and not overwhelming, and that allows for reorganization rather than reliving of past experience.

Self-Regulating Bodily Arousal

Because a hallmark of both PTSD and complex traumatic stress disorders is persistent physiological dysregulation, attention to regulating arousal must be a key feature of any effective treatment for trauma. Allowing clients repeatedly to access feelings common to traumatic experience, such as fear, horror, helplessness, anger, and shame, without the ability to modulate the reactions or "put the brakes on" (Rothschild, 2000), is of little therapeutic benefit: Overwhelming emotions and autonomic dysregulation only tend to exacerbate the symptoms. Dysregulated arousal subsequent to trauma tends to occur both situationally and habitually, is not always tied to specific images or events, and is easily interpreted by traumatized individuals as a sign of threat in the here-and-now environment. For the client to experience a somatic sense of safety in the present, the autonomic nervous system must be stabilized and the capacity for optimal arousal developed. In sensorimotor psychotherapy, the therapists help clients to regulate arousal by carefully tracking physical sensations for signs of dysregulation, by asking questions that direct attention to relationships between bodily responses and narrative content, by teaching clients to recognize the physical signs that indicate dysregulated hyper- or hypoarousal, and by encouraging them to experiment with specific somatic interventions that promote regulation. In this way, clients experience confidence in their bodies as a resource rather than a hindrance or a threat, and are able to develop a sense of mastery over what were overwhelming autonomic states driving their posttraumatic symptoms.

Sensorimotor Memory Processing

As memories come up spontaneously in session or are deliberately accessed for therapeutic memory processing, the sensorimotor psychotherapist approaches work with memories not by "talking about" them exclusively, but by first helping the client become mindful of how that experience has been "organized" in mind and body. As individuals respond to events, *what they actually experience or remember* is a function of the unique interaction of their thoughts, feelings, body sensations, perceptions, and movement impulses. For example, individuals might first perceive something, then react to it physically, then have a thought or a feeling. Together, these stimuli organize the "feeling of what happens" (Damasio, 1999). Even different individuals who have been exposed to the same traumatic event have different subjective experiences of it; hence, their organization of the experience will differ (Terr, 1992). Human beings develop "procedurally learned" habits of responding: They react to all future experience with the most adaptive combination of automatic cognitive, emotional, motor, visceral, and behavioral reactions learned from *past* experience.

Traumatic memories often are encoded implicitly in the form of images, visceral and muscular sensations, movements and impulses, smells, sounds, feelings without words, and autonomic responses, as well as articulated emotions, thoughts, and life narratives. The focus in sensorimotor psychotherapy is on studying and then reorganizing how the traumatic event has been encoded in the body and mind, so that the memory can be experienced as "finally being over, in the past," rather than "still happening" or "impossible to get over."

Mindful awareness of bodily reactions to the recall of traumatic events may also contribute to the prevention of inadvertent retraumatization during work with traumatic memories. A client is encouraged to become curious rather than fearful as the therapist evokes mindfulness by querying the client as to emerging thoughts, emotions, sense perception, body sensation, and movements that accompany the recall. As the client learns to recognize how the trauma has been encoded in mind and body, and then is helped to implement techniques that somatically reorganize it, the client is supported in experiencing the threat as "finally over." The sense of finality or closure can be achieved in a number of different ways: For example, a client whose traumatic experience ended at age 6 subsequently experienced her mother's inability to tolerate hearing what had happened as a signal that she (the child) could no longer speak of it. The sense of "It's over now" for her resulted from her therapist's encouragement to notice what it felt like in her body to sense the therapist's attuned presence and ability to tolerate hearing what happened.

Action and Movement

Trauma-related symptoms are reflected in both mobilizing (fighting, fleeing) and immobilizing (freezing, collapsing) physical reactions and impulse. With ongoing threat, when fight or flight and other mobilizing defensive responses are ineffective, these must be inhibited and movement impulses must be frozen or subdued to enhance survival. For example, during a rape, attempting to fight or to flee could provoke more injury. In a violent family environment, a child's healthy defensive actions could lead to more violence: For both the rape victim and the child, it may be safer and more effective to be immobilized, quiet, and frozen.

Thus, in treatment, *action and movement* can be effective targets for treatment intervention. Even when immobilization is the only survival option, the impulses to actively defend remain, as urges concealed within the body long after the original trauma is over (Levine, 1997; Ogden et al., 2006). The "actions that wanted to happen" might include pushing away, hitting out, kicking, raising an arm in self-defense, leaving the situation, calling for help, screaming "No," fighting back, or standing one's ground. Aware that these impulses to act remain encoded in the body as truncated, incomplete body sensations and preparatory movements, the therapist carefully tracks the client's body for signs of those incipient action impulses, as well as movements that reflect immobilizing defenses, such as freezing (body held stiffly, eyes widened) or collapsing in submission (head down, gaze averted, spine slumped, tonic immobility). When these responses are noted, the therapist intervenes to help the client reorganize habitual defensive physical patterns to be more effective, active, and expansive.

The most powerful uses of movement involve asking clients to observe their own spontaneous, small, preparatory movements that signal larger actions "that wanted to happen" and then to repeat or even exaggerate those. When subtle signs of mobilizing responses are noted (e.g., lifting the hand, making a fist), the therapist helps the client first to notice and then mindfully and deliberately to carry through the physical execution of this new action, until a sense of mastery rather than discharge is achieved. For example, a young woman who had been molested by a photographer was observed to lift her hands slightly as she talked about her passive, mute, frozen response to his advances. Noticing this gesture, the therapist asked whether she would be willing to repeat the movement again as an experiment and observe what happens. Each time the client repeated the movement of lifting her hands up, she instinctively oriented to her left side, saying, "This feels like keeping him away." Repeated movements of holding her hands up, as if to block the unwanted intrusion, gradually resulted in feelings of greater solidness and safety in her body.

SENSORIMOTOR PSYCHOTHERAPY IN PHASE-BASED COMPLEX TRAUMATIC STRESS DISORDER TREATMENT

Because of its focus on the psychophysiological reorganization of traumatic experience, rather than on the recall or abreaction of memories, sensorimotor psychotherapy is appropriate and effective during all three stages of phase-oriented treatment. With its unique ability to increase access to somatic and cognitive resources, and to stabilize autonomic responses, sensorimotor interventions are particularly useful during Phase 1 stabilization (Ford et al., 2005; Steele & van der Hart, Chapter 7, this volume).

Sensorimotor Psychotherapy During Phase 1 Stabilization: Composite Clinical Case

> Jeanette entered therapy soon after an alcohol relapse and suicide attempt precipitated by months of out-of-control autonomic arousal. At the very first session, the therapist gently interrupted each time the arousal escalated, asking Jeanette to take a breath and just attend to the feeling of her feet on the ground. Each time Jeanette became activated, the therapist would again slow the pace, offering psychoeducation to explain the need for attention to autonomic arousal and mindful noticing. Next, the therapist taught Jeanette to observe the somatic signs of increasing activation and to respond somatically by standing up, orienting to the room, walking around, or placing a hand over her heart until her heart rate stabilized. Thus, Jeanette was taught to slow down and "put on the brakes" to experience mastery over her reactions.

Sensorimotor Psychotherapy During Phase 2 Memory/Emotion Work

Sensorimotor psychotherapy's emphasis on dual awareness of mind–body reactions can help to maximize safe, effective processing of memory. By accentuating the use of newly acquired somatic resources and skills learned in Phase 1 to regulate autonomic arousal and maintain a connection to present time, attention is given to both memory processing and relapse prevention. The sense of mastery over overwhelming experience achieved in this way is further enhanced when frozen or submissive responses are replaced by empowering ones brought to effective completion through movement interventions (Ogden et al., 2006).

> For example, Miriam, a victim of a home invasion and sexual assault, had been unable to sleep through the anniversary of this event for years. On the day before the anniversary, she described to her therapist the distress associated with her inability to defend herself: "I'm so ashamed I just gave in." The therapist noticed a slight movement in Miriam's hands. Recognizing this movement as potential preparation to defend, the therapist asked Miriam to repeat her words and movements. This time, her hands came up, so that they formed a "stop" gesture. Repeating the movement again, Miriam experienced an impulse to shout, "Go away!" She was invited next to push against a pillow held by the therapist—while both repeated the words, "Go away!"—until she reported feelings of power and solidity in her body. As she made meaning of this transformation in her responses to the memory, Miriam was also helped

to understand how her "submission" was in fact a defensive response that effectively enabled her not to enrage her assailant further. That anniversary, after 22 years, Miriam reported with great glee that she had finally slept soundly through the night. In the weeks that followed, she experienced increasing relief and a heightened sense of self-understanding and self-compassion that challenged the shame and self-blame she had experienced previously.

Sensorimotor Psychotherapy During Phase 3 Integration Work

Phase 3 work focuses on overcoming core phobias that prevent full resolution of trauma: the phobias of normal life, change and exploration, and healthy connection to others, including the ability to be intimate (D. Brown, Chapter 6, this volume). In this phase, sensorimotor work focuses equally on the body and on discovering and changing cognitive distortions (e.g., "I do not deserve an intimate relationship" or "I can't be normal") and corresponding physical habits (e.g., failure to sustain eye contact or inability to tolerate physical touch). As clients attempt to master these challenges and fully resolve their posttraumatic symptoms, habitual somatic responses are often reevoked: autonomic dysregulation, impulses either to avoid or to act out, and frozen or hyperactive movement impulses. Often, therapist and client discover that the old responses are fueled by trauma-related cognitive schemas that activate the body's survival responses and defenses. At this phase, the emphasis is on "homework," on practicing new, more adaptive responses that challenge trauma-related cognitive distortions and facilitate fuller engagement in normal life.

> For example, although Evelyn now reported few traumatic stress disorder symptoms, she still avoided self-disclosure and emotional intimacy with others, even with her partner of 17 years. Asked to imagine sharing ordinary day-to-day feelings, Evelyn felt a tightening in her chest and an intrusive thought, "I'll be humiliated," which she associated with "hiding." Her therapist asked, "Is there an image or memory that goes with those words?" Spontaneously, an image came to mind: Evelyn was trying to tell her mother about her fear of being left with her abusive stepfather, only to be criticized for being "too sensitive" and "disrespectful." Emotions of sadness emerged as Evelyn felt a connection to the little girl she had been in that frightening environment, and the therapist encouraged her to feel the sensations of sadness and pain in her body, "to stay with them," and just to notice "what it feels like to tell someone right here, right now." Evelyn reported feeling relief and lightness, as if a weight had lifted: "Right here, right now, it's OK to share my feelings," she reminded herself. "I don't have to hide." As Evelyn was able to apply this learning by disclosing to her partner more about both her needs for closeness and her past history of abuse, the emotional intimacy between them deepened, and Evelyn was able both to verbalize and physicalize her love and attachment to her partner.

COMPOSITE CASE EXAMPLE:
A SENSORIMOTOR PSYCHOTHERAPY SESSION

"Annie," a 55-year-old married mother of two grown sons, has a history of chronic childhood trauma, including severe neglect, physical and emotional abuse, childhood pornography, and incest. Like many patients with complex traumatic stress disorders, she carries a number of diagnoses: PTSD, attention-deficit/hyperactivity disorder, major depression, and dissociative identity disorder. In the past few years, she has had difficulty holding jobs, because her symptoms overwhelm her capacity to be fully engaged, to think clearly, and to tolerate normal stress and interpersonal stimulation. Prior to coming for sensorimotor psychotherapy, Annie had a 10-year course of treatment with a therapist who focused almost exclusively on the retrieval and abreaction of trauma memories. Although Annie became deeply attached to the therapist, her symptoms and functioning worsened over the 10 years. In her treatment with Janina Fisher, the focus was initially on Phase 1 stabilization and skills building through somatosensory awareness and self-regulation and, more recently, on overcoming her phobia of the traumatic memories.

In this session, Annie arrives for her session literally trembling, reporting feelings of fear and hopelessness.

ANNIE: (*tearfully*) I don't think you understand. I'm *alone*, all alone in that horrible lonely house. I have no friends anymore. I just want to *die!*

THERAPIST: That loneliness is *so* painful, isn't it? When you say those words, "I'm alone, *all alone*," what happens inside?

ANNIE: My heart is racing—my chest feels tight—my stomach is in knots ...

As Annie speaks of feeling so painfully alone, past and present are merged: Her stable family and home life are forgotten as she interprets the body sensations and emotions as evidence that something is terribly wrong with her present environment.

THERAPIST: I wonder if we could try something. ... Notice what happens in your body when you say those words again, "I'm so alone."

ANNIE: The tightness gets worse, especially along my sides. I feel like I'm in a vise—I'm so scared! (*Becomes tearful again.*)

THERAPIST: I wonder if we could study what happens in your body when you "let go" of those thoughts to just attend to the feelings and sensations—would that be OK?

ANNIE: (*Lowers her eyes, indicating a turn of her attention inward.*) Well, my heart isn't just racing—it's pounding. Like a hammer: ba-ba-boom, ba-ba-boom ... I can feel my lower lip trembling. But now it's settling a little bit as I talk about it.

Often, this resolution or settling of the body sensations and arousal often accompanies the client's ability to attend to experience with mindful dual consciousness in the context of therapist's affect-regulating co-attunement (Schore, 2003a, 2003b). Next, the therapist facilitates a reorganization of trauma-related patterns via the use of "mindful experiments"; that is, the conscious and voluntary execution of a new movement, word, gesture, or response that is then studied to evaluate its effect (Ogden et al., 2006). Experiments do not have to "succeed": They are exploratory, meant to gather information and challenge habitual tendencies, as discussed below.

THERAPIST: I'm wondering if you would be willing to try an experiment ... Notice what happens when I make this movement.... (*Reaches out her hand to indicate connection with Annie, nonverbally challenging her perception of aloneness.*)

ANNIE: My heart beats faster. I can feel all the muscles along my sides tighten up—it's *worse*. I don't want to be alone, but it's not safe to be with someone either.

THERAPIST: Yes, it's not safe to be alone, and it's not safe to be with people either. Would you be willing to try another experiment? Notice what happens if you make a boundary with your hands.... (*Holds both hands up in a "stop" gesture, demonstrating the boundary to Annie physically.*)

ANNIE: I can feel the relaxation immediately! But, almost as soon as I say that, I start to have thoughts that now I'll be *more* alone, and I want to cry again.

THERAPIST: So, it doesn't feel safe to have connection *or* to have a boundary. (*Annie nods.*) Let's try both at once, and just sense whatever feels right. ... (*Models putting up one hand in a "stop" gesture and reaching out with the other.*)

ANNIE: (*After some experimenting, she makes "stop" movement with dominant hand and reaches out with the other.*) This feels better. My heart is slowing down now, my stomach is untwisting—things are relaxing a little more.

THERAPIST: So, just *enjoy* that feeling! When you have a boundary, it actually feels safer to reach out to others and let them reach out to you.

ANNIE: Sure does! But I'm sick of living this way—spending all my time trying not to be overwhelmed! I want to understand and change it.

THERAPIST: I wonder if you would be willing to "rewind the tape" back to when you first started to feel these feelings and sensations.... When was that, do you recall?

ANNIE: It actually started a few days ago.... I took the dogs out at dusk, and I was walking in the woods, noticing the beautiful fall light, and then I suddenly got panicked! I literally ran home, and sat and trembled for the next few hours!

This illustrates the paradoxical experience of normal daily life for so many survivors of trauma: Annie is engaged in enjoying her walk and the fall light on the trees when suddenly an intrusion of memory precipitates related physical reactions and emotions. In this case, the memories that came up were implicit memories, not clearly identifiable as "memory": body sensations, autonomic arousal, impulses to run, and emotions of fear and panic.

THERAPIST: As you recall noticing the fall light and then the feelings of panic, is there an image or memory that goes with those?

Notice that the therapist evokes only a "sliver" of memory rather than asking Annie to discuss the events in detail. In sensorimotor psychotherapy, the event memory is a vehicle for evoking the organization of that memory in the body. Rather than processing memories using narrative recall, they are processed "bottom-up": first, the body sensations and movement impulses, then the emotions and cognitive meaning making.

ANNIE: The image that comes up is Halloween night—I'm young, and I'm all by myself outside, and this lady is coming over to me with a smile. [The "nice lady" took advantage of Annie's isolation to take her away to a man who used her in a child pornography ring.] As soon as I see the image of her face, my heart starts racing, and I can feel shaking and trembling all through my body—I want to run, but I can't.

THERAPIST: What happens in your body as you recall that?

ANNIE: I can feel my heart starting to beat really fast, and there is this strong muscular pull in my chest and stomach, like I'm going to double up in pain.

THERAPIST: You know, sometimes muscle tension can be a precursor to movement. Notice how the tension would like your body to move ...

ANNIE: It's somehow connected to my legs. ... The pull would bring my head down and my legs up over my chest. Wow! It wants me to curl up into a ball—I just want to huddle and wait for it to be over. (*Makes a motion as if to collapse to the floor.*)

THERAPIST: (*continuing to mirror Annie's words*) Yes, your body wants to huddle and wait for it to be over.... And what happens as you say those words?

ANNIE: I can feel the pull to curl up getting stronger! This is really weird—it was so long ago—but my body is still waiting for it to be over! No wonder I isolate.

Once Annie observes the relationship between her thoughts and body experience, she becomes more curious about the "huddle and wait for it to be over" response that has been driving her symptoms of agoraphobia and social phobia.

THERAPIST: (*recognizing the opportunity to introduce alternatives to the passive defense of "huddling and waiting for it to be over"*) I wonder if your body ever wanted to move in a different way, a more active way. Just sense that: Is there is any other action that "wants to happen" right now? Does your body want to push away? Hit out? Kick? Run away?

ANNIE: Yes, what my body *needs* is a new action that says, "You *don't* have to huddle and wait for it to be over! You don't have to go with that woman at all!"

THERAPIST: What happens when you say, "I *don't* have to go with her!"?

ANNIE: I want to run—I want to leave.

THERAPIST: How is your body telling you that?

ANNIE: My feet want to take a step—it's amazing: I felt so frozen before.

THERAPIST: Notice what happens if your legs and feet take one step ...

ANNIE: (*Stands and takes a step, noticing herself doing it.*) That small step felt so effortful, like I was fighting with the wish to huddle up! Let me try another one.... (*Takes a step.*) That definitely felt a little easier. I feel more solid—I realize how much strength I have in my legs and body. (*After taking several steps, Annie is quieter and more serious as she begins to make sense of her symptoms and anticipate more adaptive options for the future.*) Wow! That is a lot to take in.... When I was triggered on that walk, my body freaked out. Everything felt threatening and desperate—it wanted to do what worked when I was a child: "Huddle down and wait for it to be over." But when I do something a little bit different, my body has other possibilities. All I have to do now, each time I'm triggered, is to notice what my body is *telling* me to do—and then do one tiny thing differently.

In this vignette, key elements of sensorimotor psychotherapy are illustrated: the close attention and attunement of the therapist to the client's physical responses; the focus on the body and on physical sensations; the direction to "just notice" physical sensations, while letting go of verbalization and cognitive interpretations; the encouragement to focus not on the details of the memory itself but on the physical impulses experienced; and the practice of interventions to reverse physical immobilization by experimenting with the completion of truncated defensive responses that result in a sense of mastery. From this body-based experience, new insights and meaning making spontaneously arise and can be integrated with the somatic experience.

SUMMARY AND CONCLUSIONS

In sensorimotor psychotherapy practice, the therapist carefully attends to the client's narrative, empathically interrupting tendencies toward either hyper- or hypoarousal before either causes dysregulation, and encouraging alternative physical actions that challenge habitual, trauma-related reactions. When clients have difficulty experiencing or observing their somatic experience, the therapist tries to determine the reason: Is the client phobically avoidant of body awareness? Or numb and disconnected? Does connecting to the body trigger shame or alarm? How can the client be helped to cultivate curiosity rather than to engage automatic phobic reactions about the body-based symptoms of the traumatic events? If clients are uneasy with the word *body*, avoiding the word itself helps to increase comfort. The use of specific language, such as *activation, visceral sensation*, or *movement impulse*, is rarely problematic for clients. Providing a concrete "menu" of words and phrases with which to label physical sensations may also be more comfortable than a general instruction about body awareness.

Normalizing somatic experience through psychoeducation or therapist modeling is often useful, especially for clients who are more comfortable with cognitive experience and verbalization. The process of reconnecting with the body should not be made effortful for clients, nor should it be dysregulating or painful. Often, capitalizing on existing somatic strengths (e.g., the ability to feel grounded, or a client's athletic ability) fortifies confidence and stimulates enthusiasm for further somatic exploration. Increasing the client's awareness of survival resources (e.g., immobilizing defensive responses that helped to ensure survival) may have the side effect of facilitating increased curiosity about and pride in the body's many built-in resources, and challenging the physical antipathy that many adult survivors experience toward their bodies.

In sensorimotor psychotherapy treatment, clients are first encouraged to learn how to simply and mindfully observe the physical sensations that accompany their emotions and cognitions; to gradually become more familiar and equally "at home" with thoughts, feelings, and bodily sensations or movements (whether that process takes a single or many sessions); and eventually to begin to experiment with and practice new, more adaptive physical actions. Over time, the trauma-related feelings and cognitions begin to reorganize as clients experience new physical responses and the sense of mastery in physical control.

Somatic interventions must be tailored to the unique needs and therapeutic goals of each client. One client might need to become more aware of body sensation and involuntary movements to better modulate autonomic activation, whereas another might find involuntary sensations autonomically dysregulating and need to work with controlled movement and physical action. Although dual awareness is helpful in and of itself, it is not sufficient simply to help clients become aware of the body: The therapist must also be familiar with effective interventions to work with sensations and movements, to regulate autonomic arousal, and to transform habitual, trauma-related patterns of response.

Focus on narrative memory can be helpful in the treatment of trauma: to understand the client's history, to design a treatment plan, and to provide clients the opportunity for a witness for their overwhelming experiences. However, to *change* the body's response to the telling of the story requires meticulous observation of clients' trauma-related procedurally learned action tendencies. Neither insight nor understanding can replace therapeutic interruption of these automatic reactions that teach clients to trust their body sensations, regulate arousal, and learn new, empowering physical actions that were impossible during the actual traumatic events. In the words of Bessel van der Kolk (personal communication, 2002), "Trauma treatment must restore a sense of safety in the body and complete the unfinished past." Rather than focusing on the verbal and narrative remembering or reprocessing of the event memories of the trauma, sensorimotor psychotherapy aims to achieve this goal by enhancing clients' ability first to witness and then to transform trauma-related somatic, cognitive, and emotional experience, until they not only achieve cognitive understanding that the past is finally behind them but also experience at a deep somatic level that they are safe now.

REFERENCES

Brewin, C. R., Dalgleish, T., & Joseph, S. (1996). A dual representation theory of post-traumatic stress disorder. *Psychological Review, 103*, 670–686.

Creswell, J. D., Way, B. M., Eisenberger, N. I., & Lieberman, M. D. (2007). Neural correlates of dispositional mindfulness affect labeling. *Psychosomatic Medicine, 69*, 560–565.

Damasio, A. (1999). *The feeling of what happens: Body and emotion in the making of consciousness.* New York: Harcourt, Brace.

Davidson, R. J., Kabat-Zinn, J., Schumacher, J., Rosenkranz, M., Muller, D., Santorelli, S. F., et al. (2003). Alterations in brain and immune function produced by mindfulness meditation. *Psychosomatic Medicine, 65*, 564–570.

Ford, J. D., Courtois, C. A., Steele, K., Hart, O., & Nijenhuis, E. R. (2005). Treatment of complex posttraumatic self-dysregulation. *Journal of Traumatic Stress, 18*(5), 437–447.

Janet, P. (1925). *Principles of psychotherapy.* London: Allen & Unwin.

Kurtz, R. (1990). *Body-centered psychotherapy: The Hakomi method.* Mendocino, CA: LifeRhythm.

Lanius, R. A., Williamson, P. C., Boksman, K., Densmore, M., Gupta, M., Neufeld, R. W., et al. (2002). Brain activation during script-driven imagery induced dissociative responses in PTSD: A functional magnetic resonance imaging investigation. *Biological Psychiatry, 52*(4), 305–311.

Lazar, S. W., Bush, G., Gollub, R. L., Fricchione, G. L., Khalsa, G., & Benson, H. (2000). Functional brain mapping of the relaxation response and meditation. *NeuroReport, 11*(7), 1581–1585.

LeDoux, J. (2002). *The synaptic self.* New York: Viking.

Levine, P. A. (1997). *Waking the tiger, healing trauma: The innate capacity to transform overwhelming experiences.* Berkeley, CA: North Atlantic Books.

McFarlane, A. C. (1996). Resilience, vulnerability, and the course of posttraumatic reactions. In B. A. van der Kolk, A. C. McFarlane, & L. Weisaeth (Eds.), *Trau-*

matic stress: The effects of overwhelming experience on mind, body, and society (pp. 155–181). New York: Guilford Press.

Nijenhuis, E. R. S., & van der Hart, O. (1999). Somatoform dissociative phenomena: A Janetian perspective. In J. Goodwin & R. Attias (Eds.), *Splintered reflections: Images of the body in trauma* (pp. 89–128). New York: Basic Books.

Nijenhuis, E. R. S. (2006). *Somatoform dissociation.* Assen, Netherlands: Van Gorcum. (Original work published 1999)

Ogden, P., & Minton, K. (2000). Sensorimotor psychotherapy: One method for processing traumatic memory. *Traumatology, 6*(3), 3.

Ogden, P., Minton, K., & Pain, C. (2006) *Trauma and the body: A sensorimotor approach to psychotherapy.* New York: Norton.

Porges, S. W. (2001). The polyvagal theory: Phylogenetic substrates of a social nervous system. *International Journal of Psychophysiology, 42*(2), 123–146.

Porges, S. W. (2003). The polyvagal theory. *Physiology and Behavior, 79,* 503–513.

Rolf, I. P. (1977). *Rolfing: The integration of human structures.* Santa Monica, CA: Dennis-Landman.

Rothschild, B. (2000). *The body remembers.* New York: Norton.

Schore, A. (2003a). *Affect dysregulation and disorders of the self.* New York: Norton.

Schore, A. (2003b). *Affect regulation and the repair of the self.* New York: Norton.

Siegel, D. (2007). *The mindful brain: Reflection and attunement in the cultivation of well-being.* New York: Norton.

Siegel, D. J. (1999). *The developing mind: How relationships and the brain interact to shape who we are.* New York: Guilford Press.

Terr, L. (1992). *Too scared to cry.* New York: Basic Books.

van der Kolk, B. A. (2002). Beyond the talking cure: Somatic experience and subcortical imprints in the treatment of trauma. In F. Shapiro (Ed.), *EMDR as an integrative psychotherapy approach.* Washington, DC: American Psychological Association.

van der Kolk, B. A. (2006). Clinical implications of neuroscience research in PTSD. *Annals of the New York Academy of Sciences, 1071,* 277–293.

van der Kolk, B. A., & Fisler, R. (1995). Dissociation and the fragmentary nature of traumatic memories: Overview and exploratory study. *Journal of Traumatic Stress, 8*(4), 505–525.

van der Kolk, B. A., McFarlane, A. C., & Weisaeth, L. (Eds.). (1996). *Traumatic stress: The effects of overwhelming experience on mind, body, and society.* New York: Guilford Press.

CHAPTER 16

Pharmacotherapy

Lewis A. Opler
Michelle S. Grennan
Julian D. Ford

Despite the several selective serotonin reuptake inhibitors (SSRIs) demonstrating efficacy in patients meeting DSM-III-R criteria for posttraumatic stress disorder (PTSD; Friedman & Davidson, 2007), clinicians working with survivors of early life and/or chronic and/or extremely horrific traumatic stressors, such as childhood abuse or genocide, have found that many of them benefit little or not at all from SSRIs. Such patients often present with complex traumatic stress symptoms and functional impairments that include not only the cardinal symptoms of PTSD (intrusive reexperiencing, avoidance, emotional numbing, and hyperarousal) but also dissociation, somatic and affect dysregulation, and altered life schemas (Herman, 1992; van der Kolk, Roth, Pelcovitz, Sunday, & Spinazzola, 2005). Therefore, pharmacotherapy for complex traumatic stress disorders must address not only PTSD symptoms but also complex affective states (e.g., shame, self-loathing, emptiness), cognitive schemas (e.g., sense of betrayal, permanent damage to the self), behavior problems (e.g., impulsivity, addictions), alterations in information processing (e.g., dissociative fugue states and amnesia, fragmented narrative memory), somatization (e.g., psychogenic pain, somatoform dissociation), and impairments in relationships (e.g., distrust).

TARGETING PHARMACOTHERAPY TO SYMPTOMS AND IMPAIRMENTS OF COMPLEX PTSD AND DISORDERS OF EXTREME STRESS (DES)

No formal diagnosis in the *Diagnostic and Statistical Manual of Mental Disorders* (American Psychiatric Association, 2000) specifically addresses complex traumatic stress morbidity. A prototype labeled complex PTSD (Herman, 1992) or disorders of extreme stress not otherwise specified (DESNOS; van der Kolk et al., 2005), proposed and tested in DSM-IV field trials, was not kept as a diagnosis. Therefore, in this chapter, we refer to complex trauma-related impairments as complex PTSD/DES. Given the absence of a formal complex PTSD/DES diagnosis, we first consider approaches developed to address existing psychiatric diagnoses that involve symptoms and impairments similar to complex PTSD/DES, often with a history of psychological trauma.

Pharmacotherapy for Borderline Personality Disorder

Many patients diagnosed with PTSD and comorbid borderline personality disorder (BPD) have experienced complex trauma and present with symptoms consistent with complex PTSD/DES (e.g., difficulties with sense of self, emotional lability, transient episodes of severe dissociation, relational instability, and impulsivity) (Kuhler & Stachetzki, 2005; van der Kolk et al., 2005). BPD has been criticized as a potentially stigmatizing diagnosis that implies intractable impairment and has been disproportionately applied to women (perhaps in part due to the greater degree of female exposure to complex trauma, and/or to biases based on sexism). Complex PTSD/DES may be both a more accurate and a less stigmatizing diagnosis that allows therapists a greater breadth of treatment options and compassion (Herman, 1992).

Nose, Cipriani, Biancosino, Grassi, and Barbui (2006) reviewed 22 randomized, placebo-controlled clinical trials evaluating efficacy of pharmacotherapy in persons with BPD. They found that although mood stabilizers did not consistently show evidence of efficacy, antidepressants were efficacious in reducing affective instability and anger but not other BPD symptoms (i.e., "impulsivity and aggression, unstable relationships, suicidality and global functioning," p. 345), and that antipsychotics did show efficacy in reducing symptoms, as well as stabilizing relationships and improving overall psychosocial functioning. Soloff (2005) described the findings of the American Psychiatric Association Work Group's *Practice Guideline for the Treatment of Patients with Borderline Personality Disorder* and noted that fewer than 50 published scientific reports could be located on pharmacotherapy of BPD. The Work Group concluded that medication has limited benefit with BPD, rarely eliminating or more than partially improving its core symptoms. Although Soloff found no evidence that pharmacotherapy can reduce the severity or frequency of the most dangerous BPD symptoms, such as the self-mutilation symptoms that are present in 70–80% of BPD cases (Gerson & Stanley, 2002), he concluded that medication can adjunctively target three BPD symptoms (impaired cognitive processing, emotion dysregulation, and poor impulse control).

At the present time, *psychotherapy integrated with pharmacotherapy* is the standard of care for BPD (Oldham, 2006), as it is for PTSD (Foa, Davidson, & Frances, 1999). The domains targeted for pharmacotherapy with complex PTSD/DES expand those for BPD to include severe substance use disorders

(SUDs), extreme intrusive reexperiencing symptoms (including dissociative flashbacks) and other symptoms of dissociative disorders, and problems with reality testing and agitation.

Pharmacotherapy for Substance Use Disorders

Clinicians historically have been hesitant to address PTSD (Ford, Russo, & Mallon, 2007a) or to use pharmacotherapy in the treatment of SUDs. Although results are mixed, recent studies suggest that the following medications may be efficacious: SSRIs for cocaine dependence (Moeller et al., 2007) and alcoholism (Pettinati, Kranzler, & Madaras, 2003); topiramate (see Table 16.1 for the brand names of the medications mentioned) for cocaine dependence (Preti,

TABLE 16.1. Generic Psychotropic Medications Referred to in the Chapter and Their Brand Names

Generic medication	Brand name
Acamprosate	Campral
Baclofen	Lioresal
Buspirone	Buspar
Carbamazepine	Tegretol
Clomipramine	Anafranil
Clonidine	Catapres
Disulfiram	Antabuse
Fluoxetine	Prozac
Fluvoxamine	Luvox
Lamotrigine	Lamictal
Modafinil	Provigil
Naltrexone	Revia
Olanzapine	Zyprexa
Paroxetine	Paxil
Prazosin	Minipress
Propranolol	Inderal
Quetiapine	Seroquel
Risperidone	Risperdal
Sertraline	Zoloft
Tiagabine	Gabitril
Topiramate	Topamax
Valproate	Depakote

2007) and, in combination with the glutamate antagonist and gamma-amin-obutyric acid (GABA) agonist acamprosate, for alcoholism (Assanangkornchai & Srisurapanont, 2007); the opiate antagonist naltrexone for alcoholism (Garbutt et al., 2005), disulfiram for alcoholism and cocaine abuse; the narcolepsy medication modafinil for cocaine abuse (Preti, 2007); the GABA reuptake inhibitor anticonvulsant tiagabine for cocaine dependence (Preti, 2007); and the GABA-related agents baclofen and valproic acid (Preti, 2007) for cocaine abuse. Research is needed to determine how best to provide pharmacotherapy that safely targets not only specific addictive disorders and substances but also subgroups of patients with SUDs that may differ genetically or psychosocially in their response to medications (Preti, 2007).

Although caution is required in addressing SUDs with pharmacotherapy, SUDs are a commonly comorbid with complex PTSD/DES (van der Kolk et al., 2005), and patients in treatment for SUDs are less likely to complete and to benefit from SUD treatment when they report complex PTSD/DES symptoms (Ford, Hawk, Alessi, Ledgerwood, & Petry, 2007; Ford, Russo, & Mallon, 2007). Histories of traumatic violence and PTSD are prevalent among individuals with SUDs, and SUDs are prevalent among adults with PTSD (Ouimette, Moos, & Finney, 2003). Women seeking SUD treatment for comorbid PTSD–SUD reported more extensive trauma histories and more severe PTSD symptoms (i.e., avoidance, emotional numbing, sleep difficulties) than women with PTSD only (Saladin, Brady, Dansky, & Kilpatrick, 1995).

Based on a growing body of empirical evidence that an SUD may result when traumatic stress symptoms lead to attempts to seek relief through the use of addictive substances, pharmacotherapy may provide a plausible and controlled alternative to assist patients with complex PTSD/DES and an SUD to manage extreme states of emotional and physical distress, and psychological and behavioral disorganization and impulsivity, without the use of addictive substances. Most adults receiving SUD treatment are neither evaluated for PTSD (let alone for complex PTSD/DES), nor offered PTSD treatment, and PTSD services are provided only after lengthy periods of substance use abstinence (Ouimette et al., 2003). Integrated complex PTSD/DES–SUD psychotherapies have been developed (Ford, Russo, & Mallon, 2007), but integrated psychotherapy–pharmacotherapy approaches are still needed for SUDs and complex TSD/DES.

Pharmacotherapy for Dissociative Disorders

Dissociation often is incorrectly described as a unitary clinical phenomenon that is a defense against intolerable emotions, or as a delimited set of discrete symptoms (i.e., depersonalization, derealization, affective or physiological anesthesia, psychogenic amnesia, fugue states, or blackouts). Persons with histories of developmentally adverse interpersonal trauma often present with a much more complex set of psychobiological impairments related to not only a reduction in their conscious awareness but also a biologically based division in their personality (Steele and van der Hart, Chapter 7, this volume). *Structural dissociation* of the personality into distinct parts—*not* "alters" or "alternative personalities," as sometimes believed—involves fundamental shifts in self-awareness, mood, memory, attitudes, and behavior that are at least partially outside the individual's conscious control (Chapter 7). PTSD symptoms of intrusive reexperiencing, emotional numbing, avoidance, and states of confusion, anger, and sleeplessness, may involve substantial dissociation (Chapter 7). Complex PTSD/DES specifically includes dissociation as a cardinal feature, but most definitions of this feature do not include the fundamental structural divisions of self that are observed clinically in these patients (Chapter 7). Therefore, pharmacotherapy strategies have not yet been developed to address the full extent of dissociation in general, and as part of complex PTSD/DES.

The International Society for Study of Dissociation (ISSD; 2005) developed a consensus set of treatment guidelines that describe pharmacotherapy as a frequently used but primarily adjunctive intervention for the treatment of the most severe dissociative disorder, dissociative identity disorder (DID). Noting that clinical trials of pharmacotherapy with patients with DID have not been reported, and that open-trial studies primarily demonstrate potential benefit of medication for alleviating symptoms of comorbid PTSD or depression, the *Guidelines* (pp. 112–113) suggest caution by clinicians:

> Medications in DID are usually best conceptualized as "shock absorbers," rather than as curative interventions. Partial responses are the rule with DID patients as well as in similar complex PTSD patients with multiple co-morbidities and dysphoria and despair based on multiple adverse life experiences. The goal is to find the best medication or medications at a given time that most effectively moderate the patient's symptoms. Not uncommonly, the DID patient will report that medications work for a while, and then stop doing so. Sometimes, these medications will work again if the patient is given them at a later time. Because of the potential for partial responses to many different medications, prescribers should be alert to the potentially negative effects of polypharmacy.

Patients with dissociative disorders, including DID, have been found to benefit from SSRIs for dysphoria, irritability, panic, and intrusive reexperiencing (and also obsessive rumination with fluvoxamine); antipsychotics for thought disorganization, agitation, intrusive reexperiencing, and irritability (but not for hallucinations, with rare exceptions); anticonvulsant agents for extreme emotion states and lability; and naltrexone for self-harm tendencies (especially if these result in a euphoric state of feeling "high"). The use of anxiolytic benzodiazepines, as with PTSD or SUDs, is considered to be appropriate for patients with dissociative disorder only for limited periods with very close supervision. When dissociative pathology presents in the form of physical symptoms that cannot be explained adequately or treated medically (i.e., somatoform dissociation), the obsessional subtype of these symptoms (i.e., hypochondriasis; body dysmorphic disorder) has shown evidence of a positive response to SSRI antidepressants; however, primarily somatic forms of somatoform disorders (e.g., psychogenic pain, conversion symptoms) have not been shown consistently to respond to pharmacotherapy (Fallon, 2004). Thus, when addressing the somatic distress often reported by patients with complex PTSD/DES, psychotherapeutic intervention may be the best approach.

Pharmacotherapy for Psychosis

Psychotic disorders such as schizophrenia have been found to respond well to pharmacotherapy, although on a highly individualized basis that is dependent on the specific medication(s) and the individual patient's psychobiological characteristics. Both neuroleptic medications and the newer second-generation antipsychotics have shown evidence of efficacy in achieving reductions or remission of psychotic symptoms. A growing body of research indicates that PTSD is often present, though underrecognized, in persons with psychotic disorders (Muenzenmaier et al., 2005). The symptoms of schizophrenia may mask those of PTSD (Butler, Mueser, Sprock, & Braff, 1996). Delusions and hallucinations may in part be the intrusive thoughts, images, and "flashbacks" that so often occur with PTSD. The negative symptoms of psychosis, such as blunted affect and social avoidance, may exacerbate or be confused with the PTSD symptoms of affective constriction and feelings of estrangement from others. Catatonic states might be confused with pathological structural dissociation (Steele & van der Hart, Chapter 7, this volume).

It is important to be sensitive to the existence of PTSD in persons with psychotic disorders, because researchers have found that the experience of being psychotic—including consequences such as hospitalization and police involvement—may be precipitants for PTSD-like or dissociative symptoms (Centofanti, Smith, & Altieri, 2005). Furthermore, other researchers have found that a significant number of psychotic disorders may actually arise as a result of a traumatic experience (Morrison, Frame, & Larkin, 2003), suggesting a complicated relationship between psychological trauma and psychosis. Childhood exposure to severe trauma has been found to be associated with increased impairment in schizophrenia (Lysaker, Meyer, Evans, Clements, & Marks, 2001). Therefore, pharmacotherapy for patients who present with symptoms consistent with complex PTSD/DES and severe mental illnesses, such as schizophrenia or bipolar disorder, should target specific complex PTSD/DES symptoms, as well as aim to reduce psychotic symptoms and generalized mood instability, and agitation/confusion. If either set of problems is overlooked or considered as only secondary, the reciprocal exacerbation of these disorders may remain a serious impediment to achieving and sustaining remission.

PHARMACOTHERAPY AGENTS AND STRATEGIES FOR PTSD: APPLICATION TO COMPLEX PTSD/DES

Given the limited scientific and clinical evidence for a rational pharmacotherapy for BPD, substance abuse, dissociative disorders, and psychotic disorders among patients who fit the clinical profile for complex PTSD/DES, a variety of pharmacological agents warrant consideration for treatment. Many of these medications have shown promise with PTSD as well; therefore, they may be useful in reducing the PTSD component, even if they have limited or unknown effectiveness with the complex PTSD/DES symptoms.

Anxiolytic Agents

Although it is generally acknowledged that benzodiazepines are contraindicated for both PTSD and complex PTSD/DES due to the potential for dependence (Gelpin, Bonne, Peri, Brandes, & Shalev, 1996), this is not true for buspirone. Whereas benzodiazepines are indirect GABA agonists, buspirone is an anxiolytic agent that works primarily as a serotonin presynaptic receptor partial agonist; therefore, it does not have the tolerance/dependence risks associated with the benzodiazepines. Duffy and Malloy (1994) found buspirone to be associated with significant improvement in reexperiencing, avoidance, and intrusion scores in their study of Vietnam War veterans. As of yet, buspirone has not been tested in clinical trials with either women or civilians with complex PTSD/DES.

Several antihypertensive medications tend to reduce adrenergic reactivity; therefore, they may be useful in treating hyperarousal in PTSD and stress reactivity in complex PTSD/DES. The alpha$_1$ receptor agonist prazosin, the alpha$_2$ receptor antagonist clonidine, and the beta receptor antagonist propranolol have shown efficacy in reducing hyperarousal and intrusive reexperiencing in individuals with PTSD, including chronic cases (Friedman & Davidson, 2007). In addition, prazosin specifically has shown great benefit in reducing the severity of PTSD nightmares, insomnia, and daytime reactivity to trauma cues in both military and civilian patient samples (Raskind et al., 2007; Taylor et al., 2006). In light of evidence that sleep problems, reexperiencing symptoms, and trauma cue-related reactivity are particularly severe among adults with complex PTSD/DES (van der Kolk et al., 2005), prazosin warrants consideration as an intervention for patients with complex PTSD/DES who report problems with hyperarousal/reactivity in sleep and during the daytime.

The potential value of adrenergic medications in reducing trauma cue-related reactivity is suggested by the results of a study by Pitman, Sanders, and Zusman (2002), who found that patients receiving the adrenergic beta blocker propranolol during and soon after emergency medical treatment for psychologically traumatic injuries exhibited less psychophysiological reactivity in response to listening to personalized trauma descriptions 3 months later than those who did not receive propranolol. This particular medication is not necessarily likely to be beneficial with complex PTSD/DES, because it was not associated with reduced risk of PTSD, and the study involved patients who had experienced a single adult psychological trauma (as opposed to the history of extensive childhood psychological trauma reported by most patients with complex PTSD/DES). However, the findings are a reminder to clinicians that addressing the trauma-related hyperarousal associated with PTSD, and the trauma-related reactivity (e.g., flashbacks, severe sleep disturbance) associated with complex PTSD/DES, is important in planful pharmacotherapy.

Anticonvulsants/Mood Stabilizers

Several mood stabilizers have been found to be effective in treating military veterans with chronic PTSD, many of whom may experience complex PTSD/ DES. Valproate has shown evidence of efficacy in several open-label trials and case reports with PTSD (Friedman & Davidson, 2007), including with military veteran patients with chronic PTSD (Fesler, 1991). Valproate's active ingredient, valproic acid, is U.S. Food and Drug Administration (FDA)–approved for the treatment of seizures, bipolar disorder, and migraines, and operates by increasing GABA activity.

Akuchekian and Amanat (2004) randomly assigned male combat veterans with chronic PTSD, who were nonresponsive to other agents, to receive either another antiseizure medication (topiramate) or placebo. After 12 weeks, the reductions in total Clinician-Administered PTSD Scale (CAPS; Blake et al., 1995) scores were 37.4% for topiramate versus 4.7% for placebo. Analysis of symptom clusters revealed significant improvement in the topiramate group for reexperiencing and arousal, but not avoidance. Given the large effect size (1.63), the chronicity of illness (mean duration = 17.9 years), and the failure of previous medication trials, these compelling results suggest that topiramate may be beneficial with trauma-related hyperarousal associated with chronic PTSD. Topiramate, FDA-approved in the treatment of seizures and migraines, is also used off-label as a mood stabilizer in the treatment of bipolar disorder. Although its exact mechanism of action is poorly understood, some of topiramate's efficacy is likely due to enhancing chloride passage through GABA-activated channels.

Dopaminergic Second-Generation Antipsychotic Agents

Bartozokis, Lu, Turner, Mintz, and Saunders (2005) compared efficacy of risperidone (a second-generation antipsychotic) versus placebo in combat veterans with chronic PTSD. Adjunctive risperidone was superior to placebo in all outcome measures, and the researchers concluded that risperidone improved the psychiatric symptoms of combat-related PTSD even in the absence of psychosis. Reich, Winternitz, Hennen, Watts, and Stanculescu (2004) found that low-dose risperidone was more effective than placebo in women with PTSD related to childhood abuse. Thus, risperidone has shown promise in treating chronic PTSD (which may, although not assessed, have been comorbid with complex PTSD/DES in some cases) in women as well as men.

Summary

Combat-related PTSD in men and early, chronic, extreme abuse in women appear to respond to treatment with buspirone; some mood stabilizers, including valproate and topiramate; some second-generation antipsychotics; and the adrenergic agent prazosin. It is likely that some women in these studies had complex PTSD/DES in addition to PTSD. Although this cannot be determined definitively with the male combat veteran samples, a history of complex trauma and complex PTSD/DES may characterize as many as 33–50% of male combat veterans in treatment for chronic PTSD (Ford & Kidd, 1998). The positive response to these medications suggests that they be therapeutic with complex PTSD/DES. Future studies must assess symptoms of both PTSD and complex PTSD/DES to prove or disprove this clinical hypothesis.

PHARMACOTHERAPY OF COMORBID PTSD: APPLICATION TO COMPLEX PTSD/DES

Mueser and colleagues (1998) assessed the prevalence of PTSD in 275 persons with severe mental illness. Although only 2% of patients had a chart diagnosis of PTSD, Mueser and colleagues found that 43% of them had PTSD. Persons with a primary diagnosis of depression had the highest rate (58%), followed by BPD (54%), bipolar disorder (40%), all other personality disorders (40%), schizoaffective disorder (37%), and schizophrenia (28%). Our approach to treatment of complex PTSD/DES co-occurring with other disorders such as bipolar disorder or schizophrenia is straightforward in principle (although never simple in practice): Where possible, we use one agent to treat both disorders. Sometimes multiple agents are required, but, if possible, an attempt should be made to use one medication that targets both comorbid conditions to avoid drug–drug interactions, side effects, overmedication, and complex medication regimens, all of which contribute to both poor outcome and nonadherence to the medication regimen.

Given that the SSRIs are approved for the treatment of depression, they are the first-line therapy for persons with comorbid depression and PTSD. However, in one study, the SSRI fluoxetine proved less effective than a psychosocial therapy, eye movement desensitization and reprocessing (EMDR), particularly with patients who had histories of psychological trauma in childhood (van der Kolk et al., 2007). Although complex PTSD/DES was not assessed in that study, the patients with childhood-onset trauma would have been at high risk for complex PTSD/DES, and they generally did not respond to the SSRIs. Therefore, whereas SSRIs are indicated for PTSD and depression symptoms

(Friedman & Davidson, 2007), their utility with complex PTSD/DES has not been established. Other antidepressants that operate on the serotonergic and/ or adrenergic systems have shown similar promise in ameliorating PTSD and depression (Friedman & Davidson, 2007) but require testing with complex PTSD/DES.

Similarly, based on evidence that the anticonvulsants carbamazepine and valproate are effective in treating bipolar disorder and may reduce PTSD symptom severity, these medications should be considered when bipolar disorder co-occurs with PTSD (Friedman & Davidson, 2007). Two other anticonvulsants, topiramate and lamotrigine, are also efficacious in many cases of bipolar disorder and have shown preliminary evidence of benefit with PTSD (topiramate specifically with intrusive reexperiencing symptoms; Friedman & Davidson, 2007). Patients diagnosed with bipolar disorder who have histories of psychological trauma, particularly childhood-onset trauma, tend to have more severe psychiatric symptoms and impairment (Leverich et al., 2002), and may have complex PTSD/DES. It is worth noting that many patients with symptoms of chronic PTSD, complex PTSD/DES, and severe dissociative disorders (including DID) are misdiagnosed with bipolar disorder before their trauma symptoms are accurately identified (Steele & van der Hart, Chapter 7, this volume). Therefore, the psychopharmacological evaluation needs to take these matters carefully into account. That said, the utility of anticonvulsant medications with the subset of patients with comorbid PTSD–bipolar disorder warrants consideration and testing.

In light of similar findings concerning the exacerbation of psychiatric symptoms by childhood-onset psychological trauma among patients with schizophrenia spectrum disorders, second-generation antipsychotics operating on the dopamine system deserve consideration for schizoaffective disorder or schizophrenia comorbid with PTSD. Quetiapine, risperidone, and possibly olanzapine (but see Butterfield et al., 2001, for negative findings with olanzapine for PTSD) should be considered as adjunctive treatments for patients with comorbid PTSD and psychotic disorders. Both quetiapine and risperidone have shown evidence of reducing symptoms of complex PTSD/DES (e.g., dissociation, aggression) (Friedman & Davidson, 2007).

CLINICAL ISSUES IN CONDUCTING PHARMACOTHERAPY WITH COMPLEX PTSD/DES

As summarized earlier, a number of pharmacological agents are available for treating the symptoms of both PTSD (alone or comorbid with other disorders) and complex PTSD/DES. However, the clinician should not rely on medication alone, because psychotherapy has been found to be the best augmentation agent for the medication. The role of medication is primarily to decrease the intensity of symptoms so that psychotherapy may proceed. Thus, pharmacotherapy primarily enables the patient to achieve greater emotional, relational, and physiological safety, stability, and well-being in augmenting psychosocial interventions targeting symptoms of complex PTSD/DES, and in applying therapeutic gains to everyday functioning (Ford, Courtois, van der Hart, Nijenhuis, & Steele, 2005; Herman, 1992).

Patients with complex PTSD/DES impairments have been found to have more difficulty in sustaining engagement and in achieving positive outcomes in psychotherapy (Ford & Kidd, 1998) and substance abuse treatment (Ford, Hawke, et al., 2007; Ford, Russo, & Mallon, 2007). However, these findings (and the clinical lore associated with such putatively "poor prognosis" disorders, such as BPD, DID, or SUD) are entirely preliminary and should serve as a reminder to the clinician that careful development of efficient and focused treatment strategies are essential for complex PTSD/DES. Anecdotally, patients presenting with complex PTSD/DES are often observed to have difficulty adhering to or responding positively to medication regimens, but this remains to be empirically demonstrated (as well as whether subsets of patients with complex PTSD/DES have differential responses to different pharmacotherapies). The extensive clinical literatures on the treatment of BPD (American Psychiatric Association, 2001) and dissociative disorders (Steele & van der Hart, Chapter 7, this volume) suggest that patients with problems similar to those seen in complex PTSD/DES may be difficult to engage or successfully treat with medication due to problems with suicidality, impulsivity, affect dysregulation, and self- and relational boundary instabilities. Rather than treating complex PTSD/DES per se, it is advisable to identify specific target symptoms or functional impairments that are both subjectively and objectively of greatest concern for each patient, and to select medications specifically to address these targets. Ideally, the clinician should carefully and regularly monitor the response of each target symptom to treatment, with attention to related indices of safety and functioning, to identify quickly instances of adverse responses to medication.

Given that past histories of abuse often lead to patients' difficulties in trusting others, including the clinicians treating them, and because side effects are by nature dysphoric, careful monitoring is particularly important with patients who may have difficulty recognizing or expressing specific iatrogenic reactions (as opposed to diffuse distress or a numbed/dissociated response). When a patient with complex PTSD/DES does not show a positive response to a targeted medication within the expected time frame of the medication's action, it is important first to determine whether adherence is a problem—and if so, to determine why the patient prefers not to take the medication, then discontinue it, or to develop a collaborative plan with the patient and caregivers or significant others that enables the patient to remember and follow through with the regimen. Some patients with complex traumatic stress disorders do not want to take medication, but they agree to do so due to a history of avoidant coping with what they perceive as the unassailable power of authority figures, such as psychiatrists, by maintaining a superficial facade of submissive compliance. Other patients with complex traumatic stress disorders are reluctant to take medications, because doing so is an uncomfortable reminder of childhood experiences during which they were coerced or seduced into using alcohol or drugs, sometimes as part of their abuse experience. Other patients have had medications prescribed based on questionable diagnoses of serious mental illnesses, and found that medications increased rather than decreased their sense of distress, confusion, and powerlessness. Additionally, some patients who have had serious problems with substance abuse or dependence may equate medication with a compromise to their sobriety. In all such cases, it is essential for the clinician to understand empathically and validate the patient's core concern(s), and to develop a plan and an explanation for pharmacotherapy that is consistent with the patient's adaptive goals, and that does not inadvertently replicate coercive, insensitive, inconsistent, critical, or frankly traumatic past experiences.

Still other patients with complex traumatic stress disorders who experienced fragmented, neglectful, or abusive early caregiving, and developed dismissive or disorganized attachment styles, may express their fear or unwillingness regarding medication in indirect or dysregulated ways, such as taking medication irregularly (often compounded by dissociative difficulties in recalling or following through with the scheduled regimen), or taking excessive amounts when symptoms are experienced as otherwise unmanageable. With the latter subgroup of patients with complex PTSD/DES, the risk of dependence and addiction, as well as of overdose, must be carefully monitored. A coordinated approach to psychotherapy and pharmacotherapy is essential to avoid the psychic splitting that can lead to countertherapeutic alliances with one provider (i.e., the "good doctor" who provides the magic cure of medications or alternatively protects the patient from the horrible violation caused by drugs) against the other(s). In a collaborative model, both psychotherapy and pharmacotherapy should emphasize how treatment can provide the patient with the psychological and biological tools to develop autonomy and self-efficacy safely within a therapeutic relationship in which the therapist does not penalize the patient by withdrawing if he or she successfully follows the regimen and becomes more functional.

Patients may also need guidance in recognizing and explicitly identifying specific adverse effects of medications. As a result of both psychoform and somatoform dissociation (Steele & van der Hart, Chapter 7, this volume), and associated emotional dysregulation, many patients with complex PTSD/DES are either unaware of their bodies' responses to medications or are terrified and preoccupied with finding even the smallest sign of a potential adverse reaction. These patients can benefit greatly from accurate information about the potential bodily reactions they may experience, conveyed in nontechnical terms that enable them to understand why uncomfortable or distressing bodily reactions may occur, without precipitating a crisis. Many patients with complex traumatic stress disorders believe (based on their own fears or misinformation that is widely available through the media and the grapevine) that medications will render them powerless, poison their bodies, or otherwise cause them further harm. Therefore, pharmacotherapy must be provided in a context of clear and full disclosure of potential adverse reactions, with reassurance that not only is no reaction too small to be discussed but also most reactions should be monitored by the patient for a sufficient period of time to determine whether symptoms are manageable or simply transient. The approach developed by Smith, Monson, and Ray (1986) for somatization disorder may be helpful when patients with complex traumatic stress disorder make frequent inquiries about medication effects as a justification for contact between scheduled visits: Setting up a planned schedule of brief telephone consultations with a trusted member of the doctor's clinical staff led to reduced contacts and fewer "side effects."

Active substance abuse disorders or drug/medication dependency poses a particular threat to adherence and to a therapeutic response to any pharmacotherapy. As discussed earlier, given the likely prevalence of these problems in complex PTSD/DES, it is essential to assess substance abuse/dependence prior to planning or implementing pharmacotherapy. Target symptoms associated with substance use or craving should be addressed immediately with pharmacotherapy and psychotherapy, and medication for other symptoms or impairments should be added only if these have not already been addressed, and after a period of stable nonuse of substances has been achieved.

If adherence is not in question, alternative medications with similar clinical indications but different biological mechanisms can be considered. For example, it may be advisable to switch from an adrenergic medication to a serotonergic or a serotonin–norepinephrine agent to address problematic irritability and mood instability secondary to hyperarousal and anxiety. Augmentation with a second targeted medication for specific purposes (e.g., adding a mood stabilizer or second-generation antipsychotic to address agitation, in addition to an SSRI for dysphoria) is another possible strategy—with caution to avoid the risks of polypharmacy.

As discussed earlier, complex PTSD/DES has been found to develop from the experience of fundamental threats to not only survival but also safety and security in primary relationships, and ultimately can best be overcome if new relationships built on trust and continuity are established. Furthermore, persons develop complex PTSD/DES due to both exposure to traumatic stressors and an inability to intervene proactively to protect themselves or others, or as a result of not having significant others respond to them. Therefore, recovery from complex PTSD/DES best occurs in the context of responsive relationships and, optimally, with the active involvement of the patient. A prescriber (whether also in the role of the primary therapist or not), even if his or her medication is "correct," can best help a person recover if a mutually trusting and respectful relationship is established, and if decision making involves all treaters and the patient. Patients who are coerced into taking medication, or who do so without having made an informed decision about the goals, rationale, and possible limitations and adverse effects of even the "correct" medication, may, by virtue of being rendered passive and uninformed, inadvertently reenact the powerless condition associated with traumatization.

Thus, we recommend that pharmacotherapy for complex PTSD/DES always take place in concert with the relational context of psychotherapy. Some patients with complex PTSD/DES may prefer not to receive medication, based on personal preferences or history (including adverse experiences in prior psychiatric treatment) or cultural values and norms (Australian Centre for Posttraumatic Mental Health, 2007). Education about empirically and clinically demonstrated potential benefits and risks of specific pharmacotherapy agents for the individual's specific symptoms of concern should enable the patient to make an informed and entirely voluntary decision. The potential benefits of alternative psychosocial therapies, and of augmenting those therapies' outcomes with specific pharmacological agents (i.e., the possible rapid enhancement of well-being and of the ability to engage productively in psychotherapy that may occur as a result of medications that reduce the intensity of distressing symptoms) also should be presented, with an opportunity for discussion. Although psychiatric practice tends generally to focus on the selection of the most appropriate medication, the therapeutic alliance is of such importance (and so often initially tenuous) with these patients (Kinsler, Courtois, & Frankel, Chapter 9, this volume; Ford et al., 2005; Pearlman & Courtois, 2005) that a counterbalance is needed in the form of considering nonbiological interventions with at least equal (if not greater) emphasis in the initial phase of assessment and treatment planning. For example, it may be helpful to state at the outset that medications are only one element of treatment, and are not a requirement unless the patient judges the benefits to be sufficient and the risks to be manageable.

Although this may obviously seem to be good practice in general, such an approach with patients who have complex PTSD/DES may convey a provider's essential willingness to be transparent and collaborative—in contrast to many patients' prior experiences of psychological trauma (and, subsequently, of invalidating treatment or confinement). The importance and actual application of a person-centered approach to pharmacotherapy for complex PTSD/ DES is illustrated by the following composite case, presented as a first-person account by Lewis A. Opler.

CASE DESCRIPTION

Into my office came 31-year-old Sara, who reluctantly agreed to meet with me at the urging of her therapist. Although neatly dressed and well-spoken, she appeared uneasy, speaking in a quiet voice and avoiding eye contact. As I took her developmental and psychosocial history, I quickly became aware of why she would be distrustful of men in general, and of a male psychiatrist in particular. As a young girl, she had been sexually molested by an uncle over the course of a year. When she finally worked up the courage to tell her parents of the abuse, they did not believe her and instead sided with her uncle. Sara had been moody and sullen for many months prior to this disclosure, her grades had declined, and her parents felt this accusation was just another part of some prepubescent troublemaking, a phase that was now getting out of hand. Frustrated by her behavior, they sent her to a psychiatrist. After speaking with her parents and completing the initial evaluation, even the psychiatrist concluded she was lying and that Sara's story of abuse was a manipulation, the result of confusion about her emerging sexuality combined with preteen dramatics intended to gain the attention of busy parents and draw attention away from her recent failing grades at school. Clearly, there was more to this case than a simple differential diagnosis: This woman had been sexually abused by a close relative and subsequently invalidated by both her parents and psychiatrist. I acknowledged this to her and said further that it was to her credit that she was still willing to consult with someone from my profession given such an adverse experience with psychiatric "treatment" in the past.

"You seem like you're at least actually listening to me," she said. "So I may come back, but I still don't know if I want to, and I certainly do not want to take any of those mind-control drugs: I'm only here because I promised my therapist I'd see you one time." I thanked Sara for her candor and told her that just because people called me a "clinical psychopharmacologist" did not mean that I would automatically recommend that she be placed on medication. Precisely because I did not invalidate or attempt to push a particular treatment without listening to her, Sara asked whether she could make another appointment, because she did have some bothersome symptoms about which she would like my opinion. However, she reiterated, she would never agree to ingesting chemicals manufactured by unscrupulous pharmaceutical companies. I acknowledged her concerns regarding the fiscal motivation of the industry and agreed to see her again at a time of her convenience. She said she would call. Sara did call a month later, sounding tearful and frantic, and asked if she could see me right away. After assessing that she had no intent to harm herself, I assured Sara that I was available and we made an appointment for the next evening. When she arrived, she looked quite depressed, describing symptoms of low energy, difficulty concentrating, and passive suicidality without intent or a plan. Upon my further questions regarding Sara's thoughts of harming herself, she reported that since her teens, she periodically had had the urge to cut herself superficially, usually when she was "just feeling really spaced out."

Sara told me that over the course of her lifetime, she had many episodes of what appeared to be severe depression. She was feeling panicked now, because "I can feel it coming on, and when it hits me it's so black that I don't know if I can live through it one more time. It's like dying, only it just goes on and on, and I wish I could die but I can't. I know this sounds crazy and I'm probably so screwed up that there's nothing anyone can do to help me, even someone as smart and kind as you. I don't deserve your help." I let Sara know that when a person experienced the molestation and later the invalidation and stigmatization of symptoms, as had happened to her, periods of very deep depression and feeling as if something was horribly wrong were some of the "unfinished emotional business" that actually could be helped by therapy. Medication could play a role by giving her enough of a medically mediated "platform" to regain her emotional equilibrium, along with a sense of hope and increased self-esteem. These, in turn, would help her in her psychotherapy.

Sara asked, "So does this mean that it's all in my head, and I'm just making up these feelings and thoughts because I'm really crazy, like my parents and that psychiatrist said?" I replied that this actually was not just a "mental" problem, and certainly not one that she was making up, but a very real change in her body, including her brain, that had occurred during the extreme stress of being abused, then being disbelieved and blamed.

> "Those experiences place a great strain on anyone's body and mind, because they are so stressful—not just the minor stressors that happen all the time, but a real challenge to your ability to survive emotionally, which you *very successfully accomplished* despite not getting the support and help you needed at the time. What this tells us is not that you're screwed up or crazy, but that you actually are very strong and very sane, so much that you were able to go on with your life. The fact that those experiences left emotional scars is due to the harm you experienced, not to any failure on your part. Our job now is to help you to heal those emotional scars by helping your body and mind get back to normal—and that is possible even many years after trauma."

She replied, "I don't know what it would be like for my body to be 'normal.' It's always so screwed up." I replied, "So we need to see if there is a medication that can help you to rediscover what your body feels like and, therefore, what your emotions also feel like, and whether you're really back to a state that is normal and healthy for you. That's what medication can do—help your body get back into balance after the imbalance that is caused by trauma and by related problems such as depression. Does that make sense?" Sara reluctantly said that this actually made a lot of sense, but she was afraid to get her hopes up.

I replied:

> "That is a good, cautious approach to take. If you are open to the possibility that the right medication might help your body get back into balance, and that being out of balance is an understandable problem for anyone who has experienced severe trauma, because your body and mind had to make major adjustments to get through trauma, then that can be our goal. I do want to ask about some other ways your body can get out of balance, as a result of both trauma and ongoing emotional strain. It is not unusual for a very resilient person to have periods of feeling not just normal energy and mood but also an excess and a kind of high, without drugs. That can be your body's way of naturally breaking out of depression, but sometimes you might get more energized than is really needed. Does that ever happen to you?"

Sara said that was exactly the case, describing brief periods of remarkable productivity, during which she was especially creative, when her mind moved quickly, she had lots of energy, and needed little sleep. At these times she was "the life of the party," as well as a charismatic leader. I told her these energetic periods sounded like hypomania, not mania, and after I described the difference between the two, she agreed. "I need to do something about these damn depressions, and I don't want to rebound so much that I'm over the top; I'm even willing to take Prozac and become a zombie, I just don't want to feel like this any longer." This statement disclosed some of the reasons for Sara's reluctance to take medication and allowed me to educate her about the likely side effects of medications, and how our goal was to make her functional and not a zombie. Additionally, to Sara's surprise, I said I did not think Prozac was a good idea, since it sounded like she had bipolar II disorder, and antidepressants alone might not help and might actually cause her moods to cycle. I went on to tell her that starting with a mood stabilizer made sense, and that lamotrigine (Lamictal) might make the most sense, being the only mood stabilizer approved for the treatment of depression in bipolar disorder. Also, I told her that some of the symptoms that were troubling her, such as feeling not just sad and "blue" but as though things were so black that she found herself spacing out or wanting to cut herself, might be related to the adaptations her body had had to make to get through the abuse.

> "These adaptations are what we call complex posttraumatic stress disorder. PTSD is a problem that occurs when a person experiences a terrifying or horrifying event, because the body mobilizes to survey the threats involved, and then it is difficult for the body to "gear down" afterwards. So PTSD often involves feeling tense or easily startled, on edge, and having difficulties with feeling relaxed enough to think clearly or to sleep. Complex traumatic stress symptoms are changes that occur when you experience trauma that also involves repeated abuse, invalidation, and lack of protection. It can include the PTSD symptoms, but it may also lead to the kind of spacing out or feeling so down and blue that you just want to hurt yourself physically to make the emotional pain more tolerable, even if that's only temporary. This may seem like an impossible problem to get over, and it certainly is a challenge, but we're finding that very specific medications can be a great help in many cases. Since there is clinical evidence that lamotrigine can help the body to regain its balance when these complex PTSD changes occur, it may address several of the goals that you've said are crucial for you."

Her response: "OK, doc, you win. Give me a prescription."

I agreed, but I wanted her to know about a rare but potentially fatal side effect called Stevens–Johnson syndrome, an adverse drug reaction involving a skin rash and fever, before sending her off with a prescription. If she still wanted to proceed with lamotrigine, I explained that starting at a low dose and increasing it slowly (by no more than 25 mg per week) were essential to minimize the risk of developing this dangerous syndrome. I gave Sara a prescription and a schedule for building the dose up to 100 mg/day over several weeks, and told her that if she developed a rash, then she needed to stop the medication and call me immediately.

A month later Sara came in; her mood was fine, but she said this was often the case with her mood swings. I agreed and said that only over time, if the lamotrigine prevented recurrence of depression, would we know that it was helpful; I also said that we might need to increase the dose, but that some people responded at 100 mg. We met 3 months later. "It's working: I've had no mood swings; I now realize that most of my life I've been cycling between depression and hypomania every few weeks." She further reported that periods of feeling "spacey," what her therapist called *depersonalization*, had lessened, as had urges to cut herself. "I have been able to actually listen to myself when I'm talking to my therapist about what's bothering me, including bad memories of the abuse and problems in life now, and I think this is really helping me to finally be truly involved in the therapy, whereas I've been holding back in the past."

I have over the ensuing years remained part of Sara's treatment team, functioning as the psychiatrist in charge of medication management. Diagnostically, I think Sara has comorbid bipolar II disorder and complex PTSD/DES. Lamotrigine is helpful for mood stabilization; hence, it is not surprising that Sara reported an increased sense of emotional presence, balance, and self-efficacy that contributes to engagement in psychotherapy and, most importantly, in life.

CONCLUSION

SSRIs are the standard of care for PTSD, but not necessarily for complex PTSD/DES. Evidence suggests that buspirone; some mood stabilizers, including valproate, topiramate, and lamotrigine; and some second-generation antipsychotics, including quetiapine, olanzapine, and risperidone, are primary agents to consider for complex PTSD/DES. For patients with comorbid PTSD, utilizing one agent that targets both disorders (e.g., SSRIs for depression and PTSD; valproate, topiramate, or lamotrigine for bipolar disorder and PTSD or complex PTSD/DES; quetiapine, olanzapine, or risperidone for schizophrenia and PTSD or complex PTSD/DES) should be tried before polypharmacy.

Although this chapter has focused on the pharmacotherapy of PTSD and complex PTSD/DES, we are in complete agreement with Foa, Davidson, and Frances (1999) that treatment should combine psychotherapy *and* pharmacotherapy. The complex impairments involved in complex PTSD/DES go well beyond any set of specific target symptoms that may be appropriately addressed by pharmacotherapy. However, in psychotherapy, as well as pharmacotherapy, targeting specific symptoms or impairments is essential in treating complex

PTSD/DES to prevent reliance on an unnecessarily complex set of treatments in an attempt to treat the "whole" disorder.

Over the next decade, we anticipate that a more targeted approach to research on pharmacotherapy, psychotherapy, and their combined use will provide clinicians and patients with more effective treatments for acute stress disorder, "standard PTSD," and complex traumatic stress disorders. In the interim period, clinicians must rely on careful observation and up-to-date awareness of the evolving research on the efficacy and safety of pharmacological agents for the specific therapeutic targets that are of particular concern with complex PTSD/DES.

REFERENCES

Akuchekian, S., & Amanat, S. (2004). The comparison of topiramate and placebo in the treatment of posttraumatic stress disorder. *Journal of Research in Medical Sciences, 5*, 42–46.

American Psychiatric Association. (2000) *Diagnostic and statistical manual of mental disorders* (4th ed., text rev.). Washington, DC: Author.

American Psychiatric Association. (2001). *Treating borderline personality disorder.* Washington, DC: Author.

Assanangkornchai, S., & Srisurapanont, M. (2007). The treatment of alcohol dependence. *Current Opinion in Psychiatry, 20*, 222–227.

Australian Centre for Posttraumatic Mental Health. (2007). *Australian guidelines for the treatment of adults with acute stress disorder and posttraumatic stress disorder.* Melbourne, Australia: Author.

Bartzokis, G., Lu, P. H., Turner, J., Mintz, J., & Saunders, C. S. (2005). Adjunctive risperidone in the treatment of chronic combat-related posttraumatic stress disorder. *Biological Psychiatry, 57*(5), 474–479.

Blake, D. D., Weathers, F. W., Nagy, L. M., Kaloupek, D. G., Gusman, F. D., Charney, D. S., et al. (1995). The development of a Clinician-Administered PTSD Scale. *Journal of Traumatic Stress, 5*(1), 75–90.

Butler, R. W., Mueser, K. T., Sprock, J., & Braff, D. L. (1996). Positive symptoms of psychosis in posttraumatic stress disorder. *Biological Psychiatry, 39*, 839–844.

Butterfield, M., Becker, M., Connor, K., Sutherland, S., Churchill, L., & Davidson, J. R. T. (2001). Olanzapine in the treatment of post-traumatic stress disorder. *International Clinical Psychopharmacology, 16*, 197–203.

Centofanti, A. T., Smith, D. I., & Altieri, T. (2005). Posttraumatic stress disorder as a reaction to the experience of psychosis and its sequelae. *Clinical Psychologist, 9*(1), 15–23.

Duffy, J. D., & Malloy, P. F. (1994). Efficacy of buspirone in the treatment of posttraumatic stress disorder. *Annals of Clinical Psychiatry, 6*, 33–37.

Fallon, B. (2004). Pharmacotherapy of somatoform disorders. *Journal of Psychosomatic Research, 56*, 455–460.

Fesler, F. A. (1991). Valproate in combat-related posttraumatic stress disorder. *Journal of Clinical Psychiatry, 52*, 361–364.

Foa, E., Davidson, J., & Frances, A. (1999). The expert consensus guidelines series: Treatment of posttraumatic stress disorder. *Journal of Clinical Psychiatry, 60*(Suppl. 16), 1–76.

Ford, J., Courtois, C., van der Hart, O., Nijenhuis, E., & Steele, K. (2005). Treatment of complex post-traumatic self-dysregulation. *Journal of Traumatic Stress*, *18*, 437–447.

Ford, J., & Kidd, P. (1998). Early childhood trauma and disorders of extreme stress as predictors of treatment outcome with chronic PTSD. *Journal of Traumatic Stress*, *11*, 743–761.

Ford, J. D., Hawke, J., Alessi, S., Ledgerwood, D., & Petry, N. (2007). Psychological trauma and PTSD symptoms as predictors of substance dependence treatment outcomes. *Behaviour Research and Therapy*, *45*, 2417–2431.

Ford, J. D., Russo, E., & Mallon, S. (2007). Integrating post-traumatic stress disorder (PTSD) and substance use disorder treatment. *Journal of Counseling and Development*, *85*, 475–489.

Friedman, M. J., & Davidson, J. R. T. (2007). Pharmacotherapy of PTSD. In M. J. Friedman, T. M. Keane, & P. A. Resick (Eds.), *Handbook of PTSD* (pp. 376–405). New York: Guilford Press.

Garbutt, J., Kranzler, H., O'Malley, S., Gastfriend, D., Pettinati, H., Silverman, B., et al. (2005). Efficacy and tolerability of long-acting injectable naltrexone for alcohol dependence: A randomized controlled trial. *Journal of the American Medical Association*, *293*, 1617–1625.

Gelpin, E., Bonne, O., Peri, T., Brandes, D., & Shalev, A. (1996). Treatment of recent trauma survivors with benzodiazepines: A prospective study. *Journal of Clinical Psychiatry*, *57*, 390–394.

Gerson, A., & Stanley, B. (2002). Suicidal and self-injurious behavior in personality disorder. *Current Psychiatry Reports*, *4*(1), 30–38.

Herman, J. L. (1992). Complex PTSD. *Journal of Traumatic Stress*, *3*, 377–391.

International Society for the Study of Dissociation. (2005). Guidelines for treating dissociative identity disorder in adults. *Journal of Trauma and Dissociation*, *6*(4), 69–149.

Kuhler, T., & Stachetzki, R. (2005). Differential diagnostics of borderline disorder and complex traumatic stress disorder. *Psychotherapeutics*, *50*(1), 25–32.

Leverich, G., McElroy, S., Suppes, T., Keck, P., Denicoff, K., Nolen, W., et al. (2002). Early physical and sexual abuse associated with an adverse course of bipolar illness. *Biological Psychiatry*, *51*, 288–297.

Lysaker, P., Meyer, P., Evans, J., Clements, C., & Marks, K. (2001). Childhood sexual trauma and psychosocial functioning in adults with schizophrenia. *Psychiatric Services*, *52*, 1485–1488.

Moeller, F., Schmitz, J., Steinberg, J., Green, C., Reist, C., Lai, L., et al. (2007). Citalopram combined with behavioral therapy reduces cocaine use. *American Journal of Drug and Alcohol Abuse*, *33*, 367–378.

Morrison, A. P., Frame, L., & Larkin, W. (2003). Relationships between trauma and psychosis: A review and integration. *British Journal of Clinical Psychology*, *42*, 331–354.

Muenzenmaier, K., Castille, D. M., Shelley, A. M., Jamison, A., Battaglia, J., Opler, L. A., et al. (2005). Comorbid posttraumatic stress disorder and schizophrenia. *Psychiatric Annals*, *35*, 2–7.

Mueser, K., Goodman, C. B., Trumbetta, S. L., Rosenberg, S. D., Osher, C., Vidaver, R., et al. (1998). Trauma and posttraumatic stress disorder in severe mental illness. *Journal of Consulting and Clinical Psychology*, *66*, 493–499.

Nose, M., Cipriani, A., Biancosino, B., Grassi, L., & Barbui, C. (2006). Efficacy of pharmacotherapy against core traits of borderline personality disorder: Meta-analysis of randomized controlled trials. *International Clinical Psychopharmacology*, *21*, 345–353.

Oldham, J. M. (2006). Integrated treatment for borderline personality disorder. *Psychiatric Annals*, *36*, 361–369.

Ouimette, P. C., Moos, R. H., & Finney, J. W. (2003). PTSD treatment and 5-year remission among patients with substance use and PTSD. *Journal of Consulting and Clinical Psychology*, *71*, 410–414.

Pearlman, L., & Courtois, C. (005). Clinical applications of the attachment framework: Relational treatment of complex trauma. *Journal of Traumatic Stress*, *18*(5), 449–459.

Pettinati, H. M., Kranzler, H. R., & Madaras, J. (2003). The status of serotonin-selective pharmacotherapy in the treatment of alcohol dependence. *Recent Developments in Alcoholism*, *16*, 247–262.

Pitman, R. K., Sanders, K. M., & Zusman, R. M. (2002). Pilot study of secondary prevention of posttraumatic stress disorder with propranolol. *Biological Psychiatry*, *51*, 189–192.

Preti, A. (2007). New developments in the pharmacotherapy of cocaine abuse. *Addiction Biology*, *12*, 133–151.

Raskind, M., Peskind, E., Hoff, D., Hart, K., Holmes, H., Warren, D., et al. (2007). A parallel group placebo controlled study of prazosin for trauma nightmares and sleep disturbance in combat veterans with posttraumatic stress disorder. *Biological Psychiatry*, *61*, 928–934.

Reich, D. B., Winternitz, S., Hennen, J., Watts, T., & Stanculescu, C. (2004). A preliminary study of risperidone in the treatment of post-traumatic stress disorder related to childhood abuse in women. *Journal of Clinical Psychiatry*, *65*, 1601–1606.

Saladin, M., Brady, K., Dansky, B., & Kilpatrick, D. (1995). Understanding comorbidity between PTSD and substance use disorder. *Addictive Behaviors*, *20*, 643–655.

Smith, G. R., Monson, R., & Ray, D. (1986). Psychiatric consultation in somatization disorder. *New England Journal of Medicine*, *314*, 1407–1413.

Soloff, P. (2005). Pharmacotherapy in borderline personality disorder. In J. Gunderson & P. Hoffman (Eds.), *Understanding and treating borderline personality disorder* (pp. 65–82). Washington, DC: American Psychiatric Press.

Taylor, F., Lowe, K., Thompson, C., McFall, M., Peskind, E., Kanter, E., et al. (2006). Daytime prazosin reduces psychological distress to trauma specific cues in civilian trauma posttraumatic stress disorder. *Biological Psychiatry*, *59*, 577–581.

van der Kolk, B., Roth, S., Pelcovitz, D., Sunday, S., & Spinazzola, J. (2005). Disorders of extreme stress. *Journal of Traumatic Stress*, *18*, 389–399.

van der Kolk, B. A., Spinazzola, J., Blaustein, M., Hopper, J., Hopper, E., Korn, D., et al. (2007). A randomized clinical trial of eye movement desensitization and reprocessing (EMDR), fluoxetine, and placebo in the treatment of PTSD. *Journal of Clinical Psychiatry*, *68*, 37–46.

SYSTEMIC TREATMENT
APPROACHES
AND STRATEGIES

The chapters in Part III follow the same model established in Part II, but they address systemic models of psychotherapy. The first chapter (17) in this section provides a bridge from individual to systemic psychotherapy, describing a one-to-one psychotherapy model, internal family systems therapy, which addresses structural dissociation based on a systemic foundation identifying and treating multiple self-states as a quasi-family system. In Chapters 18–20, respectively, couple, family, and group treatment models and approaches are described in some detail. As in Part II, the approaches are applied to simulated, composite client interactions and transcripts.

CHAPTER 17

Internal Family Systems Therapy

Richard C. Schwartz
Mark F. Schwartz
Lori Galperin

An individual's sense of self both assimilates and adapts to significant elements of his or her developmental experience and attachment environment. When phase-appropriate challenges are blended with adequate stability and attunement from key caregiver(s), the child's sense of self can grow, spurred on by the ability to explore the environment and increasingly to function independently of the attachment figure but clearly able to return to the secure base in times of stress, loss, and overstimulation.

In contrast, when children are raised in an environment that lacks attachment security with the key caregiver(s), they are less able to explore and to develop their self-capacities. When exposed to experiences that exceed their personal capacities and resources, overload occurs, and self-development is replaced by anxieties about attachment and the development of survival strategies. Whether they occur in childhood or later, traumatic experiences, events and relationships, by definition, overwhelm the organism's ability to absorb and integrate them. They are "too much" at a variety of sensory levels. They inundate. Cognitively, they shatter existing frameworks and are difficult to reconcile. Experientially, they engender helplessness. Often, their implicitly contradictory aspects generate an irreconcilability that necessitates the maintenance of disparate, mutually exclusive "realities."

This need for the coexistence of contradictory realities, emotions, and beliefs has been cited as one cause of the splintering of the mind into subpersonalities, or alters, that characterize dissociative identity disorder (DID). On the one hand, the predominant assumption has been that complex trauma creates multiplicity. On the other hand, some trauma theorists, most notably Watkins and Watkins (1988), have posited that people are naturally multiple, and that trauma does not create what they call ego states but instead creates powerful separations and conflicts among the preexisting elements of multiplicity. The approach described in this chapter, the *internal family systems (IFS) model* (Schwartz, 1995), shares the natural multiplicity perspective of Watkins and Watkins, and finds that clients of all ilk can readily identify and begin to work with their subpersonalities, or what IFS calls their *parts*. Most traumatized clients are particularly adept at this process, because their parts stand out in bold relief. Although many therapists who work with complex traumatic stress disorders are aware that their clients often describe relatively autonomous parts of themselves, they do not explore that inner territory for fear of further fragmenting or dysregulating their clients.

That fear is realistic. Many chronic trauma survivors already seem quite unstable. Their attachment histories have prevented the healthy resolution of accumulated traumas, so they contain reservoirs of pain and shame that become the affect they desperately try to regulate or avoid. To do so, they develop coping mechanisms, such as isolation and extreme self-sufficiency, avoidance/dissociation, self-injury, eating disorders and substance abuse, in an attempt to keep the pain at bay. When, however, a traumatic stressor occurs that cannot be managed by such strategies, clients often find themselves in ongoing stress response syndromes of repeated cycles of numbing and intrusion, along with hyperarousal (the classic triad symptoms of posttraumatic stress disorder) (Horowitz, 1997) and, typically, depression and mounting hopelessness and despair. These cycles are often characterized by more extreme strategies, such as increased bingeing on food, sex, drugs, or alcohol; starving; self-harm or reenactments of the original trauma; or suicidal thoughts or actions.

Given this profile, it is understandable that many trauma therapists' efforts, especially in the initial stages of treatment, are designed to stabilize clients by teaching alternative coping skills, focusing on symptom reduction, and creating a safe, trusting relationship. When clients talk about their parts, it is often about the ones that are highly critical of them and persecutory, that take them out of control in the various ways mentioned earlier, or are hurt and desperate. The prospect of further unleashing additional instability by having the client focus on those *parts* seems counterproductive. In addition, the therapists who do overcome their fear and try to work with these inner communities of subpersonalities often find themselves in escalating power struggles with their clients' extreme parts or see their clients suffer frightening forms of inner backlash after emotion-laden sessions.

Despite these challenges, many trauma therapists continue struggling to find ways safely to enter clients' inner lives and bring healing and harmony. They seek a nonpathologizing map that empowers clients to help them navigate within these delicate inner ecologies. With that goal in mind, Richard Schwartz began applying the systems thinking that he learned as a family therapist to clients' inner families of subpersonalities in the early 1980s. He found that, particularly with complex traumatic stress disorders, getting clients to coerce or rationally convince their extreme *parts* to change only made those parts more resistant or extreme. Once he was able to shift away from a mind-set of control and instead became, and helped clients become, curious about their parts and why they did what they did, he learned that the parts acted almost like parental children in a family. Many of the most seemingly destructive parts were constrained in their extreme roles by (1) their perceived need to protect other parts, (2) their polarization with still other parts, and (3) the extreme beliefs and emotions accrued from their attachment and trauma histories (what in IFS language is labeled their *burdens*). In other words, just as in family therapy, many parts could not change in isolation, because they often felt like their extreme role was necessary to the client's survival. As in external families, before one member of the inner family can change, the therapist must work with the network of relationships in which that family member is embedded, and help the part release its burdens.

So it seemed that these *protector parts* needed to be relieved of the responsibility of containing and protecting the highly *vulnerable parts* that carried the pain of past traumas and betrayals. Those vulnerable parts seemed to be frozen in time during the hurtful episodes, causing clients to strive to forget about them and to keep them, along with their beliefs and the affect they contained, locked away. They carried the volatile affect that clients tried so desperately to avoid or regulate. Schwartz called these vulnerable and disowned parts the *exiles*, and tried to help clients access and help them, so that the protectors could be relieved of their duties. However, he found that in many cases, once clients focused on those exiles, they became overwhelmed by the affect and memories, and were pulled back in an abreaction, into those hurtful past episodes in what sometimes seemed like regressions. In addition, following those emotional sessions, clients would suffer vicious attacks from inner critics, would not return to therapy, or would have dangerous somatic, self-harm, or addictive reactions.

Having inadvertently harmed clients in that way, Schwartz became committed to learning from clients the rules of inner systems and to respecting those rules. In the process, he found that when approached respectfully, even seemingly destructive and intransigent parts were not what they seemed, and instead were valuable subpersonalities that had been forced into extreme, protective roles. Also, there were ways to help clients access these exiles, without becoming overwhelmed by them. When that was possible, clients asked those parts to tell their stories, and clients could compassionately witness what had happened to the parts in the past, when they accrued the burdens. When parts felt fully witnessed, they could release the burdens—extreme beliefs and emotions—that kept them locked into their roles, and would transform into their natural, valuable states.

Schwartz also found that as clients focused on and thereby separated from their parts, they would often spontaneously and suddenly enter a state that today might be called *mindfulness*. Clients would manifest curiosity about parts that seconds before had intimidated them, would see them with clarity rather than distortion, and would feel compassion for them, whereas earlier they had hated them. While in that state, clients would begin to relate to their parts very differently and seemed to know how to help them feel safe and understood. This empirical observation, that just beneath the surface of complex trauma clients' parts lay an unharmed *Self* containing the necessary resources for clients to transform their own inner systems, was astounding, because it ran so counter to much of Western developmental psychology and psychotherapy. This confidence that such a Self exists and can be accessed, often surprisingly quickly even in clients with complex traumatic stress disorder, is a hallmark of IFS therapy. In addition to becoming mindful, clients in the state of Self became active inner leaders that their parts came to trust, leading to internal integration and healing.

IFS MODEL

Parts

To further organize these tenets of IFS, the model posits that the mind's natural state is to have subpersonalities, each containing valuable qualities and talents. Traumas and attachment injuries transform these parts from their valuable and healthy states into protective or highly vulnerable states that can be destructive and interfere with the client's life in ways described earlier. This transformation causes clients (and many of their therapists) to confuse the parts with their extreme manifestations and, consequently, to battle, ignore, or try to eliminate them (i.e., they confuse the parts with the burdens the parts carry, not realizing that once parts release their burdens, they can return to their original functional states).

Exiles

Some of the clients' most devastated parts are exiles that experienced attachment injuries and traumas. These tend to be the client's most sensitive, spontaneous, innocent, playful, child-like parts that, after having been hurt, carry burdens of pain, betrayal, shame, shock, and disbelief. They often assume that they are worthless and to blame and at fault for how they were treated. More often than not, they are frozen in time during hurtful or traumatic episodes. Exiles often appear to clients as desperately needy or as disengaged, rejecting, inner children, in a manner that parallels the anxious or avoidant attachment styles of external children. After these parts are injured (or burdened), the trauma client "adds insult to their injury" by dissociating from them to maintain distance or control. They are locked away in what often appear in clients' imagery as inner caves or abysses, and most clients fear them to the point of never wanting to feel them again. Clients have good reason for this. Anytime one of these parts has been upset by a life event and, consequently, breaks out of exile, clients feel as if they are consumed by the flames of emotion, and they enter the part's dark world, becoming immobilized, depressed, desperately needy, and highly vulnerable. They feel as if the traumatic events are happening again in the present. These exiled parts contain the dreaded affect that trauma clients spend their lives trying to manage and regulate.

Two Kinds of Protectors

To keep exiles from emotionally "breaking out," trauma clients have other parts that try to protect them from life events that could trigger the exiles, and from the feared affect whenever it is aroused. For this reason, in IFS, these parts are called *protectors*. One set of protectors has responsibility for preempting anything that might upset exiles. These are called *managers*, because they strive to manage clients' performance, appearance, relationships, and every aspect of their lives to keep them safe. In trauma clients, they are often the hyperaroused, fearful parts that are always scanning for and anticipating danger. They are also the perfectionist inner self-critics who try desperately to get the client to look and behave in ways that seem normal, so they will not be hurt. Or they criticize to destroy confidence so that clients will not take any risks. Managers also keep clients chronically numb and dissociated to manage their inner environments, so that they do not feel the events of the outside world.

The other set of protectors is necessary because, despite the best efforts of the managers, exiles still get triggered. Whenever a client begins to feel an exile's flames of emotion, there is a frantic rush to get out of that state immediately. *Firefighter* parts jump into action to douse the emotional fire with either a mood-altering substance or other distracting activity designed to redirect the client until the fire burns itself out. Firefighters tend to be impulsive, reactive, and in trauma clients, can seem irrational and self-destructive. Firefighters are behind client behaviors, such as bingeing on alcohol, drugs, sex, or food. They drive activities such as self-cutting, suicide attempts, risk taking, explosions of rage, and sudden dissociation or withdrawal.

Again, managers and firefighters are both protective parts that share the goal of keeping exiles at bay. The primary difference between them is the point in the internal sequence in which they operate. Managers preempt the triggering of exiles. Firefighters act after an exile has become upset.

Self

Because many clients with complex traumatic stress disorders have such severe histories and symptom profiles, and because they often are thoroughly shut down or highly emotionally labile (or alternate between the two), it is easy to believe they have weak egos and need a great deal from the therapist. *The most important discovery of the IFS model is that within such clients exists an undamaged essence that, once accessed, can become an effective leader of their internal and external worlds.* This is called the *Self*, and most trauma clients are scarcely aware of its existence, because it is obscured by their other parts. When, as a child, the client's Self was not able to protect him or her from being traumatized or abused, the parts lose trust in its leadership and assume instead that they have to take over and protect the system. The restoration of parts' trust in Self-leadership is a major thrust of IFS. When enough parts of a client come to trust that it is safe to separate—to shift out of their position of dominance—the client will spontaneously and rapidly manifest the qualities of good leadership associated with the Self. These qualities include what are called the *eight C's of Self-leadership*: curiosity, compassion, calm, clarity, confidence, courage, creativity, and connectedness. Clients then begin to relate to their parts in ways that help the parts unburden their extreme emotions and beliefs, and lead to transformation.

SKEPTICISM, CLINICAL OBSERVATION, AND EMPIRICAL SUPPORT

Understandably, many trauma therapists have trouble accepting the existence of such a Self in their clients because of the assumption that to contain such qualities, clients had to have received at least good enough parenting during critical periods in childhood. From that perspective, it makes no sense that clients with horrific histories and pathological presentations would already have such a Self. As therapists, we have had to struggle for years with our own skepticism about this assertion before accepting it.

Unfortunately, at this time, no well-constructed outcome studies testing the IFS model and methods have been completed; however, several are currently in progress. One of them, led by Nancy Shadick of Harvard Medical School, is using IFS with 30 patients with rheumatoid arthritis and contrasting that to a control group. A second, led by Helen Reiss and Cathy Kerr, also at Harvard, will use brain scans to evaluate changes in 20 depressed patients compared to 20 controls. A third study, led by Shelley Haddock at Colorado State, is also studying the effects of IFS with a group of depressed students compared to a control group receiving treatment as usual (TAU) at the counseling center.

Until the results of these studies are in, skeptical clinicians are left to test these assertions within their own practices. Our hope is that they will find, as we did, that clients shift dramatically and suddenly in the direction of Self once key parts are willing to separate. The same testing process is possible for the assertion that parts are not what they seem. Thus, until the outcome studies are complete, the best evidence for the efficacy of IFS is from empirical observations in clinicians' offices.

IFS THERAPY FOR CLIENTS WITH COMPLEX TRAUMATIC STRESS DISORDERS

Self of the Therapist

One way to understand IFS therapy is to realize that a client's parts become securely attached to the client's Self in a process that parallels the attachment process between a loving parent and an insecure or disorganized child. For that to happen, however, the client needs access to the therapist's Self. *It is important to emphasize that the degree to which the therapist can embody his or her Self, rather than leading from his or her own protective parts, is the degree to which the IFS techniques will be effective.* This is particularly challenging for many complex trauma clients, because they have protectors who trust no one and will test or provoke therapists who get too close. At the same time, clients' exiles desperately want closeness and may idolize or become highly dependent on the therapist. In addition, the dangerous activities of their firefighters are likely to engage therapists' fearful, controlling parts.

Maintaining personal Self leadership with such clients is easier when the therapist does not view their jarring shifts from one extreme state to another as evidence of severe pathology or therapeutic failure. If the therapist instead understands that such shifts are manifestations of the client's highly burdened and protective parts, and also trusts that the client's Self is present just beneath the surface, it is easier to not overreact. Trauma clients are extremely sensitive to self-protective parts in their therapists and will react in kind, so the potential for therapist–client escalations of conflict is high and always damaging to clients.

In IFS training, a great deal of time is spent teaching the therapist to do *self–IFS therapy* before each session, so that "therapist" parts step back and allow the Self of the therapist to be present. This strategy results in a large decrease in traditional resistance and greater openness to healing. Because with IFS the client's Self is the one working with the client's inner parts, the therapist functions as a collaborator who "knows the territory" and is like a guide or partner. Because of this collaborative stance and the availability of the Self of the therapist, IFS treatment is less subject to the intense transference, projection, or dependence that can characterize work with complex trauma clients. A safe, trusting therapeutic relationship is crucial to success, but the primary healing relationship is between the client's Self and his or her parts.

Steps of IFS Therapy

As a client describes his or her problems, the therapist helps the client identify the parts involved by asking about emotions or thoughts surrounding the problem. After the client responds, the therapist can reflect what the client said, adding the phrase, "so part of you feels _____, is that right?" For example, "So part of you is constantly afraid, and another part ridicules you for that, is that right?"

After identifying several parts, the therapist asks the client whether there is one part in particular that he or she would like to begin to get to know and to help. If the client selects what might be an exile, then the therapist asks to work first with parts that do not want the client to go near that part, because as it is important to begin working first with protective parts before going to exiles. The IFS therapist has great respect for a client's protectors and helps the client get to know and befriend protectors first, before requesting permission to approach exiles. After the client focuses on the protector and locates it in his or her body, the therapist asks the client how he or she feels toward the part. The client's answer tells the therapist how much Self is present versus other parts that are polarized with the target part. For example, if the client says, "I don't like it because it criticizes me all the time," then the therapist knows to instruct the client to ask the part that does not like it to relax and "step back." Following that, as the polarized part separates its emotions from the client, the client will feel an internal shift or will not, if the part is not ready to do so.

The therapist works with this separating process until—in response to the question "How do you feel toward this part?"—the client gives an answer that in tone and content sounds like the Self is present to some degree. Common Self-led answers include "I'm curious about it," "I wonder why it's so upset," and "I feel sorry that it has to do this." The client then begins to know the protector from a place of genuine curiosity and even empathy. Because of this, the protector will often reveal that it is protecting exiles. The therapist then helps the client ask for permission to help those exiles, and addresses the protector's fears about granting that permission.

For clients with complex traumatic disorders, the process we have just described may take many sessions. In such a client, polarized parts are reluctant to separate and trust the client's Self. They fear the part the client is trying to get to know and often believe that their presence is all that keeps the client from disaster. Often the therapist needs to talk directly to these parts about their fears, before they will step back and allow access to the client's Self. Often the biggest fear that protectors have is that the client will be overwhelmed by the exile's emotions. It took years to discover the simple solution to that problem. If exiles agree in advance to not overwhelm as the client gets close, then they will abide by that agreement and, in the client's mind, he or she can get close enough to hold and comfort exiles without being totally flooded by them and their emotions. When this process is described to protectors, they often seem to know that it is possible and will give permission to proceed with approaching the exile(s). This discovery has allowed IFS therapists to work safely with highly delicate inner systems.

Once permission is granted, the client focuses on the exile and forms a trusting relationship with it. Next the client asks the part to show what it wants him or her to know about where it got its emotions and beliefs. What parts seem to need to release their extreme beliefs and emotions (their burdens) is to have the client compassionately witness what happened to them, then to enter the scenes in which they are frozen, rescue them, and bring them to a safe place. After that has been done for an exile, the client then asks whether the exile is ready to unload the emotions and beliefs it got from those experiences. Parts usually answer affirmatively. Once unburdened, parts usually feel lighter, but sometimes they also feel empty. For this reason, they are encouraged to invite needed qualities to enter them, a process that seems to consolidate the unburdening process. Finally, to integrate this change into the larger system, the exile's protectors are invited to meet it and see that it is no longer so vulnerable, and they are encouraged to find new roles now that they no longer need to be so protective. Often, at that point, those protectors will submit to the same steps toward unburdening that the exile underwent.

This *unburdening process* is another contribution of IFS to the work with complex traumatic stress disorders. It is important that when trauma therapists encourage clients to access their exiles, they not only witness the emotional expressions of those parts but also encourage the parts actively to unload their burdens. If that is not done, trauma clients who open the door to their exiles will show the decline in functioning over time that has characterized that work, because they released the toxic emotions and beliefs carried by the exiles *into* the larger system rather than moving them *out* of the system.

The goals, then, of IFS therapy with complex trauma clients are as follows: (1) to help clients unburden all their extreme parts, so they can shift out of their manager, firefighter, or exile roles and become harmonious members of a flexible internal family; (2) to restore the parts' trust in Self-leadership; and (3) to relate from Self to the outside world. As this process unfolds, clients report feeling more unitary and integrated despite still having differentiated parts of which they remain aware. They also find that their symptoms remit, and they feel more confidence and harmony in their relationships. Creating secure internal attachments allows people to create secure external attachments.

TRANSCRIPT OF AN IFS SESSION

The following is the first half of an IFS session with a Vietnam War veteran who complained of being emotionally numb most of his life because he feared his rage. Early attachment injuries had combined with his Vietnam War experiences to produce chronic PTSD and complex traumatic stress disorder. Previously, he had several sessions during which he was introduced to the IFS model of therapy and became comfortable with the idea of parts and of focusing his attention internally. In this session he decides to deal with his chronic emotional numbness.

As is true here, the internal work of IFS usually begins when a client focuses on a part and describes feelings toward that part. Most clients initially state that they do not like or are afraid of the part they select. According to the IFS understanding, however, it is not the client's Self that is angry or afraid, because the Self would not feel those kinds of emotions toward parts. Instead, IFS theory assumes that those expressions come from other parts of the client that are polarized with the part on which the client is focused. The client asks those other parts to separate internally, until the client's Self emerges and begins to dialogue with the original part.

The initial focus in the case presented here is on the manager part that numbs the client, with the therapist's intention of appreciating its protective function and getting its permission to work with the rage being held in an exile part. IFS differs from some other trauma therapies in its approach to stabilization. As soon as severe symptoms or impulses (firefighters) appear, IFS therapists try to access the feared part, so the client can experience that it is not so scary and that it can be transformed. Therapists do not avoid these parts or try to make the client feel more grounded first. Firefighters are only dangerous when they have no hope for alternative ways of handling the feelings to which they react. We seek them early to give them hope and to elicit their cooperation.

CLIENT: It's the anger that concerns me the most. I get angry and the fear of what I could do shuts everything down, so I'm just kind of numb. I spent so many years feeling numb after my brother died that I don't feel human at times because of this numbness.

THERAPIST: Let's start with that numbness. Go ahead and focus on it, and see where you find it in your body or around your body.

CLIENT: (*Closes his eyes and is silent for a minute.*) It feels like a shroud around my heart.

THERAPIST: And how do you feel toward it?

CLIENT: (*keeping his eyes closed*) It's one of those things that I can appreciate, yet I really want it to be gone.

THERAPIST: Let's see if the part that wants it to be gone can step back a little bit, so we can just get to know it a little better and maybe help it.

CLIENT: OK.

THERAPIST: And how do you feel toward it now?

CLIENT: I understand it. I understand what it's trying to do.

THERAPIST: Let it know that. Tell it what you understand about what it's trying to do and see if it agrees with that.

CLIENT: It agrees that it doesn't want me to go over the edge and its there to protect me from going crazy or throwing things or hitting somebody. It protects me from the rage.

THERAPIST: So how are you feeling toward it now as it tells you all that?

CLIENT: Disappointed in myself, because after 57 years I should be able to deal with rage without having to shut down or need anything to protect me from it.

THERAPIST: So is there a critical part of you that's come in now?

CLIENT: Yeah.

THERAPIST: Let that critic part know that we can see that it's trying to help, too. See if it would be willing to step out and be patient and wait, and we'll check with it later.

CLIENT: It's very hesitant but willing to try.

THERAPIST: That's all I'm asking. And it can watch and come back if it feels the need. We're just asking for some space for a little while.

CLIENT: Yeah, it can do that.

THERAPIST: So how are you feeling now toward that shroud around your heart?

CLIENT: A caring fondness.

THERAPIST: Great. So let it know that you have a lot of fondness for how hard it's worked to protect you all this time, and just see how it reacts to that.

CLIENT: It feels very appreciative.

THERAPIST: So it trusts now that you care about it and appreciate what it's done?

CLIENT: Yeah.

THERAPIST: So ask it if we could go to the rage and help it feel better. ... If it didn't have to carry so much rage, would this shroud have to work so hard to protect you from it?

CLIENT: That's a definite no. It wouldn't have to work so hard. It could relax and take in the sunlight.

THERAPIST: So what it would like to do is relax and take in some sun. Is it OK with the numbing part for us to go to that rage, without the rage taking over? We would just get to know the rage better and help it unload some of that stuff.

CLIENT: Oh, this one is really hesitant on that.

THERAPIST: I understand that it's been terrified of that rage since Vietnam, so it would be a big leap of faith to do this. But I just want it to know that I've done this a lot with people who have tremendous rage, and we can do this in a safe way and we can actually help that enraged part not have to stay in that state.

CLIENT: It is really willing.

After lots of reassurance from the therapist, the shroud part gives permission to go to the rage. Before that happens, however, it is important to help the client access his Self, so that he relates to the rage from a place of confidence and curiosity. To achieve this, the therapist has to convince other parts that are afraid of it to relax.

THERAPIST: If it's possible, then, I'd like you to start by having the enraged part go inside a room and you're outside the room looking in through a window. If that doesn't work, it is OK, but if it is possible, that's a good way to start.

CLIENT: OK.

THERAPIST: And do you see it in the room or just sense it in there?

CLIENT: (*with fear in his voice*) It's like dark spirits just bouncing off walls. There are many of them.

THERAPIST: And as you look at them through the window, how do you feel toward them?

CLIENT: Afraid.

THERAPIST: OK, but they're contained in the room, right?

CLIENT: Yeah.

THERAPIST: So we'll keep it like that for a while, so everybody can relax. Let's see if the parts that are afraid of them can go into a safe, comfortable room and trust you and me to deal with these spirits.

CLIENT: It doesn't want to go.

THERAPIST: Ask it what it's afraid will happen if it trusts us.

CLIENT: It's just so afraid of what will happen if the spirits take over.

THERAPIST: So tell it that we're not going to let them take over. That's not what this is about. We're gonna get to know them, but from outside the room, so we're not going do anything dangerous. But it's important that we do it when you're not afraid of them, because it turns out that they can't do anything dangerous if you're not afraid of them. So if the ones that are afraid could go into another room, that would be great, and just trust you and me.

CLIENT: It would be willing as long as it has the final say in terms of danger.

THERAPIST: Totally, it has the final say. We're not going to do anything without consulting with it.

CLIENT: It's going into the other room and standing by the window.

THERAPIST: So now how are you feeling toward these spirits now?

CLIENT: (*with confidence*) Kind of curious.

As the frightened part steps back, the client is able spontaneously to access more of his Self, reflected in his calm tone of voice and his saying that he is now curious about the rage. This discovery, that trauma clients often can access this state of Self as soon as their parts open space for it inside, is the hallmark of IFS therapy with trauma. Once extreme firefighters sense the client's Self, they often feel the safety necessary to shift toward vulnerability. Then the client's Self may be overwhelmed by all the emotions the vulnerable exiles carry that had been obscured by the firefighter.

THERAPIST: So from outside the room, tell them you're curious about them and see what they want you to know about themselves.

CLIENT: (*breathing deeply and visibly upset*) It's bringing up some really bad times I had no control over and that affected me.

THERAPIST: OK, is it too much to handle?

CLIENT: I still want to try.

THERAPIST: Well, tell them to slow it down a little bit. We're gonna get to all that. Tell them to just relax a little bit. We just want to get to know them better first. Tell them that we get that they're carrying all that stuff and that we really want to help them with it. See how they react to hearing that.

CLIENT: (*calmer now*) What I hear them say is "it's about time, we're tired."

THERAPIST: Yeah, it is about time. Are they still bouncing around?

CLIENT: It almost seems like they've stopped to take notice.

THERAPIST: Just again reassure them that we're here to help them. We may not be able to help them all today, but this is the beginning of a process that will help them all.

CLIENT: They're very interested.

In most trauma resolution therapies, containment, affect modulation, and titration techniques are taught—often extensively—before trauma is approached. A significant contribution of the IFS model is the discovery that trauma-based parts, if asked, actually possess the ability to modulate the flow of emotion and content to the client, thereby enabling the client not to become flooded, thereby allowing the Self to maintain a healing presence. For this reason, there is less need to teach clients how to handle their traumatic affect.

THERAPIST: To do this right, it's best to do one at a time or a group that is connected to a certain scene in the past at one time, so they can talk among themselves and figure out who should go first. Is there one or a group of them?

CLIENT: There's a group, and they seem to be around my brother and his death.

THERAPIST: How do you feel toward them now?

CLIENT: I just want to talk to them.

THERAPIST: Is it OK if that group comes out of the room and comes closer to you?

CLIENT: Yeah.

THERAPIST: First, let's consult with the part that said it was afraid. See if it's OK with this.

CLIENT: It's more willing to be open since they're settled down and aren't flying all over the place.

THERAPIST: Then let's bring out that group that's connected to your brother and see how many there are.

CLIENT: There's one senior and numerous younger ones.

THERAPIST: And you're feeling some caring for these guys?

CLIENT: Yeah.

THERAPIST: So let them know that you care about them, and just do that until they start to trust it.

CLIENT: OK.

THERAPIST: Ask if they trust you to care about them.

CLIENT: Yeah, they know.

Heavily burdened parts want the client to know what happened to them, to have their stories witnessed, and sometimes they try to show the scenes as soon as possible, because they have waited so long. It is important, however, to take the time to establish a trusting relationship between the parts and the client's Self first, before the witnessing begins. Once the client's Self and the injured parts really connect, the witnessing can proceed, and the client often experiences a lot of affect, without it causing backlash reactions from the protectors.

THERAPIST: OK. Would you be up for learning what they need you to know about your brother?

CLIENT: Yeah.

THERAPIST: Then ask them to show you everything they need you to know about what happened with your brother. But ask them also if they are willing to not totally overwhelm you with their feelings as they show you, so you can be with them without blending with them, and see if they're OK with that.

CLIENT: Yeah.

THERAPIST: Then, tell them to go ahead.

CLIENT: When they brought my brother back, I was at Camp Pendleton and I flew back to Illinois for his funeral, and I remember that for 3 days I stood at the head of his casket at attention in my dress blues and I didn't move. And at the cemetery, when they played taps, I cried so hard inside, but no tears came out. And then, riding back to the house, my Grandmother had said, "I wonder if he felt any pain," and I remember my mother screaming, and all I wanted to do was just rip my uniform off and run.

Many parts are frozen in time during the traumatic event, and it is important to help them leave the past for the safety of the present. One aspect of what renders loss traumatic is the aloneness and isolation that accompanies it; when "stuck" parts emerge from their isolation, they experience a reparation of sorts. When the client's Self enters the scene, its connection to that inner, younger part creates a safe framework in which the burden can at last be experienced and released.

THERAPIST: Yeah. OK. I'd like you to enter that scene and be there with that young man in the way he needed at the time. Whatever he needs, you just be there with him.

CLIENT: He needs to cry.

THERAPIST: Can you help him see that it's safe to cry?

CLIENT: I got to take him out of the uniform.

THERAPIST: Yeah, do that.

CLIENT: (*Immediately starts sobbing intensely for several minutes.*)

THERAPIST: Is it OK to feel all this?

CLIENT: Yeah.

THERAPIST: Then tell him it's OK and to let you feel as much as he needs you to.

CLIENT: (*between sobs*) It's almost as if there's a light. And even though the pain is tremendous, there is a brighter point later. He went down on his knees and just doubled over in tears.

THERAPIST: And how are you being with him?

CLIENT: I'm just holding him and telling him it's OK. Oh God, that feels good. It just feels like the weight is coming off.

THERAPIST: So let's just see if he'd like to leave that time and place and come with you to a comfortable place.

CLIENT: He needs to stay there a little longer.

THERAPIST: That's just fine. So tell him to let you know what he needs back there.

CLIENT: It just feels so good to have the Marine out of him. He feels human and it's OK to cry.

THERAPIST: Does he want to do anything with that uniform?

CLIENT: He doesn't want to put it back on. He doesn't want to have to see it again.

THERAPIST: How does he want to get rid of it?

CLIENT: I have a special place to take it to. I love Canyonlands out in Utah and the cliff dwellings, and I go there quite a bit and I think that would be a good spot to put it for the spirits of the canyons.

THERAPIST: How's he doing now?

CLIENT: Oh, he's feeling very good. Still sad, but it's like a tremendous weight is gone.

THERAPIST: Is he now ready to leave that time and place?

CLIENT: Yeah.

In this case, giving up the uniform constitutes an unburdening. Most clients' parts are quite willing to unload the extreme emotions and beliefs that are the result of the traumas (their burdens) once they feel fully witnessed. The obstacles to full witnessing are the fears of the protective parts being overwhelmed by reexperiencing events and feelings that were overwhelming at the time of the trauma, and that have resulted in a lifetime of (attempted) avoidance that impeded processing and resolution. The impact of unburdening is usually immediate and dramatic—in the direction of relief and increased lightness. When a part unburdens, it is released from its extreme role and can rapidly transform. Clients often say that the part suddenly seems lighter, looks different—stronger, older or younger—and wants to do something totally unrelated to its former role. In the remainder of the session (too long to include here), the client brings the young man out of the funeral scene to Canyonlands, where he leaves his Marine uniform and further unburdens some other parts frozen in earlier childhood scenes. The video of the whole session is available on the website selfleadership.org.

CONCLUSION

This session illustrates the difference that can be made by partnering with the client's Self, who then works with his or her parts to address complex traumatic stress symptoms. The major differences are as follows: First, clients are helped to take on the role of their own internal parents, creating an intrapsychic climate of intimacy by forming a secure, empathic, compassionate relationship with their parts. This leads to increases in clients' ability to experience their parts as trusting in Self leadership (e.g., protective parts come to trust that they no longer have to dominate, because there is another leader in there who can handle things internally and externally). Clients become more confident that they can deal with a variety of life challenges in an integrated manner, secure that if they experience their parts as feeling a sense of hurt, then they (acting as the integrative parent-like Self) will move to heal this hurt rather than be left feeling fragmented, abandoned, or locked out emotionally. As the integrative Self, the client also develops the capacity to help parts correct the trauma-related beliefs they carry by reassuring them, for example, "The fact that they hurt you doesn't mean that you are bad." As parts unburden the extreme beliefs and emotions accumulated from multiple psychological traumas, clients become less reactive and develop a new internal working model (Bowlby, 1969) about self, and both internal and external others, that permits intimacy with others, breaking their lifelong histories of isolation and loneliness. Also, clients no longer have to rely on their extreme methods of affect regulation, such as addictions or rage, because they no longer fear the affect (their *exiles*) or feel overwhelmingly burdened by trauma-related affect. The ultimate goal of IFS therapy is the restoration of the capacity for secure attachment, first internally and then externally. As parts are able to tell their stories and feel witnessed by Self, clients achieve a more integrated narrative with increased coherence and personal meaning. Losses are acknowledged, and grieving is encouraged, without the neurovegetative depression that comes from pathological intensification.

Second, therapists come to trust that there is a Self with whom they can partner, even in clients with highly symptomatic complex traumatic stress disorder; thus, they can enjoy the treatment process. Relieved of the responsibility for providing key insights, interpretations, homework assignments, or coping skills, therapists can help their own worried, striving manager parts to relax and allow their Selves to be therapeutically present with clients. Once they help clients embrace rather than fight their suicidal, addictive, or explosive firefighter parts, therapists can further relax, knowing that those extreme parts have allied with their healing efforts. IFS provides a model for therapists to understand not only the disparate emotions and states of mind of their clients but also their own internal family systems. In so doing, therapists may be better able to work with the parts within themselves, which is particularly important when conducting therapy with clients whose internal fragmentation and traumatic stress impairments often trigger a sense of fragmentation and stress for the therapist (see Pearlman & Caringi, Chapter 10, this volume). Thus, IFS provides a basis for therapists, as well as their clients, to grow in the therapy experience.

In conclusion, the IFS model brings a number of innovations to trauma-based psychotherapies. The greatest of these is that clients experience "Self-healing" facilitated by the therapist. Clients' parts achieve a secure relationship with Self, ending internal civil wars and self-hatred, and they find they can work on their own, outside the session. In addition, the client's Self does the witnessing and can tell the injured parts exactly what they needed to hear in the past (in contrast to the therapist, who can only guess what the client needed to hear), thus correcting primary process cognitions. Clients come to trust themselves, a process that is likely to be more empowering than externalizing primary trust to the therapist. This process may also significantly reduce or provide a therapeutic basis for working through resistance and transference reactions. Addictive clients may begin to experience healthy guilt about revictimizing injured parts. Also, injured parts typically carry enormous wisdom, so listening to them provides greater intuition and further prevents repeating dangerous reenactments. Finally, as mentioned, unburdening is hypothesized to create a completion of the trauma and reintegration of split-off parts, which clients experience as the relief they need to participate more fully in life experiences. When clients are triggered, instead of relapsing, they learn to go to the part within themselves that is upset and help it. Experiences, such as marriage or sex, that in the past could reliably cause some symptom remission may become less overwhelming. Ultimately, the goal of IFS is to enable clients to become more Self-led and Self-secure as opposed to parts-dominated and symptomatic.

REFERENCES

Bowlby, J. (1969). *Attachment and loss: Vol. 1. Attachment.* New York: Basic Books.

Horowitz, M. (1997). Stress response syndromes. *Hospital and Community Psychiatry,* *37,* 241–249.

Schwartz, R. C. (1995). *Internal family systems therapy.* New York: Guilford Press.

Watkins, J. G., & Watkins, H. (1988). The management of malevolent ego states in multiple personality disorder. *Dissociation, 1,* 67–72.

CHAPTER 18

Couple Therapy

Susan M. Johnson
Christine A. Courtois

Complex developmental traumatic stressors that occur in the context of an insecure or chaotic relationship between an infant and a primary caregiver often include recurring episodes of abuse and neglect over the course of childhood, both within and outside of the family. Psychological trauma experienced at the hands of a key attachment figure, on whom a child depends for a basic sense of safety and connection, has a pronounced impact on the developing child's self-identity and self-worth. If opportunities for change or repair via other relationships are not available, resultant negative models of self and others tend to be stable over the lifespan (Klohnen & Bera, 1998; McCann, Sakheim, & Abrahamson, 1988). These identity and relational prototypes and associated strategies for the regulation of emotion come into play in the various aspects of adult relationships, including bonding, emotional intimacy, and sexual interaction. *In this chapter, we address the impact of complex traumatic stress disorder on adult intimate partner relationships and describe a form of therapy, emotionally focused therapy (EFT) for couples, that addresses the needs of couples when one or both partners has such a history.* Over the last 25 years, EFT has developed, with extensive observation, analysis, and research, as a modality for couple therapy (Johnson, 2004, 2008), as well as individual therapy. More recently, it has been applied to the treatment of couples in which one or both partners have been traumatized, and the trauma has negatively impacted the couple's relationship (Johnson, 2002).

EFT FOR COUPLES

EFT has been used in clinical practice with traumatized clients in distressed relationships for over 20 years in a hospital clinic, a couple and family institute, and a university training clinic. Many of these individuals had experienced a basic "violation of human connection" (Herman, 1992, p. 154) and exhibited symptoms associated with complex posttraumatic stress disorder (PTSD)/disorders of extreme stress (DESNOS; Herman, 1992) and/or borderline personality disorder (BPD). EFT has extensive empirical substantiation as an effective treatment modality for couples (Johnson, Hunsley, Greenberg, & Schindler, 1999), including evidence of the stability of positive effects over 2 years in persons at high risk.

Research results suggest that EFT helps to reduce depression, and a preliminary empirical investigation of the application of EFT to complex developmental trauma, in this case in child sexual abuse (CSA) survivors, has been undertaken with positive results (MacIntosh & Johnson, 2008). This study, in which 80% of the sample was identified as exhibiting symptoms associated with complex PTSD, examined the impact of 20 sessions of EFT in a small sample ($N = 10$) of female CSA survivors and their partners. Survivors had suffered severe, chronic intrafamilial sexual abuse and had received prior individual therapy for their difficulties. Many of the partners had also experienced significant trauma. Posttreatment, half of the couples reported clinically significant increases in relationship satisfaction, as measured by the Dyadic Adjustment Scale (DAS), and decreases in trauma symptomatology, as measured by the Trauma Symptom Inventory and Clinician-Administered PTSD Scale (see Briere & Spinazzola [Chapter 5, this volume] for description of these measures).

A preliminary study is also in progress at the Baltimore Veterans Administration (VA) hospital using EFT with war veterans with chronic PTSD superimposed on complex developmental trauma, many of them having been abused as children. In this practice setting, it became very apparent that a terrible spiral occurs for these clients: Distress in their primary relationship perpetuates the effects of psychological trauma and triggers negative coping strategies. These maladaptive coping strategies in turn compound the effects of having experienced trauma in the past, then feed back into and exacerbate the effects of current problems with traumatic stress. For example, when a husband withdraws from his wife and numbs himself with alcohol to blunt his PTSD symptoms and to avoid his feelings (in general and about the relationship), paradoxically, his nightmares and flashbacks may worsen, and his sense of efficacy may deteriorate. Needless to say, his wife is affected by both the withdrawal and numbing, and by the intrusive reexperiencing. The partners usually become increasingly estranged and unavailable as comfort to each other.

These studies, although preliminary, are extensions of a body of research that attests to the efficacy of EFT for couples. In general, findings support the clinical refinements that have been formulated over many years of EFT applied to traumatized couples, including the following: The therapist must move slowly, containing and processing emotions, and using explicit strategies to maintain what Briere (1997) calls the *affective edge*. Intentional risks must be structured with very gradual increases in the level of affective challenge; dissociation and numbing must be monitored and addressed in the moment, and new strategies for coping developed; education concerning trauma is crucial, especially for the nontraumatized partner; and the "enemy" in the relationship is explicitly framed as the echoes of trauma and the negative interaction cycle that create insecurity and isolation in the relationship rather than comfort and support.

EFT APPLIED TO COUPLES
WITH COMPLEX DEVELOPMENTAL TRAUMA

The following characteristics make EFT particularly suited for couples in which one or both partners have experienced complex developmental trauma:

1. Interventions in EFT and the process of change are explicit and systematic, and several studies of the process of change detail key interventions and predictors of recovery from distress in EFT. In the chaos of a distressed relationship that is further complicated by the shadow of the "dragon of trauma," EFT offers the therapist a clear map for intervention (Bradley & Furrow, 2004; Johnson, 2002).

2. EFT explicitly addresses the impact of emotion on the quality of close relationships. Affect regulation, processing, and integration are central to all posttraumatic stress difficulties. Affect dysregulation in complex forms has been shown to be predictive of poorer psychosocial treatment outcome (Ford & Kidd, 1998).

3. EFT is based on a clear and research-based conceptualization of adult bonding (Johnson, 2003; Mikulincer & Shaver, 2007). The relevance of attachment theory to the trauma field has long been recognized. As noted by van der Kolk, Perry, and Herman (1991) and reflecting the seminal work of Bowlby (1969), the best predictor of trauma recovery is not trauma history per se but whether it is possible to seek comfort in others who offers solace and a safe haven. As they do with other life stresses, interpersonal relationships have been found to moderate and mediate the relationship between CSA and long-term distress (Runtz & Shallow, 1997; Whiffen & Aube, 1999), a finding that no doubt applies to other forms of childhood trauma and maltreatment. EFT directly addresses the security of the bond between survivors and their partners, and how insecurity actively perpetuates the long-term effects of trauma or, conversely, how increased security can provide a healing environment.

4. EFT is an experiential humanistic approach that is deliberately collaborative and focuses on validating and affirming clients. This nonpathologizing approach is essential and particularly restorative in a client population whose self-blame, stigmatization, and other negative cognitions have been found to mediate adjustment after trauma (Coffey, Leitenberg, Henning, & Turner, 1996) and to cause profound changes in schemas about self and others in the world, usually in a negative direction (McCann & Pearlman, 1990).

EFT for couples has been used effectively with heterosexual and same-sex couples, whether married or not. It is also applicable in the treatment of culturally diverse couples, because its foundation, attachment in primary relationships, has been found to be a universal feature across cultures and in all human and mammalian species (Mikulincer & Shaver, 2007). As noted by L. S. Brown (Chapter 8, this volume), therapy for the traumatized, whether individual, dyadic, or familial, must further be individualized and tailored to individual cultural and diversity needs, and this is also considered in EFT.

Although individual therapy has traditionally been considered the best treatment modality for persons with complex trauma disorders (Courtois, 1999, 2004), problems in ongoing intimate and other relationships are key aspects of this disorder (Pearlman & Courtois, 2005). Survivors' relationships are inevitably colored by the experience of wounds delivered at a vulnerable age by those on whom they relied and needed the most. CSA survivors, for example, report more current relationship problems than do nonsurvivors and are often unable to depend effectively on their partners (DiLillo Guiffre, Tremblay, & Peterson, 2001; Rumstein-McKean & Hunsley, 2001). In fact, they often choose as partners those who interact in ways that are familiar to them (i.e., partners who are unreliable or unresponsive, like the original caregivers). If, however, they find a partner with a more secure attachment style, the relationship can help them change in ways that lead to more personal and interpersonal security known as *earned security*.

The past focus on the individual treatment of survivors has, at times, been at the expense of relationships with partners and children. When abuse and individual recovery receive primary or exclusive emphasis, relationships may be neglected and founder as a result. Johnson (2002) and other couple therapists (Davis, 1991; Maltz, 1991) have criticized the overuse of individual therapy at the expense of couple or family work and have suggested that all modalities should be considered for use, either sequentially or concurrently. Including couple and family modes of interventions in the treatment of trauma allows therapists to address directly the quality of these key relationships and how trauma cues, such as numbing or irritability, impact such relationships. Survivors are redirected from a focus that is exclusively self-involved and taught new relationship skills. Partners of survivors are taught to be active allies in their partners' healing process. Couple therapy provides an ideal opportunity to clarify and revise survivors' negative models of self and others, and constrained affect regulation strategies and patterns of engagement with key others *in the context in which they occur.*

ATTACHMENT AND ITS SIGNIFICANCE IN THE CONTEXT OF COMPLEX DEVELOPMENTAL TRAUMA

Attachment theory, first elucidated by John Bowlby (1969, 1988), is a developmental theory of personality and a theory of love, but it is also a theory of psychological trauma and the impact of isolation, neglect, and emotional star-vation on the developing personality. Bowlby and others recognized that sepa-ration from primary caregivers and lack of human contact over even a short period of time during critical periods of psychosexual development could have severe personal and relational consequences. A significant body of research that has accumulated over the last half-century supports the major tenets of attachment theory (Mikulincer & Shaver, 2007):

1. Attachment is an innate and primary motivating force for human beings. The *attachment behavioral system* is an inborn regulatory system with important implications for personal development and social behavior. Sustained connection with caretakers and significant others is in the interest of survival; thus, it is significant in the evolutionary process and not a pathological dependency that should be outgrown in childhood.

2. *Proximity maintenance* depends on the responsiveness of the care-taker and on the fact that infants over time develop an *attachment bond* to a primary *attachment figure*. The quality of interactions with attachment figures during times of stress and need is the major source of differences in attachment system development and functioning. *Secure attachment* (when attachment figures are consistently available and responsive) has been found to support the child's self-regulatory capacities in a variety of domains (i.e., affective, biological, cognitive, interpersonal, and identity and self-worth). Security in the primary relationship allows the child, and later the adult, to be confident about accessibility to and connection with the loved one. The child has a secure base and safe haven from which to function in the world: This allows the child the freedom to explore, confident that he or she has support and sustenance when needed.

Attachment security also offers children models of how to approach other relationships with confidence and to develop reciprocal interactions with oth-ers. Later, as partners and parents, they can accept any protests at their unre-sponsiveness or "neediness" shown by their loved ones and are more likely to respond empathically. This translates into stronger, more flexible people and happier, more responsive relationships. Secure adults tend to have better close relationships, and to self-disclose and assert themselves easily; to use com-munication skills, such as metacommunication during conflict; to have a more articulated, positive, and coherent sense of self (Johnson, 2002); and to be more resilient in the face of stress (Mikulincer, Florian, & Weller, 1993).

3. In contrast, unavailable, abusive, or rejecting attachment figures cause distress and anxiety to develop, resulting in the child's development of *sec-ondary attachment strategies* to compensate: *hyperactivating strategies* based on anxiety and attempts to gain needed attachment, *deactivating strategies* based on avoidance of connection and self-reliance, or a combination of both strategies, termed *disorganized or fearful avoidant* (described below) (Main & Hesse, 1990). Hyperactivated anxious children tend to move into demanding, controlling, and pursuing roles in adult relationships. Avoidant, dismissing,

deactivated children, as adults, move into distancing and withdrawn stances. Fearful avoidant children and adults move between these two.

In the worst-case scenario, the caregiver directly and repeatedly abuses the child and/or does not respond or protect him or her from abuse by others, creating an environment that is markedly unstable and unpredictable (Solomon & George, 1999), and inherently dissociative and dissociogenic (Lyons-Ruth & Jacobvitz, 1999), with the caretaker inconsistently alternating between the extremes of attentiveness and appropriate response on one hand, and neglect and disregard on the other. The attachment figure becomes, at one and the same time, a source of fear and the potential solution to fear, making the adoption of a coherent strategy for dealing with stress and separation impossible for the child. Although the *resultant disorganized/dissociated* or fearful avoidant style has been labeled *disorganized*, it is in fact an organized strategy on the part of children attempting to cope with environmental and caretaking inconsistency, and the most common attachment strategy in those who have experienced severe and recurrent child abuse (Alexander, 1993; Shaver & Clarke, 1994). This disorganized, fearful style is associated with low self-worth and self-confidence, leading to distressed relationships that in turn serve constantly to trigger and reinforce a negative sense of self, traumatic memories, and poor coping strategies. It is also associated with less personal and interpersonal flexibility and resilience.

Subsequent studies of attachment in adult relationships have painted a clear picture of how secure and insecure attachment styles play out in interactions with loved ones at moments of disconnection, when attachment needs are primed (Mikulincer & Shaver, 2007). The creation of a secure attachment, in which a survivor can have a new emotional experience of connection and feel safe enough to explore emotional responses and attain affirming attention and comfort, has always been part of traditional trauma treatment (Courtois, 1988, 1999; Herman, 1992; McCann & Pearlman, 1990). The creation of such a relational context was considered to occur primarily in the therapeutic alliance. In couple therapy that has as its focus the processing of emotion and the creation of secure connection, this task is now extended in part to the survivor and his or her partner. *This relationship is the natural healing arena for posttraumatic problems of emotion regulation and interpersonal relatedness, especially problems that result from psychological traumas inflicted in the past by primary attachment figures.*

Next, we outline the EFT couple model and change processes, and show how they are applied to individuals with complex traumatic stress disorders and their partners.

ELEMENTS OF THE EFT COUPLE MODEL

The EFT couple model (Johnson, 2004) combines a focus on the self of each partner and the relational system, and how the partners define each other.

The therapist focuses on how partners first construct their moment-to-moment experiences, then their moment-to-moment patterns of interaction. A snapshot of an EFT therapist includes the therapist helping a client identify a poignant moment in which, for example, she could not accept her partner's offer of love and support, and piece together this experience in a new way. The therapist also focuses on expanding marginalized aspects of this experience, then using this new formulation as the basis for a new interaction with the other partner. So a client who might begin by simply turning away and refusing to look at her spouse, or by making a cynical remark about how anyone who trusts is pathetic, is then able to come to a place where she can tell her partner how afraid she is that if he comes close, he will "see" her. Her fear is that he might then feel the disgust she feels for herself and reject or abandon her in ways that happened in the past. The therapist then works with the partner, building on his empathy to encourage responding in a caring, reassuring way. *The tasks of EFT are always to identify, expand, and further process key emotional experiences, and to restructure negative interactions into responses that are more positive, thereby moving the relationship toward a more secure bond.*

The three stages of EFT, as applied to couples facing problems related to histories of developmental trauma, are very similar to the stages in the change process for trauma treatment outlined by Ford, Courtois, van der Hart, Nijenhuis, and Steele (2005). They are (1) safety through the deescalation of negative cycles and stabilization; (2) the creation of new interactions that restructure the relationship into a more secure bond that supports a positive sense of self, and in which partners can stand together against the "dragon of trauma"; and (3) consolidation and integration, in which partners can actively problem-solve and integrate the changes made in therapy into their everyday lives (Johnson, 2002). Special considerations apply when initiating therapy with couples in which trauma is part of the history of one or both partner. In brief, these include the following:

- The need to liaise with an individual therapist who is working with the client(s) to ascertain the stage of treatment and coordinate the couple and individual therapies.
- Careful assessment of the issue of possible violence, because one of the aftereffects of trauma is a loss of affect regulation and a tendency toward rage and aggression. Any physical aggression must end before couple EFT can safely begin. Emotional and verbal abuse (including neglect and abandonment) become foci of EFT.
- The need to address directly the question of how survivor clients deal with posttraumatic reactions and feelings. Is there a tendency to self-harm or attempt suicide? Is there a tendency to self-medicate through drugs and alcohol? If so, the therapist has to help create specific safety practices that both partners endorse, that is, sequences of mutually agreed-upon coping strategies to contain dysregulated emotion and to curb these behaviors. In some cases, individual treatment of substance abuse or other major addiction (i.e., alcohol,

drug, sex addiction) and/or self-injury/suicidality must precede or occur simultaneously with the individual and couple therapy.

• Addition of an educational aspect on the nature of traumatic stress to the traditional EFT couple model. It is often the case that both partners have little or no knowledge about psychological trauma and its effects, and may not recognize associations between prior trauma and problematic behavioral and emotional sequences. Additionally, the spouse/partner often knows only the barest of facts about the survivor's past experiences of abuse or other developmental trauma (if any information at all), whether it is a civilian massacre witnessed by a peacekeeping soldier or repeated rape by a stepbrother during childhood. Often, survivors avoid disclosing past trauma because of shame and for fear of being seen as bad, or being labeled crazy and abandoned as a result (this may have happened in the past if survivors disclosed, so these fears may be warranted). Moreover, many developmental trauma survivors do not feel entitled to care and comfort, nor do they know how to seek it. When they do talk about past traumas, they tend to do so in a diluted and sanitized manner. Because spouses often also know very little about the effects of trauma, naturally, they may take many traumatic stress responses and relational reenactments as personal slights. Therefore, the therapist must provide specific education about trauma and its personal and interpersonal repercussions, and assist the traumatized partner to disclose his or her experience accurately, without the usual minimization. The therapist further helps the partners outline the specific moments when traumatic stress reactions occur in their relationship and gain control of these stress reactions to begin developing alternative response scenarios.

• Tailoring the goals of therapy and the length of the therapy process to the needs of each couple. In research studies, EFT has been conducted in 10–12 sessions. When working with survivors of trauma (especially of the complex developmental sort, in which the attachment style is likely to be fearful/avoidant or disorganized/dissociative) the pace is slower, and temporary setbacks are planned for and expected. Treatment may take up to 30 or more sessions and may need to be concurrent with individual treatment. The goals of therapy must also be sculpted to fit the specific needs of the couple. For example, a CSA survivor may want a more controlled form of sexuality and may work on sexual issues at a slower pace than a partner who has never been so traumatized (Maltz, 1991). However, partners who can be open about these kinds of issues are most often able to deal with them in a way that promotes their satisfaction and intimacy.

• Finally, the alliance with the therapist, and that therapist's ability to create a safe haven in the therapy session—always the foundation on which EFT interventions rest—is even more crucial with survivors and partners. Rifts in the alliance are to be expected, monitored, and actively mended. The EFT therapist attempts to be genuine and transparent, and to remain open to learning from every couple in every session. This is even more crucial in complex developmental trauma cases, in which the therapist is acting as a relationship process consultant, and a model and catalyst for change.

EFT INTERVENTIONS

The focus of the intervention and the specific intervention varies depending on where partners are in the change process. In Stage 1, the focus is on identifying and deescalating negative cycles of interaction, and accessing underlying security-oriented affect. The therapist repeatedly *reflects the process of interactions and frames negative cycles* (e.g., "demand and withdraw") as the "enemy" that keeps both partners on guard and off balance with each other, and helps to maintain traumatic stress symptoms. The therapist uses *evocative questions, reflection, and interpretation* to expand reactive emotions to include the more vulnerable affect that underlies them (e.g., to expand reactive anger into underlying sadness and attachment fears). The therapist then encourages the partners to share these core emotional responses in structured guided interactions or enactments with each other, which usually involve various forms of fear of loss, abandonment, or rejection, and grief and hurt. The therapist also *reframes key responses in terms of attachment needs and fears, and as the aftereffects of trauma.* At the end of a successful Stage 1, partners are able to be more kind to and generous with each other and can view the negative interactive cycle and traumatic stress reactions as their mutual enemies (rather than as solely the problem of one partner or the other). Despite this initial progress, the attachment bond between them is still insecure and needs strengthening.

In Stage 2, the focus is on restructuring interactions to introduce and reinforce more secure attachment. The therapist works toward reengaging more withdrawn partners and helping more critical, blaming partners to "soften," that is, to ask from a position of vulnerability that their attachment needs be met. When both partners are then accessible and responsive, bonding interactions of comfort and reassurance begin to define the relationship as a safe haven and a secure base. The couple then enters the final stage of therapy. The therapist reflects new patterns of interaction, and encourages the partners to create a coherent narrative of how their relationship became distressed and how they repaired it. The couple can then problem-solve ways to prevent incursions of negative interaction patterns and traumatic stress into their relationship in the future.

Throughout treatment, the EFT therapist *privileges emotional responses*, viewing them as organizing interactions between the partners, much the way music organizes a dance. When working with survivors, there are also times when the therapist helps to contain chaotic, dysregulated, and overwhelming emotional responses, such as intense reactivity and flashbacks (e.g., see Johnson & Williams-Keeler, 1998), and to deconstruct negative responses, such as shame. Not uncommonly, the spouse is able to respond to a survivor in a more loving and compassionate way than the survivor can initially allow or accept. This compassion begins to act as an antidote to negative emotions, such as shame, while validating the self and the worth of the wounded partner.

Emotion is seen as a high-level information-processing system that communicates to an individual and to others that individual's needs and motives, and supports a stronger sense of self-esteem. Emotion also plays a central role in the creation of meaning. It is a physiological, as well as psychological, experience that organizes action and responses to others. Negative emotion is reframed in the context of cycles of distress, traumatic stress, and attachment, then it is restructured, often by including marginalized elements, whereas "new" emotional responses (e.g., fear of hurt and longing for comfort and reassurance) are used to develop new, positive interactions between partners.

Throughout the process, the EFT therapist focuses on the most present and poignant emotions that arise, including those most salient in terms of attachment needs and fears, the nonverbal gesture, or the "hot" image. The therapist also hones in on the emotion that seems to organize problem interactions or, alternatively, has the potential to organize positive ones. For example, the therapist might highlight the look of sadness and compassion on a husband's face when his partner says that she "interrogates" him out of feelings of abandonment fear, not out of contempt. Fear is addressed extensively in EFT, primarily because it tends to become an especially absorbing emotional state that overrides other cues, and constricts and constrains both information processing and interpersonal responses. Clients caught up in fear often strike out or flee, or appear frozen and complain about not being able to think or react. Attachment longing, or its mirror opposite, the pain of isolation and fear of loss, is also used to prime new behaviors, such as risk taking and asking for caring responses. Emotion is designed to reorganize behavior rapidly in the interests of survival and the fulfillment of basic needs. Attachment longing and fears play a part in the establishment of negative cycles of interaction, but they can also be essential in moving out of such cycles.

We now discuss the core interventions used in EFT to reprocess emotional experience are as follows (Johnson & Denton, 2002).

Close Tracking and Reflecting of Emotional Experience

Example: "Could you help me understand? I think you're saying that you 'stay on the surface,' as you put it, because this feeling of hopelessness comes up when you think of talking about how lonely you feel. And now there is another piece to this that makes you want to throw up your hands like you just did? If you talk about your needs, you are afraid that you will not only feel more alone, but you will also be told how demanding and impossible you are. Am I getting it?"

Main functions: Focusing the therapy process; building and maintaining the alliance; clarifying emotional responses that underlie relational positions.

Validation

Example: "You feel so alarmed right now that you can't even focus. When we're that afraid, we can't even concentrate, is that it? And you had to learn to stay vague and kind of numb. It was the only way to grasp a little safety. It was a way of saving your life in your family, wasn't it?"

Main functions: Legitimizing responses and supporting clients to continue to explore how they construct their experience and their interactions; building the alliance.

Evocative Responding

Examples: "What's happening right now, as you say that?"; "What's that like for you?"; "So when this occurs, some part of you just wants to rage, fight and attack—to never let anyone hurt you again?"

Main functions: Using open questions to expand the stimulus, bodily response, associated desires, and meanings or action tendency implicit in an emotional response; expanding elements of experience to facilitate the reorganization of that experience; formulating unclear elements of experience, and encouraging exploration and engagement.

Heightening Deeper Emotions: Using Repetition, Images, Metaphors, or Enactments

Examples: "Could you say that again, directly to her, 'I can't let you in'?"; "This is so difficult for you, like stepping off into space, so terrifying."; "Can you turn to him and tell him, 'It's too hard to ask. It's too hard to ask you to hold me and help me feel safe'?"

Main functions: Highlighting key experiences that organize responses to the partner and new formulations of experience that reorganize the interaction. With trauma survivor clients, it is also crucial to "slice risks thin" and to pace interventions carefully. Survivors often need considerable acknowledgment of the valid blocks and fears about engaging with their deeper emotions, before they can begin to do so.

Empathic Conjecture or Interpretation

Example: "You turned your head. It is almost as if you were turning away from this feeling—like you don't want to touch it, to own it. It feels wrong, unacceptable almost, is that right? You don't want to know this, to feel this way?"

Main functions: Clarifying and formulating new meanings, especially regarding definitions of self (including accepting disowned and/or uncomfortable emotions) and relational positions. It is important when working with emotions for the therapist to repeat interventions, often multiple times, and to "slice emotions" into small components, because difficult emotions take longer to process, to be congruent with the affect (e.g., to speak of sadness in a soft voice, and to use simple language and simple images). The best images of all are the ones generated by the clients themselves.

Core interventions to restructure interactions in EFT follow.

Tracking, Reflecting, and Replaying Interactions

Example: "So what just happened here? John, your wife told you that she loved you deeply and that she needs you. But you looked away and told her that she is too 'demanding.' Then you went on to explain in a distant voice that if she had to ask for this, you were obviously messing up and failing her ... that you were not perfect and that this was the only thing that saved your life in Nam. You are listening for judgments and looking for the safety of perfect performance all the time? Yes? And you do not see the love in your wife's face. So then she gave up and turned her chair away. Then you looked up and said, 'See, she is going to leave me. And then I will just shoot myself.'"

Main functions: Slowing down and clarifying steps in the interactional "dance"; replaying key relational sequences, so that partners begin to see how they construct this dance.

Reframing in the Context of the Cycle, Trauma, and Attachment Processes

Example: "You freeze because you feel like you're right on the edge of stepping into all that helplessness; because she matters so much to you, not because you don't care."

Main functions: Shifting the meaning of specific responses and fostering more positive perceptions of the partner.

Restructuring and Shaping Interactions

Examples: "Can you tell him, 'I promised myself never to be open and so easy to hurt again. You don't get to devastate me again'?"; "Can you tell him directly, 'I am so afraid, I have to hold you at a distance just to breathe—can't let you close—feel like I have no skin—so raw'?"; "Can you ask him, please? Can you ask him for what you need?"

Main functions: Enacting present positions, enacting new behaviors based on new emotional responses, and choreographing specific change events. Specifics of these interventions are presented in greater detail in the text by Johnson (2002) and the EFT couple therapist training manual by Johnson and colleagues (2005). The following case study illustrates how EFT interventions can be deployed in a systematic, yet individualized, manner during each stage of couple therapy.

CASE STUDY: WHERE ARE YOU, ANYWAY?

Shane and Mary, a couple in their mid-50s, had been married for about 25 years when they entered therapy for relationship problems that escalated after her recent treatment for breast cancer. Mary revealed in an assessment session that she also had nightmares and regular "flashes" of her father and brother abusing her physically and sexually. These had worsened since her cancer treatment. She spoke of using physical exercise to "numb out." She needed extreme structure to cope and had developed many household rules that "just had to be obeyed if people want to live with me. If not, they should move out." When their children, now grown and living on their own, were small, Mary had been diagnosed with depression and "possible PTSD" by a psychiatrist, and had received a "few" therapy sessions focusing on the abuse in her family and its effect. She had learned that the main effect of her past was that she "did not trust people." Mary disclosed that she tended to be very reactive with coworkers and family members. She could be emotionally volatile when she believed that others were not considering her or her needs. Mary also did not like her body and, since her mastectomy, had refused to look at herself in the mirror or undress in front of her husband. She blamed her body for having developed cancer, believing it to be an external sign of her internal "badness."

Shane, a very successful manager, lost his job just as his wife was diagnosed with breast cancer, was having difficulty finding full-time employment, and was in individual therapy and on medication for depression. He reported spending most of his time searching for a new job and woodworking in his basement, partially to avoid interacting with Mary. He described a childhood in which family members were very distant, and his only experience of satisfying closeness had been with Mary, while they were courting. He expressed worry about Mary's cancer prognosis and that she did not let him support her. Furthermore, with his job loss and no prospect of a replacement, he felt like a failure as the family breadwinner.

During the formal assessment, Shane endorsed an avoidant style and Mary, a fearful avoidant style on the Relationship Questionnaire (Bartholomew & Horowitz, 1991). They both received a very low score on a measure used to assess marital satisfaction, indicating that they were severely distressed. Despite this, both Shane and Mary appeared committed to their relationship, although they complained of being "exhausted" by the tension and their spats. Both were highly intelligent and at times very aware of their dynamics; however, like many distressed couples, Shane and Mary understood the problem in terms of each other's shortcomings.

Their interactions would play out as follows, in a pattern that was apparent from the first session: Mary would first rail at her husband for his distance and weep at her "loneliness"; however, if Shane did express any feeling for her, she would give long intellectual digressions to the effect that relying on others was a sign of "weakness" and "stupidity." Mary would critically attack Shane and point out his inability to follow the "rules of the house" and his lack of caring for her. Shane distanced himself, concurring bitterly that he was "probably useless," and that he would sometimes shut down to avoid everything for days on end. Mary would then feel abandoned. As she recalled, no one, including her mother, had ever protected her.

Mary had disclosed her abuse to Shane before they married. He had tried to comfort her then but later stopped after developing the belief that she hated him for being a man and for wanting to be sexual with her, and that the abuse had "poisoned" their sexual relationship. During their entire relationship, their sexual encounters had been very short and usually took place in the dark. Following the mastectomy and chemotherapy, sexual interactions became virtually nonexistent, a concrete expression of their emotional estrangement and Mary's alienation from her postmastectomy body. Mary was able to articulate that a key recurring difficulty for her was when Shane would recoil from physical touch when she offered or sought it. She would initially feel "rebuffed," then would become defiant and angry. Since her mastectomy, Mary felt "less than" as a woman, and felt that Shane rejected physical contact because she was now physically defective. Mary had moved out of their bedroom and spent less time at home.

Their "angry critical complaint/distance and dismiss" cycle occurred repeatedly. Mary denigrated Shane as incompetent in relationships, "cold," and "rejecting." Shane was silent or expressed hopelessness, stating that he might as well "shut down" or leave to get some "peace." Mary repeatedly mentioned that Shane had let her go alone to her chemotherapy sessions or refused to pick her up at the hospital. He agreed that he had done this, but that she had told him explicitly that she did not need his help and would go alone. He had felt helpless to support her.

The first task of the EFT therapist is to create a safe, secure base in therapy by validating and legitimizing both partners' experience and their positions in the relationship. The therapist clarified her role as a process consultant who would work collaboratively with both partners to help them see how they became "stuck" in certain patterns of interaction that left them both feeling defeated and alone. She also acknowledged the extra "sensitivity" that Mary had to deal with as a result of being abused and unprotected by those she had counted on, and how Shane had been given no map to closeness by his distant upbringing, so he would naturally "shut down" when he did not know what to do. As the opportunity arose in session, the therapist linked emotional responses and interaction moves to the echoes of trauma and Mary's experience of relationships as a "minefield," where she needed to be on guard, ready to take control or to numb out and survive alone.

As noted earlier, in Stage 1 of EFT, the goal is to capture, reflect, and reframe the negative interaction cycle between the partners. Shane responded very well to the view that both were caught in a demand–withdraw dance. This provided an antidote to his self-denigrating view that he was "useless" at relationships and also lessened his resentment at this wife, whom he came to see as also being "stuck" in this negative dance. The therapist contained negative emotions and responses with reflection and validation, for example, interrupting Mary's criticism of Shane by focusing on Mary's experience of her anger (secondary reactive emotion), then gradually exploring Mary's experience with her and naming her more primary underlying panic at abandonment. Her conflicting messages of "Come here/Where are you, then?" and "Go away/I do not and will not need you" were made explicit and their legitimacy was validated in terms of Mary's abusive past. Shane was able to own his withdrawal, and his sadness and shame at being unable to "do things right," and to reveal new information to Mary; for example, he *had* wished to accompany her to chemotherapy but had accepted her refusal to allow this as punishment for past "failures."

As the process of the steps in their dance and the attachment emotions— the music of this dance—became clear, they were able to slow down, reflect on their negative patterns, and begin to see into each other's pain. They began actively to frame their "negative cycle" as their joint problem. An educational element concerning the effects of trauma on the ability to trust and accept needs or to ask for those needs to be met was repeatedly included as opportunities arose in sessions. Attachment needs for comfort and connection were validated and normalized. Mary began to understand in a new way that her expectations of others and emotional volatility were part of her traumatic history, and she agreed to be referred to an individual therapist who worked with trauma in a way that was compatible with EFT.

In Stage 2 of EFT, the goal is to restructure each person's attachment-oriented responses and build a new positive cycle of attuned connection. In this case, this would also provide an antidote to Mary's panic and volatility, and Shane's hopelessness and withdrawal. In this stage, each partner is encouraged to move into a new way of engaging with and integrating emotions, formulating relationship needs, and responding to the other. The more withdrawn partner is first encouraged to shift into a new level of engagement. For Shane, this involved being able to access and to own his deeper emotions and, with the therapist's help, communicate them to Mary. He was able to talk of how his fear of failure, exacerbated by his job loss and her cancer diagnosis and treatment, induced such a sense of hopelessness and shame that as soon as his wife showed any sign of being upset, he simply shut down. He now understood that his wife then felt shut out and alone when he withdrew. His "recoil" from her touch, he noted, was due to fear. Shane had never been confident sexually, and he assumed that he had failed in that realm as well.

As Shane began to talk openly about his fear of Mary's rejection, he also began to formulate his needs. He told her that he felt "oppressed" by her rules and did not want to try and live by them any longer. He also told her that he wanted to learn to be close, but that she had to be less "confusing." He could not move closer when he was told to keep his distance, when told that he was not needed, then castigated for not coming close. With the therapist's help, Mary was gradually able to tune into and accept Shane's disclosures. The following excerpt gives a flavor of working with the attachment consequences of trauma and a survivor's resultant *fearful avoidant* and dysregulated attachment style. It shows a piece of the shift from a controlling, demanding position to an open acknowledgment of attachment fears and needs on Mary's part. The therapist "unpacks" a key response, Mary's response to Shane's recoil, and helps Mary deepen the emotion around this to create new interactions that communicate attachment needs.

SHANE: There are so many triggers—times when I get judgment or confusing messages from you. I never know when you will get upset with me. But I am tired of keeping my head down and freezing up. I'd like some comfort between us, without all the tension. I am starting to understand in a new way how hard it is for you to trust me, and how the shadow of your dad is always there between us.

THERAPIST: When Shane talks about how he knows this is hard for you, you want him to know that letting yourself even think about or want that closeness is like a "minefield," it's so dangerous, yes? (*Mary nods tearfully.*) To survive you had to be "strong" and in control, try to make the rules, and not let that softer feeling of needing comfort creep in. Is that right? (*Mary nods again. She has used all these terms before in previous sessions.*) So when you hear him say he wants comfort between you?

MARY: Of course, I like it. But I feel so alone that part of me doesn't believe him.

THERAPIST: How do you feel as you say this? What signals does your body give you? [evocative questioning]

MARY: Right now, I want to run. Maybe it's fear. I have to take care of me.

THERAPIST: Yes. During chemo, when he didn't take care of you, when you couldn't ask for that, you said you felt sad and hurt and angry; but you also protected that soft scared part of you by showing you could cope on your own. [repeating primary emotions to heighten engagement and clarify attachment dilemma]

MARY: I will not ask. He should have known. He should have just come.

THERAPIST: It's too hard to ask—to feel that need? It's scary—you want to run instead. What would have happened if you had felt those softer feelings of fear and asked him to come and take care of you?

MARY: (*Her face shifts from angry to sad.*) I'd have gotten his withdrawal—shut down—recoil routine. He wouldn't be there. So, if I am so much of a judge—well, maybe I am. If he can't live by my rules, he can just move out. I am fine on my own.

THERAPIST: (*in a very soft, slow voice*) You are? We talked about how sad and scary it is to be so alone. How you get mad to get him to hear you—how alone you feel. But wanting and asking for closeness is too scary, hum ... [exploring at the edge of Mary's experience in the moment]

MARY: It's fine. I'm used to it. (*Looks up at the therapist.*) Guess it feels bad. (*Gets tearful.*) OK, so it's terrifying. My body says run, he'll turn away. Better to just try to stay in control. If I reach ... let my guard down and believe ...

THERAPIST: And he turns me down, turns away, shuts me out—then I will die inside?

MARY: (*Weeps.*) I don't want to feel that weakness, it's too hard. And he won't listen. He will laugh at me. [In a previous session, she had recalled how her father laughed when he found her crying after her brother had assaulted her.] He'll step back.

Shane and Mary repeatedly revisited moments in which his lack of confidence and fear of failure made it hard for Shane to respond, and her hunger for and opposing fear of connection played out. They also had to explore how Mary's cancer had evoked vulnerabilities and attachment needs in each of them in ways that previously had been private and unspoken, exacerbating Shane's sense of helplessness, loss, and fear of further loss, and Mary's attachment fears. The effects of cancer treatment had also exacerbated Mary's sense of shame about her body, and this, and its impact on their sexual life, had to be addressed. They also had to address how Shane's job had affected his identify and deepened his sense of failure and helplessness.

Mary offered a classic example of how abuse by an attachment figure can create a relational double bind, in which neither distance nor connection can be tolerated. Once partners understand that their loved one has simultaneous needs for and contradictory fear of closeness and fear of abandonment, often they can offer care and protectiveness. At the end of treatment (25 sessions) this couple scored just above the cutoff for distress on a measure of relationship adjustment. Shane no longer reported feeling as depressed, and Mary's anxiety symptoms had largely abated. They still became caught in demand–withdraw at times but were able to exit from this pattern and reconnect much more easily. Their sexual life was still narrowly defined, but they were able to hold and comfort each other.

CONCLUSION

In EFT treatment, clients are enabled to identify and connect with the previously overwhelming emotions associated with old traumas, and the attachment dilemmas set up by those traumas. They are helped to engage with those emotions at a "working distance" (Gendlin 1981), ordering and reshaping them into new meanings and new responses. This process resembles individual trauma therapies; the difference is that in EFT, *the newly integrated emotions can then evoke new responses in interactions with a partner*. They can be used to shape positive cycles of connection and a more secure attachment bond.

Couple therapy with partners whose symptoms are associated with complex trauma disorders is never easy. As this case illustrates, the attachment perspective offers an invaluable guide to client problems and the creation of potential antidote experiences. The experiential model of change offers a clear set of procedures for working with and regulating emotion. An integration of these two factors in couple therapy allows the therapist to address effectively perhaps the two main issues in complex trauma disorders, affect regulation and attachment behaviors.

REFERENCES

Alexander, P. C. (1993). The differential effects of abuse characteristics and attachment in the prediction of the long-term effects of sexual abuse. *Journal of Interpersonal Violence, 8*(3), 346–362.

Bartholomew, K., & Howowitz, L. M. (1991). Attachment styles among young adults: A test of a four-category model. *Journal of Personality and Social Psychology, 61,* 226–244.

Bowlby, J. (1969). *Attachment and loss: Vol. 1. Attachment.* New York: Basic Books.

Bowlby, J. (1988). *A secure base.* New York: Basic Books.

Bradley, B., & Furrow, J. (2004). Toward a mini-theory of the blamer softening event. *Journal of Marital and Family Therapy, 30,* 233–246.

Briere, J. (1997). Treating adults severely abused as children: The self-trauma model. In D. A. Wolfe (Ed.), *Child abuse: New directions in prevention and treatment across the life span* (pp. 177–204). Thousand Oaks, CA: Sage.

Coffey, P., Leitenberg, H., Henning, K., & Turner, T. (1996). Mediators of the long term impact of child sexual abuse. *Child Abuse and Neglect, 20,* 447–455.

Courtois, C. A. (1988). *Healing the incest wound: Adult survivors in therapy.* New York: Norton.

Courtois, C. A. (1999). *Recollections of sexual abuse: Treatment principles and guidelines.* New York: Norton.

Courtois, C. A. (2004). Complex trauma, complex reactions: Assessment and treatment. *Psychotherapy: Theory, Research and Practice, 41,* 412–426.

Davis, L. (1991). *Allies in healing: When the person you love was sexually abused as a child.* New York: Harper Perennial.

DiLillo, D., Guiffre, D., Tremblay, G., & Peterson, L. (2001). A closer look at the nature of intimate partner violence reported by women with a history of child sexual abuse. *Journal of Interpersonal Violence, 16,* 116–132.

Ford, J. D., Courtois, C. A., van der Hart, O., Nijenhuis, E., & Steele, K. (2005). Treatment of complex posttraumatic self-dysregulation. *Journal of Traumatic Stress, 18,* 437–448.

Ford, J. D., & Kidd, P. (1998). Childhood trauma and disorders of extreme stress as predictors of treatment outcome with chronic posttraumatic stress disorder. *Journal of Traumatic Stress, 11,* 731–761.

Gendlin, E. (1981). *Focusing* (2nd ed.). New York: Bantam Books.

Herman, J. L. (1992). *Trauma and recovery.* New York: Basic Books.

Johnson, S. M. (2002). *Emotionally focused couple therapy with trauma survivors: Strengthening attachment bonds.* New York: Guilford Press.

Johnson, S. M. (2003). Attachment theory: A guide for couple therapy. In S. M. Johnson & V. E. Whiffen (Eds.), *Attachment processes in couples and families* (pp. 103–123). New York: Guilford Press.

Johnson, S. M. (2004). *The practice of emotionally focused couple therapy: Creating connection*. New York: Brunner/Routledge.

Johnson, S. M. (2008). Emotionally focused couple therapy: Creating secure connection. In A. S. Gurman (Ed.), *Clinical handbook of couple therapy* (4th ed., pp. 107–137). New York: Guilford Press.

Johnson, S. M., Bradley, B., Furrow, J., Lee, A., Palmer, G., Tilley, D., et al. (2005). *Becoming an emotionally focused couple therapist: The workbook*. New York: Brunner/Routledge.

Johnson, S. M., & Denton, W. (2002). Emotionally focused couple therapy: Creating secure connections. In A. S. Gurman & N. S. Jacobsen (Eds.), *Clinical handbook of couple therapy* (2nd ed., pp. 221–250). New York: Guilford Press.

Johnson, S. M., Hunsley, J., Greenberg, L., & Schindler, D. (1999). Emotionally focused couples therapy. *Clinical Psychology: Science and Practice, 6*, 67–79.

Johnson, S. M., & Willams-Keeler, L. (1998). Creating healing relationships for couples dealing with trauma. *Journal of Marital and Family Therapy, 24*, 25–40.

Klohnen, E. C., & Bera, S. (1998). Behavioral and experiential patterns of avoidantly and securely attached women across adulthood: A 31 year longitudinal study. *Journal of Personality and Social Psychology, 74*, 211–223.

Lyons-Ruth, K., & Jacobvitz, D. (1999). Attachment disorganization: Unresolved loss, relational violence and lapses in behavioral and attentional strategies. In J. Cassidy & P. R. Shaver (Eds.), *Handbook of attachment: Theory, research, and clinical applications* (pp. 520–554). New York: Guilford Press.

MacIntosh, H. B., & Johnson, S. M. (2008). Emotionally focused therapy for couples and childhood sexual abuse survivors. *Journal of Marital and Family Therapy, 34*, 298–315.

Main, M., & Hesse, E. (1990). Parent's unresolved traumatic experiences are related to infant disorganized attachment status. In M. T. Greenberg, D. Cicchetti, & E. Cummings (Eds.), *Attachment in the preschool years* (pp. 161–182). Chicago: University of Chicago Press.

Maltz, W. (1991). *The sexual healing journey: A guide for survivors of sexual abuse*. New York: HarperCollins.

McCann, I. L., & Perlman, L. A. (1990). *Psychological trauma and the adult survivor: Theory, therapy, and transformation*. New York: Brunner/Mazel.

McCann, I. L., Sakheim, D. K., & Abrahamson, D. (1988). Trauma and victimization: A model of psychological adaptation. *Counseling Psychologist, 16*(4), 531–594.

Mikulincer, M., Florian, V., & Weller, A. (1993). Attachment styles, coping strategies, and posttraumatic psychological distress. *Journal of Personality and Social Psychology, 64*, 817–826.

Mikulincer, M., & Shaver, P. R. (2007). *Attachment in adulthood: Structure, dynamics, and change*. New York: Guilford Press.

Pearlman, L. A., & Courtois, C. A. (2005). Clinical applications of the attachment framework: Relational treatment of complex trauma. *Journal of Traumatic Stress, 18*(5), 449–459.

Rumstein-McKean, O., & Hunsley, J. (2001). Interpersonal and family functioning of female survivors of childhood sexual abuse. *Clinical Psychology Review, 21*(3), 471–490.

Runtz, M. G., & Shallow, J. R. (1997). Social support and coping strategies as mediators of adult adjustment following childhood maltreatment. *Child Abuse and Neglect, 21*, 211–226.

Shaver, P., & Clarke, C. L. (1994). The psychodynamics of adult romantic attachment. In J. Masling & R. Borstein (Eds.), *Empirical perspectives on object relations theory* (pp. 105–156). Washington: DC: American Psychiatric Association Press.

Solomon, J., & George, C. C. (1999). *Attachment disorganization.* New York: Guilford Press.

van der Kolk, B. A., Perry, C., & Herman, J. L. (1991). Childhood origins of self-destructive behavior. *American Journal of Psychiatry, 148,* 1665–1671.

Whiffen, V. E., & Aube, J. A. (1999). Personality, interpersonal context, and depression in couples. *Journal of Social and Personal Relationships, 6,* 327–344.

CHAPTER 19

Family Systems Therapy

Julian D. Ford
William Saltzman

The individual, group, and couple psychotherapy approaches presented in other chapters in this book may be of direct benefit not only to patients with complex traumatic stress disorders but also indirectly to their entire families. However, the psychosocial challenges to the family having a member with complex traumatic stress disorder impairments may alter the family system in profound ways that are not readily addressed without direct family involvement in psychotherapy. If families are helped to restore the functionality of all their relationships, including but not limited to the relationships with the traumatized member, then they may more effectively contribute to (and not inadvertently undermine) that troubled member's recovery and healthy adaptation. Moreover, although complex traumatic stress disorders are not "contagious," it is not uncommon for multiple family members to have been directly or indirectly affected by psychological trauma and, by definition, this has occurred when the trauma is intrafamilial (e.g., incest, domestic violence).

Therefore, this chapter provides an overview of family systems therapy approaches to complex traumatic stress disorders, including clinical illustrations of two empirically based models of family therapy designed or adapted to address complex traumatic stress sequelae. Case vignettes from each family therapy approach demonstrate how family systems interventions can assist children and adults in families with complex traumatic stress disorders.

RATIONALE FOR FAMILY THERAPY WITH POSTTRAUMATIC STRESS AND COMPLEX TRAUMATIC STRESS DISORDERS

Family members are deeply affected and family relationships tend to be profoundly altered when any family member experiences psychological trauma and develops posttraumatic stress disorder (PTSD; Schumm, Vranceanu, & Hobfoll, 2004; Smith & Fisher, 2008). It is stressful at best, and overwhelming and demoralizing at worst, to live with a family member who is troubled by and attempting to avoid feeling distress associated with memories or reminders of traumatic experiences. The impact of PTSD on the entire family, including earlier (e.g., parents, grandparents) and current (e.g., spouse/partners, siblings, children) generations, is profound and potentially debilitating. It is rare that a family member's PTSD (or resultant behavior) causes other family members to be "traumatized" themselves: Abuse or family violence is not caused by PTSD. However, the strain on family members who attempt to care for and cope with another member who, due to PTSD, interacts with intense and unpredictable hyperarousal or emotional numbing, detachment, and avoidance, can be substantial. The burden of caring for and witnessing the traumatic memories and reactions of a family member may cause adults or children in the family to feel significant distress and a sense of helplessness (i.e., vicarious traumatization; Pearlman & Caringi, Chapter 10, this volume).

The adverse effects of psychological trauma and traumatic stress disorders on the family are particularly profound when they result from abuse, abandonment by caregiver(s), severe neglect, domestic violence, or death or gruesome injury due to community violence, war, or terrorism. People in the same family often have different levels of actual or perceived exposure to traumatic events, and different types and degrees of traumatic stress problems (Saltzman, Babayon, Lester, Beardslee, & Pynoos, 2008). Family members' reactions to traumatic events also are influenced by risk and protective factors, including history of psychological trauma or loss; early life relationship with caregivers; psychological and behavioral problems, temperament, and intellectual functioning; and personality, social support, and community and family resources (Pat-Horenczyk, Rabinowitz, Rice, & Tucker-Levin, 2008). As a result, the family members to whom a traumatized person looks for help and protection when exposed to psychological trauma are likely to have different needs and courses of recovery, whether they were directly or indirectly affected by a psychological trauma (Layne et al., 2008). When these differences lead to dysynchrony in the nature and timing of posttraumatic reactions and recovery among family members, heightened levels of stress, discord, and alienation may occur within the family (Saltzman et al., in press) at a time when family cohesion is most needed by all affected family members (Hawkins & Manne, 2004).

If psychological trauma occurs as a result of the actions of a parent or caregiver(s), all family relationships may be altered, not just those with the offending or neglectful caregiver(s), as a result of the profound issues of trust, protection, and responsibility raised by intentional intrafamilial trauma (Courtois, 1988). Nonoffending caregiver(s) and other family members (e.g., siblings) may experience abuse or violence as psychologically traumatic because they are witnesses or collateral victims, or due to a sense of shock and vulnerability, or guilt, shame, and bereavement, as a result of having failed to prevent the traumatic events. Abuse perpetrated by persons outside the immediate family may lead children to feel isolated from or rejected by their family as a result of social stigma and a sense of helplessness (at times compounded by family members' reactions of denial or nonsupport), and caregivers and other family members may experience a sense of guilt, shame, and victimization (particularly if the perpetrator was a trusted individual, or if family members believe they should have known and prevented the abuse). If the psychological trauma involves family, family members (including children) often feel guilty for failing to prevent harm to caregiver(s) or other family members. All of these sequelae may be mediated by ethnic/cultural and other meanings systems (see L. S. Brown, Chapter 8, this volume).

Spousal relationships also are substantially impacted when either or both partners, or a child suffers traumatic stress problems. This in turn can reduce spouses' abilities to effectively support their children when traumatic stressors occur. Spousal relationships and parenting are crucial sources of support and recovery for every family member in the wake of exposure to psychological trauma. Conversely, when parents respond to the stress of a traumatic experience with hostility, anger, anxiety, and conflict, the family environment can exacerbate trauma-related symptoms for family members and for the family system. When a family encounters particularly severe stress (e.g., in a conflictual divorce or due to domestic violence), the risk for parenting practices to be negatively influenced by irritability, insensitivity, and harshness also is high. Additional factors (e.g., parental history of psychological trauma, or mental health or addiction problems) can exacerbate the disruption of parenting practices. Parental experience of traumatic stress symptoms tends to interfere with parents' ability to maintain family routines and roles (Jordan et al., 1992; Ruscio, Weathers, King, & King, 2002). Children depend on their parents to provide emotional support, role modeling, and physical safety and/ or security precisely by keeping family routines and roles intact. Thus, when parents experience traumatic stress symptoms, their children may have difficulty managing their own reactions to the traumatic stressors. This appears to be true not only for children directly victimized by a traumatic event but also for those who simply have been told about a family member's violent or traumatic experience (Saltzman et al., 2008). Parental withdrawal, overprotectiveness, or preoccupation with trauma are relational factors that may indirectly exacerbate a child's traumatic stress symptoms (Scheeringa et al., 2007). Meiser-Stedman, Yule, Dalgleish, Smith, and Glucksman (2006) found parental depression to be positively correlated with posttraumatic stress symptoms in their children.

A child's traumatic stress experiences or reactions also may be traumatic for the parents. Parents may develop posttraumatic stress symptoms based on their child's experiencing potentially traumatic stressors, regardless of whether the parents have been directly exposed to the traumatic event itself (Cohen, 2008). Psychological trauma affects the entire family system, potentially across many generations (Horenczyk et al., 2008). Children of traumatized parent(s) are at greater risk of developing PTSD or related psychological difficulties than other children if they are exposed to psychological trauma themselves (Brand, Engel, Canfield, & Yehuda, 2006). Evidence indicates that a risk factor for PTSD—reduced resting cortisol levels—may be transmitted genetically from mothers with terrorism-related PTSD to their 9-month-old babies (Brand et al., 2006).

On the positive side, family relationships also are indispensable to the traumatized person's recovery, because they simultaneously provide essential support for the restoration of emotional security, physical safety, and hope, and for the resumption of healthy growth and development in the wake of psychological trauma. Children, adolescents, and even adults often look to parents, siblings, and other adult relatives as a source of support during a variety of potentially traumatic situations, including life-threatening illness, unexpected loss of a loved one or close friend, violence in the family or community, and disasters and traumatic accidents. In these circumstances, children in families characterized by chaos, disorganization, anger, emotional detachment, anxiety, or depression are at increased risk of PTSD, whereas children in families that are cohesive, caring, and emotionally involved are more likely to recover (Saltzman et al., 2008).

EVIDENCE BASE FOR FAMILY THERAPY WITH PTSD AND COMPLEX TRAUMATIC STRESS DISORDERS

Meta-analytic studies have found family based treatments to be more effective than treatment as usual (TAU) and at least as successful as individual psychotherapies for a variety of psychological disorders (Diamond & Josephson, 2005). Couple therapy interventions based on behavioral (Rotunda, O'Farrell, Murphy, & Babey, 2008) or cognitive-behavioral (Monson, Schnurr, Stevens, & Guthrie, 2004) approaches to altering conflicted, avoidant, addictive (e.g., substance abuse) or nonsupportive interaction patterns have shown promise in pilot studies (i.e., no control group or comparison therapy) with military veterans with PTSD and their partners.

However, conjoint family therapy for the treatment of adults with PTSD (Lebow & Rekart, 2004; Walsh & Rothbaum, 2007) or disorders involving complex traumatic stress impairment (e.g., pathological psychoform or somatoform dissociation, affect dysregulation, or profound interpersonal and spiritual alienation) has not been studied scientifically. One randomized clinical trial (RCT) compared a low intensity (i.e., four to eight sessions over a 9- to 18-month period), family-based grief therapy to routine care with families of terminally ill adult patients. This family therapy had limited benefit and primarily only with "sullen" or "hostile" families (Kissane et al., 2006).

The strongest evidence for the efficacy of family therapy for traumatic stress disorders is provided by studies with families of traumatized toddlers and preschool- or early elementary school-age children of relational/psychodynamic (child–parent psychotherapy [CPP]; Van Horn & Lieberman, 2008) and cognitive-behavioral parent management therapy (parent–child interaction therapy [PCIT]; Eyberg & McDiarmid, 2005). Neither CPP nor PCIT was originally developed for traumatized children, but both have been used clinically with families of children who have been maltreated or exposed to traumatic violence. CPP guides the caregiver of a traumatized toddler or young child toward developmentally appropriate, responsive, and nurturing attitudes and behavior, while interacting with the child (Van Horn & Lieberman, 2008). In RCTs, CPP has been shown to be superior to case management plus TAU in achieving sustained reductions in PTSD symptoms and behavior problems in preschool children who witnessed domestic violence (Lieberman, Ghosh Ippen, & Van Horn, 2006; Lieberman, Van Horn, & Ghosh Ippen, 2005) and in enhancing the likelihood of secure attachment in the parent–child dyad and in maltreated toddlers' and preschoolers' beliefs about parents (Toth, Maughan, Manly, Spagnola, & Cicchetti, 2002). Other relationally focused family therapy models for incestuous (Giaretto, 1982; Maddock & Larson, 1995; Sheinberg & Fraenkel, 2001; Trepper & Barrett, 1989) or dissociative (Benjamin & Benjamin, 1992) families have shown promise clinically but not been validated in systematic research studies.

PCIT is a highly structured educational intervention in which parents are coached by the therapist, while they play with their child, to consistently reinforce prosocial behavior and to ignore aggressive, impulsive, or noncompliant behavior. One RCT showed that a modification of PCIT for low-income, physically abusive parents and their children was more effective than a parenting group in reducing harsh, punitive, and nonresponsive parent behaviors and preventing additional charges of abuse during the following 2–3 years. Evidence that PCIT may also reduce maltreated children's behavior problems and parenting stress was found in a quasi-experimental study (Timmer, Urquiza, Zebell, & McGrath, 2005), although maltreated children showed less favorable change than nonmaltreated children, and the parents frequently (64%) dropped out of therapy when behavior problems were severe. PCIT uniquely focuses on assisting abusive parents to reestablish healthy relationships with their children, whereas other approaches, such as CPP, are used primarily with nonoffending parents.

Brief family-based cognitive-behavioral therapies (CBTs) for families of adolescent survivors of cancer (Kazak et al., 2004) and young children newly diagnosed with cancer (Kazak et al., 2005) have been shown to be superior to routine palliative care in reducing some PTSD symptoms for adolescents and their fathers (but not their mothers), and anxiety and PTSD symptoms for both mothers and fathers of newly diagnosed pediatric cancer patients. The intervention called the Surviving Cancer Competently Intervention Program (SCCIP), involved a single day, with four sessions (both single-family and multifamily groups) for the adolescent survivors and their families, and three sessions in a single-family format for the families of newly diagnosed children with cancer.

CBTs for child and adolescent PTSD usually include a component involving parents or other adult caregivers (Stallard, 2006). For example, Kolko (1996) compared individual and family-based CBT to community-based services in work with physically abused children (ages 6–13 years). Individual CBT involved separate sessions for both parent and child, whereas family-based CBT included members of the entire family together. Community-based services involved education about parenting and homemaking skills provided in the home. Individual and family-based CBT resulted in more substantial reductions in PTSD, emotional and behavioral problems, and parent-to-child violence following therapy and at a 1-year follow-up assessment than did community services. The specific value of parental involvement was more clearly demonstrated by Deblinger, Lippmann, and Steer (1996), who found that involvement by the nonoffending mother in trauma-focused CBT was associated with greater reductions in PTSD symptoms among sexually abused children than when the parent was not directly included in the therapy. At 6- and 12-month follow-up assessments, not only the sexually abused children but also their adult caregivers reported substantially improved PTSD and depression symptoms following trauma-focused CBT, but not when only the child was treated with a supportive psychotherapy (Deblinger, Mannarino, Cohen, & Steer, 2006).

With the exception of CPP for traumatized young children and their caregivers, none of these approaches to family therapy was developed or adapted for complex traumatic stress disorders. The only outcome measure in CPP clinical trials that falls within the domain of complex traumatic stress disorders is toddlers' secure versus disorganized attachment. Perhaps the closest approximation to family therapy for complex traumatic stress disorders is an approach to marital and family therapy developed for borderline personality disorder (BPD) (Kreisman & Kreisman, 2004). The SET (support, empathy, truth) model of marital and family therapy for BPD is psychodynamically based. The therapist addresses the impact of emotion dysregulation, suicidal and other crises, and "acting-out" behavior on the spouse/partner and other family members, while assisting them and the identified patient in developing empathic understanding of each other and more honest supportive communication. However, neither the SET model nor any other family or couple therapy for BPD has been scientifically evaluated.

Although all of these family- or couple-based psychotherapies seek to improve the trust and communication between family members, only CPP, SCCIP, and the relational therapies for incestuous families explicitly use a family systems approach to treatment. CCP helps the caregiver and child experiment with new roles (e.g., the caregiver as facilitator and guide rather than disciplinarian or detached outsider) and perspectives on each other's thoughts and emotions (e.g., helping the caregiver to empathize with the child's developmentally appropriate fears and aspirations). SCCIP purposively "joins" with family members by aligning with their primary goals, and working toward developing ways that family members can mutually support one another.

FAMILY SYSTEMS MODELS:
DESCRIPTION AND APPLICATION
TO COMPLEX TRAUMATIC STRESS DISORDERS

Family systems approaches to psychotherapy aim not just to change individual family members but to restructure, rebuild, or restore healthy family relationships. Family therapy for PTSD has been described as aiming either to repair the family system or to enhance the available social support utilized by the family (Riggs, 2000). Family systems models attempt to facilitate the following features of family relationships related to cohesive, respectful, trustworthy, responsible, and caring communication and emotional connections: (1) the development of role expectations and behavioral "rules" that are explicit; (2) open and sensitive discussion of troubling past experiences ("myths" and "secrets"); (3) a balance of individuality and togetherness ("relational boundaries"); (4) strong but inclusive leadership by parents ("family hierarchy"); (5) respectful and affectionate approaches to communication; and (6) effective family problem solving.

Family Roles

A family member who is affectively dysregulated, dissociated, debilitated by persistent unexplained or treatment-refractory physical problems, emotionally detached or explosive, and psychologically and spiritually demoralized may take on roles in the family, such as a perpetually dependent "identified patient," the family "scapegoat," an unpredictably destructive "toxic" perpetrator, or an "invisible" outsider. Other family members often take on complementary roles, such as the "rescuer," who unsuccessfully attempts to "save" or "cure" the traumatized family member; the "enabler," who acquiesces to the troubled family member's anger, coercive demands, or impulsive behaviors; the "protector," who attempts to keep both the traumatized member and other family members from being harmed emotionally or otherwise by the traumatized member's behavior; or the "rock of strength," who tries to take care of everyone else's needs in the family. Such family roles are not explicitly defined or assigned, but generally are well known to all members and assumed to be immutable, because they rarely change and seem to be necessary to cope with family members' traumatic stress impairments.

Rules

As a counterpart to implicit family roles, family members develop unspoken expectations as a result of coping with persistent stress, turmoil, and disappointment associated with complex traumatic stress disorders. These implicit and pervasive expectations become fixed in the form of "rules" that make interactions predictable, albeit dissatisfying and demoralizing. Trauma-based "rules" might include "Don't have feelings," "Don't treat abuse as real," "Don't tell,"

"Whatever you do, don't upset [traumatized family member] or else he'll lose it and there will be hell to pay for all of us," "Other family members have to put their needs aside and do whatever [traumatized family member] needs or demands because she was abused," "He [traumatized family member] can't control the urges to [use substances, get in fights, do risky impulsive behaviors] because he has PTSD" or "She should just stop overreacting to everything, and grow up, and not be such a burden for all of us," and "We can't go out anywhere because he gets so upset that it ruins it for everyone" (see Courtois, 1988).

Family Myths and Secrets

Family roles and rules tend to be based on beliefs that have taken on the status of both *myth* (i.e., a putatively incontrovertible truth about the family or the traumatized member that has become an integral part of the "story" of the family or the person's history) and *secret* (i.e., something that one or several family members hide from other family members, often due to a sense of guilt, shame, or remorse, or due to fear or distrust concerning the reactions that would result should the secret be known). Complex trauma often leads to secrets (e.g., the very fact of abuse, or the identity of a perpetrator, may be hidden) and may also lead to a sense of betrayal, abandonment, or violation of trust that can result in family members' harboring other secrets (e.g., an extramarital affair in reaction to infidelity or violence by the spouse; "alliances" between a nonabusing parent and her children not to tell an abusive parent things that might lead to angry reprisals or further abuse). Secrecy may become a way of life for survivors of childhood developmental trauma, such that they keep innocuous, as well as very important, facts about themselves or others, or thoughts and feelings, hidden in their adult life.

Family Hierarchy and Relational Boundaries

Troubled families often are disorganized in terms of their intergenerational hierarchy (i.e., older generation(s) serving as role model(s) and leader(s) for subsequent generations) and boundaries in relationships (i.e., maintaining a balance between closeness in the emotional connections between family members, without extreme overinvolvement [enmeshment], and autonomy and self-determination for each individual, without emotional detachment by or rejection of any member). The distress associated with complex traumatic stress disorders may lead parents to act more like children and children to take on a pseudo-adult demeanor and sense of responsibility (the "parentified" child and role reversal). Sexual or physical abuse that occurs within the family involves a fundamental breakdown of family hierarchy and relational boundaries: Parent(s) are harming or failing to protect their children; children are forced to be too intimate with, and to distance and protect themselves against, the very people with whom they should be safest and emotionally close but not enmeshed.

Family Communication and Problem-Solving Styles

Families differ in the openness and flexibility (vs. rigidity), mutuality (vs. coercion and authoritarianism), and emotional responsivity (vs. detachment or rejection) of their styles of communicating and solving problems. Living with a complex traumatic stress disorder, whether one's own or that of a family member, tends to lead communication and problem solving to become rigid, coercive and controlling, and emotionally detached or rejecting, because these styles are adaptive in life and death emergencies, and developmental traumas can lead a child to adopt (or an adult to fall back upon) a mentality and coping style dominated by desperate attempts to survive, no matter what the cost.

EVIDENCE-INFORMED FAMILY THERAPY MODELS FOR COMPLEX TRAUMATIC STRESS DISORDERS

With the exception of CPP, no family therapy modality has been validated scientifically for the treatment of PTSD or complex traumatic stress disorders. Therefore, with very young traumatized children (i.e., infants, toddlers, preschoolers), CPP is the treatment of choice to reduce traumatic stress symptoms, and to enhance the parent–child relationship and the security of the child's attachment working models. There also is recent evidence to suggest that trauma-focused cognitive-behavioral therapy (TF-CBT) (Cohen, Mannarino, & Deblinger, 2006) may be feasible and beneficial with traumatized young children (Scheeringa et al., 2007).

PCIT has shown promise with abusive parents and their children, as has SCCIP with families in which a child has cancer. Both interventions emphasize structured behavioral skills to enhance parents' ability to be responsive to their child's emotions and to assist their child with behavioral problems (typically, anger, impulsivity, and oppositionality in PCIT, and a mix of less severe externalizing and internalizing [e.g., anxiety, isolation, regression] problems in SCCIP). SCCIP includes brief family engagement interventions, but PCIT does not. These family-based therapies may be useful on a selective basis with complex traumatic stress disorders.

A family-based therapeutic intervention integrating cognitive-behavioral therapy (CBT) and family systems therapy (FST) has been developed for adolescents with PTSD or complex traumatic stress disorders (Faust & Katchen, 2004), although this model has not been described in sufficient detail to be replicable or scientifically validated. Structural (Minuchin, 1974) and strategic (Madanes, 1990) variations of FST are utilized to help the entire family to identify and change problematic roles, rules, relational boundaries, and communication patterns. CBT with the traumatized child includes parental psychoeducation and *in vivo* fear reduction exercises. While described as applicable with "complicated posttraumatic stress reactions" (Faust & Katchen, 2004), CBT-FST appears to focus primarily on addressing PTSD symptoms.

Two recently developed models were designed to enhance family self-regulation as a treatment for complex traumatic stress disorders. Both models aim to shift family members' perspectives from blaming or excusing traumatized family members (the so-called "identified patient") to working together to improve every member's self-regulation and the family system's ability to react to internal and external stressors in a regulated rather than reactive manner.

FAMILY SYSTEMS TRAUMA AFFECT REGULATION: GUIDE FOR EDUCATION AND THERAPY (FS/TARGET)

A family systems adaptation of the self-regulation-based TARGET intervention for complex traumatic stress disorders (Ford & Russo, 2006) provides the entire family with psychoeducation about the biology of traumatic stress (and addiction, when applicable). FS/TARGET also teaches all family members a skills set for anticipating and managing stress reactions in ways that support both self-regulation by each member and the family's overall ability to develop roles, rules, boundaries, and communication and decision-making patterns that promote self-regulation.

FS/TARGET therapists address several key teaching points and therapeutic goals/challenges in every session to organize family systems intervention in a systematic manner paralleling the sequence of self-regulation components (the "FREEDOM steps") taught by TARGET.

1. *Focusing*: In addition to beginning, ending, and periodically interjecting into each session a brief exercise designed to enhance purposeful self-reflective attention (the "SOS" for "focusing"), the FS/TARGET therapist's first guiding question is: How does each family member achieve and sustain focused attention, and what are the specific verbal and nonverbal behavioral signs for each family member that distinguish between states of focused self-regulation and stress reactivity? To provide a strength-based model encouraging family members to view themselves and each other as capable of self-regulation and to support one another in doing so, FS/TARGET therapists observe and highlight for the family examples of each member being well regulated.

2. *Recognizing stress triggers*: FS/TARGET integrates the identification of specific cues that serve as "triggers" for family members' stress reactions (including all family members, not just the traumatized children). The multidimensional family therapy tenet of facilitating nonblaming and direct communication between all family members "in the moment" in each therapy session (Liddle, Rodriguez, Dakof, Kanzki, & Marvel, 2005) provides family members with a model and specific nonjudgmental language for being aware of, talking openly about, and being more sensitive to the precise cues that elicit stress reactions. Whereas a parent might describe "everything she does" as a "stress

trigger" when feeling angry, hurt, helpless, and confused by the behavior of an adolescent daughter, the therapist guides the parent toward recognizing specific nonverbal (e.g., a certain "look" or tone of voice) or verbal (e.g., certain words that connote a lack of respect or compliance) triggers. When each person's specific stress "triggers" are understood by all, family members can be helped to anticipate and prevent or manage trigger interactions, thereby shifting their view of each other from globally stress-inducing to understandably stress reactive.

3. *Identifying main Emotion states (and distinguishing these from reactive emotion states)*: To address the alternating extremes of emotional under- and overexpression that often characterize families with traumatized children, FS/TARGET engages all family members in a dialogue and learning process designed to enable them to distinguish between emotion states that are primarily a reflection of stress reactivity and those that are more grounded and grounding. Dysregulated emotion states involving either hyperarousal (e.g., rage, terror, disgust, contempt) or hypoarousal (e.g., guilt, despair, shame, dissociative emotional emptiness) are identified in family interactions, redefined as useful signals that triggers are occurring, and relabeled as specific emotions (instead of as global distress, hopelessness, helplessness, or annoyance). Family members are assisted in defining and recognizing nonreactive emotion states (i.e., not driven by a sense of unspoken threat), that instead are expressions of a sense of security, accomplishment, or positive anticipation (e.g., interest, excitement, happiness, love, pride, appreciation, dedication). This shift is described as focusing on "main" (i.e., core) rather than "reactive" (i.e., stress-based) emotions.

4. *Evaluating thoughts to identify main thoughts versus reactive thoughts*: Building on the distinction between "stress reactive" and core ("main") emotions, family members are assisted in cataloguing the thoughts that are driven by stress reactivity (i.e., a sense that something is wrong and must be fixed, stopped, or prevented) and recognizing or creating alternative or "reframed" thoughts that express their "main" (or core) beliefs, values, and hopes, and that enable them to shift from reactive to "main" emotion states. Rather than challenging the reactive thoughts as irrational or inappropriate, the potentially adaptive aspects of these thoughts are explored and used as the kernels from which to build or identify "main" thoughts that preserve the person's core ideas, beliefs, hopes, or intentions but reduce the reflexive, threat-based, inflexible, and impulsive quality of the original "reactive" thoughts. In so doing, the therapist is family members' role model for how cognitively to contain and reshape extreme emotions and thoughts, while using the sense of being "focused" as their shared goal (rather than seeking to reject or eliminate "dysfunctional" emotions or thoughts).

5. *Defining main goals (and distinguishing these from reactive goals)*: Extending the stress-reactive versus self-regulated ("main") emotions and thoughts to goals, FS/TARGET engages family members in a reexamination of their personal and collective goals to ensure that the goals reflect their core

priorities. Goals based on stress reactivity are examined and validated as adaptive if traumatic events occur, and the core goal(s) embedded in reactive goals are highlighted. Borrowing from multidimensional family therapy (Liddle et al., 2005), FS/TARGET therapists define therapeutic goals for each session in a behaviorally specific manner (e.g., What is specifically different for each client at the end of this session that reflects enhanced self-regulation?).

6. *Options for small positive steps toward the immediate main goal*: Again borrowing from multidimensional family therapy (Liddle et al., 2005), the FS/TARGET therapist helps family members to identify behaviorally specific actions they can take or paradigm shifts in their intentions or interpretations that provide each of them with a greater range of helpful emotions or behavioral choices (e.g., What goals are blocked or unrealized by current patterns of behavior or family interaction? What change does each client want, and how can he or she take a small but personally meaningful [to other family members as well as to him or her] behavioral or mental step toward that change?).

7. *Making a contribution*: How can family members recognize that by managing stress reactions in a self-regulated manner, they provide irreplaceable instrumental and moral support to every other family member, and often to other persons as well? It is crucial that children and parents recognize that they can be positive contributors to their family simply by handling stress reactivity in ways that increase the safety, trust, security, and hopefulness of other family members, and that parent(s) realize that they are "the medicine" (Liddle et al., 2005) when they assist their children in learning to self-regulate by serving as role models for self-regulation in the face of stressors.

Simulated Case Vignette Transcript

To illustrate application of FS/TARGET to the treatment of youth with complex traumatic stress disorders, the following simulated case vignette provides a sample of interventions with a single mother, her 15-year-old daughter from a prior relationship, and her 4- and 8-year-old daughter and son from a more recent relationship that ended 6 months earlier, when the older daughter (M) reported an incident of physical assault by her stepfather. M was described by her mother as oppositional defiant at home since the age of 11. M accused her stepfather of emotional and sexual abuse at that age, but her mother had attributed the behavior to M's "jealousy" toward her stepbrother and stepsister. M was born out of wedlock when her mother was 16 years old, and both lived with the maternal grandparents (with the truth of M's parentage kept hidden) until her mother left home to marry M's stepfather, when M was 6 years old, and brought the child with her. When therapy began, M's mother had called the police numerous times because M had stolen from her, was associating with friends who used drugs, were several years older, and had dropped out of high school. Placement in a foster home was being recommended by the juvenile probation and child protective services professionals working with the family, because there had been no improvement in M's "beyond parental control" behavior, and M's mother was fearful that M would get pregnant and run away to live with one of the young men with whom she associated.

After six initial assessment and stabilization sessions in which the therapist helped M and her mother to reframe their conflicts as mutually escalating stress reactivity, several altercations occurred between M and her mother, with the mother calling the police and M being arrested and placed in a juvenile detention facility. The following excerpts are from the next conjoint session:

THERAPIST: I'm glad to see you again after what I'm sure has been a stressful period for all of you.

MOTHER: (*Sighs, looks at* M *with a combination of annoyance and resignation.*) I don't think my daughter really wants to be a part of this family. She just wants her own way.

M: (*Looks off into space with no expression, then looks down at her hands.*)

THERAPIST: I can see that you're each in a reactive state, so we need to deal with the triggers for each of you right now to help you get back in focus. (*turning to the younger children*) How about if you two help us by showing us how you are good at being really focused with the books and art stuff over on this table? Could you do that? That's great, we need you to just have fun and be really focused on whatever you like there, while your mom and M and I have a talk to help them get focused, too. So we'll all work on being focused, and we'll check in with you, so you two can show us how you do it, OK? (*Turns back to the mother, while* M *intently watches her younger brother and sister play.*) I can see how much you want M to be a part of this family, but I think your stress alarm is keeping you stuck in reactive feelings and thoughts. I can understand why you might be feeling very reactive, as a parent who loves your daughter and wants her to be safe and happy, and also not to make mistakes like ones that you feel you made at her age. Even though you're certainly feeling some reactive feelings, including maybe feeling hurt or worried when you think that M isn't going to be safe or be a part of the family, would it be fair to say that love and hope for M are your main feelings underneath? It must be hard to get to those main feelings, and main thoughts like what you value about M and your relationship with her, when you're having these understandably strong reactions.

MOTHER: Well, wouldn't any parent feel like this if she had a daughter who was disrespectful and selfish? She *is* making the same mistakes I made, and she's just as pig-headed as I was when I thought I knew everything as a teenager. Look what happened to me!

THERAPIST: You want M to be open-minded and thoughtful about her choices, not stubbornly or impulsively doing things that aren't really what she wants or needs. Sounds like that's not easy for you to do, either, even now, so maybe it's more that you and M both are very strong willed and emotionally intense, and that can look "pig-headed" or impulsive, but it's really just needing not to be controlled by your stress reactions. And you're working very hard to stay focused on making a good life for yourself and your children. As a single, working mother, that's a lot of stress—especially when you had to choose to protect your children instead of staying in your marriage—that took a lot of courage and a real focus on doing the right thing.

MOTHER: I know I should have ended that relationship a long time ago, when M said he was being abusive, but I just didn't know what to do or who to believe. (M *looks up intently at her mother.*) I never wanted my daughter or any of my children hurt, but I didn't know it was so bad, until the time when I left M with him while the kids and I visited my family. As soon as M told me what happened, I said that's it, enough, he's out. I won't let anyone hurt my daughter. (*Looks tearfully at* M.) I wish she could stop being angry at me and accept that I really love her and will do whatever it takes so she's OK.

THERAPIST: (*turning to M, who looks down and away again after a pause*) Is it a trigger for you when your mom says things that might sound like she thinks you're the problem and maybe doesn't want you to be in this family? I'm not hearing your mom saying that exactly, but that could be what you're hearing now—or what you might have felt for a long time if you didn't know how to get your mom to understand how bad things were.

M: (*Pauses, looks intently at her mother, who has her eyes closed, then looks down, nods yes.*)

THERAPIST: (*Turns to the younger children, who have stopped their previously active play and are looking wide-eyed at their mother and sister.*) Well this is some important stuff we're talking about, and I see that you two want to be sure that it all gets worked out OK. I'll make sure your mom and sister figure out how to make this OK, if you could just help by showing us how to focus again. That's what I'm doing with your mom and sister, but since you two already are very good at focusing, it would be a very big help if you remind us how to be focused. You should focus on stuff that you like, like those books and toys and drawing, and that will help us focus really well on the talking we're doing. How does that sound, is that a good plan, Mom? (*Mother refocuses on the younger children, smiles, and nods yes.*) Great, thanks, you guys, for being such a good help to us by showing us how you focus. (*The younger children smile and resume play.*) So I think maybe some of those really bad times are still bothering each of you, and you haven't known how to get your focus, together as well as individually, back on your main feelings and thoughts and goals. There are two ways to do that: One is to take some time, not a lot, but some sessions, and just deal with the triggers and reactive emotions and thoughts that didn't get dealt with entirely in past stressful situations. I can help you do that in a way that is hard work but doesn't dredge up all the old stuff—just the specific triggers and reactions that you don't want to be bothered by all the time now. I can do that privately with each of you and both of you together, but we'll need to do that when the younger kids aren't here, because it's really adult or young-adult talk and not something that they are old enough to be involved in. Is that something you'd each be willing to do with me, maybe in some sessions in the next several weeks?

MOTHER AND M: (*Silently look pensive, then sigh and look accepting, and nod yes.*)

THERAPIST: OK, the other way we can do right now, while you're both more focused than you were when we started—did you notice that? (*Pauses.*) You're both very good at getting focused when you just do an SOS—slow your thoughts down, get oriented to what's really important to you, and then start thinking or doing things that give you more personal control— and I see the younger kids are very good at focusing in their own way, too. (*Everyone looks over at the younger children, who are playing happily and intently.*) So what we can do to help you both deal with the triggers and reactive feelings and thoughts that are coming between you is to talk about a recent situation where you lost your focus, but we need to focus on figuring out the specific triggers right then for each of you, and how you tried to keep your focus, so you can do that again and maybe be able to succeed a little better in keeping your focus when something similar happens.

M: OK, how about the argument that happened between us last night, when M took my phone and then wouldn't admit it. After I told her I couldn't trust her if she kept doing that, she turned around and didn't get up to go to school this morning. How about that?

THERAPIST: (*Turns to M*) OK if we talk about that? Here are the ground rules: We're not just going to focus on what you did or didn't do. We'll include that, but we're also going to talk about how your mom got triggered and what she did or didn't do to be focused. The goal is for each of you to be able to keep your focus better, not to blame or punish anyone.

M: (*Looks at her mother, smiles.*) That would be different. I usually get blamed and punished.

MOTHER: (*Looks affronted, turns to the therapist, who calmly gives her a look of curious interest.*) I think a parent has to hold her daughter responsible and set limits. I don't call that blame and punishment. Am I supposed to just give up and let her do anything?

THERAPIST: You each make a good point. So it's important to M not to be blamed or punished, and it's important to Mom to be able to expect responsible behavior and set some limits. Those are good "main" goals, except M, I think that tells us more about what you don't want than what you do want in your relationship with your mom. If she isn't blaming or punishing you, do you just want her to let you do anything and totally leave you alone?

M: Sometimes, yes. (*Turns to Mom, smiles.*) But no, not really. I know I can't just do what I want all the time and I need to be responsible, but I try to do that and she doesn't notice except when she gets stressed out, and then I'm always the one she blames.

THERAPIST: So what's your main goal in your relationship with your mom and your life; what do you want her to do, and what do you want for yourself?

M: (*Pauses.*) I just want her to notice when I do good things, and not send me away. (*tears*)

MOTHER: (*tears*) That's what I want, too, really. I never want you to go away, and I know I need to be better at noticing what you do that's good, so you know I think you're great and I love you. I just get so stressed and worried. ... I know I shouldn't have such high expectations for M. I do want her to be able to be a girl and not have to be an adult and miss out on all the fun and freedom of being a teenager, but these days that seems to mean doing things that kids never would have dreamed of when I was that age—smoking marijuana, staying out to all hours, having a car of her own. It's just not what I think is right—it's really dangerous for her because the drug use gets her depressed.

THERAPIST: Let's just slow down and take a moment to get focused, Mom. M seems very focused and is listening very carefully, so it's important that she hears your "main" feelings and goals right now, and that you do, too. The reactive feelings and thoughts are important, but we don't want them to take your focus away from what you really feel and want.

MOTHER: (*after an extended pause*) OK, you're right, it's just hard. M always thinks very deeply about things, and she says she understands why I worry, but that I should trust her and that I shouldn't try to keep her a child when she needs to grow up and be her own person. She's like me in that way; she wants her mom to trust her. And I want to, but I'm afraid I've failed her and, because of that, she's going to shut me out and just do whatever she wants—or thinks she has to—like I did when I was her age.

THERAPIST: So things happened to you when you were M's age or younger that made you feel unsafe or unprotected, and you shut people out and just did what you felt you had to.

MOTHER: (*Looks down, tearful.*) It's not something I talk about, and it was different back then. The expectations were different and some things could happen that you had to just keep secret. I thought I'd dealt with all that, and I don't want M to have that happen.

THERAPIST: Sometimes feelings from bad experiences can get triggered even if you've tried to put the memories behind you, and if that interferes with your focus when you really want to do the right thing—as a parent, or as a 15-year-old—and when you don't want it to turn into a conflict or hurt someone you care about, whether you're the daughter or the mother, then you may have dealt with it very well but just did not quite finish by putting it all into focus so you know how to deal with triggers when they come up again now. I think that's what comes between you both now, more than anything else. M, do you sometimes have feelings or even memories that are from the past but all of a sudden can really bother you now? Maybe that's when you do things like taking stuff from your mom, which you know you shouldn't, and don't even really want, but those feelings can just take your focus away and you're not really choosing you're just reacting.

M: (*crying softly*) All the time, every day. I don't know why I do things like that when I really don't want to. I just feel like I have to do it, and I do. That's not really what I'm like. I'm not really a liar or a thief, but I just stop thinking and feeling when I do that.

THERAPIST: So even though you two are very different in some important ways, you share an ability not to just think but to care very deeply, and to know that those you love always are with you and won't let you down. We can work on that, if it makes sense to both of you that the challenge is to focus on what turns on your inner stress alarms, and deal with that, so you can be focused the way you want and really are capable of. That won't change everything, but it might give you back your most valuable resource: your ability to use your mind to focus, to make good decisions, and to feel good even when you're stressed.

Summary

In FS/TARGET, family members together learn skills for self-regulation. By identifying both types of functioning—the "reactive" and the "main" (regulated)—in therapeutic interactions and in daily experiences, FS/TARGET helps family members see that they have a shared and solvable challenge—to regain or maintain self-regulation—rather than separate, intractable dilemmas. FS/TARGET can include trauma memory reconstruction (as illustrated by preparatory comments by the therapist in the vignette), but the emphasis is on helping all family members use the FREEDOM foci to reexamine current and past experiences reflectively in a manner that models, provides guided practice, and leads to shifts in affective state that reinforce all family members' increasing commitment to achieve self-regulation.

FAMILIES OVERCOMING AND COPING UNDER STRESS (FOCUS)

The FOCUS program is unique in providing a structured approach for delivering trauma-focused family therapy that is at once rich with detail and therapeutic activities, and sufficiently flexible to accommodate families of different ethnicity and culture who present with various levels of need and traumatic stress disorder severity. A number of individual and family assessment measures are administered initially and throughout the treatment to monitor ongoing trauma and loss exposure; symptoms of posttraumatic distress; depression and anxiety; functional impairment; and family cohesion, support, and communication. These assessments help to specify the sequence and number of sessions needed to accomplish the program goals.

FOCUS is generally delivered over eight sessions: the first three sessions with the parent(s), the fourth and fifth sessions with the children, and the last three sessions with the entire family. The FOCUS program is not intended for crisis intervention and should be applied after acute stabilization has taken place. For example, in the case of medical, disaster, or other acute traumas, initial outreach is provided to the family in the hospital, and arrangements are made to meet after the immediate medical crisis has been resolved and ongoing or rehabilitative treatment is in place.

The FOCUS program aims to improve child outcomes (reducing posttraumatic stress, anxiety, and depression symptoms, while improving functioning in key domains) by targeting key intermediate outcomes, both familial (improve family communication and cohesion) and parental (improve communication and support between parents, facilitate consistent care routines and parenting practices, and maintain developmentally appropriate expectations for child reactivity and recovery). The model underlying this intervention, an integration of psychoeducational, narrative, and cognitive-behavioral theory, builds on previous research that demonstrates the potential of improving child adjustment by increasing family coping skills, promoting positive parenting skills, enhancing parent–child communication, and reducing parental emotional distress.

The FOCUS intervention is based on the earlier UCLA Trauma/Grief Program, which has been shown to reduce primary trauma-related symptoms and improve school and interpersonal functioning among participants (Saltzman et al., 2008). The FOCUS model also incorporates elements of an intervention for families with parental depression, which has shown both short- and long-term effectiveness in changing attitudes, behaviors, and interactions, and in reducing the long-term risk of mental health problems among children (Beardslee, Gladstone, Wright, & Cooper, 2003). The FOCUS model also incorporates portions of an intervention for HIV-affected mothers and their children, which has demonstrated improvements in emotional and behavioral adjustment and sustained, long-term improvements in key functional domains (Rotheram-Borus, Lee, & Lester, 2004). FOCUS has several core therapeutic elements: (1) psychoeducation regarding psychological trauma and developmentally appropriate expectations for children and adolescents, (2) enhancement of individual and family coping skills, and (3) development and sharing of individual and family psychological trauma narrative time lines.

Psychoeducation

Prior studies have shown that trauma-focused psychoeducation including information about expected reactions to trauma and course of recovery, when linked to coping skills enhancement, can help to ameliorate posttraumatic symptomatology in adolescents (Saltzman, Pynoos, Layne, Steinberg, & Aisenberg, 2001). In the current program, psychoeducation is provided separately and collectively to parents, children, and the family as a whole. Psychoeducation regarding trauma and loss is woven throughout all of the sessions in the guise of factual information, feedback from assessments, and activities designed to heighten personal and interpersonal awareness. Feedback is provided from initial and ongoing assessments of trauma history, symptoms, and functional indices for individual family members, along with measures of overall family functioning. Information on expected reactions to trauma based on age and developmental level is then customized to the family's specific symptom and functional profile, and prioritization of current concerns. Family members and the therapist then draw upon this information to craft family goals collaboratively. The therapist helps parents understand how family traumas or loss and parental distress may be linked to breakdowns in family cohesion, communication, care routines, and key parenting activities. On the positive side, family strengths, adaptive coping responses, and available resources are highlighted.

Individual and Family Coping Skills

The FOCUS program is designed to identify and build on the strengths and adaptive coping strategies already present in the family. It starts by helping the parents and the family identify and prioritize current concerns, difficulties, and situations that evoke trauma-related reactions in one or more family member. Families then explore what they do individually and collectively to help themselves feel better and function better. This discussion begins an ongoing dialogue in which family members report on difficulties and trauma or loss reminders encountered during the week, and how they coped with them. The clinician also offers them new coping strategies to add to their existing "toolkit," such as relaxation and breathing techniques, communication and interpersonal awareness skills, cognitive techniques designed to interrupt distorted and harmful ways of thinking, and problem-solving strategies. Skills are learned in sessions and practiced in homework. Individual skills, built in an incremental fashion, focus first on monitoring and articulation of feeling states, on identifying the internal and external "triggers" or reminders that contribute to these changes, then on selecting one or more behavioral responses or strategies to deal productively with the distress.

Individual and Family Trauma Narrative Time Lines

Perhaps the most novel element of the FOCUS program is having individual family members develop their own narratives of trauma or loss events and share them with the rest of the family through a graphic "time line." This exercise is important, because family members usually have different levels of exposure and experiences in traumatic events. This is true even if family members were all present during the same distressing events. Individual discrepancies are based on differences in proximity and perceived threat, prior trauma and loss history, comorbid psychopathology, and gender and personality characteristics. These differences can be extreme when one family member has had severe trauma exposure (e.g., parental experience of combat trauma, or a child's experience of sexual or physical abuse).

As a result of their different experiences and reactions, family members typically have very different psychological needs and courses of recovery. These differences may lead to increased family conflict, decreased empathy and understanding between family members, and decreased family support and tolerance. This becomes especially problematic, because most families do not have in place mechanisms of discourse that permit open discussion and acknowledgment of these differences. In many cases, family members frame their silence as a way of protecting each other from worry or from what they perceive as an additional burden on family members who already are under duress. This was the case for a mother of a 16-year-old boy whose friend was shot while standing next to him at a bus stop after school. The boy and his family did not understand why their mother became increasingly anxious and depressed over the months following the incident, nor why she could not get out of bed and demanded to know her son's whereabouts at all times. During a family session 6 months after the shooting, the mother revealed that before she was married, she was standing next to her uncle when he was shot and killed during an armed robbery in a small downtown store. She had never told her husband or family about this experience and was insistent that she should not do so even now, when the memory and related fears were activated by her son's similar experience. Clearly, it was very important that the mother understand how her previous trauma heightened her reactions in the current case, and equally important that her family make sense of her seemingly extreme reactions, and be supportive of her very different course and timetable for recovery. Mutual understanding and appreciation of differences can reduce family stress, increase support, and foster individual and family recovery. As illustrated in the case example, only by bringing these discrepant experiences and reactions to family members' attention in an appropriate manner can the family resources be enlisted fully in the tasks of support and recovery.

To provide a safe and structured means for family members to develop and share their personal narratives within the family and, ultimately, to develop a consensual "family narrative" of the traumatic event(s), guidelines are developed for eliciting these narratives from children and adults. To facilitate the sharing and contrasting of experiences, a graphic approach using a "narrative time line" is developed. Parents and children (generally age 10 and older) are shown how to graph out their single or multiple trauma and loss experiences via a chart that shows time on the horizontal axis and intensity of distress on the vertical axis. Once instructed, clients are usually able to map their experiences on the time line themselves. Younger children are directed to use art and drawing to convey their experiences and to assemble their narrative on a game board that tracks chronology via a colorful and winding path. Parental narratives are elicited during the first "parents only" sessions. In most cases, a parent learns new aspects of his or her partner's objective and subjective experience from the narratives. It can also be helpful to use the narrative time line to track prior trauma and loss experiences that the parent or family has encountered. Helping parents appreciate the cumulative load of multiple or repeated stressful experiences can enhance understanding of the individual and family reactions to the current traumas. For example, in working with a family that had lost a daughter in a car accident, it was pivotal to track the prior experiences of both parents, who had endured serial hardships and traumatic events their country of origin, El Salvador, during the civil war, and during the course of their immigration to the United States.

During the latter parts of the parental sessions, the clinician focuses on the ways that differences in parental experiences and reactions, and subsequent misunderstandings, may contribute to current difficulties and breakdowns in marital communication and parenting tasks. In fact, by maintaining the primary focus on the family and on the children's welfare rather than on marital issues, parents are much more open and willing to engage in the therapeutic work. It is also important to spend time preparing the parents for the family sessions. This involves clarifying which portions of the parental narratives should be shared with the children, how to respond appropriately to children's questions and concerns, and how to take a leadership role in the family sessions via good listening and supportive engagement. Child narratives are elicited during the following two sessions by incorporating art and play activities to provide developmentally appropriate means of representing the children's experience. In preparation for the family sessions, children are helped to identify the specific concerns and questions they want to discuss at that time.

The final sessions of the program are family meetings. After a summary of the major family traumatic events, usually provided by the clinician, the children are invited to share their narratives. The parents then comment and contrast their experiences of the same events. Later sessions are dedicated to discussing significant differences among family members regarding their experiences, perceptions, attributions, and reactions. As appropriate, any misattributions or distortions identified during the sharing of narratives, especially those regarding issues of blame, guilt, or shame, need to be addressed by the family. Structured activities are then used to help the family develop a consensual family narrative, and "healing theory" about the traumatic events (Figley, 1989). The final session is devoted to identifying, prioritizing, and engaging in family problem solving for current difficulties, and plans for upcoming and continuing family stressors.

CONCLUSION

Family-based and family systems models for treating complex stress disorders are still in the formative stage of development, with much room for innovation and a substantial need for scientific testing and validation (Walsh & Rothbaum, 2007). However, family-based therapeutic interventions (and couple therapy; Johnson & Courtois, Chapter 18, this volume) provide a unique way to address both the self-regulation (e.g., FS/TARGET) and trauma memory reconstruction (e.g., FOCUS) goals of recovery from complex traumatic stress disorders, while drawing upon, and enhancing, the ameliorative resources of the traumatized person's family and the traumatized family's internal and external support systems.

REFERENCES

Beardslee, W. R., Gladstone, T. R. G., Wright, E. J., & Cooper, A. B. (2003). A family-based approach to the prevention of depressive symptoms in children at risk: Evidence of parental and child change. *Pediatrics, 112,* e119–e1310.

Benjamin, L., & Benjamin, R. (1990). An overview of family treatment in dissociative disorders. *Dissociation, 5,* 236–241.

Brand, S., Engel, S., Canfield, R., & Yehuda, R. (2006). The effect of maternal PTSD following *in utero* trauma exposure on behavior and temperament in the 9-month-old infant. *Annals of the New York Academy of Sciences, 1071,* 454–458.

Cohen, E. (2008). Parenting in the throes of traumatic events: Risks and protection. In D. Brom, R. Pat-Horenczyk & J. D. Ford (Eds.), *Treating traumatized children: Risk, resilience, and recovery* (pp. 72–84). London: Routledge.

Cohen, J. A., Mannarino, A. P., & Deblinger, E. (2006). *Treating trauma and traumatic grief in children and adolescents.* New York: Guilford Press.

Courtois, C. A. (1988). *Healing the incest wound: Adult survivors in treatment.* New York: Norton.

Deblinger, E., Lippmann, J., & Steer, R. (1996). Sexually abused children suffering posttraumatic stress symptoms: Initial treatment outcome findings. *Child Maltreatment, 1,* 310–321.

Deblinger, E., Mannarino, A., Cohen, J., & Steer, R. (2006). A follow-up study of a multisite, randomized, controlled trial for children with sexual abuse-related PTSD symptoms. *Journal of the American Academy of Child and Adolescent Psychiatry, 45,* 1474–1484.

Diamond, G., & Josephson, A. (2005). Family-based treatment research: A 10-year update. *Journal of the American Academy of Child and Adolescent Psychiatry, 44*(9), 872–887.

Eyberg, S. M., & McDiarmid, M. D. (2005). Parent–child interaction therapy. In A. M. Gross & R. S. Drabman (Eds.), *Encyclopedia of behavior modification and cognitive-behavior therapy* (Vol. 2, pp. 940–944). Thousand Oaks, CA: Sage.

Faust, J., & Katchen, L. B. (2004). Treatment of children with complicated posttraumatic stress reactions. *Psychotherapy: Theory, Research, Practice and Training, 41,* 426–437.

Figley, C. R. (1989). *Helping traumatized families.* San Francisco: Jossey-Bass.

Ford, J. D., & Russo, E. (2006). A trauma-focused, present-centered, emotional self-regulation approach to integrated treatment for post-traumatic stress and addiction. *American Journal of Psychotherapy, 60,* 335–355.

Giaretto, H. (1982). *Integrated treatment of child sexual abuse.* Palo Alto, CA: Science & Behavior.

Hawkins, S., & Manne, S. (2004). Family support in the aftermath of trauma. In D. R. Catherall (Ed.), *Handbook of stress, trauma and the family* (pp. 231–260). New York: Brunner/Routledge.

Jordan, B. K., Marmar, C. R., Fairbank, J. A., Schlenger, W. E., Kulka, R. A., Hough, R. L., et al. (1992). Problems in families of male Vietnam veterans with posttraumatic stress disorder. *Journal of Consulting and Clinical Psychology, 60,* 916–926.

Kazak, A., Alderfer, M., Streisand, R., Simms, S., Rourke, M., Barakat, L., et al. (2004). Treatment of posttraumatic stress symptoms in adolescent survivors of childhood cancer and their families. *Journal of Family Psychology, 18,* 493–504.

Kazak, A., Simms, S., Alderfer, M., Rourke, M., Crump, T., McClure, K., et al. (2005). Feasibility and preliminary outcomes from a pilot study of a brief psychological intervention for families of children newly diagnosed with cancer. *Journal of Pediatric Psychology, 30,* 644–655.

Kissane, D., McKenzie, M., Bloch, S., Moskowitz, C., McKenzie, D., & O'Neill, I. (2006). Family-focused grief therapy. *American Journal of Psychiatry, 163,* 1208–1218.

Kolko, D. J. (1996). Clinical monitoring of treatment course in child physical abuse: Psychometric characteristics and treatment comparisons. *Child Abuse and Neglect, 20*(1), 23–43.

Kreisman, J., & Kreisman, J. (2004). Marital and family treatment of borderline personality disorder. In M. McFarlane (Ed.), *Family treatment of personality disorders* (pp. 117–148). Binghamton, NY: Haworth Press.

Layne, C. M., Beck, C., Rimmasch, H., Southwick, J., Moreno, M., & Hobfoll, S. (2008). Promoting "resilient" posttraumatic adjustment in childhood and beyond. In D. Brom, R. Pat-Horenczyk, & J. D. Ford (Eds.), *Treating traumatized children: Risk, resilience, and recovery* (pp. 13–47). London: Routledge.

Lebow, J., & Rekart, K. N. (2004). Research assessing couple and family therapies for posttraumatic stress disorder. In D. R. Catherall (Ed.), *Handbook of stress, trauma and the family* (pp. 261–279). New York: Brunner/Routledge.

Liddle, H. A., Rodriguez, R. A., Dakof, G. A., Kanzki, E., & Marvel, F. A. (2005). Multi-dimensional family therapy. In J. Lebow (Ed.), *Handbook of clinical family therapy* (pp. 128–163). New York: Wiley.

Lieberman, A. F., Ghosh Ippen, C., & Van Horn, P. (2006). Child–parent psychotherapy. *Journal of the American Academy of Child and Adolescent Psychiatry, 45,* 913–918.

Lieberman, A. F., Van Horn, P., & Ghosh Ippen, C. (2005). Toward evidence-based treatment: Child–parent psychotherapy with preschoolers exposed to marital violence. *Journal of American Academy of Child and Adolescent Psychiatry, 44,* 1241–1248.

Madanes, C. (1990). *Sex, love, and violence.* New York: Norton.

Maddock, J. W., & Larson, N. R. (1995). *Incestuous families.* New York: Norton.

Meiser-Stedman, R. A., Yule, W., Dalgleish, T., Smith, P., & Glucksman, E. (2006). The role of the family in child and adolescent posttraumatic stress following attendance at an emergency department. *Journal of Pediatric Psychology, 31,* 397–402.

Minuchin, S. (1974). *Families and family therapy.* Cambridge, MA: Harvard University Press.

Monson, C., Schnurr, P., Stevens, S., & Guthrie, K. (2004). Cognitive-behavioral couple's treatment for posttraumatic stress disorder: Initial findings. *Journal of Traumatic Stress, 17,* 341–344.

Pat-Horenczyk, R., Rabinowitz, M., Rice, A., & Tucker-Levin, A. (2008). The search for risk and protective factors in childhood PTSD. In D. Brom, R. Pat-Horenczyk, & J. D. Ford (Eds.), *Treating traumatized children: Risk, resilience, and recovery* (pp. 51–71). London: Routledge.

Riggs, D. S. (2000). Marital and family therapy. In E. B. Foa, T. M. Keane, & M. J. Friedman (Eds.), *Effective treatments for PTSD: Practice guidelines from the*

International Society for Traumatic Stress Studies (pp. 280–301). New York: Guilford Press.

Rotheram-Borus, M. J., Lee, M., & Lester, P. (2004). Six year intervention outcomes for adolescent children of parents with HIV. *Archives of Pediatrics and Adolescent Medicine, 158,* 742–748.

Rotunda, R., O'Farrell, T., Murphy, M., & Babey, S. (2008). Behavioral couples therapy for comorbid substance use disorders and combat-related posttraumatic stress disorder among male veterans: An initial evaluation. *Addictive Behaviors, 33,* 180–187.

Ruscio, A. M., Weathers, F. W., King, L. A., & King, D. W. (2002). Male war-zone veterans' perceived relationships with their children. *Journal of Traumatic Stress, 15,* 351–357.

Saltzman, W. R., Babayon, M., Lester, P., Beardslee, W., & Pynoos R. S. (2008). Family-based treatments for child traumatic stress: A review and current innovations. In D. Brom, R. Pat-Horenczyk, & J. D. Ford (Eds.), *Treating traumatized children: Risk, resilience, and recovery* (pp. 240–254). London: Routledge.

Scheeringa, M. S., Salloum, A., Armberger, R., Weems, C., Amaya-Jackson, L., & Cohen, J. (2007). Feasibility and effectiveness of cognitive-behavioral therapy for posttraumatic stress disorder in preschool children. *Journal of Traumatic Stress, 20,* 631–636.

Schumm, J. A., Vranceanu, A., & Hobfoll, S. E. (2004). The ties that bind. In D. R. Catherall (Ed.), *Handbook of stress, trauma and the family* (pp. 33–50). New York: Brunner/Routledge.

Sheinberg, M., & Fraenkel, P. (2001). *The relational trauma of incest: A family-based approach to treatment.* New York: Guilford Press.

Smith, D. K., & Fisher, P. (2008). Family systems. In G. Reyes, J. D. Elhai, & J. D. Ford (Eds.), *Encyclopedia of psychological trauma* (pp. 277–278). Hoboken, NJ: Wiley.

Stallard, P. (2006). Psychological interventions for post-traumatic reactions in children and young people: A review of randomised controlled trials. *Clinical Psychology Review, 26,* 895–911.

Timmer, S. G., Urquiza, A. J., Zebell, N. M., & McGrath, J. M. (2005). Parent–child interaction therapy: Application to maltreating parent–child dyads. *Child Abuse and Neglect, 29,* 825–842.

Toth, S. L., Maughan, A., Manly, J. T., Spagnola, M., & Cicchetti, D. (2002). The relative efficacy of two interventions in altering maltreated preschool children's representation models: Implications for attachment theory. *Development and Psychopathology, 14,* 877–908.

Trepper, T., & Barrett, M. (1989). *Systemic treatment of incest.* New York: Brunner/Routledge.

Van Horn, P., & Lieberman, A. (2008). Using dyadic therapies to treat traumatized children. In D. Brom, R. Pat-Horenczyk, & J. D. Ford (Eds.), *Treating traumatized children: Risk, resilience, and recovery* (pp. 210–224). London: Routledge.

Walsh, S. S., & Rothbaum, B. O. (2007). Emerging treatments for PTSD. In M. J. Friedman, T. M. Keane, & P. A. Resick (Eds.), *Handbook of PTSD: Science and practice* (pp. 469–496). New York: Guilford Press.

CHAPTER 20

Group Therapy

Julian D. Ford
Roger D. Fallot
Maxine Harris

The experience of clinical practitioners and trauma survivors over the past 50 years or more indicates that many of the potentially therapeutic factors identified with group therapy for a variety of psychiatric and psychosocial disorders (Yalom & Leszcz, 1995) are applicable to traumatic stress disorders. On a practical level, group therapy is more efficient and can be offered more broadly than individual psychotherapy, a fact that is financially relevant in the increasingly cost-sensitive fiscal climate of managed health care. With the parallel increase in awareness and identification of complex traumatic stress disorders and the role of psychological or developmental trauma in the etiology and course of many psychiatric disorders, group therapy is a practical way to provide traumatic stress interventions to large numbers of trauma survivors.

Group therapy offers a direct antidote to the isolation and social disengagement that characterize posttraumatic stress disorder (PTSD) and complex traumatic stress disorders. Being in a group in which safety, respect, honesty, privacy, and dedication to recovery are the norm provides unique opportunities for trauma survivors to see and hear, and to be seen and heard by, other persons who also struggle (albeit each in their own unique way) with the anxiety, fear, shame, guilt, alienation, loneliness, and a sense of powerlessness and of being permanently damaged that is profoundly demoralizing and isolating for many trauma survivors (Courtois, 1988; Mendelsohn, Zachary, & Harney, 2007). In group therapy, it is possible to find one's authentic voice and reclaim one's memories and sense of self, as well as to discover a peer group that is supportive and nonexploitive. These crucial features of psychological and interpersonal growth, individuation, and bonding often have been lost, stunted, or have never developed as a result of growing up in physically and psychologically dangerous circumstances (e.g., abuse, violence, loss).

Group therapy provides additional opportunities for learning that experiences of many trauma survivors have been denied as a result of having been exposed to developmentally adverse interpersonal trauma (Ford, Courtois, van der Hart, Nijenhuis, & Steele, 2005). Group therapy members experience a range of emotions, and receive guidance and role modeling in identifying, differentiating, labeling, and modulating these emotions from group facilitators and other group members. Lack of emotion regulation skills and basic knowledge about how emotions work, and how they can be usefully managed, are critical deficits for many persons with complex traumatic stress disorders (Courtois, 1988; Ford et al., 2005). Skills for modulating bodily arousal that have been compromised in complex traumatic stress disorders may be addressed in group therapy processing and experiential exercises, in which members share experiences that alternate between creative self-expression and grounding or centering themselves. Group therapy also provides education about, and opportunities to observe and practice, several other social-cognitive skills that often are either not in the repertoires of persons with traumatic stress disorders or not accessible to them when experiencing traumatic stress reactions (e.g., problem solving, assertive communication, active listening).

Group therapy also provides a forum for education about topics that often are assumed to be understood but actually are rarely well explained. Trauma survivors may know that PTSD is a disorder that they "have," but not know the specific symptoms that constitute PTSD (or trauma-related disssociative, somatoform, anxiety, mood, or personality disorders), and why symptoms develop and persist in the wake of psychological trauma. They may assume that no one else has similar confusing or troubling bodily reactions, emotions, thoughts, and behavioral impulses and inhibitions. They may also think that these symptoms reflect a deficiency or illness rather than being the product of expectable and relatively automatic biopsychosocial attempts to survive extreme threat that were adaptive in traumatic experiences but do not adapt well to ordinary life.

The interpersonal dynamics in group therapy often bring to the fore complex relational dilemmas with which members have struggled for much of their lives and that are exacerbated by experiences of developmental trauma. Both anxiety-based and more primal "selfobject"-related transference enactments (Kohut & Wolf, 1978) often occur in the group therapy process; the latter particularly occur with participants who present with characterological problems associated with personality disorder diagnoses and developmental trauma-related complex traumatic stress disorders (Grossmark, 2007). For example, a profound sense of abandonment and betrayal by parents and family members may be enacted in dramatic interactions in which the "protagonist" unconsciously relates toward group leaders and members as if they were the fantasized versions of those key people. Sarol-Kulka (2001) described how these often initially unpredictable and chaotic selfobject transference enactments tend not only to override the classic progression of group process (which she observed in group therapy with "neurotic" participants) but also lead to opportunities for therapeutic reflection and the reparation of psychic wounds over many group sessions. Consistent with these observations, Whewell, Lingam, and Chilton (2004) observed the development of intense and rapidly shifting emotional connections and disconnections among and by members with the leader of an empathically and psychodynamically oriented psychoeducational "reflective borderline group therapy." Whewell and colleagues reported evidence of reductions in self-reported interpersonal sensitivity, affectively triggered impulsivity, and hostility by participants who attended a 20-session cycle of this group therapy.

RESEARCH ON GROUP PSYCHOTHERAPY AND PSYCHOEDUCATION WITH TRAUMA SURVIVORS

Group psychotherapy and psychoeducation are widely used with adults, adolescents, and children who have been exposed to psychological trauma and are experiencing posttraumatic distress (Kanas, 2005; Ready & Shea, 2008). Group therapy also is used in the treatment of individuals with complex traumatic stress disorders in the aftermath of childhood maltreatment and trauma (Lundqvist, Svedin, Hansson, & Broman, 2006; Najavits, Gallop, & Weiss, 2006), childhood (DeRosa & Pelcovitz, 2008; Kagan, 2008; Saltzman, Layne, Steinberg, & Pynoos, 2006) and adult exposure to domestic or community violence (Fallot & Harris, 2002; Mendelsohn et al., 2007; Morrissey et al., 2005), traumatic military service (Ford & Stewart, 1999), and civilian exposure to disaster, terrorism, war, genocide, or torture (Blackwell, 2005; Raphael & Wooding, 2006). Group therapy for traumatic stress disorders has been used in both inpatient and outpatient settings.

Despite the breadth of its application to traumatic stress reactions and disorders, group treatment for trauma survivors has not been extensively evaluated in rigorous randomized clinical trial (RCT) research, and the scientific evidence of its efficacy is limited but growing (Committee on Treatment of Posttraumatic Stress Disorder, 2007). With adults, outcomes of group therapy for PTSD have been reported in studies with civilian survivors of childhood abuse; with multiply traumatized women, with concurrent chronic mental illness, experience of domestic violence, rape, traumatic accidents, and traumatic bereavement; and with military veterans.

With women survivors of childhood sexual abuse (who often present with chronic complex traumatic stress symptoms), outcomes of group therapy provided in either extended (e.g., 46 sessions over a 2-year period; Lundqvist et al., 2006) or brief (e.g., 12–15 weekly sessions) (Wallis, 2002; Wolfsdorf & Zlotnick, 2001), have been reported for several theoretical models. Psychodynamic (Lundqvist et al., 2006), supportive (Classen, Koopman, Nevill-Manning, & Spiegel, 2001; Talbot et al., 1998; Wallis, 2002), affect management (Frisman, Ford, Mallon, Lin, & Chang, in press; Wolfsdorf & Zlotnick, 2001), or trauma memory disclosure (Classen et al., 2001; Lubin & Johnson, 2008; Lubin, Lori, Burt, & Johnson, 1998) group therapy approaches have been shown to be associated with improved functioning and adaptation, with follow-up assessments as long as 2 years after completing group therapy. One RCT compared supportive ("present-focused") and memory processing ("trauma-focused") group modalities to a wait list and found both group modalities to be associated with reductions in self-reported dissociative and sexual symptoms, vindictiveness, and nonassertiveness, as well as with less risk of being revictimized (38 vs. 67%; Classen et al., 2001). Another study that compared 10 sessions of individual or group psychotherapy in women who had experienced childhood sexual abuse found group and individual therapy to be associated with comparable benefits; however, half of the women sought additional treatment during the study, suggesting that neither therapy fully addressed their needs (Stalker & Fry, 1999). Three studies showed psychodynamic (Lundqvist et al., 2006) and supportive (Morgan & Cummings, 1999) therapies to be associated with symptomatic and functional improvements in women with histories of childhood sexual abuse, and adults with histories of other types of psychological trauma (Wallis, 2002). With HIV-positive men and women, group therapy focused on coping skills and resources was associated with self-reported improvements in traumatic stress and behavioral problems (Sikkema et al., 2004). With incarcerated women, group therapy based on dialectical behavior therapy (Jackson, Nissenson, & Cloitre, Chapter 12, this volume) was associated with self-reported improvements in PTSD and depression symptoms, and reduced interpersonal problems compared to a treatment as usual (TAU) cohort—although 45% of the group participants dropped out, compared to 28% of the controls (Bradley & Follingstad, 2003).

With adult civilian survivors of violence, group therapy is widely used but infrequently evaluated scientifically. Two models for group therapy for women with co-occurring disorders—Seeking Safety for co-occurring substance use disorders (SUDs) and PTSD (Najavits, 2002) and the Trauma Recovery and Empowerment Model (TREM), originally for co-occurring severe mental disorders and PTSD (Fallot & Harris, 2002)—have been found to be associated with symptom reductions and improved psychosocial functioning. Seeking Safety been found to be efficacious in randomized trials in women with co-occurring PTSD and SUD (Hien, Cohen, Miele, Litt, & Capstick, 2004), and with adolescent girls with PTSD (Najavits et al., 2006), but the intervention was delivered as an individual therapy and not as a group therapy in those studies.

In women who were sexually assaulted as adults, a specialized, brief cognitive-behavioral group therapy for insomnia associated with PTSD, imagery rehearsal therapy (IRT), has been found to be more effective than a waitlist condition in reducing nightmare frequency and PTSD symptom severity (Krakow, Hollifield, et al., 2001). IRT was associated with similar outcomes and reduced sleep impairment, anxiety, and depression, and increased sleep quality in an open-trial study of adult crime victims with PTSD (including a small subsample of men; Krakow, Johnston, et al., 2001). More recently, an open trial of IRT with 11 Iraq-deployed U.S. Army combat soldiers, who had experienced a traumatic event and related nightmares within the past month, demonstrated substantial reductions in nightmare frequency, PTSD symptoms, and overall distress in 64% of the participants (Moore & Krakow, 2007). An independent replication with an adaptation of IRT, which includes systematic trauma memory Exposure work (using nightmares as the focus), Rescripting of nightmares, and Relaxation Training for sleep hygiene (ERRT; Davis & Wright, 2007), found that after a three-session intervention, adult survivors of traumatic accidents and assaults reported reduced PTSD and depression symptoms and fear of sleep, and improved sleep compared to a randomized control group that reported no changes. At a 6-month follow-up. 84% of the treatment completers reported no nightmares in the past week.

Although clinical models have been described for group therapy with disaster or terrorism survivors, no empirical outcome studies have been reported (Foy & Schrock, 2006).

With military veterans diagnosed with chronic PTSD, Schnurr and colleagues (2003) conducted a large ($N = 360$) RCT comparing 35 sessions, conducted over a year-long period, of a group version of exposure therapy and a supportive "present-centered" group therapy. The two models were equally effective in reducing PTSD symptom severity, although only 38% of participants reported as much as 15–20% improvement, and most still met criteria for severe PTSD after therapy. The exposure-based group therapy had a higher dropout rate during weekly treatment phase (23%) than present-centered therapy (13%). Ready and colleagues (2008) modified exposure-based group therapy to provide more opportunities therapeutically for participants to recall traumatic memories, both at home and in group sessions. In a field trial with 102 male veterans, clinically significant reductions in PTSD symptoms occurred (based on both therapist and patient reports) and were sustained, with few therapy dropouts.

With children and adolescents, outcomes of group therapy for trauma survivors have been reported in a variety of populations and settings. A school-based weekly, 10-session cognitive-behavioral group therapy (cognitive-behavioral intervention for traumatized students, or CBITS) was shown in an RCT to result in more improvement in PTSD and depression symptoms and social functioning than a wait-list condition with inner-city sixth graders (Stein et al., 2003). The group included psychoeducation about PTSD; teaching and practice of coping and self-management skills; and a brief, structured retelling of trauma memories. A briefer (eight-session) bilingual adaptation of CBITS was well accepted by school personnel and students, and achieved comparable reductions in PTSD and depression symptoms with third- to eighth-grade inner-city Latino children (Kataoka et al., 2003).

Deblinger, Stauffer and Steer (2001) reported that cognitive-behavioral groups were more efficacious than supportive therapy groups in an RCT in reducing sexually abused girls' intrusive reexperiencing symptoms and their mothers' negative reactions to the abuse. Twelve published nonexperimental studies of group therapy in girls with histories of sexual abuse have shown evidence of increased self-esteem and active coping, and reduced anxiety and depression when the focus was on skills for safety and interpersonal effectiveness, and cognitive reappraisal, or on client-centered or psychodrama methods (Avinger & Jones, 2007), but mixed success with conduct problems (see Tourigny, Hebert, Daigneault, & Simoneau, 2005, for positive results) and less success than individual therapy (Trowell et al., 2002).

CLINICAL PARAMETERS FOR GROUP THERAPY WITH COMPLEX TRAUMATIC STRESS DISORDERS

As described earlier, several approaches to group therapy for adults with chronic or complex traumatic stress disorders or similar conditions (e.g., complicated bereavement) have shown promise, with no clear evidence favoring any modality. As we illustrate in the group therapy transcript below, most modalities provide psychoeducation, support, cognitive-behavioral therapy (e.g., reframing, examining fixed beliefs, developing helpful self-talk), and narrative therapies (e.g., examining connections between traumatic past events and current distress or dissociation, and between current and past ways of coping, in discussion or journal writing).

Groups may have an "interpretive" psychodynamic focus (Piper, Ogrodniczuk, Joyce, Weideman, & Rosie, 2007), but more commonly, group therapy for complex traumatic stress disorders tends to take a supportive (e.g., Piper et al., 2007) or "process" (Alexander, Neimeyer, Follette, Moore, & Harter, 1989) or combination (education and process; e.g., Lubin et al., 1998; Whewell et al., 2004) approach, which provides group members with specific information, validation for their feelings, assistance in reflecting on and reframing thoughts and beliefs (e.g., schemas about self and others), and encouragement to consider alternative behavioral choices that may be especially beneficial for people with developmentally adverse interpersonal trauma histories (Courtois, 1988), because it explicitly focuses on strengths and solutions. This approach includes the development of a support system within the context of the group (based on the development or the refinement of interpersonal skills—especially important with individuals who have been misused extensively by others and are extremely mistrustful of others—rather than on the kinds of deficits or defenses that often are exploited and accentuated when a person is victimized by abuse or violence). One study with trauma survivors demonstrated that a supportive/process approach was particularly beneficial for patients with prior therapy experience (Follette, Alexander, & Follette, 1991). When traumatic bereavement is an issue, mutual support also appears to be particularly important (Marmar, Horowitz, Weiss, Wilner, & Kaltreider, 1988).

Although there is no clear and firm determination of whether to encourage explicitly the retelling of specific memories of psychological traumas in group therapy, or how to structure this to be optimally beneficial without iatrogenic reactions (not only for the discloser but also for group members who may experience traumatic stress as a result of other members' intense disclosures), some approaches include it as a mandatory part of the treatment and offer a method for distress modulation and containment (e.g., Lubin et al., 1998; Ready et al., 2008). Lubin and colleagues' (1998) novel approach also includes a "public testimony" component as part of "graduation" from group, in which group members describe memories of psychological trauma to selected friends and family members whose role is to acknowledge these experiences nonjudgmentally and express their unconditional acceptance of the survivor on both a personal basis and more broadly and symbolically, as stand-ins for society at large. This intervention is designed to enable group members to rejoin their community psychologically, with the explicit acceptance of others whom members might otherwise fear would blame, disbelieve, or discount them or their past traumatic experiences. Alternatively, the exposure-based group therapy developed by Ready and Shea (2008) provides, in a different manner, repeated opportunities for group members to develop a sense of confidence in their own ability to recall and make sense of traumatic memories, and in other persons' (i.e., group leaders and members) ability to hear these memories supportively.

Schnurr and colleagues (2003) found that including "exposure" therapy in groups was *not* more effective, and led to higher dropout rates than a here-and-now, focused problem-solving approach. More recently, in military groups with PTSD, Ready and colleagues (2008) reported greater success with exposure therapy that included more preparation and support for between-session practice, so the jury is still out about how and with whom to incorporate intensive trauma memory retelling into group psychotherapy. Trauma survivors consistently affirm the importance of being able to find "my voice" and tell "my story" in a respectful and validating peer group, as a source of internal clarity, hope, and empowerment, as well as belongingness and worthiness to be accepted by other people (Fallot & Harris, 2002; Mendelsohn et al., 2007). Therefore, the opportunity to disclose and to reflect carefully on key memories (including but not limited to traumatic experiences), and to support other group members in doing so, is likely to be of benefit to group members if they can do so without a sense of being too overwhelmed or too out of control to recover with the support of the therapist and the group. This approach may be seen as a group adaptation of graduated exposure that follows from safety, skills building, and cognitive reframing, and that specifically builds in the support of other group members as a major component of narrative development and emotional processing.

As illustrated in the transcript below, several potential approaches help participants "titrate" the emotional intensity of group participation. One method explicitly models and teaches emotion regulation skills (e.g., Bradley & Follingstad, 2003; Ford & Russo, 2006; Wolfsdorf & Zlotnick, 2001), beginning in the stabilization phase of therapy and continuing through the second phase of memory work (Ford et al., 2005). Another method embeds memory work in a context of building a complete personal life story or narrative that includes but is not limited to traumatic experiences (Fallot & Harris, 2002; Ford & Russo, 2006; Lubin & Johnson, 2008; Mendelsohn et al., 2007). A third approach that provides a detailed structure for memory work includes sufficient practice in and outside of group sessions to permit members to experience a sense of mastery of previously avoided anxiety or fear (Ready et al., 2008) as well as of grief and shame (Ford & Russo, 2006).

The severely dysregulated trauma survivor is a particular challenge for group therapy. In supportive or interpretive groups for adults with traumatic grief (Piper et al., 2007) or interpersonal therapy groups for women with chronic PTSD secondary to childhood abuse (Cloitre & Koenen, 2001; Courtois, 1988), the presence of a group member with poor object relations or borderline personality disorder (BPD) (especially uncontrolled reactivity and aggression) has been shown to be associated with diminished outcomes for *all* group members. In addition, Cloitre and Koenen (2001) noted an "anger contagion" phenomenon, whereby *all* members of groups with a member diagnosed with BPD reported increased anger following the group therapy. These findings are consistent with those of Follette and colleagues (1991), who reported that women with sexual abuse histories who had experienced more severe molestation, or had higher initial levels of psychological distress or depression, had poorer outcomes than other participants in both supportive open-format groups and in structured dyadic discussion groups. Therefore, pretreatment modalities might be of benefit to individuals who have difficulty with group interaction. It is also necessary to consider that group participation is not possible for some developmental trauma survivors who may have difficulty because they feel overstimulated and dysregulated in social groups or when listening to and experiencing the emotions associated with other trauma survivors' distressing recent or past experiences. These individuals may only be able to tolerate individual treatment, at least initially and possibly permanently, and might find even a very affectively contained form of individual therapy overwhelming, unless their information load and affective intensity in therapy is carefully titrated by the therapist (e.g., empathic validation; using a relatively affectively neutral approach of a primarily educational and/or supportive intervention).

These are indirect indices of severity of traumatic stress–related dysregulation but, along with the finding that women with lower education also responded less favorably, the results suggest that women who have difficulty with psychosocial self-regulation may require particular therapeutic attention in group therapy. Whether this is the case for men is not clear, because only the Piper and colleagues (2007) study included men, and they represented only 21% of the participants. However, results of a study of intensive residential treatment (primarily group therapy) for chronic PTSD with male military veterans, consistent with this view, indicated that those with poorer object relations had a poorer treatment response and dropped out more often (Ford, Fisher, & Larson, 1997). To the extent that confrontational or conflict/arousal-evoking interventions are used (e.g., "interpretive" therapy; Piper et al., 2007), a group composed of members with uniformly high levels of object relations and emotion regulation abilities appears indicated, regardless of gender.

Group psychotherapy is not recommended as a primary treatment modality for patients with severe dissociative symptoms or dissociative disorders (International Society for the Study of Trauma and Dissociation [ISSD], 2005, p. 111). However, there is no evidence that these are negative prognostic factors for group therapy engagement, retention, or therapeutic response (Ford & Stewart, 1999; Lundqvist et al., 2006). Group therapy is considered an indicated intervention for many persons with dissociative disorders (including dissociative identity disorder [DID]; ISSD, 2005) if the affective intensity of group processing and participant disclosures is carefully titrated by the leader(s). Classen and colleagues (2001) found that both memory processing and a present-centered approaches to group therapy with women survivors of childhood sexual abuse were associated with improvements in dissociation, as did Wolfsdorf and Zlotnick (2001) in their affect management group therapy.

Keys to effective engagement and alliance formation/maintenance in group interventions with severely dissociative participants include (1) knowing how to identify subtle as well as obvious, instances of dissociative alterations in personality and awareness (Steele & van der Hart, Chapter 7, this volume); (2) skill in "grounding" participants when they or other group members are significantly dissociating (e.g., sensorimotor strategies; Fisher & Ogden, Chapter 15, this volume); and (3) the ability to "gently confront" dissociative defenses (Scott, 1999, p. 35) and acknowledge rather than challenge dissociated parts of the self if these structural splits emerge (e.g., in the form of dissociative flashbacks or intrusive memories, as well as in more obvious [e.g., DID "alters"] shifts in self-state; Steele & van der Hart, Chapter 7, and Schwartz, Schwartz, & Galperin, Chapter 17, this volume).

Group members with co-occurring SUDs or severe mental illness (SMI) also may experience periods of behavioral, emotional, or interpersonal dysregulation and crises (i.e., relapse, suicide attempt, self-injury) that pose threats to their safety and are stressful for other group members. An integrated rather than fragmented approach to treatment and care coordination is essential in these cases, as is illustrated by the findings of the Women, Co-Occurring Disorders, and Violence multisite study, in which participants reported greater benefits following comprehensive, integrated, trauma-informed service interventions (e.g., TREM, Seeking Safety, Addiction and Trauma Recovery Integration [ATRIUM], and similar models; Veysey & Clark, 2004) than when core services were delivered in separate interventions or by several providers (Morrissey et al., 2005).

The integration of clinician guidance and peer support in group therapy may be especially challenging when participants are deeply distrustful of persons who have roles of authority and as caregivers (Courtois, 1988) and whose attachment styles are insecure and/or dysregulated. This is likely to be especially true for those participants who also long to be rescued by idealized, powerful individuals and relieved of the burden of responsibility of having been placed in a parentified role in relationship to caregivers and other victims (e.g., their siblings), or those who never expect consistent support from others. Working through the complex emotional dilemmas and tragedies associated with having experienced betrayal, abandonment, or rejection as the result of maltreatment, violence, or neglect can be either overwhelming or therapeutic for group members, depending on the therapist's ability to titrate the intensity for each member.

THE TRAUMA RECOVERY AND EMPOWERMENT MODEL

The TREM (Fallot & Harris, 2002; Harris, 1998) approach to group therapy is an integrative model that was originally designed for and by women (and later adapted for men) with chronic traumatic stress, and comorbid psychiatric and substance abuse problems. TREM utilizes a combination of therapeutic methods derived from interpersonal, relational, client-centered, cognitive-behavioral, and psychodynamic models, including (1) psychoeducation about psychological trauma, PTSD, and recovery from complex trauma sequelae; (2) teaching of skills for cognitive reappraisal, self-efficacy, mood and arousal regulation, and interpersonal effectiveness; (3) mobilizing peer validation and support; and (4) assisting clients in developing an understanding of their lives to foster hope and change. The TREM model (see Table 20.1) for group treatment of persons with complex traumatic stress disorders is illustrated in the following composite transcript based on several TREM groups.

TREM Group Therapy Transcript

"Feeling Out of Control" is the topic addressed in the fifth (and final) TREM session that deals specifically with ways to manage what feel like "out of control" traumatic stress symptoms. In this session the focus is on helping women to identify and learn strategies for coping with intense feelings that threaten to overwhelm and disorganize their capacities for self-regulation.

The session begins with an acknowledgment by the leader of the challenges that arose and the strengths that group members displayed in the last session. The leader also encourages members to identify positive reactions, so they will feel ready to master this week's topic.

LEADER 1: Welcome back, everyone. I'm glad to see that everyone made it back this week. I know that last week's session was difficult, and I think the group did some great work tackling the issues of blame and forgiveness. Does anyone have thoughts about those issues or any experiences during the week where that work was especially relevant or helpful?

TABLE 20.1. Trauma Recovery and Empowerment Model (TREM) for Group Therapy

TREM core assumptions

- Some current difficulties may have originated as legitimate, even courageous, coping responses to traumatic events.
- Repeated childhood trauma deprives women of the opportunity to develop certain life skills.
- Trauma severs connections to one's family, one's community, and oneself.
- Women who have been abused repeatedly feel powerless and unable to advocate for themselves.

TREM group content

- Twenty-nine sessions—each with specific topic, goals, and guiding questions
- Four main parts of the intervention
- Part One: Empowerment (9 sessions)
- Part Two: Trauma Recovery (10 sessions)
- Part Three: Advanced Trauma Recovery Issues (8 sessions)
- Part Four: Closing Rituals (2 sessions)

TREM group structure

- Eight to 10 group members with histories of physical and/or sexual abuse
- Two or three women coleaders
- Weekly 75-minute sessions
- Maximally inclusive: women diagnosed with severe mental disorders, substance use disorders, co-occurring disorders
- Wide range of settings (mental health, substance abuse, criminal justice, domestic violence, homeless shelters, other social services)
- Typically offered as part of a comprehensive system of care, but can stand alone

TREM trauma recovery skills

- Self-awareness
- Self-protection
- Self-soothing
- Emotional modulation
- Relational mutuality
- Accurate labeling of self and others
- Sense of agency and initiative taking
- Consistent problem solving
- Reliable parenting
- Possessing a sense of purpose and meaning
- Judgment and decision making

Group members are assisted in recognizing and accepting powerful feelings that have been intensified by trauma experiences to enable them to move in the direction of acquiring a sense of mastery and control of their emotions rather than feeling overwhelmed by them. The leader asks questions to engage group members immediately in the discussion and to help them to identify and accurately label their emotions, and to begin healthy problem solving by also identifying the triggers for and the consequences of stress reactions.

LEADER 2: Today we are going to be talking about feeling out of control, but we're not going to stop there. We're going to help each other come up with some healthy ways to cope when we are confronted with those all-too-familiar feelings of being overwhelmed. This topic is especially important for trauma survivors, because traumatic stress can lead people to go through their lives feeling right on the edge of an emotional meltdown. Sometimes it seems as if even the smallest event can send us over the edge. When trauma first occurs, feeling flooded and overwhelmed by feelings that are unmanageable or even impossible to comprehend is natural. Now, in today's life, we need a way to understand and manage those feelings when they arise, so that we can get on with things we want to do in our lives. What are your feelings when you're really stressed?

PARTICIPANT 1: I never feel happy, just frustrated or bored. Then, when I'm stressed, it gets really bad and I feel like I'm going crazy, like I just can't take it.

PARTICIPANT 2: Sometimes I feel at the end of my rope, too, but I have noticed that since I've been coming to these sessions, I've felt happy once in a while. It never lasts, though.

PARTICIPANT 3: You have to have something to feel happy about before you're gonna feel happy. I feel lonely most of the time, because people don't want to be around me. I'm a downer.

LEADER 2: It's pretty easy to focus on unpleasant feelings and doubt that positive feelings, like being happy or feeling loved or liked, are possible or can last. When you've experienced trauma and losses and disappointments, negative feelings are your body and mind's way of trying to protect you, to keep you from getting hurt again. Positive feelings can seem very scary, because it's hard to trust that something bad won't happen if you let yourself feel good.

PARTICIPANT 2: Exactly. I feel safer feeling bad. When I start feeling happy, I get scared, like I don't deserve to feel good and I'm going to be punished or laughed at or made fun of.

PARTICIPANT 3: Yeah, I'd rather be lonely than let anyone hurt me more. I guess that's my way of protecting myself. If I'm a real downer, people leave me alone, or if I get suicidal, then they have to take care of me even if they wish I'd just drop dead and stop bothering them.

LEADER 1: Trauma makes feelings really hard to trust, because people have been untrustworthy, and that can make you unsafe or really hurt. Trauma also makes feelings seem like there's nothing you can do to control them. You just have to put up with them, even if you don't really want to feel bad. We can't make unpleasant feelings just disappear, but would you be interested in learning some ways that you can have some say about your feelings, so they don't get out of control and leave you feeling overwhelmed and powerless? That would be a good way to get out of the trap that trauma creates, where you feel powerless. If you can have some control of how strong your feelings are, that would be a real strength, a way to have some power.

PARTICIPANT 2: I don't really believe that's possible, but I'd like to hear about it. My feelings just run my life, especially when they get overwhelming. I wish I could have some control of them.

The leader builds on this initial discussion by providing a rationale for the session that continues the theme of trauma education. Group members are given an understanding of where these powerful feelings may have begun that does not leave them with the sense that the feelings are somehow their fault, or that they are bad people because they cannot control their emotions. They are also given a rationale for their paradoxical feelings (e.g., "I feel safer feeling bad" or "I can't accept good feelings because I don't trust that they will last"). The rationale also alerts members that this session will not be a chance to dwell on or relive powerful negative feelings; instead, it will be an opportunity for focusing on present-day strategies for recognizing feelings before they get out of control, and for managing out of control feelings.

LEADER 2: OK, let's start then with the first step in being able to keep emotions from getting out of control. It isn't by trying to get rid of or ignoring your feelings, although that often is what people try to do. (*Several group members nod knowingly.*) Let's try a better way. Let's be like emotion detectives and look for clues that can help us figure out why emotions get out of control, and what we can do to stop that. So tell me, what does being out of control feel like for you?

PARTICIPANT 1: What are you talking about, it feels like being out of control, crazy, you know.

LEADER 1: Be more specific: How does your body feel when your feelings are out of control?

PARTICIPANT 1: My whole body changes. I feel hot and tingly all over.

PARTICIPANT 2: I know what you mean. I'm like a volcano that is just ready to blow.

PARTICIPANT 3: For me, it's like an energy rush. Everything inside is racing at maximum speed.

LEADER 2: Can you say more about that, because I think those images are real important.

PARTICIPANT 3: Well, it's just like I said. I can't slow down, but it's all on the inside.

LEADER 2: Great—that's a wonderful distinction!

PARTICIPANT 1: I can relate. I'm exploding inside. I just have to punch something, or cut myself.

PARTICIPANT 4: I'm just the opposite. When I'm out of control, I just shut down; I go on remote.

PARTICIPANT 5: For me, it's all about anger. I feel just full of rage and I know if I had a gun or something, I would just want to blow somebody's head off, and sometimes it don't really matter who it is. Just whoever gets in my way. You better not be in my way when I'm like that.

PARTICIPANT 6: I hear that. Don't be asking me for a cigarette when I'm feeling uptight, because I just might bite your head off. Especially if you're a man, oh my!

LEADER 2: (*following some general laughter from the group*) You can see how intense these feelings sometimes are. This ties in with what we talked about last week—self-destructive behaviors. Anger can feel so overwhelming that you're tempted to do something you might regret.

The leader reminds members that this current discussion ties in with what they discussed previously. Such integrative comments emphasize that this intervention builds on past learning. Each session does not stand alone, and connecting ideas from different sessions provide a model for making mental connections that help group members to develop this skill.

LEADER 2: Other reactions to feeling out of control that any of you have experienced?

PARTICIPANT 7: I just think I am going crazy and nobody understands me. Which really is true.

PARTICIPANT 8: I just feel scared, and then I want to give up, because I think, "What's the use?"

LEADER 1: These are all important responses, and before we move on to the next question, I want to take a minute and look at all the different ways you can feel out of control. Some people talked about how their bodies felt, hot or numb. For others, out of control was more of an emotion, like being scared or angry. And for some others it came in the form of an idea, like "I'm crazy" or "Nobody understands me." Being out of control can be felt in your body, in your emotions, and even in the beliefs you have about yourself. It's important to understand how being out of control feels for you personally, because you might try one way to cope, if your body is affected, and another way, if it's your beliefs that seem to be running away.

LEADER 2: So what happens when you're feeling out of control, if you don't just stop and shut down, or punch something or cut yourself?

PARTICIPANT 2: You *don't* want to know. She just gets so mad and hopeless that she'll take it out on somebody, or so depressed that she wants to kill herself. That's what *I* do if I can't let it out when I feel that worked up. Then I don't feel anything anymore, like I empty my insides out.

PARTICIPANT 4: Yeah, I don't want anyone else to get hurt like I have. I'd rather just go away.

PARTICIPANT 5: I'll get revenge if they do me wrong. That makes me feel better. They deserve it. I don't go looking for trouble, but if you bring it to me, then we're going the whole distance.

The leader identifies a constructive theme in these intense statements: Rather than a focus on the defensive anger, the focus is on the desire for justice and to prevent harm.

LEADER 2: So each of you actually is thinking and working really hard to contain that inner explosion, and you're looking for a way to vent that won't hurt anyone except you, or the wall, or someone who has hurt you. You're working very hard to make things fair and protect innocent people from harm. Have I got that right? Is that true for other group members, too, maybe in different ways? Are you looking for a way to release the pressure inside without hurting anyone else who doesn't deserve it—even if you hurt yourself or get yourself in trouble?

PARTICIPANT 6: I never thought about it that way. Sounds too good to be true. I'm not that good.

LEADER 1: You sure? We're not giving out gold stars, just trying to understand things as they really are. As we've discussed, trauma leads people to devalue themselves, and that's not fair.

PARTICIPANT 5: It may not be fair, but I'm no angel. I don't hurt myself by accident. I *need* to hurt myself when I feel that bad. If I don't, I *will* explode and then people *do* get hurt real bad.

PARTICIPANT 6: *Real* bad. They took my children away because I kept hitting them, couldn't stop.

PARTICIPANT 1: I don't want to lose my daughter. She's my reason for living. I need to not ever hit her, but I don't know what else to do when she makes me so mad.

LEADER 1: So the dilemma is how to turn down the pressure you feel inside and not hurt *anyone*, because you know how bad it is when people hurt other people. If only it were possible to do that without having to hurt yourself. I know that may sound impossible, but let's look at this carefully together. When you're feeling really out of control, it's like having trauma happen all over again, even if it's not really true. Then it's really hard to stop and figure out what's going on, and what you need so you can be safe and feel better.

PARTICIPANT 6: I don't even know what being safe or feeling better means when I feel that way.

LEADER 2: Right, but you just described what it takes to keep emotions, and actions, from being out of control: knowing that you're safe and being able to think about what's going on and figure out what you need to do. That's what we're going to work on in today's group.

One leader again reframes extreme and hopeless statements to draw out the wisdom of the group members. Then the other leader further surprises group members by highlighting how they already are doing very constructive things to be in control of their emotions. This strength-based and solution-focused approach can stimulate creative thinking and discussion.

LEADER 1: You may find this surprising, but I've observed in this group that each of you actually has the skills. It's just very hard to remember to use them—or even that you have them—when stress brings back the trauma feelings of being unhappy, alone, scared, and powerless. But you deserve to be able to use those skills. You've worked very hard at learning them, and trauma shouldn't deprive you of what you've earned.

PARTICIPANT 3: You're saying that I actually know how to feel safe and how to figure out ways to deal with problems, but I'm too stressed to do it? I must be a real basket case.

PARTICIPANT 1: Girl, if you can do that stuff, you are *no* basket case. But I need to see some proof that any of us can do that. I never feel safe, and I blow up or give up whenever I have a problem, and from what I can see, every other woman in this group is just like me.

LEADER 2: So let's look for some proof. Let's look at how each of you actually does help herself to feel—and be—safe, and how each of you actually solves very tough problems every day! We'll be talking about this more later on in the session, but can anyone think of something you might do in the moment to avoid that self-destructive lashing out or hurting yourself?

The leader also uses the opportunity to do some preliminary problem solving. Even though strategies for coping will be addressed in greater detail, the leader does not end the discussion with the dysfunctional response of acting out violently.

PARTICIPANT 5: I just walk away, get myself out of the situation before things get out of control.

PARTICIPANT 3: I wish I could do that, but I end up running into a wall when I try to walk away. Someone or something always knocks me down when I try to do the right thing.

PARTICIPANT 6: At least you try. It takes a strong heart to walk away when you been dissed.

LEADER 2: Right! It's real important to remember that there are alternatives, sometimes very simple alternatives, to letting a feeling run away with you.

They may have a price, like dealing with other people's reactions when they want to fight and you walk away. That takes strength.

LEADER 1: Maybe it's just a little easier to make the choice that you really want instead of just having your emotions get out of control. Like, if you know that you're likely to get triggered, maybe it won't just sneak up on you. So what triggers each of you to feel out of control?

PARTICIPANT 1: Whenever I see a child being abused, I get so angry I can barely control myself.

PARTICIPANT 2: Me, too. Only I feel that way even if it's an adult or even a pet. I just can't stand to see someone hurt and taken advantage of.

PARTICIPANT 6: Children are innocent. They should not be abused. It makes me real mad, too.

PARTICIPANT 3: What about when the system say you a bad mother or a bad person, and then won't let you make things right? Or when your own boyfriend does that to you? That's a trigger.

PARTICIPANT 5: Sure is! Especially if he sleeping with some other tramp, and putting you down!

LEADER 1: Those are some serious triggers. Each one makes sense, and it's also real strong when it's connected to painful or terrible things that have happened to you—to trauma. You probably felt some of that same anger when you were being abused, but you couldn't express it, so now you feel it in response to seeing abuse or betrayal in the present.

PARTICIPANT 1: I never thought of it that way, but you're right. That's what I like about this group. Some of this stuff starts to make sense.

PARTICIPANT 6: Well, I think I would feel that way no matter what. It's just not right.

PARTICIPANT 2: Yeah, but you wouldn't get so worked up about it except what happened to you.

PARTICIPANT 6: So I'm a crazy woman who can't control her feelings because I had trauma.

PARTICIPANT 2: No, girl, that's not crazy. It's just extreme. You so *extreme* because you had trauma, even when you right, you take it to the extreme. Gotta be some way to be less extreme.

PARTICIPANT 6: I hear you, OK, I don't mean to be extreme, but I figure that just the way I am.

LEADER 1: It's the way you learned to be, because of the trauma.

Having drawn a specific connection between past trauma and current responses, the leader makes the current reaction understandable to participants and helps them to challenge long-standing beliefs about what is "wrong" with them. This offers a reframing of pathologizing messages that label such responses as purely "symptomatic" or as overreactions.

PARTICIPANT 2: I get triggered if someone tries to take advantage of me. Like, if someone charges me more for something than they should, or if my daughter tries to manipulate me into babysitting for her. I feel trapped, like I'm just going to lose it.

LEADER 2: Can see how this connects to your trauma history? Abuse is the ultimate experience of being taken advantage of, so it makes sense that many triggers for feeling out of control are about people being hurt or taken advantage of, or having their trust betrayed. And then if people tell you, or you tell yourself, it's because something's wrong with you, that's really unfair.

PARTICIPANT 8: That's all I ever hear. It's my problem. I'm the problem. I can't take anything. I got too many triggers, and I don't know how to handle any of them.

PARTICIPANT 6: That's not right, it's not you. You the one trying to do the right thing. You take a *lot* and you still trying to do the right thing. I respect that.

LEADER 1: (*to participant 8*) Can you hear that respect, for you? Can you let yourself feel that?

PARTICIPANT 8: Maybe. I hear it. (*to participant 6*) I don't mean to dis what you saying, it's just hard to think anything good about me when all I been told is I'm the bad one.

PARTICIPANT 6: I hear you on that. To me, you the good one.

PARTICIPANT 3: For me, I get triggered when I feel ignored. If I'm trying to say something and someone interrupts me or, say, they turn away and start talking to someone else. I just freeze inside. I might even go numb, like I'm catatonic or something.

PARTICIPANT 7: Well, we're listening to you now, and you're making a lot of sense. I don't talk much, because I'm used to being ignored or talked over. This group's the only place I think it is safe to talk, without getting dissed or ignored.

Group leaders summarize key themes for the session up to this point— to help group members pause, reflect, and remember what they're learning— before moving on.

LEADER 2: Many of you may have had the experience when you were abused of trying to tell your story to someone you thought could help. Maybe you tried to talk to a relative or a teacher, or someone from church. If that person didn't listen, for whatever reason, you probably felt helpless and abandoned, like you had nowhere to turn. It's not surprising that similar feelings are triggered now if someone doesn't give you the attention that helps you feel heard. But don't ever forget, though, that "that was then and this is now." You've grown, and you have more ways of making yourself heard, and finding people who will listen, than you did when you younger.

Throughout this session, the leader ties participants' comments to experiences of trauma. Many of the present-day triggers for feeling out of control originated during experiences of abuse. Now, similar situations in a woman's present life trigger those same intense feelings of being out of control. The leader attempts, in this cognitive restructuring, to make current responses understandable and at the same time suggest that the extreme helplessness one felt as a child need not be carried forward into adulthood. The initial feelings may be similar, but the options for coping successfully are greatly enhanced by understanding how feelings make sense.

PARTICIPANT 4: Maybe this sounds crazy, but I get triggered when I'm bored. I just can't stand that feeling of time on my hands and there's nothing to do and nowhere to go. I go crazy.

PARTICIPANT 5: I know what you mean; I use when I'm bored. But you know what they say: "The Devil looks for idle hands." If you bored, it's one more step 'til you in trouble.

PARTICIPANT 2: You go to meetings? That's why I go to meetings every day, because it helps with being bored, and it keeps me from going back to drinking or smoking weed.

LEADER 1: Hold on for a minute 'cause I think we are getting ahead of ourselves. Going to meetings is a great strategy for coping with feeling out of control in general, but I want to go back to this feeling of boredom, because I think that's real important. What do you mean when you say you're bored? What's happening when you feel bored?

PARTICIPANT 5: I know for me I get afraid of being alone with my own thoughts. I say I'm bored, but I just want to run away from me. I'm bored because I bore myself with my stupid thoughts.

PARTICIPANT 4: Yeah, I know about those thoughts. When I just sit with my thoughts, the pain and the memories start coming back. That scares me, so I gotta do something if I start those thoughts.

PARTICIPANT 7: It's not bored, it's that trauma stuff all just spilling out. Bored is no problem. You just do something interesting. But nothing is interesting when those thoughts get started.

LEADER 1: Thank you! I think it's real important to call things by their right name. Maybe sometimes boredom is really a fear of the thoughts and feelings we hold inside ourselves. And some of the using and running is a way to avoid feeling some of those things from the past.

LEADER 2: Other times, when we say we're bored, I think it means not feeling anything. That's being shut down to avoid the pain of troubling thoughts, feeling empty, like nobody is home.

PARTICIPANT 1: I wasn't gonna say it, but you're right. I space out, I go away, then I say I'm bored, but I'm really not there. You're saying that's to escape bad feelings and thoughts?

LEADER 2: Does that make sense? Going away in your mind or losing track of where or who you are, losing time—we sometimes call it dissociation—can be ways to escape that people learn to do, without even realizing it, when they have to cope with trauma growing up. When that happens, it's a way of protecting yourself, but you don't get to be in control, so that can make you feel more powerless over your own mind instead of helping you feel safe.

PARTICIPANT 3: I do that, too. So my mind is out of control because of trauma, and I'm never gonna be able to stop my mind from just going away when it wants to?

LEADER 1: No, your mind is actually in control, and you're using a mental skill you just didn't know you had. The important thing is to learn how you can choose when—or whether—to go away mentally, and then do it when you choose instead of on automatic pilot. That's not dissociation, that's deciding how to focus your mind, and if you need to focus away from where you are, then you can do that. We'll be working on ways to choose what your mind focuses on, so that your mind doesn't have to go on automatic pilot.

Having paused the conversation to help the group accurately label the feeling of boredom or emptiness and to briefly explain dissociation, the leaders again summarize connections between trauma-based triggers and overwhelming or shut-down affect, so that intense or absent feelings are more understandable and, therefore, less overwhelming. The discussion then turns to active problem solving about ways to anticipate and manage extreme feeling states.

LEADER 1: It's interesting to see how many different triggers there are for feeling out of control. What's really important is to recognize that these feelings do have specific, here-and-now triggers. Sometimes women feel as if these feelings just fall out of thin air, and in a way that makes them even scarier. If you think a feeling could just come on you, with no cause at all, you might feel anxious all the time. But there is a trigger for these feelings, and the more we can identify those triggers, the more we can learn ways to cope with them so they have less power.

LEADER 2: Let's return to the question of positive ways to bring an emotional storm to an end.

PARTICIPANT 1: I really try to avoid anything that makes me see red. Sometimes I'll just turn my cell phone off, so that I have no intrusions. I know I have to be careful about isolating myself, but I really don't want to explode, and isolating isn't as bad as blowing up.

LEADER 1: These strategies have some very different consequences. Sometimes they are totally positive, but other times, like what you just pointed out, the consequences are mixed.

The leader highlights the fact that actions have consequences, so members are best prepared for stressors if they consider the up- and downside of all their options.

PARTICIPANT 2: I exercise when I feel out of control. It really helps me feel calm inside. I think I'm burning off all that extra energy that has me revved up.

PARTICIPANT 3: I know what you mean. I like to take a walk. Just get outside, so I can breathe.

LEADER 2: These can be helpful strategies when feeling out of control involves "hot" feelings like anger, but what about when feeling out of control is the more numbed or shut down variety?

PARTICIPANT 4: Then I try to focus myself. I write in my journal or else I tell myself something positive, like I'm a good person and I've been through this before, so I can get through it again.

LEADER 2: Pausing to reflect on your thoughts and write them in a journal, or positive thoughts about yourself, can really help keep feelings from becoming shut down or too extreme.

PARTICIPANT 5: I just tell myself that this too will pass. Whatever I'm feeling will not last forever, and I keep telling myself to be patient and it will be over.

LEADER 1: It sounds like some of those words of comfort are what you would have liked to have heard from a parent when you were hurting a long time ago. It's great that you can now give that comfort to yourself. This reminds me of some of the strategies we came up with when you made those "comfort cards" with positive messages for yourself several sessions ago.

PARTICIPANT 2: I still have mine. I have it up on the refrigerator. I look at it all the time to remind me what I can do, and that I deserve good things and good people in my life.

PARTICIPANT 6: I got so mad I tore mine up, but then I really missed it, so I made another one.

LEADER 2: Having a comfort card is a way of treating yourself right, and you don't have to be perfect to have one, so you can always make new ones or keep going back and adding ideas for how to take care of yourselves when things get too intense.

The leaders once again illustrate the connections among sessions and the opportunity that group members have to learn from upsetting experiences and to modify choices they regret. They then move on to address potential immediate challenges for group members, to anticipate possible situations in which regaining a sense of inner control may be crucial.

LEADER 2: I wonder if anybody has a current situation dealing with feeling out of control that the group might be able to help her with.

PARTICIPANT 3: My roommate drives me *crazy*. Wants to talk all the time. I try to listen to my music or turn on TV, but she just keeps yapping. Anger is building inside me, and I'm afraid I'll lose it, and then the counselors will throw me out, and *I'll* be the one to end up on the streets.

PARTICIPANT 1: Have you told her how she is making you feel?

PARTICIPANT 3: No.

PARTICIPANT 1: Well, you could try explaining to her that her talking is driving you up a wall. Maybe she doesn't realize it, and she thinks she's being friendly.

LEADER 1: That is just a great example of how sometimes we don't feel that we have the right to say what's on our mind in a direct way. Remember when you were being abused, nobody cared what you thought or how you felt, so you may have learned that speaking up directly for what you need and telling someone what's bugging you isn't even an option.

The leaders use the opportunity afforded by this question to assist members with some current and immediate problem solving, again connecting current behavior with learning that occurred when coping with victimization. Members help each other reevaluate beliefs related to guilt or self-blame by recognizing that they coped as best they could during childhood, and they now have choices and strengths that can help them to feel and actually be more in control.

SUMMARY AND CONCLUSION

Group psychotherapy and psychoeducation provide an important complement to the individual, family/couple, and pharmacotherapy approaches to treatment of complex traumatic stress disorders. Further clinical experimentation and rigorous research are needed to address clinician's questions, such as how best to deploy (e.g., concurrently, sequentially) group and other intervention modalities with persons who have had different types and severity of exposure to developmental or other forms of psychological trauma and complex traumatic stress disorders. Clinical strategies for engaging and maintaining therapeutic boundaries and processing in groups in which some (or many) participants present with intense affective and interpersonal instability are also in need of further refinement, building upon the foundation established by cognitive-behavioral (e.g., Davis & Wright, 2007; Najavits, 2002; Ready et al., 2008), psychodynamic (e.g., Sarol-Kulka, 2001; Whewell et al., 2004), and integrative (e.g., Classen et al., 2001; Ford & Russo, 2006; Harris, 1998; Lubin & Johnson, 2008; Stalker & Fry, 1999) models for group treatment of adolescents and adults with traumatic stress disorders. Group therapy for survivors of complex trauma is particularly attentive to the healer's creed: First do no harm. In so doing, group therapy may provide an emotionally and objectively safe context in which participants can experience and resolve the psychosocial dilemmas that complex trauma has caused in their lives (Scott, 1999).

REFERENCES

Alexander, P., Neimeyer, R., Follete, V., Moore, M., & Harter, S. (1989). A comparison of group treatments of women sexually abused as children. *Journal of Consulting and Clinical Psychology, 57*, 479–483.

Avinger, K., & Jones, P. (2007). Group treatment of sexually abused adolescent girls: A review of outcome studies. *American Journal of Family Therapy, 35*, 315–326.

Blackwell, D. (2005). Psychotherapy, politics and trauma. *Group Analysis, 38*, 307–323.

Bradley, R., & Follingstad, D. (2003). Group therapy for incarcerated women who experienced interpersonal violence: A pilot study. *Journal of Traumatic Stress, 16*, 337–340.

Classen, C., Koopman, C., Nevill-Manning, K., & Spiegel, D. (2001). A preliminary report comparing trauma-focused and present-focused group therapy against a wait-listed condition among childhood sexual abuse survivors with PTSD. *Journal of Aggression, Maltreatment and Trauma, 4*, 265–288.

Cloitre, M., & Koenen, K. (2001). The impact of borderline personality disorder on process group outcome among women with posttraumatic stress disorder related to childhood abuse. *International Journal of Group Psychotherapy, 51*, 379–398.

Committee on Treatment of Posttraumatic Stress Disorder. (2007). *Treatment of posttraumatic stress disorder.* Washington, DC: National Academy of Science.

Courtois, C. A. (1988). *Healing the incest wound: Adult survivors in therapy.* New York: Norton.

Davis, J., & Wright, D. (2007). Randomized clinical trial for treatment of chronic nightmares in trauma-exposed adults. *Journal of Traumatic Stress, 20*, 123–133.

Deblinger, E., Stauffer, L., & Steer, R. (2001). Comparative efficacies of supportive and cognitive behavioral group therapies for young children who have been sexually abused and their nonoffending mothers. *Child Maltreatment, 6*, 332–343.

DeRosa, R., & Pelcovitz, D. (2008). Group treatment for chronically traumatized adolescents: Igniting SPARCS of change. In D. Brom, R. Pat-Horenczyk, & J. D. Ford (Eds.), *Treating traumatized children: Risk, resilience, and recovery* (pp. 225–234). London: Routledge.

Fallot, R. D., & Harris, M. (2002). The trauma recovery and empowerment model (TREM). *Community Mental Health Journal, 38*, 475–485.

Follette, V., Alexander, P., & Follette, W. (1991). Individual predictors of outcome in group treatment for incest survivors. *Journal of Consulting and Clinical Psychology, 59*, 150–155.

Ford, J. D., Courtois, C., van der Hart, O., Nijenhuis, E., & Steele, K. (2005). Treatment of complex post-traumatic self-dysregulation. *Journal of Traumatic Stress, 18*, 437–447.

Ford, J. D., Fisher, P., & Larson, L. (1997). Object relations as a predictor of treatment outcome with chronic PTSD. *Journal of Consulting and Clinical Psychology, 65*, 547–559.

Ford, J. D., & Russo, E. (2006). A trauma-focused, present-centered, emotional self-regulation approach to integrated treatment for post-traumatic stress and addiction. *American Journal of Psychotherapy, 60*, 335–355.

Ford, J. D., & Stewart, J. (1999). Group psychotherapy for war-related PTSD with military veterans. In B. H. Young & D. D. Blake (Eds.), *Approaches to group psychotherapy with PTSD* (pp. 75–100). San Francisco: Taylor & Francis.

Foy, D., & Schrock, D. (2006). Future directions. In L. Schein, H. Spitz, G. Burlingame, & P. Muskin (Eds.), *Psychological effects of catastrophic disasters: Group approaches to treatment* (pp. 879–903). Binghamton, NY: Haworth Press.

Frisman, L. K., Ford, J. D., Lin, H., Mallon, S., & Chang, R. (in press). Outcomes of trauma treatment using the TARGET model. *Journal of Groups in Addiction and Recovery*.

Grossmark, R. (2007). The edge of chaos. *Psychoanalytic Dialogues, 17*, 480–499.

Harris, M. (1998). *Trauma recovery and empowerment*. New York: Free Press.

Hien, D., Cohen, L., Miele, G., Litt, L., & Capstick, C. (2004). Promising treatments for women with comorbid PTSD and substance use disorders. *American Journal of Psychiatry, 161*, 1426–1432.

International Society for the Study of Trauma and Dissociation. (2005). *Guidelines for treatment of dissociative identity disorder in adults*. Northbrook, IL: Author.

Kagan, R. (2008). Transforming troubled children into tomorrow's heroes. In D. Brom, R. Pat-Horenczyk, & J. D. Ford (Eds.), *Treating traumatized children: Risk, resilience, and recovery* (pp. 255–268). London: Routledge.

Kanas, N. (2005). Group therapy for patients with chronic trauma-related stress disorders. *International Journal of Group Psychotherapy, 55*, 161–165.

Kataoka, S., Stein, B. D., Jaycox, L., Wong, M., Escudero, P., Tu, W., et al. (2003). A school-based mental health program for traumatized Latino immigrant children. *Journal of the American Academy of Child and Adolescent Psychiatry, 42*, 311–318.

Kohut, H., & Wolf, E. (1978). The disorders of the self and their treatment. *International Journal of Psycho-Analysis, 59*, 413–425.

Krakow, B., Hollifield, M., Johnston, L., Koss, M., Schrader, R., Warner, T., et al. (2001). Imagery rehearsal therapy for chronic nightmares in sexual assault survivors with post traumatic stress disorder. *Journal of the American Medical Association, 286*, 537–545.

Krakow, B., Johnston, L., Melendrez, D., Hollifield, M., Warner, T., Chavez-Kennedy, D., et al. (2001). Open-label trial of evidence-based cognitive behavior therapy for nightmares and insomnia in crime victims with PTSD. *American Journal of Psychiatry, 158*, 2043–2047.

Lubin, H., & Johnson, D. R. (2008). *Trauma-centered group psychotherapy for women*. New York: Routledge.

Lubin, H., Lori, M., Burt, J., & Johnson, D. R. (1998). Efficacy of psychoeducational group therapy in reducing symptoms of posttraumatic stress disorder among multiply traumatized women. *American Journal of Psychiatry, 155,* 1172–1177.

Lundqvist, G., Svedin, C., Hansson, K., & Broman, I. (2006). Group therapy for women sexually abused as children. *Journal of Interpersonal Violence, 21,* 1655–1677.

Marmar, C., Horowitz, M., Weiss, D., Wilner, N., & Kaltreider, N. (1988). A controlled trial of brief psychotherapy and mutual-help group treatment of conjugal bereavement. *American Journal of Psychiatry, 145,* 203–209.

Mendelsohn, M., Zachary, R. S., & Harney, P. A. (2007). Group therapy as an ecological bridge to new community for trauma survivors. *Journal of Aggression, Maltreatment and Trauma, 14,* 227–243.

Moore, B., & Krakow, B. (2007). Imagery rehearsal therapy for acute posttraumatic nightmares among combat soldiers in Iraq. *American Journal of Psychiatry, 164,* 683–684.

Morgan, T., & Cummings, A. (1999). Change experienced during group therapy by female survivors of childhood sexual abuse. *Journal of Consulting and Clinical Psychology, 67,* 28–36.

Morrissey, J., Jackson, E., Ellis, A., Amaro, H., Brown, V., & Najavits, L. (2005). Twelve-month outcomes of trauma-informed interventions for women with co-occurring disorders. *Psychiatric Services, 56,* 1213–1222.

Najavits, L. M. (2002). *Seeking safety: A treatment manual for PTSD and substance abuse.* New York: Guilford Press.

Najavits, L. M., Gallop, R., & Weiss, R. (2006). Seeking Safety therapy for adolescent girls with PTSD and substance use disorder. *Journal of Behavioral Health Services and Research, 33,* 453–463.

Piper, W., Ogrodniczuk, J., Joyce, A., Weideman, R., & Rosie, J. (2007). Group composition and therapy for complicated grief. *Journal of Consulting and Clinical Psychology, 75,* 116–125.

Raphael, B., & Wooding, S. (2006). Group intervention for the prevention and treatment of acute initial stress reactions in civilians. In L. Schein, H. Spitz, G. Burlingame, & P. Muskin (Eds.), *Psychological effects of catastrophic disasters: Group approaches to treatment* (pp. 481–503). Binghamton, NY: Haworth Press.

Ready, D. J., Brown-Thomas, K. R., Worley, V., Backscheider, A. G., Harvey, L. C., Baltzell, D., et al. (2008). A field test of group based exposure therapy with 102 veterans with war-related PTSD. *Journal of Traumatic Stress, 21,* 150–157.

Ready, D. J., & Shea, M. T. (2008). Group therapy. In G. Reyes, J. D. Elhai, & J. D. Ford (Eds.), *Encyclopedia of psychological trauma* (pp. 301–303). Hoboken, NJ: Wiley.

Saltzman, W., Layne, C., Steinberg, A., & Pynoos, R. (2006). Trauma/grief-focused group psychotherapy with adolescents. In L. Schein, H. Spitz, G. Burlingame, & P. Muskin (Eds.), *Psychological effects of catastrophic disasters: Group approaches to treatment* (pp. 669–729). Binghamton, NY: Haworth Press.

Sarol-Kulka, E. (2001). Group dynamics in psychotherapy of patients with personality disorders. *Archives of Psychiatry and Psychotherapy, 3,* 31–41.

Schnurr, P. P., Friedman, M. J., Foy, D. W., Shea, M. T., Hsieh, F. Y., Lavori, P. W., et al. (2003). Randomized trial of trauma-focused group therapy for posttraumatic stress disorder. *Archives of General Psychiatry, 60,* 481–489.

Scott, W. (1999). Group therapy for survivors of severe childhood abuse: Repairing the social contract. *Journal of Child Sexual Abuse, 7,* 35–54.

Sikkema, K., Hansen, N., Tarakeshwar, N., Kochman, A., Tate, D., & Lee, R. (2004). Clinical significance of change in trauma-related symptoms following a pilot group intervention for coping with HIV/AIDS and childhood sexual trauma. *AIDS and Behavior, 8,* 277–291.

Stalker, C., & Fry, R. (1999). A comparison of short-term group and individual therapy for sexually abused women. *Canadian Journal of Psychiatry, 44,* 168–174.

Talbot, N., Houghtalen, R., Cyrulik, S., Betz, A., Barkun, M., Duberstein, P., et al. (1998). Women's safety in recovery. *Psychiatric Services, 49,* 213–217.

Tourigny, M., Hebert, M., Daigneault, I., & Simoneau, A. (2005). Efficacy of a group for sexually abused adolescent girls. *Journal of Child Sexual Abuse, 14,* 71–93.

Trowell, J., Kelvin, I., Weeramanthri, T., Sadowski, H., Berelowitz, M., Glaser, D., et al. (2002). Psychotherapy for sexually abused girls. *British Journal of Psychiatry, 180,* 234–247.

Veysey, B., & Clark, C. (Eds.). (2004). *Responding to physical and sexual abuse in women with alcohol and other drug and mental disorders.* Binghamton, NY: Haworth Press.

Wallis, D. A. N. (2002). Reduction of trauma symptoms following group therapy. *Australian and New Zealand Journal of Psychiatry, 36,* 67–74.

Whewell, P., Lingam, R., & Chilton, R. (2004). Reflective borderline group therapy: The patients' experience of being borderline. *Psychoanalytic Psychotherapy, 18,* 324–345.

Wolfsdorf, B., & Zlotnick, C. (2001). Affect management in group therapy for women with posttraumatic stress disorder and histories of childhood sexual abuse. *Journal of Clinical Psychology, 57,* 169–181.

Yalom, I., & Leszcz, M. (1995). *The theory and practice of group psychotherapy* (5th ed.). New York: Perseus.

Conclusion

The Clinical Utility of a Complex Traumatic Stress Disorders Framework

Julian D. Ford
Christine A. Courtois

This book has addressed a fundamental question that confronts every clinician and clinical researcher who treats or studies people who have experienced the effects of psychological trauma: Does identifying a history of complex psychological trauma and complex reactions (labeled here as complex traumatic stress disorders) make a meaningful difference in clinical conceptualization and assessment, psychological and psychopharmacological treatment, and professional practice management and self-care?

We believe the answer is "yes." Distinguishing between complex trauma and other forms of psychological trauma, and between complex traumatic stress disorders and posttraumatic stress disorder (PTSD) as currently defined in the text revision of the fourth edition of the *Diagnostic and Statistical Manual of Mental Disorders* (DSM-IV-TR; American Psychiatric Association, 2000), makes a *substantial* difference in clinical assessment and treatment. Each chapter in this book provides support for this view by describing evidence-informed approaches to the assessment and treatment of complex traumatic stress disorders. Taken together, these chapters provide for clinicians who treat traumatized clients a knowledge base that builds upon but substantially extends the concepts and tools previously available within the traumatic stress field. Thus, each chapter in this book is a valuable illustration of what the clinician can gain by understanding complex traumatic stress disorders. Whether a complex trauma framework will enhance the outcomes of treatment for persons whose posttraumatic reactions transcend those found in the currently available criteria for PTSD remains an empirical question—but one that is being actively tested in research by many of the authors who have contributed to this book. Therefore, in this Conclusion, we highlight some of the ongoing controversies, unresolved issues, and as yet unanswered questions about complex traumatic stress disorder and its definition, assessment, and treatment that remain to be studied scientifically and addressed through innovations in clinical practice.

In this book, *complex psychological trauma* has been defined as experiences or events that (1) are repetitive, chronic, or prolonged; (2) involve harm, such as physical, sexual, and emotional abuse and/or neglect or abandonment by parents, caregivers and other ostensibly responsible adults; and (3) occur at developmentally vulnerable times in the person's life, especially over the course of childhood, and become embedded in or intertwined with the individual's development and maturation. Complex posttraumatic sequelae (or reactions) that comprise *complex traumatic stress disorders* have been defined as including the conditions, states, features, and phenomenology experienced by individuals in the aftermath of exposure to complex psychological trauma. We use this inclusive terminology to indicate our understanding that reactions may be quite mixed and variable in their expression, presentation, and duration; may vary in degree of severity; and may manifest at subclinical levels that do not always reach a threshold required to meet criteria for a formal diagnosis or disorder. Nevertheless, in this book, we have referred to the aggregate of these reactions, including those identified by clinicians and researchers as the most common (i.e., severe problems with self-regulation and relationships due to stress responses that dysregulate body physiology, cognitive and emotional processing, self-awareness and consciousness, and interpersonal security; Herman, 1992; van der Kolk, 2005).

Although there is substantial controversy concerning whether these complex traumatic stress reactions constitute a singular disorder warranting a distinct diagnosis (van der Kolk & Courtois, 2005), we refer to them as *complex traumatic stress disorders* for the purpose of parsimony. This is not to say that all who suffer complex trauma histories go on to develop all of these symptoms with sufficient severity to constitute a complex traumatic stress disorder; as is true for psychological trauma generally and for PTSD, it is likely that survivors of complex trauma have range of symptoms at levels of chronicity and severity that are quite individual (e.g., see Ford, Stockton, Kaltman, & Green, 2006). Additionally, we wholeheartedly agree with those who emphasize including the person's strengths, resilience, personal resources in all cases as important in understanding the variability of adaptations to complex trauma (Chapter 9, this volume).

As a result of the multiplicity of traumatic antecedents and the range of traumatic stress reactions, symptoms, and impairments that follow, individuals with complex traumatic stress disorders have proven very difficult to assess accurately, diagnose, and effectively treat. As is evident from the descriptions of assessment and treatment approaches in this book, a variety of options are available to clinicians who treat these disorders. These models share a common emphasis on sequencing treatment in phases that were first articulated by Pierre Janet and later adapted for complex traumatic stress disorders by Judith Herman (1992; see also Courtois, 1999, 2004; Ford, 2005). However, the greatest challenge facing clinicians often is not how to treat stress reactivity or affective/anxiety disorder symptoms, but instead when and how to address severe dissociative disorders (see Chapters 7 and 17), self-harm and suicidality (see Chapters 7, 9, and 20), addictive and eating disorders (see Chapters 12 and 20), and posttraumatic difficulties and traumatic reenactments in relationships (see Chapters 17–20). These coping mechanisms are often the reason for seeking treatment, along with posttraumatic symptoms such as flashbacks, numbing, and hyperarousal, and associated features of anxiety and depression. Thus, the clinician is challenged in terms of where and how to begin, and how to sequence and titrate the treatment, and even in terms of attempting to develop a healthy and well-boundaried therapeutic relationship, because many of these clients are especially mistrustful of authority figures (e.g., due to attachment insecurities and transference reactions, in which clinicians are experienced as stand-ins for abusive or neglectful parents and caregivers). These clinical challenges extend to the clinician's practice management (Chapter 9), countertransference (Chapter 9), and vicarious traumatization, and personal and professional self-care (Chapter 10). *Although familiar to experienced mental health professionals in general, the challenges posed specifically by working with clients with complex trauma histories and complex traumatic stress disorders warrant special attention, as well as the need to be highlighted in the training of new professionals and in collaborative relationships with professionals from other fields.*

CLINICAL ASSESSMENT

As described in Chapters 3 and 4 in terms of general practice principles, and Chapters 5 and 6 in terms of specific clinical assessment tools and methods, clinical assessment of clients with complex trauma histories should not only include a detailed history of their trauma history and review of their Axis I and II psychiatric symptoms but should also attend to competencies and problems in the domains of self-regulation of identity, emotion, memory, decision making, behavior, physical health, relationships, and guiding beliefs and expectancies. Psychometric assessment of complex clinical cases has come to rely on sophisticated interviews and procedures, and a variety of measures that extend beyond the symptoms of specific psychiatric disorders, including PTSD and its comorbidities. Identification of the features of complex traumatic stress disorders and their possible developmental origins and psychobiological mechanisms (Chapters 1 and 2) has led to the development of interview and self-report measures that enable the clinician to understand how the client processes bodily and affective responses, memories and appraisals, decisions and action plans, ways of being in relationship to other people, and spirituality (Chapters 5 and 6).

Thus, a conceptual focus on the domains identified by syndromal models of complex traumatic stress disorders (i.e., self-development, relational capacity, self-regulation, and dysregulation), in addition to the symptoms of PTSD and comorbid diagnoses, has provided a basis for an expanded clinical assessment repertoire. Additionally, studies and conceptual models describing the ontogenetic development of self-regulation of affect and cognitive/somatic information processing in childhood consistently point to the importance of having responsive and self-regulated caregiver(s) as the platform and scaffolding for acquiring these two core sets of competencies (Ford, 2005; Schore, 2001; Siegel, 2001; see Chapters 1–3 and 6, this volume). The result of such facilitative early life relationships with caregiver(s) tends to be a combination of a lasting sense of secure attachment and an ability to process bodily and affective feelings, and to utilize cognitive processes effectively—precisely the opposite of the dysregulation of core beliefs and self-regulation competencies associated with complex traumatic stress disorders. Therefore, a metamodel of complex traumatic stress disorders focusing on problems in self-regulation implies that clinical assessment of attachment history (including disruptions due to neglect, abuse, family violence, or other adversities or traumatic stressors) and inner working model and attachment style (e.g., secure vs. insecure/fearful/disorganized; see Chapter 6, this volume, for a review of attachment styles and validated or promising clinical assessment tools) are important, in addition to assessing PTSD and comorbid psychiatric disorders. When attachment and self-regulation are systematically assessed, psychotherapeutic approaches that address these domains (e.g., Chapters 7, 9, 11, 14, 15, and 17–20) can be targeted specifically to clients with these impairments, potentially enhancing psychotherapy effectiveness and efficiency.

Although a complex trauma framework implies that more than PTSD and comorbid Axis I or II diagnoses should be addressed in clinical assessment (Chapters 1, 5, and 6), including a range of self-regulation and attachment-related impairments, it is not clear that a unified syndrome of complex traumatic stress disorders (e.g., disorders of extreme stress not otherwise specified [DESNOS], developmental trauma disorder [DTD]) is necessary or even desirable to achieve thorough assessment and treatment planning. If a single syndrome is prematurely reified, clinical assessors may overlook the potential efficiency of first screening for specific target symptoms/impairments before investing the time and effort required to assess a full clinical condition systematically (see Chapter 5). There also might be a tendency to assume mistakenly that all clients who are "diagnosed" with complex traumatic stress disorders necessarily fulfill all of the criteria and require an identical therapeutic approach, which clinical experience (Chapters 3, 4, and 8) and research on the sequelae of complex trauma (Chapters 1 and 2) demonstrate is not the case. Thus, whereas a syndromal model, such as DESNOS or DTD, reminds us of the importance of the full range of potential self-regulation and attachment symptoms and impairments when assessing clients with complex trauma histories, symptom- or domain-specific clinical assessment measures are essential for both screening and in-depth assessment at this stage of the field's development. Additionally, clinical experience has demonstrated that assessment may need to be repeated, ongoing, or initiated throughout the course of treatment, as indicated by the client's presentation. Symptoms and problems not evident initially may emerge over the course of treatment, often as an adaptive response to the development of trust in the therapeutic relationship and to therapeutic attention to or resolution of other problems.

PSYCHOTHERAPY

The psychotherapy chapters in this book demonstrate that, in addition to several forms of cognitive-behavioral therapy (CBT) and its constituent elements (e.g., anxiety management, behavior analysis, cognitive processing, imagery reconstruction, exposure therapy; Chapters 12–13), several other much less widely recognized approaches for the treatment of PTSD have shown promise in studies of the treatment of clients with complex posttraumatic impairments (Chapters 7, 11, 14–15, 17–20). Spurred in part by a need to be applicable to clients with complex traumatic stress symptoms and impairments, CBT research and clinical practice is emphasizing the need to build a relational base to support clients who have serious deficits in emotional, bodily, cognitive, and interpersonal self-regulation (Chapters 12 and 13). Extending CBT from targeting PTSD to a broader focus on affective–somatic–cognitive regulation, as well as PTSD, is likely to be challenging logistically for the psychotherapist, but it is less complicated than attempting to coordinate CBT for PTSD with another (or with several other) evidence-based therapies for comorbid disorders. A movement toward integrative (or "hybrid") therapy models for clients with PTSD and comorbid Axis I or II disorders, already well underway, reduces the burden on therapists and clients of multiple concurrent or sequential therapies, for example, for PTSD and comorbid depression (e.g., Markowitz, 2008), PTSD and substance use disorders (Ford & Russo, 2006; Najavits, 2002), schizophrenia (Mueser et al., 2001), and borderline personality disorder (Wagner & Linehan, 2006). When clinical assessment indicates that PTSD and a single comorbid Axis I or II psychiatric disorder are the full extent of a client's psychopathology, these dual comorbidity treatment models provide an efficient and thorough approach for clinicians.

However, it appears that simply delivering PTSD-focused psychotherapies, such as CBT, with complicated clinical cases of PTSD in the real world is sufficiently difficult to lead to poorer adherence and lower levels of utilization of CBT techniques than are optimal, even by well-trained psychotherapists (Zayfert, DeViva, Becker, Pike, Gillock, & Hayes, 2005). In cases of "simple" comorbidity (i.e., PTSD and a single comorbid disorder, as described earlier), an expanded version of CBT (e.g., Chapters 12 and 13) may be the solution. Of course, complicated clinical cases often involve multiple comorbidities (including both full and subthreshold Axis I or II diagnoses). In these cases, although attention to the symptoms involved in the comorbid conditions is important, it may be more clinically feasible to focus psychotherapy on core mechanisms, such as dysregulation of bodily–affective–cognitive–interpersonal functioning, and core issues, such as shame-based beliefs about self and others, and limited self-regulatory and interpersonal skills. Indeed, some approaches to CBT are taking that tack (Chapters 12 and 13).

In addition, shifting focus from PTSD and comorbidity to a complex traumatic stress disorders formulation based on self-regulation and attachment styles offers the possibility of a wider range of psychotherapies, including experiential and emotion-focused therapies (Chapters 7, 11, 14–15, and 17–20), therapies for somatoform and psychoform dissociative fragmentation of information processing (Chapters 7, 11–15, and 17–19), and therapies that aim to enhance clients' relational working models (Chapters 7, 11–15, and 17–20) and interpersonal support systems (Chapters 11 and 17–20). The clinical reality that self-dysregulation and attachment disorganization problems tend to be intertwined for many clients with complex trauma histories (rather than occurring as distinct and readily separable symptoms) suggests that a comprehensive traumatic stress disorder perspective may be of greater utility as a guide to psychotherapy than a conceptual model that treats the symptom domains as discrete. However, for the purposes of monitoring therapeutic outcomes, specific measures of each domain of symptomatology are essential to identify where improvement actually has occurred, and where additional or modified treatment is necessary (Chapters 5 and 6).

PHARMACOTHERAPY

Pharmacotherapy for complex trauma survivors begins with a careful evaluation of their PTSD and comorbid psychiatric disorder symptoms, as described in Chapter 16, this volume. Differential diagnosis may be quite difficult even when a careful evaluation is conducted. Identifying specific target symptoms or areas for change is crucial in all approaches to pharmacotherapy, because the myriad psychotropic agents available have different specific mechanisms, effects, and side effects. Therefore, even if the framework for conducting pharmacotherapy with a client with a complex trauma history is based primarily on a PTSD plus comorbidity(ies) model, the complexities of symptom presentation within single psychiatric disorders (let alone across comorbid disorders) are sufficient to require a more individualized protocol than one size fits all.

When problems with dysregulation of affect–body–cognition–relatedness threaten to undermine not only the client's functioning but also adherence to a pharmacotherapy regimen, a complex traumatic stress disorders framework identifying specific targets in those domains also is necessary. For example, a client may be reluctant or even phobic about ingesting medication due to sexual abuse or domestic violence experiences involving coercion, drugging, and violation of bodily integrity; these posttraumatic reactions may manifest in the form of dissociative forgetting or preoccupation with otherwise manageable bodily reactions to medications. Therefore, pharmacotherapy is likely to be feasible—let alone beneficial—only if the treatment provider(s) work with the client to develop a rationale and a set of realistic expectancies within the context of a therapeutic alliance. As the case example in Chapter 16 illustrates, the development of a truly collaborative approach to pharmacotherapy—although optimal for all clients—is essential with complex trauma survivors. To the extent that this can be done by focusing on the benefits of addressing specific PTSD, complex PTSD, or psychiatric comorbidity symptoms or impairments with medication, a PTSD-plus-comorbidity framework may be sufficient for the client and clinician—so long as the full range of potential complex trauma sequelae are included (Chapters 5 and 6). Thus, a syndrome perspective on complex traumatic stress disorders may have less utility for pharmacotherapy than for psychotherapy, consistent with the widely accepted approach to psychiatric pharmacotherapy of targeting specific symptoms rather than purely focusing on global diagnoses (Chapter 16).

PRACTICE MANAGEMENT
AND CULTURAL COMPETENCE

Often, clients with complex trauma histories bring unique challenges to the therapeutic relationship. It is not uncommon for some clients with the most severe self-dysregulation or attachment disorganization symptoms to reenact conflictual relationship in ways that may have "burned out" a number of therapists over the course of many years of treatment, and to enter any new treatment with profound mistrust and even aggression toward the clinician. The relational dilemmas that clients with complex trauma histories tend to bring into treatment—as fears (e.g., "You, like everyone else—including past therapists—will abandon and abuse me"), wishes (e.g., "Never leave me"), expectations (e.g., "If you care, you will always be available to me when and as I need you"), rage and hostility (e.g., "I have to pay to get you to care about me"), and traumatic transferences and projective identifications (e.g., "You *are* neglecting and abusing me")—pose a powerful and complicated challenge for the therapist (see Chapters 9–10 and 17–20). Sustaining a safe and therapeutic (i.e., trusting, open, inquisitive, flexible) interpersonal environment for the treatment requires attention to the past (i.e., the client's history of complex trauma and attachment experiences, and of interpersonal and therapeutic problems and successes), the present (i.e., a working alliance based on a shared understanding of the treatment process, interventions, and goals), and the future (i.e., a shared understanding of the realistic possibilities for goal attainment within a specific time frame and for the means of ending of treatment). A combination of straight talk, therapeutic boundaries, and responsive empathic listening is needed to accomplish those goals with clients who often reenact traumatic "dramas" in the therapist–client relationship (Chapters 9–10). Addressing symptoms of PTSD and comorbid psychiatric disorders (e.g., Chapters 12, 13, and 16), as well as self-regulation and attachment/ interpersonal problems (e.g., Chapters 14–15 and 17–20), also provides therapist and client with a constructive focus for developing a collaborative working relationship.

However, when that strategy does not succeed—or if it has been attempted in prior treatment episodes with only partial or transient remission—or, even more importantly, when the client's unsafe or therapy-interfering behavior does not respond (or has not responded in the past) to it, it is crucial to have a systematic way to shift the therapeutic frame to address disorganized attachment and dysregulation of emotion, body, cognitive, and interpersonal functioning. A common alternative is to recommend supportive psychotherapy or palliative pharmacotherapy for the putatively "untreatable" or "impossible" client. However, a complex traumatic stress disorders perspective implies that many of these clients are far from "untreatable," if treatment is designed and delivered in a manner that helps them with self-regulation skills and attachment security. Dialectic behavior therapy was developed as a constructive response to this dilemma with parasuicidal clients with borderline personality disorder (Wagner & Linehan, 2006; Chapter 13, this volume). Therapy models described in this book enable clinicians to address self-dysregulation and attachment disorganization with education, skills training, and a relational approach that is informed by research on developmental neurobiology and traumatology (Chapter 2), as well as trauma-informed cultural competence (Chapter 8).

With these psychotherapy and pharmacotherapy models, and this knowledge base, the clinician treating clients with complex trauma histories should be less likely to feel stymied or defeated when faced with symptoms that otherwise are difficult to account for or treat with traditional diagnostic and treatment models. To the extent that a clinician is able to assess the specific symptom domains associated with self-dysregulation and attachment disorganization, a complex traumatic stress disorders syndromal perspective is not necessarily needed. However, the symptom-by-symptom approach to conceptualizing, assessing, and treating clients with complex trauma histories may lead clinicians to focus on managing discrete symptoms that may be difficult to address effectively or empathically in isolation. For example, it is a very different perspective to view a client as needing to reduce the frequency and intensity of pathological dissociative symptoms than as needing help with dissociative forms of dysregulated body functioning, self-identity, relational trust, and emotion and information processing that originated in traumatic and neglectful early life experiences. In the latter case, treatment does not simply target dissociative symptoms but addresses an intertwined multimodal network of problems with self-regulation and disorganized attachment working models. Thus, a complex traumatic stress disorders framework may facilitate a whole-person, client-centered approach to delivering psychotherapy, which may increase the clinician's therapeutic competence.

PROFESSIONAL SELF-CARE

Vicarious trauma can occur when a clinician helps any client with PTSD, because there is no form of PTSD that involves negligible or easily psychically metabolized trauma experiences. The therapist's experience of vicarious trauma is well recognized by clinicians who have treated clients with chronic or comorbid PTSD. They often find themselves profoundly affected and transformed in significant personal and interpersonal ways (Chapter 10). However, when a client's entire life and development—or large and formative portions thereof—have occurred in a context shaped by developmentally adverse interpersonal trauma, the therapist faces a particularly difficult professional and personal challenge in providing a safe and secure, empathic relational environment (Chapters 9–10) in which the client can disclose the often overwhelming, unfinished emotional business that continues to be deeply troubling (Chapters 8–10). In this sense, the client with a history of complex trauma is likely to come to therapy with an unstated (and often unrecognized even by him- or herself) hope that the therapist somehow can provide emotional stability and psychological understanding that will transform inchoate distress into a knowable and solvable set of problems—as well as the wish that the therapist has some "magic" that no one (or almost no one) else has had or has been willing to share to make life seem livable and worth living, and the fear that there is no such magic or no one generous enough to bestow it. This combination of a complex traumatic history and equally complex (biologically based; Chapter 2) psychosocial adaptations to survive those traumas creates a highly emotionally charged tension in the client's relationship with the therapist (paralleling but often exceeding that which exists in the client's other important relationships).

The challenge for the therapist is to use information-processing and emotion regulation skills (e.g., awareness of often subtle and rapidly fluctuating bodily [Chapter 15], emotional [Chapters 14, 17, and 18], and contextual [Chapters 11 and 13] reactions that may lead to fragmented consciousness [Chapters 7 and 17] on the part of the therapist him- or herself in the midst of therapy sessions or during the course of episodes of psychotherapy) to serve as a coregulator (i.e., nonverbal role model and guide; not a surrogate or replacement parent or caregiver) (Schore, 2001) with whom the client can experientially learn how to self-regulate in the face of persistent stress reactivity based on chronic survival adaptations (Chapter 2).

One practical implication of an self-regulation/attachment metamodel of complex traumatic stress sequelae is that it is important distinguish empathy in the therapeutic sense (i.e., the self psychology or Rogerian definition of *empathy* as taking the client's perspective seriously and understanding the client's experiences, current and past, from the client's frame of reference) from the lay concept of empathy (which is less intentional and based more on sympathetic resonance). The latter is more consistent with a conceptual framework based on PTSD and comorbidity, because that metamodel emphasizes symptom reduction rather than self-reflective self-regulation. That symptoms-based focus may lead therapists to experience difficulty in maintaining therapeutic boundaries, and in recognizing and managing personal stress reactions, countertransference, or vicarious trauma, because change in clients with complex trauma histories is particularly likely to occur in a nonlinear fashion (Ford, Courtois, van der Hart, Nijenhuis, & Steele, 2005). Phases of therapy often shift out of the apparently optimum order as the client recursively reworks earlier issues in new ways and at greater depth. Therapists could use this as a way to think about "processing" their own reactions: If they pay attention to their emotional reactions and thoughts in therapy primarily as "noise" to be kept to the lowest possible volume, then they may feel great sympathy or compassion for a client, which may be draining and lead to increasing distress if the client's progress in terms of symptom reduction is halting or erratic. However, if therapists view themselves as role models and coregulators for the development of self-regulation by the client, and reflect upon their own reactions and the client's disclosures in terms of the meaning these have, both from their own and from the client's perspective, then this may enhance their sense of emotional and cognitive integration and their psychological "presence" in, and satisfaction with, therapy.

CLINICAL RESEARCH

Research on assessment and treatment of complex posttraumatic conditions, whether framed as chronic PTSD with multiple comorbidities/subtypes or as self-regulation–based complex traumatic stress disorders, is still at an early stage. Most psychiatric, psychosocial, and specifically PTSD-related assessment instruments have been normed and validated with only community samples (an important first step; Chapter 5, this volume) or mildly to moderately impaired clinical samples (e.g., outpatient or university counseling center cohorts). In this respect, assessment measures for severe PTSD comorbidities (e.g., borderline personality disorder, chronic substance dependence, schizophrenia) tend to be better validated for persons with complex trauma histories and severe psychosocial impairments than are measures of either PTSD or complex traumatic stress disorders, with some exceptions (e.g., Trauma Symptom Inventory, Structured Interview for Disorders of Extreme Stress; Pelcovitz et al., 1997; Chapter 5, this volume). Verifying that measures intended to operationalize the clinical sequelae of complex trauma are in fact valid assessments of those biopsychosocial impairments for each clinical subpopulation remains a key research agenda.

Similarly, the psychotherapy models that have been developed to treat PTSD tend not to have been tested with clients with chronic PTSD plus multiple comorbidities or externalizing problems (Spinazzola, Blaustein, & van der Kolk, 2005), and only rarely tested with outcome measures that address the complex posttraumatic sequelae (see Chapter 12, this volume). Most therapies that have been developed or adapted for clients with complex posttraumatic impairments have not been validated in randomized clinical trial studies (for exceptions, see Chapters 12–14, and 20). Thus, research is needed to determine whether PTSD psychotherapies can effectively address complex traumatic stress impairments (see Chapter 12) and whether psychotherapies primarily designed to treat complex traumatic stress impairments are efficacious, effective, and cost-effective.

There is no research base for practice management or cultural competence in clients with complex trauma histories, and very little research has been done on vicarious trauma (Dalenberg, 2008). Studies are needed that actually assess therapists using validated measures of the hypothesized effects of vicarious trauma on their own spirituality, beliefs, and functioning (e.g., adapting measures developed for clients with PTSD or complex posttraumatic impairments to be applicable to therapists' attachment style, competencies, and difficulties with affect regulation and information processing), as well as with indirect indices, such as therapists' health problems, use of health care or counseling, worker's compensation, problems in intimate relationships, and so forth. Such studies should take into account therapists' variable personal histories of traumatic or psychological difficulties, amount and types of work with trauma survivors, and the immediate (e.g., right after intense sessions) and long-term effects (e.g., over periods of months or years, including while still treating survivors and after no longer doing so), and whether doing comparably intense psychotherapy with clients with other disorders has comparable effects. For example, empathic engagement, as rated objectively from therapy tapes or by the client, is posited to be inversely related to vicarious trauma/countertransference (Chapter 10). Research is needed to clarify how empathic engagement in the treatment of complex traumatic stress disorders affects or is affected by factors such as therapy model, caseload, clinical training, professional support, and therapist personal factors, such as temperament, personality, trauma history, and life stresses.

SUMMARY

It is our hope that the innovations in clinical conceptualization, assessment, and treatment described in this book will inspire this and future generations of psychotherapists and scientists to develop, validate, and utilize these and additional innovative approaches carefully to help clients with complex trauma histories. As clinicians and clinical scientists, it is our responsibility to provide these clients (and their families and communities) with realistic hope that their often chronic and treatment-refractory disorders can be overcome and healed. We have the privilege of offering the assistance and empathic understanding that has been needed by, but often denied to, survivors of complex trauma. With this privilege comes the obligation to develop and provide assessment and treatment approaches that honor and support the resilience of trauma survivors as they carry on with their lives and enrich the lives of their families and communities.

REFERENCES

American Psychiatric Association. (2000). *Diagnostic and statistical manual of mental disorders* (4th ed., text rev.). Washington, DC: Author.

Courtois, C. A. (1999). *Recollections of sexual abuse: Treatment principles and guidelines*. New York: Norton

Courtois, C. A. (2004). Complex trauma, complex reactions: Assessment and treatment. *Psychotherapy: Theory, Research, Practice and Training, 41*, 412–426.

Dalenberg, C. (2008). Countertransference. In G. Reyes, J. D. Elhai, & J. D. Ford (Eds.), *Encyclopedia of psychological trauma* (pp. 166–170). Hoboken, NJ: Wiley.

Ford, J. D. (2005). Treatment implications of altered neurobiology, affect regulation and information processing following child maltreatment: *Psychiatric Annals, 35*, 410–419.

Ford, J. D., Courtois, C. A., van der Hart, O., Nijenhuis, E., & Steele, K. (2005). Treatment of complex post-traumatic self-dysregulation. *Journal of Traumatic Stress, 18*, 437–447.

Ford, J. D., & Russo, E. (2006). A trauma-focused, present-centered, emotional self-regulation approach to integrated treatment for post-traumatic stress and addiction: TARGET. *American Journal of Psychotherapy, 60*, 335–355.

Ford, J. D., Stockton, P., Kaltman, S., & Green, B. L. (2006). Disorders of extreme stress (DESNOS) symptoms are associated with interpersonal trauma exposure in a sample of healthy young women. *Journal of Interpersonal Violence, 21*, 1399–1416.

Herman, J. L. (1992). Complex PTSD. *Journal of Traumatic Stress, 5*, 379–391.

Markowitz, J. (2008). Interpersonal psychotherapy. In G. Reyes, J. D. Elhai, & J. D. Ford (Eds.), *Encyclopedia of psychological trauma* (p. 367). Hoboken, NJ: Wiley.

Mueser, K. T., Rosenberg, S., Friedman, M. J., Gorman, P., Drake, R., Vidaver, R., et al. (2001). Developing effective treatments for posttraumatic stress disorder among people with severe mental illness. *Psychiatric Services, 52*, 1453–1461.

Najavits, L. M. (2002). *Seeking safety: A treatment manual for PTSD and substance abuse*. New York: Guilford Press.

Pelcovitz, D., van der Kolk, B., Roth, S., Mandel, F., Kaplan, S., & Resick, P. (1997). Development of a criteria set and a structured interview for disorders of extreme stress (DESNOS). *Journal of Traumatic Stress, 10*, 3–16.

Schore, A. (2001). Effects of a secure attachment relationship on right brain development, affect regulation, and infant mental health. *Infant Mental Health Journal*, *22*, 7–66.

Siegel, D. (2001). Toward an interpersonal neurobiology of the developing mind. *Infant Mental Health Journal*, *22*, 67–94.

Spinazzola, J., Blaustein, M., & van der Kolk, B. (2005). Posttraumatic stress disorder treatment outcome research. *Journal of Traumatic Stress*, *18*, 425–436.

van der Kolk, B. A. (2005). Developmental trauma disorder. *Psychiatric Annals*, *35*, 401–408.

van der Kolk, B. A., & Courtois, C. A., (2005). Editorial: Complex developmental trauma. *Journal of Traumatic Stress*, *18*(5), 385–388.

van der Kolk, B. A., Roth, S., Pelcovitz, D., Sunday, S., & Spinazzola, J. (2005). Disorders of extreme stress. *Journal of Traumatic Stress*, *18*, 389–399.

Wagner, A. W., & Linehan, M. M. (2006). Applications of dialectical behavior therapy to posttraumatic stress disorder and related problems. In V. M. Follette & J. I. Ruzek (Ed.), *Cognitive-behavioral therapies for trauma* (pp. 117–138). New York: Guilford Press.

Zayfert, C., DeViva, J., Becker, C., Pike, J., Gillock, K., & Hayes, S. (2005). Exposure utilization and completion of cognitive behavioral therapy for PTSD in a "real world" clinical practice. *Journal of Traumatic Stress*, *18*, 637–645.

Afterword

Bessel A. van der Kolk

Over the past two decades, vast amounts of knowledge have accumulated about what we call "complex trauma," a psychiatric condition that officially does not exist, but which possibly constitutes the most common set of psychological problems to drive human beings into psychiatric care. In some respects, we have emerged from the dark ages. Back in 1974, when I was studying for my Board examinations, Freedman and Kaplan's *Comprehensive Textbook of Psychiatry* stated that "incest is extremely rarely, and does not occur in more than 1 out of 1.1 million people" (Henderson, 1975, p. 1536). Over 30 years ago, this leading textbook of psychiatry still stated that

> there is little agreement about the role of...incest as a source of serious subsequent psychopathology. The father–daughter liaison satisfies instinctual drives in a setting where mutual alliance with an omnipotent adult condones the transgression.... The act offers an opportunity to test in reality an infantile fantasy whose consequences are found to be gratifying and pleasurable... such incestuous activity diminishes the subject's chance of psychosis and allows for a better adjustment to the external world... the vast majority of them were none the worse for the experience.

During the 1970s, case reports of sexual abuse and incest started to appear in the medical literature and today we know that, each year, 3 million children in the United States are reported to Child Protective Services for child abuse and neglect. Though it is difficult to come up with exact figures, the best estimate is that there are approximately 150,000 new cases of childhood sexual abuse each year (Putnam, 2003). A host of studies over the past two decades have shown how wrong Henderson's statement about aftereffects was: Childhood sexual abuse and other forms of maltreatment are now known to consistently lead to severe problems with self-regulation, ranging from psychological and behavioral problems such as extreme fluctuations of anger and anxiety to impaired immunological functioning and changes in coordination, balance, and cognitive development. Numerous epidemiological studies have shown how early adverse experiences increase the individual's chances to grow up depressed, hooked on alcohol and drugs, engaged in self-destructive activities, suffering from numerous medical illnesses, and with deeply unsatisfactory interpersonal relationships. Our research during a 1-year window of the entire Medicaid population of the Commonwealth of Massachusetts showed that the most common problems for children in psychiatric care were trauma-related disorders, and that adults with histories of chronic childhood trauma in the mental health system had more frequent hospital admissions and were more expensive to treat than people with any other psychiatric condition (Macy & van der Kolk, 1999).

Today we know that being dependent on hostile or severely misattuned caregivers interferes with the brain development necessary to become a focused, thoughtful, and well-regulated human being. Early exposure to danger molds the brain to be vulnerable, to make a person more irritable, impulsive, suspicious, and compelled to engage in fight-or-flight reactions. In reaction to abuse and neglect, the brain is programmed to a state of defensive adaptation, which enhances survival in a world of constant danger, but at a terrible price.

Over the past few decades we have learned a great deal about brain development and how exploration and play in the context of secure attachment promote intelligence, collaboration, curiosity, and mental flexibility. In contrast, fear interferes with self-regulation, imagination, and empathy for self and others. Since the central nervous system matures in a use-dependent fashion (Perry, 2002), the brain areas that are most intensely stimulated in a growing child develop most vigorously: safe children develop imagination, play, and curiosity, while terrified children cultivate strong alarm systems, defensive postures, and warning signals.

Play and exploration are critical stimulants for optimal brain development (Panksepp, 1998). Brain maturation in a safe context promotes the development of executive functioning, which includes an individual's learning to anticipate the feelings and reactions of the people around him or her and the capacity to modulate his or her impulses. Children progressively become less reactive, less impulsive, and more "thoughtful" as they make increasingly complex appraisals of the world around them. Eventually well-developed brains contain minds that can make decisions that incorporate a variety of points of view—an internal representation of themselves within the continuity of past and future, and the capacity to imagine a variety of different outcomes, depending on what action they decide to take.

Since the time of Hughlings Jackson (1958), it has been known that fear, danger, and other forms of excessive arousal deactivate higher brain areas that promote a flexible response to the environment. Stress, fear, and uncertainty stimulate activity of the brainstem, while predictable, attuned rhythmical interactions with other members of our species stimulate the development of brain areas related to safety, play, and exploration.

If children are well cared for, they learn how to deal with frustration with active assistance from caregiving adults who help them modulate their arousal levels—by defining the problem, showing them how to do things, taking over when they cannot do the task themselves, and holding and rocking them when they are distressed. By means of attunement and mirroring by caregivers, children gradually learn to deal with frustrations and disappointments without kicking, screaming, or otherwise taking their misery out on those around them. Secure children also learn to deal with aggravation without feeling that this is proof that they are evil, inadequate, or doomed. Persistent fear activates primitive self-preservation systems in the brain at the expense of those involved in play and exploration. This interferes with learning to regulate arousal. Arousal modulation is essential for being able to imagine a variety of options and for feeling empathy for oneself and for others.

It is a sad reality that as our society in general and our profession in particular have become more and more technically proficient and knowledgeable about brain development, we often seem to lose track of the context in which human beings develop and thrive. Science has clearly supported what most human beings instinctively know: that secure attachment bonds are essential for the proper development of optimal cognitive and interpersonal functioning.

Remarkably, even though research has shown that the majority of psychiatric inpatients have histories of having been molested, abused, or abandoned by a caregiver, and even though the consequences of adverse childhood experiences constitute the single largest public health problem in the United States (Fellitti et al., 1998) and, likely, worldwide, there is enormous resistance to place the care and feeding of developing human beings where it belongs: at the forefront of our attention. There continues to be vastly more funding for studying the genetic components of mental illness, and for relatively obscure disorders such as obsessive–compulsive disorder, than for preventing and treating the long-term effects of child abuse and neglect (van der Kolk, Crozier, & Hopper, 2001).

Child abuse and neglect are tragically common. Despite the fact that research has repeatedly demonstrated that human beings who are exposed to betrayal, abandonment, and abuse by their caretakers suffer from vastly more complex psychobiological disturbances than human beings who are victims of earthquakes and motor vehicle accidents (van der Kolk, Roth, Pelcovitz, Sunday, & Spinazzola, 2005), our diagnostic system continues to lump all trauma-related symptomatology under the category of "PTSD." Clinicians have always dealt with patients with complex trauma histories. For more than a century, people like Pierre Janet, Morton Prince, Sandor Ferenczi, and Leonard Shengold have provided us with luminous case descriptions and treatment reports about these patients. Reading them can be as fresh and illuminating as the best work of our contemporaries. However, what is new is the contribution by the brain sciences to a more precise understanding of the nature of the damage caused by chronic developmental trauma. The evolving knowledge about the biological underpinnings of the injuries caused by child maltreatment also invites us to explore, and to possibly radically expand, treatment directions for the future.

In the 1980s, Arthur Green and Dorothy Otnow Lewis wrote the first papers that documented that many abused children had evidence of neurological damage, even when there were no reports of head injury (Teicher, Tomoda, & Andersen, 2006). In a study by Robert Davies and colleagues of 22 sexually abused patients, 77% had abnormal brain waves and 36% had seizures (Ito, Teicher, Glod, & Ackerman, 1998). This was the first concrete evidence that human abuse and neglect affect the development of vulnerable brain regions. Subsequent research has shown that when traumatized individuals are reminded of traumatic experiences, there is increased activation in brain regions that support intense emotions and decreased activation in brain regions involved in (1) the integration of sensory input with motor output, (2) the modulation of physiological arousal, and (3) the capacity to communicate experience in words (Rauch et al., 1996). The research by Martin Teicher, Michael DeBellis, Ruth Lanius, Paul Plotsky, and many others has begun to delineate a constellation of brain abnormalities associated with childhood abuse. The results are quite consistent across studies: When a person is in a persistent low-level fear state, the primary areas of the brain that are processing information develop differently. Frightened people are dominated by subcortical and limbic activity. As a result, they tend to base their appraisal of what is happening on nonverbal information such as facial expressions, gestures, and arousal states.

Alarm states erase people's sense of time: In brain scans one can observe decreased activation of these cortical areas when subjects are exposed to reminders of their traumatic experiences (Hopper, Frewen, van der Kolk, & Lanius, 2007; Lanius, Williamson, & Densmore, 2001). Cut adrift from internal regulating capabilities of the cortex, the brainstem acts reflexively, impulsively, and aggressively to any perceived threat. In alarm states, contemplation of the consequences of one's behavior is almost impossible. Because the brain areas responsible for executive functioning go offline under threat, frightened people loose touch with the flow of time and the knowledge that every sensation has a beginning, middle, and end—they get stuck in a terrifying, seemingly never-ending present. As a result, they are desperate for immediate relief, and delayed gratification is difficult, if not impossible.

The documentation of these abnormalities goes a long way in explaining why traumatized individuals usually have little idea what upsets them so much, and have so little control over their reactions. One needs a well-functioning left prefrontal cortex to know one's feelings and grasp the effects of one's actions. Not really knowing what one feels and having no idea how one's actions affect other people go hand in hand with blowing up in response to minor provocations, with automatically freezing when frustrated, and with feeling helpless in the face of trivial challenges. To observers who do not understand that reminders of the past activate terror-inducing physical sensations, these emotional reactions appear bizarre, and the behavior reprehensible and in need of control and suppression.

The foundation of self-experience is grounded in the capacity to identify and utilize physical sensations (Damasio, 1999). When infants have upsetting sensations, they use their facial expressions, body movements, and vocal cords to ensure that their caregivers stop what they are doing and do whatever it takes to change the way the infants feel. Most caregiving interactions are able to change children's sensations and restore their inner balance. When moving and crying fail to elicit a caring response, children change their strategy. Crittenden (1998) and Fosha (2003) have described three ways in which children learn to cope with consistently unresponsive caregivers. One is "feeling but not dealing": getting stuck on a continuous alarm or defeat response that does not significantly change even when people around them seem to respond appropriately. No amount of care seems to be able to provide a sense of safety and comfort. These children seem to be stuck in a continuous state of alarm which becomes independent from actual threat. The second adaptation is "dealing but not feeling": coping by shutting down. When this occurs, the children continue to be able to function despite adequate caregiving by learning to ignore physical sensations and warning signs. They develop "alexithymia," in which they are plagued by unpleasant physical sensations that are disconnected from emotional experience. Emotions lose their function as warning signals. These individuals cannot use their feelings to adjust how they relate to other people and are prone to respond to stress with physical problems. The third form of coping has been called "neither feeling nor dealing," the sort of disorganized response that is most common in abused and neglected children who end up in residential treatment centers and in chronic psychiatric care.

When parents and children can freely use language to communicate what they see and hear, and when children are encouraged to name and reflect on all aspects of reality, they will learn to name what they see and articulate what they need. However, when reality is terrifying and experience is denied, children have trouble putting their inner world into communicable language. As Bowlby (1990) said, "What cannot be communicated to the (m)other cannot be communicated to the self" (p. 61). Research shows that lack of verbal interaction with caregivers, or the deliberate denial of certain aspects of reality, leads to decreased intelligence, decreased school performance, loss of focus, and increased dissociation (Pollak, Cicchetti, & Klorman, 1998).

Traumatized individuals have more selective development of nonverbal cognitive capacities. People raised in the vortex of violence have learned that nonverbal information is more critical for survival than words. Ruth Lanius and her colleagues (Hopper et al., 2007; Lanius et al., 2001) have shown that chronically traumatized individuals have decreased dorsolateral and medial prefrontal activation, particularly when under stress. These are the areas in the brain that endow human beings with the uniquely human imagination and with the capacity to think of themselves and the world around them with continuity over time.

IMPLICATIONS FOR CLINICAL
ASSESSMENT AND TREATMENT

Over the past two decades, there have been significant advances in the assessment and treatment of complexly traumatized people. Many of these have their foundation in the increased understanding of how trauma affects the developing brain and self-perception. Contemporary neuroscience research suggests that effective treatment needs to involve (1) learning to modulate arousal, (2) learning to tolerate feelings and sensations by increasing the capacity for interoception, and (3) learning that after confrontation with physical helplessness, it is essential to engage in taking effective action.

Describing traumatic experiences in conventional verbal therapy runs the risk of activating implicit memory systems, that is, trauma-related physical sensations and physiological hyper- or hypoarousal. The very act of talking about one's traumatic experiences can make trauma victims feel hyperaroused, terrified, and unsafe. These reactions only aggravate posttraumatic helplessness, fear, shame, and rage. In order to avoid this situation, chronically traumatized individuals are prone to seek a supportive therapeutic relationship in which the therapist becomes a refuge from a life of anxiety and ineffectiveness, rather than someone to help them process the imprints of their traumatic experiences. Learning to autonomously modulate one's arousal level is essential for overcoming the passivity and dependency associated with a fear of reliving the trauma.

Most clinicians agree that being able to regulate affective arousal is critical to being able to tolerate effective trauma processing therapy. In recent years, there has been an increasing awareness that people have built-in ways of regulating themselves. Interestingly, there is little in the Western tradition that cultivates this inborn capacity—there always has been a tendency to believe that one can lead "a better life through chemistry." In Western cultures, alcohol traditionally has served as the primary way of dealing with excessive arousal and fear. During the past century, alcohol was gradually condemned as a way of coping, and psychopharmacological agents were increasingly substituted to help disturbed people "get a grip." However, in other, largely non-Western cultures, there are long traditions of cultivating the capacity to regulating one's physiological system. Examples are chi qong and tai chi in China, yoga in India, and drumming in Africa. All of these self-regulatory practices involve the activation of the 10th cranial nerve, the vagus nerve, which, as Darwin (1872/1898) already pointed out in *The Expression of the Emotions in Man and Animals*, is the principal pathway to emotion regulation between brain and body.

Contemporary research is beginning to support the notion that breathing, moving, chanting, tapping acupressure points, and engaging in rhythmical activities with other human beings can have a profound effect on physiological arousal systems. Clinicians are gradually learning that bodily sensations that have become dulled by avoidance of painful stimuli need to be reawakened and activated in order to help clients regain a sense of pleasure and engagement. Our initial studies utilizing yoga for complex trauma have been very promising (van der Kolk, 2006), and we are hopeful that this work will be just the beginning of the exploration of effective body-based self-regulatory practices.

Interoceptive, body-oriented therapies can directly deal with a core clinical issue in PTSD: Traumatized individuals are prone to experience the present with physical sensations and emotions that are associated with their traumatic past, and act accordingly. For therapy to be effective, it is useful to focus in on the patient's physical self-experience and increase his or her self-awareness, rather than to focus exclusively on the meaning that people make of their experience—their narrative of the past. If past experience is embodied in current physiological states and action tendencies and the trauma is reenacted in breath, gestures, sensory perceptions, movement, emotion, and thought, therapy may be most effective if it facilitates self-awareness and self-regulation. Once patients become aware of their sensations and action tendencies, they can set about discovering new ways of orienting themselves to their surroundings and exploring novel ways of engaging with potential sources of mastery and pleasure.

One of the most robust findings of the neuroimaging studies of PTSD is that, under stress, the higher brain areas involved in "executive functioning"—planning for the future, anticipating the consequences of one's actions, and inhibiting inappropriate responses—become less active. In particular, a well-functioning medial prefrontal cortex is essential to the extinction of conditioned fear responses (Morgan, Romanski, & LeDoux, 1993), by suppressing the stress response mediated by the hypothalamic–pituitary–adrenal axis. The fact that the medial prefrontal cortex, the brain region most implicated in interoceptive awareness, can directly influence emotional arousal has enormous clinical significance, since it suggests that the practice of mindfulness can enhance control over emotions.

Maybe one of the most profound lessons of the last 50 years has been that trauma that once was outside, and played itself out in a social setting, becomes lodged within people's internal experiences, in the very sinew and muscles of their organism. Deeply learning to tolerate, approach, befriend, and nurture one's deepest sensations and emotions becomes the greatest task of therapy. Clinical experience shows that traumatized individuals, as a rule, have great difficulty attending to their inner sensations and perceptions—when asked to focus on internal sensations, they tend to feel overwhelmed or they deny having an inner sense of self. When they try to meditate, they often report becoming overwhelmed by being confronted with residues of trauma-related perceptions, sensations, and emotions; feeling disgusted with themselves, helpless, or panicked; or experiencing trauma-related images and physical sensations. Trauma victims tend to have a negative body image—as far as they are concerned, the less attention they pay to their bodies, and thereby their internal sensations, the better. Yet one cannot learn to take care of oneself without being in touch with the demands and requirements of one's physical self. In the field of traumatic stress disorders treatment, a consensus is emerging that, in order to keep old trauma from intruding into current experience, patients need to deal with the internal residues of the past. Neurobiologically speaking, they need to activate their medial prefrontal cortex, insula, and anterior cingulate by learning to tolerate orienting and focusing their attention on their internal experience, while interweaving and conjoining cognitive, emotional, and sensorimotor elements of their traumatic experience.

Traumatized individuals need to learn that it is safe to have feelings and sensations. If they learn to attend to inner experience, they will become aware that bodily experience never remains static. Unlike at the moment of a trauma, when everything seems to freeze in time, physical sensations and emotions are in a constant state of flux. Traumatized persons need to learn to tell the difference between a sensation and an emotion (How do you know you are angry/afraid? Where do you feel that in your body? Do you notice any impulses in your body to move in some way right now?). Once they realize that their internal sensations continuously shift and change, particularly if they learn to develop a certain degree of control over their physiological states by breathing and movement, they will viscerally discover that remembering the past does not inevitably result in overwhelming emotions.

Lazar and colleagues (2005) at the Massachusetts General Hospital completed a functional magnetic resonance imaging study of 20 people engaged in meditation that involved sustained mindful attention to internal and external sensory stimuli and nonjudgmental awareness of present-moment stimuli without cognitive elaboration. They found that brain regions associated with attention, interoception, and sensory processing, including the prefrontal cortex and right anterior insula, were thicker in meditation participants than in matched controls. It has been proposed that by becoming increasingly more aware of sensory stimuli during formal practice, meditation practitioners gradually increase their capacity to navigate potentially stressful encounters that arise throughout the day. Lazar and colleagues' study lends support to the notion that treatment of traumatic stress may need to include becoming mindful, that is, learning to become a careful observer of the ebb and flow of internal experience, and noticing whatever thoughts, feelings, body sensations, and impulses emerge. In order to deal with the past, it is helpful for traumatized people to learn to activate their capacity for introspection and develop a deep curiosity about their internal experience. This is necessary in order to identify their physical sensations and to translate their emotions and sensations into communicable language—understandable, most of all, to themselves.

After having been traumatized, people often lose the effective use of fight-or-flight defenses and respond to perceived threat with immobilization. Attention to inner experience can help them to reorient themselves to the present by learning to attend to nontraumatic stimuli. LeDoux and his colleagues (Morgan et al., 1993) have demonstrated that the lateral nucleus of the amygdala is the critical anatomical structure in the formation of conditioned fear memories. Specifically, animals who respond actively to threats divert the flow of information from the lateral amygdala to the motor circuits of the brain involved in active coping, which prevents the establishment of conditioned endocrine and behavioral responses (Amorapanth, LeDoux, & Nader, 2000).

LeDoux and his colleagues showed that when rats are given the option of physically escaping from a traumatic stimulus, they lose their conditioning even after a conditioned fear response is well established. This work suggests that action diverts the flow of information from the lateral nucleus of the amygdala. According to LeDoux and Gorman (2001, p. 1954):

> By engaging these alternative pathways, passive fear responding is replaced with an active coping strategy. This diversion of information flow away from the central nucleus to the basal nucleus, and the learning that takes place, does not occur if the rat remains passive. It requires that the rat take action. It is "learning by doing," a process in which the success in terminating the conditioned stimulus reinforces the action taken.

The implications of this research are clear: Traumatized individuals need to engage in action that is pleasurable and effective, particularly in response to situations where in the past they were helpless and defeated. In our trauma center, we have a very active theater program for chronically traumatized adolescents that now has officially been declared an "evidence-based treatment," and we collaborate with programs such as Impact/Model Mugging to help traumatized people regain a sense of pleasure and competence as they take affective action (Kisiel et al., 2005; Macy et al., 2004).

We have rediscovered that traumatic memories are fragmented. Trauma is not primarily remembered as a story, but is stored in mind and brain as images, sounds, smells, physical sensations, and enactments. Our research showed that talking about traumatic events does not necessarily allow mind and brain to integrate the dissociated images and sensations into a coherent whole. Techniques other than figuring out, talking, and understanding have proven to be enormously helpful in the integration of these fragments of the traumatic past. In the early years of psychiatry, clinicians primarily used hypnosis for this purpose, but as yet we have no research to show how effective hypnosis was in accomplishing this.

Of course, one of the greatest challenges is that complex trauma is a condition that does not exist as a formally acknowledged disorder within the mental health field—with the partial exception of the European guidebook to medical diagnoses, the *International Classification of Diseases*, which includes a diagnosis of "enduring personality change after catastrophic experience" (F62.0). Despite valiant efforts to integrate complex time of diagnosis in DSM-IV (and attempts to do this again for DSM-V under the rubric "developmental trauma disorder" [van der Kolk, 2005]), these patients do not have a diagnostic home, and therefore there is no real possibility that organized psychiatry and psychology can study people with complex trauma in a coherent fashion. As long as the various symptoms from which traumatized individuals suffer are relegated to seemingly disconnected diagnoses such as PTSD, ADHD, bipolar illness, attachment disturbances, borderline personality disorder, and depression, it will be very difficult to systematically and scientifically study the full range of possible interventions to help human beings with complex trauma histories gain control over their lives.

Clinicians attempting to describe and understand the problems confronting patients who have complex trauma histories have had to go beyond the standard interview measures and diagnostic categories provided by the psychiatry profession. There is a remarkable array of psychometrically robust assessment measures that can help in this endeavor, as Briere and Spinazzola have thoroughly summarized in Chapter 5, on assessment of complex trauma sequelae. There also are frameworks for conceptualizing and developing treatment goals for complex traumatic stress disorders, as illustrated in the book's chapters on developmental neurobiology (Ford, Chapter 2) and emerging practice guidelines (Ford & Cloitre, Chapter 3; Courtois, Ford, & Cloitre, Chapter 4).

It is ironic that, despite the fact that people with complex trauma histories probably make up the bulk of patients seen in mental health centers, they remain nameless and homeless. In an age of the genome project and highly evolved epidemiological methods and neuroimaging techniques, the treatment of chronically traumatized individuals fundamentally continues to play itself out on a village level of oral traditions and anecdotes. The profound clinical wisdom that results from intimate exposure to chronically traumatized people continues to be largely anecdotal, and transmitted in supervision sessions, small conferences, and informal discussions among colleagues. Because dissociation is of little interest to mainstream psychology and psychiatry, it is not being studied systematically. Because affect regulation and its vicissitudes are not central to our scientific work, it is relegated to yoga studios, martial arts classes, and meditation centers. Because self-hatred and disgust are not understood as developmental inevitabilities after abuse and neglect, they are relegated to the realm of religion rather than the realm of science.

REFERENCES

Amorapanth, P., LeDoux, J. E., & Nader, K. (2000). Different lateral amygdala outputs mediate reaction and actions elicited by a fear-arousing stimulus. *Nature Neuroscience, 3*, 74–79.

Bowlby, J. (1990). *The making and breaking of affectional bonds*. Boston: Routledge.

Crittenden, P. M. (1998). The developmental consequences of childhod sexual abuse. In P. K. Trickett & C. J. Schellenback (Eds.), *Violence against children in the family and the community* (pp. 11–38). Washington, DC: American Psychological Association.

Damasio, A.R. (1999). *The feeling of what happens: Body and emotion in the making on consciousness*. New York: Harcourt Brace.

Darwin, C. (1898). *The expression of the emotions in man and animals*. London: Greenwood Press. (Original work published 1872)

Felitti, V. J., Anda, R. F., Nordenberg, D., Williamson, D. F., Spitz, A. M., Edwards, V., et al. (1998). The relationship of adult health status to childhood abuse and household dysfunction. *American Journal of Preventive Medicine, 14,* 245–258.

Fosha, D. (2003). Dyadic regulation and experiential work with emotion and relatedness in trauma and disorganized attachment. In M. F. Solomon & D. J. Siegel (Eds.), *Healing trauma: Attachment, mind, body, and brain* (pp. 221–281) New York: Norton.

Henderson, D. J. (1975). Incest. In A. M. Freedman, H. I. Kaplan, & B. J. Sadock (Eds.), *Comprehensive textbook of psychiatry* (2nd ed., p. 1536). Baltimore: Williams & Wilkins.

Hopper, J. H., Frewen, P., van der Kolk, B. A., & Lanius, R. A. (2007). Neural correlates of reexperiencing, avoidance, and dissociation in PTSD: Symptom dimensions and emotion dysregulation in responses to script-driven trauma imagery. *Journal of Traumatic Stress, 20,* 713–725.

Ito, Y., Teicher, M. H., Glod, C.A., & Ackerman E. (1998). Preliminary evidence for aberrant cortical development in abused children: A quantitative EEG study. *Journal of Neuropsychiatry and Clinical Neuroscience, 10,* 298–307.

Jackson, J. H. (1958). Evolution and dissolution of the nervous system. In J. Taylor (Ed.), *Selected writings of John Hughlings Jackson* (pp. 45–118). London: Stapes Press.

Kisiel, C., Blaustein, M., Spinazzola, J., Swift, C., Zucker, M., & van der Kolk, B. A. (2005). Evaluation of a theater based youth violence prevention program for elementary school children. *Journal of School Violence, 5*(2), 19–36.

Lanius, R.A., Williamson, M., & Densmore, D. (2001). Neural correlates of traumatic memories in posttraumatic stress disorder: A functional MRI investigation. *American Journal of Psychiatry, 158,* 1920–1922.

Lazar, S., Kerr, C., Wasserman, R., Gray, J., Greve, D., & Treadway, M. (2005). Meditation experience is associated with increased cortical thickness. *NeuroReport, 16,* 1893–1897.

LeDoux, J. E., & Gorman. J. M. (2001) A call to action: Overcoming anxiety through active coping. *American Journal of Psychiatry, 158,* 1953–1955.

Macy, R. D., Behar, L., & Paulson, R., Delman, R., Schmid, L., & Smith, S. F. (2004). Community-based, acute posttraumatic stress management: A description and evaluation of a psychosocial–intervention continuum. *Harvard Review of Psychiatry, 12,* 217–228.

Macy, R. L., & van der Kolk, B. A. (1999). [A survey of the Medicaid population of Massachusetts, 1999]. Unpublished raw data.

Morgan, M.A., Romanski, L. M., & LeDoux, J. E. (1993). Extinction of emotional learning: Contribution of medial prefrontal cortex. *Neuroscience Letters, 163,* 109–113.

Panksepp, J. (1998*). Affective neuroscience: The foundations of human and animal emotions.* New York: Oxford University Press.

Perry, B. D. (2002). The neurodevelopmental impact of violence in childhood. In D. H. Schetky & E. P. Benedek (Eds.), *Principles and practices of child and adolescent forensic psychiatry* (pp. 221–238). Washington, DC: American Psychiatric Publishing.

Pollak, S., Cicchetti, D., & Klorman, R. (1998). Stress, memory, and emotion: Developmental considerations from the study of child maltreatment. *Development and Psychopathology, 10,* 811–828.

Putnam, F. W. (2003).Ten-year research update review: Child sexual abuse. *Journal of the American Academy of Child and Adolescent Psychiatry, 42*, 231–240.

Rauch, S., van der Kolk, B. A., Fisler, R., Alpert, N., Orr, S., Savage, C., et al. (1996). Symptom provocation study using positron emission tomography and script driven imagery. *Archives of General Psychiatry, 53*, 380–387.

Teicher, M. H., Tomoda, A., & Andersen, S. L. (2006). Neurobiological consequences of early stress and childhood maltreatment: Are results from human and animal studies comparable? *Annals of the New York Academy of Sciences, 1071*, 313–323.

van der Kolk, B. A. (2005). Developmental trauma disorder: Toward a rational diagnosis for children with complex trauma histories. *Psychiatric Annals, 35*, 401–408.

van der Kolk, B. A. (2006). Clinical implications of neuroscience research in PTSD. *Annals of the New York Academy of Sciences, 1071*, 277–293.

van der Kolk, B. A., Crozier, J., & Hopper, J. (2001). Child abuse in America: Prevalence, costs, consequences and intervention. *Journal of Aggression, Maltreatment, and Trauma, 4*, 9–31.

van der Kolk, B. A, Roth, S., Pelcovitz, D., Sunday, S., & Spinazzola, J. (2005). Disorders of Extreme Stress: The empirical foundation of a complex adaptation to trauma. *Journal of Traumatic Stress, 18*, 389–399.

Index

Page numbers followed by *f* indicate figure, *t* indicate table